What Is a Person?

What Is a Person?

*Rethinking Humanity, Social Life, and the
Moral Good from the Person Up*

CHRISTIAN SMITH

THE UNIVERSITY OF CHICAGO PRESS CHICAGO AND LONDON

The University of Chicago Press, Chicago 60637
The University of Chicago Press, Ltd., London
© 2010 by The University of Chicago
All rights reserved. Published 2010.
Paperback edition 2011
Printed in the United States of America

20 19 18 17 16 15 14 13 12 11   2 3 4 5 6

ISBN-13: 978-0-226-76591-4 (cloth)
ISBN-13: 978-0-226-76594-5 (paper)
ISBN-10: 0-226-76591-1 (cloth)
ISBN-10: 0-226-76594-6 (paper)

The University of Chicago Press gratefully acknowledges the generous support of the
University of Notre Dame toward the publication of this book.

Library of Congress Cataloging-in-Publication Data

Smith, Christian, 1960–
    What is a person? : rethinking humanity, social life, and the moral good from the person
  up / Christian Smith.
        p.   cm.
    Includes bibliographical references and index
    ISBN-13: 978-0-226-76591-4 (hardcover : alk. paper)
    ISBN-10: 0-226-76591-1 (hardcover : alk. paper)   1. Persons. 2. Philosophical
anthropology.
    I. Title.
    BD450.S558 2010
    128—dc22

                                                                                    2009041981

FOR ERIN

Contents

Acknowledgments

Having completed the writing of this book and now looking back on the manuscript, I see that some of its tone suggests an existential vantage point of real confidence, security, and power in the world. I realize that this is a privileged position in which an author might feel himself or herself. I also know that not all possible readers will share such a perspective or even be sympathetic toward it. In principle, such a difference should not impeach a book's argument for readers from other perspectives, especially this book's, which makes claims about the unified reality that all of us share. In fact, this book is the product of many years of uncertain dissatisfaction, intellectual struggle, frustrated wrestlings with a variety of professional routines, and a slow and halting learning process about possible alternative approaches to sociology—a learning process that is far from complete. The product here, rather confident in tone, may thus mask the struggling process that brought it to fruition. Most important in this long process of struggle and learning were the many valuable intellectual and practical assistances I received from an immense number of generous persons. Steve Vaisey, Chris Eberle, Trish Snell, Keith Meador, George Thomas, and Kraig Beyerlein have been great conversation partners over the years, colleagues with whom I have been able to hash out many issues found in this book. Peter Bearman, Jim Moody, Bert Hodges, Russ Bishop, Bruce Herman, Dan Dehanas, John Tyson, and Stan Gaede also deserve thanks for conversations that proved helpful in forming my thinking developed in the pages that follow. Numerous people read part or all of this book's manuscript at different stages of completion and provided feedback, including Trish Snell, Chris Eberle, Nick Wolterstorff, Steve Vaisey, Brad Gregory, Brian Brock, Douglas Porpora, Bill Hurlbut, Don Miller, Jeff Schloss, Jim Heft, Dallas Willard, Steve Smith, George

Thomas, John Evans, Michael Evans, Omar Lizardo, Jessica Collett, Warren Brown, Jon Turner, Don Browning, Michael Emerson, Michael Lindsay, Michael Young, Mark Regnerus, Chris Pieper, Charles Stokes, Nicolette Manglos, Jeremy Ueker, Alasdair MacIntyre, Todd Whitmore, Erika Summers-Effler, Monique Gregg, Philip Reed, Joseph Rabbitt, Emily Stetler, Austin Murphy, Chris Morrisey, Brandon Vaidyanathan, Andy Crouch, and Rebecca McCumbers. The intellectual fingerprints of Terence Cuneo are also found in various parts of what follows. They all—including those who do not agree with my case—have my deepest appreciation. In particular, Snell, Wolterstorff, Eberle, Gregory, Brock, Porpora, Pieper, Summers-Effler, Evans, Evans, Heft, Vaidyanathan, Collett, Hurlbut, and Lizardo provided extensive written and oral critical comments on my manuscript that were extremely helpful. In addition, I enjoyed three days of beneficial discussion and feedback at the May 2008 "Critical Realism and Human Personhood" workshop at Notre Dame, whose helpful participants included Iddo Tavory, Mucahit Bilici, Michael Evans, Chris Pieper, Nicolette Manglos, Chuck Stokes, Dan Dehanas, Juan Carlos Esparza, Avi Astor, Jeffrey Dill, Jennifer Barrett, Katie Hoegeman, Margarita Mooney, Kyle Longest, Steve Offutt, Gary Adler, Alessandra Gonzalez, Carol Ann MacGregor, Christine Sheikh, Amy Adamczyk, Conrad Hackett, Kristin Geraty, and Tricia Bruce. Sincere thanks I return to each of these people for their generous and varied contributions to this book. The seeds of many of the ideas in this book were sown during discussions in a five-week summer seminar I led at Calvin College in 2001, for which I am grateful to Susan Felch and the Calvin seminars program for making possible and hosting. This book also grew out of discussions in a conference I held on human personhood at Sea Island, Georgia, in May 2007. Participants in that conference not already named above include Mark Berner, Joe Davis, Steve Hitlin, Michael Perry, David Sikkink, and Brad Wilcox. Kimon Sargeant, Arthur Schwartz, Chris Stawski, and Jack Templeton of the John Templeton Foundation deserve thanks too for awarding me a planning grant on the nature of human personhood in the social sciences, which became the platform on which this book was written. None of these people, however, as the customary disclaimer runs, holds any responsibility for any of its inadequacies, problems, or weaknesses.

Introduction

What are humans? One would think that of all the personal and scientific subjects we study the one we would be most interested and proficient in understanding would be ourselves, human beings. Should we not be quite transparent to ourselves? Yet it is not obvious that we humans actually do understand ourselves as beings very well. I am not the first to observe that, of the many mysteries in the universe, we humans are perhaps the most mysterious of all to ourselves.[1] Even the social sciences, for all their sophistication in certain ways, have not helped us much to understand clearly the nature of our own species, humanity as such. Or so I believe. The social sciences are good at describing and analyzing human activities, cultures, institutions, social relations, and social structures. But that is not the same thing as actually understanding human beings per se, what we are, our constitution and condition. I will argue in the pages that follow that the social sciences have been frequently unhelpful in our search for self-understanding as a particular kind of existent and acting being. This seems to me most certainly true of my own discipline, sociology. I also find few in sociology who are particularly interested in engaging such questions directly. Perhaps the mystery we are to ourselves makes us uneasy. Perhaps the question seems too unscientific. And yet the wise have challenged us for millennia in different ways with the charge, "Know Thyself." This I seek to do.

1. Among many perceptive observers, see, for example, Walker Percy, *Lost in the Cosmos* (New York: Farrar, Straus and Giroux, 1983); and Charles Chesnutt (*The Marrow of Tradition* [1901; Ann Arbor: University of Michigan Press, 1969], 233) states, "The workings of the human heart are the profoundest mystery of the universe." For a sense of the difficulty of tackling the question philosophically, see Eric Olson, *What Are We? A Study in Personal Ontology* (New York: Oxford University Press, 2007).

Why Inquire about Human Being?

Many in sociology may reply that they are not interested in understanding human beings per se, that they are concerned instead about explaining or predicting aspects of cognitive, cultural, organizational, social, political, or economic worlds.[2] My first reply is that this book's inquiry is not merely about abstract philosophical anthropology or personal self-exploration. The question animating this inquiry has relevance for social science research and scholarship. There is no social science analysis that does not at least implicitly assume some model of the human to help underwrite its explanation. Therefore, the better we understand the human, the better we should explain the social. While few social scientists need to devote their careers to studying human nature, our scholarly works will still benefit by investing some time and energy into investigating the question, what are humans? My second reply is that we social scientists are not merely scientists. We are all human beings too, more fundamentally human persons, in fact, than we are sociologists or psychologists. So, inquiring into the nature of our very own selves as a particular kind of being should matter. Impoverished is he who can predict economic trends but who does not well understand his own self.

Four related considerations motivate this book. Two have to do with disjuncts that exist between the image of humans in many of our social science theories and our actual personal experiences and commitments as human creatures. And two are more abstractly theoretical. First, while many of our social science theories are interesting and do illuminate particular dimensions of human social life, I am not convinced that we as people actually find ourselves well represented by them. When we look at the models of the human operative in, say, exchange theory, social control theory, rational choice, functionalism, network theory, evolutionary theory, sociobiology, or sociological Marxism, we may recognize certain aspects of our lives in them. Otherwise the theories would feel completely alien and implausible to us. But I suspect that few of us recognize in those theories what we understand to be most important about our own selves as people. Something about them fails to capture our deep subjective experience as persons, crucial dimensions of the richness of our own lived lives,

---

2. My examination of all ten sociological dictionaries, handbooks, and encyclopedias in the reference section of the main library at the University of North Carolina at Chapel Hill reveals not a single reference to "person" in any entry, chapter, or index.

what thinkers in previous ages might have called our "souls" or "hearts."[3] That itself is not a fatal flaw for such theories. But it does raise questions about such an apparent mismatch between scholarly theory and personal experience.

The second, related disjunct that helps motivate this book concerns the gap I see between the depiction of human beings in many of our social science theories and the moral and political beliefs and commitments that many social scientists embrace. Most social science scholars I know are personally committed—some passionately so—to human rights, social justice, equality, tolerance, and human emancipation. Behind those commitments stands a moral belief in the innate, inalienable dignity and value of human persons. The disconnect I see is that few of the social science theories we employ in our disciplines model human beings in ways that justify or account for these humanistic moral and political beliefs. Few representations of the human in social science theories make it at all clear why such objects should be bearers of rights, equality, or self-determination. If anything, much theory portrays humans as essentially governed by external social influences, competing socially for material resources, strategically manipulating public presentations of self, struggling with rivals for power and status, cobbling identities through fluid assemblies of scripted roles, rationalizing actions with post hoc discursive justifications, and otherwise behaving, thinking, and feeling in ways that are commonly predictable by variable attributes and categories according to which their lives can be broken down, measured, and statistically modeled.[4] Perhaps all this is true. But that picture does not obviously justify belief in human rights, social justice, equality, tolerance, and emancipation. I think it often does not and cannot. Some social scientists might be willing to live with that kind of intellectual and moral tension, even schizophrenia. I prefer to think harder about ways our social scientific, moral, and political views of

---

3. See Edward Reed, *From Soul to Mind: The Emergence of Psychology from Erasmus, Darwin, to William James* (New Haven, CT: Yale University Press, 1997).

4. Consider, too, Ivan Pavlov's early, related view of social science as endeavoring to gain controlling power over people's behavior: "Mankind will possess incalculable advantages and extraordinary control over human behavior when the scientific investigator will be able to subject his fellow men to the same external analysis he would employ for any natural object, and when the human mind will contemplate itself not from within but from without." Pavlov, "Scientific Study of the So-Called Psychical Processes in the Higher Animals," in *Lectures on Conditioned Reflexes* (1906; New York: International Publishers, 1967), 95.

human beings might better correspond with and reinforce one another.[5] That, too, is one of the purposes of this book.

At this point, some readers may simply reply that science, morality, and politics are separate matters that need not have anything to do with one another. I do not see why that is or should be so. Just because science, morality, and politics are not identical does not mean they can or should be radically separated to go their merry, incompatible ways. In these as in most human concerns and practices, the commitment to coherent knowledge about what is true and real is a good to prize. Fragmentation and schizophrenia are not. I think that when social scientists work with professional theoretical depictions of the human that are at odds with their personal, moral, and political views of the human, something else unintentional is going on: the influence of a powerful background assumption about social science—namely, the model of naturalistic positivist empiricism[6] that demands that the social sciences emulate the natural sciences. Social scientists like me need not be ideologically committed to this belief for it to shape our suppositions and instincts. When it does shape us, we start to disconnect theory from reality, the descriptive from the normative, fact from value, human explanation from human experience. We become more committed to looking professionally like the science of physics—or actually to our often-misguided vision of what physics is—than to best understanding and explaining our subject of study as it actually exists and operates. Those moves are natural for us modern scholars to make. But, when it comes to things human, they are misguided and unhelpful. They lead us, for one thing, to scholarly theories of human beings that do not

5. For an effort similarly attempting to relate the moral imperatives of personalism to political theory, see Thomas Rourke and Rosita Chazarreta Rourke, *A Theory of Personalism* (Lanham, MD: Lexington, 2005).

6. Here we meet a crucial distinction between empiri*cism* as a philosophical belief and being empiri*cal* as a method. These are not at all the same thing. My argument in this book is resolutely against empiri*cism* (also sometimes stated as being antiempiri*cist*), in that I reject the philosophical belief that valid human knowledge is always and only obtained through sense perceptions of observed evidence gained through experience and ideally through deliberate experimentation—and thus a priori ruling out the role of reasoning, as well as perhaps innate ideas, intuition, or, in principle, revelation. My argument, however, fully affirms the need for science to be empiri*cal* as one of the defining characteristics of natural and social scientific work. We need all of the empirical evidence we can gather for our reasoning minds to use in larger processes of understanding and explanation in order to better grasp a reality not all aspects of which are empirically observable. The meaning of this should become clear as the book's argument develops.

fit with our own, real, personal, moral, and political views about human beings. This book is an attempt to theorize the human in a way that might pull those divided views more closely together.[7]

A third consideration about the adequacy of much existing sociological theory also motivates this book. Central to the entire discipline of sociology—and important in most social sciences more generally—is the notion of social structure. Theorists in recent years have made helpful strides in conceptualizing what social structures are.[8] We have been less successful, however, I think, in explaining the sources or origins of social structures in the first place. What actually gives rise to the social structuring of human life? Much of sociology simply takes social structures for granted and focuses instead on how they shape human outcomes. That is legitimate as far as it goes. But sociology should also want a solid theoretical account of the sources or origins of social structures, one of its core concepts. Many general theoretical approaches offer no such account. Others do but their accounts are arguably incomplete or debatable. My view is that a good theory of the origins of social structures needs to be rooted in a larger theory about the nature of human persons. Attempting to develop and articulate such a theory is also one of the purposes of this book.

The fourth factor motivating this book concerns our deep contemporary uncertainties about the human self and person. In the wake of the postmodernist critique from the humanities and in the face of the rapidly growing power of biotechnology and genetic engineering in the natural sciences, many people today stand uncertain about the meaning or lucidity of the very notion of a coherent self or person, unclear about what a person essentially is or might be whose dignity might be worth preserving,

7. Erizim Kohák ("Selves, People, Persons: An Essay in American Personalism," in *Selves, People, and Persons: What Does It Mean to Be a Self?* ed. Leroy Rouner, Boston University Studies in Philosophy and Religion [Notre Dame, IN: University of Notre Dame Press, 1992], 17–35) addresses the question from the perspective of Bostonian personalism, explained in chapter 2. See Hans Jonas, *The Phenomenon of Life: Toward a Philosophical Biology* (Chicago: University of Chicago Press, 1966), for an exploration of how mind, action, and moral responsibility are rooted in organic, phylogenetic existence.

8. William H. Sewell Jr., "A Theory of Structure: Duality, Agency, and Transformation," *American Journal of Sociology* 98 (1992): 1–29; Anthony Giddens, *Central Problems in Social Theory* (Berkeley and Los Angeles: University of California Press, 1979); Giddens, *The Constitution of Society* (Berkeley and Los Angeles: University of California Press, 1984); Pierre Bourdieu, *Outline of a Theory of Practice* (Cambridge: Cambridge University Press, 1977); Margaret Archer, *Realist Social Theory: The Morphogenetic Approach* (New York: Cambridge University Press, 1984).

as technological capabilities to reconfigure the human expand.[9] Responding to this cultural and technological context and the challenge it presents,
numerous scholars have written recently about the history, meaning, and
nature of the human self and person.[10] The social sciences appear to have
contributed little to this reflection, however, sociology perhaps least of
all. I do not pretend to have an approach that speaks to all of the issues
raised by our contemporary uncertainties about the self and person. But
I believe that the theoretical perspectives I develop here do make some
significant contributions to the conversation and helpfully correct some of
the more problematic tendencies in current discussions.[11]

9. For a taste of such uncertainty about persons from a postmodern perspective, for those
who are not already overfed by it, consider as one among myriad possible examples this offering: "The disappearance of the self . . . is most immediately related to our subject, person. . . .
The problem is that the person as a self is dispersed and disseminated over a range of experiences. . . . The subject is disseminated beyond itself in realities that are not under its control
even though the primary reference of experience remains in the notion of the self as subject.
The postmodern person is an amalgam of the person of philosophies of being and philosophies of consciousness without either the transcendent unity of being or the transcendental
unity of apperception in consciousness. Who is this person?" Charles Winquist, "Person,"
in *Critical Terms for Religious Studies*, ed. Mark C. Taylor (Chicago: University of Chicago
Press, 1999), 232.

10. See, for example, Jerrold Seigel, *The Idea of the Self: Thought and Experience in Western Europe since the Seventeenth Century* (Cambridge: Cambridge University Press, 2005);
Raymond Martin and John Barresi, *The Rise and Fall of Soul and Self: An Intellectual History
of Personal Identity* (New York: Columbia University Press, 2006); Jürgen Habermas, *The
Future of Human Nature* (Malden, MA: Polity Press, 2003); Richard Sorabji, *Self: Ancient
and Modern Insights about Individuality, Life, and Death* (Chicago: University of Chicago
Press, 2006); Roger Lundin, *From Nature to Experience: The Search for Cultural Authority*
(Lanham, MD: Rowman and Littlefield, 2005); Wilfred McClay, ed., *Figures in the Carpet:
Finding the Human Person in the American Past* (Grand Rapids, MI: Eerdmans, 2007); Marya
Schechtman, *The Constitution of Selves* (Ithaca, NY: Cornell University Press, 2007); Ronald
William Dworkin, *The Rise of the Imperial Self* (Lanham, MD: Rowman and Littlefield, 1996);
Louis Pojman, *Who Are We? Theories of Human Nature* (New York: Oxford University Press,
2006). The larger project on human personhood from which this book springs might engage
works in cultural studies, feminist theory, law, normative political theory, and other strands
of philosophy addressing the nature of personhood, including, for instance, Pheng Cheah's
Inhuman Conditions: On Cosmopolitanism and Human Rights (Cambridge, MA: Harvard
University Press, 2007), Alain Badiou's *Theory of the Subject* (London: Continuum, 2009), and
Ann Cudd and Robin Andreasen's *Feminist Theory: A Philosophical Anthropology* (Hoboken, NJ: Wiley-Blackwell, 2005)—though doing so is beyond the possible scope of the already
long present book.

11. Yet another way to understand the purpose of this book is as a reply to a problem that
I posed for myself in another book, *Moral, Believing Animals* (New York: Oxford University

In a book about personal being I wish to keep the personal relevance of the question from disappearing. What are humans? At first glace this question may indeed seem an abstract, grandiose speculation. But in most general and personal terms it is among one of the more important questions we face in our lives. The answer we give—whether reflectively or by default—helps to determine our view of our own selves, our lives, our very being and purpose, and of what makes a good society. Few people today, including scholars, seem to spend much time consciously pondering the question, "what actually *are* we?" We need to attend to more pressing matters. Yet none of us can finally avoid, at a personal level, one way or another, answering the question. For the choices, trials, routines, crises, practices, and tragedies of human life require some assumptions and beliefs about human being to inform or guide our decisions, responses, and commitments. Consider the range of possibilities at the broadest, most philosophical and religious levels. Are we simply self-conscious animals improbably appearing for a moment in a cosmos without purpose or significance? If so, that has implications for life, which even ordinary people can work out. Or are we rather illusions of individuality destined to dissolve into the ultimately real Absolute? That would make a difference. Are we instead really materially acquisitive hedonists or carnally desiring sensualists who have nothing higher to which to aspire than the gratifications of possessions and physical sensations that we can use our money and relations to consume? Or maybe only bodies with capacities to define by means of the exercise of will and discourse our identities through self-description and re-description? Or perhaps are we children of a personal God, whose perfect love is determined to rescue us from our self-destruction in order to bring us into the perfect happiness of divine knowledge and worship? Or maybe something else? The differences matter for

---

Press, 2003) but that I was not able to answer there. My argument in that book—to which I mostly continue to subscribe—led me by page 88 to question whether a proper understanding of the human condition, particularly its constructionist dimension, should lead us to become cultural and moral relativists or even nihilists. That was a cliff off of which I was not willing to jump at the time, thankfully. I offered in a few pages some tentative responses to that problem and simply lived with the loose ends. But I was not satisfied with the hesitant, underdeveloped answers that I had floated there. So I continued to read and think about the problem and have since become convinced that one of the possible answers that I mentioned on pages 90–91—critical realism—does in fact help to provide an intellectually sound response to the relativism problem over which I had made myself stumble. The present book is in part an attempt to work out why and how that might be accomplished.

how life ought to be lived, how *we* ought to live, as individuals and as a society.[12] And ultimately we have no choice but to adopt some position, even if by default our culture adopts it for us. I think we ought to want to embrace a position that is deliberately considered and believed for good reasons.

The worldviews to which I have just alluded, in order to set this inquiry in its broadest context, are mostly drawn from the realms of philosophy and religion. But this book will not be primarily philosophical or religious, at least as those are normally conceived. My aim will be more modest than exploring the meaning of life and the cosmos. I am a sociologist who dabbles in other disciplines, including philosophy and social theory broadly considered. So I approach the guiding question of this book from a social theoretical standpoint, particularly as it relates to specific sociological theories. I intend to work within the disciplinary boundaries of sociology and am not, strictly speaking, attempting to engage philosophers or anthropologists directly on their own turf. However, in what follows I do draw upon certain philosophical perspectives—as all social scientific theories of course ultimately do. I find that philosophy and the metatheoretical discussions it facilitates help to build bridges to other disciplines tangential to sociology but which are worth better engaging in interdisciplinary discussions. Even so, I will recurrently come back in my argument to specific social scientific theories as references in relation to which to make sense of the theory of human being that I develop here. I will in particular be examining the views of human persons that are implicit and explicit in social constructionism, network structuralism, and the standard approach of variables sociology. Social science will never be far from view, even if this book is not strictly social scientific, as *scientific* is normally understood.

Much has been written over millennia about human beings and human nature. What might I add to increase understanding, to provide some "epistemic gain?"[13] There is nothing new under the sun. And so the case I

---

12. Roger Trigg, *Ideas of Human Nature: An Historical Introduction* (Malden, MA: Blackwell, 1999); Louis Pojman, *Who Are We? Theories of Human Nature* (New York: Oxford University Press, 2006); Peter Loptson, *Theories of Human Nature* (Peterborough, ON: Broadview Press, 2006); Leslie Stevenson and David Haberman, *Ten Theories of Human Nature* (New York: Oxford University Press, 2004); Leslie Stevenson, *The Study of Human Nature* (New York: Oxford University Press, 2000); Martin Hollis, *Models of Man: Philosophical Thoughts on Social Action* (Cambridge: Cambridge University Press, 1977).

13. Charles Taylor, *Sources of the Self* (Cambridge, MA: Harvard University Press, 1989), 72.

build contains no particularly novel ideas. In what follows, I mostly weave together certain perspectives and insights that others have already expressed. Still, as I have written elsewhere, I believe that in the course of carrying on collective discussions over time about interesting and important concerns, it is sometimes helpful to have distinct positions restated anew.[14] Such restatements can help to move arguments along in productive ways. Furthermore, while the intellectual resources I bring to bear to develop my argument—critical realism, personalist theory, and antinaturalistic phenomenological epistemology—are not original, they are also not widely known and appreciated in American academia, particularly in the social sciences. I hope to help change that in part through developing the argument that follows.

Initial Clarifications

I am exploring in this book the specific question, what are humans? I should be clear about what I mean by the word "are," so as not to be confusing. Trying to do so very quickly entangles us in much larger discussions of ontology, epistemology, and the philosophy of social science. Further along I will more thoroughly unpack what I have to say. For present purposes, I will simply state the following. By asking the question, what are humans? I am first of all assuming that human beings have a specifiable nature, that there is a real quiddity or "whatness" about human personhood that can be known.[15] I say this intentionally and fully aware that such a claim is contentious in some circles. That, however, is precisely one of the points of contention I wish to engage.

It has become fashionable in recent decades under an "antiessentialist" banner to deny anything common or fixed or natural in or about human beings.[16] This has been a somewhat understandable but unfortunate

14. Christian Smith, *Moral, Believing Animals: Human Personhood and Culture* (New York: Oxford University Press, 2003), 4.

15. "Quiddity" being the essential quality that makes something what it is, etymologically originating in Medieval Latin as *quidditās*, deriving from the Latin *quid* (what) and *-itās* (-ity), or "what-ity."

16. For one among many possible examples, see Stephan Fuchs, *Against Essentialism: A Theory of Culture and Society* (Cambridge, MA: Harvard University Press, 2001). For a minority counterview, see Steven Pinker, *The Blank Slate: The Modern Denial of Human Nature* (New York: Penguin Books, 2002).

intellectual move. I do believe there is some important element of truth in antiessentialist claims. But many versions of anthropological antiessentialism are often unclearly formulated and recklessly stated, in ways that I think are often confusing and sometimes simply ridiculous and self-defeating. Furthermore, the nugget of truth in recent antiessentialist arguments that is worth affirming had already been said quite well before by other theorists. Besides, the antiessentialist position of course assumes or is itself an answer to the very question I wish to raise—and a dubious answer at that. It therefore hardly seems reasonable for antiessentialists to champion their particular answer to the question and then, on the ground that the question itself is out of line, turn around and deny others the chance to try to answer it differently. Here, then, is my position on this point. Human beings do have an identifiable nature that is rooted in the natural world,[17] although the character of human nature is such that it gives rise to capacities to construct variable meanings and identities, which does complicate matters. My purpose in this book is to construct a theoretical model of the ontology of the nature of human being. That human nature is complex does not make an inquiry into what humans "are" pointless and naive, but rather only more interesting.[18] What is pointless,

17. Defining *nature* and therefore *natural* is notoriously difficult. This book is not about parsing out the meanings of those words, although I here clarify my usage. In this sentence, by *natural* I mean simply of the material or physical universe. However, the view of nature and the natural in this book's larger argument includes both material and immaterial realities (i.e., I am not a strict metaphysical materialist). I am saying, then, that nature comprises not only material but also immaterial realities—both are part of the natural. Examples of natural immaterial realities, by my account, are noncorporeal dimensions of human persons, memories, and many kinds of causal forces. To be clear, however, by *natural immaterial* in this book I do not mean *God*—which is where many dubious minds seem immediately to go when they hear the word *immaterial*—because God, in my understanding, is radically transcendent and so not bound by nature's space, time, material being, or laws. I also do not mean anything supernatural or paranormal or otherworldly, such as ghosts. This book is about human persons, which belong to the natural order. Consistent with that frame, however, the immaterial realities discussed here include something like human *souls*. But by that I simply mean the noncorporeal dimensions of human persons, which, again, belong to the natural world; by souls I do not mean spectral ghostly substances floating somewhere within material bodies. Readers with an aversion to the word *soul* are welcome to substitute for it the word psyche, spirit, atman, or whatever else captures the essential meaning. What matters in the end is not a particular word per se but rather getting right the theoretical ideas that represent the reality in question.

18. University of Durham (UK) anthropologist Michael Carrithers rightly states matters this way: "Is there in fact a fundamental, shared human nature? In one perspective, there must

in my view, rather, is to continue supporting disciplines that have, through their rhetorical excesses, dissolved away their subjects of study. Let others who believe they have something durable to investigate do so.

Against my position, I know that some readers (of a different variety from the antiessentialists) will push back by saying that the goal of theory is not primarily to accurately represent reality with words. The goal of theory instead, they will say, is to help explain and predict observable outcomes and events. And if to do that with success we need to make assumptions about humans that we know are oversimplified or even untrue, then we should. Among those in this camp are scholars known as theoretical instrumentalists. Thus, for instance, we know that people are not actually predictably self-interested, do not always hold stable sets of preference orderings, and often do not act to maximize their material benefit given their resources. However, this view believes that if making those assumptions enables us to statistically model economic behavior with high predictive power, then those are the assumptions we should make. My reply is that this view has simply started off with the wrong assumptions about the purpose of science and theory. Already the critical realist position—which I introduce more systematically in chapter 2—insists on establishing a different framework. It is not, in fact, the purpose of theory to help science predict observable outcomes and events. That supposition is the fruit of positivist empiricism, which we should toss into the dustbin. It may not even be the central purpose of theory to help science explain observable events, even though explanation understood differently is crucial to science. The point of science is to understand as accurately as possible what reality is and how it works. Theory is the conceptual tool we use to model the structures and causal mechanisms present in reality at different levels, whether directly observable or not. Thus, what we should want to know about human being is what is actually real about human being. And we are

---

be, for the very perception of diversity depends on its being a diversity of something. To be a species suggest that there are traits that we all share. . . . I start by asking the question: Given the diversity of human forms of life, what must be true of humans in general? . . . The sense of the phrase 'in general' [is]: we want to know not about each individual variant of human life, but about the ground on which all the variants are built. . . . An explanation of variability . . . must account for the very possibility of those different forms of life. It must show what all humans must share in order to be able to create diversity." Michael Carrithers, *Why Humans Have Cultures: Explaining Anthropology and Social Diversity* (New York: Oxford University Press, 1992), 3–5. Also see Eliot Deutsch, "The Comparative Study of the Self," in *Selves, People, and Persons*, ed. Rouner, 95–105.

misguided if we settle for the making of simplistic and inaccurate assumptions about the human in order to try to predict empirically observable events. At least that is the position of critical realism I am adopting.

Another line of objection to what I am setting up could be that, methodologically, science requires simplification, yet my project seems to be heading in the direction of increased complexity. Did not the fourteenth-century Franciscan friar, William of Occam, give us "Occam's razor," the principle that, all else being equal, we should make the fewest assumptions and rely on the fewest postulates and conceptual entities possible? Ought not our theories to be governed by the dictates of parsimony, so that we "shave off" with that razor as many nonessentials to explanation as feasible? *Pluralitas non est ponenda sine necessitate*—entities should not be multiplied unnecessarily. Why am I proposing to complexify sociology with what coming chapters will show to be critical realism's knotty terminology, personalism's subjective notions of human personhood, and the intangibles of phenomenological experience let in the door by Charles Taylor's antinaturalistic epistemology?

My answer is that Occam's razor is useful is far as it goes, but it should not be allowed to go too far. In response to it we might ask two questions. How can we compare rival explanations when all else involved is in fact not equal? And what counts as making for a "better" sociological explanation in the first place? The answers will be determined in part by the philosophy of social science we initially bring to the table. Critical realism asks us to discover our best account of what is true about reality. If it turns out that human and social reality is quite complicated, as in fact it does, then Occam's razor does not authorize us to hack away toward oversimplification for the sake of parsimony. What critical realism suggests, instead, is that the principle of parsimony must be balanced by the principle of "sufficient complexity." That means we ought to be willing to theorize with enough complexity to capture the important features of the real world that we are trying to understand. True, we should not proliferate theoretical concepts unnecessarily. But we should allow in as many theoretical entities as are needed to model and explain human and social reality well. This is, in fact, exactly what the natural sciences have had to do as they have come to better understand physical reality—the more apparent relative simplicity of classical physics, for instance, had to give way to, or at least be put into perspective by, the greater complexity of quantum mechanics and general relativity. In fact, if we look at the complexity of what contemporary physicists and cosmologists are currently theorizing to explain the universe (e.g., superstring theory, dark matter, wormholes, M-theory, etc.), one realizes in comparison that much of the social sciences have—in their "physics-envy" effort to live up to their often erroneous view of the natural sciences on which they want to be modeled—gone overboard with Occam's razor. B. F. Skinner was an outlandish case in point, we see now in retrospect. But there are many today still operating out of the same general paradigm of naturalistic scientism that gave rise to Skinner's program. The result is that much of the social sciences, informed by positivist empiricism, give us views of human persons and social life that are too simplistic. At root, naturalistic positivist empiricism has misled us. We need to discard it in favor of critical realism or something better.

The inquiry of this book, therefore, will not focus primarily on the frequency of and correlations among things we observe empirically that humans do. Rather, it will attempt to focus on the real ontological nature of human being—again, on what people *are*, however messy that may turn out to be. I am aware that such an inquiry will be considered by many in the social sciences and humanities to be quite odd, if not entirely impossible, irrelevant, or lunatic.[19] My reply is simply that I believe those objections are coming from paradigms that need to be seriously edited if not abandoned. In any case, when I survey the social sciences today, I am not so awed by what they have achieved that I feel obliged to ditch this inquiry because some there will balk at my project or claims. The social sciences could use some new, more adequate assumptions and frameworks. And I am willing, however tentatively, to try to venture the offering of something like that here.

Finally, I will in this book repeatedly make claims that certain things "are real." By this I mean simply those things that exist, are genuine elements of the totality of what is. But by what criteria can we determine whether something is real or not? I have already said that being of material substance does not entirely define what is real. Although all things with physical substance are real, not all real things have physical substance. Some immaterial things are real—including certain human mental objects (including reasons, intentions, and values), certain social facts (including a

19. As Mark C. Taylor writes, "For interpreters schooled in postmodernism and post-structuralism, the seemingly innocent question, 'What is . . . ?' is fraught with ontological and epistemological presuppositions that are deeply problematic." Taylor, ed., *Critical Terms for Religious Studies*, 6. I understand Taylor's problems, yet believe they stem from erroneous and unwarranted thinking within his own postmodernist framework.

variety of social and cultural structures), and, I believe, certain normative facts (including the one upon which all of science is built, namely, that it is better to know and believe what is true rather than what is false).[20] I have also said that certain things that are real are not visible to direct human observation, that not everything real is empirical (observed) or even actual (what happens in the world when real capacities are activated, even if we do not observe them). Reality has a deep dimension often operating below the surface of empirical experience. To think otherwise is to commit what critical realists call the "epistemic fallacy," namely, to reduce what is to what we can empirically observe. That is a debilitating move.

So if existing in the form of material substance or being visible to direct human observation are not the criteria for determination of the real, what is? Here I follow the critical realist lead in conceptualizing the real primarily, though not exclusively, according to a *causal* criterion instead of an exclusive perceptual or materialist criterion.[21] Most of the real, in short, possesses ordered and structured causal capacities to behave, under certain conditions, according to particular tendencies that exert influences that bring about changes in material or mental phenomena. The real may consist of material things, such as chemicals and hurricanes, or of nonmaterial entities, such as structures of memory or identity or personhood. What matters in establishing their reality, in most cases,[22] is their possessing or being endowed with some properties, mechanisms, forces, charac-

20. See Charles Larmore, *The Morals of Modernity* (Cambridge: Cambridge University Press, 1996), 89–117; also see Russ Shafer-Landau, *Moral Realism: A Defense* (New York: Oxford University Press, 2003). Roy Bhaskar writes: "That truth *is* a good . . . is not only a condition of moral discourse, it is a condition of any discourse at all. Commitment to truth and consistency apply to factual as much as to value discourse; and so cannot be seized upon as a concealed (value) premise." Bhaskar, *The Possibility of Naturalism* (New York: Routledge, 2000), 63). Joseph Margolis, a nonreductive, antidualism materialist who takes emergence seriously, makes a similar argument in *Persons and Minds: The Prospects of Nonreductive Materialism* (Dordrecht: D. Reidel, 1978).

21. Bhaskar, *The Possibility of Naturalism*, 12; Margaret Archer, *Realist Social Theory* (Cambridge: Cambridge University Press, 1995), 14. Perception plays an important role in the larger practices of science, but must be supplemented by theoretical conceptualizations and mental operations of inference and attribution. Also see Margaret Somers, "'We're No Angels': Realism, Rational Choice, and Relationality in Social Science," *American Journal of Sociology* 104, no. 3 (1989): especially 743–45.

22. I have said that the causal criterion is the primary "though not exclusive" means of defining the real, that a capacity to exert causal effects is what determines the reality of things "in most cases." This stopping short of establishing causality as the single condition defining reality reflects my being amenable to, though not settled about, the possibility—as a result

teristics, powers, tendencies, or interactive relations capable of producing causal effects in the world.[23] Entities that do are real; they are the things that constitute the intransitive objects of scientific inquiry.[24] They exist and operate objectively, whether or not we are aware of them or understand or conceptualize them well. The task of science, both natural and social, in all of this is to identify these real entities and their structures and causal powers and to learn how they operate in ways that produce events in the world. To do this, we rely on a combination of our theoretical conceptualizations that mediate our experiences of the data of events, our observations of patterns of events happening at the empirical surface of reality, and our cognitive reasoning abilities of inference and attribution[25] to connect what we see at the surface with what is real operating beneath the surface. Fundamental "retroductive" questions running through all such inquiry are: What must be real and operative, even if it is not observable, in order to explain the events we observe? What cannot be eliminated without making the object of inquiry cease to exist as it does?

What Follows

The first two chapters present my opening case for critical realist personalism. Chapter 1 advances and develops the core of my argument about human personhood. I argue that human beings as they exist in the world embody a particular constitution—they have a human nature rooted in nature more broadly. Human bodies interacting with their environments give rise through emergence to a constellation of powerful physical and

---

of Nick Wolterstorff's prodding—that a small number of real entities may possess no causal capacities—numbers, for example.

23. To be clear, throughout this book I refer to causal capacities and causal mechanisms, which are not the same things. Causal capacities concern powers or abilities that belong to real entities but which may or may not be exercised in various circumstances. Causal mechanisms are (usually unobservable) processes and forces exerted, through the triggering of combinations of various causal capacities, to produce particular facts, events, or other outcomes in the world.

24. Below I will qualify this discussion by introducing an important distinction between two fundamentally different kinds of reality, following philosopher John Searle (*The Construction of Social Reality* [New York: Free Press, 1995]) in calling them brute reality versus institutional reality; but the emphasis on a causal criterion of reality here, which applies to both brute and institutional reality, is an adequate point of departure for the present.

25. Including the logical operations of retroduction and abduction, which I explain later.

mental capacities. Those capacities endow humans as real causal agents capable of intentionally affecting outcomes in the world. Those causal capacities interact in complex ways to give rise through emergence again to the "higher" level reality of human personhood. Personal being subsists irreducibly at a level of existence that transcends the lower level elements that sustain it, being characterized by properties, abilities, and qualities unique to human personhood proper. In short, human persons are actual, new realities existent in the world and universe, what we might even think of—if we were not so allergic to the term—as embodied soul-like realities, emergent from the material world from which they arose.[26] It is those characteristics of the reality of personhood that we have in mind when we call human beings *persons*, when we do not call rocks, flowers, or cats *persons*. That is, an ontologically real—though not absolute—dividing line exists between that which is personal and that which is not personal, between an "I," a "you," and an "it." This understanding of human personhood as a particular kind of creature provides, I hope to show later, the link to the normative and moral (and thus political) in human life and society.

Crucial in all of this is the recognition of the essentially *socially interactive* nature of human constitution and the emergence of personhood. Corporeal bodies in material environments alone cannot give rise to normal human persons. Personhood is dependent in emergent origin and continuation upon intersubjective social interaction, communication, and communion with other human persons. Human persons are irreducibly socially constituted, even though at lower levels of reality they are composed of particles of matter. This, too, is a fact of nature that in the realm of human life creates a link between the descriptive and the normative, fact and value, the scientific and the political—the implications of which I will try to unpack in later chapters.

Chapter 2 introduces three key theoretical perspectives that I bring to bear as intellectual resources to develop the argument in this book: critical realism, personalist theory, and an antinaturalistic phenomenological epistemology. I am reluctant to jump into such abstract background issues so early in a book. But little of my argument will make sense or have a chance of persuading readers if I do not explain the three background theoretical perspectives that frame and inform my case. Chapter 1 will have already drawn heavily on them. So I find it necessary to provide at least

---

26. See footnote 30 below for elaboration.

an introductory outline of these three theoretical resources sooner rather than later. Readers who find the material difficult to work through should not be deterred from pressing on into the rest of the book. Grasping the assumptions and arguments in chapter 2 will pay off in understanding the case made in every other chapter.

Chapters 3 through 5 turn in a critical mode to evaluate from the perspective of critical realist personalism other important theoretical and methodological approaches in the social sciences, particularly in sociology. As a means to hammer out the theory I want to develop in this book, I critically engage the three significant paradigms of social constructionism, network structuralism, and variables analysis. Chapter 3 examines, from the perspective of critical realist personalism, theories of social constructionism, a significant perspective in sociology that has important implications for personhood. This chapter describes and critiques the social constructionist perspective, focusing especially on problems in what appear to be strong versions of that theory. It analyzes the misguided theoretical moves that led to strong social constructionism's problems and poses an alternative approach in order to develop a social constructionist theory coherent with critical realist personalism. Toward that end, chapter 3 explores how human knowledge might be deemed true even though it is culturally and conceptually mediated, describes different meanings and modes of reality needed to be distinguished by a realist(ic) constructionism, and reflects on the implications of the foregoing for our broader understanding of personhood. By the end of chapter 3, we will have begun to fill out what exactly is "real" and "personal" in critical realist personalism and why that matters. Between chapters 3 and 4 I redirect my attention in a brief excursus about the basic epistemological question of our human ability to know things that are true and to make statements that are true—both of which I consider within the realm of human possibilities.

Chapter 4 moves on to examine the theories and analytical commitments of network structuralism. Here, again, I describe the distinctive approach of this paradigm, identify what is valuable in it, and critique what is problematic about it from the perspective of critical realist personalism. My purpose is to evaluate an important analytical approach in sociology and to sharpen the understanding of critical realist personalism. Chapter 5 carries out a similar critical engagement with the dominant form of scholarship in the social sciences today: variables analysis. I argue that variables analysis is beset with serious problems but, when properly framed theoretically and conducted in ways consistent with that sound theoretical frame, the variables approach may provide a useful tool in efforts to understand and explain the social world.

Chapters 6, 7, and 8 turn toward more theoretically constructive ends. Chapter 6 develops an account of the ontological nature and causal sources of social structures in human life. I focus on the reality of human finitude and limitations and their importance to a theory of social structure. Human personhood and its capacities as described must also be understood as operating within natural limits, constraints, and bounds. Humans are profoundly finite creatures, in both body and mind. The tensions arising between human capacities and human limits—between the vastly capable and severely finite in human life—give rise through emergence to creative patterns of lived practice that often solidify into what we call social structures. Social structures are not agreed upon contracts made by autonomous exchange partners, nor are they illusions of facticity appearing falsely to socially constructed and constructing actors as more real than they are. Social structures are real entities with causal powers generated through emergence from the tension created between human capacities and limits as given by the nature of the real world. In this way, the reality of the social again impinges powerfully on human life and personhood in ways that create potential links between the analytical and the normative, between fact and value, between social science and the moral and political good.

Chapters 7 and 8 shift away from sociological theory proper toward moral philosophy and philosophically informed social theory concerning what is good in human life, how and why it is that humans have dignity, and what the moral implications are for building good social structures. In chapter 7 I develop an account of what is good in light of the proper teleological ends of human personhood, elaborating an essentially Aristotelian account of moral virtues, character, and discernment. I first seek to blunt the force of the traditional "is-ought problem" and argue against that concern that we can indeed know what we as humans ought to think and do significantly in part by understanding what is true about reality. The understanding of human personhood advanced in chapter 1 and developed through the rest of the book thus in the end informs our knowledge about what the good in life consists of, how people ought to live, and what a good society looks like. In chapter 8 I advance and defend the personalist insistence on the fact of human dignity, rejecting skeptical views of the reality of human dignity. I develop an account of human dignity that relies on the crucial notion of personal emergence that I think neither shares the standard vulnerabilities of capacities-based theories of dignity, on the one hand, nor relies necessarily on (though is compatible with) theistic accounts of dignity that in theory guard against those standard vulnerabilities, on the other hand. My approach relocates the ground of dignity not in human capacities per se but in the reality of personhood, which exists with characteristic and irreducible properties at a higher level of reality than human capacities. I then attempt some additional intellectual moves to safeguard the dignity of humans whose personhood is undeveloped, damaged, or significantly deteriorated through immaturity, injury, malformation, disabilities, or old age. Finally, I close by indicating ways that the natural dignity of human persons suggests implications for social scientific understanding, thus helping to reconnect fact and value.

A few last specific comments on what follows before jumping in. First, in subsequent chapters I engage and evaluate a variety of sociological and other theorists, some of whom will strike readers as extremists operating on the intellectual fringe. These are people who seem to be playing what Harry Collins and Steven Yearly call "epistemological chicken"—as if they were accepting dares to see who can take intellectual matters to increasingly extreme and risky positions.[27] Am I showing myself to be crazy by arguing with crazy people? Am I silly for criticizing silly arguments? No. First of all, with few exceptions, the scholars I engage are not crazy and their arguments are far from silly. As I hope to show, these are very smart people who simply make wrong arguments because of the erroneous and misleading presuppositions from which they being their thinking. They deserve to be engaged in order to identify the underlying sources of their mistakes so that we can think more clearly. Furthermore, whether or not the ideas I critique in this book are crazy or silly, they still remain subtly influential today among many sane and serious other people. Even if the ideas I criticize seem to be out on fringes, they shape the perspectives and thoughts of more reasonable people—scholars, students, and nonacademics alike—and still influence more moderate academics who would never directly subscribe to their more radical programs. It is not so easy to disassociate fringe theorists from more moderate positions that remain—knowingly or not—within the orbit of their large influence. We need, I argue in what follows, to become more aware of the intellectual lineages and logics that often connect both fringe and moderate versions of theory and scholarship and, in some cases, to make decisive intellectual

27. Harry Collins and Steven Yearley, "Epistemological Chicken," in *Science as Practice and Culture*, ed. Andrew Pickering (Chicago: University of Chicago Press, 1992), 301–27. Thanks to Omar Lizardo for suggesting this image to me.

breaks that allow us to head in new, more fruitful directions. By helping to break from certain extremist influences, I hope to contribute toward "cleaning up the middle" of a great deal of mainstream scholarship that otherwise possesses real value.

Second, while the approach of this book is often critical, its larger purpose is actually constructive and affirmative. My goal is to articulate what I think is a better account of not only what sociology ought to do but also what sociology often already actually does well but does not always realize or have an adequate language by which to name it. The significance and value of much smart and important sociological scholarship is, in my view, often obscured by many of the impoverished terms and frameworks of contemporary mainstream sociology. We sell ourselves short and underestimate our disciplinary capacities by presupposing the wrong philosophies of science and neglecting to take seriously the nature of the human subject. My hope is that this book, as an exercise in retrieval[28] and recasting, will provide an alternative theoretical context and language by which better to identify and appreciate what is truly good in sociology and steer away from what is not so good. It is also worth noting that in developing the argument of this book, I rely on thought-experiment kinds of examples that philosophers tend to use and also on more concrete examples from social life that sociologists tend to reference and appreciate. I ask my sociological readers to indulge the thought-experiment illustrations, whether or not they are philosophically inclined, because I think they make points important for sociologists to grasp.

Third, it is worth acknowledging up front that matters such as the nature of human personhood are not only complicated but also in many ways ultimately mysterious. We will not be able to dissect personhood as we dissect frogs or represent it with statistical equations the way we do certain physical forces and processes. What we are addressing is not an "it" but rather a thou, a you, an I. There is a mystery of being here[29] that we may know tacitly or better in certain ways other than social theory and philosophy. People may have long plumbed the depths of the nature of persons through story, poetry, and parable not only because humans in the past were more "primitive," but also perhaps because those modes of understanding and communication access truths that discursive analysis cannot. At some point in our exploration, the subject/object of inquiry becomes

---

28. This approach is shaped by Charles Taylor's *Sources of the Self.*

29. Gabriel Marcel, *The Mystery of Being* (South Bend, IN: St. Augustine's Press, 1950).

ineffable. Analytical writing ceases to be able to express what is real and what we know about it. That should not count as failure. That does not mean the inquiry is futile. That does not make it any less scholarly than any other reasoned, systematic inquiry. It simply signals something important about the nature of personhood under consideration, the need for inquiry and its mode of conduct to be governed by the nature of the subject in question, the limits of science when it comes to the human, and the epistemic humility we need in seeking to understand reality. Declaring ineffability when matters truly are ineffable is not an intellectual cop-out. It is a humble acknowledgement of reality as it actually exists and of our finite humanity in grasping it. All of that said, however, I intend to do my best to plumb the character of personhood in the mode of social theorizing and analytical description as deeply as I can take it.

Fourth, examinations of the nature of human personhood raise a host of practical moral and ethical questions that are particularly relevant at the margins of life—at the start and end of human life and in the midst of life when human organisms are damaged. American culture in recent decades has been wracked by difficult conflicts—over abortion, stem cell research, physician assisted suicide, euthanasia, and so on—related to these marginal cases. Chapter 8 in this book does begin to develop an argument that has implications for those issues. But the vast majority of this book is not concerned with marginal cases of personhood. Rather, to achieve best this book's central purpose, which is to engage sociological theory—not medical ethics and bioethics—I intentionally focus on the most self-evident cases of the most fully developed expressions of human personhood. The chapters that follow concentrate on the most obviously robust, fully expressed versions of personhood, and on descriptions of human persons at the height of their normal development and functioning. That less disputable, less contentious version of the person is what best enables me to make my case about sociological theory.

Finally, in all of this, to reinforce points already made, the case I will develop is resolutely realist ontologically, antireductionistic methodologically, and antifoundationalist epistemologically. It is naturally bent toward opposing naturalism, positivism, and scientistic empiricism. But it is also hostile to strong versions of constructivism, idealism, postmodernism, and relativism. My position is, on the one hand, that a reality exists independently of our consciousness of it, which science is often well positioned to understand; yet also, on the other hand, that human life involves a crucial dimension we must recognize and account for, which all but the most recent generations of intellectuals of our species have called "soul," "heart," or "spirit." Human beings, I will suggest, are free, ensouled creatures of a particular kind, with the kind of nature about which we must get over our mental and emotional difficulties admitting if we hope possibly to understand ourselves.[30] Yet humans are also material, embodied animals, nurtured and sustained in a physical world governed by causal powers and laws and their natural effects that we cannot simply deconstruct away. When it comes to the human, therefore, reductionistic moves toward either the physical or the mental, the material or the ideal, the corporeal or the spiritual are unacceptable and self-defeating. Humans are embodied souls who can only be well understood and explained in light of that complex reality.

30. To be perfectly clear, such a view has no necessary connection with religion, ghosts, substance dualism, or immortality after death—one could be a total secularist and believe in the soul as defined here. Sorting through various historical, philosophical, theological, and scientific understandings of what a "soul" (or *psyche*, spirit, *jiva*, atman, and such—depending on the particular culture that is seeking to describe what I think is the same human reality) is or might be would require writing an entirely separate book, if not a series of books, which I do not intend to undertake. Nor for purposes of this book do I need to adopt and defend one definitive position about the soul or resolve the many debates and problems associated with the long history of thinking about the soul. I do, however, take a broadly realist rather than an actualist or ontogenetic approach to soul. This means I understand the soul as being and having a single, definite nature in continuity across all stages of life, which unfolds and can be and is expressed differently across the entire life course. That contrasts with viewing the soul as a higher-end aspect of human experience that comes into being developmentally and is exercised or instantiated in an actual state of consciousness or through the actual exercise of powers. With that frame in mind, suffice it for present purposes to say that by a personal soul I mean something like the mysterious though real and vital principle of life—of vital operations in living beings—that endows each particular life with organization and integrated unity, continuity, identity, and direction, thereby providing specificity, integration, and developmental direction to each particular being. The soul by this account, as it relates to this book, is a quality and reality existing ontologically prior to and formative of the matter and parts of the person—something like Aristotle's form of the body. Souls do not come into existence—even emergently—as a result of parts operating in certain ways in temporal development. Rather, soul is the initial and primordial life-organizing and constituting principle that defines, sustains, and directs the temporal unfolding and developing of parts and selves. In short, *agere sequitur esse*—action follows being. It is also inaccurate, on this account, to say that humans "have" souls; rather, we *are* souls, embodied souls (see Ric Machuga, *In Defense of the Soul: What It Means to Be Human* [Grand Rapids, MI: Brazos Press, 2002]). Finally, while I would not claim that all arguments against the soul are necessarily self-defeating, I would suggest that the making of such arguments reveals the reality of the soul of those who make them. Thus, as strange as soul talk is for most social scientists, it is hard for me to imagine a reasonable account of the person that could deny the reality of human souls as defined here.

PART I

Initial Arguments

CHAPTER ONE

The Emergence of Personhood

In this chapter I explain what the reality of human personhood is and how it is constituted. To do this, I first explain the crucial concept of emergence. Then I describe a set of human causal capacities that are emergent properties of the human bodies existing in their natural and social environments. Following that, I explain how those emergent properties interact to compose an emergently new, real, and central aspect of human being: personhood. I then define what I mean by *person* and elaborate some of the features and implications of my account.

Emergence against Reductionism

It is impossible to understand properly the world or ourselves as human beings without understanding the idea and reality of emergence.[1] Emergence refers to the process of constituting a new entity with its own particular

---

1. The recent literature on emergence includes Phillip Clayton and Paul Davies, *The Re-Emergence of Emergence: The Emergentist Hypothesis from Science to Religion* (New York: Oxford University Press, 2006); Nancey Murphy and William Stoeger, *Evolution and Emergence: Systems, Organisms, Persons* (New York: Oxford University Press, 2007); Michael Polanyi, "Emergence," in *The Tacit Dimension* (1966; Gloucester, MA: Peter Smith, 1983), 29–52; Berth Danermark et al., *Explaining Society: Critical Realism in the Social Sciences* (New York: Routledge, 2002); Margaret Archer, *Realist Social Theory: The Morphogenetic Approach* (Cambridge: Cambridge University Press, 1995); R. Keith Sawyer, "Durkheim's Dilemma: Toward a Sociology of Emergence," *Sociological Theory* 20, no. 2 (2002): 227–47, especially 232. Peter Berger and Thomas Luckmann's notion of the dialectic—through externalization, objectification, and internalization—might be interpreted as a protoemergentist model. Berger and Luckmann, *The Social Construction of Reality: A Treatise in the Sociology of Knowledge* (Garden City, NY: Anchor Books, 1966).

characteristics through the interactive combination of other, different entities that are necessary to create the new entity but that do not contain the characteristics present in the new entity.[2] Emergence involves the following: First, two or more entities that exist at a "lower" level interact or combine. Second, that interaction or combination serves as the basis of some new, real entity that has existence at a "higher" level. Third, the existence of the new higher-level entity is fully dependent upon the two or more lower-level entities interacting or combining, as they could not exist without doing so. Fourth, the new, higher-level entity nevertheless possesses characteristic qualities (e.g., structures, qualities, capacities, textures, mechanisms) that cannot be reduced to those of the lower-level entities that gave rise to the new entity possessing them. When these four things happen, emergence has happened. The whole is more than the sum of its parts.[3]

This may sound abstract and complicated, but emergence happens all the time in our everyday lives. The reality that we routinely live in is composed of many levels of emergent phenomena and properties. A simple example will help to get us started in seeing this. Among the elements in the periodic table on the wall of any chemistry classroom are hydrogen and oxygen. These two elements can exist separately as H and O and,

2. Emergence, to be clear, is antidualistic, against dualism. It is a strategy or method designed to explain the existence of very different qualities and features in a reality that is understood to be unified, not dualistic.

3. Hodgson's fascinating history of the concept of emergence in social science traces its roots to the thinking of Hegel, Marx, Engels, Comte, and Mill. The term *emergence* was first developed in the last quarter of the nineteenth century by the philosopher George Lewes and later (the 1920s and 1930s) by the evolutionary biologist Conwy Lloyd Morgan, who in turn influenced others, including Alfred Whitehead at Harvard and Thorstein Veblen at Chicago. Through Veblen and his student Wesley Mitchell, the idea of emergence significantly shaped the Keynesian macroeconomics of the interwar period. Talcott Parsons was somewhat influenced by Whitehead on emergence, though his use of the idea was not systematically developed. The dominance of logical positivism and growing empiricism, however, marginalized the influence of emergence theory until Michael Polanyi, Karl Popper, and Ernst Mayr revitalized the idea in the latter half of the twentieth century. From there, developments in chaos theory, complexity theories of order from chaos, computer simulations revealing the emergence of order and other higher level properties in complex systems, and the ideas of "bifurcation points" and "butterfly effects" further validated the idea of emergence and undercut reductionism. Geoffrey Hodgson, "The Concept of Emergence in Social Science: Its History and Importance," *Emergence* 2, no. 4 (2000): 65–77. For an argument that emergence was central to all of Durkheim's theorizing, see R. Keith Sawyer, "Durkheim's Dilemma: Toward a Sociology of Emergence," *Sociological Theory* 20, no. 2 (2002): 227–47.

when they do, possess certain characteristic properties. Both, for example, help to inflame fires. However, we also know that when two hydrogen molecules combine with one oxygen molecule, something new comes into existence: water, H_2O. Water cannot exist apart from the hydrogen and oxygen that compose it, but is entirely dependent upon them simply to be. However, in their combination, the hydrogen and oxygen give rise to a truly new thing that is quite unlike either H or O, whether taken alone or as a sum of the separate parts H and O. Water, for example, has the characteristic of wetness, while hydrogen and oxygen do not. Water, furthermore, has the capacity to extinguish fires, while H and O feed fires. Water is the emergent reality brought about by a particular combination of hydrogen and oxygen. Water is very real and unique in its existence. It is composed of definite substances. But it is irreducible to that of which it is composed. Literally and truly something new has come into existence that is more than the sum of its parts. "The emphasis is not on the unfolding of something already in being but on the outspringing of something that has hitherto not been in being."[4]

Emergence is also evident at the subatomic and atomic levels up to the molecular and chemical levels. Three quarks, which are fast moving points of energy, when related to one another by the force of gluons, compose protons and neutrons, depending on the combination of up quarks and down quarks. The interaction of protons and neutrons with electrons in particular ways through positive and negative electrical charges constitutes through emergence the existence of atoms. Atoms are characterized by particular structures and properties unique at the atomic level that are not existent in the mere sum total of their subatomic parts. It is from the *relation* or *interaction* of parts—not merely the parts themselves—that emergent properties have existence. From there, we know that different kinds of atoms combine through the interactive sharing of electrons to form molecules. As emergent entities existing at a new level, molecules

4. C. Lloyd Morgan, *Emergent Evolution*, 2nd ed. (London: Williams and Norgate, 1927), 112. Mayr extends this idea to the notion of unpredictability in suggesting that the characteristics of a complex system "cannot (not even in theory) be deduced from the most complete knowledge of the components, taken separately or in other partial combinations. In other words, when such systems are assembled from their components, new characteristics of the new whole emerge that could not have been predicted from a knowledge of the components." Ernst Mayr, "How Biology Differs from the Physical Sciences," in *Evolution at a Crossroads: The New Biology and the New Philosophy of Science*, ed. David Depew and Bruce Weber (Cambridge, MA: MIT Press, 1985), 58.

also reflect particular characteristic structures and capacities, depending on their type—that is, upon the relationships of the parts that compose them—that are not directly reducible to the sum total characteristics of their parts. The formation of water molecules is one example. From this level, chemical substances emerge through various interactions of different molecules of elements. Furthermore, depending on the amount of energy present in these substances, the same chemical entities can take solid, liquid, or gaseous forms. Again, the distinctive qualities of solidness, liquidity, and gaseousness are not present in the atomic particles that compose the substances but are emergent properties from particular kinds of relationships among the particles. A reductionistic perspective would assert that things like gold and radon and silicon consist merely of so many protons, neutrons, and electrons of particular sorts. But by trying to understand entities by reducing them to their component parts existing at lower levels, reductionists miss what are often the most important qualities of things, their irreducible emergent properties.[5] As Michael Polanyi observed, "You cannot derive a vocabulary from phonetics; you cannot derive the grammar of language from its vocabulary; a correct use of grammar does not account for good style; and a good style does not provide the content of a piece of prose. . . . It is impossible to represent the organizing principles of a higher level by the laws governing its isolated particulars."[6]

My examples of emergence so far have operated at very low levels of reality. But emergence happens at every level of the real, including massive systems of regional and planetary force. Take hurricanes, for example. Water molecules in particular ocean regions are transformed into vapor

5. It is crucial here to distinguish *reductionism* from *reduction*. I am not here opposing *methodological* reduction (the partial decomposition of elements at one level into parts at a different level for purposes of systematic analysis) per se, which is an essential aspect of science when appropriately done; my argument rather contradicts both *ontological* reductionism, which fails to acknowledge and understand the complexly stratified nature of reality, and *causal* reductionism, which routinely seeks to explain facts and events by more basic features and causes operating at lower levels. See Geoffrey Hodgson, "The Concept of Emergence in Social Science: Its History and Importance," *Emergence* 2, no. 4 (2000): 73.

6. Polanyi, *The Tacit Dimension*, 36. The reductionistic analogue in the discipline of economics is evident in the "microfoundations revolution" of the 1960s and beyond, which rebuffed much of Keynesian macroeconomics. S. A. T. Rizvi, "The Microfoundations Project in General Equilibrium Theory," *Cambridge Journal of Economics* 18, no. 4 (1994): 357–77. More generally, see L. Udéhn, *Methodological Individualism: A Critical Appraisal* (Uppsala, Sweden: Uppsala University Reprographics Centre, 1987).

by heat energy and move spatially upward in massive volumes of moist air, creating bands of cumulonimbus clouds, which are deflected by the Co-riolis effect (generated by the earth's rotation) to form a whirling cylinder. This rising air is replaced below by new air rushing in from surrounding spaces, creating strong winds. Condensing water vapors in the rising moist air give off immense amounts of heat energy, fueling the system's power, which produces torrential rain, hail, and high winds. Thus, the simple mo-lecular elements of air and water, interacting under particular conditions of heat energy and planetary motion, give rise at the meteorological level to the new, emergent reality we call the hurricane. The ontological system and causal powers of a hurricane exist as real at their own level, with great effect. An average single hurricane lasts ten days, extends at one time over hundreds of miles, produces more energy than a nuclear explosion, and produces winds of up to 150 miles per hour—enough, in some cases, to cripple the economies of entire countries. To a reductionist, hurricanes are nothing more than air and water vapor in particular energy states. But, as anyone who has ever lived through a hurricane knows, hurricanes are real weather-system entities possessing emergent properties that are irreduc-ible to the sum total of their constituent parts. Reductionism misses the most important facts about hurricanes, because it is blind to emergence.

My examples of emergence so far are also all of a natural type. That is, the processes that give rise to their emergent properties inhere in the causal capacities of nature and the natural laws that govern them and so do not require intentional intervention by sentient agents to make them happen.[7] Emergence can also happen by design, however, as the intended outcome of intentional intervention by purposeful actors. People can, for instance, arrange particular elements of matter together in ways that compose entirely new entities characterized by novel causal powers. The

---

7. The so-called Copenhagen interpretation of quantum mechanics in physics, as I under-stand it, suggests, to the contrary, in theory at least, that observation itself affects the subject of study at certain levels of reality, namely, that measurement causes a change in the state of the measured particle. This interpretation is widely accepted among quantum mechanics physi-cists but remains contested by alternative accounts. See James Cushing, *Quantum Mechan-ics: Historical Contingency and the Copenhagen Hegemony* (Chicago: University of Chicago Press, 1994). Christopher Norris, a former postmodernist writer and now confirmed critical realist, offers an introductory critical realist response to quantum mechanics in his, "Critical Realism and Quantum Mechanics: Some Introductory Bearings," in *After Postmodernism: An Introduction to Critical Realism*, ed. José López and Garry Potter (New York: Athlone, 2001): 116–27.

computer on which I am writing this sentence, for example, is just such
an emergent entity. Viewed reductionistically, my computer is little more
than a collection of small pieces of plastic, metal, silicon, other miscel-
laneous materials, and electrical energy. But through emergence, those
pieces of material and energy give rise to another single entity with amazing capabilities: the computer. The emergent properties of my computer
have existence not because they inhere in the component parts that compose them. They do so because those component materials are related to
one another by careful design to work together as a single system in order
to produce those properties. The visual, informational, and computational
abilities of my computer are new realities, yet not present in the sum total
of the inputs of which my computer is constituted. It is only through their
systemic relationships that those amazing abilities have being. The novel
reality takes existence not through the parts but through their relationships and interactions. Reality is thus significantly constituted through
relationality, not merely composition.

Emergence also explains the reality of social structures and institutions. I examine how and why this happens in depth in chapter 6. But a
simple illustration of an emergent social fact may be helpful. Consider any
system of social inequality—say of racial segregation. Through the interactive relations over time of individual people (whom our model assumes
are seeking security, status, and material advantage), certain categories of
difference become culturally defined (e.g., skin color, continent of origin)
by which categorical groups are distinguished (e.g., white, Indian, black).
Through the exercise of symbolic and material exclusion and coercion,
these come to enjoy different types and amounts of socially valued goods
(e.g., access to productive capital, use of best facilities, access to higher
education). This, then, brings into existence particular social structures
of relations and difference that possess new causal capacities—to segre-
gate, allocate, control, legitimate, socialize, and otherwise socially reproduce itself—that operate at the distinctively *social* (not individual) level
through the ongoing interaction of all of the parts. Note that—contra the
view of strong methodological individualism and atomism—those causal
capacities are not present in the mere sum total of the parts and cannot be
adequately explained by reducing the system to its component elements,
because the social structure is a real emergent product of the *relationality*
of parts and not simply the features of each part added up. In the end, such
emergent social realities can possess immense powers of "downward causation" to influence the consciousness and actions of the individual people
from which they emerge—often in ways that may not be consistent with

the natural, rational, or even actual interests or desires of many of the people involved. This is because social systems and structures are emergent facts, existent above the individual or personal level, at the higher level of the social. Studying when, how, and why this operates is the central task of the discipline of sociology.

Examples of emergent realities of many types and at many levels could be multiplied. We could discuss living cells as singular emergent realities with new causal powers composed of but not reducible to the chemical and subcell constituents that compose them. We could note how particular kinds of cells combine to make specific bodily organs as new biological entities with their own causal abilities—the human eye, for instance. We could observe how from the systemic interaction of various organs and other tissues single bodily organisms—our own human bodies, for example—exist ontologically, endowed with their own causal capacities that are irreducible to the organic components of which the bodies consist. From bodies, human causal capacities are made real, such as language use, as I describe below, from which the reality of personhood emerges.[8] At yet a higher level, from the ongoing interaction of human persons, social structures and institutions emerge, as I describe in chapter 6. Such examples of emergence rising through higher and higher levels of reality could be proliferated. The underlying point is that reality is not flat. And explanation is not always best achieved through reductionistic methods. Much that is real enjoys characteristic properties and capacities at one level and yet not explicable in terms of the characteristics and capacities present at the levels below and from which the higher-level realities above are composed. Through the relation or interaction of component parts, entirely new realities have existence.[9]

    8. Joseph Margolis makes a similar argument in *Persons and Minds: The Prospects of Nonreductive Materialism* (Dordrecht: D. Reidel, 1978). Margolis writes about personal capacities and persons themselves as "culturally emergent" out of "material embodiment" (7–9). Also see Hans Jonas, *The Phenomenon of Life: Toward a Philosophical Biology* (Chicago: University of Chicago Press, 1966).

    9. These arguments notwithstanding, social theorists do not share a consensus about emergence. Émile Durkheim believed in emergence while Anthony Giddens, for example, appears not to, along with most strict methodological individualists. Compare Durkheim, *The Rules of Sociological Method* (London: Macmillan, 1983), 39–40 to Giddens, *The Constitution of Society* (Berkeley and Los Angeles: University of California Press, 1984), 171–72. Some theorists who are not comfortable with emergence as a strong ontological claim prefer a weaker approach described as *supervenience*, which allows for a moderated form of reductionism and maintains the ontological precedence of the micro over the macro level. See, e.g., Kieran Healy, "Conceptualizing Constraint: Mouzelis, Archer, and the Concept of Social Structure,"

To help understand the concept of emergence I have represented it in graphic form in figure 1. Such pictorial representations can help us grasp concepts about abstract realities that words may have difficulty conveying. At the same time, pictures like these risk oversimplifying and misleading as much as providing insight and understanding. For instance, the idea is presented as taking place in four phases, but in truth at least three of those phases often normally happen together, simultaneously and continually.[10] For this reason I have called them *analytic*—as opposed to temporal— phases. Furthermore, as I explain next, the "levels" of the entities existing and emerging in the process represented in figure 1 are not spatially distinct, as if emergent entities and properties exist at a higher altitude than the parts from which they emerge. No, the levels discussed are *analytic* levels, which, to make it more abstract, we might also call dimensions, with the entire process happening in what we might call multidimensional unified space. Moreover, the arrows running in a clockwise circle through the analytic phases could suggest that emergence operates as a recurrent cycle in which a completed phase 4 returns matters to their original state at the start of phase 1. But that, too, would be wrong. "Upward" emergence brings new entities into ontological being that possess capacities of maintenance and reproduction that keep them existing at their higher levels for long periods of time. No cycle needs to return to the beginning to complete a rotation. With such cautions in mind, figure 1 offers an analytical breakdown of the emergence process: interactive parts at the lower level give rise to new, emergent entities at a higher level that entail new properties and capacities, including often the capacity to act with downward causation to transform the parts from which the emergent entity

Sociology 32, no. 3 (1998): 509–22; R. Keith Sawyer, "Emergence in Sociology: Contemporary Philosophy of Mind and Some Implications for Sociological Theory," *American Journal of Sociology* 107 (2001): 551–85; Alexander Rosenberg, "On the Interanimation of Micro and Macroeconomics," *Philosophy of the Social Sciences* 6, no. 1 (1976): 35–53; Jaegwon Kim, "Supervenience as a Philosophical Concept," *Metaphilosophy* 21 (1990): 1–27.

10. Phases 1–3 normally happen simultaneously in time. Phase 4—downward causation—may (but need not) take place temporally after emergence has happened. For example, a group of people may form, out of the members of their group, a club to pursue a particular interest. Once formed, the club becomes an emergent social institution with properties and capacities greater than the sum of its parts, even though it is completely and continually reliant on all of its parts to be what it is. Five years later, however, a set of upstart members might use the authority structure of the club to expel the founding members, in which case an emergent causal capacity of the social institution created through emergence would have acted with downward causal capacity to change some of the parts that had theretofore constituted the emergent institution.

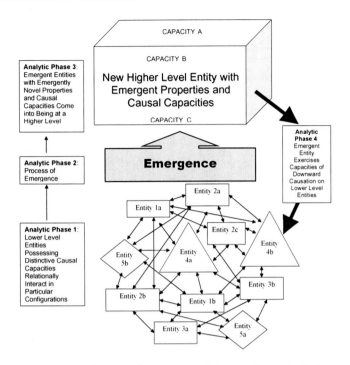

FIGURE 1. A simple model of upward emergence and downward causation in four analytic phases.

arose. The transformation of two-dimensional rectangles, triangles, and diamonds through emergence into the three-dimensional box is intended to signify the added complexity and powers of the reality that comes into being through emergence.

Before going any further, I must emphasize two crucial clarifications. First, to be plain from the start, the critical realist language of *higher* and *lower* should *not* be read literally as referencing spatial relations or evaluatively as judgments of better and worse. Higher is a metaphor highlighting "movements" of emergence through different strata of the real. This can be simplified by thinking in terms of an "upwardly moving" process, in keeping with established critical realist discourse. The truth, however, is something more like multiple dimensions of the same reality in space and time, with each level of reality nested, embedded, or constituted directly within each of the others, such that we might also or otherwise speak of multidimensional unified spaces. Second, it is crucial to remember that we are observing *ontological* emergence, not necessarily temporal development. In some cases, ontological emergence happens through temporal development. But in other cases it does not. Living organs, for instance, do not come chronologically before organisms—quite the opposite, actually; biologically, humans are organisms at the single cell stage well before they develop differentiated organs. Stated differently, in at least some cases, ontology (being) stands prior to ontogeny (the developmental life history of a particular organism), such that the actuality of the latter is fully dependent upon the reality of the former. Thus, emergent realities can begin to exist simultaneously with the lower-level parts out of which they are constituted. So, when I use phrases such as "gives rise" and "comes to exist," those may but do not necessarily denote a temporal or diachronic process happening between time^1 and time^2. Those always mean that the emergent is constituted as such—again, in multidimensional unified spaces, often with ontological synchronization—by the interaction of its parts.

Some of what I have written above needs, at the risk of repeating myself, a bit more unpacking. I said, for instance, that we need to understand both the idea and the reality of emergence. By the latter, "the reality," I mean first that emergence is real, it happens objectively in that which has being, regardless of whether we realize it in our minds or not. By "the idea" I mean that, since emergence is real, we will do well to grasp the concept of it in our thinking so that we can perceive emergence, understand it, and comprehend its broader implications for knowledge and explanation of our reality. Understanding the idea enables us to see its reality more clearly and thoroughly, which in turn permits us to apply the insight in new ways toward greater understanding of reality. Not believing in emergence does not make emergence not real. Emergence remains an essential dynamic of reality whether we realize it cognitively or not. But if we do think it, then we are better able to see, understand, and explain it operating in reality, because our minds are better tuned to the reality that exists independently of our minds.[11]

I also referred above to higher and lower "levels" of reality that I said different entities occupy. What do I mean by that? Just this: reality, again, is not flat. Reality is stratified. It exists and operates, in fact, on many levels, each of which is governed by structures, processes, and tendencies appropriate to its own level. The reality in which we live and participate (and of which we are partly composed) involves at the very least these

11. I am aware of the controversial epistemological issues raised by such claims and will address them below; meanwhile, I make no apologies for these claims. For now, see John Searle, *The Construction of Social Reality* (New York: Free Press, 1995), 199–226.

many stratified levels: subatomic, atomic, molecular, chemical, biological, physiological, zoological, ecological, meteorological, mental, social, global, galactic, and cosmological. At each of these levels different dynamics and mechanisms operate to cause to happen what actually does happen at that level. This is why we have the different scientific disciplines of physics, chemistry, biology, meteorology, physiology, psychology, sociology, astronomy, and so on. Different disciplines need to focus for analysis and explanation on the subject matters that pertain to their own levels of analysis. The tools of psychology are useless for doing particle physics because they are designed to understand an objectively different level of reality. Biology is not very helpful for directly explaining the character of interactions within human groups; that is the level of reality that sociology is properly equipped to explain. What this means for emergence is that the operation of phenomena at one level of reality often gives rise to new entities and operations at higher levels. What emerges above is fully dependent upon that from which it emerged below. But the emergent entities exist and function at higher levels than those elements that give rise to their emergence.

At the same time, it is important to understand that all of these different levels are connected. Biology of course has to do with chemistry, which has to do with physics, and so on. And—crucial for my larger point— one of the important ways that different levels of reality are connected is through emergence. Subatomic-level dynamics give rise to atomic-level processes that are dependent upon the subatomic dynamics but are not reducible to them. They have their own structures, dynamics, and laws that require a different disciplinary focus to understand. Likewise, biological processes at one level give rise ontologically to physiological phenomena at an entirely different level. From the combination of cells come bodily organs, which are completely dependent in existence upon the cells that combined to make them. But ontologically emergent from those combinations of cells are bodily organs—brains, hearts, glands, livers—that possess their own structures and causal capacities. Thus, while a brain depends for existence upon the cells that make it up, from the combination of those cells emerges a new entity, a brain, which has capacities to do things infinitely beyond what the simple sum total of all of the cells themselves could do.[12]

12. Furthermore, we must remember, in at least the biological realm, in an important sense the subsidiary parts are actually not properly *parts* at all *apart from* the whole they help

I have repeatedly spoken about characteristic qualities of emergent entities being "irreducible to" and "unable to be reduced to" the lower-level entities that give rise to them. What does that mean? To be *reducible*, in the way I use the term, means that some property observed at one level can be fully accounted for and explained by properties, structures, or dynamics operating at a lower level. When one breaks an entity down into its component parts, everything about the original entity can be found in the sum total of those parts. Some things in our reality are like this. A sack of chicken feed, for instance, contains a mixture of soybean meal, cracked corn, fish meal, and other ingredients, which we can break down into these component parts that are listed in print on the sack. The chicken feed is nothing more than the addition of these ingredients together in certain proportions. Nothing new of importance happens in the mixing. The content of the sack does not possess properties over and above those of its distinct ingredients when separated and placed next to one another. By feeding the mixed ingredients of the sack to chickens, for example, compared to feeding the same proportion of ingredients separately, chicken farmers are not able to double their egg production. The whole is not more than the sum of parts. For this reason, we can properly understand the sack of chicken feed reductionistically by breaking it down into its component parts. The interaction or relationship of those parts does not give rise to any new, nontrivial causal capacities.[13]

But many things are not like chicken feed in this way. Emergent things are not. It is true, to give another example, that Claude Monet's *Water Lilies* (*The Clouds*) consists of nothing more than dabs of different colored paint on a canvas.[14] But because of the particular arrangement of those dabs of paint, Monet has produced not simply a piece of canvas with dabs

---

to compose and into which they are integrated—such that the lower-level entities are finally dependent upon the higher-level organism to have and sustain their own life and identities.

13. This is parallel to the difference in chemistry between mixtures and compounds. Trivial new capacities include things like the ability of feed suppliers to sell the ingredients as "feed" instead of "ingredients of feed" and making the feeding of chickens easier for chicken farmers. Nothing about the feed, however, has changed by combining the ingredients.

14. I draw this example from French impressionism, aware that in painting that movement actually has some affinity with the subjectivistic constructionism I critique in chapter 3—in its interest in expressing subjective visual sensations of light on objects perceived by the artist's eye rather than in recreating exact, photograph-like depictions of the realistic forms of subjects—because it nevertheless helps to illustrate the key matter of parts and wholes involved in understanding emergence here.

of paint on it. Monet has produced for us *a painting*, a unique picture, a cognitively recognizable and culturally meaningful representation of a reality, a new entity with its own characteristics and capacities to cause effects in the world. One of the emergent causal capacities of those particularly arranged dabs of paint is the ability to evoke certain emotions in people who view the painting, such as warmth or serenity. Neither the recognizable and meaningful picture nor the capacity to evoke emotions is present in the dabs of paint totaled up. It is through Monet's particular relational arrangement of those paint dabs that a unique picture emerges possessing particular characteristics and capacities that can cause experiences in observers. To say that Monet's *Water Lilies* (*The Clouds*) is reducible to many dabs of colored paint on a canvas would be to say that all of the characteristics and capacities we observe in the painting are present in the sum total of all the dabs of paint and the piece of canvas. To say that about this painting would be to make oneself a reductionist in relation to it. And to do this would be misguided. For the characteristics and capacities of the painting are irreducible to the paint and canvas. Thus a reductionistic approach is mistaken when it comes to emergent entities.

Reductionism is often evident in the phrases *only really* and *nothing but*—as in the assertion that the human body is *nothing but* a whole lot of oxygen, carbon, hydrogen, nitrogen, calcium, phosphorus, sulfur, sodium, magnesium, and trace amounts of copper, zinc, selenium, molybdenum, fluorine, chlorine, iodine, manganese, cobalt, iron, lithium, strontium, aluminum, silicon, lead, vanadium, arsenic, and bromine. It is in fact true that human bodies are composed of these and only these elements. Without these elements we would not have human bodies. But this is a different claim than saying the human body is "nothing but" a collection of these elements. That is a move that various authors have rightly disparaged as "Nothing Buttery."[15] When it comes to persons, Francis Crick—the codiscoverer, with James Watson, of DNA structure—is a reductionist when he writes, "You're nothing but a pack of neurons."[16] The MIT robotics researcher Rodney Brooks is also reductionistic when he writes in a chapter titled "We Are Not Special" that "the body consists of components that interact according to well-defined . . . rules that ultimately derive from

15. The coining of the phrase has been attributed variously to G. K. Chesterton, C. S. Lewis, and Donald McKay, among others.

16. Francis Crick, *The Astonishing Hypothesis* (New York: Charles Scribner's Sons, 1994), 3, 11.

physics and chemistry. . . . We, all of us, overanthropomorphize humans, who are after all mere machines."[17] I reject such views in this book. The counter to reductionism is emergence. What emergence enables us to see is that all of those elements come together in a very particular combination to create a new entity, the human body, which possesses characteristics and capacities irreducible to the elements from which the body emerged. Without understanding the reality of emergence, all scientific endeavors are vulnerable to the reductionistic program. Institutionalized group behavior is really nothing but individual behaviors added together. Intentional altruistic actions are really nothing but behavioral compulsions driven by biologically selected upon altruistic genetic dispositions. Psychology is ultimately really nothing but biology. The mind is finally nothing but physical, neurological brain activity. Pornographic photos are ultimately nothing but some dots of ink on paper. Etcetera, ad nauseam.[18]

Stated another way, the reductionism of Nothing Buttery is guilty of erroneously mixing up the function of distinct questions and answers. Sometimes we want to know, *what is this?* A different question we sometimes ask is, *what is this made of?* A third, related but distinct question is, *what is this capable of doing?* Each of these questions relates to but is not identical with the other. A particular object may be a bucket of garden soil. It is made of clay, sand, decomposing organic matter, water, air, and other substances. It is capable, under certain conditions, of supporting the growth of plants—even though all of its ingredients separated out and piled on top of each other cannot do that. Reductionism is the bad habit of trying to answer the "what is this?" question by asking the "what is this made of?" question, as if the "is" of the "this" is never more than the "what" that it is "made of." To a reductionist, therefore, a Zen garden is nothing more than sand, gravel, rocks, and some organic plant matter. And a football game is simply twenty-seven people (some wearing black and

17. Rodney Brooks, *Flesh and Machines* (New York: Pantheon, 2002), 173, 175.

18. The radical constructivist Heinz von Foerster provides an example: Sight, taste, touch, smell, and other sensory receptors, he says, "are all 'blind' as to the quality of their stimulation, responsive only to their quality. Although surprising, this should not come as a surprise, for indeed 'out there' there is no light and no color, there are only electromagnetic waves; 'out there' there is no sound and no music, there are only periodic variations in the air pressure; 'out there' there is no heat and no cold, there are only moving molecules with more or less mean kinetic energy, and so on. Finally, for sure, 'out there' there is no pain." Von Foerster, "On Constructing a Reality," in *Inventing Reality*, ed. Paul Watzlawick (New York: Norton, 1984), 46.

white striped shirts) running around on a 57,600 square foot plot of grass chasing a leather-covered, air-pressurized rubber bladder. Zen gardens and football games are composed of such things. But that is not all that they are. And what about the "capable of doing" question? To answer, sometimes we need to know what something is made of and sometimes we need to know what something is. Are the little particles my landscaper spread across my yard while I was away able to feed all the plants in my lawn, able to feed the grass but kill the weeds, or not able to feed anything but only to kill insects? To know that, I need to know if the small particles I see are made of the chemical compounds that compose fertilizer, weed and feed, or insecticide. In this case, "what is it made of?" answers the question "what can it do?" By contrast, finding out what my lawn mower is made of (steel, plastic, etc.) does nothing to tell me what it as a single object is capable of doing. Only by understanding the emergent entity that my lawn mower is, including its emergent properties, can I know that it is capable of cutting my grass (and slicing my garden hose or foot, if I am not careful). Sometimes we use other bodies of knowledge to work from "what is this capable of doing?" to answering the "what is this?" and "what is this composed of?" questions. For instance, it is after the naive senator's staffer has tasted the white powder that arrived in an envelope in the senator's morning mail—and we his colleagues see what it does—that we come to know whether it was cocaine, anthrax, or confectioner's sugar. And it is after we see someone strap it on her back, jump out of a plane, and float to the ground that we realize the small fabric-covered bundle is a parachute.

Nothing Buttery often thinks itself smart and elegant. Is it rarely either, however, or enlightening. For Nothing Buttery tends to flatten reality down to one level, the lowest level known, ultimately, and seeks to explain everything else it observes in terms of the laws operating at that lowest level. From this arises, for example, the aspiration of some to identify the single theory or equation that will explain and predict all of reality.[19] But will we really have learned much insightful, interesting, important, or satisfying about, for instance, the dynamics of international conflict if tomorrow a brilliant mathematical physicist were to hit upon the single

---

19. See Stephen Hawking, *The Theory of Everything: The Origin and Fate of the Universe* (Beverly Hills, CA: New Millennium Press, 2002); Brian Greene, *The Elegant Universe: Superstrings, Hidden Dimensions, and the Quest for the Ultimate Theory* (New York: Norton, 1999); John D. Barrow, *Theories of Everything: The Quest for Ultimate Explanation* (New York: Oxford University Press, 1990).

equation that explains everything? Not in the least. International relations operate at their own level according to their own processes and dynamics.

Nothing Buttery, it turns out, is something like a man watching a classic silent film that is being projected onto a huge theater screen. The man is seated against the front wall on which the screen is hung. He insists, because he is watching from a 3-degree angle to the screen, that a classic silent film is not showing, but rather that some incomprehensible lights are merely jumping around on a very thin vertical line on the wall against which he is seated. The problem, of course, is not that a silent movie is not showing. The problem is that this silly viewer has taken an a priori position that compresses the two-dimensional screen down to nearly one, vertical dimension. The right response, if we are interested in what is real, is not to agree with the poorly seated viewer because, true enough, an incomprehensible line of lights is all he can see. The correct response is to change his position so he is able to view the full width of the theater screen and so to see the film showing. Likewise, to perceive, appreciate, and understand reality as it actually is, we human inquirers need to position ourselves cognitively to see and understand the concept of emergence that is happening in reality. Only then will we be able to grasp the multileveled, multidimensional, complex, rich, interesting nature of what is real.[20] Only then will we, for present purposes, have a hope of understanding ourselves well as human beings.

Another aspect of reality that emergence enables us to see and appreciate is the distinct but related idea and reality of "downward causation." Downward causation, like emergence, assumes a stratified, multileveled reality. But whereas emergence reflects an upward movement of ontological development, downward causation signals a descending dynamic of causal influence. Downward causation, as I am using it, means that higher-level entities, by virtue of the emergent characteristics and capacities proper to their level and nature, sometimes possess the ability to act causally back down upon entities operating at lower levels of reality.[21] Thus, not only

20. Francis Fukuyama, *Our Posthuman Future* (New York: Farrar, Straus and Giroux, 2002), 162–66.

21. My meaning here is close to Donald Campbell's meaning of "downward causation": Campbell, "'Downward Causation' in Hierarchically Organized Biological Systems," in *Studies in the Philosophy of Biology*, ed. F. J. Ayala and T. Dobzhansky (New York: Macmillan, 1974), 179–86; Campbell, "Levels of Organization, Downward Causation, and the Selection-Theory Approach to Evolutionary Epistemology," in *Scientific Methodology in the Study of Mind*, ed. E. Tobach and G. Greenberg (Hillsdale, NJ: Erlbaum, 1990), 1–17.

can lower-level phenomena combine or interact to give rise to genuinely new phenomena through emergence, but at least some of those emergent phenomena become as a result causally capacitated to influence entities and processes operating at lower levels. The physical human brain, for example, gives rise through emergence to capacities for higher-level affective and mood experiences, including, for instance, depression. And extended depression, we have come to learn, has the causal capacity to influence the physical operations of the brain. Our brains thus serve as "mutable maps" controlled in part by our minds: "There is a capacity for local plastic change in the structure of the healthy human adult brain in response to environmental demands."[22] Emergent properties of personhood can also give rise through relational conflict to life stress. In turn, stress can exert downwardly causal forces on the physiology of nervous, endocrine, and digestive systems that alter chemical reactions, hormone and blood flows, and protein synthesis.[23] The emergent causal power acts back downward on that from which it was given rise. Further along in my argument I will explain why downward causation is important for properly understanding ourselves as human beings—which of course is what all of this theory is about. For now, it is enough simply to introduce the basic idea.

In addition to the downward causation just discussed, there is another way worth noting that reality does not always and everywhere work upwardly through emergence: that is through the downward and outward

22. Quote from Eleanor Maguire et al., "Navigation-Related Structural Change in the Hippocampi of Taxi Drivers," *Proceedings of the National Academy of Science* 97 (2000): 4398–403; Michael Merzenich, "The Power of Mutable Maps," in *Neuroscience: Exploring the Brain*, ed. Mark Bear, Barry Connors, and Michael Paradiso (Baltimore: Lippincott Williams and Wilkins, 2001), 418. Also see Bogdan Draganski et al., "Changes in Grey Matter Induced by Training," *Nature* 427 (2004): 311–12; Andrea Mechelli et al., "Structural Plasticity in the Bilingual Brain," *Nature* 431 (2004): 757; Christo Pantev et al., "Increased Auditory Cortical Representation in Musicians," *Nature* 392 (1998): 811–14; Thomas Elbert et al., "Increased Cortical Representation of the Fingers of the Left Hand in String Players," *Science* 270 (1995): 305–7; all cited in Homes Rolston III, "Human Uniqueness and Human Dignity: Persons in Nature and the Nature of Persons," in *Human Dignity and Bioethics* (Washington, DC: President's Council on Bioethics, 2008), 140–41.

23. Eric Kandel, James Schwartz, and Thomas Jessell, *Principles of Neural Science* (New York: McGraw-Hill Medical, 2000), 1028; Steven Rose, *Lifelines: Biology, Freedom, Determinism* (New York: Allen Lane, 1997); R. Nowak, "Men Behaving Badly: It's Not Just Women Who Suffer from Hormonal Ups and Downs," *New Scientist* 2 (2002): 4; see Michael Carolan, "Society, Biology, and Ecology: Bringing Nature Back into Sociology's Disciplinary Narrative through Critical Realism," *Organization and Environment* 18, no. 4 (2005): 397.

forces of entropy and related forces. The natural capacities of reality do entail great powers to move upwardly to higher levels of complexity and capability. But that upward movement tends to press against other natural, oppositional forces of resistance, corrosion, breakdown, disintegration, chaos, diffusion, deterioration, and loss. The second law of thermodynamics—stating that the entropy of isolated systems will tend to increase over time to approach maximum values at equilibrium—works powerfully in a variety of ways throughout the natural and social worlds. Things fall apart. Resistance must be overcome. Therefore, fully to understand the exercise of causal powers of any sort requires a larger appreciation of the relevant "entropic" forces that condition, resist, confuse, or limit them. Our larger theoretical visions ought not to model reality as simply smooth and unobstructed movements of progressive development toward ever-higher levels of complexity, capacity, and functionality. There is always a relevant tension, resistance, dissolution, challenge, or struggle to be met.

Human Capacities

Having established the idea of emergence, we are ready to return to the question of human personhood. The next step in my account is to show that a series of real, distinct, interrelated causal capacities are emergent from the human body, particularly from the human brain, as it operates in its material and social environment.[24] By *causal* capacities I mean that these powers endow humans with the ability to bring about changes in material or mental phenomena, to produce or influence objects and events in the world. Humans share many similarities of basic genetics and body structure with other primates, to whom we are most closely related biologically. But many of these causal capacities are distinctively human in extent, intensity, and quality, and so set humans uniquely apart from these and other animals.[25] The causal capacities I describe do not themselves

24. Greater social scientific attention to the body might do well to attend to the work of Mary Douglas, who theorizes links between the human body and the social body, particularly in the former's giving rise to "natural symbols" operative in social life. Douglas, *Natural Symbols* (New York: Routledge, 1996); Douglas, *Purity and Danger* (New York: Praeger, 1966).

25. Still, statements about similarities among species based on genetics are tenuous exactly because of the way new properties and capacities arise emergently. Humans and yeast, for example, share many basic genes—approximately 60 percent of yeast genes can be replaced by their human homologues and the organisms will still function. Even among closely related species there may be tiny differences with enormous effects, such as in size or behavior.

constitute human personhood. Personhood is emergent from them. But they do form some of the key elements from which, as they interact, human personhood is emergent. These causal capacities thus mediate between the real human body and real human personhood.

The mechanisms of emergence, we must remind ourselves, can sometimes be a mystery. We can be sure that the causal capacities I am about to describe do in fact emerge from human bodies as they interact with their environments. But exactly how they do so is not entirely transparent. We know that the brain, collaborating with other body parts and genetic information, is the organizing and controlling organ for most of these processes. And neuroscience can often identify specific areas of the brain that are involved in the function of the following causal capacities. But how the brain interacting with the rest of the body gives rise to the mental capacity to, for example, creatively imagine possibilities that do not yet exist, is absolutely mysterious. Much that is real and important is not visible or perhaps humanly comprehendible. For present purpose, what matters most is simply the recognition that these human causal capacities do exist as emergent from the human body living in its natural and social environments.[26] What then are these capacities? I mention thirty, although there are no doubt others that matter.[27] After briefly describing them next, I sort through how they may be grouped together and which may depend upon others for their own emergence.

The first is the capacity for *consciousness*, which humans also share with many living creatures. Much that exists in reality is not conscious. My mailbox, for instance, is not conscious. But the operation of the physical matter that composes brains and bodies of humans and most other

---

Although there is no doubt that they are biologically most closely related, humans and chimps actually have notable differences in the arrangement and regulation of genes. Note, too, that changes in quantity can give rise to changes in quality—as is ubiquitously evident in biology, especially neurobiology, as well as in nuclear physics, where a critical mass, for instance, may trigger a chain reaction. Thanks to Bill Hurlbut for emphasizing these points to me.

26. For one phenomenological account, see Vincent Shen, "'Person' as the Central Concept in the Human and Social Sciences: An Interpretation of Edmund Husserl's Thought on the Human Person in *Ideen II*," in *Human Dignity*, ed. Miloslav Bednar (Washington, DC: Council for Research in Values and Philosophy, 1999), 215ff.

27. Martha Nussbaum enumerates a list of ten capacities, two of which have two subcapacities, which are: life; bodily health; bodily integrity; sense, imagination, and thought; emotions; practical reason; affiliation (interaction and self-respect); life with other species; play; and control over one's environment (political and material). Nussbaum, "Human Dignity and Political Entitlements," in *Human Dignity and Bioethics* (Washington, DC: President's Council on Bioethics, 2008), 377–78.

animals somehow gives rise to subjective awareness of existence. As conscious creatures, humans are able to take in, be attentive of, and respond to external data. Consciousness at a basic level means that humans can exist in a state of being that is sentient, wakeful, alert, aware, attentive. Humans also possess what we might think of as involuntary capacities. One is to live in part out of a state of *unconscious being*. Not all of the desires, feelings, beliefs, dispositions, and goals that govern people's affect and actions are immediately accessible to their conscious inspection. Part of the normal human being's personality and motivational structure exists "below the surface" of awareness and recognition—even if they are shaped by ongoing conscious processes. This we call the unconscious, the depths of which in its influence on complex behavior appear to be extensive among humans.[28]

Among their basic mental abilities, humans possess the natural capacity to *understand the real properties of quantity, quality, time, and space*. This ability provides humans with the basic ordering and representational categories for understanding the crucial features of the real environment about which human perception provides information. As conscious animals, humans are also capable of *mental representation*, of forming cognitive depictions of reality. In this ability, humans represent mental images for themselves of objects or states of affairs in the world other than themselves, depictions that are *about* something or directed *at* something.[29] This cognitive representation is a basic building block of most other causal

28. A better developed critical realist personalism will have to theoretically elaborate the human unconscious, a task that fits well critical realism's readiness to analyze nonmaterial and non-directly-observable entities—since even nonpsychoanalytical neuropsychologists claim to be finding evidence for unconscious processes—though space does not permit that theoretical elaboration here. Suffice it to clarify that I do not mean to suggest that the unconscious operates independently of ongoing conscious processes—clearly the latter helps to produce the former, as indicated by the two-directional arrow in figure 2 between conscious awareness and unconscious being. Furthermore, it could be that many of the capacities located in the conscious life of humans in these pages may have equivalents in unconscious life. Finally, whatever conscious-unconscious "splitness" or "cleftedness" exists naturally in humanity will require theorizing beyond my capacity here; however, that issue may relate to and help to explain the problem of "brokenness" that is raised but also undertheorized in this book.

29. Philosophers often call this *intentionality*, but because of the confusion of meaning between this definition of intention and the different meaning of intention as intended purpose (not to mention other meanings of the word *intension*), I will use the term *representation* here. See John Searle, *Intentionality: An Essay in the Philosophy of Mind* (Cambridge: Cambridge University Press, 1983); Searle, *The Construction of Social Reality* (New York: Free Press, 1995), 6–7.

capacities discussed here. The causal capacity of *volition* also derives from the normally functioning[30] human body and brain. Humans are able to will, to desire, to aspire to, to set something as a wanted goal or purpose. Rocks do not desire, nor do computers or corpses. But humans can and do, and the character of human volitional wanting takes on a unique subjective quality that cannot be eliminated from experience or reduced to another quality or capacity. Volition is profoundly its own phenomenon that powerfully shapes human experience.

In addition to these positive, active abilities, humans also possess, as I have said, passive or involuntary capacities. Another of them is the human capacity to live in a state of *practical consciousness*. By this I mean the ability to "go on" in life, executing a host of functional behaviors but without consciously thinking about why and how one is doing it or perhaps even being aware that one is doing it.[31] Michael Polanyi described this crucial

---

30. Throughout this chapter especially, and as an important background assumption of this book in general, stands the idea of "normal" humans and persons, meaning humans or persons who are not seriously damaged physically and mentally and have not seriously deteriorated in their functional capacities. By this definition, while most humans on the earth are normal, humans in comas, those with extreme disabilities, and Alzheimer's patients, for instance, would be not normal. They would still be humans and, I argue, persons. But they would not be normal human persons. This particular meaning and the idea of statistical normalcy are not identical; however, empirical instances of the two overlap a great deal. I realize that my use of the word *normal* in this context is potentially hazardous, as it could give rise to numerous possible unfortunate misunderstandings. But to be clear on at least one point, *normal* here is not intended to stigmatize nonnormal humans or exclude them from the community of persons enjoying all of the rights pertaining thereto—quite the opposite, as we will see in chapter 8. Still, it is simply not possible effectively to examine the issues addressed in this book without somehow distinguishing between what is normal and what is seriously damaged and deteriorated. To lump every case of genetically human being into the category human or person without possessing ideas distinguishing the normal and nonnormal destroys crucial analytical categories and comparisons and ultimately collapses into mere nonevaluative descriptions of what is, as if every case were the same with no distinctions to be made between them. However, there is no reason to have to go there; we simply need to avoid missteps along the way. No reasonable reader actually believes that every living, genetically human being is normal. If that were so, then words like *damaged, malformed, pathological,* and *deranged* would be meaningless and useless when applied to human bodies or persons. So, although the idea of nonnormal humans or persons may be unpleasant, such are empirically real, and the language to distinguish them from normal humans and persons is analytically essential for present purposes.

31. Steven Vaisey, "Socrates, Skinner, and Aristotle: Three Ways of Thinking about Culture in Action," *Sociological Forum* 23, no. 3 (2008): 603–13; Giddens, *The Constitution of Society*, xxiii.

aspect of human understanding and living as "tacit knowledge," explaining the importance of the fact that "we can know more than we can tell."[32] The actions of practical consciousness are habituated, "automatic-pilot" behaviors that demand little cognitive effort to complete. This is a very important human ability to perform.

Human beings are also emergently capacitated to *assign causal attributions*. Humans have the ability to perceive, intuit, or analyze both the relations among events and the natural causal powers of entities in order to understand the real operations of cause and effect. Humans first of all possess the cognitive category of real world causation, and they are often able to apply it to understand the operation of influences and outcomes in life. They are thus able to understand mentally not only that the world operates in certain ways but also how and why the world operates causally as it does.

Furthermore, human beings are capable—by virtue of numerous other capabilities—to engage in *interest formation*. That is, they are able amid myriad possibilities to identify and rank those states, conditions, and experiences they believe will serve their well-being or the well-being of others they prize, which they desire to attain for themselves and those others. By forming such interests, people personalize their larger value schema in application to their own lives, drawing out the implications of their general value structures for their personal selves.

Human beings are also naturally capacitated to feel deep, complex, and intense *emotions*. Humans do not merely feel bodily fear, pain, and pleasure, as many animals do. Human animals are able to enjoy and suffer extremely profound, complicated, and overwhelming affective events of feeling, emotion, mood, sentiment, and passion happening in their bodies and subjective mental states.[33] Moreover, whatever their origins, human emotions are not simply reactive behavioral aids to physical survival. They spring from and redound through deep wells of human subjectivity with profound consequences for perception, motivation, and behavior.

32. Polanyi, *The Tacit Dimension*, quote from p. 4.

33. Jonathan Turner, *Human Emotions: A Sociological Theory* (New York: Routledge, 2007). Fear, anger, happiness, sadness, surprise, and disgust are primal emotions. See Paul Ekman and W. V. Friesen, "The Repertoire of Nonverbal Behavior: Categories, Origins, Usage, and Encoding," *Semiotica* 1 (1969): 49–98; Robert Plutchik, "A General Psychoevolutionary Theory of Emotion," in *Emotion: Theory, Research, and Experience*, vol. 1, *Theories of Emotion*, ed. Robert Plutchik and H. Kellerman (New York: Academic Press, 1980), 3–33.

Moreover, normal humans are causally capable of complex and extensive *episodic and long-term remembering*. Humans do not simply live in the present. Their brains and bodies are somehow capable of storing and retrieving an immense amount of images, associations, knowledge, reminiscences, and other memory contents that provide powerful links to the temporal past and which they carry into the future for recollection and cognitive reimaging. Memory enables people cognitively to live in the past, to learn from history, to sustain a sense of continuity of reality over time.

Humans possess the natural causal capacity to experience *intersubjective understanding*. Philosophers struggle to explain how intersubjectivity can actually work, given the nonidentity of different people's egos. But however it does work, humans clearly do have the ability to at least somewhat correctly understand the subjective beliefs, thoughts, emotions, desires, intentions, goals, interests, moods, and meanings of other people. Without such intersubjective understanding, human life could simply not function at the level that it does—most human behaviors would have to be controlled by hardwired instincts from which it would be difficult to deviate, or else human actions would be reduced to the most basic of functional behaviors capable of being coordinated by creatures incapable of comprehending one another's internal states and intentions. One of the mysteries of human being is the ability of different subjects to connect in intersubjectivity.

Humans are furthermore capable of remarkable feats of *creativity*, innovation, and imagination. Humans are not stuck working with what already exists. They can imagine that which does not yet exist and use their creative imaginations and other capacities to bring that nonexistent entity into being. Through downwardly causal processes of the brain,[34] people can mentally innovate in order to visualize, dream, invent, connect, conceive, and envision ideas, possibilities, and images that do not yet exist in reality. In this way, humans have the ability to originate genuinely

---

34. Neuroscientist Joaquín Fuster writes about a "difficult to define" "emergent property" of the brain: "As networks fan outward and upward in associative neocortex, they become capable of generating novel representations that are not reducible to their inputs or to their individual neuronal components. Those representations are the products of complex, nonlinear, and near-chaotic interactions between innumerable elements of high-level networks far removed from sensory receptors or motor effectors. Then, top-down network building predominates. Imagination, creativity, and intuition are some of the cognitive attributes of those emergent high-level representations." Fuster, *Cortex and Mind: Unifying Cognition* (New York: Oxford University Press, 2003), 53.

new behaviors, ideas, material artifacts, and meanings from old thoughts, materials, practices, and significances. Humans can also engage in creative "transposition," by which I mean the novel application of one cognitive map or schema that is normally employed in one domain of thought or life for analogous use in a quite different domain—for example, extending the idea of political freedom to develop the ideas of economic or moral freedom. This human capacity for creativity and transposition thus emancipates humanity from the extant and opens up human futures to immense possibilities of originality and innovation.

As a consequence of the operation of much of the foregoing, humans also enjoy the capacity to be the *efficient causes of their own actions and interactions*.[35] People are not simply passive objects upon which other forces act. Humans are able to cause their own acts. People can mobilize their representational beliefs, memories, interests, desires, emotions, values, moral commitments, and identities to decide with a significant degree of free will on certain courses of action and then to put them into motion. People's actions, in other words, can often be rightly understood as significantly, though not completely, caused by the people who are acting.

Humans enjoy capacities for inventing and employing *technology* to manipulate the material world by fashioning various devices, utensils, tools, machines, and other material apparatuses to augment their bodily powers of motion and force. In this way, numerous human mental abilities take form in and recreate the material world. Humans are also capable more broadly of engaging in *material cultivation and development*. This capacity draws upon human abilities of creativity, interest formation, technology, future planning, and even aesthetic judgment in order not only to perform discrete actions but also to develop more complex, ongoing life projects enhancing human social and cultural survival and flourishing. The product of this capacity is not merely a tool or artifact but instead

---

35. I rely here on Aristotelian terms to denote by "efficient cause" the agent as the immediate force or precursor that actually brings an event about, which causes certain results; this is distinguished from material, formal, and final causes. This is consistent with Anthony Giddens's view that "one of the distinctive things about human beings, which separates us from the animals, is that normally we know what we are doing in our activity, and why. That is to say, human beings are concept-bearing agents, whose concepts in some part constitute what it is that they are up to, not contingently, but as an inherent element of what it is that they are up to. In addition, human actors have reasons for their actions, reasons that consistently inform the flow of day-to-day activities." Giddens, *Social Theory and Modern Sociology* (1987; Cambridge: Polity Press, 1991), 2–3.

complex systems of material harvesting, fabrication, production, and improvement—all broadly conceived. This capacity entails projects engaging and reconstructing the natural, physical world, such as systematically
gathering material resources, harnessing various natural sources of power,
systematizing food supply, and so on, through farming, animal husbandry,
craftwork production, the construction of settlements, and so forth.

Humans are also capable of profound *self-transcendence*, that is, of
passing beyond their own interests and concerns in order to be attentive
and present to nonpersonal objects and especially to other persons. Humans can engage other and different matters of import, those of other
people, for instance, of better understanding the world around them, of
the possible significance and purposes of life and the world. Of course all
conscious creatures transcend themselves in some ways in being aware of
a reality beyond themselves. But human self-transcendence is extraordinary, first because of the great subjective depths of self-concern humans
experience beyond which their self-transcendence rises, and second because of the intensity with which humans can devote themselves to things
above and beyond themselves. This self-transcendence thus creates immense possibilities for devotion to other people, ideas, and projects in the
material world.

Among these many human capacities I am recounting is also the ability
to create, grasp, and communicate *meanings*. By this I intend to denote the
ability mentally and emotionally to draw connections between different
entities in ways that generate import and significance for people. Meaning
is a primal or first-order fact of human existence that is difficult to define
precisely. Yet the making of meaning is real, important, and ineliminable
in human life. The world and its parts do not simply exist for people functionally or at face value. They have significance.

Another key causal capacity related to mental representation and
meaning is the human ability for *symbolization*. In ways apparently lacking in other animals on earth, humans are able to extensively use some
ideas or objects to represent other ideas or objects and their attributes,
meanings, and emotional associations. People are capable of employing
signs to represent meanings and ideas they wish to signify to themselves
and others.[36] Scratches of ink on a piece of paper can stand for a word
that represents a material or conceptual thing; colored pieces of cloth can

36. For a nonsocial scientific work, see Terrence Deacon, *The Symbolic Species* (New
York: Norton, 1988).

represent the history, purpose, and destiny of an entire nation; a hand gesture can stand for a disposition of disrespectful hostility toward another person; perpendicularly crossed pieces of wood can represent the boundless love of God. Very closely related to the human ability for symbolization is the capacity for *language use*. By this I mean the capacity for complex, constructed systems of vocabulary, grammar, and syntax expressed in speech and texts that communicate ideas, questions, commands, exclamations, and other types of speech acts to other language users. Humans are unique in the capacity for complex language use. Moreover, humans also possess the emergent capacity to compose and recount *narratives* as a particular formation of communicated meanings. Narratives are a particular genre of accounts consisting of ordered sequences of connected events, situations, and actions—involving settings, actors, conflicts or problems, and resolutions—that point to some significant larger conclusion or meaning. In short, narratives are stories with a point of meaning.

Humans are furthermore capable of *valuation*. People possess the mental equipment and propensity to assess in fairly abstract terms the relative goodness, rightness, worth, merit, importance, or virtue of various objects, situations, beliefs, or behaviors. Through valuation, people develop evaluative mental schemas that transcend specific cases and situations they use to discriminate levels of relative desirability. By means of valuation, humans are thus able to create normative differentiations in the world of experience that help to inform their perceptions, decisions, and actions.

Humans possess the emergent capacity to *anticipate the future*. By employing their capacities for causal attribution, memory, and creative imagination, people are able—often fairly accurately—to "think ahead" in order to project outcomes of different courses of action that have not yet happened. People can mentally play out ahead of time alternative real world scenarios resulting from diverse sets of causes as pictures in their minds, estimating ranges and probabilities of consequences.

Many human capacities also facilitate another distinctive human ability, the capacity for *identity formation*. People are not merely conscious creatures behaving in the world. They also have reflexive perceptions of themselves as more or less unique creatures representing particular configurations of character, personality, psychological structure, and social location that are relatively durable, defining of self, and behavior-guiding. Identities are self-understandings derived from occupying particular, stable locations in social, behavioral, mental, and moral space that securely define who and what somebody is, for themselves and for others. Every normal human animal rejects being a some*thing* and drives mightily to be a some*one*. Achieving this requires the successful exercise of forming personal and social identity.

Moreover, human beings possess the causal capacity for *self-reflexivity*. That is, people are able to make themselves the objects of their own reflection and evaluation. In this way, humans are not only conscious animals but also, importantly, are self-conscious animals.[37] People are not merely aware of the world they live in but also of themselves as objective beings living in that world. This capacity for reflexivity helps to foster a subjectivity and responsible self-control that is crucial to human experience.

Humans, uniquely, also enjoy the causal capacity for *abstract reasoning*. Humans do not simply respond behaviorally to external stimuli, but are capable of exercising cognitive faculties—like categorization, generalization, comparison, analogizing, logical induction, deduction, retroduction, and abduction—that enable them to reflect, calculate, and analyze abstractly and deliberatively in ways that inform their understanding and decision-making.

Humans are causally capable of *truth seeking*, that is, of distinguishing what is reality and truth from personal preference and desires. Many animals can form perceptions of the world that inform their behavior. The human animal seems especially susceptible, however, to having its perceptions biased by its interests, desires, and preferences. We are more likely to see and believe what we want to see and believe than what we do not want to—social psychology studies have clearly shown this. But humans are nevertheless also able to and sometimes motivated to transcend their powerful interests, desires, and preferences in order to seek out and know what is true and real, for its own sake, regardless of the possible negative implications for their own selves. This awareness of the existence of an objective truth or reality that might diverge from what appears to be or is in one's interests, and the seeking to know it for its own sake, is an important aspect of our human being.

Related to but distinct from valuation is the human capacity for *moral awareness and judgment*. By *moral* I mean an orientation toward understandings about what are right and wrong, good and bad, worthy and un-

37. Mark Leary, *The Curse of the Self: Self-Awareness, Egotism, and the Quality of Human Life* (New York: Oxford University Press, 2004), 3–21.

worthy, just and unjust, which are not established simply by our desires, decisions, or preferences, but instead believed to exist apart from them, providing standards by which our desires, decisions, and preferences can themselves be judged.[38] We human animals are moral animals—I suggest here as I have argued at length elsewhere[39]—in that we possess a capacity and propensity unique among all animals not only to have desires, beliefs, and feelings, but also to have the ability and disposition to make moral evaluations of our desires, beliefs, and feelings, which hold the potential to transform them. Human persons are capable of existing—indeed I believe are incapable of not existing—in a morally oriented reality in this way. Humans also possess the capability of *forming virtues*. That is, humans have the capacity to purposefully integrate a variety of their beliefs, desires, and actions into stable dispositions and habits to think and act in certain ways under certain circumstances in order to foster lives of greater happiness and moral goodness. Humans intentionally form and learn virtues as a means to counteract tendencies toward what are considered to be vices and moral faults, such as cowardice, vanity, selfishness, laziness, and foolishness. Humans appear recurrently to form and attach importance to virtues such as courage, wisdom, moderation, humility, justice, self-control, and kindness.

Humans have the capacity for *aesthetic judgment and enjoyment*. This ability entails the critical distinguishing at a sensory-emotional level of differences in attractiveness, beauty, appropriateness, or tastefulness. The focus of aesthetic judgments and enjoyments may be natural and designed objects, performances, sceneries, images, narratives, or musical or other sounds.

Finally, humans possess the capacity for *interpersonal communion and love*.[40] Building upon many other capacities—especially emotional experi-

38. Here I closely follow Charles Taylor, who describes morality as involving "discriminations of right and wrong, better or worse, higher or lower, which are not rendered valid by our own desires, inclinations, or choices, but rather stand independently of these and offer standards by which they can be judged." Taylor, *Sources of the Self* (Cambridge, MA: Harvard University Press, 1989), 4.

39. Christian Smith, *Moral, Believing Animals: Human Personhood and Culture* (New York: Oxford University Press, 2003).

40. "Communion" derives from the Latin *communio*, which denotes "sharing in common" (itself derived from *com-* + *ūnus*, meaning oneness or union). The related Greek term, κοινωνία, is typically translated as "fellowship." The term *love* descends from Old English, Old High German, and Old Aryan languages as well as Latin, variously involving meanings of precious, dear, pleasing, and desire. More on love below.

ence, volition, intersubjective understanding, self-transcendence, reflexivity, moral awareness, and virtue formation—humans are able to enter into social relationships with other humans that are characterized by profound depths and intensities of mutual understanding, empathy, attachment, solidarity, devotion, affection, and commitment to the other's well-being. The results of such relations—which can be expressed in friendship, among blood relatives, in small communities, and in sexual relationships—can be ineffable. But normally entailed are intense experiences of intimacy, affection, bonding, agreement, sharing, self-giving, and, at times, altruistic self-sacrifice.

What it means to be a normal person, then, is related to (though is not defined only by) the fact that humans ordinarily possess at least these thirty causal capacities—and no doubt others—for subjective and objective human activity. We humans possess these capacities together as the natural emergent properties of our embrained bodily selves living in our material and social environments. We can ontologically describe normal humans one way, therefore, as animals endowed with at least the causal capacities for the subjective and objective activity described here. Some other animals do possess some of these capacities, but usually at much lower levels of function and intensity. Other of these capacities are unique to human existence. Note, to be clear, I am not saying that the mere collection of these capacities is what makes for personhood. Persons are emergent from—not simply the sum total of—these and likely other human capacities. Personhood exists at a higher level of the human than a mere list of capacities. Still, those capacities are the basic facts out of which normal personhood exists emergently at a higher level.

The thirty capacities are not alike in how basic, central, or complex they are in human life or to what objects they are referenced, expressed, or engaged. I have sorted out the capacities by these differences, as I understand them, in table 1. The most basic and central capacities begin at the bottom, from which capacities work their way upward toward more complex, higher-order ones at the top. Higher capacities are dependent for their existence and functioning upon combinations of more basic capacities below them. The most basic human capacities—conscious awareness and unconscious being—I label "existence" capacities. They comprise the core up and out from which all else develops. They give rise to "primary experience" capacities, which in turn produce a set of more complex "secondary experience" capacities. Out of these experience-oriented capacities develop a host of what I am calling "creating" capacities, which involve

TABLE 1 **Analytical organization of human capacities by centrality, complexity, and primary exercise or expression of engagement**

Centrality/ Complexity of Capacity	Specific Human Capacity	Engages Subjective Self	Engages Social Relationships	Engages Material World
Highest Order Capacities ↕	30. interpersonal communion and love	X	X	
	29. aesthetic judgment and enjoyment	X	X	X
	28. forming virtues	X	X	X
	27. moral awareness and judgment	X	X	X
	26. truth seeking	X	X	X
	25. abstract reasoning	X	X	X
Creating Capacities ↕	24. self-reflexivity	X		
	23. identity formation	X	X	
	22. anticipate the future	X	X	X
	21. valuation	X	X	X
	20. compose and recount narratives	X	X	
	19. language use	X	X	
	18. symbolization	X	X	X
	17. create, grasp, and communicate meanings	X	X	
	16. self-transcendence		X	X
	15. material cultivation and development		X	X
	14. inventing and employing technology		X	X
	13. creativity, innovation, and imagination	X	X	X
	12. acting as efficient causes of own actions and interactions	X	X	X
Secondary Experience Capacities ↕	11. inter-subjective understanding	X	X	
	10. episodic and long-term remembering	X	X	X
	9. emotional experience	X	X	X
	8. interest formation	X	X	X
	7. assigning causal attributions	X	X	X
Primary Experience Capacities ↑	6. practical consciousness	X	X	X
	5. volition	X	X	X
	4. mental representation	X	X	X
	3. understand quantity, quality, time, and space properties	X	X	X
Existence Capacities	2. conscious awareness	X	X	X
	1. subconscious being	X	X	X

various sorts of innovations, extensions, novelties, and other creative and imaginative developments within the self, in relation to other humans, and engaged with the material environment. The downwardly pointing arrows on the left indicate that higher-level capacities often possess the ability to exert causal forces or influences on the more basic capacities below them. For instance, moral awareness can influence valuation, which can in turn shape emotional experiences, which in turn again can influence volitions. Up from all of these emerge what I view as capacities of the highest order—in complexity, dependent, and practice—involving abstracting, truth, morality, virtues, aesthetics, communion, and love.[41]

Continuing to study table 1, the three right-hand columns indicate the objects that each capacity normally engages, whether the interior subject self of the capacity's human possessor, social relationships with other humans, or features of the nonhuman material world. We see that, while some capacities tend to focus on one or two objects—for instance, self-reflexivity focuses primarily on the self—most capacities engage the self, other humans, *and* the material environment, even if they do so in different ways. For example, emotional experiences occur "within" the subjective self and typically have to do with meaningful interpretations of bodily sensations produced through particular kinds of interactions with the social and material world. This widespread engagement across the three object domains does not tell us that the three named objects are the wrong indicators of important differences across the capacities. They are. What this tells us is that the exercise of most human capacities enmesh humans with many dimensions of reality—the internal and external, the self and other, the alive and inert, the tangible and intangible, the social and material. Most relevant from a sociological perspective, however, is that every listed capacity engages social relationships with other humans. Even the most basic capacities of conscious awareness and unconscious being touch on social relationships with other people. This we might interpret as evidence in partial support of Émile Durkheim's "social epistemology,"[42] which takes a distinctively sociological approach to explaining not only what humans are and how they behave but also what they can and do know—a theory of knowledge on which I also partly draw to critique

41. This table is offered not as the definitive, complete accounting of the order of human capacities but a possible initial conceptual ordering subject to revision and development.

42. Anne Rawls, "Durkheim's Epistemology: The Neglected Argument," *American Journal of Sociology* 102, no. 2 (1996): 430–82.

strong social constructionism and develop an alternative approach to human knowing in chapter 3.

To further illustrate some of the relationships among the human capacities enumerated in this chapter, figure 2 depicts many—though certainly not all—of their upwardly emergent and downwardly dependent relations (the dashed arrow lines are the same as the solid arrow lines except they cut through capacities texts). To be clear, the arrows, levels, and relations represented here are not intended to be exhaustive and definitive but conceptually illustrative of the general idea—further research and thinking could no doubt much better specify the elements of this figure more accurately and thoroughly. We see again that capacities crucial for the emergence of personhood work upwardly from the most basic existence capacities through experience and creating capacities to the highest order capacities. Relations among capacities are complex, generally moving "upward," though sometimes are reciprocal. In other words, central human capacities are highly interdependent and interactive. I have not necessarily captured all of the dependency and emergence relationships here. And it would take many pages to explain each of the relationships depicted with arrows here, which I will not attempt, in the interest of progress on the larger argument. Worth pointing out, however, I think, is the centrality of three capacity nodes here. Most capacities are linked to others with between two and seven arrows. But the causal capacities to act as the efficient cause of one's own actions and interactions, for human creativity and innovation and imagination, and for self-transcendence are tied to other capacities by a larger number of arrows—at least as I have presented it—by ten, eight, and eight, respectively. Particularly crucial, then, in the middle level of creating capacities seem to be the human ability as agents proactively to make things happen in the world, to think and act creatively, and to transcend the concern with one's self in order to seriously engage other people and concerns in the world. This observation of persons as creative actors with outward life projects to pursue fits with the larger picture of personhood that I am developing in this book. It also helps to call into question certain social theories and methods that centralize language as the source of all human life, that focus strictly on structures of social relations at the expense of actors with agency, and that fragment persons into bearers of values on different variables that are treated as the real agents in social life. Chapters 3–5 address those concerns from the standpoint of the critical realist personalism developed throughout this book. At present, however, the key concern is to note the variety, complexity, interdependence, emergence, and creative

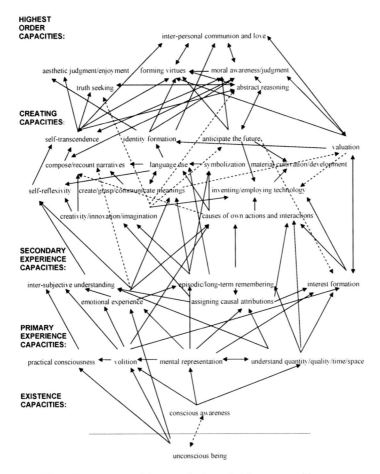

FIGURE 2. Upwardly emergent and downwardly dependent human capacities.

action-oriented nature of the many capacities that help to define human life and from which, I will argue below, human personhood emerges.

Before moving forward, a few last clarifications about these human capacities are warranted. First, I am not saying that the use or expression of the human capacities named above has been constant throughout human history, that humans are somehow everywhere and at all times the same in how these capacities are employed. Everything human is of course historically and culturally conditioned. Modern people, for instance, appear much more oriented toward plumbing the depths of personal subjective inwardness than were many premodern peoples.[43] But that itself does not change the fact of the existence of the natural human capacity for subjective self-consciousness. Many causal capacities exist in reality without being activated and expressed. Others, by their very nature, can be expressed in a variety of ways. So the fact that we observe human variability across history and cultures with regard to the expression of some of the abilities I have enumerated does not undermine the fact that humans qua humanity naturally possess these capacities.[44] Such capacities are real, are rooted in nature, and are as a collection distinctively human.

Second, I need to underscore the profoundly social preconditioning and character of the thirty capacities. The capacities named above are the natural endowments of distinct people with minimally normally functioning bodies and lives, to be sure. But that is only because all normal people are born into and grow up and live their lives within communities of other people. Functioning human capacities presuppose functioning human social life. None of the capacities identified above would have a chance to develop normally, much less flourish, apart from regular and intense social interaction with other humans who are also exercising their natural capacities. Most if not all of the capacities are themselves by nature highly socially oriented. They are exercised not to sustain isolated, atomized individuals but to bond people together in social relationships—in keeping with the socially oriented nature of their own personhood, as described below. So whenever we think about the capacities of single persons, we need to remember that they are very socially and interactively rooted, nurtured, oriented, and functional.

43. See, for example, Taylor, *Sources of the Self*; Ian Watt, *The Rise of the Novel* (Berkeley and Los Angeles: University of California Press, 2001). We should not overestimate the subjectivity of modern people compared to premoderns, however, since plenty of ancient literature—such as the Hebrew Psalms and St. Augustine's *Confessions*—reveals the potential for profound depths of subjective reflexivity.

44. This, then, is the answer to the anthropologist who claims an inability to identify "essential" human characteristics based on the observed variability in expressions of human life in different cultures: critical realism would have us focus on the existence of natural capacities, whether or not they are always and in every circumstance activated; simply because members of some tribe do not exhibit strong tendencies toward abstract thinking, say, does not mean that they do not possess the natural capacities to do so under circumstances that would activate those tendencies. In theory I might even say that certain powers in reality exist about which we have not yet become aware because the conditions that would give rise to them have not yet occurred, though this is abstract speculation.

Finally, we also need to register the fact that these human capacities can be and often are used for ill and not for good. My introduction of the thirty capacities in the previous pages cast them in a fairly positive light, emphasizing the many impressive and sometimes-admirable things they enable humans to do. But we must always acknowledge that every human power, however impressive, can be directed toward good or bad ends. Our human capacities can always be negatively as well as positively charged. They can be used for "win-lose" as well as "win-win" outcomes. Humans use their capacity for long-term memory, for instance, to keep promises, but also to hold grudges, feed melancholy and depression, and nurture desires for revenge. We deploy our technological abilities to save millions of lives in clinics and hospital operating rooms, but also to send millions in enemy, stigmatized, or scapegoat groups to their deaths. It is important, therefore, not to view human capacities in too consistently a rosy or romanticized light. That itself would be to turn away from reality. Often, we know, people and groups use their capacities for their own good and at the real expense of others. Any account of personhood therefore needs to attend to the realities of personal egoism and ill will as well as to the related social dynamics of exclusion, exploitation, coercion, and oppression. I will revisit these themes from time to time throughout the following chapters. In chapter 7 I also examine in greater depth their larger significance for understanding the good in human life and society.

Human Personhood

The thirty human causal capacities are the stuff out of which human personhood exists emergently. Recall that, through natural processes of emergence, elements at one level of reality interact or relate in particular configurations in ways that give rise to new, ontologically real entities at higher levels of existence possessing characteristics and capacities that are irreducible to the lower-level elements that compose them. This is how human persons, in the sense I mean, are composed. The causal capacities I have enumerated above interact with one another, and certainly with other natural human powers that I have not named, and with the external environment in particular ways that emergently constitute a new human reality, the reality of personhood. Normal human persons, then, we can understand as higher-order, emergent beings existing through the interactive functioning of specific, lower-order, human causal capacities, which, when related in operation in those ways, sustain personhood. In this way, the normal human person is dependent upon the causal powers that constitute him or her, which themselves are entirely dependent upon human brain and body. Yet personhood subsists as real ontological being, as its own existent actuality with its own causal capacities, not reducible to the lower-level entities that emergently compose it. In short, human persons and personhood are not epiphenomenal appearances that can be dissolved by making reductionistic moves toward lower, allegedly more real levels of reality.[45] Human persons are fully real, in all of their properties, structures, powers, and existence.

I am not able to specify the exact relational configurations through which the many human causal capacities interact to give rise emergently to personhood. At this level of reality, such interactions are not subject to mathematical formulation or modeling or even precise verbal description. Many such things remain a mystery to the human mind. Brain scientists call understanding and explaining this emergence from the brain of the personal self with self-awareness, identity, agency, and responsibility "the Holy Grail of neuroscience."[46] But this lack of exact knowledge about the interactive or relational conditions that give rise to personhood is not troubling. Much in science remains mysterious, yet we nevertheless rightly place confidence in it and work with our limited knowledge of it. We know, for instance, that gravitational force is real and operative, and we can formulate equations to represent its strength, but ultimately we do not know how and why gravity works. It simply does. Similarly, we know that some objects are living while others are not, and we can define the living by certain characteristics (growth, adaptation, reproduction, etc.), but how it is that nonliving matter (carbon, H_2O, etc.) transcends its nonlife to "leap" into the qualitatively different realm of life remains mysterious. Yet somehow it does. And then sometimes the life of the living stops, such that the same material substances become dead. It is therefore sufficient,

45. Joseph Margolis is very strong on this point as well, although our respective accounts do not agree on every point of discussion; see Margolis, *Persons and Minds: The Prospects of Nonreductive Materialism* (Dordrecht: D. Reidel, 1978).

46. Bear, Connors, and Paradiso, eds., *Neuroscience: Exploring the Brain*, 434. Francis Fukuyama writes, "There is a hierarchy of levels of complexity in science, with human beings and human behavior occupying a place at the uppermost level. . . . It would be surprising if the process of 'emergence' didn't play an important part in explaining how humans came to be human. . . . We are complex wholes rather than the sum of simple parts." Fukuyama, *Our Posthuman Future*, 164, 171.

for now at least, simply to understand that human personhood, as its own
distinctive reality with its own particular characteristics, has existence by
emergence through the sustaining interactive operation of lower-level human causal capacities.

What then is a person?[47] By *person* I mean a conscious, reflexive, embodied, self-transcending center of subjective experience, durable identity, moral commitment, and social communication who—as the efficient
cause of his or her own responsible actions and interactions—exercises
complex capacities for agency and intersubjectivity in order to develop
and sustain his or her own incommunicable self in loving relationships with
other personal selves and with the nonpersonal world. That, in any case,
is what a normal person is, a person who has developed normally. This is
an unwieldy concept, but the unpacking of each element of it in the following pages should help to make it more understandable. The reader will
immediately note that many of the causal capacities named in the previous
section show up in this definition. However, by the key phrases *center of*
and *in order to* I mean to fuse those elements together into a single, coherent, existent life that is not simply a jumbling together of component parts
but a distinct personal being. It is not that capacities like embodiment,
self-reflexivity, and durable identity somehow in personhood "emerge
out of themselves"—which is impossible—but that they are drawn up
through the "centeredness" of personhood into an integrated function-

---

47. My thinking as expressed in the following pages has been informed and shaped in vari-
ous ways by the following personalist and related writings: Emmanuel Mounier, *Personalism*
(Notre Dame, IN: University of Notre Dame Press, 1952); Jacques Maritain, *The Person and
the Common Good* (1946; Notre Dame, IN: University of Notre Dame Press, 1966); Maritain,
The Collected Works of Jacques Maritain, Volume 11 (Notre Dame, IN: University of Notre
Dame Press, 1996); Maritain, *Man and the State* (Washington, DC: Catholic University of
America Press, 1951); Martin Buber, *I and Thou* (New York: Charles Scribner's Sons, 1970);
Alistair McFadyen, *The Call to Personhood* (Cambridge: Cambridge University Press, 1990);
Rufus Burrow, *Personalism: A Critical Introduction* (St. Louis: Chalice Press, 1999); Michael
Polanyi, *Personal Knowledge: Toward a Post-Critical Philosophy* (Chicago: University of Chi-
cago Press, 1958); Karol Wojtyla, *Person and Community* (New York: Peter Lang, 1993); John
Crosby, *The Selfhood of the Human Person* (Washington, DC: Catholic University of America
Press, 1996); Crosby, *Personalist Papers* (Washington, DC: Catholic University of America
Press, 2003); Borden Parker Bowne, *Personalism* (Boston: Houghton Mifflin, 1908); Thomas
Williams, *Who Is My Neighbor: Personalism and the Foundations of Human Rights* (Washing-
ton, DC: Catholic University of America Press, 2005); Eileen Cantin, *Mounier: A Personalist
View of History* (New York: Paulist Press, 1973); Joseph Amato, *Mounier and Maritain* (Yp-
silanti, MI: Sapientia Press, 1975); Taylor, *Sources of the Self.*

ing at a higher ontological level. The whole, again, is more than the sum of its parts, even as the parts are entailed in the whole. Furthermore, the lower-level parts are causally influenced by the higher-level whole that, by virtue of its "center" acts downwardly upon them. In any case, wholes do have their parts, at least analytically speaking, and for purposes of analytic understanding I should unpack my definition and explain better what I mean by some of its terms.

Persons, first and foremost, are *centers of* something. This is absolutely crucial. It means that persons are not mere conglomerations, inventories, or compilations of diverse features. At the core of the person is a centering, interior focal point of personal being, consciousness, and activity. Persons exhibit structures of internal organization that provide a hub or nucleus of coherence and a continuity of awareness and action. It is not that persons are perfectly unified, harmonized, or consistent internally. We are not. Personal being involves certain degrees of internal disconnection, disjuncture, and lack of integration between parts. People's structures of belief and patterns of behavior, for example, do not always consistently add up. But those disconnections always operate relative to what for all normal persons is a more dominant controlling center of coordinated mental and physical activity. If such an organizing personal center of coherence and direction were not prevailing, the very idea and experience of disconnection and lack of integration would be meaningless. It is only against the governing center of personhood that elements of internal disjuncture can be recognized and problematized. Being centers also does not mean that unconscious activity does not also govern human actions. Unconscious activity clearly does also govern human actions. But neither does the real unconscious eliminate the fact of personal centeredness. A moment's reflection by (presumably not mad) readers on their own subjective experience of personhood will validate this point about the person being and having a "center of" coordinated awareness and activity. Indeed, it is precisely the breakdown of such a "center of" in the forms of multiple personality disorder, schizophrenia, and other psychotic thought and identity disorders that we judge that human personhood is being threatened by pathological, person-damaging forces. The normal person, by contrast, operates primarily out of a deep, single, centered nucleus of being, self-governance, and self-direction.

What, then, are the properties that characterize the "center" that the person has and is? First, the person is a *conscious* center. Objects lacking any consciousness—boulders, cars, fungi—cannot be personal. Persons are. It is not necessary that persons be continuously conscious to sustain personal existence. Sometimes persons sleep without dreaming, sometimes they are knocked unconscious, and sometimes they slip into comas. But they remain persons nonetheless. What matters in personhood is the capacity for consciousness and perhaps its occasional exercise or future promise thereof.[48] In order to be personal, however, human consciousness requires not mere awareness but the *reflexive* awareness of self-consciousness. To be a person is in part to be able to gain enough distance from oneself to make oneself the object of one's mental gaze, to look inward. It is not simply to be a knower, but to know that one is a knower in a way that this reflexive self-awareness can condition one's knowing, not only about the external world but also about oneself. This capacity is a human universal, insofar as all humans "have a concept of the person in the psychological sense. They distinguish self from others, and they can see the self both as subject and object."[49] Through reflexivity, persons enter into deliberative and evaluative conversations with themselves as internal dialogue partners in ways that facilitate responsibility and potential for self-transformation.[50]

Human persons are also always *embodied*. While much of my definition of the person emphasizes the intangible, mental, subjective, "spiritual" aspects of human being, none of that ever exists apart from the corporeal materiality of living flesh and blood. My theory of emergence elaborated above necessitates that. Human persons are always unified beings of existent duality. They are all the time both material body and immaterial "soul" existent in singular unity.[51] This view of personhood as united duality is reflected in classical definitions of the person. Aristotle, for instance, defined the person as a "rational animal," indicating both immaterial cognition and material embodiment. And Boethius and Aquinas[52] taught that *de persona et duabus naturis*, in defining the person as "an individual

---

48. This is a point of grave contention among philosophers, theologians, and medical ethicists over which I do not want to bog down at this stage, so I make my general point and leave certain specifics open.

49. Donald Brown, *Human Universals* (New York: McGraw-Hill, 1991), 135.

50. See Margaret Archer, *Structure, Agency, and the Internal Conversation* (Cambridge: Cambridge University Press, 2003).

51. See Introduction note 30, p. 22.

52. Complicating matters here, however, is the fact that both Boethius and Aquinas taught that angels are also persons, though for present purposes I limit the scope of discussions to humans and set aside the question of the possibility of immaterial bodies.

substance of a rational nature."[53] I agree with the general ontology suggested by these definitions, if not the definitions themselves. Human persons are always embodied. Exactly how the material and immaterial dimensions of personhood relate to each other I will leave to philosophers to debate.[54] For present purposes, I need not take a particular position, other than to note that my account, which emphasizes emergence and duality, rejects the extremes of substance dualism and reductive physicalism.[55]

Persons, I am suggesting, are also *self-transcending*. Again, by this I mean that, although persons as "centers" experience profound depths of

53. In the wake of the Enlightenment, and particularly of German idealism, however, definitions of person began to lose the importance of the body; thus John Locke, for example, defines the person as "a thinking intelligent being, that has reason and reflection, and can consider itself, the same thinking thing, in different times and places; which it does only by that consciousness which is inseparable from thinking and seem to me essential to it." Locke, *Essay concerning Human Understanding* (1690), book 2, chapter 27. Even the philosophical animalist Eric Olson is happy to define the person in terms of "being rational, intelligent, and self-conscious." Olson, *What Are We? A Study in Personal Ontology* (New York: Oxford University Press, 2007), 9. Benedict Ashley describes person as "embodied intelligent freedom," in Benedict Ashley, Jean Deblois, and Kevin O'Rourke, *Health Care Ethics* (Washington, DC: Georgetown University Press, 2006), 39.

54. Some of the current alternative accounts are reductive physicalism, nonreductive physicalism, emergent dualism, and substance dualism. See, among the vast literature, for instance, Jaegwon Kim, *Physicalism, or Something Near Enough* (Princeton, NJ: Princeton University Press, 2005); Marleen Rozemond, *Descartes's Dualism* (Cambridge, MA: Harvard University Press, 1998); Margolis, *Persons and Minds*; Warren Brown, Nancey Murphy, and H. Newton Malony, eds., *Whatever Happened to the Soul?* (Minneapolis: Fortress Press, 1998); Malcolm Jeeves, *From Cells to Souls—and Beyond: Changing Portraits of Human Nature* (Grand Rapids, MI: Eerdmans, 2004); Ric Macuga, *In Defense of the Soul: What It Means to Be Human* (Grand Rapids, MI: Brazos Press, 2002).

55. The notion of embodiment is growing in importance in numerous fields in social science and the humanities—not all ways of which, however, agree with where I go in this book—as represented by Elizabeth Teater, *Embodied Geographies: Spaces, Bodies, and Rites of Passage* (New York: Routledge, 1999); George Lakoff and Mark Johnson, *Philosophy in the Flesh: The Embodied Mind and Its Challenge to Western Thought* (New York: Basic Books, 1999); Simon Williams and Gillian Bendelow, *The Lived Body: Sociological Themes, Embodied Issues* (New York: Routledge, 1998); Raymond Gibbs, *Embodiment and Cognitive Science* (Cambridge: Cambridge University Press, 2006); Evan Thompson, *Mind in Life: Biology, Phenomenology, and the Sciences of Mind* (Cambridge, MA: Belknap Press of Harvard University Press, 2007); Francisco Varela, Evan Thompson, and Eleanor Rosch, *The Embodied Mind: Cognitive Science and Human Experience* (Cambridge, MA: MIT Press, 1992); Chris Frith, *Making Up the Mind: How the Brain Creates Our Mental World* (Hoboken, NJ: Wiley-Blackwell, 2007); Shaun Gallagher, *How the Body Shapes the Mind* (New York: Oxford University Press, 2006).

subjective reflexivity and self-concern, persons are also capable of passing beyond themselves to be attentive and present to nonpersonal objects and especially to persons other than themselves. To transcend means to pass beyond a point, to cross a threshold to another place—from the Latin, *transcendere*, which means "to climb over, to surpass," from *trans* (beyond) and *scandere* (to climb). Human persons have the ability to pass beyond a concern with themselves to engage other and different concerns, those of other persons, of better understanding reality, of the possible meanings and purposes of life and the cosmos.[56] To repeat, in some sense, all conscious creatures transcend themselves insofar as they are consciously aware of a reality beyond themselves. But human self-transcendence is exceptional. Nonsentient objects do not have selves to focus on or transcend—dirt, trees, and airplanes simply are what they are. Many conscious animals do have selves of sorts but appear to live primarily within and for their selves. Cats, for instance, are creatures acutely aware of their environments but—with the exception of felines taking care of their kittens—cats generally exist in and for themselves. Because cats are not personal in the way that humans are personal, we do not expect them to transcend themselves and so do not morally judge them to be "selfish," even though they are normally quite self-centered. Human persons are different, however. By virtue of their personhood, persons are quite able to climb past themselves to attend to and devote themselves to that which is beyond themselves. According to personalist theory, the ultimate form of self-transcendence is love for and communion with other persons.[57]

I have characterized persons as particular kinds—conscious, reflexive, embodied, self-transcending—of "centers of" existence and activity. But of what exactly are they centers? Four things, as I am theorizing persons here. First, persons are centers of *subjective experience*. As persons participate in and observe through their senses the world in which they live, they encounter events, states, situations, and interactions that impress upon them various sensations, thoughts, feelings, and other mental and bodily responses that register and elicit responses subjectively in their conscious awareness. The subjective nature of the experiencing concerns the

---

56. See Douglas Porpora, "The Caterpillar's Question: Contesting Anti-Humanism's Contestations," *Journal for the Theory of Social Behaviour* 27, no. 2 (1997): 243–63.

57. For one among many examples: "All meaningful knowledge is for the sake of action, and all meaningful action is for the sake of friendship." John Macmurray, *The Self as Agent* (Amherst, NY: Humanity Books, 1957), 15.

"inward" nature of the perceived and processed qualia, sensations, and feelings. Although it is difficult to express and explain, persons simply "occupy" and operate "out from" a perceiving and reflexive consciousness that has what can only be described as having an "internal" or "inward" and "private" quality to it. This private quality is a human universal.[58] As persons we experience ourselves as having an "inside" of thoughts, feelings, beliefs, desires, and so on that are not accessible to objective observation unless and until we express them through means of communication; and even then it can be impossible to convey the actual qualia of our experience to others. This is the dimension of our personhood that concerns subjective experience. What matters for and about persons is that they exist and operate as self-controlling centers that coordinate, interpret, actively make coherent sense from, and formulate responses to the mass of perceptual data the human body takes in. What also matters about persons is that they do not simply perceive and react to stimuli behavioristically—they actively experience and process their perceptions cognitively, affectively, volitionally, and evaluatively in a subjectively inward place of personal existence. And that provides personal existence a particular depth, complexity, and richness of interiority that is lacking in nonpersonal forms of life.

Persons are also centers of *durable identity*. Insofar as persons are self-reflexive, as subjects they also can understand themselves as objects existing in larger natural and social worlds. Within those worlds, personal beings are capable of relating intersubjectively with other personal beings, not as things ("its") but as reciprocating persons ("yous"). Personal beings, we shall see, are also "incommunicable"—that is, unique and irreplaceable selves, not exchangeable specimens of a more general human stock.[59] This means that persons can, must, and do know *who* they are, that they can and do represent to themselves and other persons the particular "I" that they as personal beings exist as. In short, persons can, must, and do have singular identities that they are capable of generating, knowing, communicating, and sustaining over time and space. Identities are the self-referencing markers by which persons comprehend themselves as distinct,

58. See Brown, *Human Universals*, 135.

59. "Incommunicability [means that a] . . . person is not able to be repeated in some sense or other by the other person, and does not share his being with them. . . . 'Incommunicability' expresses individual being by means of an antithesis to what is general or universal." Robert Spaemann, *Persons: The Difference between "Someone" and "Something"* (New York: Oxford University Press, 2006), esp. 34–40, 41, 44.

incommunicable selves amid a world of selves and nonselves. And persons are a particular kind of existent being that have self-governing centers that actively work to create, communicate, and sustain their own stable identities throughout the course of changes in their own experiences.

Persons are also self-governing centers of *moral commitment*. As I have written at length elsewhere and mentioned above, one ineliminable feature of human personhood is possessing a moral orientation that creates moral differentiations in the world through beliefs and judgments about what are good and bad, right and wrong, just and unjust, worthy and unworthy.[60] Crucial to these beliefs and judgments is the fact that they are understood as grounded not in our own desires, decisions, or preferences, but are believed to exist apart from these, providing normative standards by which our desires, decisions, and preferences can themselves be judged. Humans possess the capacity and propensity not only to have desires, beliefs, and feelings, but also the capacity and disposition to make moral evaluations of our desires, beliefs, and feelings, which opens the potential to change them. One cannot be a human person without also being a moral creature. One cannot live as a functioning human agent or sustain a personal or social identity without locating oneself in moral space.[61] Persons are the particular kind of existent creatures that are self-governing centers of moral perception, evaluation, judgment, and commitment. Persons are not the passive object recipients of the consequences of moral influences, but the active, involved, responsible subject participants of moral thought, order, and behavior. Persons and only persons are the subjects and agents of their moral lives.

Finally, persons are self-governing centers of *social communication*. Many personalists insist that persons are not "individuals," when the latter is understood as discrete, self-contained, autonomous, self-existent selves. Personalism thus rejects the human image constructed and promoted by individualistic liberalism, libertarianism, social contractarianism, rational choice theory, and exchange theory. Persons do not exist first as self-contained selves who subsequently engage and exchange with other selves in order to secure some outcome or consume some benefit. Persons, instead, are originally, constitutively, and inescapably social, interactive, and communicative in origin and being. Sociality helps constitute the essential character of personhood. For starters, the human bodies from

60. Smith, *Moral, Believing Animals.*
61. Taylor, *Sources of the Self.*

which personhood emergently arises into ontological being are not only produced by but essentially *are* the commingling of two preexistent human bodies through the intimate meeting of personal relation. Furthermore, the necessary condition of the full expression of personhood emerging from any human body is that the body from which personhood is developing be embedded for years in sustained networks of human social and personal relationships of communication, interaction, nurturance, instruction, support, challenge, and belonging.[62] Socially isolated human selves prove to be emaciated selves and underdeveloped persons. Rich, interactive communication among persons is that which gives rise to and sustains robust personhood. As active participants in these larger interactive webs of communication, persons are capable actors of intersubjective discourse, self-governing centers of social communication, and proactive agents of reciprocal relations and shared understanding. Literally, to be a person *is* in part to communicate with other persons toward the exchange of self and mutual understanding.

Personalism takes the emphasis on social communication one step further, however. From a personalist perspective, persons are not simply social creatures. Nearly everyone grants as a truism that humans are naturally social. But wolves, bees, hyenas, and ants are also highly socially interactive. Social communication does not make for personhood. What humans experience in their social interactions that sets them apart as persons is the relating at a deeper level of intersubjective understanding, what some personalists call "communion." Personalist theorists define communion as a type of shared human existence and reciprocal action that advances the personal fulfillment of those involved through relationships of mutual confirmation and affirmation. Communion involves the mutual giving of personal selves as gifts of fellowship and love for the good of each person concerned.[63]

Ontologically, persons are centers of subjective experience, durable identity, moral commitment, and social communication. These are crucially defining features of personhood, markers of unique personal existence constituting one type of real in the larger reality. These central aspects of the personal, however, culminate in another critical dimension

62. Alasdair MacIntyre, *Dependent, Rational Animals* (Chicago: Open Court Press, 1999).

63. Williams, *Who Is My Neighbor: Personalism and the Foundations of Human Rights*, 140–42.

of personhood, namely that persons are *the efficient causes of their own responsible actions and interactions*. A central characteristic of personal being is possessing the capacity to cause one's own actions and interaction. Humans everywhere, in every culture, understand that persons are at least in part responsible for their own actions.[64] Inanimate and nonsentient entities do not possess this ability. Coal burns not because it causes itself to burn, for instance, but because someone or something else burns it. Earthworms burrow through dirt not because they choose among alternatives to do so, but because automatically by nature that is what earthworms do. Nonpersonal sentient animals can and do function as the efficient causes of their own actions and interactions, but they do so within much more behavioristic parameters of stimuli and response, not in the meaning-laden terms that comprise significant actions. Thus, a bear is not wrongly thought of as its own cause of the difference between its roaming up a hill alone in search of berries versus working the rapids of a river among rival bears in search of fish. But the self-determinants of those behaviors operate at fairly primitive levels and are heavily conditioned by genetically grounded instincts interacting with determining stimuli-response mechanisms. So when the bear wanders into our blueberry patch and destroys our crop, we may get angry and frustrated, and we may complain to the county's animal control office that the bear is "responsible" for the damage it caused. But we will not hold the bear responsible for a choice to eat our blueberries in the same way we hold responsible a human person who did the same thing. There are severe limits on the causal responsibilities of nonpersonal sentient objects. It is only personal beings who enjoy robust capacities to be the efficient causes of their own responsible actions and interactions.[65] That is why we put persons on trial for crimes, but not bears. Bears do not commit crimes. Bears do not engage in meaningful actions. Bears merely behave.

All of this directly relates to the next aspect of personhood, namely that persons *exercise complex capacities for agency and intersubjectivity*. What do these terms mean? Agency is the human capacity to employ intention, deliberation, and choice to make decisions and to impose them on the

64. Humans universally "do not see the person as a wholly passive recipient of external action, nor do they see the self as wholly autonomous. To some degree, they see the person as responsible for his or her actions. They distinguish actions that are under control from those that are not. They understand the concept of intention." Brown, *Human Universals*, 135.

65. In Steven Lukes's words, humans have a particular ability "to act otherwise." Lukes, *Essays in Social Theory* (New York: Columbia University Press, 1977), 6–24.

surrounding world. Agency contrasts with unreflective, deterministic, causal processes involved in various natural forces. Human agency operates in contexts where outcomes are underdetermined. Human persons can then play an intentional role as agents by influencing which outcomes become actual. Intersubjectivity is the existence of a state of mutually understood or shared cognitions, affects, meanings, evaluations, or desires between two or more persons. Intersubjectivity involves the mutual understanding of cultural definitions of situations, of the meanings of actions, and of the content of intentions, thoughts, emotions, and wants. It consists of the making accessible to other persons the content of a self's subjective experiences and dispositions. Intersubjectivity is not automatically given. It must be achieved. The primary vehicles for the accomplishment of intersubjectivity are language and other forms of communicative symbolic interaction, the uses and meanings of which are publicly shared, not privately owned. Persons, then, are those existent beings possessing the causal capacities for agency and intersubjectivity and exercising them to accomplish particular purposes.[66]

What are the particular purposes that persons exercise their capacities for agency and inter-subjectivity to accomplish? My definition begins to answer this by saying, "in order to sustain his or her own incommunicable self." Personhood is emergent from the interactive operation of a host of human causal capacities, which themselves are rooted in the natural human body. But once emergent as existent realities, persons by nature become active participants in their own self-creation and continuation. Persons—as living, organic, "spiritual" selves—must be sustained, nourished, cultivated. And persons themselves are the most important agents in their own personal sustenance. A central project of every person, then, is the sustaining of themselves as personal selves.[67] Life for persons is about

66. For an argument about how this relates to Searle's *Construction of Social Reality* book, see Mariam Thalos, "Searle's Foole: How a Constructionist Account of Society Cannot Substitute for a Causal One," *American Journal of Economics and Sociology* 62, no. 1 (2003): 105–22. Jürgen Habermas also makes important sociological contributions to the centrality of language in human life and society.

67. This statement here is descriptive, although, as I argue in chapter 7, it entails a normative claim within it. In fact, I argue in that chapter below that the descriptive and the normative cannot actually be separated in these matters. What I mean, then—the significance of which will only become clearer at the end of this book—is that persons as a matter of descriptive fact are purposefully oriented and as a matter of normative fact have particular purposes that are proper to their being.

more than physical survival and security—although, insofar as persons are embodied souls, bodily survival and security are essential aspects of sustaining personhood. Life is about developing, protecting, and continuing into the future one's personal self.

Herein is a key point of connection between my account and other sociological theories that stress individual interests and desires, particularly utilitarian-based rational choice theory. I said above that a fundamental human capacity is interest formation. I have now said that a central element of my account's definition of a person is the personal project of developing and sustaining an incommunicable, person self. Packed into that project of self-development and sustenance are, it turns out, strong elements of rational egoism, self-interest, desire, competition, and choice. No reasonable sociological theory can deny or ignore the fact that we live in a world of scarcity and that this scarcity matters for human action and social structure. Furthermore, characteristic human perceptions, emotions, and behaviors—anxiety, hoarding, excluding others, and so on—tend to accentuate and exacerbate those scarcities. My account of personhood emphasizes relationships of self-giving and, we will see below, the learning of virtues that help overcome some of the problems of rational egoism. But my account also does not ignore the evident fact that most humans endemically (which is not to say universally) desire greater material possessions, experiences, statuses, and security than they often possess— in fact my account is theoretically perfectly consistent with this. I do firmly resists the reductionistic aspiration of utilitarian-based social theories to oversimplify the complexities of personhood and personal life— including self-transcendence, identity, morality, and communion—into rational exchanges toward maximizing material goods. But personal life also does consist, among other things, of a great many purposive exchanges—sometimes calculated, often self-centered—toward the end of sustaining the personal self. That fact is built into my larger personalist account, in this very recognition that to be a person in a world of many kinds of scarcities is to act to develop and sustain one's personal self in ways that include the pursuit in social contexts of material and other goods through exchange and struggle. In the final two chapters I advance a theoretically coherent approach for dealing morally with this fact.

I have already said that an "incommunicable" self is one that is unique, that cannot be repeated or replaced by a replica or interchangeable specimen of the general type. No person can be exchanged for another. Particularity is indispensable to personhood. Each personal self is exactly their

own being and not another. This each person understands him or herself
to be. This is why when a particular person dies, something unique and
irreplaceable is lost. It is also why if we were either to encounter another
person who is exactly our self or to morph ourselves into a perfect copy
of another person this would provoke a personal identity crisis. But this
does not happen, because persons are naturally incommunicable selves, a
central task for whom is to sustain their own incommunicability. Finally,
the selves that are doing this work of sustaining are normally "his or her,"
male or female. Persons are always sexed and, following as a cultural inscription of meanings, gendered in one way or another.[68] There are no
asexual or suprasexual human persons. This is so because persons are
naturally always embodied, and bodies are naturally always sexed and,
by acts of human construction, gendered. Indeed, according to some personalists, differences in sexuality are a crucial aspect of the distinctions
among personal selves that create possibilities for certain crucial kinds
of interpersonal communion—although such a position is not essential
for my larger account. Suffice it to say that persons embody particularity
of many sorts, but including always the particularities of sex and gender.
In this embodied definition of persons, we move helpfully away from the
Enlightenment's notion of the person as emphasizing almost exclusively
their rational minds.

The incommunicable selves that persons act to sustain are not existent
entirely for their own sakes. For to be a person is to be both embodied
in a material world and living in social relationships with other personal
selves. Thus persons, as I am defining them, sustain their selves "in loving
relationships with other personal selves and with the nonpersonal world."
Communicating in relationships is not something that persons do for instrumental reasons after they are established as selves, but it is the very
activity that helps to constitute persons as persons in the first place and is
a central purpose of personal life.[69] "All actual life is encounter," wrote

68. The biology is sometimes not decisive, to be sure, as, depending on how one defines
male and female, there is a spectrum of possible variation and ambiguity even of genital structures as well as a range of abnormal combinations of sex chromosomes, which medicine generally considers an expression of pathology and searches for a cause and a cure.

69. Macmurray, *The Self as Agent*; Harold Oliver, "The Relational Self," in *Selves, People,
and Persons: What Does It Mean to Be a Self?* ed. Leroy Rouner, Boston University Studies
in Philosophy and Religion (Notre Dame, IN: University of Notre Dame Press, 1992), 37–51;
also see Lawrence Cahoone, "Limits of the Social and Relational Self," in *Selves, People, and
Persons*, ed. Rouner, 53–72.

the personalist philosopher and protosociologist Martin Buber.[70] Meeting, sharing, engagement, fellowship, and communion are constituting activities of personhood—not functional means or afterthoughts. They are among the very fundamental goals of personal life. Personal communication is not simply a means. It is also an end, insofar as persons are ends and communication constitutes persons. But note that I am not merely suggesting that any kind of social relationship or communication defines human personhood. Particular kinds of relationships, especially those involving love, are what matter. By "love" I do not mean feelings of attraction—which tend to be oriented to the gratification of the self. Instead, by "loving," I mean relating to other persons and things beyond the self in a way that involves the purposive action of extending and expending of oneself for the genuine good of others—whether in friendships, families, communities, among strangers, or otherwise.[71] Human persons are such that their very selves are centered in and grow out of relationships of genuine care for each other that are not purely instrumental but require genuine giving of the self in love in various ways for the good of others.[72] Furthermore, as embodied creatures in organic form—not incorporeal ghosts—persons not only relate interpersonally with other selves but also as material animals engaged in their material environments. Physical work, play, cultivation, touching, movement, labor, healing are all essential elements of personal existence. Of course, interpersonal communication and engagement with the material world often go together, as most of the latter takes place for most people in social activity. The kind of relationships with the nonpersonal world proper to human persons is also one of love— that is, of respect, care, understanding, appreciation, and protection.

---

70. Buber, *I and Thou* 62.

71. Love is not a term commonly referenced in sociology but I find it unavoidable for talking about personhood—yet also difficult in contemporary American culture, given its common assumptions and outlooks about love. The Greeks differentiated at least three types of love, as *phileo, eros,* and *agape*—the former concerned the companionship shared in friendship, the second physical and sexual attraction, and the latter a purely altruistic love enacted solely for the well-being of the loved. Love is appropriately expressed differently in different kinds of relationships. Love, for instance, can be expressed even to strangers, through respect for them and the just protection of their dignity and rights.

72. Considering in a thought experiment what human persons and life would be like if they were completely devoid of all kinds of love helps validate the ineradicability of love from the nature of personhood and social life, and therefore—given my phenomenological epistemology described in the following chapter—its legitimate use in theoretical discourse.

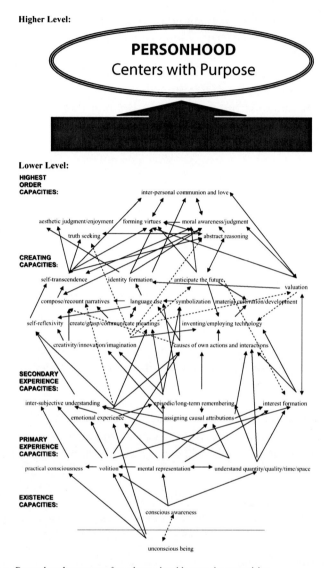

FIGURE 3. Personhood emergent from lower-level interactive capacities.

Having taken my concept of person apart and looked at it piece by piece, let me now put it back together. A normal person is a conscious, reflexive, embodied, self-transcending center of subjective experience, durable identity, moral commitment, and social communication who—as the efficient cause of his or her own responsible actions and interactions—exercises complex capacities for agency and intersubjectivity in order to

develop and sustain his or her own incommunicable self in loving relationships with other personal selves and with the nonpersonal world. This is a
mouthful. But I think it conveys some of the depth and complexity of the
character of personhood. A representation of this model is presented in
figure 3.

One last substantive observation before moving on: my account of personhood in this chapter described persons—as I also at first described
human capacities—in a fairly positive light. The creature described above
portrays an ideal representation of a person—well capacitated, adjusted,
adequately coherent, balanced, empowered, and sociable. We know, however, that the human reality is more complicated than that. Not all is quite
that well. Things can be quite bad, in fact. Sometimes in human life, both
personally and socially, things are downright awful. I think this gives us
a crucial clue for pursing the task of this book. If we want to understand
human persons and social life adequately, we will have to account not only
for powerful capacities and conditions of personal thriving but also what,
for lack of a better word, we might call brokenness. Humans seem broken[73] and the world seems broken. Empirical observations of other people,
the daily news, and often our own phenomenological experiences of ourselves as selves tell us that we humans characteristically suffer some kind
of brokenness or disorder or alienation that prevents the realization of
our completeness, perfection, integration, and wholeness.[74] Every culture,

73. The psychologist Mark Leary argues in *The Curse of the Self* that human self-
awareness gives rise to capacities of planning, decision making, self control, self evaluation,
introspection, and perspective taking—all of which serve beneficial functions in human life.
But, Leary notes, "the self is not an un-mitigated blessing. It is single-handedly responsible for
many, if not most of the problems that human beings face as individuals and as a species. . . .
The mental capacity that is responsible for many of the best aspects of being human also
underlies our most serious deficiencies and problems." According to Leary, for example, the
human capacity for self-awareness is primarily responsible for self-preoccupation, distractions
from real life, choking under pressure, insomnia, many sexual dysfunctions, beating ourselves
up, unfairly judging others, worry, fear of death, jealousy, shame, depression, self-importance,
interpersonal conflict, violent reactions to ego threats, dangerous risk taking, defensiveness,
and suicide. Thus, some of the very powers and abilities that bless humans with personal selves
turn out also to curse humans with a host of troubles and problems. Leary, *The Curse of the
Self: Self-Awareness, Egotism, and the Quality of Human Life* (New York: Oxford University
Press, 2004), 21.

74. It is difficult, in my view, based on the evidence, to resist the conclusion that no human is exempt from susceptibility to such moral brokenness. Humanity, of course, comprises
people of personal character ranging across a colossally wide moral spectrum. Some people
live lives of astonishing love, service, integrity, virtue, and humanity; others pursue lives of
reprehensible malevolence, self-centeredness, and destruction. Most of the rest of us live

philosophy, and religion has developed some account or other of what I am calling *brokenness*, conceptualizing it as ignorance, faults, wrongness, error, darkness, injustice, deviance, misdirection, evil, alienation, or some other idea that recognizes and addresses the problem raised here. Not to do so, I suggest, would be, literally, to be out of touch with reality—because something like brokenness is part of our reality. A great many social institutions, a good deal of personal experience, and very many movements for social and cultural change are all about wrestling with the thing I am calling brokenness. I do not wish to quibble about the specific labels by which we might name it.[75] Nor am I prepared to argue whether brokenness is an essential or accidental feature of reality.[76] The present point is merely that in some significant way or other, things with humans are not entirely right, together, peaceful, and functional. All is not well. Things often don't work the way they should. For one reason or way or another, something like brokenness seems to be part of the past and current hu-

---

somewhere mucking around in the middle of this moral spectrum. Neither extreme—of perfect goodness or absolute evil—is realized by any person. Rather, history and experience suggest that Alexander Solzhenitsyn was right when he observed that "the line separating good and evil passes not through states, nor between classes, nor between political parties either, but right through every human heart, and through all human hearts. This line shifts. Inside us, it oscillates with the years. And even within hearts overwhelmed by evil, one small bridgehead of good is retained. And even in the best of all hearts, there remains an un-uprooted, small corner of evil." Solzhenitsyn, *The Gulag Archipelago Two* (New York: Harper and Row, 1975), 615–16. The world is not populated with a certain number of angels, on the one hand, and a balance of beasts, on the other. Instead, the burden humans live under seems to be something like that of being "angel/beasts," in various degrees of combination (see Bruce Cockburn, "Burden of the Angel/Beast," *Dart to the Heart*, Columbia Records, 1994).

75. Scientists in various contexts might prefer terms such as *fragmentation, failure of coherence, imperfection, conflicting impulses*, and *intrinsic disorder* to describe the reality discussed here.

76. My initial inclination, however, is to say that brokenness is neither essential nor accidental, exactly. I would rather follow a line of thought suggesting that every existence of unbroken reality creates (neither exactly essentially nor accidentally) the inescapable *possibility* of brokenness, just as every affirmed "yes" carries with it an implicit, potentially expressible "no"; every shining of light brings into possibility (though not necessarily actuality) of a shadow through the obstruction of light; every real capacity and power involves the possibility of its abuse; and every act of freedom is open to misuse, even of the sort that can lead to oppression and slavery. Such an approach would suggest that the existent reality we occupy inescapably entails the *risk* of brokenness, but not necessarily its actual inevitability or essential, natural, inevitable reality. In fact, in the world we experience, the possibility of brokenness has been actualized. In which case, brokenness is a fact, but one that is neither essential nor accidental to reality, but rather an actualized possibility.

man condition.⁷⁷ At the personal level, this brokenness can take the form
of an incoherence of self, of a lack of internal integration, an inability to
realize a robust sense of wholeness as persons. At the interpersonal level,
brokenness is experienced in a host of ways, including endemic misunderstanding, hostility, hatred, estrangement, deceit, alienation, violence,
and murder. And at the social level, brokenness is expressed in institutional dysfunction, injustice, corruption, exploitation, and a host of other
social ills that people bemoan, resist, and sometimes fight.⁷⁸ Oftentimes

77. Few academic scholars and even fewer social scientists have used such normative language in their works, but that is beginning to change. The number of scholars, including social
scientists, publishing with secular presses about human evil, vice, and moral corruption has
recently increased rapidly, a sampling of whose works from a much larger related literature includes Roy Baumeister, *Evil: Inside Human Violence and Cruelty* (New York: W. H. Freeman,
1999); Arthur Miller, *The Social Psychology of Good and Evil* (New York: Guilford Press,
2005); Michael Shermer, *The Science of Good and Evil* (New York: Owl Books, 2004);
Margaret Breen and Richard Hamilton, *This Thing of Darkness: Perspectives on Evil and
Human Wickedness* (Kenilworth, NJ: Rodopi, 2003); Margaret Breen, *Minding Evil: Explo-
rations of Human Iniquity* (Kenilworth, NJ: Rodopi, 2005); Arne Vetlesen, *Evil and Human
Agency: Understanding Collective Evildoing* (Cambridge: Cambridge University Press, 2005);
Steven Bartlett, Eric Zillmer, and Irving Greenberg, *The Pathology of Man: A Study in Hu-
man Evil* (Springfield, IL: C. C. Thomas, 2005); Aaron Beck, *Prisoners of Hate: the Cognitive
Basis of Anger, Hostility, and Violence* (New York: Harper, 2000); James Waller, *Becoming
Evil: How Ordinary People Commit Genocide and Mass Killing* (New York: Oxford University
Press, 2002); Solomon Schimmel, *The Seven Deadly Sins* (New York: Oxford University Press,
1997); Ervin Staub, *The Roots of Evil: The Origins of Genocide and Other Group Violence*
(Cambridge: Cambridge University Press, 1992); Ilham Dilman, *The Self, the Soul, and the
Psychology of Good and Evil* (New York: Routledge, 2005); M. Scott Peck, *People of the Lie*
(New York: Touchstone, 1998); Charles Ford, *Lies! Lies! Lies! The Psychology of Deceit* (Ar-
lington, VA: American Psychiatric Publishing, 1999); Willard Gaylin, *Hatred: The Psychological Descent into Violence* (New York: Public Affairs, 2003); Rush Dozier, *Why We Hate* (New
York: McGraw-Hill, 2003); Michael Eric Dyson, *Pride—The Seven Deadly Sins* (New York:
Oxford University Press, 2006). Even a naturalistic sociobiologist such as Edward O. Wilson
is not averse to recognizing moral brokenness in humans: "A person who gains nothing . . . in
order to reduce [the fitness] of another has committed an act of *spite*. The action may seem
sane, and the perpetrator may seem gratified, but we find it difficult to imagine his rational
motivation. We refer to the commitment of a spiteful act as 'all too human'—and then wonder
what we meant. True spite is a commonplace in human societies. . . . Human beings are [also]
unique in their capacity to lie to other members of their own species." Wilson, *Sociobiology*
(Cambridge, MA: Harvard University Press, 1975), 117, 119.

78. Our normal vocabulary affirms that human life—however rich with dignity, beauty,
accomplishment, goodness, and love—is also fraught with a depressing diversity, extent, and
intensity of troublesome vice and moral failure. Consider, for instance, the realities that the
following words describe: selfishness, conceit, rapacity, hatred, violence, insensitivity, bigotry,

personal, interpersonal, and social brokenness are tied together in knotty, complicated ways. This recognition of such brokenness need not veer us off into philosophy or religion. The reality of the brokenness of persons and the world are relevant for sociological theorizing. A great deal of human social life consists of our attempts to cope with ourselves as human persons, individually and collectively. And part of what we have to cope with is the problematic, selfish, injurious, dark side of personal human life. We need to factor brokenness into our scholarship if we hope to understand what persons are, how they should be understood in social life, where social structures come from, what the critical purpose of social science is, and how we all might go about thinking about what is normatively good when it comes to human personal life and society. About this I will have more to say as we move ahead.

Centers with Purpose

What are the unique emergent properties and capacities of personhood? I have said that emergent properties and capacities do not exist in the lower-level parts out of which they arise. They belong to the higher level of that which is emergent. But many aspects of personhood just described

lying, ruthlessness, contempt, disloyalty, murder, abuse, fraud, malevolence, deceit, oppression, terrorism, malice, egoism, rape, apathy, animosity, ridicule, estrangement, guile, betrayal, bitterness, persecution, revenge, entrapment, genocide, bullying, envy, wickedness, lynching, injustice, coldness, stalkers, poverty, greed, intolerance, callousness, humiliation, atrocity, backbiting, rage, robbery, resentment, vindictiveness, snobbery, assault, meanness, insult, cynicism, wretchedness, tyranny, misogyny, torture, jealousy, cheating, massacre, scorn, mendacity, cowardice, duplicity, intimidation, indignity, hostility, viciousness, self-destruction, indifference, cruelty, manipulation, molestation, exploitation, battery, hard-heartedness, identity theft, unfaithfulness, slavery, acrimony, smugness, nastiness, lying, double-cross, bribery, embezzlement, executions, sadism, vice, brutality, suicide, spite, pitilessness, disdain, piggishness, ingratitude, rudeness, dishonesty, vanity, destitution, dehumanization, degradation, prejudice, stinginess, belittling, treachery, intimidation, shame, and heartlessness. Brokenness in humanity comes in many forms. To this list of nouns and verbs we can add a list of adjectives, also describing troublesome and sometimes repellent features of human persons: petty, churlish, defensive, snide, pompous, cutting, unpleasant, nasty, jealous, inpatient, insufferable, odious, self-seeking, severe, detestable, irritable, miserly, predatory, overbearing, dishonorable, grasping, sullen, self-righteous, boorish, underhanded, conceited, scornful, insincere, rude, corrupt, uncaring, disgraceful, vile, repugnant, surly, hostile, merciless, self-important, devious, repellent, beastly, supercilious, capricious, loutish, disgraceful, grudging, cynical, tiresome, insufferable, offensive, rancorous, false, dishonorable, anxious, rotten, menacing, craven, joyless, hurtful, invidious, morose, vengeful, degenerate, and dishonest.

seem similar to the capacities from which I say personhood emerges. So what is new in emergent personhood that does not exist in the human capacities? The primary answer is: *centers with purpose* of a particular kind. First, centers. My group of lower-level human capacities enumerated above does not entail an organizing or integrating center. The capacities are merely a list of various abilities, powers, or potentialities. With emergent personhood, however, dependent upon their interactive relations, a new and unique *center of subjective experience* has being. That center acts as the personal core or heart that integrates, coordinates, and directs those capacities in new, purposeful ways. The exercise of each capacity is then connected to and guided by that personal center. Without the center there is no person. The personal center emerges as a distinct reality with novel properties and capacities that help constitute the real person. But what exactly is a personal center? That is not easy to say. I could talk about brains and consciousness and subconsciousness for a long time.[79] But at some point in the process of reasoned exploration of personhood, personal centers are ineffable. Beyond some point we cannot describe them well with prose, much less represent them with mathematical equations. But that does not make them any less real or important. No normally functioning persons can reasonably deny that they operate in living their personal lives out of something like what I am calling a center of subjective experience. Our personal centers remain absolutely central. Of course, oftentimes the most real and crucial things in life are also the most inexpressible. This is not a comment about the significance of the things themselves but about the variety of kinds of human experience, understanding, and expression and their natural limits.

Second, purpose. Most of the human capacities from which I say personhood emerges are powers or potentialities, largely neutral toward particular ends.[80] In general terms, they are not in themselves directed to one specific purpose or goal—any more than a wood log carries in itself the purpose of burning in a fire or becoming a beam supporting a roof or

79. While we normally think of self-governing centers as concerning conscious awareness, and they largely do, we should not conceive of centers in strictly rationalist, Cartesian terms; personal centers of the sort I mean can and do also involve dimensions that operate below conscious awareness.

80. This neutrality should not be absolutized, however, since many basic human capacities are shaped with perceptual and conceptual biases ordered toward particular ends. For example, humans see colors in discrete categories rather than as a blended continuum and have auditory biases that allow us to discriminate phonemes. Thanks to Bill Hurlbut for corrective balance on this point.

something else. The log can be used for either, but it needs a purpose from outside itself to actualize its potential. Likewise, individual human capacities can be directed toward many different goals. But they themselves do not specify and motivate the purpose they might achieve. However, when from the many interacting human capacities real persons emerge, those capacities do come to have real purposes, a genuine "in order to." That purpose is to develop and sustain the person's own incommunicable self in loving relationships with other personal selves and with the nonpersonal world. That purpose is the natural and objective project of being a person.[81] Note that this personal purpose is much more than and qualitatively different from the mere sum total of the lower-level capacities from which it emerged. Merely adding the capacities together could not have produced the purpose. It requires a certain kind of relational interaction among the capacities for the emergent purpose to be. Of course the features of many of the lower-level capacities from which personhood emerges are crucial for enabling the purpose to be pursued and achieved—the purpose could not be engaged without those capacities. But the capacities per se, either singly or together, do not carry within themselves their own directive purpose. They need the larger emergent purpose of personhood to direct them to its end.

The purpose and the center, note, are crucially interdependent, both functionally and ontologically. Purposes presuppose intentionality. The purpose needs the center in order to be constituted, pursued, and achieved by an intentional, coherent somebody. Centers exist for intentions. The center needs the purpose in order to be itself a center *for* something and not merely to exist without end or sense. Neither can be nor do without the other. With persons, being entails becoming. And becoming presupposes being. The purpose-endowed center of personal existence has a natural narrative quest,[82] the telos of personhood. And the quest itself is only even conceivable and viable because of the existence of a personal center. To eliminate purpose breaks apart the center. To deny the center eliminates purpose.[83]

---

81. By "natural" here, I mean rooted in given human ontology, not cognitively produced by humans; by "objective" I mean belonging to reality whether or not humans are conscious of it.

82. Alasdair MacIntyre, *After Virtue* (Notre Dame, IN: University of Notre Dame Press, 1981); Taylor, *Sources of the Self*.

83. A variety of modern antihumanistic schools of thought have shown us this last point.

Now, I am fully aware that the ideas developed in the previous paragraphs are anything but broadly accepted in the sciences and humanities today. That is exactly why I have written them. Why make a case for something everyone already thinks? But to help dubious readers to continue entertaining my account, it is worth pausing to consider possible objections. First, one may object that persons are not or do not have centers of subjective experience, that whatever we humans are is disjointed, fragmented, confused, transient, de-centered. My first response is to ask who or what it is that is raising this objection and what obligation I have to respond to it. I presume the objection is coming from a person who is working with a perspective that is coherent, meaningful, and brought to bear on the discussion for a purpose. If so—by virtue of the fact that they are and I am the kind of persons that I have described in the pages above—I am obliged to answer. But if the objection is coming from a source that is disjointed, fragmented, confused, and transient, the status of the objection as presumably a reasonable question deserving reply is highly uncertain. When a stranger addresses us with a question, our normal first response it to try to reply helpfully; however, when we realize that the stranger is a child playfully babbling gibberish or an escaped mental hospital patient who is talking nonsense, we no longer feel obliged to answer the given question but instead ignore it and respond to the stranger from a different frame of reference. The same holds in the present case. If human "persons" really are essentially disjointed, fragmented, confused, transient, and de-centered, then it is not clear that anyone needs to take the objection seriously. In short, the kind of objection to my account deserving a reasoned response presupposes the very kind of center-with-purpose persons described by my account to which this objection is objecting—the objection seems self-defeating, a "performative contradiction."[84]

Nevertheless, let us take the objection seriously and see how it helps to clarify matters. By stating that we persons are centers of subjective experience, I am not claiming that our personal centers are perfectly integrated, balanced, harmonized, and functional. In most cases, we are adequately so but not completely so. There is empirical variance of personal coherence within the reality of our being personal centers. Most people are reasonably well centered but have room for increased integration and coherence.

84. Jürgen Habermas, "Discourse Ethics: Notes on a Program of Philosophical Justification," in *Moral Consciousness and Communicative Action*, trans. C. Lenhardt and S. W. Nicholsen (Cambridge, MA: MIT Press, 1990).

But when we encounter cases at extreme points in that variance toward a lack of coherence, when persons reflect radical disintegration, imbalance, or dysfunctionality of self, what do we say? That such cases are entirely normal persons, too? No. We say that such cases are indeed persons but tragically abnormal or damaged persons. These are persons, for example, who suffer conditions of mental illness and disabilities, such as multiple personality disorders, obsessive-compulsive disorder, and other psychopathologies.[85] Even so, in such cases personal centers still exist, and other persons who care hold out the hope for enhancing the coherence of those centers, even if only marginally. Radically damaged persons, to be clear, have not ceased to be persons. But they are damaged. And to deny the gap between the normal and the damaged is unhelpful. So, back to the point, we can and must bring to the center of our account of personhood the fact that persons are centers of subjective experience. But this does not force us to claim that any of us is perfectly centered, that we have achieved complete personal coherence, balance, and integration. We have not. This fact is part of what provides our personal centers with purpose. For to pursue and achieve our purpose as persons itself significantly entails the quest toward greater coherence and integration of ourselves as centers. This is constitutive of developing and sustaining our own incommunicable selves in loving relationships with other personal selves and with the non-personal world. More on that and on its moral implications in chapter 7. For now the point is that we ought not to reject the idea that persons are centers simply because our phenomenological experience is that none of us is perfectly centered. That *is* our experience. But we do not need perfection and completeness in order to still have the reality and centrality of ourselves as centers that constitute our real personhood. Indeed, the very gap between what we actually are and potential completeness is part of what is presupposed *in* our very personal purpose, which also constitutes our personhood. The alternative response to our existential situation of incomplete and imperfect centeredness, of declaring that we humans do

85. I am aware that for some of my sociological colleagues such mental pathologies are not the challenge to coherent personhood; their main objection is rather some form of situationalism—perhaps especially of dramaturgical or social psychological theories—in which persons are essentially defined by situations or chains of situations in which they find themselves. My reply is that situations do much to form people's identities and actions but are incapable of constituting or radically altering the personhood of people per se, except in the broader realities of social dependence and influence that I spell out in this book that are consistent with my theory.

not have or are not centers—that we are fictions of personal selves that
are mere sites of transient, confused, incoherent, disjointed sense experiences—is, I think, unwarranted and self-defeating. And so I set that objection aside.

A second possible objection to my account of persons as centers with
purpose is that people do not entail or possess any natural or objective
purpose. The idea is that any purpose or purposes that humans perceive
themselves to have are invented and imposed from outside of the naturally given world by the socially constructed world—they are contingent
cultural products, social constructions of "reality" that are not really objectively real. By this objection's account, all I am doing in my personalist
account is projecting upon "persons" a purpose I think is real (or *want* to
be real, since shared reason tends to dissolve into individual desire) but
which is not so. This is a serious objection requiring a serious response. A
much fuller addressing of the issues embedded in this objection is forthcoming in chapters 3 and 7. For now, the following responses will have to
suffice. First, we should note that the objection contains an inescapable
commitment to the idea that something is real. In this case, what is real is
that objective purposes are not real, that reality for humans is naturally and
objectively not purposeful. So the difference between my account and the
objection's account is not about whether certain things concerning humans
are real. The difference is about whether what is real for humans—or, by
my account, persons—includes a natural, objective purpose or not. If the
objection is true, then we do not have any natural or objective purpose,
but only take to be our purpose social constructions that we mistakenly
take to be real but that are contingent, relative, perhaps even arbitrary. In
which case, a kind of relativism sets in and it becomes unclear why the objection even matters any more (the self-defeating problem again). The objection and anyone's taking it seriously presupposes that included among
the goods or purposes of human life is to know what is real, to seek that
which is true, to dispel illusions, to conform the beliefs of our minds to the
nature of the reality that is external to our minds. If those purposes do not
matter, then this entire discussion, including the objection, is pointless. We
should bury ourselves within the social constructions we find most attractive for whatever reasons and enjoy them while we can. But that is wrong.
These purposes do matter. And so we struggle through these issues. But,
if so, both sides agree that humans confront at least some nonarbitrary
purposes with which to engage. At which point the central force of the
objection is blunted. What is left is to have a reasoned discussion about

the nature of real, objective purposes for humans. And that is what I am attempting to do in this book.

My second response to this second objection is—in the spirit of the phenomenological epistemology and retroductive reasoning that I explicate in the next chapter—to ask the reader to try to imagine what it would be like to be a person without any purpose. Expunge purpose in life entirely from one's existence. What then would we have? To begin, the possibility is nearly if not entirely impossible to imagine. That itself tells us something. But let us imagine it as best we can. Picture an absolutely purposeless human existence, pure human being entirely lacking in meaningful human becoming.[86] What would that look and feel like? Such a life would be inert, pointless, and pathetic. It would not be a life worth having or living. It hardly seems human.[87] Of course, sometimes people are confused about their life's purpose. But that does not mean they do not have one, only that they do not know what it is—otherwise the very phrase "confused about" would be nonsense, unless we think it reasonable to be confused about nonexistents. We also sometimes take breaks and vacations in order to escape from the demands and routines of our larger life's purposes. Sometimes people want to "vegetate." But such forms of intentional purposelessness are always encompassed and legitimated by life's real larger purposes. Whether people recreate so they can work better or work so they can recreate better, some purpose or other is still always present and guiding. Now, this observation does not validate the purpose specified by my account as the true, objective purpose of personhood. My point is merely that purpose cannot be eliminated from human existence without eviscerating human existence. Human life will always entail purpose in order to be human. And this is a clue to something important. That recognition also puts us in the position to focus on the key question: Is the purpose—which humans perceive themselves to have to possess simply to live a human life—natural and objective to us or is it socially constructed and embraced by or imposed on us? In short, do we compose our human purpose or does our human purpose compose us? The right answer, I think and will argue, is that we humans socially construct the huge variety of

86. By *meaningful* I denote not the becoming of mere biological growth but of purpose, which always involves significance.

87. To the skeptic who asks, "So what? Reality is reality whether it works for us or not," I point ahead to Taylor's phenomenological epistemology: the fact that we simply cannot in fact live our basic lives without purpose authorizes us to include purpose among our scientifically useful explanatory concepts and accounts.

ways that we go about seeking to pursue and accomplish our purpose, but that we do *not* socially construct our purpose *itself*. The purpose is a natural and inescapable property of personhood, objectively existent of human awareness of it, properly given as a purpose for all persons. That purpose, again, is to develop and sustain our own incommunicable selves in loving relationships with other personal selves and with the nonpersonal world. The significance of and justification for all of this should become clearer as the argument of the book unfolds. In particular, the moral and political implications of all of this I address directly in chapter 7.

A third possible objection to my account of persons might acknowledge that persons do exist and that they do entail both centers and purposes but claim that neither of the latter is particularly crucial for defining or constituting personhood. Such a claim would not deny the elements with which I am working, but merely suggest that I wrongly emphasize what matters most about personhood. If so, then I have claimed to be fundamental what is actually secondary. Such an objection may want instead to emphasize human rationality, choice making, dutiful obedience to moral laws, relationship to God, or some other believed constituent of personhood. To respond well to such an objection, I would have to hear the entire specific argument spelled out. Lacking that, I can only reply as follows. There are many features of human personhood for which we need to account. I may have missed some of those features in my account. Different thinkers may also disagree about how to order or prioritize the various dimensions of personhood for which we all think we need to account. I do not claim that my theory is infallible, so I am open to alternatives that promise to increase our understanding and insight. That said, however, I do not at present see how it is possible to develop a robust and phenomenologically resonant account of persons that does not emphasize persons as centers and as having purpose. Critical realism instructs us to attend to emergent properties and capacities constituted by the relational interaction of lower-level entities at new, higher levels of existence. Persons, I believe, are not simply one species of animal reflecting a unique trait, such as rationality or duty before the moral law, which makes them personal. Personhood is an emergent reality existing with its own particular characteristics and capacities proper to the reality of the person. To the best of my ability to discern, crucial to that reality is being a particular kind of center with a particular purpose. I cannot imagine, as mentioned above, removing either center or purpose from the person and still having anything like persons as we know them, with each living their own personal lives. So, in principle, I am interested in hearing more persuasive accounts of the person. Meanwhile, I develop the best account that I am able based on the knowledge, experience, and insight I possess.

Finally, one last important point. Grasping the notion of centers with purpose forces us to revisit the idea of emergence discussed above in order to introduce a key distinction between two types of emergence that is crucial for understanding the nature of persons. Emergence, I suggest, operates in one of two ways. The first we might call "proactive" and the second "responsive."[88] The difference between them concerns whether the agency generating and guiding the interactions of lower-level parts that constitute the emergent reality belongs to the emergent reality itself or is external to it. With proactive emergence, the emergent entity itself involves some governing agency and power to cause the development and behavior of the relationally interacting parts on which the emergent entity is dependent for being. With responsive emergence, by comparison, some agent other than the emergent entity causes parts to interact relationally, which then constitutes the emergent entity. A simple example of *responsive* emergence is Monet's painting mentioned above. The painting's picture is an emergent reality consisting of more than the sum of it paint-dab parts and possessing causal powers to effect changes in those who view it, such as feelings of serenity. But the emergent picture was not the agent that caused the dabs of paint to create the painting. Monet was the agent. The picture exists through emergence because another agent, Monet, arranged dabs of paint that relate in such a way to produce an emergent picture that he knew would be perceived in a certain way by the viewer. Emergence, using my term, is responsive insofar as it exists as a response to the operations achieved by another's agency. In short, responsively emergent entities are the *objects* of emergent processes and outcomes caused and guided by another agent or force.

By contrast, proactive emergence involves cases in which the agency of the emergent operations resides in the emergent entity. Here the emergent entities are the *subjects* of the emergent processes and outcomes on which they depend. Take, for example, the emergent bodily life of a dog. The dog's bodily organism as a single whole is emergent from the relation of its various body parts and could not exist apart from them. But those

88. Alternatively, one could label these *immanent* versus *contingent*. My reservation about the existing terminology is that *proactive* sounds a bit too voluntaristic, as if proactively emergent entities have to work to become emergent.

body parts were developed and coordinated in the first place by the dog's life organism. Before the parts ever existed, the dog existed at first as a single cell organism. And that organism contained within itself the capacity as a self-governing and self-developing agent of life, of its *own* life, to draw on nourishment, develop its parts, and coordinate them together in such a way as to produce emergently the normal, mature dog organism that it becomes. Dog ontology (real being) was the agent of dog ontogeny (organic development). This is one example of *proactive* emergence, in that the primordial core of the emergent entity was the proactive agent causing its emergent existence. In this case, the agency consisted of the dog's life principle or energy operating through genetic causal DNA processes. Clearly, to mark the conceptual contrast, the dog as emergent entity did not come to exist because some other agent caused its parts to develop and come together. A kennel owner, for instance, did not assemble dog parts to produce an emergent dog organism for a pet owner. The agency behind the emergence adheres in the emergent entity.

Recall that emergence does not need to be a temporally sequential process moving developmentally from parts to wholes. This means that emergent wholes and constituent parts can exist from the start simultaneously in time (indeed, primal versions of wholes can in some cases precede parts in time). Developing emergent wholes can be the proactive efficient-cause agents of their own temporal development. When thinking about proactive emergence, we should picture densely compacted bundles of vitality, coded direction, and perhaps intelligence unfolding their own natural abilities and tendencies through developmental processes. As the parts complexify, so does the whole. Think analogously of an oak tree growing from an acorn. Think of a green caterpillar encapsulating itself in a chrysalis and soon emerging as an orange butterfly. No other agent makes these happen. The entities contain the causal powers and directions to develop in these ways. Importantly, the developmental process does not produce the emergent entity, but instead the other way around. Nor, again, does another agent cause the developmental process but rather the emergent entity itself.

Here is how all of this connects with our present purposes. Human persons are *proactively*—not responsively—emergent realities. Persons are not subsequent products of purely physical processes, the final outcomes of a temporal series of events governed by other agents at the end of which persons emerge. To the contrary, ontologically, personhood adheres in the human from the start—even if in only the most nascent, densely

compacted form possible—acting as the causal agent of its own development. This is part of what makes personhood what it is—namely, comprising a self-subsistent, self-governing center of being, direction, and
purpose. This is also where the human agency comes from that good sociological thinking rightly works to acknowledge and theorize. This too is
why people are never the mere passive consequences or products of social
forces—whether as cultural dopes, network nodes, identity constructions,
or anything else—however powerful social forces are. This very proactive,
not responsive, nature of personal emergence makes personhood not a
possible, optional, high-end addition or accessory in human existence but
rather fundamental and ineradicable in and for human being itself. That
is not to say, for instance, that human bodies are persons—that would be
a reversion to a reductionistic, flatter-reality mentality. The real, including the human reality, is complex and stratified, existing and operating at
least in part through emergence and downward causation. Human bodies, capacities, and persons are in reality intimately connected but are not
identical. The theoretical and practical importance and implications of
keeping these separate are many, some of which the following chapters
will make more apparent.

Conclusion

The larger significance of this model of personhood will become clearer
in future chapters as I contrast it with other theoretical notions of the
human that I believe at least partly fail to adequately represent the nature of personhood. My main goal for now is to underscore these key
ideas: Something that we not only call ourselves but also live in reality
as—persons—exists as real objects among all of that which is.[89] Those
real, existing persons possess definite, identifiable characteristics, tendencies, capacities, and orientations that mark them as particular kinds of
creatures among a host of other kinds of creatures, as personal in contrast
to nonpersonal. Many of those personal characteristics involve particular
qualities that are, in their depth and intensity, exclusive to persons: re-

89. As Paul Ricoeur says, "The concept of person, just as that of physical body, is held to
be a primitive concept, to the extent that there is no way to go beyond it without presupposing it in the argument that would claim to derive it from something else." Ricoeur, *Oneself as
Another* (Chicago: University of Chicago Press, 1992), 31.

flexivity, self-transcendence, self-identity, morality, causal self-direction, communion, responsibility. And at the heart of the emergent fact of personhood is the reality of our being centers with purpose. While many of these features and qualities inescapably involve dimensions of subjectivity, interpretation, and humanistic description, they are not, for those reasons, any less real or consequential in the operation of human life. If we want to understand the human, we must take the human into account.[90]

I wrote in the introduction that I hope in this book to set out an account of human personhood that resonates with our lived experience as human beings better than many social science theories do, that more coherently connects to and justifies the moral and political commitments that many social scientists embrace, and that explains the origins of social structures more adequately than most sociological theories do. My strategy in trying to fulfill those hopes, as I explain in the next chapters, is to develop a personalist understanding of the human, beginning with the model I have elaborated in this chapter. I am doing so within the philosophy of science framework provided by critical realism, and justified, I think, in some of my arguments about what to take as ontologically real in the human by an antinaturalistic phenomenological epistemology. The task of future chapters will be to develop the approach begun here to try to make good on fulfilling the intellectual and moral aspirations that animate this book. In chapters 3 through 5, I compare this personalist account of the human with the visions embedded in three sociological theoretical alternatives. Before doing that, however, I need to provide a more solid theoretical account of the approach I am advancing in this book. I turn next to that task.

90. See John Searle, *The Rediscovery of Mind* (Cambridge, MA: MIT Press, 1992). A little known fact is that modern law—since the 1886 Supreme Court case *Santa Clara County v. Southern Pacific*—treats corporations as "legal persons," such that corporations enjoy many of the same rights as natural persons. This application of the concept of *person* to corporations as legal institutions raises numerous theoretical and possibly moral issues that are beyond the scope of this book to address but include the context of inquiries into which I hope this book might contribute.

Key Theoretical Resources

This book's argument relies directly upon three key intellectual resources that I presuppose and marshal to develop my theory of personhood: critical realism, philosophical personalism, and an antinaturalistic phenomenological epistemology. I have already drawn upon these resources to make my case in the previous chapter. Before pressing on, it seems prudent to stop and examine these theoretical resources more explicitly and systematically in order to be clear about the sources of my argument for critical realist personalism. The larger case I develop in this book may raise various theoretical objections from different readers, particularly those who do not understand the theoretical assumptions underwriting it. In order to minimize such dissent and keep the focus on the critical and constructive case I develop, I seek here to anticipate and answer such objections and to deepen our understanding of critical realist personalism by laying out my basic theoretical presuppositions that inform it. This theoretical material is somewhat dense and abstract, but is essential to grasp, ultimately, for making sense of my case in this book. The following pages summarize some dense theoretical material through which readers are encouraged to wade before moving on—with the promise that it will pay off in greater understanding of my larger argument and of the purpose and nature of social scientific inquiry and human personal life.

Critical Realism

Critical realism is a postpositivist and post-Winchean[1] philosophy of (social) science that was expressed originally in the form I appropriate here

---

1. Post-Winchean means having assimilated the insights but worked past the shortcomings of Peter Winch's seminal work, *The Idea of a Social Science and Its Relation to Philosophy*

by the British philosopher Roy Bhaskar and that is currently being developed by various scholars, especially in England and Scandinavia, including Margaret Archer, Andrew Sayer, Andrew Collier, and Mats Ekström.[2]

(London: Routledge, 1958)—or, to use an even less felicitous phrase, it means post-post-Wittgensteinian (but see Phil Hutchinson, Rupert Read, and Wes Sharrock, *There Is No Such Thing as a Social Science: In Defense of Peter Winch* [Surrey, UK: Ashgate, 2008]).

2. The following discussion draws upon Roy Bhaskar, *A Realist Concept of Science* (London: Verso, 1997); Bhaskar, *Critical Realism* (New York: Routledge, 1998); Bhaskar, *The Possibility of Naturalism: A Philosophical Critique of Contemporary Human Sciences* (London: Routledge, 1979); Andrew Collier, *Critical Realism: An Introduction to Roy Bhaskar's Philosophy* (London: Verso, 1994); Berth Danermark et al., *Explaining Society: Critical Realism in the Social Sciences* (New York: Routledge, 2002); Andrew Sayer, *Realism and Social Science* (New York: Sage, 2000); Sayer, *Method in Social Science: A Realist Approach* (New York: Routledge, 1992); Margaret Archer, *Realist Social Theory: The Morphogenetic Approach* (Cambridge: Cambridge University Press, 1995); Margaret Archer et al., eds., *Critical Realism: Essential Readings* (New York: Routledge, 1998); Justin Cruickshank, *Realism and Sociology: Anti-Foundationalism, Ontology, and Social Research* (New York: Routledge, 2002); Philip Gorski, "Social 'Mechanisms' and Comparative-Historical Sociology: A Critical Realist Proposal," in *The Frontiers of Sociology*, ed. Björn Wittrock and Peter Hedström (Leiden: Brill, 2009); George Steinmetz, "Odious Comparisons: Incommensurability, the Case Study, and 'Small N's' in Sociology," *Sociological Theory* 22, no. 3 (2004): 371–400; Jon Frauley and Frank Pearce, eds., *Critical Realism and the Social Sciences* (Toronto: University of Toronto Press, 2007); José López and Garry Potter, eds., *After Postmodernism: An Introduction to Critical Realism* (New York: Continuum, 2005); Margaret Archer, *Being Human: The Problem of Agency* (Cambridge: Cambridge University Press, 2000); David Harvey, "Agency and Community: A Critical Realist Perspective," *Journal for the Theory of Social Behavior* 32, no. 2 (2002): 163–94; George Steinmetz, "Critical Realism and Historical Sociology," *Comparative Studies in Society and History* 40, no. 1 (1998): 170–86; Peter Manicas, *A Realist Philosophy of Social Science* (Cambridge: Cambridge University Press, 2006); Andrew Collier, "Critical Realism," in *The Politics of Method in the Human Sciences: Positivism and Its Epistemological Others*, ed. George Steinmetz (Durham, NC: Duke University Press, 2005), 327–45; Stephen Kemp and John Holmwood, "Realism, Regularity, and Social Explanation," *Journal for the Theory of Social Behavior* 33, no. 2 (2003): 165–87; Douglas Porpora, *The Concept of Social Structure* (New York: Greenwood Press, 1987); Porpora, "Four Concepts of Social Structure," *Journal for the Theory of Social Behavior* 19, no. 2 (1989): 195–211; Sam Porter, "Critical Realist Ethnography," in *Qualitative Research in Action*, ed. Tim May (London: Sage, 2002); Douglas Porpora, "Social Structure: The Future of a Concept," in *Structure, Culture, and History: Recent Issues in Social Theory*, ed. Sing Chew and J. David Knottnerus (Lanham, MD; Rowman and Littlefield, 2002), 43–59; Porpora, "Cultural Rules and Material Relations," *Sociological Theory* 11, no. 2 (1993): 212–29; Porpora, "Sociology's Causal Confusion," in *Revitalizing Causality: Realism about Causality in Philosophy and Social Science*, ed. Ruth Groff (New York: Routledge, 2007); Ray Pawson, *A Measure for Measures: A Manifesto for Empirical Sociology* (London: Routledge, 1989); Mats Ekström, "Causal Explanation of Social Action: The Contribution of Max Weber and of Critical Realism to a Generative View of Causal Explanation in Social Science," *Acta Sociologica* 35 (1992): 107–22; David Harvey, "Agency

Critical realism seeks to offer a constructive framework for understanding science that is alternative to both the positivist empiricist paradigm, on the one hand, and constructivism, postmodernism, and certain versions of the hermeneutical perspective, on the other. The struggle between these two broad alternatives, advanced in different times in different forms, has left the social sciences deadlocked in a debate that cannot be resolved within its own terms. Critical realism seeks to transcend that sterile impasse by articulating a coherent, third-way alternative. I believe critical realism succeeds in this and so I wish to advance it further in American sociology. For present purposes, I believe critical realism opens a window for understanding the human in more illuminating and satisfying ways than do rival approaches.

I cannot here adequately, much less fully, explain critical realist philosophy. Readers interested in learning more will have to explore the many relevant works on critical realism beyond this book. For present purposes, it will have to suffice simply to note briefly some of its key ideas, some of which I have and will more fully explain and employ in other chapters.[3] Critical realism's central organizing thought is that much of reality exists independently of human consciousness of it; that reality itself is complex, open, and stratified in multiple dimensions or levels, some of which come to exist through the crucial process of emergence; that humans can acquire a truthful, though fallible knowledge and understanding of reality through various forms of disciplined conceptualization, inquiry, and

and Community: A Critical Realist Paradigm," *Journal for the Theory of Social Behavior* 32, no. 2 (2002): 163–94; William Outhwaite, *New Philosophies of Social Science: Realism, Hermeneutics, and Critical Theory* (New York: St. Martin's Press, 1987); Peter Manicas, *A History and Philosophy of the Social Sciences* (Hoboken, NJ: Wiley, 1989); George Steinmetz and Ou-Byung Chae, "Sociology in an Era of Fragmentation," *Sociological Quarterly* 43, no. 1 (2002): 111–37; Douglas Porpora, "Recovering Causality: Realist Methods in Sociology," in *Realismo Sociologico*, ed. A. Maccarini, E. Morandi, and R. Prandini (Genoa-Milan: Marietti, 2008). Margaret Somers offers a somewhat more pragmatically driven approach in her "'We're No Angels': Realism, Rational Choice, and Relationality in Social Science," *American Journal of Sociology* 104, no. 3 (1998): 722–84. The term *critical realism* appears to have first been coined in 1920 by D. Drake, *Essays in Critical Realism* (London: Macmillan, 1920). Others who in various ways subscribed to schools of thought identified as critical realism include Roy Wood Sellars, George Santayana, Arthur Lovejoy, Bernard Lonergan, and T. F. Torrance, among others. For recommendations on how as a novice to learn critical realism, see http://www.nd.edu/~csmith22/criticalrealism.htm.

3. Helpful dictionaries of critical realist terminology can be found at Mervyn Hartwig, *Dictionary of Critical Realism* (New York: Routledge, 2007); http://www.raggedclaws.com/criticalrealism/index.php?sitesig=WSCR&page=WSCR_060_WSCR_Glossary.

theoretical reflection; that (social) science is rightly concerned with, first, identifying what is real and, second, understanding and explaining real causal capacities, mechanisms, and processes that operate in reality to produce various events and outcomes of interest (rather than discovering allegedly law-governed regularities among observable events or, for social scientists, merely interpreting meanings that actions have for actors); and, finally, that knowledge and understanding of the truths about reality position knowers to critically engage the world in normative, prescriptive, and even moral terms in ways that may overcome the traditional fact-value divide and intentionally try to shape the world for the better.

In critical realism, to spell out a few specifics, *ontology* (the study of being) is prioritized over *epistemology* (the study of what and how we can know)—a move that feels alien to us moderns and postmoderns who naturally prioritize epistemology, but which we nevertheless must make presuppositionally to get anywhere worth going in science. That which is cannot be immediately constrained by limits on the knowable of it. First we come to terms with what we believe is and what it is like, then we examine the possibilities for knowing about it. According to critical realism, the real is not coterminal with the empirical. So, we must distinguish among the three aspects of the *real*, the *actual*, and the *empirical*. The real is what exists—material, nonmaterial, and social entities that have structures and capacities. The real exists whether we know or understand it. The real possesses objective being apart from human awareness of it. The actual, by contrast, is what happens as events in the world, when objects that belong to the real activate their powers and capacities. The actual happens in time and space, whether we experience it or not. The empirical, by contrast, consists of what we experience, either directly or indirectly. Thus, what we observe (the empirical) is not identical to all that happens (the actual), and neither is identical to that which is (the real). The three must not be conflated.

Also, as I have said, not everything that is real is observable, since reality possesses a "deep" dimension operating below the surface of direct human apprehension. Critical realism thus opposes strict empiricism, such as what David Hume advanced in claiming that "as the science of man is the only solid foundation for the other sciences, so the only solid foundation we can give to this science itself must be laid on experience and observation."[4] If we want to understand reality, we must open our minds to the

---

4. David Hume, *A Treatise of Human Nature* (1739–40; Oxford: Oxford University Press, 1975), xvi.

fact that not all of it is observable.[5] At the most minute end, for example, the smallest bits of matter are not humanly observable, yet we use reliance on what we can observe, reasoning minds, theoretical coherence, and observable trace effects of the unobservable to reason through retroduction toward believing that they do exist. At the supercosmic end, cosmologists are now seriously positing the reality of such things as parallel universes, multiverses, alternative timelines, and such—none of which are observable—to best explain through retroduction the universe as we do observe and understand it.[6] Again, as I have mentioned, reality exists with its own objective structures and dynamics independently of human cognition of it—people do not construct reality but only construct more or less well their meaningful beliefs about and interpretations and understandings of reality. The point of science, then, is to conform the shape of our minds to the nature of the reality that exists beyond (but also including) our minds. We can do this because reality embodies a structured order and operation that is not merely the construction of our minds. Further, scientific knowledge is *fallible* but is *not all equally fallible*. Contra empirical realism, scientific knowledge never perfectly corresponds to reality. Contra strong constructivism, scientific knowledge is not hopelessly relativistic in merit. We must live with the fact that we never have perfect human knowledge of the real. Still, some accounts of the real are identifiably better than other accounts. Again, it is the job of human knowing generally and science specifically to engage the process of sorting through the merits of different accounts.

Human knowledge has both *intransitive* and *transitive* dimensions that should not be conflated. The former concerns the real objects of scientific knowledge, the latter the content of our human knowledge of those objects in reality. The transitive aspects of knowledge are (fallible) social products that change over time. The intransitive aspects of knowledge may be social products (e.g., real social structures) but often they are not social products (e.g., atoms, stars, etc.). The key points are that

5. The words of Hamlet may thus apply well to many of us: "There are more things in heaven and earth, Horatio, than are dreamt of in your philosophy." William Shakespeare, *Hamlet*, Act I, Scene 5.

6. For starters, see Bernard Carr, *Universe or Multiverse* (Cambridge: Cambridge University Press, 2007); Paul Steinhardt and Neil Turok, *Endless Universe: Beyond the Big Bang* (New York: Doubleday, 2007); David Deutch, *The Fabric of Reality: The Science of Parallel Universes and Its Implications* (New York: Penguin, 1998); Alex Vilenkin, *Many Worlds in One: The Search for Many Universes* (New York: Hill and Wang, 2006).

the intransitive usually does not depend upon the transitive for its being, and that the transitive can change without changing the intransitive object that is the focus of its attention. Further, objective reality is by nature not *flat* but *stratified*, existing on multiple, though connected, levels, each of which operates according to its own characteristic dynamics and processes.[7] We live in a multilayered reality, it turns out, and our framework for understanding reality must be attuned to that fact—a point discussed in the previous chapter. Reductionistic scientific explanations are typically misguided and should be resisted, because they artificially flatten what is a stratified reality—critical realism is thus strongly *antireductionistic*. The best way to understand and explain something is usually at the level of reality at which it exists, not by reductionistically decomposing it into its component parts at a lower level. Again, this is a view I already began to unpack in chapter 1. Furthermore, the combination or interaction of two or more phenomena at one level often gives rise through *emergence* to new phenomena at a higher level, which possess characteristic properties and capacities that are irreducible to their constituent parts at the lower level from which they emerged. New forms of reality emerge from lower forms and comprise properties and capacities that are more than the sum of the parts from which they are made. This point will be particularly important for my argument and, like the previous two, has already appeared in the previous chapter.

Causation is real. Causality has to do with real causal capacities and mechanisms, not with the association of regular sequences of observed events. Thus, the Humean "successionist" theory is rejected in favor of causal realism emphasizing the natural causal powers of entities. Causes exist, adhering in the capacities of different aspects of reality to make things happen, even though we cannot often see that. Humean skepticism about and redefinition of causation is interesting but misguided. Furthermore, causes are context-dependent tendencies exerting varying degrees of strength on outcomes, not universal laws of consistent influence that

7. In fact, there very well may be more levels or dimensions of the totality of reality than those on which humans can get purchase through normal or even any means within our power, just as there are certain frequencies of sound and specific ranges in the spectrum of light that the human ear and eye cannot naturally hear or see. In such cases, we may need to employ indirect means of observation and human reasoning to infer their real existence; or perhaps such realities have their own capacities to make their existence known to humans under certain conditions; or perhaps most or all humans will simply never know about those dimensions of reality.

are either *always* or *never* operative. The same causal forces may help to produce a host of different kinds of social outcomes. And different causal forces may produce similar classes of social outcomes.[8] Scientific inquiry as a project should be concerned more with the structured properties of causal relations and mechanisms than with the regularity of observable sequences of events—theorizing unobserved causal dynamics is what the best of science actually does and is more important than measuring the strength of association between variables.[9] The latter is done primarily in service to the former. Again, the focus is more on the nature of the real than on the events of the empirical. Not only are material objects real, but many (at least partially) nonmaterial, emergent phenomena, such as social structures and human cognition, are also real, insofar as they possess emergent, durable, causal power. Reality can be nonmaterial. We must also distinguish between closed systems versus open systems in reality, each of which requires a different scientific approach. In closed systems, generative mechanisms can operate in conditions of isolation from the influence of other mechanisms, enabling the scientist more precisely to isolate causal relations and make predictions. In open systems, many generative mechanisms operate in complex combinations and interactions that cannot be cleanly isolated and identified, making causal analysis and prediction more difficult if not sometimes impossible. Closed systems are associated with many[10] of the natural sciences, and open systems are associated with the social sciences and with some natural sciences. All things

8. Critical realism entails a major shift in thinking about causality, which unfortunately I cannot further develop in the present discussion but about which much of importance has already been published. See, for starters, Porpora, "Recovering Causality: Realist Methods in Sociology," in *Realismo Sociologico*, ed. Maccarini, Morandi, and Prandini; Porpora, "Sociology's Causal Confusion," in *Revitalizing Causality*, ed. Groff; Manicas, *A Realist Philosophy of Social Science*; Danermark et al., *Explaining Society*, 52–53, 56, 59, 74; Sayer, *Method in Social Science*.

9. See Gorski, "Social 'Mechanisms' and Comparative-Historical Sociology," in *The Frontiers of Sociology*, ed. Wittrock and Hedström; Steinmetz, "Odious Comparisons," 371–400. For treatments of mechanisms that are not critical realist, see Peter Hedström and Richard Swedberg, eds., *Social Mechanisms: An Analytical Approach to Social Theory* (Cambridge: Cambridge University Press, 1998); Doug McAdam, Sidney Tarrow, and Charles Tilly, *Dynamics of Contention* (Cambridge: Cambridge University Press, 2001); Robert Merton mentions social mechanisms in his "The Self-Fulfilling Prophecy," in *Social Theory and Social Structure* (Glencoe, IL: Free Press, 1957), 43–44.

10. Although not all and in all ways; certain fields of biology, for example, have difficulty creating experimental closure.

humanly social operate in open systems, making the task of social science more difficult. A pure "unity of science" assumption drawn from positivism is thus rejected in favor of an acknowledgment that the social sciences are in crucial—though not all—ways distinct from the natural sciences. Because social phenomena are always intrinsically meaningful to and for both those who constitute them (people) and those who seek to understand and explain them (social scientists), following on Peter Winch we see that social science necessarily has a *hermeneutical* dimension that requires the interpretive work of cultural understanding. Yet interpretive social science cannot, on these grounds, as has been typical of some previous hermeneutic perspectives, reject causal analysis, since causality is real, meanings are embedded in a causally operative reality, and meaningful cultural reasons possess causal powers for humans. All social science has an interpretive aspect, but not all that the social sciences study consists of meanings requiring interpretation. Therefore, hermeneutical sociology does not need to reject the causality of "science" in social science, since doing so presupposes the false strong division between *naturwissenschaften* and *geisteswissenschaften* maintained historically by both positivism and German hermeneutics.

We should be far more prepared than positivist empiricism has allowed us to be to engage not only in deduction, induction, and statistical inference, but also in *retroduction*. Retroduction is the thought operation reconstructing the basic conditions for anything to be what it is, providing knowledge of the properties that are required for a phenomenon to exist. Retroduction thus recurrently asks the question, "What must be true, even if we cannot observe it, for what we believe exists to be what it is?" The larger goal of science is to produce generalizable claims. Generalizations, however, from a critical realist perspective, should more concern transfactual conditions of reality than universal laws or probabilistic inferences to populations. Ideographic study, as normally conceived today,[11] is thus rejected as underachieving, while nomothetic science in its usual positivist forms is rejected as misguided in its view of laws, empiricism, and determinism. Social science should seek to generalize. But its generalizations should focus on the structured and causal nature of the real, not so much on the regularity of events. As to method, socials science should embrace methodological pluralism, transcending old assumptions that

---

11. However, if by idiographic we simply mean that individual events or persons can be causally explained, then critical realism is idiographic.

have given rise to the sterile quantitative versus qualitative divide, and instead focusing on the choices involving "extensive" versus "intensive" methods driven pragmatically by the particular subject and question under study. Whereas critical realism is principled on questions of ontology, it is pragmatic on questions of method. Within the critical realist framework of knowledge, methods should be applied that are most appropriate for the precise subject of study and the questions researchers ask about it. Finally, by conceiving itself as *critical* realism (instead of so-called empirical realism or scientific realism[12]), this approach signals a particular orientation. What "critical" intends to communicate about this realism is its antifoundationalist character, its fallibilist understanding of science as a socially situated human practice, its resistance to modernity's absolute separation of fact from value, and its readiness to engage in normative critical theory without (because of its ontological realism) collapsing into ideology and crass academic political activism.

Through the development of a coherent framework reliant on these commitments and beliefs, critical realism seeks—successfully, I think—to transcend a host of unhappy dualisms that have long divided the social sciences. In summarizing only the first of three intellectual resources informing this book, I have already offered a lot of abstraction packed into a few paragraphs. That will have to do for now as the outline of one of the perspectives that is crucial in developing the argument that follows. Some of the ideas noted above may give some readers some clue as to what critical realism is and where I want to go with it. Other readers will have to wait until other chapters unpack and deploy these ideas more clearly.

Personalism

The second intellectual resource on which I draw to develop my argument about the nature of human being is the philosophical perspective known as personalism. Describing personalism is more difficult than summarizing critical realism because as a framework of thought it is more amorphous, and its historical articulation has been more varied and intermittent. Personalism is a broad philosophical school of thought that

---

12. Or what Isaac Reed—in, I think, a largely off-the-mark critique of critical realism—calls *strict realism*, "Justifying Sociological Knowledge: From Realism to Interpretation," *Sociological Theory* 26, no. 2 (2002): 101–29.

developed most clearly as explicit intellectual movements in two different contexts: in continental Europe in the early twentieth century
and in Boston, Massachusetts, in the late nineteenth and early to mid-
twentieth centuries. The European movement, which developed particularly, though not exclusively, among Catholic intellectuals,[13] was crushed
by the rise of the Nazis in the 1930s and 1940s. The American personalist
movement, not subject to the same threats, evolved more freely into a
fifth generation of theorists. Leaders in the European personalist movement included Emmanuel Mounier, Martin Buber, Jacques Maritain, and
Gabriel Marcel. Personalist leaders in the United States included Borden
Parker Bowne, George Holmes Howison, John Wesley Edward Bowen,
and Edgar Sheffield Brightman.[14] The intellectual roots of personalism
in both Europe and America go back, in various and sometimes indirect
ways, to a variety of famous and less famous thinkers.[15] More recently, personalist theorists have included the older Jacques Maritain, expatriated
to the United States; the Hungarian chemist turned philosopher Michael
Polanyi; the Polish phenomenologist Karol Wojtyla; and the American

13. Personalism has strong affinities with theism, although that connection is not necessary; there are, for instance, according to the personalist scholar Rufus Burrow Jr., both
atheistic and pantheistic versions of personalism, reflected in the writings of John McTaggert
and William Stern. Burrow, *Personalism: A Critical Introduction* (St. Louis: Chalice Press,
1999), 36–40. Also see H. Stuart Hughes, "The Catholics and the Human Condition," in *The
Obstructed Path: French Social Thought in the Years of Desperation, 1930–1960* (New York:
Harper and Row, 1968), 65–101; J. B. Coates, *The Crisis of the Human Person: Some Personalist Interpretations* (London: Longmans, Green, 1949).

14. See Burrow, *Personalism: A Critical Introduction*; Paul Deats and Carol Robb, eds.,
The Boston Personalist Tradition in Philosophy, Social Ethics, and Theology (Macon, GA:
Mercer University Press, 1986); Albert C. Knudson, *The Philosophy of Personalism* (New
York: Abingdon Press, 1927); Ralph Flewelling, "Personalism," in *Twentieth-Century Phi-
losophy: Living Schools of Thought*, ed. Dagobert Runes (New York: Philosophical Library,
1943); Leroy Rouner, ed., *Selves, People, and Persons: What Does It Mean to Be a Self?* Boston
University Studies in Philosophy and Religion (Notre Dame, IN: University of Notre Dame
Press, 1992); for a detailed analysis of the European intellectual roots of idealist personalism
that counters some of the Boston personalists' account of that history, see Jan Olof Bengtsson,
The Worldview of Personalism (New York: Oxford University Press, 2006).

15. These include, in various ways, Aristotle, Athanasius of Alexandria, Gregory the
Great, Peter of Nyssa, Thomas Aquinas, Maine de Biran, Søren Kierkegaard, Friedrich
Heinrich Jacobi, Immanuel Kant, Rudolph Hermann Lotze, Friedrich W. J. Schelling, Max
Scheler, Nicholas Berdyaev, Charles Renouvier, John Henry Newman, Maurice Blondel,
Étienne Gilson, Henri Bergson, Marcel Péguy, and Karl Jaspers.

philosopher John Crosby.[16] Other more contemporary writers develop-
ing various aspects of personalist theory include Paul Ricoeur, Emmanuel
Levinas, Thomas Williams, Stephen Evans, Alistair McFadyen, Richard
Bayer, Martin Luther King Jr., Hans Urs von Balthasar, John Zizioulas,
Peter Maurin, Dorothy Day, Thomas Rourke, John Macmurray, Robert
Spaemann, and Rosita Chazarreta Rourke.[17]

The rise of personalism must be properly understood in its intellectual, social, and political context. European personalism sought to offer
an alternative to the liberal individualism that had transformed Europe
during the eighteenth and nineteenth centuries by emphasizing the person
over the individual and community solidarity over atomization. Indeed,
personalism insists on speaking of people as "persons" instead of "indi-

16. Jacques Maritain, *The Person and the Common Good* (1946; Notre Dame, IN: University of Notre Dame Press, 1966); Michael Polanyi, *Personal Knowledge: Toward a Post-
Critical Philosophy* (Chicago: University of Chicago Press, 1958); Karol Wojtyla, *Person and
Community* (New York: Peter Lang, 1993); Wojtyla, *The Acting Person* (Dordrecht: D. Reidel,
1979); John Crosby, *The Selfhood of the Human Person* (Washington, DC: Catholic University
of America Press, 1996); Crosby, *Personalist Papers* (Washington, DC: Catholic University
of America Press, 2003). Also see John O'Malley, *The Fellowship of Being: An Essay on the
Concept of Person in the Philosophy of Gabriel Marcel* (The Hague: Martinus Nijhoff, 1966).
Wojtyla, the Polish philosopher, later became Pope John Paul II.

17. Paul Ricoeur, *Oneself as Another* (Chicago: University of Chicago Press, 1992);
Emmanuel Levinas, *Totality and Infinity* (Pittsburgh: Duquesne University Press, 1969);
Thomas Williams, *Who Is My Neighbor: Personalism and the Foundations of Human Rights*
(Washington, DC: Catholic University of America Press, 2005); Richard Bayer, *Capitalism
and Christianity: The Possibility of Christian Personalism* (Washington, DC: Georgetown University Press, 1999); Alistair McFadyen, *The Call to Personhood* (Cambridge: Cambridge Uni-
versity Press, 1990); C. Stephen Evans, *Preserving the Person: A Look at the Human Sciences*
(Downers Grove, IL: InterVarsity Press, 1979); see Lewis Baldwin and Walter Muelder, *God
and Human Dignity: The Personalism, Theology, and Ethics of Martin Luther King, Jr.* (Notre
Dame, IN: University of Notre Dame Press, 2006); Hans Urs von Balthasar, "On the Concept
of Person," trans. Peter Verhalen, *Communio* 13 (Spring 1986): 18–26; Robert Spaemann,
Persons: The Difference between "Someone" and "Something" (New York: Oxford University
Press, 2006); John Zizioulas, *Being as Communion* (Crestwood, NY: St. Vladimir's Seminary
Press, 1985); Garth Baker-Fletcher, *Somebodyness: Martin Luther King, Jr. and the Theory
of Dignity* (Minneapolis: Fortress Press, 1993); Rufus Burrow, *God and Human Dignity: The
Personalism, Theology, and Ethics of Martin Luther King, Jr.* (Notre Dame, IN: University of
Notre Dame Press, 2006); Dorothy Day, *Selected Writings* (Maryknoll, NY: Orbis, 1994); John
Macmurray, *The Self as Agent* (Amherst, NY: Humanity Books, 1957); Thomas Rourke and
Rosita Chazarreta Rourke, *A Theory of Personalism* (Lanham, MD: Lexington, 2005). Also
see Kevin Schiesing, "A History of Personalism," unpublished paper, Acton Institute, Grand
Rapids, Michigan; Peter Maurin, *Easy Essays* (Chicago: Franciscan Herald Press, 1984).

viduals" because the former involves natural social ties and obligations
while the latter suggests atomistic autonomy. Personalism in Europe and
America also arose in part as a response to the intellectual movements
of materialism, determinism, and positivism that had so influenced the
nineteenth century variously through Karl Marx, Auguste Comte, Charles
Darwin, Claude Adrien Helvétius, and others. The Boston school of personalism was also reacting against the absolute idealism in the Hegelian
tradition, the implications of which it believed were depersonalizing.
European personalism came to its fullest fruition in a particularly turbulent socioeconomic and political context of Europe of the 1930s and
1940s, which shaped the character of its expression. The personalism of
this era attempted to raise an intellectual bulwark against both collectivist communism and National Socialism, the tides of which were sweeping
across Europe, by emphasizing the centrality of the person over the state
and economy, and human freedom over totalitarianism. As it happened,
Nazism overran that bulwark and repressed and scattered the personalist movement. For Mounier's struggle in the personalist movement and
support of the French Resistance he suffered years of suppression by the
Vichy regime, censorship, an imprisonment, a hunger strike, and multiple
heart attacks—the third of which he died from at age forty-five.[18] Buber
resigned his professorship at the University of Frankfurt in 1933 in protest
of Hitler's coming to power, was persecuted by the Nazis, and finally left
Germany in 1938 to live in Jerusalem. Maritain was displaced from France
in 1940 to live his war years in exile in the United States. Nazism thus effectively broke up the European personalist movement. As for Boston
personalism, its influence in U.S. philosophy during the twentieth century has for various reasons been limited. Yet I believe the personalism of
the early twentieth century—particularly the realist personalism of Europe, more than the more idealist personalism of Boston[19]—bequeaths an

18. Eileen Cantin, *Mounier: A Personalist View of History* (New York: Paulist Press,
1973), 5–18.
19. The idealism native to Boston personalism—believing that "all reality is in some sense
personal"—is, I believe, misguided and incompatible with the critical realist beliefs in the
stratification of reality and in emergence developed in this book, even if its instinct in resisting
materialism was correct. On idealist personalism, see Flewelling, "Personalism," in *Twentieth-
Century Philosophy: Living Schools of Thought,* ed. Runes; Paul Deats, "Introduction to
Boston Personalism," in *The Boston Personalist Tradition,* ed. Deats and Robb. The "all reality"
quote is from Flewelling, "Personalism," 324.

intellectual and moral legacy, despite ambiguities and problems, that is worth retrieving, amending, and developing today.[20]

The central idea in personalism relevant for my argument is deceptively simple. This is the belief that human beings are *persons*. I realize that to many this will seem no more enlightening than saying that dogs are canines. But it is not that straightforward. To claim that humans are persons, to develop what it means to be a person, and to take that personalist viewpoint seriously in our social scientific work is more consequential and challenging than it first appears. To believe that humans are persons, not something else, and to grasp the meanings and ramifications of that belief, is to stake out a position among rival positions that is neither self-evident nor universally shared or reflected in academic scholarship. Of course, *person* is a word we use in our discourse pervasively and without much thought. But an exploration of the meanings of "person" reveals that it involves significant, distinctive substantive content that carves out a view of humanity that is different from other, seemingly viable positions.[21] It actually means something quite momentous to say that humans are persons while ferns and baboons are not.

To claim that humans are *persons* is to say that humans are something qualitatively more than and different from what many alternative views construe humans to be. Such a claim believes that there are characteristic qualities of human being that cannot be reduced to the elements of other, nonpersonalist realities. Personalism claims more for and about humans, we will see, for example, than the model of humans as fundamentally rational, self-interested, exchange-making calculators of costs and benefits—a common model in the social sciences. It believes there is more to the human than being the constituents of functional social orders,

20. I distinguish, however, what I seek to develop here from a movement originating in the 1980s called "Economic Personalism" and associated with the Acton Institute of Grand Rapids, Michigan, which—in its apparent semilibertarian economics and particular theory of the primacy of culture—appears to be at odds with the historical personalist tradition on which I am building. See Anthony Santelli Jr. et al., *The Free Person and the Free Economy: A Personalist View of Economics* (Lanham, MD: Lexington, 2002); Patricia Donohue-White et al., *Human Nature and the Discipline of Economics* (Lanham, MD: Lexington, 2002); Gregory Beabout et al., *Beyond Self-Interest: A Personalist Approach to Human Action* (Lanham, MD: Lexington, 2002).

21. For enlightening histories and explorations of the meaning of the word *person*, see Arthur Danto, "Person," in *The Encyclopedia of Philosophy, Volume One* (New York: Macmillan, 1972); and Kenneth Schmitz, "Reconstructing the Person: A Meditation on the Meaning of Personality," *Crisis* 17, no. 4 (1999): 26–29.

which are the agents of action, who fulfill their roles in order to meet the requisite needs and goals of those ordered systems.[22] Personalism claims something different and more than the postmodern view of humans as discursively constructed positions of shifting identities pieced together in the flux of variable meanings and power relations. It also conflicts with the view that humans are nothing more than corporeal sites though which regimes of power express themselves through bodily discipline. Personalism says more about the human than the version of interactionist theory that characterizes people as essentially strategic, dramatic presenters of performances driven by culturally specified scripts. It also conflicts with the sociobiological and evolutionary psychology model of humans as essentially biological carriers of "selfish" genetic material that has been naturally selected upon for its superior reproductive fitness and that seeks to perpetuate itself through behavioral determination. Personalism claims that human beings are more than egos struggling to manage the id in the face of the superego. These are some of the models of human being that are available—and in some cases highly influential—in contemporary institutions of science and higher learning. To take a strong personalist view that humans are persons is to set oneself in tension, if not at odds, with many other perspectives. Some of those models may be harmonized with personalism, when understood nonreductionistically. But some of them are incompatible with personalism. Thus, when we say that someone is a person, we are, whether we know it or not, claiming a great deal about human nature that may or may not be obvious or taken seriously in the sciences and humanities.

What, then, do I mean by "person?" In the previous chapter I defined the person as a conscious, reflexive, embodied, self-transcending center of subjective experience, durable identity, moral commitment, and social communication who—as the efficient cause of his or her own responsible actions and interactions—exercises complex capacities for agency and intersubjectivity in order to sustain his or her own incommunicable self in loving relationships with other personal selves and with the nonpersonal world. The defining qualities of personhood in this approach demarcate persons from all things nonpersonal as existing on two different levels of

22. In the sphere of political theory, personalism is analogously incompatible with the collectivist theory that humans are subordinate components of the nation or state, the primary unit of reality, into and for the larger interests and purposes of which the lives and interests of any number of single humans may be subsumed and consumed.

being, which separate every self who is a "you" from everything else that is an "it." This personal/nonpersonal split, which I believe rightly "divides nature at its joints" in crucial though not all ways, helps to define a fundamental characteristic of the human social world that I think social scientists must recognize and for which they must provide an account. In Wojtyla's words, personalism expresses "a belief in the primordial uniqueness of the human being, and thus in the basic irreducibility of the human being to the natural world."[23] It is worth better exploring what it means to be a person and what the consequences are for social scientific knowledge if humans are persons. That is what I attempt to do in drawing on philosophical personalism in the other chapters in this book.

Antiscientistic Phenomenology

Finally, I rely in developing my argument in this book on a particular phenomenological account of warranted knowledge that gives priority to certain features of experience that it claims are indispensable for making sense of our lives. That account is what I understand to be the antiscientistic[24] phenomenological epistemology articulated by the philosopher Charles Taylor in his book *Sources of the Self*. Michael Polanyi's *Personal Knowledge* also influences what follows. Explaining this account will take some effort but, again, it is worth laying out before moving on.

We have long been taught by a particular view of science to doubt the reliability of our lived experience as human persons to tell us true things about reality. This view of science has taught us that personal perception and experience are subjective, biased, and idiosyncratic and often produce misleading appearances, particularistic perspectives, and false models of reality. We see the sun moving, for example, but science tells us that really the sun is standing still—it is the earth that is moving. We think we have freely chosen our political attitudes, but then we are told that most of the

23. Wojtyla, "Subjectivity and the Irreducibile in the Human Being," in *Person and Community*, 211.

24. Taylor views his approach as antinaturalistic, and in the sense that he means it, I agree. However, I wish to apply his viewpoint in a more narrow fashion by opposing not naturalism broadly but naturalistic scientism specifically. There are forms of naturalism, Omar Lizardo has helped me to see, that are compatible with critical realism, and my account here can be understood and embraced from a certain naturalistic framework. So, while I reference naturalism in the following I focus especially on scientism.

variance in our attitudes can be explained by ten demographic variables in multiple regression analyses that are driving them. Therefore we ought not to trust our personal, subjective, phenomenological experiences to tell us truth about reality. Rather, we should trust the methods and findings of naturalistic sciences, or perhaps social sciences that are modeled on the natural sciences, as the final authority explaining reality.

Three background assumptions inform naturalistic scientism's view of science. The first is the ontological assumption of materialism, that what exists consists of physical matter, the forces of energy that animate matter, and the natural laws inherent in matter and energy that govern them. Everything is material nature. Immaterial entities that are not examinable by physics and chemistry—such as meanings, values, moral facts, and certainly things "spiritual"—do not exist.[25] The second assumption concerns perspective and authority, namely, the premise that the natural sciences are neutral and objective, which is good and reliable, compared to personal human perception and experience, which are biased and subjective, and so problematic and untrustworthy. The third assumption built into naturalistic scientism's claims concerns right method—namely, that the best way to understand and explain anything is through reductionist analysis. The true properties and dynamics of any subject are best revealed by breaking the subject down into its component parts existing at lower levels to disclose the more primary elements constituting the subject. This reductionistic move points downward to explain, shifting toward increasingly elementary levels of reality.

These three background assumptions—materialism, objectivity, and reductionism—justify naturalistic scientism's discounting of people's phenomenological experience as a guide to valid and reliable knowledge about reality, including about human life. They empower naturalistic scientism as the source of right knowledge, authorized to trump rival claims to understanding and explanation. The model for properly understanding the human and the social is natural science, not anything "humanistic" or subjectively based. Our personal, lived, subjective perceptions and understandings need to give way and be conformed to the claims of

25. Thus, for example, the early twentieth-century behaviorist psychologist John B. Watson wrote, "Consciousness . . . has never been seen, touched, smelled, tasted, or moved. It is plain assumption just as unprovable as the old concept of the soul. And to the behaviorist the two terms are essentially identical, so far as the metaphysical implications are concerned." Watson, *Behaviorism* (Chicago: University of Chicago Press, 1929), 14.

naturalistic scientism and naturalistic social scientism. This view is widespread and deeply rooted in modern people's assumptions and beliefs. Even many people who know nothing about the history and philosophy of science have absorbed from the cultural atmosphere many of naturalistic scientism's suppositions and instincts.

Following Charles Taylor and others, however, I believe that when it comes to understanding the human world, naturalistic scientism's framework is inadequate. We have good reasons to doubt its picture of human persons and the knowledge of them it generates. We also have good reason to think that there is much important to learn about ourselves as human from our own best perceptions and experiences, even those that are personal and subjective. I rely in part on Taylor's phenomenological epistemology—or at least my reading of it—to build my argument about the nature of human personhood in this book. Because this approach runs so strongly against the grain of us moderns who are so shaped by naturalistic scientism, it is worth devoting more than a little space here to presenting it. In so doing I quote liberally from Taylor, since he has made the original strong case.

The starting point of this phenomenological approach that opposes naturalistic scientism is that terms of our experience that we cannot live without to best "make sense" of our lives provide legitimate and important clues about what is real. To be clear, the "terms" that Taylor is specifically defending in his argument are *morality* and *value*, though his argument can easily be extended to make sense of other aspects of human experience, such as personhood, to which naturalistic scientism is often blind. So, when it comes to explaining human life, even social scientifically, the unavoidably personal experience of living life cannot be radically separated off as providing untrustworthy knowledge. As persons, all we have is our best personal knowledge about the world we live in, gained through a variety of methods, including but not limited to naturalistic science. Since reality is a unity, terms we need to make sense of our own experiences cannot automatically be cordoned off from informing the narrower task of scientific inquiry and explanations.[26]

26. Thus, Charles Taylor asks, "What better measure of reality do we have in human affairs than those terms which on critical reflection and after correction of errors we can detect make the best sense of our lives? 'Making the best sense' here includes . . . allowing us best to understand and make sense of the actions and feelings of ourselves and others. . . . These requirements are not yet met if we have some [naturalistic] theoretical language which purports to explain behavior from the observer's standpoint but is no use to the agent in making sense

But what does it mean, "not to be able" to do without a term to make sense of life? Taylor explains, "I mean that this term is indispensable to (what now appears to me to be) the clearest, most insightful statements of the issues before me. If I were to be denied this term, I wouldn't be able to deliberate as effectively, to focus the issue properly—as, indeed, I may feel . . . that I was less capable of doing in the past, before I acquired this term."[27] And which kind of "terms" ought we to rely upon? Exactly those terms we employ to make sense of a wide range of life experiences and explanations, which seem indispensable for making life the most clear and understandable to us as it can be, for which over time we seem not to be able to find better substitutes. This approach is what Taylor calls "the BA Principle," BA meaning "best account."[28] Included in the category of indispensable terms, according to Taylor, are the idea of morality, values, and human dignity—none of which is tangible but each of which seems to us nonetheless inescapably real.

Taylor then argues that we are entitled to grant epistemic authority to the terms of our best accounts, those that provide greatest insight in focusing issues as best as we are able and for living our lives. Of course, best accounts rely on human perceptions and judgments, but that is all anyone ever has to go on anyway. There is no way or reason to back away from our larger trust in our phenomenological experience and the best accounts to which they give rise as we sort through our unique experiences as persons and together as communities. There exists no autonomous, experience-

---

of his own thinking, feeling, and acting." Taylor, *Sources of the Self* (Cambridge, MA: Harvard University Press), 57. Also see Polanyi, *Personal Knowledge: Toward a Post-Critical Philosophy*; various works by Maurice Merleau-Ponty, such as "Phenomenology and the Sciences of Man" (1958), in *The Primacy of Perception*, ed. James Edie (Evanston, IL: Northwestern University Press, 1964), 43–95; Vincent Shen, " 'Person' as the Central Concept in the Human and Social Sciences: An Interpretation of Edmund Husserl's Thought on the Human Person in *Ideen II*," in *Human Dignity*, ed. Miloslav Bednar (Washington, DC: Council for Research in Values and Philosophy, 1999); E. Rae Harcum, *A Psychology of Freedom and Dignity* (Westport, CT: Praeger, 1994).

27. Taylor, *Sources of the Self*, 57.

28. "The terms we select have to make sense across the whole range of both explanatory and life uses. The terms indispensable for the latter are part of the story that makes best sense to us, unless and until we can replace them with more clairvoyant substitutes. The result of this search for clairvoyance yields the best accounts we can give at any given time, and no epistemological or metaphysical considerations of a more general kind about science or nature can justify setting this aside. The best account in the above sense is trumps. Let me call this the BA principle." Ibid., 58.

independent standpoint or foundation of evaluation by which to more objectively judge our own experiences and the best sense we can make of them. Attempts to do so have led to irresolvable forms of skepticism. True, we recurrently learn that some of our prior beliefs and accounts were wrong, that alternative accounts are better, and so we change our perceptions, thinking, and interpretations about important matters. But we always do that by struggling through experience and hitting upon better accounts of them, not by asking some allegedly neutral scientific principle that is alien to our phenomenological experience to tell us true things that overrule our best accounts.[29]

As a result, theories and terms that falsify our lived experience and are impossible to live with ought finally to have no epistemological authority for or trump what by our best accounts seems real to us. Why exactly ought we to trust our own phenomenological experience? Taylor answers:

> This is . . . an exploration of the limits of the conceivable in human life. . . . The aim of this account is to examine how we actually make sense of our lives, and to draw the limits of the conceivable from our knowledge of what we actually do when we do so. But what description of human possibilities, drawn from some questionable epistemological theories, ought to trump what we can descry from within the practice itself as the limits of our possible ways of making sense of our lives? After all, the ultimate basis for accepting any theories is precisely that they make better sense of us than do their rivals. If any view takes us right across the boundary and defines as normal or possible a human life which we would find incomprehensible or pathological, it can't be right.[30]

Therefore, naturalism cannot discard what is indispensable for living as mere (unreal) appearance, unless its rival account provides "epistemo-

---

29. Taylor writes, "The idea that we ought to prescind altogether from this background confidence of purchase [of phenomenological perception] is . . . unjustified. . . . This would mean checking the trustworthiness of this confidence against something else. But this something else would have to be quite outside the perceivable, and thus gives us an impossible task. Classical epistemology was always threatening to drive into this cul-de-sac and therefore fall into the despair of skepticism. Of course . . . our confidence *on a particular occasion* might be misplaced. But we discover this only by shifting out of one purchase into another, more adequate one. . . . The most reliable . . . view is not one that would be grounded quite outside our intuitions, but one that is grounded on our strongest intuitions, where these have successfully met the challenge of proposed transition away from them." Ibid., 75.

30. Ibid., 32.

logical gain" in making better sense of our lives.[31] We ought to reject, in other words, social science concepts and theories that may predict some observed empirical association, but that we could not fit into the actual living of our lives, no matter how otherwise elegant or impressive they appear.[32]

For these reasons, naturalistic scientism's project is often inappropriate when applied to humans, who involve real phenomena for which naturalism is not able to account. Belief in the absolute unity of science—that is, the belief that the same kind of (naturalistic) science is needed for human and social life as for the natural world—is therefore at least partly wrong, since different subject matters require qualitatively different kinds of

31. "This kind of indispensability of a term in a non-explanatory context of life can't just be declared irrelevant to the project to do without that term in an explanatory reduction. The widespread assumption that it can comes from a premise buried deep in the naturalist way of thinking, viz., that the terms of everyday life, those in which we go about living our lives, are to be relegated to the realm of mere appearance. They are to be taken no more seriously for explanatory purposes than the visual experience of the sun going down behind the horizon is in cosmology. But this assimilation is untenable. We can see excellent reasons why my perception of the horizon at sunset ought to be sidelined in face of the evidence of, e.g., satellite observations. But what ought to trump the language in which I actually live my life? This is not (quite) a rhetorical question, because we do sometimes offer accounts of what people are about in their likes, dislikes, deliberations, and so forth which purport to be more perceptive, shorn of certain delusions or limitations of vision that affect the people themselves. But these [alternatives] are also terms in which the individuals can live their lives. Indeed, we frequently offer them to the people concerned as an improvement on their own self-understandings. What is preposterous is the suggestion that we ought to disregard altogether the terms that can figure in the non-explanatory contexts of living for the purposes of our explanatory theory." Ibid., 57–58.

32. "Theories . . . which declare 'phenomenology' to be irrelevant on principle are based on a crucial mistake. They are 'changing the subject,' in Donald Davidson's apt expression. What we need to *explain* is people living their lives; the terms of which they cannot avoid living them cannot be removed from the explanandum, unless we can propose other terms in which they could live them more clairvoyantly. We cannot just leap outside of these terms altogether, on the grounds that their logic doesn't fit some model of 'science' and that we know a priori that human beings must be explicable in this 'science.' This begs the question. How can we ever know that humans can be explained by any scientific theory *until* we actually explain how they live their lives in its terms?" And again: "Our understanding has been clouded by the naturalist epistemology and its focus on the natural science model. . . . But if our . . . ontology springs from the best account of the human domain we can arrive at, and if this account must be in anthropocentric terms, terms which relate to the meanings things have for us, then the demand to start outside of all such meanings, not to rely on our moral intuitions or on what we find morally moving, is in fact [simply] a proposal to change the subject." Ibid., 71.

sciences (although, where the unity of science view is correct, in my [but not Taylor's] view, is believing that the purpose of both the natural and social sciences is to understand and explain causally what is real and how and why it operates or acts as it does).[33] Taylor elaborates:

> Of course, the terms of our best account will never figure into a physical theory of the universe. But that just means that our human reality cannot be understood in the terms appropriate for this physics. This is the complement to the anti-Aristotelian purge of natural science in the seventeenth century. Just as physical science is no longer anthropocentric, so human science can no longer be couched in the terms of physics. Our value terms purport to give us insight into what it is to live in the universe as a human being, and this is a quite different matter from that which physical science claims to reveal and explain. The reality is, of course, dependent upon us, in the sense that a condition for its existence is our existence. But once granted that we exist, it is no more a subjective projection than what physics deals with.[34]

In order to gain a revealing perspective on these matters, Taylor suggests that it is helpful to "turn the tables" by seeing that naturalistic scientism's premises are often driven not by the real epistemic gain they provide—which is scant when applied to human doings—but instead by the very

33. Thus, unity-of-science views of methodology, such as that reflected by Baruch Spinoza here, are rejected: "I shall consider human actions and desires in exactly the same manner, as though I were concerned with lines, planes, and solids" (Spinoza, *The Ethics*, Part 3, [1677; New York: Dover, 1955], 129); instead, I endorse a view closer to that of Robert Redfield: "In most of social science, human nature is itself a part of the method. One must use one's own humanity as a means to understanding. The physicist need not sympathize with the atom, nor the biologist with his fruit flies, but the student of people and institutions must employ his natural sympathies in order to discover what people think or feel and what the institutions mean." Redfield, "Social Science among the Humanities," in vol. 1 of *Human Nature and the Study of Society* (Chicago: University of Chicago Press, 1949), 52; and of Florian Znanieki: "In contrast with the natural scientist, who seeks to discover an order among empirical data entirely independent of conscious human agents, the student of culture seeks to discover any order among empirical data which depends upon conscious human agents, is produced, and is maintained by them." Znanieki, *Cultural Science* (1952; Urbana: University of Illinois Press, 1963), 132. But again, the natural and social sciences are not different from each other when it comes to their goals; both seek to know what is real and to understand and explain causally how and why it behaves or acts as it does—it is simply the case that to understand and explain causally in the social sciences, one must take seriously things like subjective meanings that are absent in the natural sciences and for which naturalism cannot account.

34. Taylor, *Sources of the Self*, 59.

kind of nonnaturalistic, "spiritual" values, commitments, and emotions that naturalistic scientism denies. Taylor thus observes: "Some naturalists propose to treat all moral ontologies as irrelevant stories, without validity, while they themselves go on arguing like the rest of us about what [moral] objects are fit and what reactions appropriate. What generally happens here is that the reductive explanation . . . which supposedly justifies this exclusion, itself takes on the role of moral ontology."[35] To overcome this ironic, "ideologically induced illusion," Taylor suggests the need to articulate the hidden values driving naturalists, to show "to what extent the real spiritual basis of their own moral judgments deviates from what is officially admitted." This is necessary, Taylor claims, because "there is a great deal of motivated suppression of moral ontology among our [naturalistic] contemporaries . . . because of the great weight of modern epistemology . . . and, behind this, of the spiritual outlook associated with this epistemology."[36] This, I think, is a huge point with enormous implications.

Further, in all scientific knowledge, it is important to realize that no particular understanding is infallible or final, that all any of us can have at any time is our best account, in which we are entitled to have real, though not absolute or unquestioning, confidence. What we are always dealing with is reducing error and searching for relatively better explanations, not finding absolute and indubitable truth. Taylor explains: "Practical reasoning . . . is a reasoning in transitions. It aims to establish, not that some position is correct absolutely, but rather that some position is superior to some other. It is concerned, covertly or openly, implicitly or explicitly, with comparative propositions. We show one of these comparative claims to be well founded when we can show that the move from A to B constitutes a gain epistemically."[37] Of course, Taylor admits, we may be wrong. But that does not mean we cannot be right. And it does not mean we have an alternative approach available that guarantees that we will be right. The only means available for determining the "bestness" of our accounts is by

---

35. Ibid., 9.

36. Ibid., 9–10. In Columbia University philosopher Charles Larmore's words, "Naturalism is . . . one of the great prejudices of our age. It is widely shared and explicitly affirmed. . . . But naturalism is far more often assumed and deployed for various purposes than examined in its own right and supported by argument. It faces, in fact, grave philosophical difficulties so serious and so obvious that only dogmatic precommitment can account for why they are rarely even acknowledged." Larmore, *The Morals of Modernity* (Cambridge: Cambridge University Press, 1996), 89.

37. Taylor, *Sources of the Self*, 72.

subjecting them to the strongest critiques and seeing whether they hold up or whether an alternative understanding or interpretation makes better sense of our phenomenological experience. We also have to subject those possible alternative accounts to critiques as well and see if adopting them will have provided us any significant "epistemic gain." Every account will naturally have its difficulties and limits, and people will disagree about them. But that does not mean they are all useless or equally valid. In any case, there is no other or better means of understanding and explaining the reality we make up and inhabit.[38]

How then do we come to our best accounts? Best accounts are arrived at by challenge, discussion, argumentation, reflection, criticism, vetting, that is, by testing against the clarity of experience, including through systematic observation and the discipline of reason. "As a result of our discussions, reflections, arguments, challenges, and examinations, we will come to see a certain vocabulary as the most realistic and insightful for the things of [the human] domain. What these terms pick out will be that which to us is real here, and it cannot and should not be otherwise. If we cannot deliberate effectively, or understand and explain people's actions illuminatingly, without such terms . . . then these are real features of our world."[39] In light of all of the preceding, human subjectivity—including values, meanings, morality, and, I shall argue, personal being—is as real as physical reality. Against people who are shaped by a naturalist-driven map of reality that view humans as ready objects of natural science living in an exclusively material universe, Taylor argues this:

> What is real is what you have to deal with, what won't go away just because it doesn't fit with your prejudices. By this token, what you can't help having recourse to in life is real, or as near to reality as you can get a grasp at present. . . . If non-realism can't be *supported* by moral [or more broadly, essential phenomenological] experience, then there are *no* good grounds to believe it at all. . . .

38. Thus, Taylor writes, "I could be wrong. . . . But I could also be right. The only way to decide is by raising and facing this or that particular critique. Is there a transition out of my present belief which turns on an error-reducing move? . . . What successfully resists all such critique is my (provisionally) best account. There is nothing better I could conceivably have to go on. Or my critics either, for that matter. So says the BA principle." Ibid., 74.

39. Ibid., 69. Richard McKeon advanced a different—clearly not critical realist—"pluralistic" account justifying a similar approach to progressively improving fallible knowledge. McKeon, *Selected Writings of Richard McKeon*, vol. 1, *Philosophy, Science, and Culture*, ed. Zahava McKeon and William Swenson (Chicago: University of Chicago Press, 1998).

In fact, most non-realists adopt an incoherent mixture of both routes, impaling themselves moderately on both horns.[40]

Therefore, "Unless we make a wild conjecture of [a naturalistic reductionist] kind, we will be disposed to accept that the world of human affairs has to be described and explained in terms which take account of the meanings things have for us. And then we will naturally, and rightly, let our ontology be determined by the best account we can arrive at in these terms."[41] Thus, immaterialities—such as personhood—can be readily and legitimately understood as real if we assume a human existence of a certain kind, as Taylor argues in pressing his case:

An essential condition of the existence of such [immaterial] properties [as morality and values] is that there are human beings in the world, with a certain form of life, and kinds of awareness, and certain patterns of caring. But these properties are no less real features of the world which does contain humans than any "neutral" properties are. The underlying conviction which makes this argument compelling could be put this way: How else to determine what is real or objective, or part of the furniture of things, than by seeing what properties or entities or features our best account of things has to evoke?[42]

As a result, beliefs and knowledge gained through retroduction—that is, identifying what *has* to be, whether visible or not, in order to account for what we have warranted reasons to believe really *is*—may be legitimate and reliable. And this may be so even about potentially nonmaterial realities, such as normative facts and values.[43]

In summary, naturalistic scientism's paradigm consistently applied to understanding human persons and social life employs the wrong type and

40. Taylor, *Sources of the Self*, 59–60, italics in original.

41. Ibid., 69.

42. Ibid., 68.

43. Taylor goes so far as to extend this principle to theism, in saying, "The belief in God, say, offers a [good] reason not in [an external, naturalistic] sense but as an articulation of what is crucial to the shape of the [phenomenologically perceived] . . . world in one's best account"; and "nothing prevents a priori our coming to see God or the Good as essential to our best account of the human moral world" (ibid., 73, 76)—although this is not a point necessary for the reader to concede in order to believe my argument about personhood. For a nontheistic antinaturalistic defense of the objective existence of normative facts, see Larmore, *The Morals of Modernity*. Also see Russ Shafer-Landau, *Moral Realism: A Defense* (New York: Oxford University Press, 2003).

level of analysis for the subject at hand. It tends to fail to recognize or account for realities that are constitutive of and universally present in human being and social relations. By definition and mission statement, naturalistic scientism cannot recognize, much less adequately understand and account for, immaterial realities, like value, meaning, morality, and personhood. So it is stuck with the misguided task of denying, reducing, eliminating, and explaining away, with terms alien to the realities themselves, that which is often most important in human life. The solution, if we are interested in understanding and explaining humans, is to keep naturalism studying the nonhuman, natural world and humans only insofar as they are also natural entities, and to open up the study of things human to more expansive approaches that make more generous assumptions, use a wider range of concepts, and accept as real a larger set of existent entities and properties. This may and often will mean accepting and embracing the reality and importance of immaterial facts. This will also entitle us to rely on categories of normal human living (when well considered) to account for and explain human life, to rely on essential features of human experience to tell us what is true about what is real. Furthermore, we will be licensed to theorize retroductively if the results help to provide us a best account of life. All of this is important and helpful for the task of answering the question of human being in a way that takes the person seriously.

Taylor's antiscientistic phenomenological epistemology, as I read it, is so highly counterintuitive for the modern—and, for different reasons, the postmodern—mind that it warrants at least the introduction I have given it here.[44] If his argument and its implications are not entirely transparent at this point, I hope they will become more so in the pages ahead.

Conclusion

The reader will no doubt have perceived the affinities among this phenomenological epistemology, critical realism, and personalism. All are decidedly antireductionistic. All are also comfortable with the notion that certain things are real even if they are not material or directly visible. And

44. For one criticism of Taylor on these matters, see Ronald De Sousa, "Seizing the Hedgehog by the Tail: Taylor on the Self and Agency," *Canadian Journal of Philosophy* 18, no. 3 (1988): 421–32; for Taylor's response, see Charles Taylor, "Reply to De Sousa and Davis," ibid., 449–58.

all trust to collective human experience and judgment, much more so than does naturalistic positivist empiricism, an authority to inform our reliable understandings of human being and life. My task in this book is to show how these perspectives, taken together, provide an account of human being that improves on its rivals.

PART II

Critical Engagements

The Reality of Social Construction

One of the amazing things about human persons is the ability to engage beliefs and ideas in ways that interact with bodies and the material world in order to creatively form patterns of actions, interactions, and collective social environments. Unlike other animals, a great deal of human social existence is not directly determined by genetic codes or instinctual species behaviors. Instead, human persons are free to use their manifold capacities for representation, belief formation, language, memory, creativity, identity development, and so on variously to shape the meanings and structures of their social existence together. The result is the immense variety, richness, and complexity of human cultures and subcultural meaning systems evident in history and the world today.

One important way that this human capacity for social creativity has been theorized in sociology specifically and the social sciences and humanities broadly has been the approach of "social constructionism."[1] Inspired by Peter Berger and Thomas Luckmann's influential 1966 book *The Social Construction of Reality: A Treatise in the Sociology of Knowledge*,[2]

---

1. Other disciplines sometimes use the word *constructivism* instead, though I will use constructionism in this chapter; some distinguish the meaning of the two terms, but that is not relevant for my concerns here.

2. Peter Berger and Thomas Luckmann, *The Social Construction of Reality: A Treatise in the Sociology of Knowledge* (Garden City, NY: Anchor Books, 1966). Other seminal early works include Thomas Kuhn, *The Structure of Scientific Revolutions* (Chicago: University of Chicago Press, 1962); and Herbert Blumer, "Social Problems as Collective Behavior," *Social Problems* 18 (1971): 298–306. Thinkers before Berger and Luckmann who helped, whether intentionally or not, prepare the intellectual groundwork in various ways for social constructionism include Giambattista Vico, Immanuel Kant, Karl Marx, Max Scheler, Karl Mannheim, Ferdinand Saussure, George Herbert Mead, Antonio Gramsci, William V. O. Quine, and Jean

scholars have in the last four decades produced vast literatures working out the social constructionist perspective in the sociology of science, culture, delinquency, sex and gender, race and ethnicity, inequality, religion, education, knowledge, medicine, social problems, and other significant fields in the discipline. As a result, the phrase, "The Social Construction of _____," has become a ubiquitous framing device for sociological and other social scientific analyses of nearly every subject conceivable. Most sociologists today seem as comfortable using the phrase "social construction" as, say, "social structure," "social stratification," or any other elementary disciplinary concept.

Something about the idea of social construction resonates strongly with the sociological imagination, namely, that much of human social life that appears to many people as "natural," taken-for-granted facts of an objective, fixed order, is not determined by the essential properties of nature but are variable artifacts of human cultural creation through social definition, interaction, and institutionalization. The social thus displaces nature in this perspective as the source of much if not all of human experience. A closely related reason why social constructionism attracts many sociologists is the ironic form of analysis that it readily engenders. Most interesting and influential sociological works are those that show that something we previously understood in one way is best *really* understood quite differently.[3] Usually the difference comes with an ironic twist. For instance, we previously thought that mental asylums were institutions provided by humane societies to care for their psychologically impaired members, until Erving Goffman showed us that asylums are essentially totalitarian concentration camps.[4] Social constructionism thus provides sociologists a powerful analytical tool to perform the assumption-upending ironic twists that make for interesting storytelling. Social constructionism also appeals to many sociologists because its unmasking of the seemingly natural as contingently constructed opens up possibilities for intentional personal and social change toward greater justice, freedom, equality, and human

Piaget. See George Hruby, "Sociological, Postmodern, and New Realism Perspectives in Social Constructionism," *Reading Research Quarterly* 36, no. 1 (2001): 48–62; and Tom Rockmore, *On Constructivist Epistemology* (Lanham, MD: Rowman and Littlefield, 2005).

3. Murray Davis, "That's Interesting! Towards a Phenomenology of Sociology and a Sociology of Phenomenology" *Philosophy of Social Science* 1 (1971): 309–44.

4. Erving Goffman, *Asylums: Essays on the Social Situation of Mental Patients and Other Inmates* (New York: Anchor, 1961).

fulfillment. As Ian Hacking has observed, social constructionism tends strongly to be "against inevitability" in suggesting about much of social life that "It doesn't have to be this way."[5] This theoretical leaning fits nicely with the personal progressive politics of most social scientists.

Social constructionism is an important instrument in the sociological toolkit. It provides one of the best theoretical devices for cultivating the sociological imagination in novices. Its capacity to "denaturalize" what are really human products provides great service in our scholarly efforts to understand what is true about reality. Speaking personally, it was Peter Berger's constructionist sociology of knowledge that got me into sociology in the first place. So I am committed to the importance of social construc- tionism. But I also think that social constructionism has somewhat run amok since Berger and Luckmann's seminal book. Not all construction- ist analyses think carefully about the implications of their claims. Social constructionism has also been influenced by other misguided schools and strains of thought, particularly poststructuralism and postmodernism.[6] As a result, social constructionism stands at risk of being driven into the ground by intellectual naïveté, half truths, rhetorical hyperbole, trendy external influences, and the scholarly rigor mortis that can set in as new, in- vigorating perspectives age into formulaic guild research programs. What follows is an attempt to try to steer away from that happening. A sizeable multidisciplinary literature on social constructionism already exists that informs my argument. I am not here adding anything earthshakingly new to it. But I lay out the following argument nonetheless because it is specifi- cally relevant to critical realist personalism and generally important for the future of good sociology and social science.

Social constructionism is often discussed as coming in weak and strong versions.[7] The weak version—which I am going to propose below to call

5. Ian Hacking, *The Social Construction of What?* (Cambridge, MA: Harvard University Press, 1999).

6. Henderikus Stam, "Introduction: Varieties of Social Constructionism and the Rituals of Critique," *Theory and Psychology* 12, no. 5 (2002): 571–76. See Norman Denzin, "Postmod- ern Social Theory," *Sociological Theory* 4 (1986): 194–204.

7. Another significant distinction is between what Vivien Burr calls macro versus micro versions of social constructionism, the former focusing more on major cultural systems con- structing knowledge structures and the latter on interpersonal interactions constructing mean- ing systems. Burr, *Social Constructionism* (New York: Routledge, 2003). Pauline Rosenau makes a distinction among postmodernists and between skeptical versus affirmative tenden- cies, which holds some relevance for this chapter's discussion. Rosenau, *Post-Modernism*

a "realist" version—sounds something like this: All human knowledge is conceptually mediated and can be and usually is influenced by particular and contingent sociocultural factors such as material interests, group structures, linguistic categories, technological development, and the like—such that what people believe to be real is significantly shaped not only by objective reality but also by their sociocultural contexts. Furthermore, there is a dimension of reality that humans socially construct, what I will refer to below as institutional facts, that is, those aspects of the real that humans think, speak, and interact into existence. This weak or realist version is an essential sociological insight crucial for understanding human persons and social reality.

The strong version, by comparison, claims something like this: Reality itself for humans is a human, social construction, constituted by human mental categories, discursive practices, definitions of situations, and symbolic exchanges that are sustained as "real" through ongoing social interactions that are in turn shaped by particular interests, perspectives, and, usually, imbalances of power—our knowledge about reality is therefore entirely culturally relative, since no human has access to reality "as it really is" (if such a thing exists or can be talked about intelligibly) because we can never escape our human epistemological and linguistic limits to verify whether our beliefs about reality correspond with externally objective reality. This strong version of social constructionism is fraught with problems. We should reject constructionism's strong version. I think that many social constructionist sociologists would, if pressed, say that they really believe in the weak version of constructionism. But for various reasons many nevertheless seem recurrently to slip into statements that appear to affirm the strong version instead. In short, many constructionist analyses are often confusing in what they claim. Perhaps this is because they are confused in what they think.

Before proceeding, I need to repeat a key point from the introduction. In this and following chapters, I engage and evaluate theorists who may strike readers as extremists operating on the intellectual fringe. Yet I am not being crazy for arguing with crazy people or silly for criticizing silly

and the Social Sciences (Princeton, NJ: Princeton University Press, 1992). All versions, however, have roots in Immanuel Kant's "transcendental idealism," which believes that the order of reality is imposed on (not read from) it by human cognitive activity; critical realism, by contrast, is grounded in Roy Bhaskar's "transcendental realism." Bhaskar, *A Realist Theory of Science* (Hassocks, Sussex, UK: Harvester Press, 1978).

arguments. Again, the scholars I engage are not crazy and their arguments are not silly. These are intelligent people who unfortunately make wrong arguments because of wrong presuppositions that deserve to be engaged in order to identify the underlying sources of their mistakes. And, again, the ideas I critique remain subtly influential among many other sane and serious people. The ideas I criticize may seems out on the fringe, but they shape the perspectives and thoughts of many more reasonable people and influence more moderate academics who do not directly subscribe to their more radical programs. It is not always easy to disassociate fringe theorists from more moderate positions that remain—knowingly or not—within the orbit of their large influence. One purpose here is to become more aware of the intellectual lineages and logics of problematic theories that often connect both fringe and moderate versions of theory and scholarship. By breaking from certain more extremist influences, I wish to contribute toward "cleaning up the middle" of a great deal of mainstream scholarship that otherwise possesses real value.

Rhetorical Slippage and Metaphysical Meltdown

One example, among very many I could offer, of the slippage and confusion of meanings resulting from the lack of clarity in sociological writing about social constructionism is a social interactionist textbook that happened to be sitting on a table in my department's reception area, with a title along the lines of *Social Productions of Reality*.[8] I picked it up, started reading, and found the following. The author's purpose is to introduce undergraduate students to the social interactionist version of social constructionism. She begins by pointing out that "a person's reactions to the world depend on how he or she defines the situation." Quite so. "Cultural beliefs and practices," she notes, "include rules about what is 'real' and what is 'not real.'" The author then explains that her book is about "how human beings learn and conform to the rules of reality in various situations," which "enable us to organize and to make sense of our experiences and to share our understanding with others." Having explained this, the author then addresses the apparently ontological question, "What is

8. Because my intention here is not to critique this particular book but simply to illustrate my larger point by referencing a real text, I have left the author unnamed and have slightly modified the title.

Humanness?" Her answer is that "humanness is a situated, interactional process . . . anchored in personal experience and embodied in emotions." To be a human, therefore, requires "empathetic understanding of highly nuanced, situated meanings." Reinforcing her general perspective, the author reminds us that "humans create and re-create meaning in interaction with one another." To this point, the author has mostly properly focused her discussion on people's reactions, definitions, beliefs, rules, understandings, and meanings. (It is true that her definition of humanness as "a situated, interactional process" appears a bit ontologically thin—humans are mere processes?—but taken in the larger context, we seem justified in interpreting this generously to mean, as she mentioned on the same page, that a "distinctive mark of our species" is *developed* through situated, interactional processes.[9])

But then her claims start to become confused. On page 12, the author states flatly that "reality is not just a codified series of facts and possibilities; it is something produced and reproduced through ongoing human activity." Reality itself thus appears metaphysically to be socially produced—although the word *just* introduces some uncertainty into the scope of this claim. Soon thereafter, however, the author switches back to a discussion of "the production of meaningful realities" and people's "definitions of themselves and . . . situations." Those references to meaning and definitions seem more realistic. But then she turns around and writes that "everyday interactions . . . constitute the basis of human existence." Surely social interactions are crucial to human life and experience, but do they "constitute the basis of human existence?" Next the author asks her readers to "ponder further the question, What is real?" So we are back to metaphysics. "By now you realize," she suggests, "that the answer depends to some extent on the rules that your culture gives you for determining real/unreal." It thus appears that reality itself is dependent on cultural rules for definition. Because, however, in the very next sentence she refers again to "'real' *knowledge*," we might again charitably interpret her to actually have meant, "the question, What *do you know or believe* is real?"

Unfortunately, in the next subsection, titled "So, What's Real?" the author quotes "Trudy the bag lady" for an epigram as saying "What is reality anyway? Nothin' but a collective hunch" (a notion she explicitly reinforces in the title of the next section) and tells us in the section's first sentence

---

9. Even so, here we see first clues of social constructionism's tendency to confuse how things happen (process) and what things are (ontology).

that " 'truth' and 'reality' are determined by the context in which they are practiced." This she follows with a few examples of cultural relativism, in which she observes that "people living in modern, Western culture act as if their reality is based on a 'natural' truth (things are the way they are because nature intended them to be that way)," whereas other cultures are different. (Let's just presume that the anthropomorphizing of "nature" here as having *intentions*, which almost no modern westerner believes, is a mere slip of the fingers on the keyboard.) The effect on the reader is to relativize a realist ontology grounded in the natural, which reinforces the hunch that the author is a strong social constructionist, not simply an imprecise writer. However, next she shifts attention away from reality per se and back to mere cultural depictions of it. "In place of the question, 'What is real?' " she invites the reader, "Try asking, 'What are some of the beliefs and practices that make up commonsense realities? . . . How do different realities depict the world and the place of humans in it?" She then discusses "the human story," "scripts we produce," and "parts we play"—all suggesting an analytic focus on cultural narratives and roles as cultural dimensions of reality, not reality itself. Yet in the closing of the introduction, the author again makes what seems to be a metaphysical statement: "Realities are social constructs that exist through shared expectations about how the world is organized."

What is the undergraduate student—for whom her textbook may be their only university exposure to sociology—to make of the author's position? For that matter, what are you and I to make of it? That people construct meaningful cultural ideas about the world that help to define for them what they believe to be real? Or that reality per se is ultimately the product of collective human construction through social interaction? She actually says both, though I suspect she really only means to say the former. But her imprecise writing makes it hard to be certain. The ideas are confused and so the argument is unclear. Had she consistently written "beliefs about reality" instead of "reality," or had she always put "reality" in quotation marks and explained what that means, all would be well. But, as it is written, in the end an undiscerning reader could very well take the author as claiming that reality is entirely a social product. Even worse, readers might be led *not even to see the difference* between the very distinct claims that "beliefs about reality are constructed" versus "reality is constructed."

I do not mean to isolate this book in particular. This kind of slippage of meanings is widespread in social constructionist writing—the above is only one example of common tendencies. Many write in ways that make it unclear what is reality, what is "reality," what is reality "for us," and what exactly those might mean. Similarly, the meanings of "person," "self," "human," "lived experience," and "subject" also undergo frequent elisions in constructionist writings. The same is true, too, when it comes to the world, the "world," worlds, "accounts of the world," etcetera. Such ambiguities and slippery connotations seem to allow writers to pitch various edgy social, epistemological, and ontological claims while leaving open an escape door of plausible deniability in case anyone detects strong constructionism lurking.

Berger and Luckmann, it is worth noting, never proposed a variety of the strong version of social constructionism in their 1966 book.[10] They were clear about this. Their specific concern was not epistemology or metaphysics, but the sociology of knowledge, as the book's subtitle makes plain. Berger and Luckmann also clearly assume that humanity has a particular, essential, natural (albeit thin) "constitution" (world-openness, a particular ontogenetic development trajectory, engagement with social order, plastic instinctual structure, etcetera) and that an objective reality exists independent of humans' consciousness of it. "Externalization" for them is the human projection of constructed meanings into that reality. Never did Berger and Luckmann conflate human knowledge about reality with reality itself or claim that the content of beliefs was entirely dependent on social processes.[11] Indeed, they were careful in defining the "reality" that is the focus of their analysis as that which humans *believe is real* by virtue of its "quality . . . that we recognize as having being independent of our own volition (we cannot 'wish them away')." Human belief about and subjective recognitions of "reality," and not objective ontological being, are front and center. Human "knowledge" they define as "the certainty that phenomena are real and that they possess specific characteristics." And it is such "knowledge" that social constructionism is invited to investigate.

10. Berger and Luckmann, *The Social Construction of Reality*; specific references for points and quotes made in this paragraph come from pp. 1, 2, 15, 104. In 2008, Luckmann explicitly identified himself as a believer in "ontological realism." Thomas Luckmann, "On Social Interaction and the Communicative Construction of Personal Identity, Knowledge, and Reality," *Organizational Studies* 29, no. 2 (2008): 280. An example of a latter, more radical constructionist who is unhappy with the "limited" nature of Berger and Luckmann's claims is Jonathan Potter, *Representing Reality* (London: Sage, 1996), see 12–13.

11. Alexander Liebrucks, "The Concept of Social Construction," *Theory and Psychology* 11, no. 3 (2001): 365–66.

"The sociology of knowledge," they write, "must first of all concern itself with what people 'know' about 'reality' in their everyday . . . lives." In order to carefully distinguish people's *beliefs about* reality from reality *itself*, Berger and Luckmann intentionally use quotation marks around "reality" and "knowledge" throughout the opening pages of the book. Then they offer this note: "If we were going to be meticulous in the ensuing argument, we would put quotation marks around ["reality" and "knowledge"] every time we used them, but this would be stylistically awkward." So thereafter the quotation marks are often, though not always, omitted. The reader is to understand, however, that the argument is about human beliefs and knowledge about reality, not about reality itself.

It appears, however, that the omitted quotation marks around "reality" and "knowledge" proved confusing to many subsequent constructionists, despite Berger and Luckmann's explicit clarification. Many, apparently, felt the need to push the envelope.[12] It is thus not uncommon to find scholars in various disciplines suggesting, if not championing, strong versions of social constructionism.[13] I offer a variety of examples here. Psychologist Jerome Bruner declares that "contrary to common sense, there is no unique 'real world' that preexists and is independent of human mental activity and human symbolic language."[14] Sociologists Bruno Latour and Steve Woolgar conclude about scientific laboratory research that "reality is a consequence rather than the cause of this [scientific] construction. . . . A scientist's activity is directed, not toward 'reality,' but toward . . . operations on statements."[15] The sociologist Harry Collins suggests "as

12. Here is where the aforementioned "intellectual chicken" gaming begins. Harry Collins and Steven Yearley, "Epistemological Chicken," in *Science as Practice and Culture*, ed. Andrew Pickering (Chicago: University of Chicago Press, 1992), 301–27.

13. I am here grouping together a wide range of people from various disciplines and with different agendas under a strong social constructionist umbrella; I do not mean to suggest that they all share the same vision, are speaking to the same concerns, or agree with one another on outlooks, simply rather that the strong constructionist mentality has been expressed by various scholars in different ways and that such arguments have diffused more broadly to have, I believe, some pernicious effects in academia and culture.

14. Jerome Bruner, *Actual Minds, Possible Worlds* (Cambridge, MA: Harvard University Press, 1986), 96. Elsewhere, Bruner writes: " 'Realities' are the results of prolonged and intricate processes of construction and negotiation deeply embedded in the culture." Bruner, *Acts of Meaning* (Cambridge, MA: Harvard University Press, 1990), 24.

15. Bruno Latour and Steve Woolgar, *Laboratory Life: The Social Construction of Scientific Facts* (Beverly Hills, CA: Sage, 1979), 237. Also see Andrew Pickering, *Constructing Quarks* (Chicago: University of Chicago Press, 1999).

an epistemological principle . . . [and] methodological imperative" that "the natural world . . . is constructed and interpreted," and so he urges "a vigorous exploration of the social construction of the natural world."[16] According to psychologist Kenneth Gergen, "There are no independently identifiable, real-world referents to which the language of social description (or explanation, for that matter) are cemented."[17] Biophysicist and engineer Heinz von Foerster states, "The environment as we perceive it is our invention."[18] The historian and philosopher Michel Foucault informs us that "in fact, [social] power produces; it produces reality; it produces domains of objects and rituals of truth."[19] Philosopher Jacques Derrida famously declared, "The text is all and nothing exists outside it."[20] Philosopher Nelson Goodman writes, "Our universe . . . consists of . . . ways [of describing the world] rather than of a world or of worlds. . . . We can have . . . no world without words or other symbols. The many stuffs—matter, energy, waves, phenomena—that worlds are made of are made along with the worlds." So as not to be misunderstood, Goodman states plainly, "We are not speaking in terms of multiple possible alternatives to a single actual world but of multiple actual worlds." "Facts," therefore, "are small theories."[21] Finally, the philosopher Ernst von Glasersfeld argues:

16. H. M. Collins, "An Empirical Relativist Programme in the Sociology of Scientific Knowledge," in *Science Observed*, ed. Karen Knorr-Cetina and Michael Mulkay (London: Sage, 1983), 91. Also see Steven Shapin, "Here and Everywhere: Sociology of Scientific Knowledge," *Annual Review of Sociology* 21 (1995): 289–321.

17. Kenneth Gergen, "Correspondence versus Autonomy in the Language of Understanding Human Action," in *Metatheory in Social Science*, ed. D. W. Fiske and R. A. Shweder (Chicago: University of Chicago Press, 1986), 143.

18. Heinz von Foerster, "On Constructing a Reality," in *Inventing Reality*, ed. Paul Watzlawick (New York: Norton, 1984), 42. Also see G. Kelly, *The Psychology of Personal Constructs* (New York: Norton, 1955).

19. Michel Foucault, *Discipline and Punish* (1977; New York: Vintage, 1995), 194.

20. Jacques Derrida, *Of Grammatology* (Baltimore: Johns Hopkins University Press, 1976), 156.

21. Nelson Goodman, *Ways of Worldmaking* (Hassocks, Sussex, UK: Harvester Press, 1978), 2, 3, 6, 97. Goodman's radical constructivism is worth additional quotation: "The dramatically contrasting versions of the world" are each "right under a given system" and operate "without even the consolation of intertranslatability among or any evident organization of the several systems in question"; thus, "the world is displaced by worlds that are but versions, with substance dissolving into function, and with the given acknowledged as taken"; as to knowledge, "Discovering laws involves drafting them. Recognizing patterns is very much a matter of inventing and imposing them. Comprehension and creation go together" (3, 7, 22).

Knowledge does not reflect an "objective" ontological reality, but exclusively an ordering and organization of a world constituted by our experience. . . . The world we experience is, and must be, as it is, because we have put it together in that way. . . . We never get to see the constraints of the world, with which our enterprises collide. What we experience, cognize, and come to know is necessarily built up out of our own building blocks and can be explained in no other way than in terms of our ways and means of building.[22]

This strong constructionism has consequences for thinking about human persons. According to Foucault, for example, the individual person is merely "a reality fabricated" by disciplinary "technology of power."[23] Sociologist Stephan Fuchs tells us that a "'person' is a variable construct of variable observers, not a natural kind, essence, or constant, and not an origin or source of all things social."[24] And psychologist and philosopher Rom Harré claims:

The singularity we each feel ourselves to be is not an entity. Rather it is a site, a site from which a person perceives the world and a place from which to act. . . . Selves are grammatical fictions, necessary characteristics of person-oriented discourses. . . . What people have called "selves" are, by and large, produced discursively, that is in dialogue. . . . Selves are not entities.[25]

These viewpoints also have consequences for our understanding of human knowledge and truth in ways that often conflate perception, belief,

22. Ernst von Glasersfeld, "An Introduction to Radical Constructivism," in *Inventing Reality*, ed. Watzlawick, 24, 30, 37. Reading Von Glasersfeld makes clear how badly tripped up intellectually he is by Vico, Kant, Hume, and others, and so how he, like so many quoted here, has ended up unnecessarily thinking themselves, through erroneous assumptions and unwarranted inferences, into philosophical paper bags from which he does not then know how to escape.

23. Foucault, *Discipline and Punish*, 194. On discursive power constructions in science, see Stanley Aronowitz, *Science as Power* (Minneapolis: University of Minnesota Press, 1988). Also see Spencer Cahill, "Toward a Sociology of the Person," *Sociological Theory* 16 (1998): 131–48; Peter Callero, "The Sociology of the Self," *Annual Review of Sociology* 29 (2003): 115–33.

24. Stephan Fuchs, *Against Essentialism* (Cambridge, MA: Harvard University Press, 2001), 64.

25. Rom Harré, *The Singular Self: An Introduction to the Psychology of Personhood* (London: Sage, 1998), 3–4, 68. Therefore, according to Harré, the substantial self disappears and the "'I' needs to have no referential function, and there need be no objective referent which guarantees that the first person is meaningful" (44). Also see Rom Harré, *Personal Being* (Oxford: Basil Blackwell, 1983); Richard Shweder and Joan Miller, "The Social Construction of the Person: How Is It Possible?" in *The Social Construction of the Person*, ed.

experience, epistemology, knowledge, and reality. For strong constructionists, "because all knowledge is language-bound, truth is forever arbitrary."[26] According to sociologist Stephen Shapin and historian and
philosopher Simon Schaffer, "as we come to recognize the conventional
and artificial status of our forms of knowing, we put ourselves in the position to realize that it is ourselves and not reality that is responsible for
what we know."[27] Von Glasersfeld likewise claims that "what is 'known' . . .
originates as the product of an active subject's activity. This activity is, of
course, not a manipulation of 'things in themselves,' that is, of objects that
could be thought to possess, prior to experience, the properties and the
structure the experiencer attributes to them."[28] Therefore, knowledge is
reduced to pure pragmatic function, since to know "is to possess ways and
means of acting and thinking that allow one to attain the goals one happens to have chosen" and "the function of cognition is adaptive and serves
the organization of the experiential world, not the discovery of ontological
reality."[29] Gergen equates "the restructuring of reality" with "symbolic
restructuring," which is made possible entirely through human reflexivity
and ability to envision alternative perspectives.[30] Linguist George Lakoff
and philosopher Mark Johnson state, "Truth is always relative to understanding, which is based on a nonuniversal conceptual system."[31] In this
framework, reality becomes pluralized, as described by anthropologist

Kenneth Gergen and Keith Davis (New York: Springer, 1985). Harré was an early realist but
later moved more in the direction of language-centered theory; to the extent that Harré still
considers himself a realist, this shows that not all realists share my view that centered personhood is a natural kind.

26. Rosenau, *Post-Modernism and the Social Sciences*, 77.

27. Stephen Shapin and Simon Schaffer, *Leviathan and the Air Pump* (Princeton, NJ:
Princeton University Press, 1989), 344.

28. Von Glasersfeld, "An Introduction to Radical Constructivism," in *Inventing Reality*,
ed. Watzlawick, 31.

29. Ernst von Glasersfeld, "Knowing without Metaphysics: Aspects of the Radical Constructivist Position," in *Research and Reflexivity*, ed. F. Steiner (Newbury Park, CA: Sage,
1991), 16; the second quote is repeated in many of von Glasersfeld's works, including Ernst
von Glasersfeld, "Constructivism in Education," in *The International Encyclopaedia of Education Research and Studies: Supplementary Volume 1*, ed. T. Husen and T. Neville Postlethwaite
(Oxford: Pergamon Press, 1989), 162.

30. Kenneth Gergen, *Toward a Transformation in Social Knowledge* (New York: Springer-
Verlag, 1982), 17–19.

31. Lakoff and Johnson in George Lakoff and Mark Johnson, *Metaphors We Live By*
(Chicago: University of Chicago Press, 1980), 226–27; Lakoff and Johnson's account of "truth"

Paul Stoller: "In a world of multiple realities, there are several paths to the apprehension of social reality. . . . Multiple realities, of course, exist within distinct and permeable universes of meaning."[32] Derrida writes, "There is no such thing as truth itself. But only a surfeit of it. Even if it should be for me, about me, truth is plural."[33] Religious studies scholar Tom Tweed writes similarly: "All theories are situated and all theories emerge from within categorical schemes and social contexts. It only makes sense to talk about reality-for-us, and questions about what's real or true make sense only within a socially constructed cluster of categories and an always-contested set of criteria for assessment."[34] Finally, religion scholar Mark C. Taylor argues:

> To ask . . . "What is religion?" assumes that religion is something like a general or even universal essence that can be discovered through disciplined investigation. From this point of view, the object of inquiry is antecedent to and a condition of the possibility of any study whatsoever. . . . But what if religion has no such essential identity? . . . What if religion has not always existed or has never existed? Recent investigators working in various fields have argued that religion is a historical phenomenon that emerges only in particular intellectual and cultural circumstances. Far from existing prior to and independently of any inquiry, the very phenomenon of religion is constituted by local discursive practices. Investigators create—sometimes unknowingly—the objects and truths they profess to discover. . . . Religion is a modern Western invention.[35]

Let us reflect critically, if briefly, on the last quote, to help identify a few of the muddles confusing many of the quotes above. First, Taylor is

(156–94) is, I believe, more generally beset by many of the problems examined in this chapter. Also see Ian Parker, "Against Relativism in Psychology, on Balance," *History of the Human Sciences* 12, no. 4 (1999): 61–78.

32. Paul Stoller, "Rationality," in *Critical Terms for Religious Studies*, ed. Mark C. Taylor (Chicago: University of Chicago Press, 1998), 250. Burr also writes, "It is important to stress the radical nature of the proposal being put forward here. . . . Social constructionism is not just saying that one's cultural surroundings have an impact upon one's psychology, or even that our nature is a product of environmental, including social, rather than biological factors. Both of these views are essentialist, in that they see the person as having some definable and discoverable nature." Burr, *Social Constructionism*, 6.

33. Jacques Derrida, *Spurs: Nietzsche's Style* (Chicago: University of Chicago Press, 1979), 103.

34. Thomas Tweed, *Crossing and Dwelling* (Cambridge, MA: Harvard University Press, 2006), 6.

35. Taylor, ed., *Critical Terms for Religious Studies*, 6–7.

unclear about what he means by "religion." He seems at times to mean the particular aspects of social worlds (rituals, beliefs, etc.) that religious studies scholars study, of whatever nature or condition it or they may happen to be. But he also seems to mean the cultural and academic conceptual category, *religion*, which people use in their everyday speech and religious studies scholars use to demarcate their subject of study. But those are not the same things. Depending on which Taylor means, we might evaluate his claims differently. If he means both at the same time or both at different times in the same chapter, then it is hard to know exactly what he is even claiming.[36] Second, Taylor erroneously suggests that if "religion" is not in possession of a general, universal, essential identity or existence, then we are wrong to think of it as having an antecedent existence creating the condition of the possibility of studying it. But that makes no sense. Many real things that do not have a general or universal or essential identity or being nonetheless do enjoy an existence antecedent to their being potentially studied, which is a condition of the possibility of studying them. I think of movies, weddings, and conferences of postmodern academics, among countless other possibilities. Third, Taylor makes an unwarranted leap from the truth about the historically and culturally situated nature of religion to his false conclusion about constructionist ontology, asserting that "investigators create the objects and truths they profess to discover." It does not follow—the premise does nothing to lead to the conclusion. In the prior quote, Tweed makes a similar leap from (rightly) observing the socially and schematically situated condition of all theories to (wrongly) concluding that we can only talk about reality relativistically as "for us" and that inquiries about truth and reality are necessarily trapped inside the bounds of our constructed and contested categories and standards of judgment. There is no reason why subjects of study cannot be historically and culturally situated in particular times and places *and* exist in reality prior to and independently of the minds of observers, possess features and capacities that observers discover in the sense of causally shaping how observers understand them, and so create the possibility that our categories and criteria of truth and reality are influenced as much by them as our perceptions of them are influenced by our prior categories and criteria. These kinds of problems of specification of meanings and development of

36. Similar ambiguities about "the world" are evident in Nelson Goodman's use of "world" and "worlds." Goodman, *Ways of Worldmaking*; Karin Knorr-Cetina, *The Manufacture of Knowledge* (Oxford: Pergamon Press, 1981), 3.

arguments not uncommon in constructionist theory generate unnecessary confusion and compromise scholarship.

I doubt that most contemporary social constructionist sociologists actually believe in the strong version, or perhaps have even carefully thought through the differences between it and the weak version. Yet many have still been influenced by the strong version, if in no other way than through the commonness of its ambiguities of meaning about the word "reality" and "worlds" that make mere flirting with strong constructionism possible. The resulting conceptual muddle in a lot of social constructionist theorizing opens up analyses in that school to claim, without much lucidity, that nearly anything and everything existent has been socially constructed. A brief review of my university library catalog turned up books with titles suggesting that the following are all the products of social construction:

Academic Computing	Intellectual Disability	Scientific Knowledge
Accidents	International News	Self
American Realism	International Politics	Serial Homicide
Ancient Cities	International Relations	Sexual Assault
Anorexia Nervosa	Liberalism	Sexual Harassment
Business Management	Literacy	Sexual Risk
Chemical Industry	Medical Practice	Sexuality
Communities	Medicine	Shared Parenting
Community Nursing	Mind	Social Class
Criminal Reforms	Moral Meanings	Social Problems
Death Penalty Executions	NAFTA	Street Gang Problems
Dementia	Nationalism	Swedish Neutrality
Democracy	Native American	Technological Systems
Deviance	Criminality	Teenage Motherhood
Disability	Nature	The Child
Disasters	Normality	The Jehovah's Witnesses
Economic Union	Nostalgia	The Korean War
Educational Leadership	Oceans	The Past
Emotions	Organizations	Therapy
Europe	Organizational Behavior	Unequal Housing Systems
Free Trade	Persons	Urban Schooling
HIV Transmission	Police Deviance	Values
Human Mind	Politics	Victims
Illness	Professional Work	Vital Statistics
Infertility	Reality	War
Information	Reproductive Outcomes	Wife Abuse
IT Systems	Satellite Systems	Written Communication

No doubt a more thorough search on books combined with a search on
journal articles and dissertations would multiply the length of this list
many times. It is legitimate to suggest that some of these items are obviously the products of social constructions—on that list I would include
moral meanings, nostalgia, and values. However, it also triggers metaphysical meltdown to suggest in any but the most tendentious way that
a number of other items on this list are the products of social construction—among these I would include Dementia, Disasters, Nature, Oceans,
Persons, Reality, and The Past. We may of course construct our own *ideas*
about and *practices* with regard to these things. But whether or not we
do, they would and will exist independently of our consciousness of them.
Stated differently, we could not possibly socially construct these things
out of existence. Between the obviously constructed and obviously not
constructed on this list sits a host of other items that may be either constructed or not constructed depending on whether we mean our cultural
beliefs and practices regarding them or the real material objects, human
events, and social structures to which our constructed beliefs and practices
relate. Few constructionist analyses seem clear about the difference. And
so confusions endure. Something in the theory and scholarship has gotten
off track.

Why Strong Constructionism Doesn't Work

The strong version of social constructionism is incoherent. The weak version is valuable and important but needs some shoring up to be coherent
and useful. Social constructionism may (or may not) work as hyperbolic
rhetorical flourish to rouse drowsy students in Social Problems classes.
It may have helped some to get published in what in the 1980s and 1990s
were avant-garde journals and book series. And it might have helped to
persuade academic deans who did not know better to think they were
advancing university education by creating new departments of cultural
studies and similar programs dependent intellectually on social constructionism. But as explanatory theories, weak social constructionism needs
some maintenance—which I will attempt below—and strong social constructionism is simply bankrupt.[37]

---

37. Helpful critical reflections on social constructionism include André Kukla, *Social
Constructivism and the Philosophy of Science* (New York: Routledge, 2000); Hacking, *The*

Social Construction of What?; Sergio Sismondo, "Some Social Constructions," *Social Studies of Science* 23 (1993): 515–35; Sismondo, *Science without Myth* (Albany: State University of New York Press, 1996); Paul Boghossian, *Fear of Knowledge: Against Relativism and Constructivism* (New York: Oxford University Press, 2006); John Searle, *The Construction of Social Reality* (New York: Free Press, 1995); Ian Parker, ed., *Social Constructionism, Discourse, and Realism* (London: Sage, 1998); Andrew Sayer, *Realism and Social Science* (London: Sage, 2000); David Nightingale and John Cromby, "Social Constructionism as Ontology," *Theory and Psychology* 12, no. 5 (2002): 701–13; Steve Woolgar and Dorothy Pawluch, "Ontological Gerrymandering: The Anatomy of Social Problems Explanations," *Social Problems* 32, no. 3 (1985): 214–27; J. R. Maze, "Social Constructionism, Deconstructionism, and Some Requirements of Discourse," *Theory and Psychology* 11, no. 3 (2001): 393–417; Liebrucks, "The Concept of Social Construction," 363–91; David Nightingale and John Cromby, eds., *Social Constructionist Psychology: A Critical Analysis of Theory and Practice* (Buckingham: Open University Press, 1999); Sayer, *Realism and Social Science*; Nigel Mackay, "Psychotherapy and the Idea of Meaning," *Theory and Psychology* 13, no. 3 (2003): 359–86; Christopher Norris, *Against Relativism: Philosophy of Science, Deconstruction, and Critical Theory* (Oxford: Blackwell, 1997); Gerald Zuriff, "Against Metaphysical Social Constructionism in Psychology," *Behavior and Philosophy* 26 (1998): 5–28; Burr, *Social Constructionism*, 178–200; Nigel Edley, "Unravelling Social Constructionism," *Theory and Psychology* 11, no. 3 (2001): 433–41; Kirsta Anderson, "Social Constructionism and Belief Causation," *The Dualist* 8 (2001): 61–71; Adelbert Jenkins, "Individuality in Cultural Context," *Theory and Psychology* 11, no. 3 (2001): 347–62; Fiona Hibberd, "Gergen's Social Constructionism, Logical Positivism, and the Continuity of Error, Part 1: Conventionalism," *Theory and Psychology* 11, no. 3 (2001): 297–321; Fiona Hibberd, "Gergen's Social Constructionism, Logical Positivism, and the Continuity of Error, Part 2: Meaning-as-Use," *Theory and Psychology* 11, no. 3 (2001): 323–46; Barbara Held, "What Follows? Mind Dependence, Fallibility, and Transcendence according to (Strong) Constructionism's Realist and Quasi-Realist Critics, *Theory and Psychology* 12, no. 5 (2002): 651–69; Hruby, "Sociological, Postmodern, and New Realism Perspectives in Social Constructionism," 48–62; Jack Martin, "Real Perspectival Selves," *Theory and Psychology* 15, no. 2 (2005): 207–24; Richard Williams and Marissa Beyers, "Personalism, Social Constructionism, and the Foundation of the Ethical," *Theory and Psychology* 11, no. 1 (2001): 119–34; José López and Garry Potter, eds., *After Postmodernism: An Introduction to Critical Realism* (London: Continuum, 2001); Liebrucks, "The Concept of Social Construction," 363–91; Thomas Schwandt, "Constructivist, Interpretivist Approaches to Human Inquiry," in *Handbook of Qualitative Research*, ed. Norman Denzin and Yvonna Lincoln (Thousand Oaks, CA: Sage, 1994), esp. 125–29; Carole Vance, "Social Construction: Problems in the History of Sexuality," in *Homosexuality, Which Homosexuality?* ed. D. Altman et al. (London: GMP Publishers, 1989); Joseph Schneider, "Social Problems Theory: The Constructionist View," *Annual Review of Sociology* 11 (1985): 209–29; Kurt Danzinger, "The Varieties of Social Construction," *Theory and Psychology* 7, no. 3 (1997): 399–416; Ian Craib, "Social Constructionism as a Social Psychosis," *Sociology* 31, no. 1 (1997): 1–15; Michael Jacobsen, "The Construction of Social Constructivism," *Distinktion* 3 (2001): 111–32; John Greenwood, *Realism, Identity, and Emotion: Reclaiming Social Psychology* (London: Sage, 1994); John Shotter, "Social Constructionism and Realism," *Theory and Psychology* 2, no. 2 (1992): 175–82. For

On a purely intellectual level, strong constructionism is incoherent
and self-defeating in numerous ways. These problems have been noted
by many already but are worth restating to be clear. To begin and most
generally, if the strong version is actually right, there is no reason to take
it seriously, because then it would be only one of many possible culturally
relative constructions of knowledge about "reality," the merits of which
we have no reliable independent standard by which to judge.[38] Someone
may wish to believe it or not for personal, aesthetic, or purely arbitrary
reasons, but, in any case, by its own account it would offer no rationally
coherent reasons with which to compel the agreement of others. Stated in
other terms, if social constructionism is correct, then the authority of the
social constructionist herself or himself is undermined by her or his own
argument, as the somewhat chastened constructionist Vivien Burr points
out: "There is an implicit hypocrisy in a social constructionism that must
assume some agentic subject—the academic—who is capable of standing outside of discourse and commentating upon it for the benefit of lay

a more polemical work, see Paul Gross and Norman Levitt, "The Cultural Construction of
Cultural Construction," chap. 3 in *Higher Superstition* (Baltimore: Johns Hopkins University
Press, 1994).

38. See, for instance, Maze, "Social Constructionism, Deconstructionism, and Some Requirements of Discourse," 393–417 ("In the very act of putting forward his theory, Gergen
is expecting his theoretical statements to be accepted as asserting something true about language and knowledge, even though the content of the statements tries to deny that possibility.
This is the classic paradox: if his theory is true, it is false," 400); Anderson, "Social Constructionism and Belief Causation," 61–71. Also see Mackay, "Psychotherapy and the Idea
of Meaning," 359–86; Held, "What Follows? Mind Dependence, Fallibility, and Transcendence according to (Strong) Constructionism's Realist and Quasi-Realist Critics, 654; Douglas
Porpora, "Methodological Atheism, Methodological Agnosticism, and Religious Experience,"
Journal for the Theory of Social Behaviour 36 (2006): 68–70. For an alternative, though in my
view unconvincing, perspective, see Barbara Smith, *Belief and Resistance* (Cambridge, MA:
Harvard University Press, 1997), especially 73–87. Gergen's replies to numerous critics also
seem to me to fail as coherent responses, which may help to explain why he also wants in the
end to reduce reasoned arguments (which I think he loses) to "deliberations about the nature
of argumentation itself" and "forms of discourse, . . . simply . . . speaking and writing used by
people on various occasions." Kenneth Gergen, "Construction in Contention," *Theory and
Psychology* 11, no. 3 (2001): 419–32; Gergen, "Constructionism and Realism: How Are We
to Go On?" in *Social Constructionism, Discourse, and Realism*, ed. Parker, 148–55. Jonathan
Potter makes the same unhelpful move in his reply to critics: "The realism/relativism debate
is a literary construction." Potter, "Fragments in the Realization of Relativism," in *Social
Constructionism, Discourse, and Realism*, ed. Parker, 28. Also see Lawrence Hazelrigg, "Were
It Not for Words," *Social Problems* 32, no. 3 (1985): 234–37.

people, who are simply subject to discourse."[39] On what grounds do academic constructionists stand outside of relativistically constructed worlds to make pronouncements that deserve to persuade others?

Some social constructionists have recognized this criticism and tried, unsuccessfully in my view, to blunt its force. Goodman, for instance, insists that "willingness to accept countless alternative true and right world-versions does not mean that everything goes." Yet his explanation as to why this might be so ends up merely suggesting that different people are not prevented from "preferring" some apparently legitimate version of reality. He then immediately slides off—in what first appears as a realist self-qualification—into what sounds like radical epistemological skepticism and nihilism, saying, "I by no means insist that there are many worlds—or indeed any" and "never mind mind, essence is not essential, and matter doesn't matter."[40] Karin Knorr-Cetina and Michael Mulkay have also tried to blunt (from the position of a more weak version of constructionism than Goodman) the "anything goes" criticism by making a distinction between "epistemic relativism" (all knowledge is socially constructed and so culturally bound) and "judgmental relativism" (all knowledge is incommensurate and so equally valid), claiming that the latter "manifestly does not follow from" the former. I find this a helpful distinction—in fact, Roy Bhaskar advanced it in the 1970s.[41] But their particular account of why the one "*in no way*" entails the other merely insists that every possible alternative construction need not be "equally successful" or "equally adequate" for "solving a practical problem," "explaining a puzzling phenomenon," or being relevant "to a specific goal."[42] The argument hinges on two strong uses of the word "equally" ("equally valid" and "equally successful"), and the criterion of evaluation is purely pragmatic. It would be very hard for anyone to show that all knowledge is "equally" successful for pragmatic purposes, so, stated in those terms, their case is unassailable.

39. Burr, *Social Constructionism*, 183.

40. Goodman, *Ways of Worldmaking*, 94, 95, 96. At the same time, Goodman then seems to agree with comedian Woody Allen's definitive assertion that "there can be no doubt that the one characteristic of 'reality' is that it lacks essence" (96).

41. Roy Bhaskar, *The Possibility of Naturalism: A Philosophical Critique of Contemporary Human Sciences* (London: Routledge, 1979), 57–58.

42. Karin Knorr-Cetina and Michael Mulkay, "Introduction," in *Science Observed*, 5–6, italics in original. For another pragmatist attempted solution to the "anything goes" problem, see Bruner, *Acts of Meaning*, 24–27. Also see Knorr-Cetina, *The Manufacture of Knowledge*, 2–3.

But stepping back to assess, we see that what Knorr-Cetina and Mulkay have successfully shown here is only that—even within social constructionism and given primarily pragmatic interests—it is not the case that "everything *always* goes." What they have not shown, even from a somewhat weak constructionist viewpoint, however, is that social constructionism does not undermine its own intellectual authority. It may not be the case with the weak version that anything goes, but it is not particularly clear either why or how, if it is true, "social constructionism sticks."[43] In other words, what they have not shown is that social constructionism can provide a social constructionist account of itself that does not reduce social constructionism to just one among many possible ways of seeing the world that may or may not be pragmatically useful or that anyone may or may not want to adopt (or ignore). In this way, the strong version is self-defeating and the weak version, if not carefully stated, tends toward self-defeat.

Furthermore, strong social constructionism is self-defeating on moral grounds. One of the appeals of social constructionism for many believers, as I noted above, is its capacity to reveal the contingent, noninevitable nature of social arrangements, by showing them to be humanly constructed and therefore, in theory, capable of being humanly reconstructed. Many social constructionists want to use their scholarly work to destabilize social systems of domination, inequality, and oppression in order to replace them with emancipated systems that are more egalitarian, participatory, and humane.[44] But that presumes the possession of real moral standards—and

43. As Kenneth Gergen must admit: "While constructionist critiques may often appear nihilistic, there is no means by which they themselves can be grounded or legitimated. They fall victim to their own modes of critique." Gergen, "The Place of the Psyche in the Constructed World," *Theory and Psychology* 7 (1997): 729.

44. Steven Seidman, for instance, writes, "I urge a shift from sociological theory as a foundational practice to narrative knowledges which unite moral advocacy and social analysis." Seidman, *The Postmodern Turn: New Perspectives on Social Theory* (Cambridge: Cambridge University Press, 1994), 9–10. Likewise, Vivien Burr writes, "When I first began to read about social constructionist ideas in the late 1980s, I was attracted, as I believe were many others, by the liberatory promise of its anti-essentialism. . . . Once this principle is accepted, the liberatory message becomes clear: if what we take ourselves and others to be are constructions and not objective descriptions, and if it is human beings who have built these constructions, then it is . . . possible to re-construct ourselves in ways that might be more facilitating for us." Burr writes about constructionists' "responsibility" and concerns about what are "good or bad ends" and about things "dangerous." Burr, "Overview: Realism, Relativism, Social Constructionism, and Discourse," in *Social Constructionism, Discourse, and Realism,* ed. Parker, 13,

not arbitrary personal inclinations—by which to judge social systems as oppressive, exploitive, just, benevolent, free, or whatever else one might believe in or oppose. But such moral standards are precisely what strong social constructionism eradicates, by denying the existence of real moral facts that are anything more than certain ideas that some people happened to have made up but which other people could very well make up quite differently. Goodman, for whom "reality is relative," provides first-rate examples of this eradication of standards, in telling us, "Truth cannot be defined or tested by agreement with 'the world'; for . . . truths differ for different worlds." Truths are thus always relative to constructed "worlds," so that, for example, the claim that " 'snow is white' is true according to a true version if and only if snow is white according to that version." Consequently, "Truth, far from being a solemn and severe master, is a docile and obedient servant."[45] From such a perspective, we can only conclude that the "truth" of the moral goodness of humane systems of freedom and equality are every bit as much the contingent social constructions as oppressive systems of domination and exclusion. Within the story of strong constructionism there is no intellectually honest way by which not only to prefer one over the other but also to rationally persuade others that they ought also to prefer it. Bruner, who is sympathetic to Goodman, recognizes the problem in this way: "If knowledge is relative to perspective, what . . . of the value issue, of one's *choice* of perspective? Is that 'merely' a matter of preference? Are values only preferential? If not, how *do* we choose between values?"[46] Gergen reveals his self-compromised moral position when he argues that "in the end it is the [moral] actions that are rationalized by meta-theory . . . that will make a difference" (notice even here that "rationalized" is more tentative than, say, "authorized" or "justified"), yet cannot say anything more strongly about that than the need to be relevant for "actions that *we index* as racist, sexist, unjust, intolerant,

---

85. Jonathan Potter writes that postmodern relativism "is used most happily against authority, against the status quo, against established versions and taken-for-granted realities." Potter, "Fragments in the Realization of Relativism," in ibid., 41. See Craig Calhoun, "Culture, History, and the Problem of Specificity in Social Theory," in *Postmodernism and Social Theory*, ed. Steven Seidman and David Wagner (Oxford: Blackwell, 1992), 244–88.

45. Goodman, *Ways of Worldmaking*, 17, 18, 20, 122. Goodman again: "Truth, like intelligence, is perhaps just what the tests test; and the best account of what truth may be an 'operational' one in terms of tests and procedures used in judging it" (120).

46. Bruner, *Acts of Meaning*, 27–28, italics in original.

and the like."[47] Racism and injustice are indexed as morally wrong for us. But what if some other person or community constructively "indexes" the social patterns behind those "wrongs" as morally acceptable—as some in fact do? The constructionist, by virtue of the innate intellectual limitations of his or her own theoretical system, has no more persuasive leverage to apply. All that remains are emotivistic assertions.[48]

The kinds of answers that constructionism has to offer are hopeless suggestions like "[I] recommend . . . that social critics draw on the cultural traditions and communities of which they are a part for their moral standards and visions. . . . They should draw on the moral traditions of these communities for standards of critique and projects of social change."[49] What this kind of nonsolution dodges, however, is the fact that many local cultures and community moralities are very morally problematic, sometimes reprehensible.[50] What about, say, certain northern African communities that torture and disfigure their own girls through female genital mutilation (sans anesthesia or the girls' consent), or neo-Nazi skinhead groups who attack racial minorities, religious sects who stone women to death for daring romances outside of their religious communities, or antisodomy laws in certain Southern states?[51] Are the moral "standards and visions" of those local communities acceptable "standards of critique" for "projects of social change?" If truth is as "docile and obedient [a] servant" for them as it is for any more humane moral system, then why not? When

47. Gergen, "Constructionism and Realism: How Are We to Go On?" in *Social Constructionism, Discourse, and Realism*, ed. Parker 154, italics added for emphasis.

48. See Alasdair MacIntyre, *After Virtue* (Notre Dame, IN: University of Notre Dame Press, 1981), 6–35.

49. Seidman, ed., *The Postmodern Turn: New Perspectives on Social Theory*, 12. Also see Seidman's confused moral argument in "The End of Sociological Theory: The Postmodern Hope," *Sociological Theory* 9, no. 2 (1991): 131–46.

50. Renato Rosaldo makes the same self-defeating moral move in Seidman's book: "Social critics work outward from in-depth knowledge of a specific form of life. Informed by such conceptions as social justice, human dignity, and equality, they use their moral imaginations to move from the world as it actually is to a locally persuasive vision of how it ought to be. Because different communities differ in their problems and possibilities, such visions must be more local than universal." Rosaldo, "Subjectivity in Social Analysis," in *The Postmodern Turn: New Perspectives on Social Theory*, ed. Seidman, 183. Rosaldo, however, provides no account as to why we should expect "locally persuasive visions" to actually represent what the world "ought to be," when in fact we have plenty of reason to believe that many local visions will not be. The moral naïveté here is stunning.

51. Laws that certain communitarians defend on the same "local community norms" grounds as those advanced by Seidman.

we are consistent about it, all that is in fact left in this approach for the making of moral commitments are personal preference, arbitrary choice, and power to enforce and impose. And that hardly seems to be the kind of world toward which most social constructionists want to move. Some constructionists seem more up-front than others about this conclusion. Education professors Egon Guba and Yvonna Lincoln, for instance, admit that within their perspective the only way to judge any construction is from the perspective of "the paradigm out of which the constructor operates," such that a specific "construction can only be judged adequate or inadequate utilizing the particular . . . paradigm from which it is derived."[52] It is not clear, however that they or other constructionists are aware of the deeply problematic moral implications of such a relativistic view.

Bruner attempted to answer his own question (above) about how to choose values, given the perspectival nature of all knowledge, without falling into utter relativism. His answer is, first, that values are packaged in "ways of life" that "constitute a culture" and so are "consequential in terms of . . . cultural community" and, second, that "the value commitments of [a culture's] members provide either a basis for the satisfactory conduct of a way of life or, at least, a basis for negotiation."[53] In short, given how socially embedded we are, we don't have much choice over values anyway, and values are "good" if they pragmatically work for us in the culture we happen to live in. But that hardly answers the problem—it either evades the question about what makes for "satisfactory conduct" in life, given the limitations of human flourishing, or it falls back into the utter moral relativism of making judgments about "satisfactory" assessable only within a particular culture's perspective. Yet many citizens of several African countries (and their emigrant citizens in other countries around the world) clearly find female genital mutilation of girls an important part of a perfectly satisfactory conduct of life—that's why they keep mutilating their girls, despite outside opposition. Then, recognizing the value conflicts that modern pluralism creates, Bruner is reduced to this: "All one can hope for is a viable pluralism backed by a willingness

52. Egon G. Guba and Yvonna Lincoln, *Fourth Generation Evaluation* (Newbury Park, CA: Sage, 1989), 143.

53. Bruner, *Acts of Meaning*, 24. Kenneth Gergen observes that "while constructionists' arguments do invite moral and political deliberations, they do not champion one ideal over another. . . . Constructionism may invite a posture of continuing reflection, but each moment of reflection will inevitably be value saturated." But what this descriptive observation again fails to address is normatively *which* values and *why* those? Gergen, *An Invitation to Social Construction* (London: Sage, 1999), 231.

to negotiate differences in world-view" in which all are "conscious as we can be about the values that lead us to our perspectives. It asks that we be accountable for how and what we know."[54] Sounds nice. But, again, this merely presumes what it purports to explain. Things like willingness to negotiate differences, voluntary reflexivity about one's perspective, and accountability for our own positions are hardly human universals. They derive from specific kinds of larger moral commitments. The question is, if we believe Bruner's constructionist story, can we explain and defend those moral commitments and the admirable behaviors they generate that he would like to enjoy? I think not. Bruner's solution may (or may not) work in parts of Cambridge, Massachusetts. But they are not very helpful—even in pragmatic terms—for most people living in most of the rest of the world. We need more reliable moral bearings than social constructionism can provide.

One final attempted solution to the social constructionists' moral relativism dilemma is simply to counter that rationality regarding moral deliberation itself is a relative social construction. So, whatever moral claims are offered in an argument are dismissed as "just another social construction." But that only makes the problem of moral knowledge, values, and commitments worse, since, in that case, it really *is* true that "anything goes." In short, social constructionism's relativism cuts both ways—not only against social systems that need deconstructing, but also against the moral commitments of the deconstructors. The only way to avoid facing this embarrassing realization is to live in a state of selective intellectual denial, smuggling into one's constructionist thinking some key moral beliefs that social constructionism flatly deny, without letting oneself notice that one is doing so. But that hardly seems commendable, at least to those who have not abandoned the value of basic intellectual coherence.

This problem of self-subversion of moral commitment is reinforced by constructionism's problematic claims and implications about truth. Many social constructionists, particularly those influenced by postmodernism, maintain that any statements of truth are inherently authoritarian, oppressive, and exclusionary. Gergen, for example, writes that "objectivity claims . . . operate to silence competing voices; the discourse of objectivity and political totalitarianism are allied."[55] Jean Baudrillard suggests truth

---

54. Bruner, *Acts of Meaning*, 30.
55. Gergen, "The Place of the Psyche in the Constructed World," 279.

claims are a form of terrorism.[56] (Never mind, again, that these themselves are truth claims!) Even weak constructionists tend to be skittish about the making of claims to truth, which seem to suggest a distasteful superiority and judgment. Many constructionists suppose that by relativizing all knowledge and truth claims, the world will become a place of more tolerant, peaceful conversations.[57] Now, it may or may not be true (oops, that word again!) in theory that some foundationalist projects that believe they have access to indubitable truths tend as a result toward authoritarianism and exclusion.[58] But that is typically more assumed than argued or demonstrated. In any case, there are not many influential thinkers today who believe in direct human access to indubitable truths grounded in definite, universal foundations. We are decades past those illusions. Critical realism explicitly advocates the *fallibility* of all human knowledge (but without sliding into relativism) and therefore motivates ongoing engagement, inquiry, and debate. In fact, nothing about realism, particularly critical realism, and its search for our best human account of truth about the real has to lead to anything but scientific humility, open considerations of plausible alternative viewpoints, and reliance on persuasion and evidence to influence minds.[59] It is only a belief in the existence of truths that are

56. Jean Baudrillard, *Simulations* (New York: Semiotext(e), 1983).

57. Gergen, for example, after having been hammered theoretically in one forum by numerous critics, advocates shifting away from direct arguments and focusing instead on the "metadiscourse" of argument and the actions arguments authorize, "to enter a new domain of dialogue," "a search for non-confrontational modes of . . . opposition that are not so acutely condemnatory" that do not presume "an inner evil" in a position or person that requires "eradication through . . . incarceration," and that pursue "inter-mingling intelligibilities." Gergen, "Constructionism and Realism: How Are We to Go On?" in *Social Constructionism, Discourse, and Realism*, ed. Parker 148, 154. One senses that Gergen here is starting to realize the actual impossibility of his own position, yet rather than simply admitting his intellectual mistakes and forsaking strong constructionism, he wants to wave the white flag to sue for a "peace with honor" that obscures the key issues about which the original conflict was waged.

58. It is worth mentioning, however, that some suggest that constructionists' statements about language actually function, ironically, as foundationalist claims of knowledge, in the sense of being a first principle on which all subsequent knowledge is built and assuredly rests. See, for instance, Held, "What Follows? Mind Dependence, Fallibility, and Transcendence according to (Strong) Constructionism's Realist and Quasi-Realist Critics," 653.

59. "To acknowledge the mind-independence of the world is to undermine, not to support, hopes of some privileged relation between discourse and the world." Sayer, *Realism and Social Science*, 41. Constructionists may feel that my argument falls below their expected standards of friendly conversation. My reply is, first, that I have paid social constructionism the respect of reading and thinking extensively over many years about the merits and possible

independent of our thinking about them that can motivate the desire to subjugate our desires, preferences, ideologies, and politics to the search for truth as best as we can grasp it. And it is only a belief that some accounts of reality are actually in fact better than others, as judged by reasonable criteria, that can motivate openness to considering new ideas and the desire to use reasoning and evidence to sort through the alternatives. If there is no truth or if all "truths" are incommensurate or equally valid within their own local communities, then what is there even to have a conversation about? For these reasons it is, if anything, more likely the relativism of constructionism that over the long run threatens openness, humility, mutual respect, and critical and constructive discussion. Andrew Collier states it well: "If there is no truth about reality independent of what anyone holds about reality, then everyone may be smugly certain that their own belief is irrefutable. . . . One could not make mistakes. Nonrealism thus licenses the dogmatist."[60] Strong constructionism tends to lead, if anything, not to friendly conversations but either to intellectual apathy (what does it matter?) or arrogant tribalism (our view is right to us, those who challenge us must have bad motives or live in a different "reality" that we can dismiss).

At least some versions of strong social constructionism face another theoretical problem. If they, particularly *certain*—though obviously not all—symbolic interactionist and discursive psychology forms, were right, then most of us would live in a world that was much more congenial to our preferences, interests, and desires. For we would all work to construct the kind of reality that we would want to live in, which would—depending on

---

problems of its perspective; and, second, that I invite responses to my arguments that aim to persuade me with reasons and evidence that I am wrong. That is as much as any school of thought can ask of others and enough for us to carry on constructive scholarly work in a pluralistic environment.

60. Andrew Collier, "Language, Practices, and Realism," in *Social Constructionism, Discourse, and Realism*, ed. Parker, 56. The critical realist sociologist Andrew Sayer quotes Hitler and Mussolini to draw the historical connection between constructionists' intellectual commitments and possible political outcomes: "There is no such thing as truth. Science is a social phenomenon and like every other social phenomenon is limited by the benefits or injury it confers on the community" (Hitler); "Everything I have said and done in these last years is relativism by intuition. . . . From the fact that all ideologies are of equal value, that all ideologies are mere fictions, the modern relativist infers that everybody has the right to create for himself his own ideology and to attempt to enforce it with all the energy of which he is capable" (Mussolini). Sayer, *Realism and Social Science*, 47. Also see William Outhwaite, "Realism, Naturalism, and Social Behavior," *Journal for the Theory of Social Behaviour* 20, no. 4 (1990): 366–77.

one's view of social structures—be significantly within our power. True, there are people out there who would like to construct worlds that serve their own interests, which could very well contradict ours. But since reality would be the contingent construction of active human agents interacting together, we each could shape our own interactions and constructions to suit our ends. The more constructionists resort to power to impose a reality, the more they slide toward a realist position without admitting it— because the imposition by power of constructed worlds could only work if there are actual points of contact in reality that provide the powerful with their leverage. Each small community of persons could then live in its preferred worlds of reality, since reality is not given but open to multiple versions of construction. The problem here, however, is that few of us live in worlds nicely suited to fulfill our preferences, interests, and desires. Life in the world is often hard and unpleasant. That is because a great deal of reality, both natural and social, exists independently of our construction, in largely fixed forms governed by the given order of the ontologically and causally real. The fact that for most of us the world is not the way we would like it to be tells us that a largely objective reality exists that powerfully affects our lives, which is much more than simply the product of human interactions. If so, then our knowledge of that reality should be shaped as much as possible by the objective nature of its being, not by our projected desires and preferences for it. That is realism.

Another way to express these and similar problems is to note that for any more-than-weak social constructionist analysis to be at all interesting requires some commitment to some accurate knowledge about some aspect of what is true about the real. Since much social constructionism denies the possibility of such knowledge, to sustain nevertheless an interesting analytical story requires surreptitiously engaging in what Woolgar and Dorothy Pawluch aptly call "ontological gerrymandering"— that is, "making problematic the truth status of certain states of affairs and explanation, while backgrounding or minimizing the possibility that the same problems apply to [other] assumptions upon which the [constructionist] analysis depends."[61] Consider, for example, a hypothetical social constructionist analysis in the social problems literature of an (alleged) growing problem of teen drug abuse. Such an analysis might seek to show that growing public fears about teen drug abuse during a specific period

61. See Woolgar and Pawluch, "Ontological Gerrymandering: The Anatomy of Social Problems Explanations," 216, 224. Also see Steve Woolgar and Dorothy Pawluch, "How Shall We Move beyond Constructivism?" *Social Problems* 33, no. 2 (1985): 159–62.

of time reflect not an actual increase in teen drug abuse but the result of an interest-driven growth in media and political attention, which work together to socially construct the "teen drug abuse problem," which leads in turn to public hysteria. If the analysis is correct, then the really interesting, ironic analytical twist of the story is that what seemed to be one thing (a real, growing problem) is *really* something else quite different (media fabrications and political interests producing public hysteria). That description could very well be the case in reality. But note this: in order for us to believe that and so for the story to be at all interesting, it *must* be the case that we actually know that rates of teen drug abuse were in fact not increasing during the period of time in question. If we do not know that, the analysis is empty and the story is uninteresting. All we know is that the media and political actors paid more attention to teen drug abuse during a period of time, perhaps because abuse was actually increasing. Boring. Yet many social constructionists want by virtue of their theoretical project to attack and defeat the very idea that we can know objectively true or reliable facts about reality. The stronger their version of constructionism, the more they attack that idea. But that itself cuts the interesting analytical legs out from under the entire constructionist story. Thus, in order for such a social constructionist analysis to be compelling, it must assume something that its perspective actively denies.[62] Rather than owning up to this elementary logical problem, however, what usually happens in specific analyses is that "the programmatic claims [of constructionism] give way to clearly discernible lapses into realism." Social constructionists become only *selectively* relativistic, smuggling in, through what Mike Michael calls "honorable fudges,"[63] the bits of realism needed to make their argument interesting.

Social constructionism can be subject to numerous other theoretical criticisms,[64] but enough said for present purposes. The irony in all of

62. But for a study on the topic of the illustration that smartly mixes realism and social constructionism, see Craig Reinarman and Harry Levine, *Crack in America: Demon Drugs and Social Justice* (Berkeley and Los Angeles: University of California Press, 1997).

63. Mike Michael, "A Paradigm Shift? Connections with Other Critiques of Social Constructionism," in *Social Constructionist Psychology: A Critical Analysis of Theory and Practice*, ed. Nightingale and Cromby, 54–55. In fact, the fudges may be dishonorable.

64. Fiona Hibberd, for instance, shows that (despite constructionism's self-presentation as the antithesis of logical positivism) social constructionism ironically shares with positivism an untenable conventionalist theory of theories, namely, that theories are nonempirical because they are not imposed upon us by nature but are adopted for nonepistemic reasons. Hibberd,

this—if I may be indulged in a bit of ironic storytelling—is that the strong constructionist perspective, which is typically energized by progressive, emancipating impulses, often turns out in the end to be an imperialistic and colonizing theoretical movement. I could well have titled this entire section "The Imperialism of Social Constructionism." For too often we see the attempt of at least some versions of social constructionism to invade and colonize whole realms, sometimes all realms, of human social life with the debunking and relativizing logic of its particular perspective and analysis. Strange as this may seem, these totalizing ambitions of constructionism uncannily resemble the Gary Becker genre of neoclassical economics, which also seeks to colonize and renarrate the entire world in its own particular image. What started off as an intellectual movement to emancipate and pluralize turns out by its own logic to compress all reality into one-dimensional, relativized, linguistic constructions.

One might wonder, given these problems, how strong social constructionism has managed to carry out its project with any degree of plausibility. Part of the answer is that social and cultural conditions were ripe in the last decades of the twentieth century for many people in particular knowledge class positions to want to believe it.[65] Another part of the answer is the error-veiling function of (I presume unintentional) logical

---

"Gergen's Social Constructionism, Logical Positivism, and the Continuity of Error, Part 1: Conventionalism," 297–321. In a companion article, Hibberd demonstrates social constructionism and logical positivism's similarity in adopting an antirealist "meaning-as-use" semantic thesis, based on the Kantian assumption that the constituents of reality are not directly knowable, leading to an incoherent reliance on realism even as reality is denied. Hibberd, "Gergen's Social Constructionism, Logical Positivism, and the Continuity of Error, Part 2: Meaning-as-Use," 323–46. Furthermore, J. R. Maze argues that Kenneth Gergen's particular appropriation of Wittgenstein's "language game" theory is behaviorist and Skinnerian insofar as language ultimately has no sense but functions as conditioned stimuli. Maze, "Social Constructionism, Deconstructionism, and Some Requirements of Discourse," 399. Richard Williams and Marissa Beyers interpret social constructionism more broadly as a form of behaviorism, and suggest that it is incapable for providing a coherent account of the origins of human intelligence. Williams and Beyers, "Personalism, Social Contructionism, and the Foundation of the Ethical," 119–34. And Jack Martin believes that strong constructionism lacks an adequate account of social and cultural change: "If sociocultural rules and practices were fully determinative of meaning, there would be no possibility of changes in meaning to accommodate novel facts or features of reality." Martin, "Real Perspectival Selves," 212.

65. See, for instance, Mike Feathersone, "Towards a Sociology of Postmodern Culture," in *Social Structure and Culture*, ed. Hans Haferkamp (New York: Walter de Gruyter, 1989); George Stauth and Bryan Turner, "Nostalgia, Postmodernism, and the Critique of Mass Culture," *Theory, Culture, and Society* 5, nos. 2–3 (1988): 509–27; Gerard Delanty, *Social Sci-*

and rhetorical slippages in a lot of social constructionist writing.[66] If we are to resist the reasoning errors and theoretical colonization by the totalizing relativism of strong constructionism, we have to do at least two things. First we need to own up to the inevitability and desirability of realism and all of the complexities that it entails—in my view, the most promising

---

ence: Beyond Constructivism and Realism (Minneapolis: University of Minnesota Press, 1997), 95–109.

66. Some of these are worth a quick mention. One common misstep in constructionist writings follows this "Unwarranted Coattail Riding" logic: "Since X is A then it is *also* Z (when A in no way entails Z)." For example, many constructionists' studies of science show that scientific findings are shaped by social and cultural dynamics not admitted by official accounts of science (so far, so good), but then conclude that the substance of the scientific findings are merely human constructions (erroneous). "To show that acceptance of a [scientific] belief as fact is the result of a complex [social] process is not to show that the fact is also the product of a social process" (Zuriff, "Against Metaphysical Social Constructionism in Psychology," 16). Scientific facts as human knowledge about reality might *both* be the result of human activity *and* descriptions of truths about reality.

Another common constructionist rhetorical lapse takes the "False Dichotomous Choice" form of: "A is not true, therefore *only* Z can be true (when B, C, D . . . W, X, or Y might very well also and otherwise be true)." Vivien Burr provides an example in her description of the antihumanism of poststructuralist constructionism. She characterizes humanism as "the idea that the person is a unified, coherent rational agent who is the author of their own experience and meaning. . . . It assumes that there is an essence at the core of an individual which is unique, coherent, and unchanging . . . [and that] the individuals' experience and the meaning it holds originates within the person." Having set up this individualistic and static caricature of humanism, Burr rejects it and declares the following "as a logical conclusion" of language-centered epistemology: "The self will be constantly in flux, constantly changing depending upon who the person is with, in what circumstances and to what purpose. . . . [This] ensures a fragmented, shifting, and temporary identity for all of us." Burr, *Social Constructionism*, 53–54. Burr illustrates the same error again when she writes, "Since the social world, including ourselves as people, is the product of social processes, it follows that there cannot be any given, determined nature to the world or people. There are no essences inside things or people that make them what they are" (ibid., 5). Of course, that conclusion does not at all follow from the premise—we could very well be produced by social processes and still possess elements of an essential nature that help to make us humans what we are; by the next page, however, it becomes clear exactly why Burr objects to the possibility of essentialism: "Essentialism traps people inside personalities and identities that are limiting for them" (6); in short, a moral commitment to emancipation is what drives antiessentialism, despite its problems, not a best account of rational deliberations and the evidence of our experience. Thus, if people are not unchanging and self-originating (A) then they must be constantly changing and fragmented (Z). A more realistic assessment is that most people are somewhere in the broad middle between these extremes—but acknowledging that would take the zing out of constructionist rhetoric.

Yet another frequent unjustified leap of reason takes the "False Incompatibility" form of, "If X is A then it is *not* B (when A and B are in fact entirely compatible)." Kenneth Ger-

version of which being critical realism. Second, we have to affirm the ontological reality of human personhood of a particular kind, which provides an intellectually sturdy basis for struggling toward more humane, free, just, participatory social systems in the first place.[67] And these, to bring us back to our larger purpose, are what this book is seeking to foster. The rest of this chapter seeks to clarify a realist social constructionist account that avoids the theoretical problems we have noted above and contributes intellectually to a theory of critical realist personalism.

Against Collapsing Distinctions

How did social constructionism get itself into such theoretical difficulty? The answer is: by collapsing a number of crucial distinctions that inhere in reality. In order to move in a more positive theoretical direction with social constructionism, we need to push a little harder against the key sources of intellectual weaknesses in much social constructionist writing, which will provide important clues about how to think more realistically about the matter. Critical realism insists that reality is complex, constituted by variable types of entities, and stratified at multiple levels. We therefore need a variety of conceptual distinctions to sustain this complexity and multiplicity in our theories of reality if we hope they will ring true with reality. The general error of which problematic forms of social constructionism are at fault is the collapsing of key conceptual distinctions and, as a result, the compressing of reality in their theoretical models into fewer dimensions than are in fact real.

A good account of the crucial conceptual distinctions we need in order to understand and represent reality suitably have been well laid out by the philosopher John Searle in his book *The Construction of Social Reality*.[68]

---

gen, for instance, in opposing notions of indubitable truth, points out, "To understand that something is the case requires the realization that it might be otherwise," from which he concludes that assertions of truth cannot be true. Gergen, *Realities and Relationships: Soundings in Social Construction* (Cambridge, MA: Harvard University Press, 1994), 9; see Maze, "Social Constructionism, Deconstructionism, and Some Requirements of Discourse," 411–12. In short, because truth (X) is dubitable (A) then "truth" is not really true (B)—when in fact truths could be (and in fact often are) both not indubitable but still meaningfully true (properly understood, which I address below).

67. See chapters 7 and 8 below on the good and human dignity.

68. Searle, *The Construction of Social Reality*.

Searle begins by distinguishing between "brute facts" and "institutional facts." The former do not require human institutions in order to exist, while the latter always do. That my wedding ring is made of gold is a brute fact.[69] That the gold wrapped around one of my fingers is a "wedding ring" is an institutional fact. Without the social institution of marriage, the thing on my finger would still be made of gold but would not be a wedding ring. What Searle is curious to understand is how institutional facts are possible and how they are structured.

To do this he introduces three other important distinctions. The first concerns the *epistemic* status of claims and hence their truth status as facts of judgment. The distinction here is between *objective* versus *subjective* epistemic statuses. An objective epistemic judgment of fact is true regardless of the attitudes, feelings, or views of any person—for example, that the campus of the University of Notre Dame in Indiana contains a building on top of which sits a gold dome. That is an objective epistemic fact that is not dependent upon your or my attitude about it to be judged true. A subjective epistemic judgment of fact, by contrast, is dependent upon people's attitudes, feelings, and views—for instance, the statement by a visitor to Notre Dame that the gold dome is magnificent. For the gold dome to in fact be magnificent in this case depends upon some subjective state of the observer, in a way that the gold dome's existence per se does not.

The second important distinction Searle makes in order to understand the nature of institutional facts concerns the *ontological* status of entities and their modes of existence. The distinction here is again between *objective* and *subjective* ontological statuses. An objective ontological fact enjoys existence independent of any perceiver or mental state—for example, that gold is a softer metal than iron. A subjective ontological fact by contrast only exists in dependence on a subjective experience or feeling of a person—for instance, if someone tried to climb the dome but slipped

69. Constructionists may counter that the particular English word *gold* is a human invention. Of course. But this is a trivial observation. The substance of which my ring is made is not a human invention—it existed somewhere in the earth before humans knew it was there or had spoken the word *gold*. Furthermore, what gold does for humans is not entirely a function of contingent human constructions but is also partially determined by natural qualities of the substance itself, especially its relative scarcity, softness, color, and shine, which makes gold universally prized among humans. Thus, when Cortés met the Aztecs, despite their cultures never having interacted before, he discovered that they too highly prized gold and also formed it into valuable crafted objects—as does every culture where gold is known.

and fell, then they would be very embarrassed and in a great deal of pain. Their embarrassment and pain would be real, but their ontological existence would be dependent on the person's subjective feelings and mental state.

The third key distinction that Searle proposes for comprehending institutional facts concerns *features* of reality. The distinction here is between *intrinsic* features and *observer-relative* features. Intrinsic features of reality exist independent of human mental states—for example, that gold consists of particular kinds of molecules and is of a certain mass. That was true before gold was ever humanly discovered, named, and prized. By contrast, an observer-related feature of reality exists because observers and users make it so—for instance, that Notre Dame's gold dome created and helps sustain an institutional identity for the university. That is a real feature of the dome, yet not intrinsic but dependent upon observers' relations to it.

The difference among these three clarifying distinctions can at first seem faint, but they are worth distinguishing.[70] The epistemic distinction concerns predicates of judgment of truth. The ontological distinction concerns kinds of entities and modes of existence. And the features distinction concerns types of characteristics of reality. Connecting them all is the underlying issue of dependence or independence on human subjective mental intention toward them—an obviously crucial issue for social constructionism. But the distinctions are not identical and so they can cut across one another in different combinations. For example, a faculty member's smiling with enjoyment at the bright morning sun reflecting brilliantly off of Notre Dame's gold dome as they walk with a student to class involves an epistemically objective fact (they did smile whether or not the student or anyone else knew or would admit it), an ontologically subjective existent (the smile would not have existed except as an experience of their subjective perceptual state in response to the sunlight), and an observer-related feature of reality (the smile added a quality of happiness to the morning for the faculty member and the student companion by virtue of their mutual recognition of the "smileness" of the pleasure-induced muscle contractions of the face—the happiness was not itself

---

70. Searle later introduces three other distinctions relevant to social constructionist theory—between agentive and nonagentive functions (*The Construction of Social Reality*, 20–23), regulative and constitutive rules 27–29), and linguistic and nonlinguistic institutional facts (60–66)—but which are not important enough for present purposes to explain here.

intrinsic to the behavior we call smiling). Other combinations using different illustrations would also be possible to elaborate.

How and why, then, has social constructionism so often run amok? By
failing to sustain the above kinds of distinctions and conflating reality in
theory into fewer dimensions than actually exist in reality. Here is what
often happens: Social constructionists begin by making the archetypical
modern move of prioritizing epistemology over ontology. All other issues and assumptions are thus subordinated to the question of how we
can rightly know anything—a question we can never answer without first
having specified some ontology. Having gotten off on that wrong foot,
constructionists then bring in an empiricist assumption and fall prey to
the "epistemic fallacy," namely, accepting the erroneous assumption that
what is real is identical with what is observable—or more accurately put,
that statements about being can be reduced to or analyzed in terms of
statements about knowledge.[71] Simply by adopting these two governing
assumptions—prioritizing epistemology over ontology and conflating
the real into the empirical—constructionists have nearly determined the
outcome of the theoretical game before their theorizing has even begun.
What is required to finalize the outcome is to add in a serious appreciation
for the fact that all human knowledge is historically and culturally situated. With those three understandings in place, the social constructionist

71. Roy Bhaskar, "Philosophy and Scientific Realism," in *Critical Realism: Essential
Readings*, ed. Roy Bhaskar et al. (London: Routledge, 1998), 27–28. Philosophical empiricism
following David Hume and the logical positivism of the early twentieth century have made
such an impression that many of us find it hard to believe that a reality could exist that is not
directly empirically observable. "Seeing is believing," we say. We thus simply equate the real
with the empirical. But this is erroneous, the presuppositional source of numerous errors. We
can only observe part of what is real. Some of the real, indeed some of the actual, is simply not
empirically observable. Again, reality, according to critical realism, comprises deep structures
of causally real entities with specific tendencies and powers that are not necessarily directly
visible. But they are real nonetheless. If so, we should not be surprised that the patterns of
social action and structures are limited and governed in certain observable ways. That is because they are influenced in part by a variety of real causal forces that impinge on human
existence. Insofar as humans participate in and have access to reality, they are able to perceive,
understand, and work with many of the features of the real. Their social constructions are thus
partly influenced by reality, and not simply the categories and meanings of inherited prior social constructions. That influence is always conceptually mediated and always incomplete. But
it is a real influence with real causal effects nevertheless. If and when, however, we insist on
conflating the real into the empirical, that is, on committing the epistemic fallacy, we obscure
to ourselves the ways that constructions are shaped by reality.

can empirically observe representations of reality that are historically and culturally situated. Per their empiricist presuppositions, those are all that constructionists can count as real. Unable to distinguish the representations of reality from objective reality (for reasons on which I elaborate shortly), the social constructionist concludes that reality is a historically and culturally relative construction. The distinction between brute and institutional facts thus collapses, so that brute facts disappear into the totality of institutional facts. As a result, the distinction between objective and subjective ontological statuses of reality caves in—all allegedly objective ontological statuses are suspected if not declared to be really subjective. With those two distinctions collapsed, the other two follow. Intrinsic features of reality are reconceived as always observer-related features. And epistemically objective judgments of truth are translated into epistemically subjective judgments. Reality as it is in complex fact is thus flattened out in constructionist theory—like a tall, multitiered wedding cake that is squashed by an inebriated and accidentally tripped reception guest into a big, splattered pancake shape on the floor. The result is interesting. But it isn't very useful or somehow itself anymore.[72]

We must insist, however, that reality is much more complex than many social constructionists construe it to be—especially reality that involves human persons. If we want to understand reality as it is, therefore, we have to understand and sustain a variety of conceptually helpful distinctions that uphold differentiations in and multiple levels of the real. To be specific, in our theorizing of brute facts we have to sustain things like objective epistemic judgments, objective ontological existents, and intrinsic features of reality. Without those we either give way to total relativism or intellectually compromise ourselves through ontological gerrymandering and fudging. We should not want to do either. But to avoid those outcomes, we have to go back and revise our presuppositions. We have to stop prioritizing epistemology over ontology. And we have to stop equating reality with the empirical. We need to become critical realists.

Pressing the critical analysis one step further, I want to continue to ask *why* intellectually social constructionism characteristically dissolves

72. The "weak constructionist" offending guest apologizes to the bride and groom and admits that not all wedding cakes are squashed pancakes. The "strong constructionist" cake-squashing guest, however, being especially drunk, denies that anything is wrong with the cake, insists that all wedding cakes, when rightly understood, are really squashed pancakelike messes, and stumbles off.

such distinctions and so squashes reality. The answer has to do with its decisively flawed theory of the relation among language, reality, and knowledge. The fatal move was adopting key elements of—or perhaps misreadings of[73]—Ferdinand Saussure's structuralist theory of language.[74] Saussure (1857–1913) was a French-speaking Swiss linguist whose ideas powerfully influenced twentieth-century linguistics and literary and social theory—particularly, for our interests, midcentury structuralist and post-structuralist theorists Roland Barthes, Louis Althusser, Jacques Lacan, Claude Lévi-Strauss, Jean Baudrillard, Jacques Derrida, and Michel Foucault. Saussure's thought is complex, and I cannot do it full justice here. Nor do I intend to adjudicate whether poststructuralists properly interpreted or actually misappropriated Saussure (in what follows, I will presume the former). Suffice it to say that Saussure directed analytical attention away from the particularities of speech (*parole*) and toward language (*la langue*) as a formal system of differential elements. The former is within the control of individual users, while the latter is a social product beyond individuals' control. Saussure developed his social theory of language in opposition to both positivist biological theories of language and referential theories of language, which stressed word meanings as driven, respectively, by the effects of hearing words spoken on bodily neural systems and by their representing natural kinds of objects in reality. Saussure argued that words in language do not receive their meaning from the properties of, effects on, or by standing for things in the world. Words, instead, derive their meaning from relational contrasts with other words, through linguistic oppositions. The connection between the signifier (spoken sound or written appearance of the word) and the signified (the concept) that together compose the sign is thus arbitrary. Signs are believed unrelated to the referents they designate and so can have no intrinsic meaning, but are the union of meanings and "sound images." For instance, the meaning of "bright" as a linguistic sign is not derived from any natural property of brightness actually in the world that causally informs that concept or the

73. Numerous critics argue that poststructuralists misinterpreted Saussure, including Maze, "Social Constructionism, Deconstructionism, and Some Requirements of Discourse," 402–4; Collier, "Language, Practices, and Realism," in *Social Constructionism, Discourse, and Realism*, ed. Parker, 48; Norris, *Against Relativism: Philosophy of Science, Deconstruction, and Critical Theory*.

74. The best analysis of Saussure's problematic influence is Raymond Tallis, *Not Saussure* (New York: St. Martin's Press, 1995).

written or spoken form of the word, but from its difference from "dim" as a contrasting linguistic sign. Nothing in the pronounced sound or written appearance of the word "bright" is determined by the meaning of the word for its users or even by the inherent nature of external reality. Reality thus does not consist for humans of natural kinds of objective entities that language reflects. So language cannot be a collection of rule-governed words representing a collection of real objects. There is a reality "out there," but the way any culture divides reality up into conceptually meaningful terms is not determined by the nature of the objective world but by the structure of the arbitrary categories of its language.

Language should thus be understood as a closed system, the coherence of which is driven not by external reference but by internal structures of arbitrary oppositions. Preexistent reality does not determine human understanding. Rather, language imposes a structure on reality that makes it understandable. Relational presence, absence, and difference are crucial in that, since what exists is determined by what is different or what does not exist, by a "network of forever negative differences." Meaning arises from difference in the interplay between signs. Thus, human communication is made possible not by reference of words to real entities but by internal consistency in the structured system of signs that are put into use in speech. Causal agency is therefore located in structure, the structure of language, and not in persons. Here, then, we have an early version of strong social constructionist theory. Within its framework, Saussure taught, the purpose of the scholar is to reveal the underlying structure of relational differences that give rise to cultural systems of meaning. In all of this, Saussure emphasized studying the structure of linguistic sign systems at fixed points in time (the synchronic) rather than changes in language over time (the diachronic). He also emphasized that words and meanings, once arbitrarily linked, become fixed in structure, so that words will always denote the same meanings.[75]

Most of the problems in untenable contemporary versions of social constructionism are traceable to the initial adoption, selective reworking, and subsequent radicalizing of Saussure's theory by poststructuralists, postmodernists, and strong social constructionists. The brief story is that

---

75. Ferdinand Saussure, *Course in General Linguistics* (1916; London: Fontana, 1974). See Anthony Giddens, *Central Problems in Social Theory* (Berkeley and Los Angeles: University of California Press, 1979), 9–48; Delanty, *Social Science: Beyond Constructivism and Realism*, 95–109; Potter, *Representing Reality*, 68–73; Burr, *Social Constructionism*, 46–56.

many twentieth-century European intellectuals, particularly in France, absorbed the central themes of Saussure's theory but rejected particular teachings and certain scholarly applications. What they embraced were Saussure's antirepresentational theory of signs, his emphasis on arbitrary assignments of meaning, his reality-constructing view of language, his de-centering of the person as causal agent, his privileging of language as determinative of the social, and his insistence on the creation of identity and meaning through difference. But they rejected and modified other aspects of Saussure. Poststructuralists traded Saussure's emphasis on synchronic analysis with a diachronic interest in the changes of language and meanings over time. They rejected his teaching about the fixed meaning of words, accentuating instead the indeterminacy, ambiguity, and multiple connotations in language and of words, the ways that meanings are continually and forever shifting. Poststructuralists also moved their substantive attention away from underlying structures of language to the more public realm of culture. Most of this was filtered through a profound pessimism that was pervasive in French intellectual circles in the late 1960s and 1970s, resulting from disillusionment with existentialism, the crisis of the French leftist movement after 1968, and the growing intellectual influence of Friedrich Nietzsche (the collapse of the socialist project after 1989 intensified this pessimism for many). As a result, a major intellectual influence on social scientific social constructionism in the 1980s and 1990s carried with it a highly skeptical, pessimistic, deconstructive posture concerning knowledge, meaning, truth, coherence, authorial intent, morality, persons, subjectivity, and history. Among constructionists more generally, that pessimism coexisted uneasily with constructionism's other optimistic proclivities for human enlightenment and emancipation—which was concentrated primarily in constructionism's symbolic interactionist "branch."

It is only against this background of poststructuralism's pessimistic revision of Saussure's structuralist theory that more recent constructionist claims like the following are intelligible: "What is communicated about events is determined, not by the character of events themselves, but by linguistic figures or forms." "No nondiscourse-dependent or transcendental rules [of truth] exist. . . . What we call the mind or reason is only an effect of discourse." "[Signs] no longer represent anything and no longer have their equivalent in reality." "All that language can do . . . is to refer to itself. Language is a 'self-referent' system;" and human institutions are "predicated on the lie that is the word."[76] If we are to back away from the severe problems in strong versions of social constructionism, we will have to come to terms with and provide an alternative to Saussure and the subsequent poststructuralists' transformation and deployment of his theory that have since shaped social constructionism.

Toward Reclaiming Realist Social Constructionism

I want to restate from the perspective of critical realist personalism what is valuable and important in social constructionism, what constructionism can and cannot do and say, and how we might adjust some of the most promising versions of its approach to be more truthful and useful. Social constructionism properly understood is not only perfectly compatible with but also indispensable to critical realist personalism. How then should we appropriately approach social constructionism?

First, let us affirm what in social constructionism is good, right, insightful, and necessary for understanding reality. Social constructionism is right that positivism is a dead-end approach to social science, which fails to produce adequate understandings of human social reality. It is also correct in claiming that foundationalist epistemologies are discredited and that impersonally objective forms of human knowledge are impossible. No human knowledge is indubitable and there is for humans no "God's eye" view "from nowhere" from which to study reality. All perceptions require active human interpretation, and language plays a huge role in human thought. Moreover, the constructionist perspective is right that many different kinds of observable physical and social "texts" underdetermine their own interpretations, making "correct" interpretations difficult and sometimes impossible—there is no guarantee of accurately grasping an author's intentions or of adjudicating between plausible alternative read-

---

76. Respectively, Gergen, "Correspondence versus Autonomy in the Language of Understanding Human Action," 143; Jane Flax, *Thinking Fragments* (Berkeley and Los Angeles: University of California Press, 1990), 35–36; Jean Baudrillard, *In the Shadow of the Silent Majorities* (New York: Semiotext(e), 1983), 19; Burr, *Social Constructionism*, 81; Anne Norton, *Reflections on Political Identity* (Baltimore: Johns Hopkins University Press, 1988), 188. Elsewhere Gergen writes that although "we cannot step outside tradition," the latter is "often [a] blinding force." In the case of his own strong social constructionism, I would agree with Gergen, though not necessarily about "tradition" generally. Gergen, "Construction in Contention," 423.

ings. Reality for humans involves a good deal of ambiguity, uncertainty, openness, and multiple possibilities of understanding. Therefore, it is correct that a great deal of what people take to be the truth is not necessarily true, and that people often think they have a lot more reason to hold their beliefs than they actually have good warrant for. Constructionism is also right in pointing out that much that is real in human social life is created by human action and interaction—rather than being preexistent and essential aspects of the natural world. Symbolic social interaction is an especially crucial part of the process of the human social constructing and maintaining of cultural worlds. In this, processes and relations are often as important as entities and structures. It is also true that most human assumptions, perceptions, thought processes, interpretations, and behavioral patterns in life are not determined by any fixed nature but are profoundly shaped by historically specific cultural systems. Certain aspects of reality do exist objectively, but not in the mode of having inherent, unchanging essential natures—it is therefore mistaken to project essentialism onto all of reality. Furthermore, different cultures often make sense of the world in very different ways. So there are different alternative approaches to viewing and evaluating the same reality.

Moreover, because constructionism is accurate in stating that human social constructions are often (wrongly) perceived by their human constructors and sustainers as ontologically natural and fixed, it is entirely correct that constructionist analyses can be humanly empowering—in that revealing the contingently constructed nature of undesirable features of social life that people previously assumed to be natural and unchanging opens up new possibilities for creative, intentional actions to change those undesired aspects of social life through challenge and reconstruction. In addition, it is definitely true that knowledge and power are often bound up together, such that jurisdiction over and acceptance of epistemologies, categories, information, and definitions of reality and of situations are usually intimately connected with issues of dominance, authority, legitimation, coercion, and control of self and others. Similarly, a tremendous amount of human knowledge is significantly shaped by particular and potentially distorting material, relational, and ideological interests. In this sense, truthful knowledge can sometimes be difficult to come by. In general, social constructionists are also right that the importance of autonomous human agency, self-generation, and self-determination are grossly overstated in most individualistic Western cultures. It is true that a great deal of importance in human consciousness and action is profoundly influenced by collectively constructed social factors and forces.

Critical realist personalism affirms all of these beliefs and in its pursuit of understanding seeks to engage what is true about human persons and social reality. None of the above contradicts realism or personalism. All of it helps to fill out our picture of the complicated, multidimensional nature of reality. In order to be clear about how this is to be understood within a theory of critical realist personalism and to shore up theoretical thinking underwriting realist social constructionism, however, it is also important to develop certain clarifications and constructive arguments.

Language Refers, Knowledge Refers

I have said that the root problem of the kind of social constructionism that is demonstrably incoherent and therefore theoretically unacceptable is a certain view of the relationship among language, reality, and knowledge. That view, I said, was inherited from Saussure and his poststructuralist revisers and absorbed more or less indiscriminately into social constructionist theorizing. My judgment was that this "linguistic turn" eventually led us into an ontological and epistemological dead end. As Pauline Rosenau observes, "If . . . language produces and reproduces its own world without reference to reality, then it is impossible to say anything definite, because language is purely an artificial sign system and cannot assure truth."[77] Is this what social science has come to? A realist social constructionism seeking a more adequate theoretical account must replace that inherited and absorbed view with a more adequate approach. My first constructive argument toward clarifying and supporting realist social constructionism, therefore, is to reassert the necessity of a plausible referential theory of language. However unfashionable such a theory may be, there is no escaping some version of it if we hope to avoid debilitating relativism. I am not a philosopher of language. Nor do I intend to develop a full-blown theory of how language refers to reality. Here I can only argue that such a theory is necessary and that it should be credible if developed well, suggest a few ideas for moving constructively in that direction, and then try to head off certain possible misunderstandings of my position.

Language works for humans not simply because concepts are tightly linked to words in structures of internal semiotic difference. It is true that

77. Rosenau, *Post-Modernism and the Social Sciences*, 79.

concepts are linked to words in systems of language. But language works
for humans also because the signs that those concepts and words compose
refer to entities in reality that possess existence independent of any linguistic influence. Language often and in many ways refers to that which is
nonlinguistic.[78] Language is not a self-contained, internally enclosed, self-
referring system of oppositions. If it were, we would not have the world
and experience that we do in fact have. We can therefore use retroductive
reasoning to establish compellingly the belief that language must refer
to nonlinguistic reality. Language is thus open to the world, an aspect of
the real, possessing the causal capacity to connect the immaterialities of
human cognition and intention to the materialities and immaterialities
of being. Linguistic truth statements are objective-reality-dependent for
their existence. As Searle notes, "Facts don't need statements in order to
exist, but statements need facts in order to be true."[79] Therefore, unless
we are interested in living in impossibly solipsistic or nihilistic worlds of
meaning in which linguistic statements and truth statuses have nothing
to do with each other, we have to bring the referent of the real back in.
We do not have to believe that all of reality consists of natural kinds that
give rise to corresponding words. We do not have to believe that qualities of reality are somehow directly reflected in concepts or words. We
do not have to believe that any language provides a comprehensive or
supracultural account of reality. We do not have to believe that the lines
between real entities and actual words are perfectly clear. But we *do* have
to believe that a reality exists independent of—and inclusive of—human
language, and that language somehow meaningfully interacts with and refers to that reality.[80] True enough, language does help to constitute a part
of reality, but not the whole of reality. Much that is real is nonlinguistic
and nonconceptual. Thus, rather than understanding reality as created by
and enclosed or trapped within the all-pervading presence of language,
we should understand language as one crucial but subsidiary part of the
all-pervasive existence of reality.

Gergen is right when from his premise he concludes, "To the extent
that the mind furnishes the categories of understanding, there are no

---

78. See Tallis, *Not Saussure.*

79. Searle, *The Construction of Social Reality,* 218.

80. See T. Norris, "Signs, Social Ontology, and Critical Realism," *Journal for the Theory of
Social Behavior* 28, no. 1 (1998): 1–24. Collier, "Language, Practices, and Realism," in *Social
Constructionism, Discourse, and Realism,* ed. Parker, 36–40.

real world objects of study other than those inherent within the mental makeup of persons."[81] He is wrong, however, in thinking that only the mind furnishes the categories of understanding. And so his conclusion is wrong. Instead, the mind works interactively with other persons interacting together with reality to formulate categories and networks of understanding. And so there are real world objects of study.[82] Similarly, when Baudrillard believes that because ultimately all representations only refer to other representations, nothing is ever authentic,[83] he does not draw a false conclusion, given his premise. Where Baudrillard is false, however, is in believing the supposition that all representations only refer to other representations. Therefore his conclusion about the impossibility of authentic knowledge is erroneous. It takes realism and referential language to rescue theorists from such plights of intellect.

What, then, of Saussure? On him, I follow Collier, who observes, "People think that Saussure has shown that words get their meaning from their relation to other words, not by reference to reality. But what he has in fact shown is that words refer to reality by virtue of their relationship with other words."[84] Saussure was partly right. But where he was crucially wrong was in eliminating the referent. What that did, among other things, was to obliterate the importance of the practical use of language in the context of life in the real world. Saussure's dichotomy of signifier and signified must be opened up into a triad to include the third element of

81. Gergen, "Correspondence versus Autonomy in the Language of Understanding Human Action," 141.

82. See James Gibson, *The Ecological Approach to Visual Perception* (Philadelphia: Lawrence Erlbaum, 1986); Gibson, *The Senses Considered as Perceptual Systems* (Westport, CT: Greenwood Press, 1983); Edward Reed, *Encountering the World: Toward an Ecological Psychology* (New York: Oxford University Press, 1996).

83. Jean Baudrillard, *For a Critique of the Political Economy of the Sign* (St. Louis, MO: Telos Press, 1981). "Authentic" here seems to mean having some basis in substantiating nonlinguistic reality. Also see W. J. T. Mitchell, "Representation," in *Critical Terms for Literary Studies*, ed. Frank Lentricchia and Thomas McLaughlin (Chicago: University of Chicago Press, 1990).

84. Collier, "Language, Practices, and Realism," in *Social Constructionism, Discourse, and Realism*, ed. Parker, 48. Andrew Sayer writes, "That A is mediated by B does not mean that A is B's product. Although all observation is conceptually mediated, what we observe is not determined by concepts." Sayer, *Realism and Social Science*, 41. See Rom Harré and Roy Bhaskar, "How to Change Reality: Story v. Structure—A Debate between Rom Harré and Roy Bhaskar," in *After Postmodernism: An Introduction to Critical Realism*, ed. López and Potter, 22–39.

the referent. In fact, as some have observed, Saussure unavoidably, surreptitiously brought in the referent in his own writings in order to make his case against referential language. Anthony Giddens, for instance, observes, "The dam that Saussure established to protect the system of *langue* from semantic and referential ties to the world of objects and events [was] continually and necessarily breached."[85] In short, Saussure needed to engage in ontological gerrymandering not to be implausible. Had the poststructuralists realized and responded honestly to that, they would have saved us a lot of confusion and trouble in the decades since. Better to have admitted our need for real world referents, come up with a most sensible account as to how that works, and thought through the larger implications.

How is it, then, that linguistic signs might both refer to referents in reality and yet not mirror or resemble them in any direct way? Collier again: "The case is just like that of the relation of a map to the area mapped. The symbols on the map do not resemble what they symbolize—a blue line represents a river that appears in reality as a muddy brown expanse. But by virtue of their mutual relations, they represent real features of the landscape. If they did not, they would not be a map of anything."[86] To affirm that terms in language *refer* does not require believing that they mirror, represent, photocopy, or embody real referents. Etymologically, "refer" means "to bear back." It thus means to be related to something other in a way that something about it is borne back to the related. For terms in language "to refer" means that they point toward external objects and events in ways that enable minds cognitively to connect meanings to referents, which in turn bear back to minds "things to which referred" that are other than language and mind—enabling minds to meaningfully link signifiers (words) and signifieds (concepts). Through such referential processes, human language and knowledge are connected, however sometimes partially and fallibly, to reality.

Another way to say this is that human language, knowledge, and experience are in most cases always *about* something. This should be obvious,

85. Giddens, *Central Problems in Social Theory*, 16–17, more generally, 13–18. Giddens and Sayer agree that a more accurate term than *arbitrary* for the relation between signifier and signified is *conventional*. Sayer, *Realism and Social Science*, 36.

86. Collier, "Language, Practices, and Realism," in *Social Constructionism, Discourse, and Realism*, ed. Parker, 48. Also see Justin Cruickshank, *Realism and Sociology: Anti-Foundationalism, Ontology, and Social Research* (London: Routledge, 2003).

but it is a point that needs reiteration in a discussion on social constructionism. The theoretical background to constructionism easily leads us to
analyze knowledge as a particular entity or process or problem regarding human minds or arising among human symbolic communicators or
interactors. Knowledge tends to be viewed as the product of closed-ended,
self-referring language systems or communicative interactions among
symbolizers. Thus, lacking both subjects and objects, many constructionists end up breaking down over how language or knowledge could connect
or refer to any nonlinguistic or cognitive reality. It does so, we must see,
by being not self-enclosed and self-referential but by being *about* other
things. Collier states the point well:

> Consciousness or experience or ... language or practice is not an entity that can
> be understood in its own right. They can be understood only in so far as they
> open up reality to us. Consciousness ... is always consciousness of something.
> Without that something it is, as Sartre says, mere nothingness. Experience is
> always an encounter with what existed before the experience and is to a de-
> gree known to us as a result of the experience. ... Experience can never be a
> thing which we can inspect as it is in itself, independently of the reality that is
> given through it. And this "aboutness" is characteristic too of practice and of
> language. ... The learning of language would not only be miraculous in the
> absence of interaction with other people, it would be miraculous if that inter-
> action were not *about* independently existing entities in a public world, which
> language too is necessarily partly about. ... Language can only be learnt by
> reference to reality.[87]

However we spell out the precise details of the account, in short, we must
proceed with a theory in which language and knowledge are understood
as referring to reality.

Humans Do Not Socially Construct Reality but Rather Primarily Beliefs about *Reality*

No humans, individually or collectively, socially construct reality, as
in its entirety—not to mention realit*ies*. Most of natural reality exists

---

87. Collier, "Language, Practices, and Realism," in *Social Constructionism, Discourse,
and Realism*, ed. Parker, 48. Also see Garry Potter, "Truth in Fiction, Science, and Criticism,"
in *After Postmodernism: An Introduction to Critical Realism*, ed. López and Potter, 183–95.

independently of our constructions, objective to our consciousness of it. What humans do primarily and most importantly construct are *beliefs about* reality—beliefs that become the building blocks for constructed institutional facts. Using Andrew Sayer's terms, humans construct "thought objects" but not "real objects."[88] From a critical realist perspective, our beliefs, once formed, become a particular aspect of reality, real existents at a specific level of being. But our beliefs about reality, including much of social reality, though real in the sense of possessing causal powers, are not substitutes for the (also real) things that the beliefs are about. With simple beliefs in hand, humans also go on to construct out of them categories, definitions, assumptions, understandings, perceptions, meanings, rules, narratives, schemas, scripts, and other complex cognitive entities shared among and sustained by people through social interaction. But all of these still exist in the realm of mental constructs, thought objects, the simplest form of which is belief.

For instance, some people believe that *people* and *skin* and *color* exist as real. They believe that different people have skin of different colors. Some also believe that human "races" exist. They believe that races are determined by the color of people's skin. They also believe that people of different races tend innately to possess, by virtue of their race, different mental, physical, and dispositional characteristics and abilities. These people furthermore believe that descriptive differences between and within such characteristics and abilities are matched to normative differences in evaluative merit or value. They therefore believe that people who belong to some races should be evaluated more highly or lowly than others because of their innate characteristics and abilities. By constructing and linking together such beliefs, humans create new ontologically existent entities—in this case, racist ideology. But all of the constructed items described so far consist only of human beliefs or related cognitive entities. They are products of our cognitive capacities, existing, as we phenomenologically experience it and as best as we can describe it, as immaterial objects "in" our minds. They are nevertheless real by virtue of our causal

---

88. Andrew Sayer, *Method in Social Science: A Realist Approach* (New York: Routledge, 1992), 46–51. This statement will have to be qualified below, however, insofar as human beliefs, once thought, become part of the real. Much of the position I am taking here, incidentally, is simply a restatement of medieval philosophy and logic that was worked out with great intelligence and precision but with which moderns have largely lost touch—a fact I find somewhat embarrassing about the current state of academic thought and discourse.

criteria of reality, however, because, although they are immaterial, they possess capacities to cause things to happen in the world. Racist ideologies can help to cause resource inequalities, group conflicts, patterned segregation, health disparities, war, and murder. When so, all of that becomes part of the actual in reality. But none of that means that reality per se or in toto has been socially constructed by humans. Again, most of reality is beyond human construction or destruction. What it is in reality that humans are actually free to creatively construct into and out of reality are primarily our *beliefs* about reality. Yet that does not diminish the importance of social constructions, because beliefs for humans are very important and causally efficacious features of life.

Practical, Embodied Activity in the Material World Is Essential to Human Knowing and Being

Social constructionism, and the "linguistic turn" generally, have focused our attention on symbolic communication, cognitive categorizations, discursive practices, definitions of situations, the signaling of meanings, and the sustaining of legitimations. What social constructionism characteristically misses is the key role of practical, embodied activity in the material world for informing human knowledge and structuring being in social life. A great deal of personal and social existence is not reducible to symbolic and discursive exchanges between interactive, meaning-oriented communicators. That is crucial in human life, of course, but not the whole of it. Human life also entails a tremendous amount of practical, corporeal engagement in, care for, fabrication with, and consumption of material reality. Human personhood cannot be conceived of, much less theorized well, apart from our bodily and spiritual dealings with materiality.[89] So much of how and what we humans know and live is derived from activities like ambulating ourselves through space, building objects, tending animals, moving things, attending to hygiene, preparing meals, wielding tools, healing bodies, organizing possessions, growing food, cleaning objects, protecting families, studying the weather, avoiding accidents, touching intimates, and all of the other myriad activities that comprise the practical (and

89. Edward Reed, *The Necessity of Experience* (New Haven, CT: Yale University Press, 1996); Andy Clark, *Being There: Putting Brain, Body, and World Together Again* (Cambridge, MA: MIT Press, 1998).

sometimes expressive) dimensions of existence.[90] Whether in preschool or the high-tech lab, these are what humans do and how they learn. This is also how Berger and Luckmann began their account of the social construction of society as an objective reality—not by positing primordial humans struggling to communicate meanings but by prototypical humans seeking, in their specific example, to build canoes.[91] The interactions, meanings, habitualizations, and legitimations come in, through, and after the practical activity.

Given this orientation, strong constructionist statements like, "People behave toward objects on the basis not of their concrete properties, but of the meanings these objects have for them" ring hollow.[92] Consider yourself running into a large pack of very hungry feral dogs while hiking alone in the woods. How would you behave toward that object? You would behave in part toward the wild pack as an object based on its concrete properties—its consisting of physically powerful, biologically motivated, socially coordinated, carnivorous hunters. You would also behave in part toward the pack as an object in response to your *own* natural properties—your

90. See, for example, Elizabeth Teater, *Embodied Geographies: Spaces, Bodies, and Rites of Passage* (New York: Routledge, 1999); George Lakoff and Mark Johnson, *Philosophy in the Flesh: The Embodied Mind and Its Challenge to Western Thought* (New York: Basic Books, 1999); Simon Williams and Gillian Bendelow, *The "Lived" Body: Sociological Themes, Embodied Issues* (New York: Routledge, 1998); Evan Thompson, *Mind in Life: Biology, Phenomenology, and the Sciences of Mind* (Cambridge, MA: Belknap Press of Harvard University Press, 2007); Francisco Varela, Evan Thompson, and Eleanor Rosch, *The Embodied Mind: Cognitive Science and Human Experience* (Cambridge, MA: MIT Press, 1992); Chris Frith, *Making Up the Mind: How the Brain Creates Our Mental World* (Hoboken, NJ: Wiley-Blackwell, 2007); Shaun Gallagher, *How the Body Shapes the Mind* (New York: Oxford University Press, 2006).

91. Berger and Luckmann, *The Social Construction of Reality*, 53.

92. Judith Howard, "Social Psychology of Identities," *Annual Review of Sociology* 26 (2000): 371. "It is no surprise that the preoccupation with the undecidability of meaning should [originally] come from scholars who study literature. . . . The distinctive feature of literature is precisely its detachment from everyday practices; it is predominantly a kind of communication that has purposes other than the achievement of some immediate practical end, though of course there are some exceptions. Even when everyday communicative action is interpreted by literary theorists, the practical contexts and ends in terms of which it operates tend to be bracketed out. Communication in everyday life is embedded in ongoing practices and material and discursive contexts. Here we would do well to note that Wittgenstein's emphasis on forms of life does not involve a retreat from the object to the idea; for him, to know a language is to be able to participate in the material form of life within which it is expressed, and which it expresses." Sayer, *Realism and Social Science*, 39–40.

survival instinct, fear, adrenalin surge, impulse to flight, and such. And you might behave in part toward the pack as an object based on meanings the pack has for you—meanings that, however, would be based primarily on the concrete properties of the object. It would have been impossible for you or me—no matter how loving of canines we might be—to have socially constructed the pack of hungry and vicious feral dogs in a way that would have compelled us to behave toward it as an object as if it were our dozing cat or long-lost best friend. Reality resists certain meanings. Material reality can only be plausibly interpreted in a limited number of ways. The test of practical adequacy helps us understand what those ways are.

One reason for the centrality of practical activity for human knowledge is the fact of judgments of truth about objects, relations, causes, representations, explanations, and factual claims that all people must incessantly make in their functional activities. These are highly contested topics in philosophy and social theory—meaning that, while temporarily immersed in those theoretical worlds, academics can fall under the illusion that judgments about reality and commitments to truth must be avoidable simply because they seem so intellectually problematic. But people every day and everywhere unselfconsciously evaluate alternative interpretations and explanations about what is real, how reality works, which factors cause what outcomes, and what truth claims can be trusted. And human persons have the natural capacities to evaluate such interpretations and explanations sufficiently well so as normally to be able to cope with the numberless demands, challenges, needs, and problems of life. Fixing a broken car, deciding what to plant and when, knowing what to do about stomach pains, choosing a financial investment, deciding whether to confront a friend about a problem, packing for a long vacation—all of these require complex processes of collecting information, assigning causation, projecting possible futures, estimating probabilities, evaluating claims, and committing to decisions. Nothing says that people's judgments are always smart, accurate, or reliable. People make mistakes. Reality can be hard to sort out. Things go wrong. Yet no living person can opt out of making such judgments. Nobody can transcend the requirement of engaging in practical activity and learning truth about reality as well as they are able. We do it all the time. If we did not, human personal and social life would collapse. This means that normal people have a great deal of reality-based experience making judgments about what is real and how things work. It also means that normal humans are well practiced at making sense of how linguistic representations of the world relate to real processes and events in the world.[93] When in social science we attempt to make judgments, inferences, retroductions, and representations about reality toward enhancing human knowledge, we are not embarking on a novel, unfamiliar activity. Science is more than spiffed-up common sense. But the fundamental processes of scientific knowledge production are not essentially alien to those required and practiced in ordinary practical activity. That should increase our confidence in our capacity to generate reality-referring knowledge.

People do not live in a world of ideas, symbols, concepts, and meanings only. People *are* material. People are surrounded by materiality. Many of the causal powers of reality operate through the material world. Materiality is as much a medium of knowledge and being for humans as is language. Most versions of constructionism accentuate perception, language, categories, definitions, symbols, meanings, rules, and discourse. But lacking the reality of materiality, those alone drive us into many hopeless intellectual cul-de-sacs found in the neighborhood of idealism. To conceive of social ontology essentially as, say, interactively shared meanings, is to miss the crucial material dimension of social reality. The physicality of human bodies, for example—including all of their natural capacities and limitations—is crucial for understanding persons and society. Bodies are not passive lumps of living flesh onto which powerful social relations inscribe their constituting meanings and orders. Human bodies come preconstituted with all manner of powers, needs, faculties, and constraints given by nature that powerfully shape the nature of social life. The other material stuff out of which we fashion the fixed, tangible structures that organize our lives is also essential for theorizing human persons and social existence. Property, buildings, roads, clothes, tools, personal belongings, public spaces, and the like are all obviously made out of physical matter.

I have suggested in this book that human persons must be understood, if they are to be understood well, as something like unities of embodied souls or ensouled bodies.[94] Here I suggest that social ontology, operating at a higher, emergent level of reality, is similar. Human social life consists of materially embodied intangible beliefs, schemas, and mean-

---

93. See Anna Wierzbicka, *English: Meaning and Culture* (New York: Oxford University Press, 2006).

94. Again, however, I would insist on this being understood within an emergent and fused, not dualistic, framework of relations.

ings. Materiality provides the "resources" that interact with the "rules" or "schemas" that together compose social structures, as both Anthony Giddens and William Sewell have suggested.[95] The long history of idealist versus materialist schools of social theory has been one of partial and complementary insight but ultimately of failure. Neither idealism nor materialism taken alone can adequately account for the reality of human society. Society is constituted of real immaterial and material elements that are fused in innumerable combinations and structures. Like the human person who is the uniting of a corporeal body and intangible soul, the higher-level reality of human social existence comprises both material and "spiritual" elements. This is why reductionism in social theory is almost always counterproductive. Understanding society requires keen attention to the mutual interplay of material resources and immaterial but real beliefs, schemas, and meanings—the latter of which are social constructions and the former are prelinguistically real objects that human constructions then reshape and arrange.

In sum, it is not simply that, as some constructionists would have it, some amorphous and innately unknowable materiality exists "out there" onto which we then project our constructed meanings, which are the truly significant and real. Rather, human meanings emerge from, respond to, and are shaped by the material and social reality in which they reside.[96] Furthermore, materiality is constituted and governed by natural laws of existence and function that operate objectively of any human mental construction about them. The laws of physics, chemistry, and biology simply are. And they are not ontologically or functionally dissociated from human social life. How humans construct their cultures, worldviews, and social systems is hardly oblivious to the powers and limitations inherent in the natural order of the material world. Social structures are significantly governed by the necessity of engaging and managing them. Thus, while human ideas and symbols are central to understanding human persons and social life, these must be understood as belonging to nature and continually interacting with the capacities and constraints of natural reality.

95. William H. Sewell Jr., "A Theory of Structure: Duality, Agency, and Transformation," *American Journal of Sociology* 98 (1992): 1–29; Anthony Giddens, *The Constitution of Society* (Berkeley and Los Angeles: University of California Press, 1984).

96. See Anne Rawls, "Durkheim's Epistemology: The Neglected Argument," *American Journal of Sociology* 102, no. 2 (1996): 430–82.

Humans Are Not Alien Observers of Reality but Are Active Participants in and of Reality

A realist account of social constructionism needs to replace the too-dominant image of humans as primarily *perceivers of* reality with the image of humans as *natural participants in* reality. The background view of the human condition informing much of social constructionism supposes humans as cut off from the real, as we have seen, as somehow exiled from the true reality within which they live, primarily because of the alleged epistemic limitations of language. This belief in our inescapably alienated condition was set up for us in part by Immanuel Kant's key distinction between "noumenal" reality and "phenomenal" reality—a disastrous move driven by a desire to preserve morality in a world of Newtonian determinism—that is, between things "as they really are in themselves" and things as they merely appear to us. Noumenal reality no doubt exists out there, this account supposes, but we humans have no good access to it because all of our knowledge is limited by our restricted capacities of empirical perceptions. The only world we can ever reside in is the world of appearances. We are separated from the world as it really is by an unbridgeable epistemic chasm. Thus we are locked off in the prison of our own perceptual disconnections from the real. Saussure's contribution to this line of thinking is also evident. These assumptions are what lead constructionists to believe that we humans have no reliable access to reality, that whatever is reality "for us" must be a product of our active minds constructing it out of our cultural categories and through social interactions for our own pragmatic purposes.

But modeling humans as essentially alienated and exiled perceivers of reality presents a false picture of our actual condition. In fact, quite to the contrary, we humans are fully *participants in* reality, a reality that is not identical to us but still fully ours. We emerge from, consist of, belong to, and are intricately connected with the totality of reality, material and otherwise. We are not aliens exiled from the real. As bodies and souls we are inescapably natural parts of multiple levels of the real. Our relation to reality is metaphorically like the ballet dancer fully involved in the troupe's dance performance, not the audience member watching it through fuzzy binoculars from the highest balcony. Thus, Andrew Sayer writes, "we are . . . influenced by physical processes extra-discursively, even if we can only come to know them discursively—for example, as in catching a virus. We are involved in the world, as one of its forces."[97] Because we belong to and participate in reality, because we "indwell" reality, as Michael Polanyi said, rather than merely observing it, over the years we develop a profound "tacit knowledge" of what reality is and how reality works. "We know more than we can tell," Polanyi observes. "It is not by looking at things, but by dwelling in them, that we understand their . . . meaning."[98] Thus, the real we seek to know is therefore not fundamentally concealed or removed from us. We are more than intimately part of it. It composes us. We participate in its natural operations. We are thus terrifically well positioned to know and understand it.

Language Is Not So Much a Confining Prison as an Enabling Medium

Social constructionists tend to view human language as imprisoning and limiting, when in fact language is empowering and enabling. Strong social constructionism often conveys an outlook on human language (and linguistic concepts in thought) as preventing people from clearly perceiving, properly understanding, adequately representing, and accurately expressing knowledge about aspects of reality. Gergen, for instance, asks, "How should we answer questions about what is 'independent of language' save through language?" and argues, "It is to pound on the walls of the house of language in hopes that we may find our way outside. Yet it is this very language that must serve as the resource for the effort."[99] That language is imprisoning in this way is not typically argued or demonstrated by strong

97. Sayer, *Realism and Social Science*, 37.
98. Michael Polanyi, *The Tacit Dimension* (Gloucester, MA: Peter Smith, 1983), 4, 18. Polanyi is brilliant on this point, which he develops to discredit both positivist science and existentialist philosophy from a realist and personalist perspective. Regarding the latter, for instance, Polanyi points out that our participation in reality means that "the existentialist claim of choosing our beliefs from zero is . . . proved absurd. . . . Thought can live only on grounds which we adopt in the service of a reality to which we submit" (xi). Regarding science, Polanyi writes, "The declared aim of modern science is to establish a strictly detached, objective knowledge. Any falling short of this ideal is accepted only as a temporary imperfection, which we must aim at eliminating. But suppose that tacit thought forms an indispensable part of all knowledge, then the ideal of eliminating all personal elements of knowledge would, in effect, aim at the destruction of all knowledge. The idea of exact science would turn out to be fundamentally misleading and possibly a source of devastating fallacies. I think I can show that the process of formalizing all knowledge to the exclusion of any tacit knowing is self-defeating" (20).
99. Gergen, "Construction in Contention," 419–32.

constructionists, but often taken for granted as presupposed fact. I fail
to see why any of this should be. We can agree with most weak constructionist statements about the centrality of language and symbolization in
human life and society and knowledge. But it is not at all clear, when it
comes to our relation to reality, why any of it should be cast in the kind of
restrictive and pessimistic light it so typically is.

If language is limiting when it comes to human connection to reality,
then so is air to sound waves when it comes to the hearing of music, or
clay to sculptors when it comes to sculpting figures. Language is a crucial—though not only—medium by which humans access, categorize,
comprehend, represent, and communicate about reality with immense
depth and complexity. Language is the vehicle that enables humans to
do all that. And it is darn good at it, though hardly perfect. Language
makes possible an incredible, powerful series of human accomplishments.
Of course "language" takes form in specific languages, each of which has
its particular capacities of expression and insight. Of course languages
cannot say and do everything in every way. Of course every conceivable
idea, idiom, representation, and perception is not possible to realize in
every language. So what? Seeing this is no more insightful or original
than admitting our human finitude. This is a new and revealing insight? It
doesn't matter that Eskimos have four or four hundred words for what I
call *snow*. It doesn't matter that English cannot express gender inflections
of meaning as French can. It doesn't matter that I sometimes cannot be
confident about the author's intended meaning in something I am reading. It doesn't matter that today we cannot grasp the meaning and reality
of some word and concept that will not be coined until the year 2087. So
what?

The fact is, such limitations notwithstanding, we humans have at our
disposal the immensely powerful means of language with which to gain
access to, makes sense of, and describe, analyze, and communicate about
reality. None of that provides a perfectly mirrored reflection of reality.
Anyone who thought it would was dreaming. Nor does any of that af-
ford "the pure given, absolute immediacy, the innocent eye" or knowledge
"in full presence" or "indubitable truth"[100] or any other superlative-but-
impossible epistemic aspiration of certain naive modern thinkers, whom
strong social constructionists and their postmodernist cousins take plea-

---

100. Goodman, *Ways of Worldmaking*, 6. See Maze, "Social Constructionism, Deconstructionism, and Some Requirements of Discourse," 402–4. The second and third terms are
Derrida's and Gergen's.

sure in deconstructing. But so what? Does that itself make language imprisoning or restrictive? Strong constructionists' somber admonitions about the limitations of language strike me as not unlike the complaints of children who, upon discovering that Santa Claus doesn't really exist, become grumpy and decide they want nothing to do at all with Christmas.[101] To say that language limits our knowledge of reality because it is historically bounded and culturally particular is like saying water limits our ability to water ski because we cannot also water ski on land or in the air or anywhere else we please. To bemoan the somewhat-constraining-precisely-because-it-is-powerfully-enabling nature of language is like deciding never to own and drive a car because sometimes cars break down. The disillusioned are only those who gullibly believed what was illusion in the first place. Isolated perfectionists are only those who cannot live with the really good, which for them is still not good enough. Why does the glass always have to be half empty? Why cannot we see and appreciate the powerful though fallible reality-connecting and expressing power of human language? Such a perspective informs a realist social constructionism more adequate to the real persons, human knowledge, and social realities we seek to understand and explain.

Humans Are Naturally Highly Capacitated

Along lines similar to the enabling powers of language, it is important to emphasize our immense human natural capacities more generally. Chapter 1 elaborated many specific human capacities that I suggested interact together and with other capacities to give rise emergently to human personhood. Many sociological theories—including social constructionism—tend to focus on one or a few such human capacities. But this is to deny the reality of the broad range of real human capacities in their fullness. Our theories should bring in and appreciate the many causal powers that humans possess and exercise in the making and living of their personal and social lives.[102]

---

101. For that matter, constructionist, poststructuralist, and postmodernist boundless celebrations on the other extreme of the (alleged) near infinite polysemy and multivalence of language also strike me as not unlike children who, upon discovering that they were not struck by lightning after eating the fifth cookie when they were only given permission to eat four, decide they might as well go ahead and eat the entire contents of the cookie jar.

102. Relatedly, see Howard Gardner, *Frames of Mind: The Theory of Multiple Intelligences* (New York: Basic Books, 1993).

One set of human capacities we should affirm is our acute and powerful perceptual abilities. Again, certain forms of social constructionism emphasize the limitations and deceptions of human perceptions. Every human capacity entails limits, failings, and errors. But much depends on what one is expecting. It is hard to live up to perfection. Yet when we step back and ponder our perceptual capacities, we realize that we are supremely well endowed not only to participate in but also to make good sense of reality. For various reasons, we humans not only exist as creatures embedded in and partly comprising a natural reality, but also possess multiple capacities very well fitted to recognizing and understanding the very reality in which we participate. That is not to say that humans are not conceptualizers, that people can get a "God's-eye" view of reality, that human perception is infallible, that theories are overdetermined by evidence, or that the knowledge in our heads and shared between us flawlessly reflects the real as if in a perfect mirror. No, because we are the kind of creatures we are, all of our knowledge is always personal, conceptually mediated, fallible, historically and culturally located, perspectival, and incomplete. But nothing in that list of conditions means that humans do not also fully participate in reality, cannot form reasonably accurate perceptions of reality, or cannot develop over time relatively accurate knowledge that is shaped by our cultural categories and also significantly by the nature of objective reality. We can and we do, because we are from, in, and of reality and posses the perceptual abilities to apprehend and understand reality.[103]

103. The importance of affirming our immense natural human capacities in a realist social constructionism raises one correction of emphasis that I think is worth making to Berger and Luckmann. The authors of the social constructionist classic, because of the existentialist philosophy background informing their approach, tend to emphasize absence, openness, and indeterminacy. People are conceived as facing a void of chaos and meaninglessness unless some deliberate structuring commitment is chosen. When Berger and Luckmann describe humans, they therefore focus attention on their natural underdevelopment, human lack of direction, absence of substantive instinctual structure, unspecialized drives, instability of behavioral conduct, and so on. "Human existence," they write, "if it were thrown back on its organismic resources by themselves, would be existence in some sort of chaos" (Berger and Luckmann, *The Social Construction of Reality*, 51, more generally 47–52). The French existentialist philosopher Jean-Paul Sartre is lurking not far in the background here. In fact Sartre is present in numerous of the book's endnotes, one of which claims that Sartre's work "is the most impressive example in contemporary philosophical anthropology of the achievement of this sociologically crucial insight" of the social character of man's self-production (196n12; other endnotes make clear the book's dependence on Sartre for numerous specific analytical terms and concepts; Edmund Husserl also provides a genealogical link between this existen-

Human Capacities Entail Natural Structures, Directions, and Limits

Immense capacitation does not mean absolute sovereignty and unconstrained ability. Capacities entail their own directional tendencies and outer limits, by virtue of the nature of the real, underlying causal mechanisms that generate them. The "yes" that a capacity speaks necessarily

---

tialism and the phenomenology that Berger learned from Alfred Schutz during his graduate school years at the New School for Social Research). Existentialism's freedom-condemned individual thrown out of a falsely safe world of fixed reality and meaning into an angst-ridden unspecificity and confronted with the nearly unbearable responsibility of creating life meaning through deliberate choice closely parallels the philosophical anthropology described by Berger and Luckmann in more social terms. The lone individual is replaced by children in need of socialization. Individual existential choice is exchanged for the social activities of language, interaction, and habitualization. The overall structure of problem and solution, however, is identical. Furthermore, those familiar with this book and with Berger's related book, *The Sacred Canopy*, will recognize that many existentialist terms show up in his writing as sociological themes—anxiety, dread, alienation, freedom, the burden of decisions, bad faith, responsibility, absurdity, nothingness, marginality, nightmares, terror, facticity, *Dasein*, consciousness, madness, death, doubt, nihilation, solitariness, theodicy, and meaning. It's all there.

For a book whose ideas were formulated in the 1950s and written in the early 1960s, this reliance on existentialism is understandable. The existentialist connection also makes for stimulating reading and some insightful analysis. But the influence of existentialism also brings with it the disadvantage of leading us to underestimate the real positive human powers and capacities that persons actually possess. There is more to the nature of human personhood than simply openness, underdevelopment, and plasticity. By demonstrating human social activity constructing reality as the answer to the given human existential problem of instinct deficiency and plasticity of consciousness and behavior, Berger and Luckmann set themselves up to miss the many natural emergent powers and capacities of human persons. We might, of course, understand human activity as arising from the creative generativity of richly capacitated humans pursuing the imperatives of personhood, as I outlined in chapter 1. Instead, Berger and Luckmann focus on fairly arbitrary "habitualizations" ("There I go again") of even solitary individuals who are driven primarily by the need to reduce uneasiness and mental overload through simplification. "Habitualization carries with it the important psychological gain that choices are narrowed," they write. "This frees the individual from the burden of 'all those decisions,' providing a psychological relief. . . . Habitualization provides the direction and the specialization of activity that is lacking in man's biological equipment, thus relieving the accumulations of tensions that result from undirected drives" (Berger and Luckmann, *The Social Construction of Reality*, 53). Such a view has proven an effective pedagogical means to introduce the ideas of habitualization, predictability, and externalization. But that has come at a cost to our theoretical understanding of the manifold natural powers and capacities of human persons. It needs correction. The correction comes through a theory that emphasizes the many powerful natural human capacities of human persons.

implies a "no" of inherently associated impossibilities and boundaries. And these natural limitations inhering in human capacities have consequences for the character of human personal and social life. Because of the natural structure of a great deal of reality, human social constructions cannot be elaborated with unlimited possibilities. The social constructionist literature tends to emphasize humans' nearly unrestricted ability to construct "reality" in any number of directions and ways. Such a view serves, among other things, the constructionist's moral commitment to the self-determining emancipation of selves from fixity and limits. The realist social constructionist recognizes the great diversity in human cultures, yet finds little appeal in hyperbolic assertions of limitless constructive potential. The most radical of social constructionists in fact walks through doors instead of walls, use the same language as those with whom they want to communicate, and hopes, like everyone else, that the future will be good instead of bad (however defined).

Comparative perspective is helpful not only to show difference but also likeness. Social constructionists focus on the diversity of human cultures. Fine. But we should also keep diversity in perspective by considering—which we rarely do—the full range of hypothetical possibilities of alternative social constructions. I suspect our tie to reality makes that difficult to imagine. But when we do, we realize that the diversity of human cultures is quite limited. There are all kinds of permutations and possibilities that are never realized, a lot of cells in the matrix of potential constructions that are empty. No existing culture, for instance, lacks a psychological concept of a person or cannot conceive of personal intention and responsibility. In no culture is sexuality an irrelevant feature of life or are babies made in any way other than eggs being penetrated by sperm. In no culture are tools considered evil. No culture constructs a reality that is absent of shelters from the elements. No culture believes children should just be left to grow up on their own. No cultural construction normalizes mating between close kin, especially mothers and sons. In no culture have status differences and divisions of labor been constructed out of existence. No culture constructs away the need for planning for the future, authority, and some sort of government and laws. No culture has constructed reality that does not include conflict. In no culture does morality, etiquette, standards of sexual modesty, and hospitality not exist. No culture does not mourn their dead. No culture has successfully constructed a property-less, inheritance-irrelevant reality. In no culturally constructed reality has dance, music, art, and play been left out of the picture.[104] The list could go on. Viewed from the vantage point of uniformity, human cultures are highly diverse. Viewed from the perspective of all the constructions humans could possibly produce, human cultures are in many crucial ways relatively similar.[105] This suggests that human social constructions are not free to invent reality as they please. This is because they are somewhat bound within limits of the conceivable and feasible by the characteristics and constraints inherent by nature in capacities existent in reality as such.

Constructionism's emphasis on nearly unlimited capabilities of social fabrication has roots in existentialism's influence on Berger and Luckmann's account of social construction, noted above. Another disadvantage of that same influence, I suggest, is its tendency to overstate the openness of the possibilities of human actions. Existentialism envisioned the solitary self thrown without choice by an absence of fixed or natural meaning or purpose into the responsibility of creating his or her own meaning through radically free choice, through the individual exercise of unfettered will and commitment. Less important than the specific content of the choice is the fact of decision, the sheer willful making, as if through a "leap," of a choice that creates authenticity and meaning. Such a philosophical backdrop leads Berger and Luckmann's sociological appropriation of it to highlight—I would say exaggerate—the unbounded possibilities of formation and expression of human social action. They briefly illustrate this point with sex: "Human sexuality is characterized by a very high degree of pliability. . . . It is pliable both in the objects toward which it may be directed and in its modalities of expression. Ethnological evidence shows that, in sexual matters, man is capable of almost

104. Donald Brown, *Human Universals* (New York: McGraw-Hill, 1991). Brown's six case studies illustrating the need to rethink cultural diversity and universals are particularly interesting; they should cause us to doubt at least some of the received academic and folk accounts traditionally justifying our descriptive emphasis on cultural diversity.

105. Consider as an analogy the physiology of human bodies. Compared to a statistically normal model of the human body, the most typical body we can imagine, actual human bodies in the world comprise an incredible diversity of size, shape, color, and texture—from which we might conclude (while staring at the sideshow freak) that when it comes to the human body nearly everything is possible. But shift the frame of reference instead to all possible conceivable remotely human bodies (think, for some assistance, of the patrons of the Star Wars (episode four) "Mos Eisley Cantina" bar, or those who come to greet Jess and May Belle at the end of the movie *Bridge to Terabithia*) and most actual human bodies in the world start to look relatively similar.

anything."[106] Undeniably true, at least if "matters" means beliefs and behaviors. But there is also a difference between what humans are *capable*
of in all possible instances and what humans *typically and recurrently
tend toward* across most instances. While the former is important to always be aware of, the latter is normally of greater interest for sociological
theory. Strong social constructionism has a penchant for accentuating the
unusual, the extreme, the "subaltern." That has its value and place. But
it also risks eclipsing the typical, the chronic, the natural in social life—
which, however prosaic, is also critical for understanding persons and
society.

Nevertheless, despite their overall balance, Berger and Luckmann reinforce their emphasis on unbounded expressions of human action in reality
production in their specific discussion of habitualization. They write, for
instance, that "social order is not part of the 'nature of things,' and it cannot be derived from the 'laws of nature.' Social order exists *only* as a product of human activity."[107] This is an overstatement. Social order cannot
be derived from the laws of nature, it is true, but that does not mean that
social order is not significantly shaped by the capacities and constraints
of nature. The conclusion that social order is "only" a product of human
activity does not follow from the observation that it cannot be derived from
the "laws of nature."[108] Berger and Luckmann also depict their hypothesized stand-ins for "Man Friday joining our matchstick-canoe builder," the

106. Berger and Luckmann, *The Social Construction of Reality*, 49. Alternatively, as
Gergen puts it, "Human biology largely serves to establish the grounds and limits of human
action. Certain functions must be fulfilled to sustain life, and there are biological limits over
performance. However, between the poles of grounding essential and physical limitations
there is virtually unlimited potential for variation." Gergen, *Toward a Transformation in
Social Knowledge*, 17.

107. Berger and Luckmann, *The Social Construction of Reality*, 52, 59, italics in original.

108. Consider this argument as well: "Humanness is socio-culturally variable. In other
words, there is no human nature in the sense of a biologically fixed substratum determining
the variability of socio-cultural formations. There is only human nature in the sense of anthropological constants (for example, world openness and plasticity of instinctual structure) that
delimit and permit man's socio-cultural formations. . . . While it is possible to say that man has
a nature, it is more significant to say that man constructs his own nature, or more simply, that
man produces himself" (ibid., 49). We should not expect a constant nature to produce variability, except in the way they indicate (plasticity, etc.). What this leaves unstated, however, is
the extent to which an essential human nature in fact produces nonvariability, how the natural
in humans gives rise to such continuity, viewed in the right perspective, across human cultures,
about which more below.

"two persons A and B," as free to behave in nearly any way. They might try to build canoes with matchsticks or something completely different. They are free to choose action in nearly any direction. Aside from the broadest bodily constraints,[109] their behaviors seem uninhibited by any external or natural governing or directives. Thus, "A and B alone are responsible for having constructed this world. A and B remain capable of changing or abolishing it." Presumably *A* and *B* could have constructed something radically different in the first place. We have reason to resist the idea that the structure and character of patterned human social relations and institutions are so dramatically open to nearly all possibilities, to be determined primarily if not exclusively by combinations of random chance and free human choice. The nature of reality and the reality of nature are more directive than that. The range of possible social constructions that humans might and do produce is more constrained by factors other than human happenstances and decisions than many constructionists seem prepared to allow.

Knowledge for Human Persons Is Always Human, Personal Knowledge

This seemingly obvious statement affirms more than a first reading might suggest. For centuries we have been led by certain Enlightenment thinkers and modern philosophers to believe that we humans might attain a kind of knowledge about reality that would transcend normal human limitations. Especially after Descartes, the expectation was sustained by many that humans could achieve objective, indubitable, absolute, general, positive knowledge. The latest version of that expectation was logical positivism. The idea seemed to have been that this kind of positive knowledge was "out there" waiting to be discovered and possessed by rational human inquirers, who could acquire and depict knowledge directly in mathematical and linguistic representations. It was as if there existed not only a reality but also a general body of the sum total of generic knowledge about reality that any knower might comprehend, which humans therefore might

109. The lack of biological directing of behaviors, they note, "does not mean, of course, that there are not biologically determined limitations to man's relation with his environment; his species-specific sensory and motor equipment imposes obvious limitations on his range of possibilities" (ibid., 47–48). That observation, however, remains entirely undeveloped in the book and, so, overwhelmed by the constant emphasis on relative social determination of behavior.

tap into from the outside. But that was a misguided model of what human knowledge is or could be.

The counterpart of the fact that human knowledge, language, and experience are always *about* something, as suggested above, is the fact that the something of which they are about is always apprehended and understood in particular modes by particular kinds of knowers. In our case as humans, knowledge is always *human* knowledge. The referents of knowledge—bodies, thunderstorms, parades—exist independently of our knowing. But knowledge is not a single, autonomous, objective entity that happens to be acquirable by humans. There is not Universal, Generic Knowledge out there for us to acquire. There is rather for humans only human knowledge—knowledge fitted for and appropriate to humans as particular beings. There appear to be other kinds of knowledge that are not human knowledge. As far as we can tell, for example, bats possess "bat knowledge" of reality—which involves, among other things, an amazing radar-based apprehension of place and movement in relation to other moving objects in space and time—that is fitted to and appropriate for bats; but we humans do not have nor particularly need bat knowledge. We might also think that God has God knowledge—a kind of intelligence, comprehension, understanding, and wisdom of a magnitude, perfection, and completeness that makes God knowledge infinitely different from human knowledge but entirely fitted to and appropriate for God. We might also contemplate dolphin knowledge,[110] angel knowledge, perhaps even Artificial Intelligence knowledge. The key to note is that each of these is qualitatively different from each other and from human knowledge yet nevertheless constitutes real knowledge about the self-same reality to which all knowledge refers—since, from a realist perspective, reality is single, unified, coherent, and significantly comprehensible by knowers. Each kind of knowledge is partial, particular, and apposite to its distinct kind of knower in particular modes of comprehension (with the exception of God knowledge not being partial and particular). The nature of knowledge, in other words, is always fitted for and to the knowing agent—knowledge is intrinsically and inescapably knower- and user-oriented. Yet this does not mean that different knowers exist in distinct realities, that the real objects of their knowing are different. Rather, the existence of particular beings in the same reality entails particular kinds and modes of knowledge for

110. Aladsair MacIntyre, *Dependent, Rational Animals* (Peru, IL: Open Court, 1999), 11–28.

them, as distinct from other sorts of knowers. Human knowledge is a kind
particularly fitted to, suited for, appropriate given the kind of being humans are—for our brains, bodies, sensory capacities, biological and social
needs, practical activities, and personal existence. That is all we humans
need for knowing. We are misguided to seek another kind of knowledge
or to criticize human knowledge because it cannot attain to the standards
imagined for some other kind of knowledge—absolute, objective, impersonal, indubitable, positive knowledge, for instance.

What, then, does it mean to say that knowledge is or should be personal? For centuries many have believed that truly reliable knowledge
was impersonal, that real knowledge and its production had to transcend
the particularities and subjectivity of personal viewpoints and interests. It
was this view that motivated the desire to achieve "objectivity" in science.
I suggest that we need to see by contrast, however, that human knowledge
is always *personal* knowledge. The Hungarian chemist turned philosopher
Michael Polanyi argues this persuasively in his book *Personal Knowledge:
Towards a Post-Critical Philosophy*.[111] The very best of science, Polanyi
shows, involves not the detachment of scientists but precisely the opposite:
their deep personal involvement. The generation and comprehension of
knowledge entails not simply the following of formal rules and procedures.
More importantly, Polanyi observed, it requires of knowers personal commitment to truth, capacities to perceive the value of potential discoveries,
active engagement in inquiry, the exercise of artful skills, reliance on tacit
understanding, the making of judgments of belief, the discernment of patterns and meanings in holistic gestalts of data, appreciation for the beauty
of the known world, provisional and wise trust in other knowledgeable
authorities, passion for and joy in discovery, and the taking of responsibility for reporting knowledge well. All of these are clearly activities of
a thoroughly *personal* nature, as Polanyi points out: "Into every act of
knowing there enters a passionate contribution of the person knowing
what is being known, and . . . this coefficient is no mere imperfection but a
vital component of his knowledge." "I must understand the world from my
personal point of view, as a person claiming originality and exercising his
personal judgment responsibly with universal intent." "Knowing [is] the

---

111. Michael Polanyi, *Personal Knowledge: Towards a Post-Critical Philosophy* (Chicago:
University of Chicago Press, 1962). For a similar statement from a somewhat more existentialist viewpoint see Søren Kierkegaard, *Concluding Unscientific Postscript*, trans. David Swenson
and Walter Lowrie (London: Oxford, 1941), 112–13.

active comprehension of the thing known, and action that requires skill";
and "Love of truth operates on all levels of mental achievement."[112] This
fact of personal knowledge applies to scientific research and to the pursuit
of practical knowledge in everyday life. For these reasons, only human
persons—and not, say, supercomputerized robots—are able to produce
new scientific and practical knowledge that is important and interesting.

Pure objectivity and personal detachment are thus not only not possible in the search for knowledge but also *totally undesirable*. "As human
beings, we must inevitably see the universe from a center lying within
ourselves and speak about it in terms of a human language shaped by
the exigencies of human intercourse. Any attempt to rigorously eliminate
our human perspective from our picture of the world must lead to absurdity."[113] The quest for objectivity, we can see in retrospect, meant well, but
it was misguided. The true good that objectivity sought to accomplish was
not really about objectivity as detached neutrality. Rather, it was about
personal commitment to seeking the *truth* about reality instead of forcing
reality to fit into our interests and biases—and that inescapably entails
personal dedication, involvement, judgment, and responsibility.

At the same time, Polanyi insisted that personal knowledge is not mere
subjective opinion, since knowledge is always accountable to shared standards of knowledge production and shaped by the objective nature of real
objects under study. Polanyi writes, "The personal participation of the
knower in all acts of understanding . . . does not make our understanding subjective. Comprehension is neither an arbitrary act nor a passive
experience, but a responsible act claiming universal validity. Such knowing is indeed objective in the sense of establishing contact with a hidden
reality." Elsewhere, he states, "Insofar as the personal submits to requirements acknowledged by itself as independent of itself, it is not subjective; but insofar as it is an action guided by individual passions, it is not
objective either. It transcends the disjunction between subjective and
objective."[114]

112. Polanyi, *Personal Knowledge: Towards a Post-Critical Philosophy*, viii, 327, vii, 300.

113. Ibid., 3. Polanyi's philosophical search for an alternative to the objectivist positivist
science into which he was first trained as a chemist was originally motivated by his horror over
the Nazi research and Soviet science he confronted in his early career, which he believed was
a rational outcome of positivism.

114. Ibid., vii–viii, 300. Also: "At all . . . points the act of knowing includes an appraisal;
and this personal coefficient, which shapes all factual knowledge, bridges in doing so the disjunction between subjectivity and objectivity. It implies the claim that man can transcend his

Polanyi was philosophically a personalist and a realist. Therefore, his personalist vision of science and knowledge fits extremely well with critical realist personalism. The objective nature of the real in relation to our human consciousness provides an independent standard of reality enabling us to be fully personal knowers without thereby sliding into complete subjectivism and relativism. Because reality is not merely our human construction, we can engage and investigate it precisely as *persons*—not as impersonal, detached, neutral observers—yet still be confident that our resulting knowledge refers to and is informed by reality such that we are capable of making truthful statements about it. In Polanyi's words, "Personal knowledge in science . . . claims to establish contact with reality beyond the clues on which it relies. It commits us, passionately and far beyond our comprehension, to a vision of reality. Of this responsibility we cannot divest ourselves by setting up objective criteria of verifiability—or falsifiability, or testability, or what you will. For we live in [responsibility to reality] as in the garment of our own skin."[115] Critical realist personalism is thus not only about modeling what humans are. It is also an epistemological perspective that overthrows positivist objectivism, pragmatist instrumentalism, and strong constructionist relativism. Personal knowledge is possible because of our manifold natural human capacities that give rise to our personhood,[116] a crucial aspect of which in turn is the responsible search for truthful knowledge about reality. Unlike the implication of much strong constructionism, therefore, it is not that we are persons because we have come to know—that is, because we have been constructed as knowing subjects by our cultural categories, languages, meanings, and symbols. Rather, we are able to know because more fundamentally we are persons. Thus, even though the emergence of personhood is dependent

own subjectivity by striving passionately to fulfill his personal obligations to universal standards" (17).

115. Ibid., 64.

116. In this sense, Foucault can be understood as partly correct when he wrote, "We are subjected to the reproduction of truth through power, and we cannot exercise power except through the production of truth" (Michel Foucault, *Power/Knowledge: Selected Interviews and Other Writings, 1972–1977* (New York: Pantheon Books, 1980), 93). From the perspective of critical realist personalism, however, the truth that humans can produce is both real and personal; the power that helps to produce it derives as much from natural human capacities as from dominant regimes of power/knowledge; and the powers we persons exercise are necessarily based upon the truth about what is real, not simply constructed "truths" imposed from outside of persons.

upon interaction in social communities of other persons, the person holds ontological and epistemic priority over language, culture, and meanings. And this is in part what helps us escape the dead ends in strong social constructionism.

Humanly Emergent Mind-Dependent Realities

I have stressed thus far the nonlinguistic, noncultural nature of most of reality—of objective real objects as opposed to constructed thought objects—in order to counter the debilitating problems in strong social constructionism and draw clear lines among reality, "reality," and reality "for us." At times I have noted that human constructions, once created, do become part of reality. But that has not been my main story to this point. Rather, I have emphasized the epistemic and ontological objectivity of the reality of brute facts and our capacity as persons to develop reliable knowledge about such facts. All of that is correct. But it now needs to be more explicitly complicated. Most products of human social construction—our beliefs, symbols, ideologies, meaning systems, and social institutions—can become, through the very act of their human construction, institutionalization, and perpetuation over time, part of reality, or at least one type or aspect of reality. Thus, the claim that humans do not construct reality is not completely accurate. Much of reality humans do not construct—the universe, continents, weather systems, trees, our bodies, worms, molecules, leptons, and so on. But one subset of reality humans actually do at least partially construct. That is our mentally grounded sociocultural reality—belief systems, normative orders, organizations, economies, civilizations, and such—that exist emergently at a higher level of the real than do persons. Within critical realist personalism's explanatory framework, human social reality is emergent as ontologically real from the relational interactions over time of human persons engaged in mental and bodily activity in the material world. Through emergence, institutional facts of social reality come into being, take on real ontological existence, and thus come to possess causal capacities to make events happen in the world.

An Ontology of Three Kinds of Reality

To be clear about what is and what is not at work in this process, however, we need to sustain some important conceptual distinctions that reflect

genuine differences in reality. John Searle's conceptual distinctions are
helpful for pulling apart distinct dimensions of reality that are too often
confusingly compressed together in social constructionist theories. For
purposes of moving forward, however, I think we can condense Searle's
distinctions into three, which also parallel Berger and Luckmann's theory:
dependently subjective reality, dependently objective reality, and independently objective reality.[117] Underlying these three distinctions are two
key variations. The first concerns whether or not the reality in question is
ultimately dependent for existence upon human minds. The second concerns whether or not the reality in question exists in reality beyond the
control of particular people.

Dependently subjective realities consist of beliefs held by persons that
are real to those who hold them but that have not been socially institutionalized. Dependent subjective realities are (mentally) *dependent* because their existence depends upon human mental cognitions—if people
did not think and believe them they would not exist. They are *subjective*
because they exist only as part of the subjective belief sets of the persons
who hold them—because they are not institutionalized, if people believing them were to cease believing in them then they would not exist objectively of the (former) believers. And yet they are part of *reality* because
they exist as real in the minds of and can exert causal influences on those
who believe them. For example, the belief of a paranoid person who is
terrified that an evil ax murderer is trailing them with intent to kill is a
dependently subjective reality. It depends entirely on the paranoid person's
mental activity, is subjectively existent (has being in their subjectivity, such
that if they stopped believing there would be no ax murderer), yet is reality for the paranoid person and so causes real emotional and behavioral
consequences in their lives. Another example of a dependently subjective
reality—not taken from the realm of mental illness—concerns the belief
of a person I know that one should always press the "stop" button on a
microwave oven before opening the microwave's door because abruptly
stopping the microwaving by opening the door during operation will
damage the functioning of the microwave oven over time. This is a real
belief dependent on a particular person's mental state (is not existent in
nonmental nature), which has not been institutionalized (thank goodness)
and so would not continue to exist in the world if I could manage to persuade the person that they are wrong, and yet which is real in the person's

117. So far as I can tell, there is no such thing as independently subjective reality, because
the nature of reality and personhood exclude it.

mind and so affects the person's cooking behaviors (and interactions with people who do not share this belief). Note that dependently subjective realities tend toward the individual and idiosyncratic (sometimes insane), since by definition they are not widely shared and institutionalized. However, in a certain, definite sense they are *reality* for those who believe in and live by them, even if there is no objective basis for believing them to be true about reality. My point here, however, is that their veritable reality is of a particular kind: dependent and subjective. This, I think, is part of the reality some people mean when they say or write "reality" in scare quotes.

The difference between a dependent subjective reality and a *dependent objective reality* is that the latter has become objective in human social life because it has been institutionalized. By "institutionalized" I mean that the beliefs have become shared and acted upon by a significant enough number of people that they (a) influence other beliefs in people's larger belief sets, (b) mobilize sustaining material resources, and (c) create patterns of human mental and bodily practices and behaviors motivated or justified by the beliefs. Institutionalization is a matter of degrees, not absolute binaries—things can be more or less institutionalized. But institutionalization, when it does occur, changes the nature of the realities in question. Consider, as an example of a dependent objective reality, "recycling" as a practice, industry, and belief commitment. When I was young, recycling did not exist. In 1965, say, there may have been thousands of people who personally believed that saving, sorting, and reusing certain parts of the trash helped to protect the world's ecology—and they might have reused their glass jars and newspapers for various practical purposes, such as for planting seeds in and mulching gardens. But until recycling was socially institutionalized, those thousands of people were engaging mere dependent subjective realities. However, in the course of a few recent decades, the belief that saving, sorting, and reusing parts of trash could help rescue "the environment" became institutionalized in complex social systems of beliefs, mobilized material resources, and routinized practices—through "consciousness raising" educational programs, economic incentives, municipal pickup schedules and drop-off centers, environmental moral commitments, recycled waste markets, and so on. As a result, even if many thousands of people who once believed in recycling came instead to believe that it was a big waste of time, energy, and money, the institutionalized recycling system would still possess objectively real existence—which is to say, recycling is now objective reality. Even so, "recycling" is an institutional fact entirely dependent on minds to exist. But because it has become institutionalized, is it no longer merely subjectively real—its reality is socially objective through belief formation, resource mobilization, and routinized practices. In Berger and Luckmann's terms, recycling has gone from being an idiosyncratic habit of some through a process of externalization to the point of objectivation requiring legitimation. Thus, my children take recycling as an obvious part of the real world, my having taught them so, which it is. But recycling's reality, we need to see, is of a particular sort: mind dependent and so socially (not naturally) existent as fact.

Both kinds of mind dependent realities must be distinguished from a third kind of reality, *independently objective reality*. This is the part of the totality of the real consisting of natural brute facts that are not dependent on human mental activities, whether individually idiosyncratic or socially institutionalized. It is the real that is independent of human subjectivity, which would exist with the same properties and operations whether or not any people anywhere thought about or believed in it. Here we can think of quarks, atoms, gravity, three-dimensional space, the passage of time, bacteria, crude oil, raccoons, hardwood, cyclones, oceans, the atmosphere, planets, stars, and galaxies. In other words, independently objective reality consists of the material elements, forces, energies, and their innumerable emergent products existing and operating at multiple levels—but *not* including human mentally and socially constructed dependent subjective and objective realities.[118] The key qualities that distinguish independently objective reality from the first two kinds of reality are its mind-independent ontology, mind-affecting causal capacity, and bounded practical performance. First, independently objective realities possess existence in reality independent of human mental activity. Second, given normal human perceptual equipment and participation in reality, they possess the natural ability to impinge upon human bodies and minds from their position of objective ontology in ways that can influence the perceptions and conceptions that human minds make and hold of reality. In short, they possess

118. The one complicating exception to the last qualification is any element of independently objective reality that is mobilized as a material resource in a process of institutionalization, in which case its natural properties are used to transform its empirical shape in order to perform new functions—for instance, crude oil is refined into plastic that is used to make curbside newspaper bins to sustain recycling. When this complicating exception happens, the material resource remains an independently objective reality in ontological being and basic natural capacity but becomes a human construction in terms of its empirical shape, practical function, and cultural meaning.

epistemically relevant construction-directive capacities. Third, different parts of independently objective reality entail specific natural powers and limits in their abilities to perform in practical activities in the material world—crude oil can do certain things, for instance, that gravity, bacteria, and hardwoods cannot, and vice versa.

Four facts are crucial in all of this. The first is that humans do not fundamentally construct (in the sense of bring into being) any of this third type of reality, because it exists independently and objectively of human activity. Humans can use their natural powers to fabricate materiality to transform the empirical shape of very small pieces of independently objective reality in order to mold them for particular kinds of functions; even so, the natural ontological being and capacities of independently objective reality are *not* humanly constructed, but only formed and employed for certain functional purposes. Second, a great deal about humans ourselves—particularly our bodies and all they entail and produce—is composed of independently objective reality and so is influenced and in some ways determined by the nature and function of independently objective reality. We are every bit the constructions of nature as anything outside of us is our construction. Third, given the ways humans are related to independently objective reality as well-equipped participants, independently objective reality has the natural capacity to shape human knowledge. This means that we humans are able to form real knowledge and understanding of reality beyond our social constructions. There is thus a recurrently completed information feedback loop operating between our rational reflections and practical activities in reality and the independently objective reality we seek to know and live in. Fourth, humans normally face significant limits on the variance with which they can construct dependently objective reality out of independently objective reality. The sky is not the limit. Independently objective reality by its own deep structures of natural characteristics and tendencies entails innumerable fixities, directions, determinations, and boundaries on even the meanings about it that humans might construct. All human belief constructions of meaning, being, and purpose must work within certain limitations set by the order of natural reality.

It helps to reinforce the last point by remembering that research has well demonstrated that human cultural constructions are profoundly dependent upon—not determined by, only dependent on—the material contexts in which they are constructed. As life goes in actuality, not every social construction is feasible. In fact, social constructions are profoundly bounded and shaped by material directives and constraints. We know, for instance, that family structures can be constructed in a variety of ways. We also know, however, that the way family structures are constructed is strongly associated with the means and relations of material production and with demographic distributions of types of bodies.[119] Whether husbands have multiple wives or wives have multiple husbands or either has only one of each, for instance, depends primarily on the relative supply or men's and women's bodies and the structure of the means of earning a livelihood—which are in turn powerfully determined by the constraints of geography, climate, and famine and by the results of war. Similarly, the construction of gender relations between men and women more generally is significantly influenced by the nature of material production of a given epoch of human history, such that constructions of equality and inequality, for instance, have very much to do with differences in the nature and structure of hunting-gathering versus agricultural versus postindustrial societies.[120] Likewise, whether or not people construct "reality" in a way that values security, discipline, and material well-being ("materialist values") as opposed to creative expression and individual autonomy ("postindustrial values") appears to depend a great deal on the nature of the economy and material conditions underlying the culture.[121] In addition, how people construct "responsible parenting" is also strongly shaped by the material resources available to families determined by social class.[122] Examples could be multiplied. The point is that the possibilities for constructing dependently objective realities are usually closely tethered to the material contexts of the independently objective realities in which the constructing happens. Karl Marx long ago made this very point in an overstated but not fundamentally sociologically incorrect way. This observation is true partly because the natural capacities and constraints built into those contexts shape how they can be constructed. It is also true because, in order to institutionalize dependently subjective realities so that they become dependently objective, the former have to be embraced by a large enough

119. George Murdock, *Ethnographic Atlas: A Summary* (Pittsburgh: University of Pittsburgh Press, 1967); Murdock, *Social Structure* (New York: Macmillan, 1949).

120. Stephen Sanderson and Arthur Alderson, *World Societies: The Evolution of Human Social Life* (Boston: Pearson, 2005).

121. Ronald Inglehart, *Cultural Shift in Advanced Industrial Society* (Princeton, NJ: Princeton University Press, 1990).

122. Annette Lareau, *Unequal Childhoods: Class, Race, and Family Life* (Berkeley and Los Angeles: University of California Press, 2003).

number of believers, whose decisions on the matter will be affected at least somewhat by tests of the practical adequacy of the beliefs when worked out in practical activity in the material world. To institutionalize dependently subjective realities also requires directly mobilizing sufficient material resources for their promotion and defense. In these ways, therefore, the nature of independently objective reality impinges upon the content of the constructions involved in dependently subjective realities.

Where strong social constructionism went wrong with all of this was in believing that independently objective reality could not inform human knowledge, so that humans have to construct reality, including the reality of the human, and in doing so are virtually unbound in freedom to construct reality as desired. Independently objective reality was thus collapsed into dependently objective reality, which some saw as having its basis in what I am calling dependently subjective reality. Humans were put in charge of reality making by strong social constructionists. But the authorization of that status was built on erroneous views of ontology, language, knowledge, and human persons. So it often lacks practical adequacy when put into practice in reality.

Causal Relations to the Real

Whether or not something exerts causal influences is, according to the critical realist theory advanced here, the primary criterion for knowing whether it is real. If something possesses causal powers, it is real—whether or not it is material or directly empirically observable. If an apparent something never exerts any causal power, we have reason to question its reality. At the same time, critical realism insists that real entities and processes may not always exert causal forces in and on the world. Causal realism does not assume consistent and universal empirical manifestation. Sometimes real causal powers lie dormant. Other times they are operative but neutralized or overridden by countervailing causal powers of other real entities and processes. We should thus view causality as real and important but also as contingently operative and discontinuously evident in complex and open systems of causal relations.

In order to help get to the bottom of the reality of social construction, it is necessary to overlay the previous section's trichotomy of ontological being—independently objective, dependently objective, and dependently subjective reality—with one further conceptual distinction, which in turn involves an additional subdistinction. The distinction concerns whether the real does or does not in particular circumstances causally influence the actual. This I will refer to as the "causal relation" of the reality to persons. The subdistinction is whether or not persons in those circumstances are or are not consciously aware of the causal realities that are or are not operative. This I will refer to as the "conscious relation" of persons to the reality. I might have also called it "phenomenological relevance." All three kinds of realities described above can—by virtue of being real—be *causally related* to the persons involved. That is to say, reality, whether mind independent or dependent and whether personally objective or subjective, can exert causal powers on objects and events in the lives of people. At the same time, whether or not different kinds of reality are causally related to persons, they may also be *consciously related*. In combination, this creates a number of potential conditions of reality, causality, and awareness— twelve total, in fact.[123] Any of the three sorts of reality outlined above may causally influence people's lives in ways of which they are consciously aware or ways of which they are not aware. The real may also not causally influence people's lives—and in that case people also may or may not be consciously related to that causally unrelated reality. That is, people may be either aware or not aware of the reality of something that is not influencing them. In the social constructionist and related literatures, these different distinctions—ontological reality, causal influence, and psychological awareness—sometimes get confused in attributions of "reality" to constructions. It is helpful therefore to sort them out.[124]

123. Admittedly, cases of dependently subjective realities that were consciously unrelated to someone, whether causally so or not, would seem to have to involve beliefs that were subconscious. For instance, a dependently subjective reality that was causally related but consciously not related to my neighbor could be his strong relational aversion to me as his neighbor as a result of repressed strong negative feelings from having been raised by a sociologist father who was hateful and vindictive; the repressed generalized negative belief about sociologists would be idiosyncratic to his subjective self yet would cause definite behavioral outcomes in his life.

124. Some thought-experiment examples may help make sense of these abstractions. Suppose that I am vaguely aware, as I am when I think about it, that somewhere in my society there exist nude beaches and wooded nudist camps and retreats in which some people are regularly involved. The beaches and woods are brute facts that are part of the independently objective real, which are in turn used by socially constructing nudists to help construct their nudist associations as institutional facts that are part of their dependently objective realities. (If no such nude beaches and retreats existed and some individuals simply wandered naked on deserted beaches and in the woods, then their interest in and beliefs about nudity would be, by my definition, mere dependently subjective realities. But that is not the case.) In this instance,

I am potentially consciously related to (if and when I think about it) but normally consciously unrelated to (because I almost never think about it), and also causally *un*related to these nude beaches and nudist associations. When in the course of writing a book I cast about for an interesting illustration of my concepts and find myself thinking that nudist associations might be a good one, I am then consciously aware that they are real. But I am normally not consciously related to American nudist beaches and associations. And, for better or worse, they also concern other people's lives, not mine, and so exert no real causal influence in my life. Nothing about my life that I can discern is different (other than now using them for this illustration) because of the dependently objective existence of nudist beaches and associations compared to a world in which they did not exist. They are no doubt very much "reality" to the nudists, but not to me, either causally or consciously, that I know of (though of course by my own argument they could be causally but not consciously related to me, as I demonstrate next).

Consider, for comparison, however, a development in my situation vis-à-vis nudism. Suppose that a new nudist swimming club gets established on the property next to mine without my knowledge—because, say, I never read the local newspaper, was out of town during the town's public hearings on nudist zoning, and in any case never remove my introverted face from my computer screen. In what sense would that club be "real" to or for me? The next-door nudist swimming club's facilities (pool, showers, volleyball court, etc.) would be independently objective realities, and the swimming club association would be a dependently objective reality. And both would exist spatially not far from me. In some sense, then, the club would be part of my larger reality. Yet under these conditions I would also be consciously unrelated to the real club, oblivious in conscious awareness of its being. In that sense it would not be "real" to me. Yet I might also very well be dramatically causally related to the nudist swimming club, despite my lack of awareness of its existence. For one thing, my objective financial net worth might be altered considerably by declining (or increasing?) property values in my area, as a result of most of the people who are buying and selling properties nearby having become aware of the nudist swimming club and factoring its existence into their market dealings. My personal ignorance of the nudist swimming club's objective existence would be irrelevant to its real causal economic influence in my life. My lack of knowledge would not negate its causally real power. In this sense the nudist swimming club would be a real "reality" in my life even though I didn't know it. Thus, aspects of the very same entity would possess ontologically objective reality in different ways (independent and dependent) and would be causally very real to me even though it would be consciously unreal to me. We see, then, that what we mean when we say that something is someone's reality or "reality" makes a big difference depending on to which of these dimensions or senses we are referring.

Of course it can get simpler. Suppose if after a few months of the club's operation I was to pick up the local newspaper, read about it, get interested, visit, and immediately join up as an active, dues-paying member. The nudist swimming club would then become both consciously and causally real for me. It would also have become a dependently objective reality for me. In all ways it would be reality to me. But suppose that after being an active member of the nudist swimming club for three months I decided that the entire experience was stupid and boring, so I cancelled my membership and turned my attention to other activities. Suppose further that my experience in the club had made no lasting impression on me and that it ended up having no impact on local property values or anything else of concern. Suppose too, however,

So what does all of this tell us? First, that reality is complicated, existing in at least three ontological modes that are determined by combinations of differences in objectivity and mind dependence. Reality of whatever mode of being is also complicated in relating to humans either causally or not and being related to by humans either consciously or not. As a result, there are many different possible meanings of the word *reality* when it comes to existence and human experience and relations. We need to be as careful as possible when we talk in social science about reality, "reality," and "our" reality. Confusions and slippages of meaning are all too easy. To say, on the one hand, that humans construct reality (per se) is a grossly misleading overstatement at best. To dismiss social constructions as not actually real, on the other hand, however, is also mistaken. Reality, it turns out, is more complicated than that. Reality contains both brute and institutional facts, mind-independent and dependent realities, existing objectively and subjectively in relation to human mental activities, which may or may not causally affect human experience, and about which humans may or may not even be aware. In some senses, all humans share the same (independently objective) reality. In other senses only people who belong to the same culture and participate in the same institutions share the same (dependently objective) reality. In yet other senses only realities that causally influence people are real in their lives. In yet other senses only realities about which people are aware are real "to them." Much of this can vary at the level of civilizations, societies, cultures, regions, subcultures, clans, and families. We see, then, the need for greater precision in our social science analyses and communications when it comes to reality.

All of this also provides us something of an agenda for social scientific research. If reality were simply a social construction then there would not be much for social science to do or say, since doing or saying much about that would merely erode the purpose and value of social science at least as normally conceived. But since reality is complex and not entirely a social construction, there is much work for social science to do. For we see that we have many relationships, contexts, situations, combinations, causal relations, processes, and outcomes to sort through. For example, within a

---

that on an almost daily basis I could hear the shriekings of people who were still members of the nearby club but that none of that really bothered or interested me at all. I would still know that the swim club was a dependently subjective reality, but it would have no causal relation to me and I would have no more than a passing conscious relation with it. It would then be part of my biographical reality but not much else to me.

realist framework the question is meaningful how mind-independent realities shape mind-dependent realities, and how mind-dependent realities
in turn shape the fabrication and deployment of some mind-independent
realities. How do shifts in belief systems refabricate material resources,
and how do changes in resources alter belief systems? We also want to
know how dependent subjective realities get transformed into dependent
objective realities. How do mind and materiality interact within specific
kinds of contexts to shape institutionalization in different directions? How
do people get "converted" into new dependently objective realities? Under what conditions do institutional facts strengthen or weaken in their
apparent objective facticity? When and how do dependent objective realities work their way into people's practical consciousness or the habitus of
a group? What effect does conscious relation to different kinds of reality,
whether causally operative or not, have on subsequent reflexive human
interactions with reality? And what are the constraints embedded in the
properties and operations of different sorts of objective reality that direct
or limit the range of social constructions made about them? How are different kinds of dependent objective realities nested within each other?—
such as the weakly institutionalized belief in Santa Claus being nested
within the strongly institutionalized belief in mass consumer purchasing
at Christmastime.

Implications for Personhood

How does all of this help to better inform our theoretical understanding
of human persons? I have examined social constructionism in some detail
because problematic versions of it corrode a sound view of the person and
because a sound account of social constructionism is necessary for theorizing the person well. I hope the first point is by now clear: strong social constructionism liquefies the person into language and so eliminates human
ontological substance and causal agency. From such a point of view, "The
[human] subject cannot be regarded as the origin of coherent action. . . .
The language that interprets objects and actions . . . constitute the subject."[125] The roots of this approach that has shaped social constructionism
go back for many decades. The stated goal of Claude Lévi-Strauss's struc-

125. Murray Edelman, *Constructing the Political Spectacle* (Chicago: University of Chicago Press, 1988), 9.

turalism, for instance, was not "to constitute man but to dissolve him."[126] Poststructuralism and postmodernism have celebrated the "death of the subject." Following in this current, Gergen claims that "neither meaning nor self is a precondition for social interaction; rather, these emerge from and are sustained by conversations occurring between people."[127] Even as reasonable a sociologist as the structural symbolic interactionist Sheldon Stryker writes, "Since both [society and persons] derive from the social process, neither society nor the individual possess a reality that is prior to or takes precedence over the other."[128] Little thought appears to be given here to explaining how this could actually work—as J. R. Maze sensibly asks, "What does the . . . word 'people' refer to? What were these entities, having no grasp of meaning and no self, at the time they entered into their first meaningful interaction, and how did they manage it?"[129] Likewise, when social constructionists declare that, "the person cannot preexist language because it is language which brings the person into being in the first place," one has to wonder who or what brought language into being if not personal human agents.[130] But we have already seen enough intellectual incoherence in strong constructionism. The bottom line here is that non-realist social constructionism eviscerates the human person ontologically and psychologically. Strong constructionists know this: "The social constructionist attack on essentialist psychology has left us with an empty person, a human being with no essential psychological characteristics," Vivien Burr, for instance, observes.[131] But such conclusions are not the result of a long, hard climb to the cold mountaintop of truth. They are rather the outcome of having taken certain wrong intellectual turns decades ago— which were deeply prepared for us centuries ago by Descartes, Kant, and

126. Claude Lévi-Strauss, *The Savage Mind* (London: Weidenfeld, 1966), 247–55.

127. Gergen, "The Place of the Psyche in the Constructed World," 739.

128. Sheldon Stryker, "Traditional Symbolic Interactionism, Role Theory, and Structural Symbolic Interactionism," in *Handbook of Sociological Theory*, ed. Jonathan Turner (New York: Kluwer Academic, 2001), 213.

129. Maze, "Social Constructionism, Deconstructionism, and Some Requirements of Discourse," 414. The same problem applies to Burr's contention that "language [is] a precondition for thought. Our ways of understanding the world do not come from objective reality but from other people. . . . The way a person thinks, the very categories and concepts that provide a framework of meaning for them, are provided by the language that they use." Burr, *Social Constructionism*, 8. The relation between people's thought as products and people's language creating thought generates an infinite regress.

130. Ibid., 47.

131. Ibid., 119.

others—which have led us into some ridiculous theoretical cul-de-sacs. Critical realist personalism helps us to turn around, see where we have steered wrong, and get back on course toward reality.

The human subject is not dead, but alive and well. Strong constructionists have attempted to think the person into oblivion. But the reality is that we humans are persons and will remain persons as long as we exist in body and soul as we have for so many millennia. Human personhood exists as ontological reality by virtue of its emergence into being through the relational interacting of our manifold natural human causal capacities. To be a person does not mean knowing everything. But it does mean knowing some things. Persons do not have access to absolute, indubitable truth. But persons can justifiably believe that some things are true. Persons are natural parts of a reality in which they participate and can know reasonably well. We persons possess the right equipment for living in and understanding the real. We are not lost in a sea of discourse, nor imprisoned by our language, nor dissolved as selves by the social that is the construction of our own hands. We are creatures of a particular kind by nature that engage in a good deal of practical activity in a material world entailing a certain structure and causal operations and who are oriented toward understanding what is true about reality as an integral part of living out our own personhood.

An important insight to learn from social constructionism about human persons concerns potent human creative capacities. Persons are the creators of much about their social worlds. Persons bring into existence many things that were not and do away with many things that were. We persons do not construct reality per se, nor are we as humans constructed by language. But we do together construct massive cultural systems of beliefs, categories, definitions, assumptions, understandings, meanings, rules, narratives, schemas, and scripts that help to form the sociocultural habitat in which we live out our lives. We also use those cognitive products to direct the shaping of materiality, to animate various kinds of material resources into productive technologies, buildings, transportation systems, communication structures, residential arrangements, material religious symbols, and artistic and recreational objects—in short, we create and sustain cultural and institutional artifacts. Through these inventive mutual formations of the material and immaterial, we human persons participate in multiple and overlapping projects of creation. We do not socially construct reality, but we do out of reality creatively construct the social and refabricate the material. And the social in turn becomes for us a part of reality. By the very act of doing so and as a result, we affirm, make possible, and pursue our personhood in its intrinsic nature.

The perspective advanced here resists not only analytical reductionism but also intellectual oversimplification and polarization. Humans, it turns out, exist in a state of dynamic tension between power and limits, action and reflection, capacity and finitude, perception and reason, truth and fallibility, ideas and materiality, knowing and not knowing, determination and freedom. The powers of the many dimensions of reality that animate and characterize human existence provide a complex, vibrant, interactive quality to persons and life. When social theories compress reality by privileging certain of these dimensions and excluding others—as they often do—we lose those dynamic interplays and end up with flat, inadequate accounts of personal and social life. Critical realist personalism, by contrast, invites us to live with and make sense of the intricacies and discomforts of our complex, dynamic, stratified, tension-animated reality.

I have defined the person as a conscious, reflexive, embodied, self-transcending center of subjective experience, durable identity, moral commitment, and social communication who, as the efficient cause of his or her own responsible actions and interactions, exercises complex capacities for agency and intersubjectivity in order to sustain his or her own incommunicable self in loving relationships with other personal selves and with the nonpersonal world. Human persons are ontologically real and causally capacitated. But we persons are not autonomous or self-sufficient. Our personhood emerges from and is sustained by our human bodies and in communities of other persons together living in pursuit of personhood—and both bodies and communities have real dependencies and needs. The human ability to socially construct, as I have described it in realist terms of this chapter, is crucially dependent upon personhood and is a crucial aspect of the ability of persons to pursue their personhood. Social construction requires us to be conscious, reflexive, embodied, self-transcending centers of subjective experience, the efficient causes of our responsible actions and interactions. Social construction thus depends on our capacities of personhood. At the same time, our social constructions help to define and sustain our *durable identities, moral commitments,* and *social communications.* As causal agents capable of intersubjective relations, our social constructions and the material infrastructures and social institutions they produce are also requirements for sustaining our own incommunicable selves in loving relationships with other personal selves and with the nonpersonal world. This is because humans need the products of our social constructions to develop and sustain our personhood and because the very act of social constructing reflects and nourishes our human personhood. We socially construct, therefore, not because we are driven to by the ordering power of language, or because our alleged natural state of existential nothingness and chaos forces us to start doing something, anything, to fabricate some sense of meaning and purpose. We socially construct because by nature we are capacitated persons whose core meaning *is* the purpose of pursuing and realizing our personhood. Not to socially construct would be not to be persons, which for us would mean not to be anything.

Social science cannot proceed on the assumption that meaning, language, interpretation, symbols, and communication are peripheral. Naturalistic forms of social science that marginalize these—positivist and utilitarian-based approaches, in particular—are inadequate and alien to reality. Meaning, language, interpretation, symbols, and communication are essential for understanding human persons and social life. Any theory of the person and society must build them into its core account. But we would be foolish to completely follow the lead of those schools of thought that have most clearly criticized the problems in positivist and utilitarian social science, particularly strong versions of social constructionism, poststructuralism, and postmodernism. Their account of the relationship among language, reality, and knowledge is fatally flawed, and the result is theoretical incoherence and lack of experiential practical adequacy. Critical realist personalism proposes a third way between the impossibilities of scholarly approaches that ignore meaning, language, and interpretation, on the one hand, and the incoherence of opposing schools that conflate reality into meaning, language, and interpretation, on the other. Critical realist personalism accounts for the meaning and language at the heart of human life yet sustains objective reality as a referent for shaping the practical adequacy and determining the truth of our meanings and linguistic understandings. Critical realist personalism therefore produces an account that is most adequate to our condition as human knowers, to the challenge of social science, and to our own experience as persons.

Addendum: Evolutionary Social Constructivism?

My theory of personhood's attempt to take seriously the human body and persons' relations not only to their social but also to their nonhuman environments obliges me to try to engage relevant scholarship bridging the social sciences to fields such as biology, cognitive psychology, and neurological science. Given my training as a sociologist in the "standard social science model,"[132] which essentially ignores biology, this is not an effortless task. David Sloan Wilson is right that the modern academy is not so much an "ivory tower" as an "ivory archipelago" consisting of hundreds of specialized and disconnected disciplines and fields that know little about one another.[133] Because I occupy one island in this archipelago, biologists and neurologists reading this book on other islands will no doubt see many theoretical lacunae and unreferenced points of connection that could be included in my argument by an author with greater expertise in multiple natural science disciplines. That is fine. They may fill us social scientists in on additional readings, theories, and insights. Meanwhile, my central task is to commend to my fellow social scientists the taking of the body and its place in nature's biological systems more seriously, even if my background resources for doing this well are slight.

Fortunately, evolutionary biologists have in recent years been wrestling with how to make useful points of connection with the social sciences and humanities,[134] and I can engage one most relevant argument in that discussion here. David Sloan Wilson is an evolutionary biologist who has a vision to unify all academic learning and liberal arts under the organizing and directive paradigm of evolutionary theory. Instead of academia and science consisting of hundreds of fragments of specialized fields operating with their highly particular presuppositions, vocabularies, and procedures, Wilson thinks, the arts and sciences should be reorganized by the master

132. Jerome Barkow, Leda Cosmides, and John Tooby, *The Adapted Mind: Evolutionary Psychology and the Generation of Culture* (Oxford: Oxford University Press, 1992).

133. David Sloan Wilson, "Evolution for Everyone," *New York Times*, April 8, 2007, 17.

134. For example, see Peter Richerson and Robert Boyd, *Not By Genes Alone: How Culture Transforms Human Evolution* (Chicago: University of Chicago Press, 2004); Robert Boyd and Peter Richerson, *The Origin and Evolution of Cultures* (New York: Oxford University Press, 2005); Terrence Deacon, *The Symbolic Species* (New York: Norton, 1998); H. C. Plotkin, *The Imagined World Made Real: Toward a Natural Science of Culture* (New Brunswick, NJ: Rutgers University Press, 2003); F. John Odling-Smee, Kevin Laland, and Marcus Feldman, *Niche Construction: The Neglected Process in Evolution* (Princeton, NJ: Princeton University Press, 2003); Marc Hauser, *Moral Minds: How Nature Designed Our Universal Sense of Right and Wrong* (New York: Ecco, 2006); Jared Diamond, *Guns, Germs, and Steel: The Fate of Human Societies* (New York: Norton, 1998); also see Richard Dawkins on "memes" in *The Selfish Gene* (New York: Oxford University Press, 1976). From a social science perspective, however, not all of this is terribly impressive or enlightening.

scientific paradigm of evolutionism.[135] For Wilson and those who share his views, this includes "evolutionizing" even the study of literature and literary criticism traditionally located in the humanities. But that field has for decades now been under the sway of social constructionists—including some of the most "anything goes" types of postmodernists, whom some critics dub "secular creationists."[136] If contemporary literary criticism can be regrounded on an evolutionary foundation, then probably any other discipline or field can be as well. Hence the publication of the recent book by Wilson and coeditor Jonathan Gottschall, *The Literary Animal: Evolution and the Nature of Narrative.*[137]

In one of that book's chapters, titled "Evolutionary Social Constructivism," Wilson argues the following.[138] The study of humans in every discipline should focus on and be organized by the issue of survival and reproduction, because human life is as much about playing "the reproduction game" as the life of any other species. The nongenetic dimensions of human life are every bit as much about evolution as are genetics. The traditional hostility between evolutionary biology and social constructivism over the extent to which human life and experience are determined versus open-ended is unnecessary. Social constructivists want to emphasize the plasticity of social life in order to help change society for the better. Recent theorizing in evolutionary biology concerning phenotypic plasticity, adaptive flexibility, and group selection accommodates the possibilities of rapid adaptive system change in certain aspects of genetic evolution, therefore allowing the same in nongenetic dimensions

135. David Sloan Wilson, *Evolution for Everyone: How Darwin's Theory Can Change the Way We Think about Our Lives* (New York: Delacorte Press, 2007).

136. E.g., David Horowitz, "Indoctrination U: Secular Creationism," *Washington Times*, March 18, 2007, B03; Barbara Ehrenreich and Janet McIntosh, "The New Creationism: Biology under Attack," *The Nation*, June 9, 1997, 11–16, for the purported constructivist belief that humans can construct reality ex nihilo.

137. David Sloan Wilson and Jonathan Gottschall, *The Literary Animal: Evolution and the Nature of Narrative* (Evanston, IL: Northwestern University Press, 2007).

138. For related arguments (oddly not referenced by Wilson), see Ron Mallon and Stephen Stich, "The Odd Couple: The Compatibility of Social Construction and Evolutionary Psychology," *Philosophy of Science* 67 (2000): 133–54; and Pieter Adriaens and Andreas de Block, "The Evolution of Social Construction: The Case of Male Homosexuality," *Perspectives in Biology and Medicine* 49, no. 4 (2006): 570–85; also see Andreas de Block and Bart du Laing, "Paving the Way for an Evolutionary Social Constructivism," *Biological Theory*, 2009, forthcoming.

of life.[139] Evolution can now account for not only long-term, slow adaptations but also rapid and nimble changes in biological and social life. Part of our inherited human genetic endowment is the capacity for rapid individual and social adaptation for better reproductive fitness in changing environments. Social constructivists therefore do not need to feel threatened by evolutionary explanations. There is a "middle ground" on which both can meet. Moreover, there is no reason why evolutionists cannot stand in solidarity with social constructivists in their moral and political aspirations to promote social change toward a better world. Evolutionists, too, can not only optimistically want a better world personally but can also make working for one consistent with their comprehensive evolutionary scientific theories. So, rather than pretending that biology doesn't matter for the humanities (or social sciences), social constructivists should look to evolutionism as a master theory to learn more about the biologically rooted directives and constraints on the human capacity to socially construct and reconstruct culture and society toward affecting social change. Since most biological and social functionality primarily has to do with the adaptive correspondence of genetically driven behaviors and the environments in which they are and are not functional, evolutionists can help constructivists and social change activists to learn which environmental situations will best match the kinds of behaviors that humans characteristically exhibit. To the extent that humans cannot change their genetics, at least they can use their cultural capacities to reform their social situations better to match their genetically inflexible tendencies toward a more functional world. Furthermore, on the specific matter of literary criticism,

139. Wilson's argument relies heavily on the definite scientific validity of a handful of recent books and theories (Plotkin, Cosmides and Tooby, Deacon, and his own work), which I am in no position to evaluate. However, especially since Wilson admits that "the study of culture from an evolutionary perspective is still in the rank speculation stage" (David Sloan Wilson, "Evolutionary Social Constructivism: Narrowing [But Not Yet Bridging] the Gap: A Reflection on Christian Smith's *Moral, Believing Animals*," *Global Spiral*, November 17, 2004, at http://www.metanexus.net/magazine/ArticleDetail/tabid/68/id/9167/Default.aspx; reprinted in Jeffrey Schloss and Michael Murray, eds., *The Believing Primate: Scientific, Philosophical, and Theological Perspectives on the Evolution of Religion* [New York: Oxford University Press]), for Wilson to persuade the world beyond biology and genetics, he will need to more clearly demonstrate that the key works on which his case hangs have been widely accepted by scholars in relevant disciplines and so can be treated as reliable building blocks of knowledge. Until then, arguments at the rank speculation stage will likely not be enough to persuade scholars in the humanities and social sciences to reframe their disciplines in the terms of evolutionary biology.

Wilson sees a close parallel between biological genetic codes and the kind of cultural narratives that end up in literature, especially literature that survives the test of time. The process of the evolution of culture generally and narratives specifically proceeds in the same way as the evolution of genetic material: variance is generated, different cultural products are tested by success in their functional adaptability, and proficient ones are transmitted as adaptive guides to life from generation to generation. Both the genes and narratives that survive are functionally adaptive for their environments and so enable people to carry on with their lives successfully. And stories themselves also have the genelike properties of helping people to cope, function, and adapt over time, by providing people with scripted guides, categories, and morals for acting out functional behaviors. Thus, evolutionism provides literary studies a coherent account grounded in the authority of the master theory of verified natural science that explains the origins, purpose, character, and development of literature. That, Wilson says, is a superior approach to understanding literature than the constructivism that assumes an instinct-deprived, biologically unconstrained humanity—not to mention an anything-goes postmodernism.

How does Wilson's story compare to the account I am developing in this book? Although I am not an "evolutionist," there is a great deal of agreement between Wilson and me. We are both realists. We have some similar intellectual interests. We agree that the primary job of any science is to causally explain. We value intellectual coherence and integration over fragmentation and incommensurability. We are skeptical about strong versions of social constructionism. We concur that human beings have a nature. We are interested in identifying the mechanisms that explain outcomes. We think that practical functionality is by no means insignificant in the ordering of social life. We believe that social science has for too long downplayed or ignored the human body and perhaps biology more broadly and should amend its ways. We both want to root the character and experience of human persons more firmly in the natural world. And I am friendly to Wilson's restatement[140] of the idea that human cultures (and perhaps other nongenetic dimensions of reality) evolve and do so along

140. The idea of cultural evolution has a long history in anthropology and (less so) sociology—one of the latest major representatives in sociology being Robert Wuthnow, *Communities of Discourse* (Cambridge, MA: Harvard University Press, 1993); Wuthnow, *Meaning and Moral Order* (Berkeley and Los Angeles: University of California Press, 1989), 186–214.

lines that parallel processes of natural selection—involving the generation of variation, selection,[141] and hereditability through transmission.

But Wilson and I seem to diverge on certain significant points, the brief
explication of which here may help to sharpen my more general account.
Most importantly, Wilson's story tends, by a critical realist's light, to be
reductionistic. He is not a crass reductionist, but is reductionistic nonetheless. Admittedly, Wilson theorizes a reality that is more multileveled
and complex than do some sociobiologists and evolutionary psychologists.
But his integrating evolutionist agenda still appears in the end to force
all aspects of every level of reality into a single evolutionary explanation.
Wilson's commitment to unite all human knowledge under evolutionism's
explanatory supremacy ends up reading to me as a compressing, totalizing
project. It's all about reproduction—literature, religion, philosophy, media, whatever. Here is where Wilson goes off track. For to believe in the
unity and coherence of reality, as Wilson and I do, does not commit one to
having to find a single analytical framework that interprets and explains
every aspect and dimension of reality by reference to one master causal
mechanism. In a critical realist world—the world I believe we actually
inhabit—reality is stratified; higher levels are emergent from lower; and
different causal properties, mechanisms, and dynamics exist and operate
at varying levels according to concerns appropriate to their own levels and
not to others.[142] The critical realist can thus fully acknowledge, appreciate,

141. Still an open question in my mind, however, is the basis upon which cultural products
are selected for transmission. It is far from clear that facilitating biological survival is the only
or even central criterion or screen determining cultural product survival.

142. The idea of emergence, as I have defined it here, plays no significant role in Wilson's
theorizing, as far as I can discern—he mentions not a word of it in his two pieces on evolutionary social constructivism (Wilson, "Evolutionary Social Constructivism," in *The Literary
Animal: Evolution and the Nature of Narrative*, ed. Wilson and Gottschall, 20–37; Wilson,
"Evolutionary Social Constructivism: Narrowing (But Not Yet Bridging) the Gap: A Reflection on Christian Smith's *Moral, Believing Animals*"; and I have not found an interest in
emergence in any of his other major works (David Sloan Wilson, *Darwin's Cathedral: Evolution, Religion, and the Nature of Society* [Chicago: University of Chicago Press, 2002]; Wilson,
Evolution for Everyone [New York: Delacorte Press, 2007]; Elliott Sober and David Sloan
Wilson, *Unto Others: The Evolution and Psychology of Unselfish Behavior* [Cambridge, MA:
Harvard University Press, 1998]). His writings more generally do not reflect critical realist
leanings. Aside from not addressing emergence and emergent properties, it appears Wilson
seems committed to empiricism as the philosophy specifying the correct standard of valid
evidence; he seems to lack the kind of epistemic fallibilism that conditions the critical realist's
confidence in theoretical explanations; and methodologically he does not seem to distinguish

and build bridges to evolutionary genetic and nongenetic adaptations when and where that is appropriate, without having to force everything always to be about reproductive fitness. Evolutionary explanations may be the main story at some levels but not necessarily all levels.[143] Especially when we reach the realities of human personhood and social structures, new, emergent causal capacities and dynamics can come to the fore that need not be bound to the dictates of survival and reproduction. The very nature of human personhood as I have described it here—particularly its reflexivity, self-transcendence, moral commitments, causal agency, responsibility, and freedom—means that persons can live, move, and have their being in ways and for reasons not strictly tied to an evolutionist's monotonic explanation of everything. Does all of that emerge from lower levels of reality that are biological and therefore evolutionarily explained? Of course. But the evolutionary reality operating at the lower level does not reach up directly to explain *everything* happening at a higher level—or even very much of it. I am confident that Wilson would be capable of fitting every piece of my account of the human person into his evolutionary explanatory system. And on some points he might be right—I am open to being shown. But to explain every significant dimension of human existence as a function of Wilson's theoretical system is, for a critical realist, unnecessarily simplistic, reductionistic, and oblivious of the complexities of a stratified reality.[144]

Perhaps this inappropriate reducing of all things human to fit the evolutionist explanation explains the fact that in the end Wilson offers very little of an actual theory about how biological genetic evolution guides or constrains cultural evolution. So far, Wilson has mostly suggested that the

between open versus closed systems of causal operations that make research in the social sciences different from in the natural sciences.

143. See Michael Carolan, "Society, Biology, and Ecology: Bringing Nature Back into Sociology's Disciplinary Narrative through Critical Realism," *Organization and Environment* 18, no. 4 (2005): 393–421; Carolan, "Realism without Reductionism: Toward an Ecologically Embedded Sociology," *Human Ecology Review* 12, no. 1 (2005): 1–20; Ted Benton, "Why Are Sociologists Naturephobes?" in *After Postmodernism: An Introduction to Critical Realism*, ed. López and Potter, 133–45.

144. Sociologists beware: without a realist philosophy of social science providing a strong ontological and causal theory of stratification, emergence, and downward causation, the social sciences are vulnerable, and increasingly so, to reductionistic moves of disciplinary colonialism by entrepreneurial thinkers in the natural sciences. Critical realism provides that theory as do neither positivist empiricism nor hermeneutical interpretivism.

reasonable potential exists to make that connection. But it is one thing to suggest that social constructivism specifically, and symbolic cultures generally, have biological roots and evolutionary parallels. It is quite another to explain how culture is bounded, shaped, directed, and governed by biology. Wilson has so far done the former but not the latter. My own belief is that neither he nor anyone else will ever do the latter. That is because culture operates at a level different from (though connected to) biology, with emergent properties and capacities proper to its own level that cannot be reduced to the elements of lower levels from which it emerges. This difference between Wilson and me mirrors a difference we also have over the nature of morality.[145] Wilson insists on reducing morality to a means of achieving utilitarian functionality enhancing reproductive fitness through group selection.[146] I believe that morality cannot (always) be reduced to such terms but is better understood as an emergent fact made possible by the capacities afforded humans by virtue of their biologically generated capacities but irreducible in character and function to a mechanism of evolutionary group reproduction. Wilson believes that my "by-product explanation" does not acknowledge important advances in theoretical knowledge about group selection and adaptation. I believe that Wilson's evolutionary survival explanation is inappropriately reductionistic and reality compacting. We can continue to debate. In the end, what will matter is not this or that new study or theory supporting one side or the other, but rather the greater adequacy of the larger philosophy of science that frames the books and theories and our accounts. I think critical realism will prove

145. Compare Christian Smith, *Moral, Believing Animals: Human Personhood and Culture* (New York: Oxford University Press, 2003) to David Sloan Wilson, "Evolutionary Social Constructivism: Narrowing (But Not Yet Bridging) the Gap: A Reflection on Christian Smith's *Moral, Believing Animals.*"

146. He continues this line of thinking in his evolutionary social constructivist writings, seeming to recognize no difference whatsoever between "a better world," social optimists' "desired outcome[s]," social "goals that are desirable," and "where we want to go" in terms of individual and social change *and* "the functional," the biologically "adaptive," and "islands of function [created] out of the sea of entropy." See Wilson, "Evolutionary Social Constructivism," in *The Literary Animal: Evolution and the Nature of Narrative,* ed. Wilson and Gottschall, 20–37. Elsewhere I have expressed my grave doubts about the ability to found a robust morality of universal rights and benevolence upon the foundation of a naturalistic evolutionary worldview. See Christian Smith, "Does Naturalism Warrant a Moral Belief in Universal Benevolence and Human Rights?" in *The Believing Primate: Scientific, Philosophical and Theological Perspectives on the Evolution of Religion,* ed. Jeffrey Schloss and Michael Murray (New York: Oxford University Press, 2009).

to be the best metatheory framing and directing our scientific work—the approach that provides the most epistemic gain—one that can recognize and make a place for all of the valuable scientific contributions that Wilson may produce without allowing his approach to become a totalizing, compressing explanatory system for every level and dimension of reality.

One final observation about Wilson's project: by legitimating the kind of reductionistic program that his unifying evolutionist agenda pursues, Wilson opens himself up as a biologist to being hoisted by his own petard by a similarly reductionistic agenda in physics. Why stop at evolutionary biology? If we really believe in causal reductionism, why not take it all down to the most basic level of scientific laws? Why should we assume that biological reproduction is *the* crucial starting point of scientific understanding? Biology, understood within a causal reductionist mentality, is merely a more complex order of the most fundamental explanatory laws, which are the ones that *really* matter, the laws of physics. By his own logic, then, Wilson's case positions evolutionary biology not as the capital of the scientific commonwealth but as merely one more provincial city connected by a system of roads all of which finally lead to the commonwealth's true capital, physics. Wilson can avoid falling into his own trap by recognizing the facts of stratification, emergence, and downward causation, which give biology its legitimate level of existence and explanation. But doing so will also then require Wilson to decompress the totalized reality his program seems to create—which, in turn, will force him to recognize human cultural and social life as operating on different, higher levels of reality than his own field of study according to emergent properties and mechanisms that cannot be reduced to those of evolutionary biology.

Excursus: Getting to Truth

Doing social science requires that we possess an account of knowledge that enables us to reasonably believe that truthful human knowledge about reality is possible. Otherwise, we are simply telling stories that we happen to like to one another and to our students. How then might human knowledge be true?[1] This excursus draws upon my arguments of the preceding chapter and develops them into an account that tries to answer this question.

After the middle of the twentieth century, the foundationalist quest for objective, positive scientific knowledge collapsed.[2] Most thinkers finally realized that humans simply cannot make theory-neutral observations of the world. All of our perceptions and knowledge are conceptually mediated. All of our observations are also necessarily and simultaneously interpretations. There simply is no universal, neutral, preconceptual, and indubitable foundation for knowledge. This, we came to see, is our true epistemic condition. Different thinkers responded to this epistemic collapse in different ways. Idealist skeptics renewed their doubts about the existence of any real world independent of our thoughts. So-called judgmental relativists conceded that a real world exists but abandoned the possibility of

---

1. I use the word *knowledge* here in the broad social scientific—not strictly philosophical—sense of beliefs about reality that people hold to be true, whether or not they actually are true. Philosophers work with a more precise view of knowledge than that, holding that knowledge is by definition true, since knowledge is simply true, justified, or warranted belief; one cannot know a falsehood, even if there is good evidence for it. In which case, the more appropriate question here would be: how might we humans achieve knowledge?

2. Foundationalism here being the epistemological project of identifying some fundamental belief or principle to serve as the basic and universal foundation of inquiry that will produce indubitable knowledge.

adjudicating between alternative accounts of knowledge of the world, since the "truth" of each account is believed to be always relative to the paradigm generating the account in the first place. So-called conventionalists redefined truth as merely that about which any community comes to consensus—truth is whatever people agree it is. So-called instrumentalists gave up any interest in truth and focused instead on the pragmatic "usefulness" of theoretical knowledge. As for neopositivists, they put their heads in the philosophical sand and fixated on more sophisticated methods, better measurements, and more empirical data collection.[3]

The previous chapter showed that social scientific social constructionism has been significantly influenced in recent decades by idealist skepticism, judgmental relativism, and conventionalism. The faith of many in the ability of objective reality to form our human knowledge about reality has been compromised if not lost. Yet we also saw in this last chapter the inherent, debilitating flaws of skepticism, relativism, and conventionalism. Those positions are not sustainable. Social science needs an alternative vision. Critical realist personalism fully acknowledges the conceptually mediated, interpretive, and theory-laden aspect of all human perception, observation, and knowledge. Yet it provides a coherent account of potentially truthful human knowledge based on a highly plausible presupposition that avoids idealist skepticism and judgmental and conventionalist relativism. The critical realist presupposition is that a structured, causally operative reality exists independently of our human consciousness of it. That eliminates idealist skepticism. The realist account of truthful knowledge based on this presupposition runs as follows.

We must begin by distinguishing again between ontology and epistemology. The first has to do with what *is*; the second, *what we can know* about it. Realism holds that a statement is true when the reality about which the statement is made is as the statement says it is. That is a view about truth and ontology. The epistemological issue, by contrast, concerns what enables us to know or believe that statements are in fact true. That has

3. Regarding the field of demography, for example, see Mayer Zald, "Progress and Cumulation in the Human Sciences after the Fall," *Sociological Forum* 10, no. 3 (1995): 470–72. The critical realist Andrew Sayer, however, astutely notes that even the simple phrase "data collection" is theoretically problematic: "The common expression 'data-gathering' should also be questioned because it suggests again that the data pre-exist their conceptualization such that they can be simply 'gathered' or 'collected.'" Sayer, *Method in Social Science: A Realist Approach* (London: Routledge, 1992), 272.

to do with adequate evidence and related factors. The important point here for realists is not to conflate ontology into epistemology. We must not commit the epistemic fallacy of relativizing reality around our challenged human knowledge of it. Reality exists independently of our knowledge of it.[4] Our task is to express statements about reality that describe it as it is. Having established that priority and orientation, the second step is to consider what counts as criteria for good indicators of truth. What entitles us epistemologically to conclude that something is true? The following briefly examines both aspects of the issue.

First, social science should aspire to understand and explain what is true about what is real. But what is truth? My answer to this directly follows the eminent philosopher William Alston's "alethic" theory of truth advanced in his book *A Realist Conception of Truth*.[5] According to Alston, a propositional statement is true if and only if what the statement says to be the case actually is the case. Reality is a certain way and our statements are true when they describe the way that reality is. When our statements describe reality as it is, we have truth. Moreover, the manner in which we reliably form true beliefs about things is significantly determined by the nature of those things.[6] Reality thus impinges upon and forms our understanding of things. This view Alston develops—I think successfully—as a superior alternative to more skeptical antirealist approaches, such as the so-called deflationary, verificationist, and conceptually relativist theories argued by Michael Dummett, Hilary Putnam, and others. An important virtue of Alston's approach is that it affirms reality and truth without presuming that humans have an unmediated or infallible access to "the facts." Its "minimal realist" theory is thus highly compatible with critical realism. Alston's account also avoids embracing a simple correspondence theory of truth, although its overall logic suggests a more sophisticated version of correspondence theory. This is not the place to elaborate the details of Alston's theory and argument beyond this brief summary. The key points for present purposes are: Truth exists. Propositions can be true.

---

4. Except, of course, that piece of reality that consists of our own knowledge.

5. William Alston, *A Realist Conception of Truth* (Ithaca, NY: Cornell University Press, 1996). "Alethic" here comes from the Greek *aletheia*, meaning "truth."

6. Note that "reliable" does not mean inerrant but, rather, following William Alston again, is based on a belief-forming mechanism that yields "mostly true beliefs in a sufficiently large and varied run of employments in situations of the sorts we typically encounter." Alston, *The Reliability of Sense Perception* (Ithaca, NY: Cornell University Press, 1993), 8, 9.

Philosophical realism justifies a belief in our human capacity to make true statements. And the truth of such statements is determined not primarily by our epistemic criteria about them (not to mention by their pragmatic usefulness) but by the nature of the reality to which the statements refer. Furthermore, this realist belief about truth holds up—in my view and that of many others—against the critiques of its antirealist rivals. We therefore need not retreat from believing that there is truth. We need not deny that our statements can be true. And we need not worry that really *we* are ultimately the ones who make things true. Truth has to do with objective reality.

Having said all of that, we need next to consider the distinct epistemological questions about reliable indicators of truth—that is, criteria by which we may judge our statements to be true. Identifying some of the challenges here is helpful. For one thing, truth statements about reality, on the one hand, and the reality about which truth statements are made, on the other, are entities that are inherently distinct in quality from each other, enough so that the former cannot mimic or replicate the latter in a simple correspondence, like cloth cut out to match the shape of a paper sewing pattern. Thought objects are qualitatively different from many real objects. Thought objects are by nature linguistic and conceptual and, in Searle's terms, ontologically subjective. Real objects, by contrast, are often material, epistemologically objective, and so possess existence and characteristics objective of human perception and discourse and subjectivity. These differences mean that the one cannot provide a facsimile of or coincide with the other. There will always be a qualitative disjuncture between reality and truth statements about reality, and therefore limits on the ability of the latter to directly represent or depict the former. John Searle explains it this way: "One of the oldest urges in Western philosophy is to think that somehow or other truth and reality should coincide. That ... if there really were such things as truth and reality, as we normally think of them, then truth would have to provide an exact mirror of reality. The nature of reality itself would have to provide the exact structure of true statements."[7] Yet this coincidence has been elusive and judged impossible to obtain. The reaction to this failure, however, has often been to decide (erroneously) that truth statements are unrelated to reality. Searle again: "When the philosopher despairs of achieving an exact isomorphism be-

7. John Searle, *The Construction of Social Reality* (New York: Free Press, 1995), quotes in this paragraph are from 175–76.

tween the structure of reality and the structure of true representation, the
temptation is to think that somehow or other our naïve notions of truth
and reality have been discredited." But this, Searle says, is wrong. "They
have not been discredited. What has been discredited is a certain misconception of the relationship between truth and reality." In other words,
truth statements and reality can and do relate importantly to each other,
but not in an isomorphic form of pictorial mirroring or coincidence:

> There is a simple and deep reason why truth and reality cannot coincide. . . . The
> reason is this: All representation, and a fortiori all truthful representations . . .
> [are] always made from within a certain conceptual scheme and from a certain
> point of view. . . . Strictly speaking, there is an indefinitely large number of dif-
> ferent points of view, different aspects, and different conceptual systems under
> which anything can be represented. If that is right, and surely it is, then it will be
> impossible to get the coincidence between truth and reality after which so many
> traditional philosophers seem to hanker. . . . In short, it is only from a point of
> view that we represent reality, but ontologically objective reality does not have
> a point of view.

One might say that it is impossible to make *personal* knowledge directly
capture and depict non-personal reality, since the personal nature of our
thought objects adds an incommensurably distinct quality to human
knowledge. Reality thus cannot be mirrored in truth statements about it
as if by simple, one-to-one correspondence—about this antiobjectivist,
antipositivist constructionists are right.

However, it does not follow from these observations that the real nature of objective reality cannot meaningfully inform the content of truth
statements. It can. The relationship between the two is not arbitrary, but,
I suggest, is transpositionally correspondent. As Andrew Sayer writes,
"There is . . . no isomorphism between language and reality in which the
former is structured like the latter, for sense is not tightly correlated with
physical characteristics. Language is not about bits of matter . . . but about
the sense the world makes to us. Nevertheless, it does not follow that . . .
[the] relation [of signs] to the world is arbitrary."[8] While thought objects
cannot directly replicate real objects, they may nonetheless correspond
in some meaningful indicative way to real objects—that is, when correspondence is understood not as mirroring but as transposing or recoding

8. Andrew Sayer, *Realism and Social Science* (London: Sage, 2000), 38.

from nonlinguistic reality to the humanly personal and linguistically conceptual. We can stop expecting truth statements to operate according to a strict mimetic theory of truth—according to which representations of truth are expected to be linguistic facsimiles or duplications of reality—without abandoning our intuitively correct belief based on phenomenological experience that many statements refer to reality in ways that are actually true or not true. The terms *coincidence, isomorphism*, and *mirroring* suggest too close a reflection between the two. However, a sophisticated correspondence theory of truth—when properly understood as recognizing that reality and truth statements exist in qualitatively different modes of being—provides a defensible account of how truth statements relate to reality.[9]

This correspondence presumes the existence of a complex set of human capacities, categories, concepts, vocabularies, and mental models. But being the kind of human creatures we are, the presumed existence of such things is perfectly justified. What *else* would knowing human persons have to work with? As I argued in the previous chapter, simply because these elements of knowledge are human and personal does not mean they are invalid, compromised, untrustworthy, or debilitating. To think so is to fall back into a foundationalist dream that wants to hold out for indubitable, neutral, positive knowledge. But, in reality, what *other* elements of knowledge would humans have to employ than things like particular languages, categories, concepts, vocabularies, symbols, and so on? Those are precisely what humans use in order to know well. It will not do, therefore, for instance, for the strong constructionist to hound the realist, by saying that all of the terms used to account for knowledge of reality are culturally specific words and concepts. Of course they are. There is nothing wrong with or problematic about that, when we understand human knowledge as appropriately human and personal. Such knowledge is clearly not unlimited, but then again nothing about human life is. Yet if the constructionist

---

9. "Just because knowledge and its referents are usually different, it does not follow that there can be no relationship between them. If we are to allow a notion of correspondence, it must involve conformability and intelligibility rather than replication." Ibid., 42. Also see Gerald Visions, *Veritas: The Correspondence Theory and Its Critics* (Cambridge, MA: MIT Press); John Searle, "Truth and Correspondence," in *The Construction of Social Reality*, 199–226; Andrew Newman, *The Correspondence Theory of Truth: An Essay on the Metaphysics of Predication* (Cambridge: Cambridge University Press, 2002); and Paul Boghossian, *Fear of Knowledge: Against Relativism and Constructivism* (New York: Oxford University Press, 2006).

is able to make real peace with the conceptual mediation and cultural specificity of all human knowledge, without erroneously deciding that those invalidate knowledge, the constructionist can reconnect language to reality and therefore to the possibility of making real truth statements.

What then enables the nature of objects in reality to form the content of human thought objects? Stated differently, what helps us epistemologically to identify good indicators of truth? At least three things. First, the tools of human perceptual equipment—touch, sight, hearing, taste, and smell—capacitate normal people in most circumstances to participate in and to accurately apprehend reality. Of course there is much in reality that can fool and mislead human empirical perceptions. But more fundamentally our perceptual capacities must be adequate to discern accurately enough what is real in order for us to know that in certain cases we *have* been fooled. Without an ability to perceive what is true about the real, the idea of being fooled or misled would be completely meaningless—the world would only ever be whatever we flatly and credulously happen to see it as. We have warrant to believe, therefore, that our human faculties of perception, when functioning properly, enable us to learn and understand things about the nature of reality that inform and shape our conceptual knowledge of it.[10]

Second, human practical activity enables people to live as part of reality and so continually to test the "practical adequacy" of their accumulated knowledge. Practical adequacy of knowledge means that we encounter outcomes in experience based on what the knowledge system would expect us to encounter. When knowledge is practically adequate, it renders experience in the world intelligible and our personal capacities functional.[11] "Realists do not need to suppose that knowledge mirrors the world," Sayer tells us. "Rather it interprets it in such a way that the expectations

10. See Alston, *The Reliability of Sense Perception.* Alston's argument is that it is eminently rational to rely on our sense perceptions as we normally do in order to form our beliefs; further, that our practice of relying on our sense perceptions in this way are reasonably, though not infallibly, reliable in forming the beliefs that are true.

11. Andrew Sayer writes, "The reduction of the issue to a simple black-and-white question of (absolute) truth or falsity does no justice to the complexity of the relation of practical knowledge to its referents. . . . Truth might be better understood as 'practical adequacy,' that is in terms of the extent to which it generates expectations about the world and about results of our actions which are realized." Sayer, *Realism and Social Science,* 43. I would amend Sayer by clarifying that truth is truth not because of practical adequacy, but rather because practical adequacy is one criterion for coming to truth.

and practices it informs are intelligible and reliable. Knowledge claims involve practical commitments, that if one does such-and-such, certain things will result."[12] Note that practical adequacy is not the same as pragmatic usefulness, which encourages a move toward instrumentalism, the theory that knowledge is (as if) "true" (only) because it is useful. Practical adequacy does not make knowledge statements true. Rather, knowledge statements satisfy the criteria of practical adequacy if, when, and because they *are* true. As Sayer notes, "Realists say useful knowledge is useful because it is true, and instrumentalists say knowledge that is called true is so merely because it is useful. . . . The [correct realist] question is not only what works, but what is it about the world which makes it work."[13] My knowledge that I should not walk off of tall buildings if I want to continue living, for example, is practically adequate because of the truth of the laws of physics and biology (gravity, acceleration, normal bodily organ function, etc.) that are objectively real and operative. Neither my believing in that knowledge nor its practical adequacy in lived experience are what make true my knowledge or its underwriting physical laws. What is true and what I know about the truth of reality, rather, are why I believe my knowledge and why it *is* practically adequate.

The third criterion for helping to discern the truth of knowledge claims is rational evaluation of the internal and external coherence of knowledge. Internal coherence concerns rational consistency within the premises and conclusions of the knowledge claim. External coherence is about consistency with other knowledge claims that we take to be true. By these criteria, the truth or reliability of internally incoherent and self-defeating knowledge systems should be viewed as highly questionable, even when they seem to comport with our empirical observations and prove useful. Externally incoherent knowledge claims also require more deliberation toward reconciliation to our larger system of beliefs before being deemed acceptable as true. If apparent knowledge A seems perfectly acceptable on its own terms yet contradicts apparent knowledge X, Y, and Z, which we already for good reasons take to be true, then A remains suspect. Evident incoherence should not be enough to quickly kill certain beliefs. It could be that a reframing of beliefs in a new and better overall framework is needed to eliminate the incoherence, which might only become appar-

---

12. Ibid., 42. Also see Cynthia Lins Hamlin, *Beyond Relativism* (London: Routledge, 2002).

13. Sayer, *Realism and Social Science*, 42.

ent after long intellectual struggle. Knowledge *A* may in fact eventually show us that *X*, *Y*, and *Z* are problematic. So we should exercise some patience and forbearance in considering seemingly self-defeating and externally incoherent viewpoints. But our presumption should be in favor of coherent belief systems and the burden of proof for acceptance placed squarely on incoherent theories. We have every right to judge the veracity of particular knowledge claims in terms of their internal rationality and their coherence of fit within what we believe to be true in our broader schemas of knowledge. Again, in the end new and apparently incoherent knowledge may call for changes in our broader schemas, but that needs to be demonstrated with clear argument and compelling evidence. Given the nature of reality and the human epistemic situation, that will happen sometimes but not commonly.

These three capacities—well-fitted perception, experience of practical adequacy, and rational evaluation of coherence—taken and exercised together mean that we humans are fitted to make, over time and through the process of lived experience, reliable judgments about what is true. The real character of reality significantly shapes the content of what humans take to be truthful knowledge for these reasons. Because of them, we can rightly discern some knowledge to be true. Reliable (but not infallible) indicators of truth, therefore, are, first, that it comports with our best observations in our experience in reality; second, that it has been extensively tested through practical activity in human life and found to be practically adequate; and third, that it is not irresolvably, internally or externally, incoherent or self-defeating over time. To repeat, these do not make truth true. They are only criteria for knowing what is true. Putting these together, what we can believe to be true knowledge is that which relies on various empirical and rational means of knowing to provide the best among rival explanations of the reality for which it seeks to account. When we are able to make an inference to the best explanation of a particular phenomenon in ways that fit our own ideas and other beliefs we take to be true, we may be epistemologically justified in calling that explanation true. Stated in Charles Taylor's terms presented in chapter 2, knowledge may be taken to be true, in part, because it provides us "epistemic gain" over alternative explanations in any focus of inquiry. Conventionalist relativism can thus be eliminated by this account. Truth is not simply what we agree to believe. Again, this does not mean that what we purport to be true knowledge is complete, indubitable, or inerrant. It is always fallible and often incomplete and less than certain. But our knowledge can nonetheless be true because in the end what makes it so is not our knowing it in a certain way but its representing reality as it is. We often do get things right, even thought we can never be entirely certain that some of our beliefs will not someday be overturned.

A simple illustration of the argument thus far might help. Reality contains a small planet that is our earth. That planet has a particular shape, objective of our mental states about it. Our earth is round. If we believed the earth was square, we would be wrong—the earth would still be round. Despite the considerable obstacle of the size of the earth relative to our perceptual abilities (prior to space travel), we humans have been able to use a combination of our limited perceptual capacities, our lived experience in practical activities, and our reasoning abilities to detect internal and external incoherence of theories in order to determine that our earth is in fact round. There was a time when different theories about the shape of the earth contended as rivals for the claim of truthful knowledge. Through a process of inquiry, argument, and elimination, over time one theory won out. Reliable, though limited evidence led us to make an inference to the best explanation about the shape of the earth. That explanation subsequently was validated in practical adequacy—when, for example, it came to activities like ocean navigation and global exploration. And it involved little if any internal or external incoherence. On these grounds, we can say with confidence that it is true that our earth is round. If the earth is round then that would be true. It could be that scientists someday refine notions of planetary shape in a way that enables us to more accurately or precisely describe the form of our earth in terms different from *round*. It could be that astronomers or cosmologists someday reframe our larger understanding in a new paradigm that revises the significance of our statement that our earth is round. In either case, we might then have epistemological warrant for believing that the new or revised description is true and the earth is not round.[14] Meanwhile, we can believe that the statement "our earth is round" is true. And meanwhile, if someone claims the earth is flat or square, we have criteria telling us this is false.[15] But in the end, our beliefs

14. Earth scientists have determined that the earth is essentially but not perfectly round, not a perfect sphere, but slightly oblate—which perfectly fits my point.

15. Another crucial means for knowing what is true about reality that this chapter does not explore, because it tends to be more relevant for singular events than natural recurrences, is testimony, that is, reports by eyewitnesses. See C. A. J. Coady, *Testimony: A Philosophical Study* (New York: Oxford University Press, 1992).

do not make true what we think is the truth—the reality to which our beliefs refer makes them true, when in fact they are. We also must have epistemic criteria for reliably judging which beliefs are true and which are not, which we do. And those are usually reliable at helping us get to truth.

Of course, again, the strong social constructionist might object by countering that the very concepts and words *earth*, *shape*, and *round* are culturally specific terms, not universals or cultural inevitabilities. This would not be wrong, merely trivial. Human knowledge is always specific and conceptual for humans. Again, what else could or should it be? Angel knowledge? Humans are creatures who are highly capacitated to know conceptually, who do not have (or need) universalistic and inevitable concepts (whatever those might be). How could humans do anything *other* than develop concepts and words that they collectively understand as referring to features of the reality in which they participate and seek to understand, test the practical adequacy of their concepts and beliefs through practical activity in the world, and solidify their confidence in a most adequate account of reality that they would then rightly take to be true? The objection that the very concepts and words used to offer a linguistically transposed corresponding description of reality are "only themselves social constructions" is thus frivolous.

All of this forces us to see, however, that human statements about truth are not, never have been, and never will be about absolute certainty. Truth is about what is. Our statements about truth are about our beliefs concerning what is. We believe certain things to be true. But we cannot verify beyond a shadow of a doubt that they are true—if by that we mean absolutely, unchangingly, positively, and indubitably true.[16] Only a particular kind of transcendent or divine perspective could do that. But that does not mean that some of our human knowledge is not true, that it does not describe or represent what is true about what is real. We can hold beliefs that are tested, compelling, and seemingly unshakable, which we rightly deem to be true. All of us, in fact, do. Again, this does not mean that our beliefs are true because we believe them so. Our belief does not make them true. We believe they are true because every capacity we possess to understand reality tells us that they are. So we believe them, justifiably so, and often accurately so.

---

16. This is part of what I meant in arguing in a previous book that humans are "believing animals." Christian Smith, *Moral, Believing Animals: Human Personhood and Culture* (New York: Oxford University Press, 2003), 45–61.

This account introduces variable degrees of confidence that we should place in our truth statements, so that we are warranted in greater confidence in some knowledge than others. Different bodies of what humans take to be knowledge more or less well describe reality, meaning that some knowledge provides a better account of the real than others. Not all accounts are equal in believability or validity. Everyone knows that. Some purported knowledge is in error and some is not. Some purported knowledge is more or less likely to be in error than other purported knowledge—even if we're not entirely sure at the moment which is. All of what we believe to be human knowledge in this framework is thus fallible, but that does not mean it is all equally wrong or right. When knowledge is evaluated well, we are entitled to consider some of it reliable and truthful. "To say that [we believe that] certain propositions are true is not to say that they are beyond improvement. It is not only that they may later be shown to be false but that, even if they are not, they may be shown to be partial rather than complete, or [to have been] integrated within a wider conceptual scheme that is flawed."[17] We can, in short, often adjudicate for truth and credibility among many (though not all) rival knowledge accounts. Thus, judgmental relativism is eliminated.

Finally, however, we might ask what to do when different truth-claiming accounts of reality conflict. The same evidence often supports what seem to be mutually incompatible interpretations of it. People can look at the same data and believe it tells us different things about reality. They may, for instance, believe that very different causal mechanisms are producing the same observed correlation among variables. What do we do then? How can we adjudicate among competing, plausible accounts of the same reality? The answer is that we must proceed with the only noncoercive option available. That is to continue to interrogate the adequacy of our ideas and explanations, to gather more evidence promising to shed new light, and to continue to hammer away at a best account of reality through collective discussion, argumentation, reflection, and criticism—in sum, again, testing our accounts against the clarity of experience through systematic observation and the discipline of reason. (That, of course, is something like what this book is attempting to do on the question of the person.)

17. Sayer, *Realism and Social Science*, 43. My addition of "[we believe that]" indicates my belief that this statement should refer to an epistemological, not ontological, point about truth. Along similar lines, also see Paul Armstrong, *Conflicting Readings: Variety and Validity in Interpretation* (Chapel Hill: University of North Carolina Press, 1990).

In due time, we may with good reason come to choose one account over others. That sometimes happens. And when it does, we are entitled to believe that we then better understand what is true about reality than we did before. In the meantime, we have no choice but to intellectually wrestle through our differences, relying on the best scholarly tools at our disposal, vigorously interrogating what we believe are our rivals' inadequate ideas, yet being open to persuasion by them.

In all of this, meanwhile, it is true that what we hold to be true could be wrong. We can learn. What else is new? As long as we are more committed to searching out what is true—as Michael Polanyi says, committed to a love of truth and joy in discovery—than to merely defending what we would want to be true, then that is the best we can and all we need to do.[18] Even then, in most cases, with enough time, when pursued in good faith, humans often can learn what is true about reality.

18. Or, in Christopher Norris's words, it is the moral obligation of science "to get things right as far as possible and not to be swayed by the pressures of conformist ideology or consensus belief." Norris, *Against Relativism* (Oxford: Blackwell, 1997), 1.

CHAPTER FOUR

Network Structuralism's Missing Persons

One of the most innovative and interesting events in sociology in the later twentieth century was the emergence and development of the new paradigm of network structuralism, sometimes also called relationalism and network analysis. Network structuralism shifted analytical attention away from individual attributes emphasized by the dominant "variables paradigm." Instead, it focuses on the overall structure of social relations in networked systems of interaction. Network structuralists argued that "variables sociology" was stuck with an atomized, individualistic, psychological ontology inappropriate for a discipline on a mission to study *the social.* The alternative unit of analysis and level of explanation, therefore, should be the structured system of social relations that comprises the real social world. Their purpose was and is not simply to describe the form of social networks but to demonstrate how overall structures of relations produce social consequences and therefore explain outcomes and events through a genuine sociologic.

The network structuralist critique of variables sociology is largely on the mark, in my view, and its alternative analytical paradigm provides an important remedy to some larger endemic problems in sociology. Important for present purposes, network structuralism is also highly compatible with critical realism. When theorized correctly, it is able to emphasize the importance of interactive relations, multileveled reality, emergent properties, and downward causation. Network structuralism is also generally, though not always, unhampered by the kind of mental idealisms that confuse social constructionists, as we saw in chapter 3, although it does employ a different version of constructionism, as we will see below. One might make a good argument that network structuralism is, among the alternatives, a naturally well-suited research program for critical realist sociology. Much in network structuralism thus commends itself to those who embrace the kind of perspective I am developing in this book. But on the specific question of the nature of human persons, network structuralism warrants further interrogation.

To be clear, I am using the modifier *network* to specify the particular paradigm this chapter examines. By structuralism I do not mean the anthropological structuralism of Claude Lévi-Strauss, the linguistic structuralism of Ferdinand Saussure, the Marxist structuralism of Louis Althusser, the "structuration" theory of Anthony Giddens, or the structural equation modeling representing structures as stable effects of causal variables measured in parameter estimates. I mean a more specific approach to social science that has been developed and led in recent decades by Harrison White, Mark Granovetter, David Knoke, Ronald Burt, Barry Wellman, Ronald Breiger, Peter Bearman, Peter Marsden, Michael Macy, Jim Moody, Bruce Mayhew, S. D. Berkowitz, Miller McPherson, Roger Gould, Nan Lin, and Stephan Fuchs, among others. This is the structuralism that is organized in the International Network of Social Network Analysis and published in *Social Networks*, *Connections*, and the *Journal of Social Structure*.

To understand network structuralism for my argument that follows, it is helpful to set it in a larger intellectual context. A great deal of science has come in the last century to emphasize explanations based not on the innate characteristics of entities but on the interactive relations among parts. Included in this shift is work in quantum physics, cosmology, evolutionary and ecological biology, linguistics, and cybernetics. On the broadest scale, this change must be understood as an ongoing development in modern science's rejection of a general Aristotelian worldview, whose explanations stressed essential being, classifications of natural kinds, innate purposes, and action and processes as movements toward natural ends. Although Aristotelian science has been generally suspect since the scientific revolution, network structuralists still detect its presence lurking in contemporary rational choice and in normative theories of action. In both, a long line of theorizing—running from Thomas Aquinas, René Descartes, Thomas Hobbes, John Locke, Adam Smith, and others, all the way down to Max Weber, Talcott Parsons, and George Homans—is viewed as positing pregiven actors pursuing natural or internalized ends as the source of social action and order. Network structuralism, by contrast, shifts our focus away from the interests of purposive agents and instead to the stable order of *relations* between concretely linked actors as the real social source of action, order, and explanation. In short, what recurrently happens *between* people, more than within or out from people, is what makes the social world go around. Building on certain intellectual resources garnered from the sociologists and anthropologists Émile Durkheim, Ferdinand Tönnies, Alfred Radcliffe-Brown, Leopold von Wiese, J. A. Barnes, Elizabeth Bott, Jacob Moreno, Siegfried Nadel, Meyer Fortes, Max Gluckman, and especially Georg Simmel, network structuralists have developed matrix datasets, graphic representations, and mathematical analyses to explain social outcomes through structures of social relations rather than variable individual characteristics.[1]

At least some network structuralists were also influenced by the idea of social construction. However, it was usually not the linguistic and culturalist schools of constructionism derived from philosophical idealism (examined in chapter 3) that was influential here. Neither Kant nor Saussure is in the background of most network structuralism. Rather, it was primarily Durkheim's distinctly *social* constructionism—the view that human identities and cognitions are the dependent products of stably patterned interactions occurring at the level of the sui generis social group—that shaped network structuralism. In this view, society is not seen as the aggregated product of acting individual agents. Rather, acting individuals are understood as the products of the social structure of network relations. Individual humans are thus constructed by causally operative relational social systems.

I have already mentioned as a source of network structuralism's development a growing dissatisfaction among many sociologists with the variables approach to sociology that dominated the discipline for decades after World War II. In reaction, by the 1970s and 1980s many creative sociological minds were searching for alternatives to what they saw as the dead ends of methodological individualism, normative sociology, and rational choice theory—all of which they believed were embodied in mainstream interpretivist sociology and in the statistical methods of variables sociology. The collapse of Parsonian structural-functionalism in the 1970s

1. For historical context, see Barry Wellman and S. D. Berkowitz, "Introduction: Studying Social Structures," in *Social Structure: A Network Approach,* ed. Wellman and Berkowitz (Cambridge: Cambridge University Press, 1988); Mustafa Emirbayer and Jeff Goodwin, "Network Analysis, Culture, and the Problem of Agency," *American Journal of Sociology* 99, no. 6 (1994): 1411–54; José López and John Scott, *Social Structure* (Philadelphia: Open University Press, 2000), 53. The American pragmatism of John Dewey has also exerted influence on some network structuralists.

only increased this motivation to find a new paradigm that would avoid the ends-means teleology of the Weberian tradition, the voluntarism of symbolic interactionism, and other problematic elements of more individualistic theories. During this era, norms, values, goals, and beliefs largely went out of style as explanatorily relevant in social science. Structure was the watchword of leading theorists.

Not all versions of network structuralism are the same.[2] Some versions are perfectly compatible with the view of the human person that I am advancing in this book. Others could be congruent with critical realist personalism with certain of their terms clarified or revised. But still other versions of network structuralism are deeply problematic when it comes to their theory of the person, at least from the perspective of critical realist personalism. My purpose in this chapter is to sort through some of these differences in order to make clear the kind of person that network structuralism requires in order to succeed. My claim is that network structuralism needs, and in fact must be presupposing, something like the kind of human person I am describing in this book. It is true that the structures of social relations are real entities with causal powers operating over and above those of persons. Yet that does not make persons the determined creations of networks or black-boxed theoretical entities without substantive content. Real relational structures and real persons are mutually dependent and implicated. If humans were not robustly persons at the personal level, then network structuralism could not work robustly at a structural level. And vice versa.

An immense literature on network structuralism—elaborating theoretical, technically methodological, and substantively analytical explorations— already exists. I could not hope to begin to fairly represent the larger agenda of, different approaches within, and major substantive findings from network structuralism. Nor do I need to do so for present purposes. Here I lay out only what is necessary to make my case about persons. But first, before exploring theories of the person in network structuralism, it will be useful to briefly describe one specific analysis of network structuralism, to provide a better initial sense of the kind of work it proposes to advance. The work I describe is not from sociologists but from

2. Network structuralists also tend to gravitate either toward more purely theoretical or empirical focuses of work, the latter network structuralists rarely lay out their assumptions about human actors explicitly but often leave them implicit and devote themselves instead to practical substantive empirical analyses.

medical researchers, published during the very month I was writing this chapter.

Researchers Nicholas Christakis and James Fowler were interested in understanding how and why obesity spreads, in an effort to explain the significant growth in overweight Americans in recent years.[3] Why and how do people gain weight? The standard "variables" approach to this question would have been to conduct a survey of a sample of individuals focusing on different factors characterizing respondents (such as age, sex, income, marital status, frequency of exercise, occupation, health status, etc.) and using multivariate regression analysis to identify those independent variables that significantly predict weight gain. Other sociologists might have conducted personal interviews with individuals about their view and experiences concerning body weight, or perhaps carried out an ethnographic study at a dieting support group. Christakis and Fowler took a different approach. They examined data collected in repeated waves between 1971 and 2003 from a densely interconnected social network of 12,067 people in one city. Their data include not only individual respondents reporting on their social relationships but also the same data collected directly from many of their reported social ties—in short, their data represent a network, not merely a sample. This enabled the researchers to identify not only individual level factors associated with obesity but also the influence on weight gain of occupying variable positions in differently structured webs of social relationships. The analysis thereby focused on the causal effects of the shape and quality of people's network ties on changes in their body weight over time. Could whom one knows, we might wonder, really affect how much one weighs? Yes. According to this study, individuals' weight gain was significantly influenced by the weight gain of other people in their social networks—apart from factors like their personal history of weight change and smoking cessation. That is, when people's social relations gained weight, they were much more likely subsequently to gain weight. Over thirty-two years of observation, the risk of becoming obese for individuals who were tied to another person already obese were 45 percent higher than would have been if obesity were randomly distributed over time. The study also found that the "social proximity" of relationships was more important than geographical proximity—the risk of gaining weight increased when the social ties in question were relationally close, as in friendships, people of the same sex, siblings, and married

3. Nicholas Christakis and James Fowler, "The Spread of Obesity in a Large Social Network over 32 Years," *New England Journal of Medicine* 357, no. 4 (2007): 370–79.

couples, but was not influenced by the spatial distance of relationships. Furthermore, when a relationship was defined by *both* parties as a friendship, the chances of weight gain influence between them was higher than when only one person in the relationship viewed their tie as a friendship. The same was true when siblings were the same sex compared to different sexes. Yet simply being a residential neighbor to someone of greater weight did not increase the chances of people gaining weight themselves. Knowing people's prior weight status and collecting and modeling data over three decades effectively controlled for possible selection effects, whereby people more individually at risk of gaining weight might seek relationships with other already heavier people or people in the process of gaining weight. What then is the causal mechanism that appeared to produce these network-influenced processes of weight gain? The study's authors believe it is the adjustment of individuals' perceived interpersonal social acceptability of weight gain within their personal webs of social relationships produced by actual obesity or weight gains in their relational ties. In other words, when one's friends and relations have gained weight, one is more likely to think it will be more acceptable to gain added weight oneself. And so one often does. Operating through the channels of network ties, then, the higher body weight of some (especially socially close) people causes an increase in the chances of bodily weight gain for those to whom they are relationally networked. In short, America's obesity epidemic appears to be spreading through social network relationships. And the variable risk of contagiousness of that epidemic is significantly affected by the structural shapes and compositions of those networks.

This example illustrates key points. Changes in people's body weight, according to this study, are determined not so much by individual characteristics or autonomous choices as by positional locations in different kinds of social networks. It is the nature of the ties between people as much or more than properties of the people that shapes the outcome in question. Such an explanation, note, is inherently more sociological than other standard methods of analysis of such matters, in that it identifies outcome-causing capacities existing in characteristics of complex social systems, not simply variable features of the individual actors who occupy those systems. It is unlikely that a typical survey, transcripts of interviews, or participant observation of a social group could have revealed the causal powers of people's structured social networks to influence body weight— such data sources usually cannot model the concrete, complex ties between people; and people are often not perceptive, consciously aware, and articulate about many such social influences shaping their lives. Network structuralism, however, is able to demonstrate such effects, empirically establishing the causal power of structures that are distinctly social. Using this general relational approach, then, network structuralists have succeeded in showing not only how and why public health problems such as obesity spread, but also things such as how and why people find jobs, join social movements and rebellions, obtain abortions, develop elite cohesion, increase family influence and power, mobilize political reforms, spread new religious movements, and a host of other sociologically interesting and important outcomes and events.[4] What I wish to focus on in this chapter are the assumptions that network structuralists make about the nature of the actors or nodes that are tied together by social networks when those are individual humans.[5] Some such accounts of actors, we will see, are compatible with the view of persons I am developing in this book and some are not. I oppose those that are not because they dissolve persons.

Versions of Network Structuralism

Network structuralists do not all think and explain similarly. Within the larger paradigm a variety of different approaches, emphases, and visions

---

4. See, for example, Mark Granovetter, *Getting a Job* (Cambridge, MA: Harvard University Press, 1974); Granovetter, "The Strength of Weak Ties," *American Journal of Sociology* 78 (1973): 1360–80; N. H. Lee, *The Search for an Abortionist* (Chicago: University of Chicago Press, 1969); Peter Bearman, *Relations into Rhetorics: Local Elite Social Structure in Norfolk, England, 1540–1640* (New Brunswick, NJ: Rutgers University Press, 1993); Debra Friedman and Doug McAdam, "Collective Identity and Activism: Networks, Choices, and the Life of a Social Movement," in *Frontiers in Social Movement Theory*, ed. Aldon Morris and Carol Mueller (New Haven, CT: Yale University Press, 1992), 156–73; Roger Gould, *Insurgent Identities: Class, Community, and Protest in Paris from 1848 to the Commune* (Chicago: University of Chicago Press, 1995); Doug McAdam, *Freedom Summer* (New York: Oxford University Press, 1988); Naomi Rosenthal et al., "Social Movements and Network Analysis: A Case Study of Nineteenth-Century Women's Reform in New York State," *American Journal of Sociology* 90 (1985): 1022–54; Rodney Stark, *The Rise of Christianity* (New York: Harper, 1997); John Padgett and Christopher Ansell, "Robust Action and the Rise of the Medici, 1400–1434," *American Journal of Sociology* 98 (1993): 1259–319. Also see Duncan Watts, "The 'New' Science of Networks," *Annual Review of Sociology* 30 (2004): 243–70.

5. Note that the specific example of networks and obesity I just described, for instance, necessitates particular assumptions about actors in order for its explanation to work—in this case, actors are assumed to be motivated in part by the normative force of social acceptability.

exist. And there are several ways of parsing out differences depending on the issue involved. Mustafa Emirbayer and Jeff Goodwin, for instance, differentiate "relational" analyses from "positional" analyses, which differ by the directness or indirectness of the ties in question.[6] They also distinguish three types of implicit structuralist models of historical explanation. "Structuralist determinists," they say, entirely ignore the possible causal capacities of purposive actors in historical change, building no systematic role for human agency in their explanations. "Structuralist instrumentalists" accept the role of human actors in history but conceptualize their significance in terms of rational, instrumental action and utility maximizing—human actors have agency but are assumed to be motivated entirely by instrumental gain. Finally, "structuralist constructionists" take most seriously the causal role of human identity, cultural expressions, and normative commitments in historical change.[7] Yet even this last model, Emirbayer and Goodwin believe, falls short of adequately comprehending the complexities of the relationships among agency, culture, and social structure.[8] I find these distinctions to be adequate for thinking about models of the human person in network structuralism and feel no need to improve upon them for present purposes. It is clear, as we will soon see, that some structuralists make no place for human persons as significant in social life. Indeed, some relationalists are explicitly out to "kill the person." Others clearly assume the importance of human actors in generating action but take for granted the rational, instrumentalist, self-interested model of rational choice, modifying it only by fitting them into the relationalist agenda. Still others take a much more irenic stance toward alternative explanatory paradigms, viewing network structuralism as one among many

6. Emirbayer and Goodwin, "Network Analysis, Culture, and the Problem of Agency," 1411–54.

7. Naomi Rosenthal and colleagues and the early work of Harrison White and collaborators are offered as examples of the first model; work by Roger Gould and Peter Bearman are said to illustrate the second model; and studies by Doug McAdam, John Padgett, and Christopher Ansell are provided as exemplars of the third approach.

8. Network sociologist James Moody (personal correspondence, August 23, 2007) has suggested a different categorization of structuralist positions on the issue of assumptions about actors, including "relational absolutists," "network universalists," "network constructivists," "network realists," and scholars who view networks as mere conduits of other social processes. These comprise a range of views, believing, on the one extreme, that relations entirely constitute persons ontologically, to the other extreme, which thinks that networks are only one among many important factors shaping social experience.

valid and complementary analytical strategies that makes room for openness to more complex models of persons—even if those models are not
explicitly developed. I count certain works of David Knoke and the early
Ronald Burt, for example, among these more open structuralists.[9]

I wish to focus later in this chapter on specific cases of the first type
of network structuralists, for whom any commonsense notion of the human person and action is most problematic. I have already written elsewhere critiquing rational choice assumptions about human motivations
and do not need to repeat myself here.[10] In any case, making headway with
network structuralists on the matter of human motivations will require
first settling some other, more basic matters about personhood. So for
now I set aside the debate about instrumentalist, self-interested, utility-
maximizing models of motivation, having already registered my dissent.
The third, most irenic approach in network structuralism I find generally
nonproblematic from the viewpoint of critical realist personalism. The
doors for ongoing debate are open there. A perfect fit there may not be,
but the multiple points of contact and an amicable posture make possible
opportunities for convergence. It is the first type of network structuralism—what we might term *antihumanist structuralism*—that critical realist
personalism opposes. What follows is an attempt to explain why this is the
case.

9. David Knoke, for instance, writes reasonably that normative and rational choice sociology "would benefit enormously from incorporating principles of the structuralist perspective
advocated in this book. The[se] dominant paradigms need not be rejected in toto, but their
theoretical maturation requires them to be embedded in contexts constituted of social relations among actors. Thus a sophisticated understanding of political action requires blending
cultural, rational, and structural constraints in complex specifications for given substantive
problems. The structural perspective should be seen as an enriching, rather than a competing,
paradigm." Knoke, *Political Networks: The Structural Perspective* (Cambridge: Cambridge
University Press, 1990), 19. Ronald Burt writes, irenically rather than imperialistically, that
"my purpose in this book is to develop a perspective that circumvents the schism between
atomistic and normative action. My argument [provides] . . . a third view intellectually bridging the two views." Burt, *Toward a Structural Theory of Action: Network Models, Perception,
and Action* (New York: Academic Press, 1982), 8. At the same time Burt seems to assume a
utility maximizing rational choice instrumentalism as his background model of motivation
(174). Also see Neil Smelser, "Social Structure," in *Handbook of Sociology* (Newbury Park,
CA: Sage, 1988), 103–29, esp. 119–20, which also assumes that human actors matter within a
network structuralist perspective.

10. Christian Smith, *Moral, Believing Animals: Human Personhood and Culture* (New
York: Oxford University Press, 2003).

Initial Theoretical Responses

It is a good structuralist principle that the character of any given part of a whole is likely to be significantly shaped by that which it opposes and is opposed by, those other parts with which it has negatively charged ties. This is certainly true of network structuralism itself, for better and worse. Much that is good in network structuralism, in my view, comes from it having smartly identified real problems in (at least certain versions of) prior social science approaches and paradigms against which it reacted. At the same time, certain theoretical positions of some network structuralists are problematic—either because they originally mischaracterized something about or reacted too strongly against the problematic approaches they rejected, swinging too far to an opposite and sometimes also problematic extreme. This is complicated by what (I think is) the fact that network structuralism has long "selected on" some of the brightest, most quirky, nonconformist minds in the discipline. To be a network structuralist was for a long time to be a dissident, an innovator, a recusant. Besides the smarts to figure out something really new and alternative, being a network structuralist took a lot of intellectual self-confidence and disdain for the normal. Harrison White reflects this when he writes that common sense is "chockablock with misleading notions. In social science the only sanity is to eschew sanity, common sanity. To be sane is by definition not to penetrate the common-sense that conceals the inner mechanisms of social reality. . . . To be sane is to question . . . only those rhetorics no longer in fashion."[11] White's book, *Identity and Control*, as a whole conveys a clear sense of such a readiness to dismiss common sense, normal science, and the apparentness of reality. This style has its potential advantages. But it also risks imperviousness to aspects of reality that happen to be plain and commonsensical. While some recent network theorists have expressed more realistic approaches,[12] I still believe the issues raised below are worth addressing.

11. Harrison White, *Identity and Control: A Structural Theory of Social Action* (Princeton, NJ: Princeton University Press, 1992), 21.

12. For instance, David Smilde, "A Qualitative Comparative Analysis of Conversion to Venezuelan Evangelicalism: How Networks Matter," *American Journal of Sociology* 111, no. 3 (2005): 757–96; Ann Mische, *Partisan Publics: Communication and Contention across Brazilian Youth Activist Networks* (Princeton, NJ: Princeton University Press, 2009); Paul McLean and Julia Adams, *The Art of the Network: Strategic Interaction and Patronage in Renaissance Florence* (Durham, NC: Duke University Press, 2007); Omar Lizardo, "How Cultural Tastes

In this chapter, I wish to demonstrate my hubris as an outsider by judging some of these clever innovators. There is, again, no way to do justice to the sophistication of their work. I only focus on the theoretical question of persons—the nodes in their networks when the nodes are individual humans.[13] To assess the arguments about persons advanced by specific network structuralists, it will help to first lay out some general positions that critical realist personalism stipulates, which will be relevant for the discussion that follows. Much of this continues themes that have been developed in previous chapters. Some is sharpened up to address concerns particular to the issue of personhood in network structuralism. Much of network structuralism can be compatible and resonant with critical realist personalism. On the particular issue of the nature of human persons, however, things get trickier. To see how and why, it is helpful to grasp the following general points.

The Either/Or Substance-Relations Dualism Is a False and Misleading Dichotomy

Many network structuralist publications that seek to open up readers to its larger perspective begin by setting up an opposition between substances and relations.[14] On the one side are placed essences, substances, discrete entities, fixed attributes, "static things," pregiven units, inert materials, and so on. These are said to be nonexistent or bad analytical starting points. On the other side are placed formal relations, network ties, resource flows, complex joint activities, patterned relationships, and information exchanges. These are said to be real and good analytical starting points. These lists of opposites are not simply distinguished from each other. They are typically opposed as conflicting, mutually exclusive, either/or alternatives.

Shape Personal Networks," *American Sociological Review* 71 (2006): 778–807; Steve Vaisey and Omar Lizardo, "Can Cultural Worldviews Influence Network Composition?" *Social Forces* (forthcoming).

   13. Network structuralism does not assume that nodes are always persons; they may instead be families, organizations, nations, or other kinds of actors.

   14. See, for instance, Barry Wellman, "Structural Analysis: From Method and Metaphor to Theory and Substance," in *Social Structure: A Network Approach*, ed. Wellman and Berkowitz; Mustafa Emirbayer, "Manifesto for a Relational Sociology," *American Journal of Sociology* 103, no. 2 (1997): 281–317; Bruce Mayhew, "Structuralism versus Individualism: Part I, Shadowboxing in the Dark," *Social Forces* 59, no. 2 (1980): 335–75; Mayhew, "Structuralism versus Individualism: Part II, Ideology and Other Obfuscations," *Social Forces* 59, no. 3 (1981): 627–48.

Mustafa Emirbayer, for example, explains sociology's "fundamental dilemma" by stating that "the key question confronting sociologists in the
present day is . . . the choice between substantialism and relationalism."
And the options in this choice, he says, are "fundamentally opposed."[15] It
is either one or the other.

But this is wrong. In fact, it is impossible. One might understand why
network structuralists have felt the need rhetorically to highlight the difference between substances and relations. But that does not make the
either/or dichotomy valid or necessary. Substances and relations are in
reality mutually implicated and dependent. There cannot be substantial
relations without substances to be related, just as in our universe most
substances depend on relations for their existence. Network structuralism
formally recognizes this in requiring that relational ties connect nodes.
But they usually emphasize the structure of formal ties, not the characteristics of the nodes. The latter are typically considered shaped or determined by the former, which is one perfectly legitimate analytical strategy
of choice. But nothing in this says that the substantial nature, content, or
attributes of the nodes are irrelevant or that taking them seriously could
not complement relational analysis. To think otherwise is to fail to appreciate the stratified and emergent nature of reality such that entities and
processes at different levels can through emergence be both distinct and
related. The either/or substance-relations dichotomy is reminiscent of the
many nineteenth-century theoretical dichotomies that have plagued sociology from its inception—material versus ideal, structure versus agency,
rational versus emotional, and so on. It may be true that attributes of individual entities cannot (fully) explain outcomes in which they are involved.
But this does not mean that a focus on relations excludes attention to the
character of the entities related. There is no reason sociology could not
take a both/and approach.

Another way to say this is that relational contexts and structures enable
and constrain, but do not create, natural capacities. Consider the humble
analogy of a corn stalk. For it eventually to produce a good ear of corn,
the stalk is absolutely dependent upon environmental conditions, including relational conditions, for success. Our corn stalk needs soil with nu-
trients, water, and sunlight. Without those, the stalk dies. But to produce
a good ear of corn, our stalk also needs to be relationally situated among
other stalks of corn in blocks of adjacent rows. This structure of plant
relationship is what best provides the pollination of all the corn stalks by

15. Emirbayer, "Manifesto for a Relational Sociology," 281, 282, 286.

one another. Lacking this pollination, our one stalk will produce poorly developed ears of corn. Not to mention that a single stalk of corn is much more likely to be broken down by a passing animal or gusty storm compared to when it grows in a field of many corn stalks. But my point here is that, while the soil, rain, sun, and pollen are necessary conditions for the production of an ear of corn, that ear itself is not the creation of those environmental conditions. It is the product of a real object, by the name (if it is sweet corn) of *Zea mays* var. *saccharata*, which possesses its own natural properties and capacities. Those properties and capacities are not *created* by soil, rain, sun, and pollen, but exist emergently by the chemical and biological substances and processes giving rise to them from a lower level of reality. Nevertheless, to realize its natural potential as *Zea mays* var. *saccharata*, our corn stalk is totally and absolutely dependent upon the "resource enablement" of soil, rain, sun, and pollen. Yet, turning that perspective around, we can equally say that for these to produce an ear of corn, they are also totally dependent upon the existence of the natural properties and capacities of *Zea mays* var. *saccharata*. The existence of all of these entities—from the genetics of the corn plant to the provision of rain—is relationally generated by many complex dynamics. But pure relationality cannot and does not create objects. Relations need substances and substances need relations. All that exists and every way it works requires both relations and substance.[16] And all of this applies to people and social networks. It could not, by the sheer nature of reality, be otherwise.

Part of the interest of some network structuralists in discounting or excluding "substantial essences," it is worth noting, relates to a larger movement in academia against "essentialism." From a critical realist perspective, the valid point in antiessentialism is that we are wrong to treat what are really culturally specific, socially constructed meanings and norms as if they were naturally fixed and fundamental characteristics. For an obvious example, assuming that all women are naturally meant to be full-time homemakers responsible for raising children, cooking, cleaning, and volunteering for the PTA is an illegitimately essentialist view of the female sex. Antiessentialism in this case insists that this particular gender norm is not a fixed feature of nature but instead a social construction of certain cultures in particular points of history, which is quite different in

---

16. In this I reject Emirbayer's assertion that "substantialism (in both its self- and interactional forms) and relationalism (or transactionalism) represent fundamentally different points of view on the very nature and constitution of social reality." Ibid., 291. Rather, they must presuppose each other.

other contexts. A great deal of the energy behind academic antiessentialism appears to issue from the moral and political commitments of people
who want to deconstruct certain cultural assumptions about "natural"
gender and sexual roles. An antiessentialism that distinguishes the culturally constructed from the naturally fixed is valid and important. But
that is a far cry from denying the existence and explanatory relevance
of natural entities with essential natures and characteristic capacities,
when and where they do exist. Valid antiessentialism is sociological insight and historical consciousness. But many in academia today—significantly influenced by problematic versions of social constructionism—are
running rampant with indiscriminate antiessentialism applied as blanket
metaphysical pronouncements that are not particularly well considered
or defensible. And this, I think, has influenced at least some network
structuralists in unhelpful ways.

The point for now is: we can make as much as possible of the explanatory power of relational analysis without having to ignore the possibility
that the substantial nature of the related nodes also matters[17]—even while
recognizing that they are also at least partly shaped by positions in relational networks in prior points of time. Not all entities are "static." Not all
attributes are fixed. Not all realities are essential. We need not be forced
by a false dichotomy into a choice between two dimensions of the real that
often are both important.

Emergence Always Requires Interacting Entities with Real Properties and Capacities

This is closely related to the previous point. A potential key commonality
between network structuralism and critical realist personalism, I have
said, is their possible shared belief in and emphasis on emergence and
emergent properties. Numerous network structuralist theorists highlight
the importance of emergence in social life. Yet some tension is evident
between their recognition of emergence and their larger agenda of focusing on structures of relations and not properties of entities. In some
cases, this is merely a matter of emphasis and attention. In other cases,
related to antiessentialist impulses, network structuralists seem actively to
deny the causal capacities of the entities that as nodes are linked by structural ties. But emergence cannot and does not occur without real entities
at a lower level possessing definite properties and capacities from which

17. See Watts, "The 'New' Science of Networks," 243–70.

through their interaction emergent properties arise. Water exists at an emergent level because hydrogen and oxygen exist at a lower level of reality. And water does not bring into existence the properties and capacities of hydrogen and oxygen. Hurricanes exist at an emergent level because moisture and heat and air exist at a lower level of reality. Hurricanes then exert tremendous causal force on the elements that give rise to them, but they could not emerge absent the preexistence of those lower-level elements and the particular substantial properties and capacities that interact to generate hurricanes. The point is that in human social life structures of social relations emerge as sui generis facts at a higher, social level of reality with the capacity to causally act back upon the lower levels. But their emergence always requires the existence of objects, including persons sometimes, at a lower level, which are endowed with particular kinds of properties and capacities, from which through their interactions the social facts emerge.

Science Must Always Be Fitted to Its Subject of Study, Not Vice Versa

The critical realism, personalism, and phenomenological epistemology that inform the approach of this book are all committed to the principle that the disciplines of science must form themselves to be appropriate to the real nature of their subjects of study, rather than beginning with an a priori notion of what "science" *must* be and then forcing their subject of study to fit that predetermined vision. The purpose of science is to understand and explain reality. To do that well requires devising modes of inquiry that are appropriately fitted to the realities under investigation. The science must be driven at least in part by the subject. One size does not fit all. Critical realist personalism demands that *social* science take seriously the reality of the person. Of course, determining how science should be properly fitted to its subject is not a simple, one-shot achievement. The proper fitting presupposes knowledge about the subject, which requires experience and inquiry to produce. Engagement in the hermeneutical circle of belief, practice, interpretation, reflection, and possible revision of belief is therefore necessary. But this also mitigates against imposing a priori visions of science that are ill-fitted for the subject of inquiry.

Network structuralism is in part a claim about the actual nature of the subject of study and the kind of inquiry needed to properly understand and explain it. I am largely persuaded. But certain network structuralists push beyond such reasonable arguments by bringing to human social life grandiose visions of social science and what it must be able to accomplish that are poorly fitted to and distorting of the actual subject of study. In such cases, scholars who otherwise argue against substantial essences iron- ically turn around and essentialize and reify sociology by insisting that it *is* and *must be* a definite kind of activity. In some such cases, the structuralist obliterates the person—a move critical realist personalism cannot accept. A key question, therefore, concerns how to distinguish between subject- appropriate and subject-distorting versions of structuralism.

The Motivations of Actors Cannot Be Disregarded

Social science cannot programmatically disregard motivations for action. Actors' motivations are one particular feature of lower-level entities that give rise to social facts. It may well be that in a variety of ways any set of particular motives proves to be inconsequential in explaining an outcome or event. Structuralists are correct that people's motives for action are of- ten unclear, conflicted, and overridden by other forces. But realizing that does not authorize social science to entirely ignore or dissolve away mo- tives. The network structuralist account of human life cannot finally avoid providing some (at least implicit) account of human motives to perform its own analyses. What is evident, however, is that this is a weak point in much structuralism.

Barry Wellman, for example, directly raises the query, "If norms are to be treated as effects [not causes], then how can analysts explain why people behave the way they do?"[18] Good question. Wellman replies by observing four different typical structuralist ways of explaining motives and behavior. Unfortunately, all of these avoid the original question or slip norms back in as explanatory variables. Some structuralists, Wellman ob- serves first, simply eliminate questions about motivations from their con- cerns. A second view admits that norms motivate behavior, but observes that norms are influenced by structural constraints. A third answer is that norms just do not explain behavior as well as structural constraints. And a fourth observes that norms are unevenly distributed in populations and acquired through network ties. This helps very little. The first response refuses to hear and answer the question. The second and fourth are so- ciologically obvious and fully congruent with the normative sociology

18. Wellman, "Structural Analysis: From Method and Metaphor to Theory and Sub- stance," in *Social Structure: A Network Approach*, ed. Wellman and Berkowitz, 34–35.

paradigm that structuralism often denounces. The third answer begs the question of what motivates the behavior that sustains structural constraints that supposedly explain better—which is another version of not answering the question.[19] Wellman and the structuralists he represents, in short, appear to have no answer to the question about motivations for behavior. And I have not found a more satisfactory account elsewhere. I suggest this is because pure structuralism that ignores the nature of the nodes cannot explain motivations for behavior without smuggling back in personal norms and interests.

The Constraining, Enabling, and Motivating of Resources
by Networks Presuppose Certain Needs, Interests, and Capacities
of the Networked Nodes

Let us take a network structuralist explanation on its own terms. Human outcomes and events are explained as functions of the structure of the network ties between actors or nodes. A primary way that occurs is by the network differentially constraining and enabling flows of resources across actors. Those resources need not be material, such as property, products, or wealth. They may also consist of information, emotional support, life opportunities, protection from punishment, or status admiration, all of which are valued and useful. Thus the systemic structure of social ties matters more than the variable traits of individuals in determining consequences.[20]

Let us suppose this is true. What must it presuppose in order to be so? It inevitably presupposes some substantive model of the actors or nodes in the network that assumes what they need, what they want, how they operate, what matters. In the case of human persons as nodes, most network structural analyses must supply at least implicit answers to questions like: Why do people want or need material resources? Why do people

19. Furthermore, the example given to validate this conclusion—drawing on the Milgram shocking experiments—is easily explained from a normative perspective as a case of conflicting norms of obedience to authorities versus care for others, and so says nothing about structural explanations trumping normative ones.

20. Peter Blau, a somewhat different kind of structuralist—who generally focused more on population sizes and interaction rates than networks—for instance, offered this strong promise: "Deterministic theorems about intergroup relations can be derived from purely structural assumptions, without any psychological assumptions." Blau, *Inequality and Heterogeneity* (New York: Free Press, 1977), 7. My point is that Blau has to make psychological assumptions.

demand resources beyond modest subsistence levels? What material resources matter and why? Why is information a resource? What must be
true about people for information to be of value? What kind of raw data
makes valuable information and to which nodes and why? What must be
true about human persons for emotional support to be a resource, and
which persons demand what kinds of emotional support? And what about
status admiration? What is it about people that makes social attention and
esteem a desired good? Why should that be the case? Stated differently,
if the persons as nodes were replaced by, say, tigers, would the structuralist explanation work just as well in particular cases? Of course not. The
explanation works only with specific kinds of actors with particular kinds
of constitutions, needs, interests, purposes, and values. Some of these are
natural—they could not be otherwise and still be human in a way that
would define the relevant resources—and some are culturally variable, at
least in their content. The point, however, is that it is not possible to perform a satisfactory structuralist analysis without presupposing something
about the nodes whose relations are structured, because the explanation
depends on an account of differential flows of resources that are only valued and useful by virtue of the constitutions, needs, interests, values, and
such of the kinds of objects which are the nodes.[21]

Nearly every resource that matters in human networks has some significant cultural meaning that helps to define it as a resource and its relative value. Money, for instance, is a constructed institutional fact, not a
universally self-evident brute fact. It therefore requires a certain kind of
nodal occupant to be involved—one with certain cultural categories, sensibilities, meanings, and experiences of socialization—for money even to

---

21. Joseph Whitmeyer convincingly makes a similar point in his 1994 article "Why Actor
Models Are Integral to Structural Analysis" (*Sociological Theory* 12, no. 2 [1994]: 153–65),
in which he demonstrates that "what social structure itself is depends on what the actor is
(or what the actors are). Thus our conceptualizations and measurements of social structure
depends on our conceptualization or model of the actor(s). This in turn implies that models
of actors are indispensable, indeed inevitable, in any sociological analysis, including structural
analysis. The pure structuralist approach is simply impossible" (153–54). Thomas Gannon
and Elizabeth Freidheim similarly write, "[Bruce] Mayhew's example of dominance in a very
simple structure implies some meanings held by members of each work triad. Since the triads
compete for gain, the research assumed some meanings about gain, goal seeking, cooperation,
and competition. Mayhew's analysis shows the errors that may follow from a stress on meaning
without structure. But neither his arguments nor his example convince us that sociology should
be the study of structure without meaning." Gannon and Freidheim, "'Structuralism' or Structure: A Comment on Mayhew," *Social Forces* 60, no. 3 (1982): 877–82, quote from 880–81.

count as a resource. Try offering $100 to a squirrel and see what happens. Many other resources—from potential mates to job offers to stock market tips to protection from schoolyard bullies—are similarly culturally constituted and appreciated. But the point is not that resources are culturally defined. The larger point is that different kinds of occupants of nodal positions will change the explanatory function and capacity of the structural analysis. So for an analysis to work, the researcher must exercise his or her personal knowledge about the particular nature of the node occupants in question. Assumptions about constitution, psychology, natural needs, potential capacities, limitations, and predispositions must be made even to get started. Some structuralists use the pecking orders among farm chickens to illustrate the logic of structuralist analysis.[22] "Like chickens, like people," Wellman quips.[23] The logic holds interestingly only as long as understood analogically. But one could not replace the people in most structuralist analyses with chickens and still find the same results. Poultry weight gain, for instance, is not a function of friendships and sex matching among siblings. The substantive nature of the nodes matters in order for the explanation to work.

Furthermore, it matters not only whether the nodes are persons or chickens or multinational corporations. For cultural reasons, it matters *what kind of persons* (when it is humans) occupy the nodes. Clearly not all persons are the same in interest and motivational structures. What to one person in a particular community is a valuable resource is to another a matter of indifference or a liability. Positions in relational networks help to define what are considered resources and how much they are valued. Who would question that? But now we have circled back to a general normative sociology that observes that people are socialized by their communities to believe and value different things—people in communities reproduce norms through socialization that sustain communities that perpetuate norms that help to shape outcomes and events. The structural network matters. But

22. White, *Identity and Control: A Structural Theory of Social Action*, 24–25, referring to Ivan Chase, "Social Process and Hierarchy Formation in Small Groups," *American Sociological Review* 45 (1980): 905–24; Chase, "Behavioral Sequences during Dominance Hierarchy Formation in Chickens," *Science* 216 (1982): 439–40; S. M. Richards, "The Concepts of Dominance and Methods of Assessment," *Animal Behavior* 22 (1974): 914–30.

23. Wellman, "Structural Analysis: From Method and Metaphor to Theory and Substance," in *Social Structure: A Network Approach*, ed. Wellman and Berkowitz, 37. The parallel between structuralist chickens and behaviorist pigeons, I think, should be too close for our comfort.

so, simultaneously, do the norms and socialization. And so, too, does the precise nature of the kind of creature that occupies the nodes of the structural network.[24] Pure formalism does not work.

Atomistic, Autonomous, Self-Directed Individualism Is a Dead Rival

Norms cannot be dismissed as causally insignificant, and many network structuralists know that. The position to which many fall back is a denial of the autonomous individual as an atomistic decision-making unit unconstrained by social context. This shifts the focus from normative motivations and interests to the character of norm and interest acquisition and pursuit. That view is right to deny. But it is also a straw man easy to knock down. Many economists may need to be reminded of this message. But few sociologists or other social scientists today actually believe in and employ a model of the person as atomistic and autonomous. Such a critique refers to the old individualist-collectivist debates that animated sociology in the mid-twentieth century.[25] But that debate was supplanted decades ago by more sophisticated approaches.[26] Still, this seems to be a key point of contention for many network structuralist arguments over recent decades. Ronald Burt writes, "An 'atomistic' perspective assumes that alternative actions are evaluated independently by separate actors so that evaluations are made without reference to other actors." Emirbayer tells us, "Relational theorists reject the notion that one can posit discrete, pre-given units such as the individual . . . as the ultimate starting points of sociological analysis." And Wellman and Berkowitz claim that normative sociology wrongly "treats persons as automata, moving like compass needles, in response to internalized norms."[27] The point may be rhetorically

24. See Joseph Whitmeyer, "Social Structure and the Actor," *Social Psychology Quarterly* 3 (1994): 177–89.

25. See W. W. Sharrock, "Individual and Society," in *Classic Disputes in Sociology*, ed. R. J. Anderson, J. A. Hughes, and W. W. Sharrock (London: Allen and Unwin, 1987), 126–56; Alan Dawe, "Theories of Social Action," in *A History of Sociological Analysis*, ed. Tom Bottomore and Robert Nisbet (New York: Basic Books, 1978), 362–417; Rajeev Bhargava, "Holism and Individualism in History and Social Science," in *Routledge Encyclopedia of Philosophy*, ed. Edward Craig (New York: Routledge, 1998), 482–88.

26. Provided in different forms by Anthony Giddens, Margaret Archer, and Peter Berger, among others.

27. Burt, *Toward a Structural Theory of Action: Network Models of Social Structure, Perception, and Action*; Emirbayer, "Manifesto for a Relational Sociology," 287; Wellman and

effective. But by now the competition for network structuralism is not atomistic individualism, but much more sophisticated approaches that account coherently for both human agency and structural influence, especially approaches that understand structure as in part culturally constituted. In any case, critical realist personalism emphatically does not model humans as atomistic, autonomous, exclusively self-directing decision makers.

Temporal Change Matters

One of the ways that some network structuralists get away with not attending adequately to the nature of their nodes or with claiming actors to be the purely dependent products of networks is by beginning their analyses with already-established network structures. The structured network is then taken for granted, and its effects on outcomes for its nodes is the point of analysis. Such approaches may take relational dynamics seriously, but they do not take temporal dynamics seriously. Human personal and social life is played out dynamically through time. And network structures themselves are formed and reformed in time. One may take a given relational structure at a particular snapshot point in time and then show how its structure determines outcomes. That is legitimate and can be revealing. But that does not account for how and why that network structure came into existence in the first place. And the more analyses attend to the creation and change of networks, to additions and subtractions of actors to and from bounded networks, the more the analyses have to provide a substantive account of the properties, motivations, and capacities *of* those actors. Locations in prior networks powerfully influence the dynamics of temporal network change. But to see how and why that should happen requires a substantive account of the actors involved in the change, including an account of the continuity that characterizes actors as they move in, out, and within networks.

Stated differently, people choose the networks into which to embed their lives as they unfold. Their choices are influenced by locations in prior networks, but not entirely so. Temporality and structural change create limited but real opportunities for persons to act as agents in the formation of their own personal lives. For example, when an author writes a book,

Berkowitz, "Introduction: Studying Social Structures," in *Social Structure: A Network Approach*, ed. Wellman and Berkowitz, 3.

he or she must decide on an intended audience, which (because no single book can be all things to all people) usually excludes other potential audiences—so that if the book is successful the author has chosen for and against certain "webs of interlocutors"[28] who will matter when it comes to future intellectual exchange, status rewards, and social association. Alternatively, when a teen graduates from high school and starts college far from home, she plays an active role in the formation of her new relational ties at college, which in turn shape her developing identity, lifestyle, and perhaps life prospects—her prior network ties that shape who she is certainly influence which college she attends and how she in turn develops her new network ties at college, but not always directly or completely. As a relationally formed self, she makes significance choices about her new networks. Choosing an audience or a new set of associates in this way is an exercise of agency in the formation and sustaining of important social networks. And here is the key: for such self-formation processes to operate in ways that are not totally random requires that the actors involved possess certain capacities and characteristics that enable them to make such choices and to sustain the continuity of self across network involvements, to bridge themselves as coherent persons between changes in network configurations. Taking time seriously, therefore, forces network structuralists to explain not only how structures powerfully form persons but also how persons actively form structures. And that requires a coherent model of the human person that can both form and sustain networks and be formed and sustained by them. Critical realist personalism provides such a model.

Brave New Structuralist World

As a means to better hammer out what critical realist personalism believes, advocates, and opposes, in the following pages I engage the arguments of four different self-identified structuralist theorists whose claims about the person—whatever the value of their other scholarship may be—are deeply problematic. Three of these, Bruce Mayhew, Harrison White, and Stephan Fuchs, are network structuralists. The last, Donald Black, is not explicitly a network scholar but nevertheless shares a similar larger structuralist outlook and clearly considers himself a relationalist. Engaging

28. See Charles Taylor, *Sources of the Self* (Cambridge, MA: Harvard University Press, 1989), 36.

Black's work will take us one step away from network structuralism, but examining his view of the human person will provide another angle on relationalism that can lead us through critical reflection back to an account of the person that will be most adequate for good network structuralism.[29] I will not be able to survey and evaluate the entire research programs of these scholars, much of which is fascinating and informative. I will focus critically on their structuralist and relationalist arguments most relevant to critical realist personalism.

Bruce Mayhew

Mayhew was an early network theorist, wrote clearly about his theoretical commitments, and explicitly engaged the question of the nature of the person. He also has influenced some network structuralists who followed him, such as Miller McPherson. Mayhew's view of human persons is unambiguously naturalistic, reductionistic, and antihumanistic. Persons are, he states, nothing but biological machines: "Human organisms are . . . information and energy processing machines. . . . The human central nervous system is a biological computer. . . . From the structuralist point of view, differences between the biological computers in grasshoppers and humans is a difference in the structure of nervous systems as empirically determined by biologists." This means, according to Mayhew, that human consciousness is irrelevant to sociological understanding: "Structuralists do not assume that people think, that people are conscious, or have a mind. . . . 'Being conscious' is an electrochemical configuration not unlike the one projected on a television screen. To structuralists, this configuration is a 'stimulation function' of the central nervous system." Consequently, social and psychological experiences and properties that most people take to be important are actually epiphenomenal: "Structuralists do not attribute social or psychological characteristics to individual humans. Rather, structuralists view individual human beings as biological organisms. . . . There are no social characteristics of individuals. . . . For structuralists, psychological phenomena do not exist." The very idea of holding a concept about oneself as a person, therefore, is mere superstition: "People who talk about self-concepts are like people who talk about witches. To the structuralist,

---

29. Black's work continues to influence current sociological analysis and theorizing, as with, for example, Bradley Campbell, "Genocide as Social Control," *Sociological Theory* 27, no. 2 (2009): 150–72.

psychology is contemporary civilization's witchcraft." Sociologists can therefore explain nothing about human life by referencing the intentions and desires of human actors. "Structuralists do not employ subjectivistic concepts such as purposes or goals in their analyses, [these are] vague notions." Mayhew ridicules sociologists who appeal to meanings, values, and desires to explain human behavior, for believing that "people have ghostly properties hidden inside their heads, properties which somehow generate action."[30] The idea that people do things because they want to or have any free will, Mayhew states, is ludicrous. It is the structures of social relations and networks that explain human social life. "Social phenomena are derivatives of social networks," he asserts, "and not individual actions." Mayhew thus quotes Jean Piaget approvingly: "Everything happens at the population level, so that the individual is nothing but a passive reflection . . . of processes which are quite independent of him."[31]

This view of the person is not an arbitrary intellectual oddity but the outcome of a set of particular presuppositions about reality and science. Because those presuppositions—naturalism, positivism, empiricism, materialism, antirealism, and reductionism—are wrong, the resulting view of the person is erroneous and, I think, dangerous. Mayhew's approach to reality and social science comes in a package that is diametrically opposed to the perspective I advance in this book. For starters, Mayhew is a naturalist and a positivist:

> I am an advocate of "hard" structuralism. . . . "Hard" structuralism rests upon the assumptions of *Naturwissenschaft* (natural science) . . . [which] takes human society—human social organization—to be a natural phenomenon, to be studied in exactly the same fashion as any natural science studies any natural phenomenon. [This] offers the possibility of constructing a science of society.[32]

30. Here Mayhew reverses the traditional skeptic's doubts. Skeptics like Hume were skeptical about sense perception, not introspection—on the latter they thought we have privileged access to the contents of our minds. It is the external world, rather, that is not directly accessible and so needs justification. Mayhew, by contrast, is skeptical about introspection but not sense perception. But his view of direct observation is naive. And if the reliability of introspection is zero, then how does Mayhew know what he believes. Thanks to Chris Eberle for pointing this out (personal correspondence).

31. Mayhew, "Structuralism versus Individualism: Part I, Shadowboxing in the Dark," 335–75; quotes in this paragraph are from 346–47, 348, 353, 357, 338.

32. Quotes from this paragraph come from Bruce Mayhew, "Structuralism and Ontology," *Social Science Quarterly* 63, no. 4 (1982): 636–37; Mayhew, "Structuralism versus Individu-

Nothing about human persons therefore requires a social science particularly suited to their study. Humans are no different from the rest of nature—they are nothing but material entities whose neural systems process energy and information. This makes a naturalistic social science possible, since every science only "studies a material world. This material world is without meaning (in the sense of purpose). This material world takes on only those meanings . . . the theorist-researcher assigns to it." Furthermore, positivist sociology seeks to establish covering laws of social life: "*Naturwissenschaft* generally operates under the covering law view of knowledge . . . [in which things] are explained by being deduced from general propositions. . . . Humans [are] one species among others. Humans are subject to the laws of nature." Thus, Mayhew observes, "Naturalists believe that a scientific, nomothetic explanation of social life can be developed." As a good positivist, Mayhew defines the prediction of events as the sole criterion of success in social science: "The only thing which concerns structuralists is a theory . . . which has maximum predictive power." Scientific knowledge must also be governed by the drive for parsimony: "Parsimony is critical to the development of any theory about social phenomena" and so nonstructuralist explanations are to be rejected because they "are less parsimonious and have low explanatory power."

Mayhew's naturalistic positivism goes hand in hand with an absolute empiricism that denies the existence of anything not directly observable. By this empiricist means, Mayhew eliminates human rationality, arguing that "the assumption of rationality does not derive from observation of what humans do. No amount of observation would show that they behave rationally."[33] Again, Mayhew maintains,

> No one has ever observed humans engaging in rationally calculated actions. . . .
> *By introspection*, certain individualist sociologists have convinced themselves
> that purposes, goals, rationality, and logic are a part of the explanation (or perhaps
> all of it) for what humans do. But they have never produced a shred of
> evidence that this is so. . . . As a method of data analysis, introspection has a
> known validity of zero [and] . . . a known reliability of zero.

---

alism: Part II, Ideology and Other Obfuscations," 629, 640; Mayhew, "Structuralism versus Individualism: Part I, Shadowboxing in the Dark," 362.

33. Quotes from the paragraph come from Mayhew, "Structuralism versus Individualism: Part II, Ideology and Other Obfuscations," 634–35, 636–37; Mayhew, "Structuralism and Ontology," 637–38.

Mayhew's empiricism, directly descended from Hume, also focuses attention not on causal mechanisms operating in reality but on events and processes as the bases of stable structures. Natural social science, he says, "studies the forms or structures which emerge in human populations and the events which stabilize or transform those structures. Like natural science generally, hard structuralism does not study 'objects' but structures and processes."

Such an empiricist epistemology forces Mayhew into an antirealism that denies the relevance of ontology. Having abandoned realism, Mayhew adopts a conventionalist doctrine of knowledge, common to positivists, that denies that knowledge is formed by reality and asserts instead that knowledge is constructed by the agreement of scientists. Reality is thus the provisional construct of science: "Questions of ontology are irrelevant to the sciences—including the social sciences. Because scientific inquiry moves from one *provisional reality* to another, questions of 'ontology' are meaningless."[34] Ironically, but inevitably, this antirealist position bunks the materialist Mayhew between the sheets of the antiessentialist bed with the strange bedfellows of idealist social constructionists. About this he is quite explicit:

> An essentialist is a theorist who believes he is studying essences, that certain things are real and out there to be studied. An analyst is a theorist who does not make such an assumption. Analysts select those aspects of the phenomena they find interesting and *themselves define* what they are studying. The analyst does not assume that he is studying essences or that he knows what social reality is.[35]

Sounding as much like the radical idealist constructionists Kenneth Gergen and Nelson Goodman, Mayhew expounds his empiricist-positivist-conventionalist version of scientific constructionism:

> The solar system is a constructed reality. . . . None of us has ever seen a solar system, a galaxy, or even an atom. All are constructed "realities." Some day we may decide that these "realities" are not as useful as others, so [they] will cease to be "real." There are no "facts" at all apart from those constructed in the research process. The only "matters of fact" relevant to scientific inquiry are

---

34. Mayhew, "Structuralism and Ontology," 634, emphasis in original.

35. Mayhew, "Structuralism versus Individualism: Part I, Shadowboxing in the Dark," 633, emphasis in original.

those pertaining to the agreement or *lack of agreement* among persons participating in the enterprise.[36]

In all of this, Mayhew—his eyes seemingly ever on Comte and Carnap—
continues to appeal to the epistemological gold standard of empirical veri-
fication. He claims, for instance, that "essentialism adds nothing to our
ability to explain or understand social life, but requires assumptions that
cannot be verified."[37] However, the self-confident Mayhew never seems
to realize that all of his own presuppositions are also empirically unverifi-
able. He could never derive or justify his own position from his own position—if what he believed were true, he could not believe it. Furthermore,
Mayhew's positivist empiricism completely flattens the real into the one
dimension of the observable. He therefore is blind to the stratification
and complexity of reality. The social world appears to Mayhew to be quite
simple. "I have not seen any evidence," he flatly confesses, "that social
reality is complex."[38] As a result, Mayhew remains fundamentally in the
dark about the nature of emergence, a concept to which he refers often
though uses wrongly. He argues, for instance, that "an emergent property
is one defined on the overall connectivity of the network, and is not, therefore, derived from characteristics of individual population elements." In
fact, emergent properties always arise out of the relational interactions
of lower-level parts possessing their own real properties and capacities.
Mayhew's denial of the significance of the characteristics of real parts or
actors, however, forces him to explain emergence as arising from relations
alone, out of connectivity per se—as if that were possible. It is like saying
that the sheer relating of nonparticular molecules makes water, regardless
of the actual intrinsic nature of the related molecules themselves. But that
is impossible, a faulty understanding of reality driven by defective presuppositions.

36. Mayhew, "Structuralism and Ontology," 634–35, emphasis in original. Fiona Hibberd
was quite right, therefore, in drawing an intellectual tie connecting idealist social constructionism and positivist conventionalist constructionism, the crucial common ground uniting
their otherwise distinct viewpoints being their shared antirealism. Hibberd, "Gergen's Social
Constructionism, Logical Positivism, and the Continuity of Error, Part 1: Conventionalism,"
Theory and Psychology 11, no. 3 (2001): 297–321.

37. Mayhew, "Structuralism versus Individualism: Part II, Ideology and Other Obfuscations," 634.

38. Mayhew, "Structuralism versus Individualism: Part I, Shadowboxing in the Dark," 630;
the next quote about emergence comes from p. 339.

What is interesting to notice about Mayhew's case, however, when one reads closely, is the fact that he continually assumes and relies on the very characteristics of persons that his argument eliminates in order to persuade us that this elimination is necessary. It is like calling someone on the telephone to tell him that your phone is broken so you can't call him. Mayhew, we have seen, insists that human personal consciousness, mind, psychology, agency, experience, desires, intentions, values, meanings, self-concepts, rationality, purposes, goals, and creativity are analytically irrelevant at best if not illusions in fact. They do not explain outcomes in social life. They are sociologically superfluous. Yet everything about Mayhew's theoretical argument presupposes and depends upon those very same features of personhood to get started. At a most general level, his whole point of writing is to rationally persuade readers of the cognitive merits of his viewpoint. As an innovative agent of intellectual change who is rooted in a particular personal self-concept and identity—"I am a rigorously scientific relational structuralist"—Mayhew relies inescapably on intersubjective intelligibility and cultural meanings to appeal to those whose minds he hopes to change. Presumably his readers are sufficiently free to change their theoretical understandings, if he succeeds—or else what is the point? Furthermore, Mayhew's scholarly program is steeped in a particular set of human values: truth, consistency, intelligibility, intellectual integrity, mental clarity, reasoned persuasion, and scientific progress. Those values are part of what motivate Mayhew's entire project.

Not only that, but throughout nearly all of his published work—despite having repeatedly mocked the idea that people do things "because they want to" or because they hold certain ideas, values, and norms—Mayhew turns around and writes in ways that presuppose the motivational importance of desires, intentions, ideas, and norms. A review of his empirical and theoretical articles, for instance, shows him repeatedly explaining his own intentions, desires, and goals. He writes, for instance, that, "we wish to understand," "we intend to show," "I like to believe," "I will select," "I will try," "we do not wish to enter the debate," "we want to include," "we wish to emphasize," "we do not want to imply," "our [model] is intended to be," "we wish to identify," "I will have to guess," "structuralists are interested in answering," "we wish to arrive," and so on.[39] For someone who

---

39. See ibid., 337, 340, 361; Bruce Mayhew and Paul Schollaert, "Social Morphology of Pareto's Economic Elite," *Social Forces* 59, no. 1 (1980): 25, 28, 38, 41, 96; Mayhew and Roger Levinger, "On the Emergence of Oligarchy in Human Interaction," *American Journal of*

believes that people's desires and purposes are irrelevant, he sure has a lot of them informing and explaining his scholarship. Furthermore, in explicating why it is that so many sociologists fail to see the truth of his insights, Mayhew employs accounts that suggest to us that his own insights cannot explain why such people fail to see their truth. For instance, Mayhew complains that most sociologists "listen in the language of individualism" and have "no shared language . . . to unite them" with structuralists.[40] He says individualistic sociology makes sense to people because it is "telling people what they already believe." It seems that the normative and cohesive force of language and beliefs for people do matter after all. In one article Mayhew talks about ordinary individuals choosing different ways to travel.[41] In another he stresses the importance of scholars exercising judgment in cautiously selecting cases to which the theory is intended to apply.[42] So, human choice and judgments do turn out to be significant. Moreover, Mayhew apparently conceives of persons in a way that enables

---

Sociology 81, no. 5 (1976): 1022, 1024, 1036; Mayhew and William A. Rushing, "Occupational Structure of Community General Hospitals: The Harmonic Series Model," *Social Forces* 51, no. 4 (1973): 455; Mayhew, Roger Levinger, J. Miller McPherson, and Thomas James, "System Size and Structural Differentiation in Formal Organizations: A Baseline Generator for Two Major Theoretical Propositions," *American Sociological Review* 37, no. 5 (1972): 630, 632; Mayhew, Thomas James, and Grant Childers, "System Size and Structural Differentiation in Military Organizations: Testing a Harmonic Series Model of the Division of Labor," *American Journal of Sociology* 77, no. 4 (1972): 750, 764, 765; Mayhew and Louis Gray, "Internal Control Relations in Administrative Hierarchies: A Critique," *Administrative Science Quarterly* 14, no. 1 (1969): 127–30; Mayhew, "Structural Sociology" (book review), *Social Forces* 63, no. 3 (1985): 851; Mayhew and Paul Schollaert, "The Concentration of Wealth," *Sociological Focus* 13, no. 1 (1980): 4, 5; Mayhew, "Hierarchical Differentiation in Imperatively Coordinated Associations," in *Research in the Sociology of Organizations*, vol. 2, ed. S. Bacharach (Greenwich, CT: JAI Press, 1983), 215, 216; Mayhew, J. Miller McPherson, Thomas Rotolo, and Lynn Smith-Lovin, "Sex and Race Homogeneity in Naturally Occurring Groups," *Social Forces* 74, no. 1 (1995): 18, 22, 41, 46 (Mayhew died in 1988—this article, drafted by him, was published postmortem by his coauthors).

40. Mayhew, "Structuralism versus Individualism: Part I, Shadowboxing in the Dark," 337, 339; the following quote comes from p. 352.

41. Mayhew, Miller McPherson, Rotolo, and Smith-Lovin, "Sex and Race Homogeneity in Naturally Occurring Groups," 18.

42. Mayhew, Levinger, Miller McPherson, and James, "System Size and Structural Differentiation in Formal Organizations: A Baseline Generator for Two Major Theoretical Propositions," 632; also see Mayhew, James, and Childers, "System Size and Structural Differentiation in Military Organizations: Testing a Harmonic Series Model of the Division of Labor," 765.

him to speak explicitly about people comprehending, conceiving, being concerned with, trying things, holding views, considering, seeing, aiming to convey, clarifying, offering proof, posing questions, defining problems, hiding, explaining, answering, evaluating, conducting discussions, being training to operate, making clean breaks, wasting time, choosing, being interested in, perpetuating confusion, feeling apprehension, holding "pet" answers, introducing strategies, focusing, developing problems, overcoming biases, insisting, bestowing rewards, concurring, holding opinions, disagreeing, viewing, setting tasks, and making errors. All of these examples come from only one of Mayhew's articles.[43] If his stated theory of social organization and behavior were correct, none of this would make sense. That is because people would not be the kind of entities for which these activities would be applicable, insofar as they involve depths and complexities of mental, emotional, volitional experience and action that Mayhew's theory denies as irrelevant if not nonexistent.

Mayhew's position is even more problematic than this, however. Numerous of his empirical analyses employ concepts that are inescapably culturally meaningful in ways that Mayhew's theory tells us is unimportant. In one article, for example, Mayhew tells us about people's "desire to maintain successful status performances," their "exposure to expenditure expectations," and rejection and acceptance of birth control proscriptions as morally wrong or right. The same article talks about religious people feeling normative pressures from church, holding attitudes toward artificial birth control, and feeling alienated from church teachings. One of Mayhew's important analytical points concerns whether marriage partners were coreligionists or not.[44] Need I point out that things such as status

43. Mayhew, "Structuralism versus Individualism: Part I, Shadowboxing in the Dark," 336–39, 345–46, 350, 352, 355–66, 368. In the companion article, Mayhew speaks of being emancipated from prejudices, offering a solution, deferring communicating ideas, extending a critique, deriving conclusions from assumptions, finding phenomena interesting, defining phenomena, locking into a view of reality, holding religious convictions, controlling life, correcting, concluding, believing, pursuing, noting, venturing, and being satisfied. Mayhew, "Structuralism versus Individualism: Part II, Ideology and Other Obfuscations," 627–30, 633, 636–42, 644. Again, these are activities of the kind of persons that critical realist personalism theorizes but not the kind for which Mayhew can account.

44. Bruce Mayhew, "Behavioral Observability and Compliance with Religious Proscriptions on Birth Control," *Social Forces* 47, no. 1 (1968): 61, 63, 65, 68, 69. Mayhew, Miller McPherson, Rotolo, and Smith-Lovin, "Sex and Race Homogeneity in Naturally Occurring Groups," 15–52 also discusses high and low status positions, which are clearly culturally (cognitively, emotionally, meaningfully) defined conditions (see especially 43–44).

positions, successful performances, expectations about financial expenditures, religious teachings on birth control, feelings of social pressure, attitudes about contraceptives, the institution of marriage, and categories such as coreligionist are not natural kinds that we can take for granted only to focus all of our attention on structural relations among actors? No, these are culturally defined, cognitively meaningful, psychologically embedded, emotionally fraught, normatively charged types, characteristics, and experiences. If we are to take these seriously, as Mayhew's analysis apparently wants to, then we need a very different sort of sociology from the kind Mayhew proposes—one that deals with consciousness, subjectivity, meanings, definitions, norms, and values. In other articles, Mayhew similarly discusses things such as occupational roles, hospitals, clinical specialization, and nurses—all of which, again, are culturally constituted and meaningful categories of the sort that Mayhew's theoretical position explicitly seeks to eliminate.[45]

In short, for someone so determined to eradicate human subjectivity, intention, meaning, and values from sociological analysis, Mayhew displays an awful lot of it in his work. This is not simply because he is inconsistent but because it is impossible to understand and explain human social life without recourse to subjectivity, intention, meaning, and values. So, even while he denies them, he has to smuggle them into his own accounts.[46] What is ironic in all of this is that Mayhew poses himself with great flair as a champion of logical consistency, telling us that "logical coherence is a *sine qua non* of any intellectual enterprise. . . . A theoretical

45. Mayhew and Rushing, "Occupational Structure of Community General Hospitals: The Harmonic Series Model," 455–62; Mayhew, James, and Childers, "System Size and Structural Differentiation in Military Organizations: Testing a Harmonic Series Model of the Division of Labor," 750–65. Whitmeyer makes the same point about Peter Blau's structuralism in his 1994 article, "Why Actor Models Are Integral to Structural Analysis," 153–65. Also see Gannon and Freidheim, "'Structuralism' or Structure: A Comment on Mayhew," 877–82.

46. Mayhew also indulges the rhetorical move of the "False Dichotomy Choice"—"A is not true, therefore *only* Z can be true (when B, C, D . . . W, X, or Y might very well also and otherwise be true)"—that we in chapter 2 observed strong constructionists employing to prop up their plausibility. For instance, he argues that if extreme analytical individualism is incorrect then (extreme) network structuralism must be correct; he also suggests that if all people do not "have the ability to calculate sophisticated probabilities in their all-powerful minds" then it must be the case that people do not act purposively or rationally. The first claims simply do not warrant the second. See Mayhew, "Structuralism versus Individualism: Part I, Shadowboxing in the Dark," 350; Mayhew, "Structuralism versus Individualism: Part II, Ideology and Other Obfuscations," 634.

position which lacks logical coherence is indefensible."[47] Mayhew's problem, however, is not that he is not smart. The problem is that he began his sociology with all the wrong presuppositions, and they forced him, despite his intelligence, into arguments and explanations that are incoherent and implausible.

In the world of contemporary network structuralism, Bruce Mayhew is a lesser-known figure than many others, in part because his untimely death in 1988 put an end to his publishing. One of the best-known network structuralists today, by contrast, is Harrison White. It is to examine his theory of persons that I now turn.

Harrison White

What is White's view of the human person? White's thinking has evolved over the years. His early work might be characterized as taking a structural determinist perspective largely ignoring human actors. His more recent work, however—especially his 1992 book *Identity and Control: A Structural Theory of Social Action*, on which I focus here—develops an approach that more explicitly addresses the nature of persons. White's account of the person begins on the first page and ends on the last. So what, from his network structuralist perspective, does he have to say? For many, it is difficult to know. White's *Identity and Control* is anything but lucid. More than a few reviewers have said the book is incomprehensible and lacking any argument. I will do my best to understand and explain White's account insofar as it is relevant for present purposes.

Here is White's view, as I understand it. Reality consists of physical matter, existing in dynamic relational fields, which conglomerates through relational structures from the most elementary particles up into more complex structures. Reality does not consist of essential entities, ultimately, but of dynamic material relations of chaos and normality, tension and equilibrium, which produces stability amid change. "There is no tiny atom and no embracing world," White says, "only complex striations, long strings reptating as in a polymer goo." Different kinds of actors evolve from this complex, dynamic physical world, and necessarily relate to one another. Actors behave in responses to the unpredictable, contingent material world they inhabit. Their behaviors are determined by biophysical directives and, for some actors, by capacities for contingent responsiveness.

---

47. Mayhew, "Structuralism versus Individualism: Part I, Shadowboxing in the Dark," 629.

The central challenge of all actors is physical survival in the material world. This necessarily produces activity oriented toward control and the formation of identities, by which of the latter White means nondetermined abilities to respond to the world. Ongoing efforts at control leave activity traces, which take the form of social processes and structures. These involve disciplines, relational ties, distinct styles, institutions, and, at the largest scale, they produce network populations. These, in turn, give rise to stories, valuations, signaling, and other stable behaviors that facilitate interaction toward physical survival. The actual features of actors involved, however, are produced by the properties of their social relations, not by any natural, intrinsic characteristics. When network-populations of actors have come together in highly particular configurations comprising certain sets of identities and modes of control, the kind of actors we call "persons" have come into being. Persons are constructed compounds or overlaps of identities—that is, somewhat stable amalgams of contingent responses to the material world that are not entirely determined by their own biophysical regularities. Historically speaking, "persons" are late creations in human history—like certain other evolutionary artifacts, such as pottery—the dependent products of particular, relatively recent social formations. Persons are derivative social constructions of network structures, not preexistent actors interacting to create network structures. Persons have some contingent substance but no real essence. They are locations of responses more than capacitated entities. They are the derivative effects of networked social existence, not the causal agents of it. Therefore, as sociologists if we want to understand the workings of human social life, we need to grant temporal and analytical primacy to structured networks and configurations of interactions, not to the actors who are constituted by them. (If all of this sounds overly abstract and abstruse, all I can say is that the book itself is much more so.)

Having summarized White as best I can, let us now see how White talks about these matters himself. White begins by arguing for the decentering of the human actor in social scientific explanation. "Effective theory of social relations," he claims, "is hindered by assuming that social action comes only from individual biological creatures—humans—as a consequence of their nature and consciousness as persons. This mirage of the person as atom breeds an obverse mirage of society as an entity."[48]

48. The quotes in this and the following two paragraphs are from White, *Identity and Control: A Structural Theory of Social Action*, 3, 4, 6, 8, 22, 23, 24, 167, 197, 212, 205. In his 2008 second edition, White includes new material that briefly addresses the question of the

According to White, the fact that (what he thinks of as) the best social sciences do not prioritize the person[49] provides a clue about the true primacy of social action over personal action: "The difficulty of the construct 'individual as person' is shown by its being shunted aside from the center of activity in each social science. . . . Work of high scientific status tends to shun the 'person' construct as polluting. This . . . suggests that social action is induced before actors, who derive from the action and need not be persons." Such a view, White notes, denies our common idea of the person: "Much of this account will challenge existing theories, and in doing so will deny what we, of the present era, take for granted, namely the construct of person." Elaborating on this point, he writes: "Much theory in social science stipulates persons, takes them as preexisting atoms. In contrast, this book builds toward the conclusion that persons develop only under special social circumstances, which come late historically. Persons should be derived from, rather than being presupposed in, basic social action." Thus, White writes, "the ordinary person, so-called, is a late and sophisticated product from the interplay of larger social formations, of populations."

A particular type of materialism informs White's theory. "In our version of the State of Nature," he says, "material productions must start the scene. Unending interactions with the biophysical environment are the distinctive constraints on action of any species. . . . The exigencies of material need in a physical world underlie much of social organization." Human social life, consistent with this naturalistic materialism, is thus modeled on atoms and molecules:

> A molecule is a spatio-temporal context which captures atoms from and using their own interactions. . . . The atoms are thereby embedded into a new level of action. . . . Let social molecules be called disciplines: They are self-reproducing

---

human person, none of which essentially alters his position described here or my critique of it—indeed, he states that his goal is to build "a foundation for sociology that does not depend upon" the "self," "consciousness," and "thinking"; that "reversion to personalism tends to cripple theory"; and "what is clear is that personalization is a dead end." Harrison White, *Identity and Control: A Structural Theory of Social Action*, 2nd ed. (Princeton, NJ: Princeton University Press, 2008), 334–35.

49. Curiously, this particular point of White's contradicts the basic claim of nearly every relational structuralist, including sometimes White himself, that the social sciences are plagued by pervasive person-centered theories—the means of the reconciling of which are not clear to me.

formations which sustain identities. . . . Social action and spaces are thus spun off from biophysical origins.

Such a model White sees as prioritizing identity over persons: "Social molecules push persons aside as being but a special case. Identity becomes the starting point." But by "identity" White does not intend what most people, including most sociologists, mean. By it he only means nonbiophysical sources of responsive action: "Identity here does not mean the common-sense notion of self, nor does it mean presupposing consciousness and integration or presupposing personality. Rather, identity is any source of action not explicable from biophysical regularities, and to which observers can attribute meaning." Thus the apparently stable ontology of persons is merely the outcome of our species' need for control to survive our physical world: "Who 'we' are is all bound up with what 'control' is in social surroundings, and also depends upon our grounding in material production and the constraints from physical space." And the "identities" created to respond to such a world are what have come together, in certain conditions, to make persons: "A person [is] a compound of identities. . . . Identities are the basis from which persons are constructed. . . . Persons should be a construct from the middle of the analysis, not a given boundary condition."

As with Mayhew above, we see that White builds a particular kind of social constructionism into this theory: "Before general theory in social science can be attained, 'persons' have to be assimilated as being but particular embodiments of a class of socially constructed actors. . . . Persons come to be generated only out of large-scale frictions among distinct network-populations." And the particular kinds of constructions that persons represent are not self-directed agents for whom purposes, rationality, goals, choices, memory, and language are crucial. Those appearances are post hoc stories invented to explain outcomes that are actually driven by other forces. Thus, White writes, "Actors . . . are social constructions in a practical and contemporaneous sense. Goals and preferences, being so changeable, are not causes, but rather they are spun after the fact as part of accounting for what has already happened." Theories of human action assuming rational decision are therefore based on an illusion: "Rational choice builds upon the myth of the person as some preexistent entity." Furthermore, persons are not the necessary basis of communication and remembrance, since persons are much more contingent than social action: "Signaling, memory . . . [and] language . . . need not come packaged as persons, in the current sense today. Such persons come into existence only in a complex stochastic [i.e., nondeterministic] environment. . . . Persons only come into existence . . . through the exigencies of a stochastic environment built on quite other principles than the valuations to which persons, once formed, continue to orient." Furthermore, the actual condition of derivative persons is one of inner fragility and dissonance:

> Persons come into existence not singly but all together, as by-products of and set within an envelope of network-population. . . . A person comes as a hybrid of ties with disciplines, a hybrid held together with stories. Any person is an uneasy balancing of disjunct identities which were triggered independently. A "person" is a continuing balancing act among distinct identities, often very disparate.

As a result, the idea that all humans hold anything substantive or essentially in common is also illusory. White quotes Erving Goffman approvingly, saying, "Universal human nature is not a very human thing."

What are we to make of White's account? If I understand it correctly, it is antihumanistic and is at odds with the critical realist personalism I am advancing in this book. However, further inspection reveals more points of contact than may at first be evident. In my view, White improves greatly on Mayhew in being arguably much less rigid, deterministic, and reductionistic. Mayhew still seems stuck in the classical physics and logical positivism of former eras, while White's view seems to me to better reflect quantum physics and contemporary antifoundationalism. Except that White has gotten particulars about the crucial issue of emergence wrong, there are many parallels between his account and critical realism's in terms of the stratification and relationality of reality. And White, like Mayhew, is correct in criticizing radical analytical individualism. White's insistence that the human parts in relational systems are powerfully influenced by the structure of the social systems, not merely by preexistent intrinsic properties, is not entirely wrong—even if this is no longer an important theoretical debate. His sense of historicity in the development of human capacities and self-understandings over long stretches of time is also completely acceptable. In all of these ways, critical realist personalism finds some affinities in White's theory and benefits from White's pointing to the centrality of relational network structures.

Nevertheless, critical realist personalism parts ways with White, as it did with Mayhew, especially on the issue of emergence, and this difference is of major consequence when it comes to understanding the person. In short, critical realist personalism insists against White that emergence always transpires through the interactions of real lower-level entities preexistently possessing their own properties and causal capacities; and that, once emergence has happened, new entities with their own irreducible properties and capacities have come to exist at a higher level of reality that are capable of acting causally both downward on lower-level and upward on higher-level entities. White is correct that much of reality is composed of parts interacting in relational fields, that humans live in a material world, that human physical survival requires identity and control, and that personhood is contingently dependent on stable social relationships for existence. But this does not mean that persons are ontologically derived from network structures, or that relational structures precede their constituent actors, or that persons do not possess their own essential ontological being. Take seriously the truths of stratification and emergence in reality, and persons immediately become capable of real ontological existence with definable features and capacities that cast them in a very different light from what White's perspective allows—without losing any of the dependency, contingency, or relationality crucial to White's account. Through emergence, persons can exist as the real substantial entities with natural powers and limits, as we experience ourselves to be, without separating ourselves from the rest of nature or adopting an atomistic theory of action.

The weaknesses in White's account are most evident in some of the metaphors he employs. One is his modeling social life on atoms and molecules. This is a potentially helpful image. But White forces the reality here to fit his preferred theoretical perspective rather than taking clues from the reality as to what his perspective ought better to be. Specifically, White skirts the fact that molecules do not create atoms. Molecules actually depend on atoms as more elementary entities to be what they are. True, no single atom can create a molecule. But that does not mean molecules make atoms. White never explicitly says they do—he uses the more ambiguous phrase that a molecule "captures" atoms. But he certainly says that relational social life creates persons, and he definitely models human social life on atoms and molecules. What we think we know about atoms and molecules tells us, if the two parallel, that relational social life does not make persons in any ontologically significant sense, even if it nurtures persons in a developmental sense. In other words, emergence does not create the parts that give rise to emergence—even if emergent properties may subsequently influence their parts—but depends upon them.

White is much less explicit than Mayhew about his underlying philosophy of social science. He does not spell it out in so many words. Still, White's writings make it clear enough that he shares with Mayhew a commitment to naturalism, materialism, antihumanism, and a Durkheimian version of social constructionism. His failure to accurately grasp the reality of emergence also undercuts any chance of embracing the kind of realism that science needs. Perhaps consequently, White's *Identity and Control* often seems to flirt with macrostructural strains of postmodernism—one senses that White has been too influenced by Foucault. Even so, White appears more solid than Mayhew on the issues of empiricism and positivism—he is simply not obsessed with direct observation, covering laws, parsimonious explanation, and the like.

Stephan Fuchs

Let us begin, as with others, by examining Fuchs's account of persons— which he spells out in his 2001 book *Against Essentialism: A Theory of Culture and Society*[50]—and then work backward to see how and why he came to such beliefs. Fuchs, like many other relational structuralists, begins by discounting the commonsensical view of persons as real entities possessing causal powers. "Common sense is essentialist," he says, "since it . . . validates persons, agency, mental states, free will, and the rest of the humanist and liberal inventory." This view, Fuchs says, inevitably hampers social science: "An obstacle to sociological advances, it seems to me, is obsession with persons and personhood, with belief, plans, goals, and intentions. . . . I am skeptical about agency, mental states, and intentions as explanations for society and culture." Fuchs instead recommends decentering the person: "A sociological science might get off to a better start without the dogma that it is persons who do, say, or mean something. We will see what happens when persons appear as outcomes of society, rather than its sources, building blocks, or rational designers. Society does not 'consist' of persons." Fuchs's strategy is to prioritize relational networks and make persons the dependent constructed products of such relations. "Network theories start with social emergence," Fuchs states, "and explain persons and actors as *constructs* that some social structures produce

50. Stephan Fuchs, *Against Essentialism: A Theory of Culture and Society* (Cambridge, MA: Harvard University Press). Quotes in the following paragraph come from 3, 5, 6, 9, 11, 16, 21, 63–64, 65, 107, 122, 125, 193, 262, emphases are in the original.

to do certain kinds of cultural work. This move turns persons into dependent variables and outcomes, not sources or origins, of society. . . . 'Person' is a variable construct of variable observers, not a natural kind, essence, or constant, and not an origin or source of all things social." Fuchs repeats this approach throughout his book, insisting that "persons and individuals are not essences and natural kinds . . . but result from relations and constructions."[51]

A series of important consequences follow. First, social networks are not explained as the result of their interacting nodes—rather, nodes are the creation of networks: "The 'master' concept is networks. . . . First come networks, then nodes. Nodes are the specific 'formats' or 'versions' that the network constructs of them—they are acquired 'identities' in the process of getting tenured in a certain network position." Again, Fuchs writes, "Relationalism in network theory treats nodes in the network as fully derivative from their connectivity. What a node is and what it does do not follow from any intrinsic properties or categorical characteristics, but from its location, position, and temporality in the network." Fuchs, in other words, views systems as causally creating their constituent elements: "A scholar is a library's way of producing more books, much as an organism is a genome's way of producing more genes. Persons do not know what they want, how to get it, and where to get it cheapest." So, in this push back against rational choice theory, persons are clearly not the causal agents of social life. A second consequence of Fuchs's theory is that the existence of persons at any point in time is fully contingent upon structures of relationships beyond persons: "Society does not consist of persons, but it can construct and observe 'personhood' in various ways, depending on time, context, and locale." Again, "the person is alive, at least in some contexts, and on some occasions. The identity of 'Harrison White' would be very upset if credit for [his theory of] 'structural equivalence' went to another person, though structural equivalence precisely destroys persons qua persons." Third, the consciousness, mental activity, and decisions that appear to go on "inside" persons are also the products of relational networks: "Mental states, natural personhood, decisions, utility. These are not natural or primordial givens, but improbable accomplishments

51. He says, "The elements are not essential building blocks . . . but sets or spaces of possibilities that are gradually narrowed down as they become embedded in patterns of interaction between elements and forces. Change the interactions and forces, and you change the elements as well" (ibid., 48).

of social structure." They therefore, fourth, cannot and do not motivate behavior—which is driven by structural forces—but merely justify it after the fact: "Personhood is [not] a ready-made unity of self-conscious beliefs and wants. Rather, some persons . . . use 'rationality' and 'decision' to make sense of what they do. Decisions are not simply acts occurring in the world, but attributions to agency, to halt causal regression." Again, fifth, Fuchs says, reasons are structurally provided, post hoc explanations: "Reasons are properties of cultures, not persons. They are standard accounts acceptable and available in a culture for making sense." Even the idea of the person is a construction invented by systems to explain events: "As a construct, 'person' is employed by some social observers, but not others, as a device for making sense and for explanations." Furthermore, even if people's reasons did cause actions, there is no way to access their minds empirically in order to relate them to explanations: "An observer cannot participate in the internal mental operations of a single person, let alone billions of them. Intimacy does not alter this fact. . . . We have no idea what goes on inside other people's minds." So reasons are explanatorily irrelevant. The sixth consequence is that the line between personal and nonpersonal objects is erased: "It does not matter whether the system is a person or a thing, since 'personhood' and 'thingness' are the outcomes, not causes, of observations, attributions, and cultural work." Fuchs is fully intentional and honest about the antihumanism inherent to his theory: "The most important commonality in systems and network theories [that I employ is] antihumanism—bidding farewell to the agency framework and its derivatives, such as intentionality, the unit act, and rational choice. These instead turn into variable attributions or outcomes of social structure. This means dropping 'person,' 'individual,' and 'actor' as foundational constructs."[52]

This is a provocative theory. It is also impossible. What leads Fuchs to want to promote it? The answer, as with Mayhew above, is a particular package of presuppositions about reality and science that inevitably

52. Fuchs's arguments about persons quoted here in the text are only some drawn from his more extended discussion, which also includes these: "Personhood is an acquired characteristic, not a constant truth about human nature. It has a history; it varies. Persons and minds are social and cultural institutions"; systems and network theories "overcome humanism and agency metaphysics in a strong move toward relationalism. 'Persons' are not the source or origin of society; rather, they are outcomes of some social networks, but not others"; and "'wants' and 'beliefs' are not internal states or attributes of personal minds, but result from observations and self-observations." Ibid., 6, 8, 124.

lead to this antipersonalistic structural antihumanism. Fuchs, being more
theoretically than empirically oriented, is entirely explicit about his basic assumptions—more so than either Mayhew or White.[53] Fuchs begins
with a strong declared belief in antiessentialism (as his title makes clear),
antirealism,[54] positivism (of a nonfoundationalist variety),[55] empiricism,
social constructionism (Durkheimian, not Kantian), reductionism,[56] and
pragmatism (Dewey and Rorty).[57] His entire project is to reconstruct
social science appropriate for a world he takes to be devoid of essential
substances, stable realities with their own causal powers, and individual
personal agents. This leads him to attribute causal powers that determine
any events or outcomes entirely to relations among positions, not at all
to, say, the normative purposes or material goals of the nodes occupying positions. In fact, any "substances" that appear to exist to observers
are explained as the mere constructions of the observers themselves. And

53. In the interest of space and flow, I will avoid extensive quotations demonstrating these
beliefs in the main text, but see especially ibid., 1–8, 12–110, 293–97.

54. Regarding realism, Fuchs's primary strategy (following Nietzsche and Rorty) is simply
to disregard all issues of metaphysical truth as quasi-problems that hinder social science and
instead turn them into variable constructs to be explained sociologically (ibid., 4–5, 71–110).
He calls this "sociologizing with a hammer," in which metaphysical puzzles "are not solved,
but dis-solved, or hammered apart. Allowing for variation converts philosophical constants
into dependent variables that covary with social structure" (8). His response to the realist
question, in short, is simply to change the question. Still, he writes in a more ontological mode
that "entities . . . are [only] pragmatic devices and summaries to account for observations, not
actual realities" (16), and that "an observation does not 'reveal' the world; rather, it becomes
part of it if, and only if, it is made. An observation does not 'disclose' the world, but adds itself
to the world" (23).

55. "Positivism culminat[es] . . . in the principle that there is nothing nonempirical or
transcendental. There is nothing absolute, universal, or foundational. Better, any universality,
including truth, is one variable degree or range. . . . In positivism, there are no natural kinds,
true essences, or final causes. Whatever exists does so not because of its inherent nature or
intrinsic properties, but because of variable relations and forces" (ibid., 69–70).

56. "One should try to reduce something to something else if this yields more powerful and simpler explanations and if the reduction can do all of the work on the level being
reduced" (ibid., 199), although Fuchs is more circumspect than most reductionists about science's current ability to use reduction effectively (199–200). Nonetheless, he writes, "Scientists
are eminently 'deconstructionist.' . . . [Science] proceeds by decomposing essences into relations between elements that are what they are only in their variable relationships" (48).

57. "Pragmatism is opposed to epistemology as such. . . . Truth is whatever 'works.' But
the pragmatic 'working' is the working of a network. . . . Truth happens in the network, not
in the world at large, although the network is part of the world as well. Truth is the internal
accomplishment of such a network, not external correspondence" (68–69).

the very act of observing creates more relational networks that generate more action. All apparent entities are viewed not as having real being but entirely as variables to be explained by network forces and relations. "There are no constants, only variables. . . . Once natural kinds are gone, everything is a matter of degree, not principle."[58] In such a world, real entities are illusions, real persons are dissolved, and real knowledge about things as they are is conventional and relative. Antipersonalism and anti-humanism are the natural outcomes of such a presupposed worldview.

Do we have good reason to accept Fuchs's account? I think not. For one thing, his theory of the relation of parts to systems is unconvincing. It is clear in this that he fundamentally misunderstands the reality and process of emergence, although he uses the term repeatedly. Fuchs has merely as-serted, but not at all shown how it could be, that nodes are the creations of networks. It is one thing to recognize that nodes are partially constituted, powerfully influenced, and often transformed by the networks in which they are embedded. It is something else altogether to suggest that networks actually construct or produce their own nodes. That is like saying that the cotton candy on the stick you are eating at the ballpark created the sugar crystals out of which it was made. Fuchs's claim is rhetorical hyperbole. Yet he is determined to assert it. The reason is that, for Fuchs to admit a proper account of emergence, his entire antiessentialist framework would start to come unglued, and he would have to retract many other claims. I have already critiqued Fuchs's kind of explanation in my discussion of White, so will not repeat that here. Suffice it to note that Fuchs falls into the same basic errors as White by misconstruing emergence and hence being similarly forced to make claims that are unsustainable.

Fuchs's theory suffers from another fatal problem, related to the dissolv-ing of nodes as substantial objects. Fuchs puts a lot of explanatory weight on culture, meaning, interpretation, explaining, and the making sense of things. The problem is that the logic of his theory contains, so to speak, a "verb" and an "object" but no "subject." The subject as agent has been eliminated as just another outcome variable. We are left conceptually with trying to make sense of a theory whose logical structure produces proposi-tions like, "the behavior was interpreted" or "the situation made sense." But interpreted or made sense to *whom*? And *why*? Why in a purely material world in which mental events are causally insignificant illusions does any-thing even need to make sense or be interpreted? Sense and interpretation

58. Ibid., 50.

have to do with meanings, with significance. But Fuchs's account has already banished those into irrelevance. At first it appears that Fuchs might have an explanation, to be found if one digs hard enough. But the shovel never hits the treasure chest. It is sand all the way down. "Observers," those who interpret and explain, turn out to be not meaning-oriented agents but networks—and very broad kinds of networks at that:

> This network is the observer. An observer is anything equipped to apply distinctions to the world. . . . "Observers" include bacteria, immune systems, frogs, lovers, and physics. An observer is not an "entity," much less a "person," but a network of related distinctions. It is this network that "observes."[59]

But how, one wonders, can a "network of related distinctions" be the kind of observer for which meanings are important? Are interpretations that make sense of significant connotations really the sort of things that are relevant to bacteria and frogs? No, meanings and sense making of the kind that require interpretation are activities relevant to sentient actors, especially to human persons of the sort I have described. Here we have, on the one hand, a highly abstract notion of observation and meaning that may work at a conceptual level internally to Fuchs's theoretical system. But—as the proliferation of quotation marks that relativize the normal meanings of the terms "observers," "entity," and "person" in the quote above suggests—this hardly explains why reality as he conceives it needs interpretation or making sense. On the other hand, if Fuchs were to dump culture, meaning, sense-making explanation, and related concepts from his theory, he would eviscerate his overall story and end up sounding a lot more like Mayhew. His is, after all, a theory of *culture* and not merely society. And so in the end we are left with interpretations without real interpreters, sense without actual sentient agents, meaning without meaning-makers and meaning-driven actors. It doesn't work.[60] Fuchs needs

59. Ibid., 18–19.
60. But to help to try to make it work, Fuchs also relies on the kind of "False Dichotomy Choice" rhetorical moves—"A is not true, therefore *only* Z can be true (when B, C, D . . . W, X, or Y might very well also and otherwise be true)"—that we have detected in others above. There are more examples to be found in his book than I can recount; here I offer only two examples. First, in order to persuade readers to reject "essentialism," Fuchs characterizes it as believing in objects being "true and constant in all possible worlds," "things-in-themselves," "exist[ing] independent of relationship, context, time, or observer," making "either/or distinctions," and operating with "static typologies," "rigid classifications," and

real human persons of the kind I describe in this book if anything like his theory is ever to get off the ground.

One wonders why Fuchs believes so firmly in his theoretical account. I suspect he reveals a clue when he speaks about sociology's lack of success as a science to date and regrettable low status among the sciences. (The openings and closings of books often give the best clues about what motivates their writing and arguments.) On the first page of his book, Fuchs, referring to "the perennial mysteries of agency, rationality, knowledge, mind, and truth," states that "sociology has more tools to solve such puzzles than any other science." Four pages later he states that standard sociology creates its own obstacles to advancement, particularly by believing that persons cause outcomes to happen. "Sociology has the tools, but not the identity," he says on the following page, "to be a great science. But it is a culture unsure of itself. When 'hard' scientists look at sociology, they see little but an ideological battlefield prone to deconstruction and antiscience. This is disappointing. The sciences have much to gain from sociology." Fuchs spends the next 325 pages developing the theory he thinks will put sociology in the high-status position he believes it deserves. Finally, the last paragraph of his conclusion says this:

> I have great faith in sociology's potential to become a great science, one that is far superior to its competitors when it comes to explaining culture, society, or even mind. Unfortunately, the discipline's strengths are not visible to other sciences, and they are obscured in sociology as well. We come across a field not to be taken too seriously. The other sciences pay very little attention to what happens in our field.[61]

"a dualistic cosmology" (ibid., 12, 13, 15). Under those conditions, nobody in their right mind is going to side with essentialism. Then, having criticized essentialism for posing "either/or distinctions," Fuchs tells us that "the opposite strategy is relationalism," which we are of course compelled to adopt. But in fact, there are multiple possible theoretical possibilities existing between Fuchs's polarized views of "essentialism" and "relationalism"— yet his argument wipes them from consideration, forcing the reader to adopt his extreme account. Similarly, Fuchs equates radical analytical individualism with humanism generally, and so concludes from the real analytical inadequacies of radical individualism (about which he is largely right) that we must therefore embrace outright antihumanism—failing to see a variety of more intermediate possibilities that sustain a nonindividualistic humanism (see p. 63).

61. Ibid., 1, 5, 6, 334.

What Fuchs wants is a theory that will turbo-charge the sociological engine to propel it above and beyond the heights that other "hard" sciences
have already reached. Fuchs, in short, has physics envy. He finds his own
people "disappointing." He hears echoes of Auguste Comte calling for sociology to ascend the throne as Queen of the Sciences. And he knows that
sociology as it currently is will never wear that crown. If sociology's best
"competitors" are "hard," then it is naturally bad if sociology is "soft,"
which it is, he believes, by wrongly assuming the ontological and causal
"realities" of human persons, agency, values, norms, purposes, and so on.
Physics, after all, does not refer to values and purposes, and look what it
has achieved.[62] Fuchs thus hopes to foment a kind of scholarly revolution
that will put sociology on top through a reaction of theoretical "chemistry"—an alchemy, really—concocting an acid mixture of antiessentialism,
nonfoundationalist positivism, pragmatism, and social constructionism
into which to submerge sociology in order to burn away its dross and
clarify and reinforce its iron strengths. In short, it is professional status
anxiety and reputational aspirations that compel Fuchs to pursue a theory
that dissolves the world as we know it and theoretically destroys the persons we are. Apparently, antihumanism is not too steep a price to pay for
disciplinary glory. Meanwhile, if I am correct, the ultimate irony is that it
is precisely the kind of culturally meaningful moral and normative considerations—the drive for success, status, respectability—that motivate
Fuchs's theory, which turns around and eradicates moral and normative
considerations as motivators of human action.

In response, I venture three hypotheses. Hypothesis 1: Anxiety about
the scientific status of sociology is a motivation that has led to the most
preposterous sociological theories ever published. Hypothesis 2: Anxiety
about the scientific status of sociology is a motivation for the kind of disciplinary scholarship that most threatens, through its antihumanism, the
moral and political status of human persons. Hypothesis 3: Anxiety about
the scientific status of sociology is strongly correlated with a failure to
understand the uniquely emergent properties of personhood that require
an appropriate kind of social science different from physics, chemistry,
and biology.

---

62. For historical context, see Charles Camic, "The Making of a Method: A Historical Re-
interpretation of the Early Parsons," *American Sociological Review* 52 (1987): 421–39; Camic,
"*Structure* after 50 Years: The Anatomy of a Charter," *American Journal of Sociology* 95
(1989): 38–107; George Steinmetz, ed., *The Politics of Method in the Human Sciences: Positivism and Its Epistemological Others* (Durham, NC: Duke University Press, 2005).

Donald Black

We have seen that positivism, reductionism, constructionism, and radical relationalism not only de-center but also often extinguish the person. I offer one more example of this in Donald Black. Among all relational structuralists, Black, a self-declared "sociological fundamentalist," is perhaps the most extreme in annihilating persons, not only analytically but also ontologically. And he does it with flamboyance. His "dream of pure sociology" requires "the elimination of people" in which "psychology totally disappears."[63] Sociology, Black asserts, "contains no assumptions, assertions, or implications about the human mind or its contents. It completely ignores human subjectivity, the conscious and unconscious meanings and feelings people experience, including their perceptions, cognitions, and attitudes." Reality is to be understood "geometrically," not from a personal perspective as personal knowledge. Concluding his theoretical article "Dreams of Pure Sociology" with a final section subtitled "The Ghost of the Person," Black proclaims,

> We obey principles we do not know and cannot change. Our actions are social, chosen no more than we chose to be born. Our ideas are social as well, attracted by the social structure of our lives. We conform to the shape of social space. Geometry is destiny.

He then poses to himself the reasonable question, "Who, then, is speaking?" His answer deserves quoting at length:

> I am the voice of pure sociology. I speak a new language. I travel social space, habitat social beings, a form of life both human and inhuman. I explore unknown locations, calculate distances in uncharted directions, measure quantities never counted. My subject is everything, I go everywhere, I live in the past,

---

63. Donald Black, "Dreams of Pure Sociology," *Sociological Theory* 18, no. 3 (2000): 343–67, quotes following come from 347, 349, 362; also see Black, *The Social Structure of Right and Wrong* (San Diego: Academic Press, 1998), 158–70. Note a special 2008 issue of *Sociological Quarterly*, Pure Sociology: A Critique and an Exchange, devoted to an evaluation of Black's sociological program. Douglas Marshall ("The Dangers of Purity: On the Incompatibility of 'Pure Sociology' and Science," *Sociological Quarterly* 49, no. 2 [2008]: 209–35) and Stephen Turner ("How Not to Do Science," *Sociological Quarterly* 49, no. 2 [2008]: 237–51) demonstrate the bankruptcy of Black's approach, overcoming, in my view, the defense of Joseph Michalski ("The Social Life of Pure Sociology," *Sociological Quarterly* 49, no. 2 [2008]: 253–74; see Douglas Marshall, "Taking the Rhetoric out of Theoretic Debate: A Rejoinder to Michalski," *Sociological Quarterly* 49, no. 2 [2008]: 275–84).

present, and future at once. I am sociology becoming itself. I study the behavior
of social life, the laws of law, the laws of art, the laws of God. I am the science
of science, the theory of theory.

Were the reader beginning by this point to suspect the possibility of the
author suffering delusions about being Nietzsche (whom Black references,
admiringly) reincarnated in sociological form,[64] Black dispels any doubts
by closing this publication with these verses of poetry:

> I myself am social, and I predict myself. I am post-personal. Post-human.
> And I am notorious.
> I killed the person.
> I am the end of the classical tradition.
> The end of Western thought.[65]

One wonders if the good citizens of Virginia are aware that their tax dollars are funding this kind of scholarship and higher education at Thomas
Jefferson's esteemed university.

I could provide more antipersonalist quotes from Black,[66] but we have
seen enough. The bottom line is that Black's sociology eradicates human

---

64. A certain megalomaniacal tone is conspicuous in Black's writings. "Let me be clear:
Much of my theoretical work enjoys so much empirical support that its validity is nearly un-
questionable." "My work may realize these ideals [testability, generality, simplicity, validity,
originality] more successfully than any body of sociological theory on any subject." "My
work . . . is different [from most sociology]. It is radically sociological. . . . My work purifies
sociology. . . . I declare independence from psychology." "Any sociological theory that ignores
any dimension of [my theory] of social space is now obsolete." "My work is shocking." "I came
to sociology and saw that it was a charade." "My work challenges morality of all kinds, official
or not. It exposes the social relativity of right and wrong. . . . But it judges nothing. It lies beyond politics, beyond jurisprudence, beyond values. . . . I took sociology seriously: I stripped
it of psychology. I stripped it of teleology. I stripped it of ontology. I even stripped it of people.
. . . My strategy had consequences I never expected: It stripped humanity itself. It reduced
human behavior to its simplest expression. It left nothing but social life. And I know now that
anyone who is not shocked by my work has not understood it. I myself am shocked." Black,
"The Epistemology of Pure Sociology," 844, 847, 850, 852, 849, 867, 869, 870.

65. Still, Black assures, "If my work is art, it is not art alone: My poems are testable."
Ibid., 841.

66. "The person had to be overthrown," Black assures us. "Only social life would survive.
And I now plead guilty to the crime of pure sociology: I assassinated the person. I do not ask
to be forgiven. . . . But wait. I too was a person. I too lost my place. Epistemologically speaking, I killed myself. What, then, happened to me? Where did I go? Who am I? I am social life."

persons. Persons do not matter, they need not exist, they explain nothing. Everything that matters is "the social," which exists ontologically in autonomy and power. Nearly every other scholar besides Black today—all "conventional scientists"[67]—stumbled about in the darkness of a pre-scientific-revolution social science, in the ignorance of "medieval sociology,"[68] pathetically still believing in human persons, mind, motivations, and purposive action. But Black has arrived to foment a social scientific revolution. He will do so by promoting his purist "dream" of a sociology that is concerned only with testability, generality, simplicity, validity, and originality.[69] Persons will be swept away by the clarity of light that this fundamentalist revolution will bring. "People do not matter." "People disappear." "The elimination of people radically simplifies human reality."[70] It certainly does—down to nothing.

As did the problematic structuralists examined above, Black has arrived at this deeply flawed, antihumanist view of the person by starting with the erroneous presuppositions of positivism, empiricism, and reductionism. Black's view is that science's goal is to predict through the discovery and application of general laws of social life.[71] Nomothetic laws are discovered entirely through empirical observation of events: "In my sociology," Black declares, "social life has no goals, purposes, values, needs, functions, interests, intentions, or anything else not directly observable by anyone."[72] He applies this view to a naive form of sociologism with the goal of increasing its "scienticity."[73] "My only excuse," he confesses, "is

---

I call the police, and I am law. I inflict pain, and I am violence. I sing, and I am music. I pray, and I am God. I write these words, and I am sociology. I obey the laws of social life, and I am greater than myself." Ibid., 870.

67. Ibid., 846.

68. Ibid., 858–59. An insult to the Middle Ages from someone clearly ignorant of the sophisticated thought of that era.

69. Ibid., 831–47; Black, "Dreams of Pure Sociology," 343–367, quotes here come from p. 351.

70. Black, "The Epistemology of Pure Sociology," 860, 861.

71. Are we surprised, then, that for his theory of science he looks to (now well outmoded) early- to mid-twentieth-century thinkers like Hempel, early Wittgenstein (the *Tractatus* era of the 1920s), Braithwaite, and Homans? See ibid., 830. Black shows little evidence that he has assimilated any postpositivist or postfoundationalist scholarship, other than Thomas Kuhn. For an incisive critique of Black's (and Blau's) view(s) of social laws, see Douglas Porpora, "On the Prospect for a Nomothetic Theory of Social Structure," *Journal for the Theory of Social Behaviour* 13, no. 3 (1983): 243–64.

72. Black, "The Epistemology of Pure Sociology," 864.

73. Black, "Dreams of Pure Sociology," 351.

that I believed the sociologists. I believed my teachers. They said sociology should be the science of social life. No one realized the destruction this would entail."[74] Along the way, Black manages to slip in a bit of Kuhnian social constructionism.[75] He also reflects some of the professional status anxiety I detected in Fuchs above, stating, for instance, that "we [in sociology] have yet to declare our scientific sovereignty," and "where is the science of social life that is truly scientific? . . . From the beginning I was disappointed by the psychological, teleological, and ideological nature of sociology. Sociology has not yet met its obligation to be sociological."[76] Altogether, such presuppositional commitments lead Black to his problematic view of persons described above.

As with the problematic theories examined above, however, Black's account is also internally incoherent and self-defeating. Like the person calling on the telephone to announce that their phone does not work, Black routinely employs terms that necessitate the existence of characteristics and capacities of human persons his theory is supposed to eradicate. To start, he confesses that he has a "dream" to promote a particular kind of sociology—meaning, he holds a strong aspiration, a cherished desire on which he has acted in writing his articles. But are not human desires eliminated? He also professes the personal identity of being a "sociological fundamentalist," which helps to explain his actions as a scholar. So, identities matter. Furthermore, in Black's theory, ideas exist, which "agents" direct to "audiences."[77] But one wonders how those fit into a Blackian universe? Black describes successful ideas as those defined as "true and important." But true and important to or for *whom*? And what must we presume about them for truth and importance even to matter? Moreover, some of Black's analyses rely on the idea of "social status," "wealth," and

74. Black, "The Epistemology of Pure Sociology," 870.

75. See ibid., 864.

76. Ibid., 850; Black, "Dreams of Pure Sociology," 345–46. (One wonders, as an aside, where "obligations" come from if Black's system is correct.) Thomas Scheff observes about Black's "pure sociology" that "the anthropologist Mary Douglas has suggested that a focus on purity has a primitive function: defending the status quo in a tribe or other group. The quest for purity . . . is deeply reactionary." Scheff, "Comment," *Contemporary Sociology* 32, no. 4 (2003): 545.

77. Black, "Dreams of Pure Sociology," 348; cites for references in the rest of this paragraph come from Black, "Dreams of Pure Sociology," 349, 357; and Black, "The Epistemology of Pure Sociology," 848–49, 851, 852, 864. Also see Donald Black, "The Geometry of Law: An Interview with Donald Black," *International Journal of the Sociology of Law* 30 (2002): 101–29.

"respectability." But, as noted above, social statuses and wealth and respectability are not objective natural kinds but the cultural constructions of persons capacitated to perceive, think about, and make evaluations of substantively meaningful ideas. How did they get into the picture? Black also talks about certain ideas being "interesting." That's interesting. If persons—indeed all purposive, sentient agents in possession of psychological capacities—have been purged, on what grounds would an idea be interesting and to whom? The same questions apply to Black's emphasis on "creativity." Furthermore, Black complains that most sociologists' treatment of "the social" have "robbed it of meaning." But that should be irrelevant, if not a non sequitur in a world in which human persons do not do anything and subjective meanings do not exist. Black's "theory of social space" also includes a "normative" dimension. But, in his larger theory, actors for whom normative orientations and motivations matter have disappeared. Black notes as well that his work is "shocking" to people because it overturns their ordinary "conceptions of reality." But how could that be or why would it matter if people and their subjective states have been eliminated as immaterial? In short, Black is incapable of describing or explaining what his scholarly project is attempting to achieve and why without recurrently relying upon terms and ideas that necessitate most of the features and abilities of human persons that Black's scholarly project is attempting to eliminate. If his theory is correct, his communication of it is badly defective, highly un-self-reflexive. But I do not think that is simply it. Black cannot communicate his project without relying on the terms and ideas he is out to eradicate for the simple reason that he is not the grandiose embodiment of "The Social" speaking Western thought out of existence, but merely a normal human person with the kind of constitution, needs, characteristics, limitations, and capacities as the rest of us. And that inescapably requires him to communicate in ways that presuppose the importance of human thought, categories, subjectivity, value, meaning, judgment, symbolic significance, interpretation, interests, creativity—and even dreams. Black's argument refutes itself and confirms a perspective more like that of critical realist personalism.

Summary

What are we to conclude from our examination of Mayhew, White, Fuchs, and Black? All four, we can acknowledge, are correct in arguing that radical analytical individualism—the methodological individualism against

which social "holists" fought, especially in the 1950s—is sociologically
bankrupt. Supposing that human persons are autonomous agents of their
own destinies, or the uninfluenced causes and aggregate constituents of
social life, is clearly inadequate. Then again, few serious sociologists today adhere to such radically individualistic views, and so our four theorists seem, in some ways, to be fighting battles that have already been
won. The problem is that, in fighting them, all four have overreacted
to individualism and swung the pendulum to the opposite far extreme.
Instead of having one old inadequate theory, they have handed us its
equally deficient converse. Better to have formulated a more nuanced,
balanced theory more adequate to reality. That, I believe, is critical realist
personalism.

But considering more carefully why these structuralist theorists overreacted and swung to their own extreme raises the key issue of theoretical presuppositions. What we have seen repeatedly is that a particular
set of belief commitments—not facts, mind you, merely prescientific
doctrines—about reality and science lead nearly inexorably to antihumanist, person-annihilating theories. Those are the intellectual package
of antirealism, positivism, empiricism, reductionism, constructionism,
and pragmatism—especially when all combined.[78] If we hope to conduct a social science that comports with our own phenomenological experiences as persons and the moral and political commitments to which
most social scientists are committed, then we must reject the presuppositional package of antirealism, positivism, empiricism, reductionism,
constructionism, and pragmatism. Instead, I think, we need to embrace
critical realist personalism, with all of the assumptions and implications it
entails.

I have said that not all network structuralists think and explain alike.
Certainly not all share the perspective on persons that Mayhew, White,
Fuchs, and Black represent. But those four are also not the only network
structuralists who seem to make assumptions about persons that critical
realist personalism finds problematic. A perusal of the structuralist literature uncovers various other dubious claims. Ron Burt tell us in his 1992
book, for instance, "You are one of the black dots in the dark grey circle."[79]
Mustafa Emirbayer, approvingly quoting Ernst Cassirer, writes, "Things

---

78. Pragmatism alone or combined with only certain other beliefs, for instance, need not
lead to antihumanism.

79. Ron Burt, *Structural Holes* (Cambridge, MA: Harvard University Press, 1992), 182.

are not assumed as independent existences present anterior to any relation but . . . gain their whole being . . . first in and with . . . relations."[80] And
Miller McPherson says, "We are a moving average of our associates."[81]
Exactly how extensively such doubtful beliefs about persons are shared
among network structuralist scholars, I do not know. But the issue is out
there and important enough to confront.

Before moving on, it must be said that in this chapter I have focused
on theoretically oriented structuralists. It is worth remembering, however,
that the majority of network structuralists are not particularly theoretically oriented but focus on applied empirical work—especially in health,
adolescence, and business studies—not frequently specifying their assumptions about the nature of actors. It is often difficult to know what they
presume about the nature of their nodes, and it should not be assumed that
theorists like Mayhew, White, and Fuchs, not to mention Black, speak on
behalf of most network structuralists. From my perspective, critical realist
personalism and network structuralism could mutually benefit from an ongoing conversation about theoretical assumptions concerning the nature,
especially the motives, of persons or other kinds of actors—whether they
be rational choice instrumentalism, identity-driven models, normatively
oriented assumptions, or otherwise. I suspect that most network structuralists presuppose a purposive actor of some sort—which would set them
at odds with the four structuralist theorists examined above—and would
profit from spelling out such assumptions more explicitly.[82] But until such

80. Emirbayer, "Manifesto for a Relational Sociology," 287.

81. Miller McPherson, personal correspondence, referring to quotation of self in his social
networks graduate seminar syllabus since 1990, referencing a paper written in 1976 and later
published as J. Miller McPherson, "Hypernetwork Sampling: Duality and Differentiation
among Voluntary Organizations," *Social Networks* 3 (1982): 225–49, but in which that exact
phrase was removed from the paper before publication.

82. One example of a primarily empirical study making its basic anthropological assumptions briefly explicit is Bearman's 1993 book, *Relations into Rhetorics: Local Elite Social Structure in Norfolk, England, 1540–1640*, in which he writes, "Necessary are models which treat
the motives of actors seriously, while not losing sight of the important long-term determinants
of structural change. . . . I show that individuals with distinctive personal biographies act
coherently with respect to the interests which arise from the structural positions they share in
local and national networks. I argue that structural positions are identity arrays, which yield
interests for purposive actors to follow. . . . I assume that people do act purposively in the
pursuit of social and material interests, and that we can only know if individuals hold given
interests by their actions. . . . Abstraction must be meaningful in terms of the motives of actors, and so sensitivity to context is fundamental. We gain little from models of action that are

a conversation and clarification is had, theorists such as Mayhew, White, and Fuchs will present themselves as the theoretical spokespeople for structuralism, which in my view is unfortunate.

Conclusion

Network structuralism is an important and valuable movement in the social sciences and beyond. Its paradigm also seems naturally fitted to critical realist personalism. Network structuralism deserves continued exploration and increased investment. But a crucial theoretical issue in it to work out—having significant explanatory but also practical moral and political implications—is the nature of the nodes assumed by network structuralist accounts. The theoretical possibilities range from something like the model described by critical realist personalism, to traditional rational choice assumptions of egoistic instrumentalism, all the way across to the antirealist, antihumanist views of people such as Mayhew, White, Fuchs, and Black. These alternatives cannot all be right. And which view among them network structuralism assumes is highly consequential.

I have tried to show that the antirealist, antihumanist perspective—and the presupposed package of positivism, empiricism, reductionism, materialism, and constructionism that underwrites it—is internally incoherent, self-defeating, and inadequate to our ineliminable phenomenological experience as persons and best understandings of the world as we know it. Beside those theoretical considerations of intellectual cogency, another more practical concern presses: network structuralism's antirealist, antihumanist model of the person flushes the reasons for human dignity, rights, respect, and rational deliberation down the toilet. They are eradicated, along with the very idea of motivating reasons itself. Such a view may today represent nothing more than an avant-garde book on a university press title list; let us hope that it stays that way. But if enough of the right (or, rather, wrong) people actually were to come to believe it and began institutionally to work out its logical social and political implications—given certain structural conditions, of course—much of what most of us cherish in life and society, as flawed as they are, could be destroyed.

---

insensitive to individual identity, and we need models that can explain individual action" (8, 11–12, 19, 178).

Certain academics may be prepared to drive over that cliff—especially if it promises to enhance the relative status of their professional discipline vis-à-vis the natural sciences. I hope I have shown that we have no good reason to go there.[83] A superior alternative on all counts is critical realist personalism.

83. Reading network structuralism, I—as a scholar of religion attuned to such matters—notice an interesting relation of some of its theory to religion. Theology, religion, faith, and even preaching seem recurrently to pop up in network structuralist theoretical writings. I find that surprising. Having noticed it, I wish here to offer a few observations and corrective remarks about religion, theology, and relational theory. Here is what I mean to convey. Mayhew writes, "The essentialist . . . is locked into a view of reality that has the character of religious conviction," and "to rely on introspection for the assumption of rationality is to rely on blind faith." Mayhew, "Structuralism versus Individualism: Part II, Ideology and Other Obfuscations," 633; the other references in this paragraph come from pp. 637, 643; and Mayhew, "Structuralism versus Individualism: Part I, Shadowboxing in the Dark," 347. He argues, "To say that a person did X because he was motivated by anger is not different from saying that he did X because he was inhabited or possessed by the god of anger (an evil spirit no doubt)." And Mayhew claims that any difference that exists between humans and grasshoppers "is not a difference to be endowed with divine qualities." Similarly, White writes, "Social science today begins, without apology, from person. Most present social science theories can be seen as exegesis on Enlightenment myths. These in turn took their presuppositions from Christian theology. Thus, the Enlightenment was formed by, even as it fought against, a theology of the soul, and the social sciences as its progeny remain enmeshed in the same presuppositions. In order to combat homiletics one needs to start in the same pulpit." White, *Identity and Control: A Structural Theory of Social Action*, 23–24; other references to White in this paragraph are from p. 197; and Harrison White, Alair MacLean, and Andy Olds, eds., "An Interview with Harrison White," April 16, 2001, unpublished paper, p. 12, also see p. 13. White reiterates a similar point elsewhere, claiming, "The ultimate fixity of the soul, carried over to hobbled social science, was a Pauline theological imperative," and "in most present social science, 'person' is instead taken as the unquestioned atom. This is an unacknowledged borrowing and transcription of the soul construct from Christian theology." In another context, White criticizes rational choice theory this way: "The whole thing is just silly, if you try to make it a religion, rational choice, it's just silly."

What about Fuchs? He writes, "Unlike religions, science is forward looking, not backward. A science cares for itself, not some social cause." Fuchs, *Against Essentialism: A Theory of Culture and Society*, 7; other references are from pp. 18, 28, 97, 199, also see 152, 252, 283. Similarly, he writes, "Unlike religion, science assumes that all observers are empirical, which means that they occur in the world." Fuchs also contrasts proper scientific observation against the primordial biblical image of human hubris—drawn from the third chapter of the book of Genesis—as "climbing up the tree of knowledge" toward reaching a "final level" found in "religion, when all rest forever in God" (except, note, that Adam and Eve did not climb the tree but only ate its fruit). Fuchs also criticizes the "elusive and opaque realm of [interpretive] practices [as] a leftover from religion and morality." Elaborating that theme, Fuchs summarizes Rorty, approvingly: "Hermeneutics is a way of paying respect to the liberal and humanist Self, admired as a knowledgeable and capable inventor and creator of the social world. The double hermeneutic is a leftover from religion. Originally hermeneutics was the decoding of sacred texts and divine messages. It remained coupled to biblical exegesis until humanism and historicism, which generalized hermeneutics into a secular philosophy. But hermeneutics never quite lost its religious bearings." This, of course, is a bad thing needing to be overcome. Finally, Black also offers the occasional negative and profaning reference to religion (references following come from Black, "The Epistemology of Pure Sociology," 862, 865, 866; Black, "The Geometry of Law: An Interview with Donald Black," 105, also see 106–7). "The behavior of God is predictable from the shape of social space," he claims. "God is a variable. . . . God is, moreover, a quantitative variable." In talking about the "epistemological shock" caused by his views, Black refers to the three archetypical historical cases commonly thought of as verifying the science-and-religion warfare model of knowledge: Nicolaus Copernicus's (in fact usually grossly exaggerated, as with the account of Galileo's—see Robert Westman, "The Copernicans and the Churches" in *God and Nature: Historical Essays on the Encounter between Christianity and Science*, ed. David Lindberg and Ronald Numbers [Berkeley and Los Angeles: University of California Press, 1986], 76–113; David Lindberg, "Galileo, the Church, and the Cosmos," in *When Science and Christianity Meet*, ed. David Lindberg and Ronald Numbers [Chicago: University of Chicago Press, 2003], 33–60; William Shea, "Galileo and the Church," in *God and Nature*, ed. Lindberg and Numbers, 114–35) persecution by the Catholic Church, Charles Darwin's (usually grossly oversimplified—see Jon Roberts, *Darwinism and the Divine in America: Protestant Intellectuals and Organic Evolution, 1859–1900* [Madison: University of Wisconsin Press, 1988]; Ronald Numbers, *Darwin Comes to America* [Cambridge, MA: Harvard University Press, 1998]; David Livingstone, *Darwin's Forgotten Defenders: The Encounter between Evangelical Theology and Evolutionary Thought* [Grand Rapids, MI: Eerdmans, 1987]) rejection by church authorities, and John Scopes's 1925 "Monkey Trial" in Dayton, Tennessee, for teaching evolution in a public school (to understand the complexities of this event, see Edward Larson, *Summer for the Gods: The Scopes Trial and America's Continuing Debate over Science and Religion* [Cambridge, MA: Harvard University Press, 1997]). About Darwin, Black contends, "In an earlier age [than the nineteenth century], he probably would have been executed." In this context, Black tells how he, for his radical views, has been branded and criticized as "alarming," "repugnant," and "crazy" for teaching "the Gospel according to Saint Donald." In criticizing the idea of intersubjective understanding, Black also claims, "The ends of people are no more observable than the ends of God." Lastly, Black has said, "The value of science has been amply demonstrated during the past several centuries. What are its competitors? Religion? . . . Science is undoubtedly the most effective means of understanding reality. It predicts and explains more facts more precisely and is easier to evaluate than any other form of knowledge."

For some reason, then, these network structuralists seem to use religion as a kind of "alter"—meaning, an ego's related opposite, not a sacrificial altar—against which to help build their theoretical case. Similarly, from an earlier era focused on Blauian structuralism, Lewis Coser stated that sociology "must search for the structurally rooted interests and values . . . if it is not to dissolve into psychological disquisitions about innate aggressiveness [or] original sin." Coser, "Structure and Conflict," in *Approaches to the Study of Social Conflict*, ed. Peter Blau (New York: Free Press, 1975), 214–15. Somehow, structures and original sin are rivals or contradictions. That is curious to me. Why should religion become the symbolic antagonist—maybe even the whipping boy—of network structuralists? Why would religion even come to mind or be cognitively relevant to these theorists?

The puzzle becomes all the more curious when one considers the fact that neither Judaism nor Christianity actually teach the immortality of the soul—a belief that some structuralists equate with an atomistic theory of human action, which they reject. The idea of the immortal soul is a product of Greek philosophy, not biblical faith. The closest thing the Bible teaches to the immortality of the human soul is the resurrection of the body, but those are extremely different ideas (Roger Olson, *The Mosaic of Christian Belief* [Leicester: Apollos, 2002], 316–21; Plato, *Plato's Dialogue of the Immortality of the Soul* [Brooklyn, NY: AMS Press, 1976]; Martin Nilsson, *The Immortality of the Soul in Greek Religion* [Mölnlycke, Sweden: Elanders, 1941]; Caroline Bynum, *Resurrection of the Body in Western Christianity* [New York: Columbia University Press, 1995]). The former posits some innate capacity for eternal existence naturally resident in the human soul. But the resurrection of the body understands all human life not as self-existent in the soul but finite, mortal, a gift from God, on whom all are dependent through resurrection for life everlasting. Without a sustaining life from God, the human condition is death. Far from modeling atomism theologically, therefore, biblical faith actually models the opposite: intimate relational ties and interactions of reciprocity between God and humans. Furthermore, the Christian Trinitarian doctrine of God leads to anything but an atomistic representation of reality. The Christian God is not some lone, solitary deity but Trinity—three divine persons of one substance in the same being (T. F. Torrance, *The Trinitarian Faith* [London: T & T Clark, 1995]). That is Christian orthodoxy. God—the ultimate and all-defining reality—*is* relationship, in essential ontological being. If network structuralism were to find an isomorphic counterpart in any religious worldview, then Christianity should be a naturally prime candidate. Yet if the recurrent contrasting and negative remarks about (especially Christian) religion that we have seen above are indicative, for some reason relational structuralist theorists seem to view religion, especially Christianity, as contrary, conflicting, rivaling their theoretical view.

Why might this be? Any answer I could give here is necessarily speculative—but perhaps still worth venturing. I do not know enough about the personal histories of our structuralist theorists to venture biographical psychoanalyses—and that would not be very sociological in any case. A more interesting explanation would set the remarks above in the larger context of American sociology's historical relation to religion in the institution of higher education (see John Evans and Michael Evans, "Religion and Science: Beyond the Epistemological Conflict Narrative," *Annual Review of Sociology* 34 [2008]: 87–105). I have elaborated this story at length elsewhere (Christian Smith, ed., *The Secular Revolution: Power, Interest, and Conflict in the Secularization of American Public Life* [Berkeley and Los Angeles: University of California Press, 2003]). The short version for present purposes, however, is that institutionally—as socially legitimate sources of authoritative knowledge—Christian religion and the social sciences have been rivals. Informed scholars now share a consensus that no necessary "warfare" between religion and science exists or has been fought, either in historical fact or conceptual logic (an immense revisionist literature has overturned the old "warfare" model in the last quarter century, only a few representatives of which to mention here are Lindberg and Numbers, eds., *God and Nature*; Lindberg and Numbers, *When Science and Christianity Meet*; John Brooke, *Science and Religion: Some Historical Perspectives* [Cambridge: Cambridge University Press, 1991]; Gary Ferngren, ed., *Science and Religion: A Historical Introduction*

[Baltimore: Johns Hopkins University Press, 2002]; Numbers, *Darwin Comes to America*). But in the history of the American institutions of science, education, publishing, and social reform, particularly, religion—mainline and evangelical Protestantism, to be more precise—originally held a controlling position in higher education, early science, publishing, and reform movements. The end of the nineteenth century saw many intense struggles by more secular actors—including leaders in the new social sciences—to displace religious authorities and control the production and dissemination of quite different forms of authoritative knowledge. In time, the secular insurgents largely succeeded in most spheres in supplanting older religious authorities. Psychology displaced pastoral counseling, anthropology displaced missionaries, social work displaced the social gospel, and sociology displaced theological ethics and moral reform movements. That experience resulted in the construction over the twentieth century of American colleges and universities as havens of secularity in a broader society still largely "awash in a sea of faith" (Jon Butler, *Awash in a Sea of Faith: Christianizing the American People* [Cambridge, MA: Harvard University Press, 1990]). It also established the social sciences, through deep cultural codings, as the structural and therefore symbolic rivals of religion. In which case, discursive work aimed at strengthening the superior authority of social science in the broader society will naturally underscore the contrast between its scientific and reliable knowledge and the superstitions and errors of religious faith. The template for such rhetorical strategies we see in Fuchs above: "Unlike religions, science is . . ."

It is understandable that scholars who intellectually came of age in an era when the old inevitable "warfare of science and religion" model was still considered credible would tend instinctively to fall back on its standard discursive strategies, exemplary historical martyrs, and symbolic drawing of rivalries in order to strengthen their theoretical hand—even if religion would seem to have nothing directly to do with the analytical strategy they wish to promote. But times have changed. The inevitable warfare model is discredited. Contemporary social scientists might exercise greater self-reflexivity, therefore, by reconsidering the bases of their claims to authoritative knowledge and alternative potential relationships between scientific scholarship and religious knowledge. More specifically, future network structuralist theorizing should at least get their religious history and theology right before attempting to draw connections among religious faith, atomistic social theory, and individualistic, psychological approaches to explanation.

CHAPTER FIVE

Persons and Mechanisms (Not) in Variables Sociology

The dominant form of analysis in the social sciences since World War II, especially since the development of user-friendly computer statistics software in recent decades, has been the statistical analysis of relationships among quantitatively measured "variables."[1] Following Herbert Blumer, Charles Ragin, Hartmut Esser, and Andrew Abbott,[2] I will refer to this general analytical approach, as I already have in the previous chapter, as *variables social science*, the *variables paradigm*, and *variables analysis*. Variables social science typically breaks down the complex reality of human social life into "independent" and "dependent variables," whose answer categories are assigned numeric values representing some apparent variation in the world. Dependent and independent variables are then mathematically correlated, usually "net of" the possible effects of other variables, in order to establish independent statistical associations between them. Important independent variables are identified as related to the dependent variable through calculations of statistical significance,

1. Anthropology, which as a discipline relies primarily on ethnography, being the major exception.

2. Hartmut Esser, "What Is Wrong with 'Variables Sociology'?" *European Sociological Review* 12, no. 2 (1996): 159–66; Andrew Abbott, "Of Time and Space," *Social Forces* 75, no. 4 (1997): 1149–82; Abbott, "Transcending General Linear Reality," *Sociological Theory* 6 (1988): 169–86; Charles Ragin, *Fuzzy Set Social Science* (Chicago: University of Chicago Press, 2000); Herbert Blumer, "Sociological Analysis and the 'Variable,'" chap. 7 in *Symbolic Interactionism: Perspective and Method* (Englewood Cliffs, NJ: Prentice-Hall, 1969), 127–39; Ray Pawson, *A Measure for Measures: A Manifesto for Empirical Sociology* (London: Routledge, 1989).

and statistical models are produced purporting to represent how certain social processes operate and produce the observed human social world.

Given the dominance of the variables paradigm in most of the social sciences, any broad examination of the nature of human persons and its relevance to social theory and explanation must address and evaluate its assumptions and common practices. We need to ask: Is this variables paradigm compatible or at odds with critical realist personalism? What exactly does variables social science presuppose about social ontology and human persons? What views about personhood and social reality does the practice of variables social science foster? Can variables social science assimilate critical realist personalism? Or, viewed differently, can critical realist personalism make use of variables analysis?

Variables social science tends not to be all that theoretically self-reflective about its assumptions concerning human actors and the nature of social reality. The disposition of the paradigm seems to draw attention to issues of precision and error in measurement, proper assumptions about the nature of variables for different forms of statistical modeling, the necessity of adequate "controls," and a host of other more technical methodological concerns. Someone with interests in the nature of human personhood is hard pressed to find much discussion about the topic within the variables paradigm literature. That itself is telling. Unlike the chapters on social constructionism and network structuralism in this book, therefore, I cannot here interpret and evaluate bodies of theoretical text about variables analysis from the perspective of critical realist personalism. This chapter will engage in some theoretical inference making in order to identify the place of personhood, causation, and other related matters in variables social science. In so doing, this exploration should not only help us to further clarify the nature and role of the person in the social sciences, but also better to evaluate the problems and promise of the analytical approach that currently dominates most of those disciplines.

The conclusions I draw below about the matter at hand are these: Variables social science is predisposed to myriad problems and is often poorly practiced in ways that reinforce problematic models of human persons and generate more than a little questionable scholarship in terms of causation and explanation. Nevertheless, variables social science is *not* an inherently defective method of analysis, as long as we understand its limits. Nor is it innately inconsistent with critical realist personalism or the production of valuable scholarship. A great deal of published variables social science scholarship is problematic in various ways, from critical realist personalism's viewpoint. But much of it need not be so. Many of the best practitioners of variables sociology are aware of the concerns described below and deal constructively with them in practice, despite the directive theoretical tendencies of the animating background positivist empiricism that so permeates the assumptions of quantitative sociology. At the same time, a great deal of variables sociology that is conducted and published seems largely oblivious to the problems described below, the background assumptions that help to create them, and alternative philosophies of social science that could turn variables analyses to better uses. My argument here is that when set within a proper theoretical framework for understanding the nature of reality and science (critical realism), and when informed by a proper understanding of human beings (personalism), variables social science can be conducted in theoretically and analytically appropriate and intellectually enlightening ways.

General Background Problems

Variables social science is beset with a host of problems—not all of which are directly related to issues of personhood—about which many practitioners seem unaware or which they simply ignore. The dominance of the variables paradigm in most of the social sciences, the authority it enjoys as the highest-status method of knowledge production, and the widespread availability of easy-to-learn statistical software packages run on personal computers together have the effect of bulldozing over most of the problems that often routinely beset variables social science. Every quarter, those problems are flattened out and covered over by fresh piles of journal articles that are churned out to keep running academia's review-and-promotion and status-competition systems. Every year, those problems are also unnoticed or minimized by new cohorts of social science graduate students who are quickly socialized into the productive practices of their competitive guilds. And yet the problems are serious and worth noting.[3]

For starters, variables social science is notoriously hung on the problem of causation. Most social science research attempts to explain facts or

---

3. For fuller treatments, see Stanley Lieberson, *Making It Count* (Berkeley and Los Angeles: University of California Press, 1985). Also see Esser, "What Is Wrong with 'Variables Sociology'?" 159–66; Paul Holland, "Statistics and Causal Inference," *Journal of the American Statistical Association* 81, no. 396 (1986): 945–60.

events by showing the causes that produced them. Causal explanation is a core goal of variables social science. Yet calculating the strength and statistical significance of associations among variables—which is ultimately all that variables analysis can do—does not and cannot establish causal influences.[4] Causal understanding is always located in and derived from our *theories* as informed by our personal substantive understandings of reality, not in or from statistical analyses. Lacking a proper philosophy of social science, however—that is, being influenced by positivist empiricism rather than critical realism—most variables analysts are caught between the horns of needing to be able to provide causal explanations and never being able to establish them definitively.[5] This dilemma is usually "resolved" by analysts either scrupulously denying any claims to causal relations or by analysts employing slippery phrases (e.g., "X *leads to* Y," "X *increases* Y," etc.) that imply but do not overtly claim causal influence. The former is not analytically satisfactory and the latter is not intellectually honest. Still, variables social science muddles on, seemingly hoping, in vain, that somehow longitudinal data or some other methodological technique will solve this problem. They can't.[6]

4. Kenneth Bollen, *Structural Equations with Latent Variables* (New York: John Wiley and Sons, 1989), 40–79; Michael Sobel, "An Introduction to Causal Inference," *Sociological Methods and Research* 24, no. 3 (1996): 353–79; John Neter et al., *Applied Linear Statistical Models* (Boston: McGraw-Hill, 1996), 9–10. The naïveté of many sociologists, however, reflecting the residual influence of positivist empiricism, is evident in simplistic mentalities that often find candid expression in introductory books, as when, for instance, John Macionis writes, "The real payoff in scientific research is determining how variables are related. . . . The scientific ideal . . . is mapping out *cause and effect*, which means a relationship in which change in one variable causes change in another. . . . Understanding cause and effect is valuable because it allows researchers to *predict* how one pattern of behavior will produce another." Macionis, *Society: The Basics*, 8th ed. (Upper Saddle River, NJ: Prentice-Hall, 2006), 15–16, italics in original.

5. For the long history of thinking about and use of causal language in American sociology, see Christopher Bernert, "The Career of Causal Analysis in American Sociology," *British Journal of Sociology* 34, no. 2 (1983): 230–54.

6. On the larger problem of causation, see Stephen Morgan and Christopher Winship, *Counterfactuals and Causal Inference* (Cambridge: Cambridge University Press, 2007); John Goldthorpe, *On Sociology* (New York: Oxford University Press, 2000), 137–60; Margaret Marini and Burton Singer, "Causality in the Social Sciences," *Sociological Methodology* 20 (1988): 347–409; Holland, "Statistics and Causal Inference," 945–60; Christopher Winship and Michael Sobel, "Causal Inference in Sociological Studies," in *Handbook of Data Analysis*, ed. Melissa Hardy and Alan Bryman (Thousand Oaks, CA: Sage, 2004), 481–504; Judea Pearl, *Causality* (Cambridge: Cambridge University Press, 2000), 331–58; Stephen Turner, "Cause,

Another problem: Variables-based analyses rarely specify the scope conditions or contextual factors within which their findings might apply. This is the result of a residual positivism lying behind the variables paradigm and the related general lack of attention to specific contexts inherent in variables social science.[7] If the goal is identifying general covering laws of social life, particular contexts are precisely what need to be ignored. In fact, samples of populations are taken from very different settings and at different times. Strictly speaking, the findings of any given analysis apply only to the specific population the sample represents and the specific time and place in which it was sampled.[8] Generalizability in this context has to do with inferences from the sample to the population from which it was drawn, *not* from a study's findings to all people or generally similar situations. No analysis can speak to its own generalizability beyond the population from which its data were collected—assuming even then that the sampling was done well. We may try to put the findings of many studies together in a meta-analysis in hopes of findings common patterns, but the problem of inductive generalizability is finally inescapable, especially

Law, and Probability," *Sociological Theory* 5 (1987): 15–40; Michael Sobel, "Causal Inference in the Social and Behavioral Sciences," in *Handbook of Statistical Modeling in the Social and Behavioral Sciences*, ed. Gerhard Arminger and Clifford Clogg (New York: Plenum Press, 1995); Jon Elster, *Explaining Technical Change: A Case Study in the Philosophy of Science* (Cambridge: Cambridge University Press, 1983); Clark Glymour et al., *Discovering Causal Structure* (New York: Academic Press, 1987); David Heise, *Causal Analysis* (New York: John Wiley and Sons, 1975), 3–35; Deborah Stone, "Causal Stories and the Formation of Policy Agendas," *Political Science Quarterly* 104, no. 2 (1989): 281–300.

7. See Henry Walker and Bernard Cohen, "Scope Statements: Imperatives for Evaluating Theory," *American Sociological Review* 50 (1985): 288–301; Henry Walker, "Spinning Gold from Straw: On Cause, Law, and Probability," *Sociological Theory* 5 (1987): 28–33; Bernard Cohen, "The Conditional Nature of Scientific Knowledge," in *Theoretical Methods in Sociology*, ed. Lee Freese (Pittsburgh: University of Pittsburgh Press, 1980), 71–110; Lee Freese, "Formal Theorizing," *Annual Review of Sociology* 6 (1980): 191–96. More generally, see George Steinmetz, ed., *The Politics of Method in the Human Sciences: Positivism and Its Epistemological Others* (Durham, NC: Duke University Press, 2005); Steinmetz, "American Sociology before and after World War II: The (Temporary) Settling of a Disciplinary Field," in *Sociology in America: A History*, ed. Craig Calhoun (Chicago: University of Chicago Press, 2007), 314–66.

8. This also involves the issue of "external validity." See Daniel Little, *Microfoundations, Method, and Causation* (New Brunswick, NJ: Transaction, 1998), 237–56; Jeffrey Lucas, "Theory-Testing, Generalization, and the Problem of External Validity," *Sociological Theory* 21, no. 3 (2003): 236–53; Thomas Cook and Donald Campbell, *Quasi-Experimentation: Design and Analysis Issues for Field Settings* (Chicago: Rand McNally, 1979), 71.

as time changes the cultures and societies in question.[9] And this creates problems, in the absence of lawlike regularities, for the accumulation of social science knowledge.[10]

Furthermore, response rates of most survey datasets upon which most variables sociology is based are troublingly low and declining with time. What was once believed to be a minimum response rate for a respectable analysis has been gradually adjusted down, as unavailable and uncooperative survey respondents have increased.[11] To the extent that nonresponses are systematically biased, our data are systematically nonrepresentative of the populations we think we are studying, and our statistical findings are in error. Yet the very nature of survey nonresponse means that there is no way to know how systematically biased our data are. And so we often fly in the dark, simply hoping for the best, and yet perhaps misrepresenting reality. For realism, that is troubling.

9. Consider as an example of this problem Bernard Berelson and Gary Steiner's 712-page tome, *Human Behavior: An Inventory of Scientific Findings*, which sets out to present fully and accurately "what the behavioral sciences know about the behavior of human beings. . . . What we here call findings might elsewhere be called . . . laws." Berelson and Steiner, *Human Behavior* (New York: Harcourt, Brace, and World, 1964), 3, 5. A great deal of what they actually presented, however, consisted of time- and place-bound generalizations (based on empirically observed associations among variables). Two examples of their laws are, "The higher a person's education or socioeconomic status, the greater the diversity of his sexual practices"(302) and "The less routinized and fragmented the work, the higher the job satisfaction" (410).

10. See Gary King, Robert Keohane, and Sidney Verba, *Designing Social Inquiry* (Princeton, NJ: Princeton University Press, 1994), 34–43; Malcolm Williams, "Generalization in Interpretive Research," in *Qualitative Research in Action*, ed. Tim May (London: Sage, 2002), 125–43; John Hughes and Wesley Sharrock, *The Philosophy of Social Research* (New York: Longman, 1997), 57–73. Lee Cronbach (of Cronbach's alpha fame) observed in 1975, "The trouble, as I see it, is that we cannot store up generalizations and constructs for ultimate assembly into a network. It is as if we needed a gross of dry cells to power an engine and could only make one a month. The energy would leak out of the first cells before we had half the battery completed. So it is with the potency of our generalizations." Cronbach, "Beyond the Two Disciplines of Scientific Psychology," *American Psychologist* 30 (1975): 123. For alternative approaches to generalizations, see Howard Becker, "Generalizing from Case Studies," in *Qualitative Inquiry in Education*, ed. Elliot Eisner and Alan Peshkin (New York: Teacher's College Press, 1990), 233–42; Florian Znaniecki, *The Method of Sociology* (1934; New York: Octagon Books, 1968), 235–331.

11. Edith de Leeuw and Wim de Heer, "Trends in Household Survey Nonresponse: A Longitudinal and International Comparison," in *Survey Nonresponse*, ed. Robert Groves et al. (New York: John Wiley and Sons, 2002), chap. 3.

The problems continue. Very many variables analyses do not contain the variables in their datasets that are needed to model the specific hypotheses and theories under investigation. Most such analyses rely on data collected by other people who did not have those hypotheses and theories in mind. Variables analyses therefore frequently rely on problematic proxy variables and measures that do not well represent the concepts they indicate. Sometimes key elements of theories are simply missing from analyses. It can be like trying to make a used car run that is missing some key parts—it may or may not work and sometimes one ends up having simply to push it down the road.

Moreover, tests of statistical significance tell us mostly about the size of our sample, not about the strength of association between variables, since sample size dramatically affects the ability to find significant differences.[12] On the one hand, real and important relationships between variables are often missed because datasets happen to contain too few sampled cases of particular kinds. On the other hand, nearly any association can be found statistically significant with a large enough sample size. Since the size of datasets is more often determined by constrained financial resources than driven by the analytical requirements of specific research questions, the statistical significance or lack of significance of associations between variables is considerably determined by factors extraneous to the logic of the research. Yet much variables scholarship seems content to report only on statistically significant variables. Few analysts examine the substantively meaningful strength of relationships between variables. This "fetishism of asterisks" leads many authors to write as if a variable being significant automatically means that it is explanatorily important, that it exerts a big influence on the dependent variable. But of course a statistically significant independent variable may be only very weakly associated with the dependent variable. Yet the obsession with significance often displaces concerns about substantive strength of relationships. As long as $p < .05$, then we have succeeded, so many seem to think.[13] Extending this problem to entire statistical models, variables sociology often seems content to judge analyses as successful that explain (as indicated by R-squares) only

12. I originally heard this idea put in this way by Chris Winship, at a talk on causation he gave at the Research Triangle Institute, Research Triangle Park, Durham, NC, in spring 2005.

13. See Stephen Ziliak and Deirdre McCloskey, *The Cult of Statistical Significance: How the Standard Error Costs Us Jobs, Justice, and Lives* (Ann Arbor: University of Michigan Press, 2008).

a few percent of the variance in their dependent variables as long as they have numerous significant independent variables.

Finally, multivariate statistical analyses of social variables that attempt to approximate the random assignment of subjects in true experiments by "controlling for" associated factors also may very well not achieve such quasi-randomness. That is because, among other reasons, the selection effects that assign people to different social locations through routine social processes may very well operate *within* the control variables themselves. We can never be sure either way. Unmeasured selectivity is by definition undetected. Yet when statistical controls cannot overcome such selection effects, statistical results may very well produce distorted and misleading findings. Believing that they have semireplicated the rigor of a natural science experiment, variables analysts may produce inaccurate and fallacious results.

I could cite numerous other problems,[14] but these suffice for now. Some of these clearly relate to matters of specific concern to critical realism, others are of broader concern for understanding reality. Certain of these problems can be solved by better-informed, more conscientious practices of variables analyses. Others are inherent to the paradigm and method and cannot be fixed. There are methodological means to address some of the problems mentioned above, but relatively few scholars seem skilled or interested enough to do so. And so a great deal of problematic variables social science continues to be cranked out by the publish-or-perish machine.

---

14. For instance, many variables-oriented scholars seem either to assume or in fact do imply that the processes examined operate with bidirectional causation when in fact they may very well work causally in only one direction. Simply because more of X means more of Y does not mean that less of X produces less of Y. Yet variables social science routinely suggests bidirectional or symmetrical causation, which can lead to problematic logical, practical, and policy conclusions. Moreover, not everything that is real or causally influential is variable— the force of gravity in physics, for instance, is not; and the cultural individualism that shapes Americans' views of personal autonomy may not be much variable either, even though it is pervasively causally powerful. Lieberson, *Making It Count*, 88–119, 223–27. In this I oppose the view expressed, for instance, by David Klein, "Constants cannot have effects. Similarly, it is . . . incorrect to assert that constants have causes. . . . The principle of variation also rules out mere existence statements or descriptions from causal assertions." Klein, "Causation in Sociology Today," *Sociological Theory* 5 (1987): 22. This is simply wrong. For numerous other problems and concerns, see Lieberson, *Making It Count*. Also see Esser, "What Is Wrong with 'Variables Sociology'?" 159–66.

The Person in Variables Social Science

What might we think more specifically about the role of *persons* in variables social science? How ought we to think of the variables paradigm if critical realist personalism is correct? On first view it seems that the variables approach has little place for the coherent, capacitated, acting person in its paradigm.[15] Persons hardly seem to exist in variables social science—they are rarely actually studied. What are studied instead are variables—which, when it comes to humans, are usually only single aspects or dimensions of persons or human social arrangements. Variables social science does not seem, on the surface at least, to conceive of human social life as consisting of persons acting and interacting within specific enabling and constraining contexts to produce certain outcomes, including emergent social structures. Rather, it appears to model social life as consisting of abstract "factors" (e.g., race, income, political party affiliation, etc.) exerting their independent causal effects to produce some variable outcome in another usually abstract factor. The standard representation of the operations of social life in this paradigm sounds like, "An increase in earnings significantly decreases percent of income given to charity," or "Each unit increase in life satisfaction leads to a 4 percent increase in the odds of marrying during the next 12 months." Taken at face value, this discourse suggests that variables, not persons, are the real social agents or actors. Persons, if anything, are simply the background medium or vehicles through which variables act or operate. Whether or not sociologists think like this, very many certainly talk like this. Such an approach takes seriously Émile Durkheim's methodological rule to "consider social facts as things."[16] Variables represent social facts—such as the existence of gendered cultures, religious differences, income inequalities, and the like—which as sui generis entities themselves cause other facts and events to occur. Real action happens between social facts, Durkheim taught, not

15. Goldthorpe, *On Sociology*, 96; Abbott, "Of Time and Space," 1149–82; James Coleman, "Social Theory, Social Research, and a Theory of Action," *American Journal of Sociology* 91, no. 6 (1986): 314–15; Raymond Boudon, "The Individualistic Tradition in Sociology," in *The Micro-Macro Link*, ed. Jeffrey Alexander et al. (Berkeley and Los Angeles: University of California Press, 1987), 61–62. For a similar argument mostly concerning *homo economicus*, see Mary Douglas and Steven Ney, *Missing Persons: A Critique of Personhood in the Social Sciences* (Berkeley and Los Angeles: University of California Press, 1998).

16. Émile Durkheim, *The Rules of Sociological Method* (1938; New York: Free Press, 1966), 14.

persons. The lives of persons are driven by social facts. Durkheim was clear about this when he characterized persons as "merely the indeterminate material that the social factor molds and transforms . . . consist[ing] exclusively in very general attitudes, in vague and consequentially plastic predispositions."[17] This is not exactly a robust view of persons as causal agents in their own right, operating emergently at their own level of reality. Persons rather channel the influences of causal social forces, which are represented if not exerted by variables. James Coleman critiqued this approach to "causal modeling" in statistics as a kind of "individualistic behaviorism."[18] Most of the best variables-oriented sociologists I know are fairly clear on thinking rightly about these matters, and thankfully do not slip into the problems that shorthand versions of variables sociology typically engender. Still, it is far from obvious that the majority of variables sociologists—those who fill up the bulk of the journals—understand and respond appropriately to these problems and concerns.

A related issue with variables social science is its fragmentation of persons and human social life into the discrete factors of abstract variables. Persons are not treated as actor units, but are sliced and diced through measurement items into a variety of bits and pieces of information that are arrayed in the cells of relational databases. What remain whole and coherent in the process are not persons but variables, which comprise data points across a range of values for every case in the file. Persons disappear from view. They are transformed into sets of distinct conceptual domains and value scores on measured variables. Here again we may see a form of reductionism at work, one that epistemologically privileges the quantifiable. Beginning from the viewpoint of variables analysis, then, what *is* a person? The answer, strictly speaking, seems to be: a conglomeration of scores on all of the variables contained in the database for one case. Of course, variables scholars do not actually experience themselves or other people in this way, and I doubt that most think about persons in these terms. But that does seem to be the view of persons that the method of the variables paradigm represents and promotes. Again, the best sociologists

17. Ibid., 106. But also see Warren Schmaus, *Durkheim's Philosophy of Science and the Sociology of Knowledge: Creating an Intellectual Niche* (Chicago: University of Chicago Press, 1994), which argues convincingly that, despite Durkheim's misappropriation by Parsons and positivists, he was in fact a realist.

18. Coleman, "Social Theory, Social Research, and the Theory of Action," 1309–35. On the connection between behaviorism and structural equation modeling, also see Otis D. Duncan, *Introduction to Structural Equation Models* (New York: Academic Press, 1975), 162–63.

keep in mind the difference between real persons and what variables sociology does to them analytically. But it is not at all clear that most sociologists have carefully considered these matters.

Furthermore, variables social science's analytical findings never come full circle back to the concrete persons about which the variable data are drawn, even when the units to which the variables refer are individual humans. No significant variable can be assumed to apply to or tell us anything about any individual case. Significant variables concern probabilities operative in the entire sample, not causal influences in particular instances. It is impossible to take the findings of variables analysis and know anything specific about how they operate in the life of any person in the sample. Merely because Julio is a case in a sample and the findings of the statistical analysis of that sample show that age, race, income, and gender, say, are significant independent variables predicting variance observed in the dependent variable of happiness, that does not mean that Julio's age, race, income, or gender influence an outcome in the dependent variable of happiness in his life as a person. It could be that all four of those variables may be, some of them may be, or none may be operative influences in Julio's life. Instead, all we can say with confidence is that those variables are significantly associated with the dependent variable *for the entire sample*.[19] We are always only talking about probabilities operative within a sample purporting to represent a population. And that does not bring our understanding back to real persons. But then, the positivist, empiricist vision underwriting most of variables social science never was interested in persons to start with, but social facts and nomothetic laws. Critical realist personalism thus encounters friction with the variables paradigm at this point as well.

One of the best-selling methodology textbooks in social science—"Babbie"—reflects all of the problems just mentioned in its presentation of what social science and theory are about:

> Social scientists don't even seek to explain people per se. They try instead to understand *systems* in which people operate, which in turn explain why people do what they do. The elements in such a system are not people but *variables*. . . . Social research involves the study of variables and the attributes that compose them. Social scientific theories are written in a language of variables, and people get involved only as "carriers" of those variables. . . . The relationship between

19. We may run our models for subsamples, but that in no way alters the present point.

attributes and variables lies at the heart of both description and explanation in science. . . . Theories describe the relationships we might logically expect among variables. Often, the expectation involves ideas of *causation*. A person's attributes on one variable are expected to cause, predispose, or encourage a particular attribute on another variable. . . . Theory has to do with the two variables . . . not with people as such. People are the carriers of those two variables.[20]

Here, then, the gateway through which huge numbers of students travel into social science research is constructed only to let in those who are ready to marginalize persons and reduce research, explanation, theory, and causation to nothing but observed relationships between variables. Critical realist personalism dissents from such a parochial, simplistic, and naive perspective that shapes not merely introductory textbooks but much of the practice of professional sociology broadly.

Consider next these issues from a moral and political perspective. Scholars working out of moral and political frameworks unrelated to the variables paradigm—for instance, political liberalism and individualism or radical socialist egalitarianism—may employ variables analyses to produce findings that inform and energize their moral and political causes. For example, a variables analysis might show that men are paid more than equally qualified and experienced women in certain labor markets, or that blacks are more likely than whites to be sentenced to longer prison terms for the same crimes. Such findings may be used by morally and politically committed scholars to inform and invigorate their activism against inequality and injustice. But it is worth noting that there is nothing intrinsic to the method or logic or apparent background ontology of the variables paradigm that could generate or legitimate the liberal or humanistic or egalitarian moral and political worldviews that animate their interests in human equality, dignity, and justice in the first place. The ontology of the person inherent to the variables paradigm could never explain or defend human equality, dignity, or justice. Those commitments have to be gotten from elsewhere. This is not a fatal problem, because such commitments *can* be gotten elsewhere. Even when those commitments are justified by other sources, however, the inherent logic of variables social science arguably works at cross-purposes with moral and political commitments to human equality, dignity, and justice. To the extent that the innate logic

20. Earle Babbie, *The Basics of Social Research*, 3rd ed. (Belmont, CA: Thomson Wadsworth, 2005), 5, 16, 18, 19, italics in original.

of the variables paradigm shapes our assumptions and outlook, when we view human social life through its lens, we are told to see that what really matters are sui generis social facts represented by abstract variables and quantified factors. Those are the true agents determining human life, the social forces that "mold and transform" humans who are only "indeterminate material." Persons disappear. But how does this ontology square with serious moral and political commitments to human equality, dignity, and justice? Are not the latter simply transformed by the variables paradigm into more dependent variables to be explained by statistically significant independent variables? To think otherwise is to believe that variables analysis is an entirely neutral and purely instrumental tool to be wielded at will in the hands of analysts motivated by quite different concerns. But that view can be naive. Social science paradigms come with their own ontological and epistemological commitments that cannot be easily discarded. Analytical methods inescapably make assumptions about reality and knowledge that over time influence how and what the analyst sees and believes. To think that we can wield the variables paradigm in the service of human equality, dignity, and justice may be, I am suggesting, working with systems of thought whose underlying ontologies are moving in opposite directions. The one seems to work at cross-purposes with the other. The variables approach is designed with certain premises in mind and perhaps might not with intellectual coherence be willy-nilly deployed to ends that make quite different presuppositions.

Using Variables Analysis in Critical Realist Personalism

All of that having been said, however, I do not believe that variables social science is a lost cause. Within a framework of critical realist personalism, variables analysis can be used with intellectual integrity to produce real analytical insights. But doing so requires some shifts in thinking and expectations about what variables analysis can and ought to be doing for us. Here I try to describe what might be involved in such a different approach.

What would a variables social science look like that was adequate to critical realist personalism? First, it would take seriously the fact that variables are not causal actors. Variables do not make things happen in the social world. Human persons do. Persons are shaped by the enabling and constraining influences of their social structures—even as social structures are also always emergent entities produced by human activity. And variables can represent aspects of social structures and relevant features of human actors. But variables do not cause outcomes. Nor do variables lead to increases and decreases in the values of other variables. Real persons acting in particular contexts in the real world do. At one level, this point is obvious. And some readers might say that I am simply playing semantics here. But within the variables paradigm as it is often practiced the point is not obvious. The best sociologists I know are not confused on this issue. But many other variables-oriented scholars I observe do not work as if they understand and believe this point. Many still speak and interpret as if variables "lead to," "produce," and "have effects on" things—in short, that variables are doers. Some may dismiss this matter by insisting that these terms are merely shorthand expressions for what is really more careful but unstated thinking. But sociologists should know better that patterns of speech employed over time in self-governing social groups tend to reify and reinforce as (subjective, observer dependent) "realities" the simpler images suggested by the shorthand rather than the more complicated, accurate thinking of which the better tend to remain aware. So, critical realist personalism asks that the interpretation of statistical results references persons when people are the units of analysis. The difference in how the numbers are interpreted is not trivial. Discourse matters.

But employing critical realist personalism requires more than simply a revised discourse for interpreting results. For unanswered in even the adjusted phrasing ("people who have . . .") is the obvious question of exactly how and why for example increased education associates with more liberal social attitudes. To what can we attribute the cause or causes linking them? Here the issue of critical realism's fundamentally parting ways with positivist empiricism over the issue of causality comes to the fore. Set against a positivist empiricist backdrop, variables social sciences misguidedly thinks that it is attempting to identify lawlike regularities that take the form of observable correlation between events—that is, in more technical terms, it is working with the constant-conjuncture-of-events view of causation theorized by David Hume in the seventeenth century, as modified by probabilistic thinking developed in statistics in the nineteenth and twentieth centuries.[21] In this view, social science scores a "nomothetic"

---

21. Peter Halfpenny, "Laws, Causality, and Statistics: Positivism, Interpretivism, and Realism," *Sociological Theory* 5 (1987): 33–36; Peter Manicas, *A History and Philosophy of the Social Sciences* (Hoboken, NJ: Wiley, 1989). For a sample of how this model has shaped recent variables analysis, consider these definitions of causation. In his widely used 1953 textbook,

success when it identifies a lawlike association between more education and more liberal attitudes that holds across a population. But that approach is misguided and fated to failure—hence the lack of social science's

---

The Design of Social Research, Russell Ackoff spoke of identifying causation by focusing on X-Y relations, stating, "There must be an environment (X) such that, when X is placed in it, Y follows. For example, there must be an environment in which an increase in education is followed by an increase in income, for education is said to be the producer [cause] of higher income. . . . If these . . . conditions hold, then X is a producer [cause] of Y." Ackoff, *The Design of Social Research* (Chicago: University of Chicago Press, 1953), 66. Herbert Simon, the influential social science polymath and eventual Nobel Prize winner, defined causality in 1957 as, "an asymmetrical relation among certain variables, or subsets of variables, in a self-contained structure." Simon, *Models of Man* (New York: Wiley, 1957), 34; also see Simon, "Spurious Correlations: A Causal Interpretation," *Journal of the American Statistical Association* 49 (1954): 467–92. Arthur Stinchcombe wrote in his 1968 book *Constructing Social Theories*, which won the ASA's Sorokin Prize for Outstanding Contributions in Sociology, that "a causal law is a statement that certain values of two or more variables are connected in a certain way. . . . A causal law is a statement or proposition in a theory which says that there exists environments . . . in which a change in the value of one variable is associated with a change in the value of another variable." Stinchcombe, *Constructing Social Theories* (Chicago: University of Chicago Press, 1968), 29, 31. In his influential 1970 book on causation, Patrick Suppes wrote, "One event is the cause of another if the appearance of the first event is followed by a high probability of the appearance of the second, and there is no third event that we can use to factor out the probability relationship between the first and second events." Suppes, *A Probabalistic Theory of Causality* (Amsterdam: North-Holland Publishing, 1970), 10. According to Wesley Burr, causal explanation "explains why variation occurs in a dependent variable. . . . A causal proposition explains that the variation occurs in a dependent variable because there is variation in a certain independent variable." Burr, *Theory Construction and the Sociology of the Family* (New York: Wiley, 1973), 20. Kenneth Bollen's 1989 book *Structural Equations with Latent Variables* defines causality in this way: "If a change in y_1 accompanies a change in x_1, then x_1 is a *cause* of y_1," (41) (more recently Bollen and Stinchcombe have emphasized social mechanisms as providing explanations of causality). Charles Ragin wrote in his 1994 text *Constructing Social Research*: "Generally, quantitative social researchers identify causation with explanation. . . . The usual sequence is: 1. a pattern of covariation is identified and the strength of the correlation is assessed, 2. causation may be inferred from the correlation, and, if so, 3. an explanation is built up from the inferred causal relationship. Another way of understanding this is simply to say that quantitative social researchers construct images by examining patters of covariation among variables and inferring causation from these broad patters." Ragin, *Constructing Social Research* (Thousand Oaks, CA: Pine Forge Press, 1994), 134. Paul Allison's 1999 textbook on regression analysis states, "There are two major uses of multiple regression: prediction and causal analysis. . . . In a causal analysis, the independent variables are regarded as causes of the dependent variable. The aim of the study is to determine whether a particular independent variable *really* affects the dependent variable, and to estimate the magnitude of that effect." Allison, *Multiple Regression: A Primer* (Thousand Oaks, CA: Pine Forge Press, 1999), 1–2, italics in original.

success in identifying the universal laws of social life.[22] Critical realism is causally realist. Causation happens. Causality is real. But causation is not a matter of lawlike conjunctions between events. That is the cul-de-sac into which epistemological empiricism has forced too many thinkers, like Hume, and where many have been stuck ever since. Causation is not a matter of associations between observables. That can only ever finally lead to a hypothetical or fictionalized causation. Causation is a matter of the operation of often nonobservable yet real powers and mechanisms that naturally exist at different levels of reality and operate (or not) under certain conditions and in particular combinations to tend to produce characteristic results.[23]

22. On the failure of the "Theory Construction" movement of the 1950s and '60s to identify the laws of social life, see Shanyang Zhao, "The Beginning of the End or the End of the Beginning? The Theory Construction Movement Revisited," *Sociological Forum* 11, no. 2 (1996): 305–18. Samples of the belief over time in the existence of social laws include the following. In his influential 1895 American sociology statistics textbook, Richmond Mayo-Smith stated, "Statistics enables us to catch a glimpse of [social] relations and hence to predicate the existence of social laws." Mayo-Smith, *Statistics and Sociology* (New York: Columbia University Press, 1895), 16. Talcott Parsons, in his foundational 1937 book *The Structure of Social Action*, wrote, "It is the universal experience of science that . . . analytical elements . . . will be found to have certain uniform modes of relations to each other which hold independently of any one particular set of their values. These uniform modes of relationship between the values of analytical elements will be referred to as 'analytical laws.'" Parsons, *The Structure of Social Action* (New York: Free Press, 1937), 36. George Homans, drawing on logical positivism's deductive-nomological model of science, argued that sociological explanations are derivations of applicable "covering laws," which he described and developed as propositions "stating a relationship between at least two properties of nature. If the properties are variables, the propositions take the general form, x varies as y." Homans, *Social Behavior: Its Elementary Forms* (New York: Harcourt Brace Jovanovich, 1974), 8. In 1987 Charles Powers argued that "the discovery of real sociological laws could be closer at hand than people realize," that "our own inhibitions are all that stop us from specifying regularities of the social universe." Powers, "In Search of Sociological Laws," *Sociological Theory* 5, no. 2 (1987): 204, 205. Powers then offered six specific examples of sociological laws, all of which are stated in the form of relationships between variables; for instance, "The level of material inequality of a society increases as a function of (a) production of surplus, and (b) concentration of surveillance and control capacity" (204). In an 1988 article, John Pratt and Robert Schlaifer "discuss the conditions under which [laws] can be observed in data," concluding that laws can only be identified when randomized experimentation shows that "a strong statistical association between y and a particular group of x's can legitimately be taken to show that the value of y is in large part determined by these x's." Pratt and Schlaifer, "On the Interpretation and Observation of Laws," *Journal of Econometrics* 39 (1988): 23, 24.

23. Philip Gorski, "Social 'Mechanisms' and Comparative-Historical Sociology: A Critical Realist Proposal," in *The Frontiers of Sociology*, ed. Björn Wittrock and Peter Hedström (Leiden: Brill, 2009); Ray George Steinmetz, "Odious Comparisons: Incommensurability,

Reality is comprised of a host of entities—material and otherwise—that possess various causal powers and capacities to make things happen in the world. Those powers and capacities are often not empirically observable, at least directly. Also, those capacities are often not always triggered or activated, and so frequently do not operate to influence anything. Yet they exist. Sometimes, under certain conditions they *are* activated and do produce certain outcomes—exactly which usually depends upon complex sets of causal interactions. A key purpose of social science, therefore, is not to look for strong correlations between empirical events, but to identify and understand the various underlying causal mechanisms that produce identifiable outcomes and events of interest. And this variables analysis can help us do. The results and findings of variables analyses will not establish causality, not to mention discover the long-sought laws of social life. Rather, they may help to isolate the activity of unobservable, theorized causal mechanisms operating under specific conditions to produce particular outcomes in the observable realm of the empirical.[24] Douglas Porpora puts it this way:

> From a critical realist perspective, regression equations are not a poor form of explanation because, properly, they are not explanations at all. Properly, a regression equation constitutes only possible evidence for an explanation, not the explanation itself. . . . Because for critical realism explanation involves mechanisms rather than laws, for critical realism, evidence and explanation become distinct. For critical realism, an event-regularity, even in the rigorous form of a regression equation, cannot serve as an explanation. It is at most one, fallible piece of evidence for an explanation. Demoting regression and other statistical techniques from explanation to evidence, critical realism has no reason to reject them as such. Of course when critical realists use statistical techniques,

the Case Study, and 'Small N's' in Sociology," *Sociological Theory* 22, no. 3 (2004): 371–400; Pawson, *A Measure for Measures: A Manifesto for Empirical Sociology*; Peter Hedström and Richard Swedberg, eds., *Social Mechanisms: An Analytical Approach to Social Theory* (Cambridge: Cambridge University Press, 1998); Mats Ekström, "Causal Explanation of Social Action: The Contribution of Max Weber and of Critical Realism to a Generative View of Causal Explanation in Social Science," *Acta Sociologica* 35 (1992): 107–22. Also see Mario Bunge, *Social Science under Debate* (Toronto: University of Toronto Press, 1998), 21–33; and James Mahoney, "Revisiting General Theory in Historical Sociology," *Social Forces* 83, no. 2 (2004): 460–62.

24. Amit Ron, "Regression Analysis and the Philosophy of Social Science: A Critical Realist View," *Journal of Critical Realism* 1, no. 1 (2002): 119–42. Also see Goldthorpe, *On Sociology*, 151–60.

they are not searching for invariant relationships independent of social context. Instead, the statistics are employed to indicate the operation of a mechanism in a particular socio-historical situation.[25]

That which is empirically observed always operates at the "surface" of reality. What matters more are the underlying causal powers and mechanisms that generate the contours of social life. And since those powers and mechanisms are not often directly observable—only their effects are observable—we can finally disabuse ourselves of the expectation that empirical variables analysis will somehow establish causal influence. It won't and we don't need it to. Instead, we need variables analysis as one tool in the larger tool kit to help us confirm or disconfirm our theories about real mechanisms by focusing particular conditions in which mechanisms appear to operate to produce observable effects.[26] The mechanisms always exist in the real world and are represented to us through the conceptual mediations of our theories. Our theories, in turn, are developed not by studying statistical output printouts but by employing our best personal, substantive knowledge as participants in reality about how reality operates.[27]

Some important implications flow from this view. The first concerns attention to causal mechanisms. In recent years many sociologists have realized the importance of identifying mechanisms that explain their statistical results. Sociologists routinely talk about mechanisms today. But that itself does not mean that variables sociology as a research program has grasped the larger issues that make mechanisms so important. If the recent attention to mechanisms is not well grounded in a compelling philosophy of science that explains why identifying mechanisms is essential,

25. Douglas Porpora, "Recovering Causality: Realist Methods in Sociology," in *Realismo Sociologico*, ed. A. Maccarini, E. Morandi, and R. Prandini (Genoa-Milan: Marietti, 2008); also see Douglas Porpora, "Do Realists Run Regressions?" in *After Postmodernism: An Introduction to Critical Realism*, ed. José López, and Garry Potter (New York: Continuum, 2001), 260–66.

26. See James Coleman, *Introduction to Mathematical Sociology* (New York: Free Press, 1964), 1–54.

27. Douglas Porpora, "Sociology's Causal Confusion," in *Revitalizing Causality: Realism about Causality in Philosophy and Social Science*, ed. Ruth Groff (New York: Routledge, 2007). Also see Tony Lawson, *Economics and Reality* (London: Routledge, 1997); Lawson, "A Realist Theory for Economics," in *New Directions in Economic Methodology*, ed. Roger Backhouse (London: Routledge, 1994), 257–85; Lawson, "Feminism, Realism, and Universalism," *Feminist Economics* 5, no. 2 (1999): 25–59; Lawson, *Reorienting Economics* (London: Routledge, 2003).

then mechanisms will always remain a post hoc, intuitive affair. Without an alternative rationale to positivism justifying a concern with mechanisms, the current attention to mechanisms could well fade into neglect, given sociology's historical record, as it is overtaken by some other fad.[28] The most noted theoretical work on social mechanisms to date points us in the right direction but does not get the bigger theoretical picture entirely right.[29] The currently most important exemplar of empirical scholarship focused on mechanisms rather than covering laws provides a good model for what an alternative social science can look like, but even this exemplar lacks a coherent larger metatheory explaining its correct analytical commitments.[30] Until positivist empiricism is explicitly identified and rejected as the operative background philosophy generating and perpetuating variables sociology, it will continue to exert its harmful influences on scholarship, even (perhaps especially) among those who do not care a hoot about philosophy. Currently much of variables sociology is trying by intuition to get to the right place, but it remains hampered by an obsolete, inaccurate positivist roadmap that recurrently leads it astray. Critical realism is the single philosophy of social science today that can tell variables sociology exactly why causal social mechanisms are crucial to its research program and how quantitative analysis can go about better understanding them. In short, we must not be lulled into an unjustified contentment or think that we have solved the causality challenge simply because so many sociologists are talking lately about mechanisms. The current mechanisms talk needs to be much better grounded in a larger philosophy that helps it make sense and that will sustain a reasoned commitment to the analysis of causal mechanisms over the long run.

The second implication concerns generalizations. Social science is (rightly) concerned with generalizable knowledge, with reliable generalizations that apply to many cases, not only to one case. But what is the nature of the general that is to be sought? What is it about reality that our generalizations ought to represent? Mainstream variables social science—following positivist empiricism—seeks generalizations in universal or regular correlations between observable events. "All else being equal,

28. See James Rule, *Theory and Progress in Social Science* (Cambridge: Cambridge University Press, 1997).

29. Hedström and Swedberg, eds., *Social Mechanisms: An Analytical Approach to Social Theory.*

30. Doug McAdam, Sidney Tarrow, and Charles Tilly, *Dynamics of Contention* (Cambridge: Cambridge University Press, 2001).

more X associates with more Y (scope condition statement missing)." Etcetera. That is the wrong approach. The correct view is that social science
seeks to identify general causal mechanisms that tend to operate to produce characteristic outcomes in a variety of kinds of contexts. What is general does not concern predictably observed events. What is general instead
concerns the underlying causal mechanisms that tend to produce events.
What success looks like, in this case, is not a growing list of nomothetic
covering laws of social life. What success looks like, instead, is a growing understanding of the underlying causal powers and mechanisms that
tend to produce various observed patterns of facts and events in human
social life. The right use of variables analyses, therefore, does not seek
generalizations represented as correlations between variables. The right
use models social conditions that demonstrate the effects of unobservable
powers and mechanisms operating to produce observable characteristic
outcomes. The generalizable knowledge that successful social science will
then have to offer will be about the most important causal mechanisms
that shape our social experiences—what they are, under what conditions
they are suppressed and activated, and how, when activated, they tend to
operate alone and in combination with other mechanisms to produce certain characteristic outcomes.

A third implication of critical realist personalism's appropriation of
variables social science concerns the critical importance of personal, substantive, experiential knowledge of the real social world on the part of
analysts for producing good social science. Misguided ideas about scientific objectivity have marginalized the personal experiences and particularistic knowledge of scholars—specific experience and viewpoints, it has
been thought, should be supplanted by the superior understanding of that
which is objective and universal. If all of the workings of the social world
were laid bare on the surface of reality for direct empirical observation
and understanding, such an approach might make some sense. But that is
not the case. We cannot rely on observation alone to understand reality.
We have to use our reasoned comprehension to grasp the real underlying
powers and dynamics that give rise to the observable. And such reasoned
comprehension is highly dependent upon, not obstructed by, the personal
experiential education, tacit knowledge, creative insight, and intuitive
awareness about the operations of reality that come through lived, personal participation in it. Scholars who were somehow to erase or bracket
off all of their personal, experiential knowledge about the world in order to
do their research "objectively" would be terrible scholars. Their scholarship

would be junk. Scientific knowledge without personal knowledge amounts to ignorant proceduralism. Personal experiences and perspectives can of course distort our visions of what is real. But we cannot solve that problem by somehow eliminating our personal, tacit knowledge gained through experiential participation in reality. We must begin with a personal commitment to truth and employ certain shared scholarly methods and communication mechanisms to attempt to reach our best truth claims. One thing this means for variables social science is that sitting in computer labs crunching out numbers *must* be balanced by more personal, experience-based field research, interviews, and participant observation that enhance our substantive personal knowledge, if we want our variables-based scholarship to live up to its potential in explanation and insight.[31]

Fourth, critical realist research programs in the variables sociology mode should break free of the myopic vision entailed in field-defined "literatures." Every study rightly converses with and builds upon previous research. The standard method, however, is for studies primarily or only to review the relevant literature in their own substantive fields that sets up their own contributions. Studies of education build on other studies of education, studies of deviance reference other research on deviance, studies of marriage build on the literature on marriage, and so on. Behind that standard approach, however, lies positivist empiricism's erroneous background assumption about covering laws of social life appropriate to their specific fields—middle-range laws—that are supposedly the nomothetic sociologist's job to discover. Assumed about such covering laws is that when it comes to various domains of social life certain observable facts and events will be associated with other facts and events. "If X then (probably) Y." However, critical realism shifts our attention away from such (fictional) covering laws and focuses us on understanding social causal mechanisms. That shift positions us to see that the same or similar underlying social mechanisms can operate *across* many domains of social life to produce analogous results. For example, the general social causal mechanism operative in the process by which homophily tends to generate segmented groups with internal homogeneity can be triggered and

31. I therefore agree with Robert Putnam's observation about the importance in social research of "soaking and poking," which, he says, "requires the researcher to marinate herself in the minutiae of an institution—to experience its customs and practices, its successes and failings, as those who live it every day do. The immersion sharpens our intuitions and provides innumerable clues about how the institution fits together and how it adapts to its environment." Putnam, *Making Democracy Work* (Princeton, NJ: Princeton University Press, 1993), 12.

made manifest in a wide range of social settings and situations. There is every reason for scholars in any field to understand all they can about the social causal mechanisms that are most relevant for their subjects of study. They can do this in part by learning how similar mechanisms operate similarly and differently in *different* domains of social life. Research programs should focus on understanding the general dynamics of key causal mechanisms that operate across that variety of social fields, instead of searching for elusive "if → then" regularities pertinent to isolated fields, such as education, deviance, and marriage. In which case, scholars from areas as diverse as, say, the sociology of small groups, race relations, religion, and occupations might pursue their shared interest by better understanding the workings of homophily as a general social mechanism as it relates to their specific interests by learning about that across fields. With the standard approach, however, everyone goes their separate way and interacts primarily with other scholars in their specific fields. Yet by broadening out from segmented substantive fields and foregrounding causal mechanisms that may work similarly in a host of social areas, scholars in different fields can work together to generate generalizable knowledge about real underlying social dynamics that explain the workings of social life more generally. In practice, this will break down some of the walls that currently silo sociologists into different fields, uniting them instead around the systematic, disciplined study of various causal mechanisms.

Finally, it is worth noting that some established statistical procedures do a better job of keeping coherent persons together as units of analysis rather than fragmenting them up into variables. Cluster analysis, factor analysis, and latent class analysis, for instance, can be used as data-reduction techniques that center on persons and seek to identify meaningful subgroups of persons in populations.[32] Qualitative Comparative Analysis

32. See, for instance, Brett Laursen and Erika Hoff, "Person-Centered and Variable-Centered Approaches to Longitudinal Data," *Merrill-Palmer Quarterly* 52, no. 3 (2006): 377–89; Bengt Muthen and Linda Muthen, "Integrating Person-Centered and Variable-Centered Analyses: Growth Mixture Modeling with Latent Trajectory Classes," *Alcoholism* 24 (2000): 882–91; J. Vermunt and J. Magidson, "Latent Class Cluster Analysis," in *Applied Latent Class Analysis*, ed Jacques Hagenaars and Allan McCutcheon (Cambridge: Cambridge University Press, 2009), 89–106; J. Vermunt, "Multilevel Class Models," *Sociological Methodology* 33 (2003): 213–39; Lisa Pearce, E. Michael Foster, and Jessica Hardie, "A Person-Oriented Approach to Classifying Religiosity," unpublished paper, University of North Carolina, Chapel Hill, 2007; Sophia Rabe-Hesketh, Anders Skrondal, and Andrew Pickles, "Generalized Multilevel Structural Equation Modeling," *Psychometrika* 69 (2004): 167–90; John Horn, "Comments on Integrating Person-Centered and Variable-Centered Research on Problems Associated with the Use of Alcohol," *Alcoholism* 24, no. 6 (2000): 924–30; Daniel Bauer,

(QCA) and Fuzzy Set analysis also provide an alternative to general linear models that view cases as coherent entities comprised of conglomerations of factors operating through conjunctural or combinational causation.[33] Combining statistical analyses with in-depth fieldwork and interviews, including an emphasis on "miniaturism," also fits the critical realist approach.[34] Critical realist personalism encourages these kinds of statistical analyses that exploit such person-centered and case-centered approaches. Beyond this, I will elaborate some rules of thumb below for conducting statistical analysis in the critical realism mode.

An Example

To try to make some of this more concrete, I provide a brief example drawn from a field I know reasonably well, the sociology of religion. My example concerns the fate of religion in the modern world and is framed at the most general level by the rival secularization and religious economies theories. For much of the history of modern sociology, it was believed that modernity would undermine the plausibility and influence of religion. That belief was advanced in secularization theory, which elaborated different explanations of how and why religious decline and perhaps extinction would occur. Some said the rational explanations of science would displace religious myths. Others suggested that a variety of state and professional organizations would take over most of the material and social functions that religion traditionally provided. Yet others argued that social, cultural, and especially religious pluralism would corrode certainty about particularistic religious beliefs or perhaps force them into the private sphere in order to avoid conflict in public life. Whatever the explanation, secularization theory predicted that more modernity—particularly as represented by science, rationality, individual freedom, institutional differentiation, market competition, and cultural pluralism—would mean less religion.

"Person-Centered Approaches to Data Analysis," paper presented at the conference on Modeling Developmental Processes in Ecological Context, Tempe, Arizona, 2004. Note that some cluster analyses simply cluster variables across persons rather than persons by their associated variables, so the right method is important.

33. Ragin, *Fuzzy Set Social Science.*

34. John Stolte, Gary Alan Fine, and Karen Cook, "Sociological Miniaturism: Seeing the Big through the Small in Social Psychology," *Annual Review of Sociology* 27 (2001): 387–413.

That view of religion and modernity, however, began to be doubted by
some in the 1980s and then was forcefully attacked in the 1990s, especially by religious economies theory. This alternative approach argued
the opposite of secularization theory, suggesting that religious practice
is a rational activity, that science and religion are not naturally in conflict,
that religious pluralism spurs entrepreneurial religious organizations to
mobilize resources, and that religious competition increases the share of
populations that are religiously affiliated. For various reasons, then, religious economies theory predicted that more modernity—as represented
by rationality, individual freedom, institutional differentiation, market
competition, and cultural and religious pluralism—could very well mean
more religion.

A great deal of scholarship in the sociology of religion in the 1990s
consisted of attempts to empirically verify or falsify one of these two
theories. They each hypothesized opposing expectations that in principle
should have been straightforwardly testable with empirical data. Much of
the most influential research in the debate employed variables analysis
to sort through the matter. And most of that presupposed—whether wit-
tingly or not—a positivist empiricist backdrop to the analyses. That meant
that investigators were looking to regular associations between variables
measuring observable facts and events to identify lawlike generalizations
about modernity and religion that would hold across populations and
cases. Does religious competition at the national level increase or decrease
levels of religious participation when viewed cross-nationally? Do higher
levels of religious pluralism in U.S. counties lead to higher or lower levels
of church attendance in those counties? And so on. The operative assumption in the research and debate was that one theory or another would
be vindicated by the empirical evidence, and that its vindicated, general,
lawlike expected associations between variables would be evident in whatever context was studied. But when all in this research dispute was said
and done, an odd thing happened. The sum total of evidence produced by
the many studies proved entirely inconclusive. A 2001 state-of-the-art *Annual Review of Sociology* chapter that analyzed 193 of the most important
pieces of empirical scholarship in the debate concluded definitively that
no definitive conclusion could be drawn.[35] Some of the studies showed one
thing, some showed another thing, and some were just unclear. Since then,

---

35. Mark Chaves and Philip Gorski, "Religious Pluralism and Religious Participation,"
Annual Review of Sociology 27 (2001): 261–81.

the debate has lost its energy. Once again, the search for a lawlike generalization about modernity and religion ended in failure.

An alternative approach to the issue—framed not by positivist empiricism but by critical realism—can explain why all of these studies as conducted and interpreted were inconclusive and can offer a constructive and illuminating way to move the larger inquiry forward. We do not need to abandon a variables approach to the matter. But we do need to conduct our variables analyses within a theoretical framework reconstructed in critical realist terms. This means the following changes. We should stop looking for generalizations in lawlike regularities of associations between observable events. We should stop thinking in zero-sum terms that either the secularization theory or the religious economies theory is true. We should stop assuming that the validity of one or another theory will be manifest similarly across different contexts. We should instead be seeking first and foremost to identify and understand the variety of underlying causal mechanisms by which aspects or dynamics of modernity influence religion, whether positively or negatively. We should expect most or all of the relevant mechanisms to exist *in potentia* within the reality comprising religion in modernity. We should expect that different specific social conditions activate or trigger different mechanisms into operative influence. We should expect the causal effect of each mechanism to be influenced by the reinforcing or neutralizing effects of other activated mechanisms. We should therefore be looking not only for independent effects of hypothesized causal influences but also for *conjunctural* and *suppressing* effects of combinations of mechanisms at work together. We should not assume that a lack of observed change in any instance means that no causal mechanisms are active, since opposing causal mechanisms might have neutralized each other. Nor should we assume that two cases that exhibit the same outcomes were produced by the same causal influences, since different combinations of mechanisms might produce similar outcomes. We should also not expect triggered mechanisms to produce similar intensities of effects in different cases, since the causal influence of such mechanisms operate only as identifiable tendencies in open systems, not consistently linear effects.

What would it look like against this critical realist backdrop for the sociology of religion to succeed in its efforts in this research program? It would look like identifying and becoming highly familiar with the inherent and interactive operations and tendencies of all of the important causal mechanisms existing in modern social structures and practices that influence the strength and character of religion. By contrast, seeking, as the sociology of religion has so far mostly done, to discover some generalizable covering laws would be viewed as misguided and hopeless. Rather than paradigms bashing each other over the head with empirical evidence purporting to validate one rival theory or the other—so common in the 1990s in the sociology of religion—critical realism would direct us to identify all of the plausible causal mechanisms suggested by all the theories. We could begin to think hard about the varying social conditions within which different mechanisms are activated, and empirically to explore the characteristic outcomes produced by different combinations of operative mechanisms. That task is much more difficult than searching for two variables that always correlate. But it is the task that is best matched to the reality in which we exist.

Framed in such terms, it suddenly becomes easy to see that the following seven distinct hypotheses, for instance, might *all* be correct in different contexts and under different conditions:

- Religious pluralism tends to corrode the certainties of believers' traditional faith who previously occupied religiously homogeneous settings.
- Religious pluralism in free religious markets tends to mobilize religious entrepreneurs into promotional activities to recruit more adherents.
- Religious pluralism provides a social setting in which religious groups that possess theological tools to sustain distinction-with-engagement will tend to thrive.
- Religious pluralism tends to exert homogenizing influences that reduce the distinctions among different religious groups, producing organizational isomorphism.
- Religious pluralism creates conditions in which religious organizations tend to seek to differentiate themselves from others in their identity and practice, in order to specialize in and target particular niche populations of the religious market.
- Religious pluralism tends to encourage more liberal, open, inclusive, and accommodating forms of religious community and practice.
- Religious pluralism tends to encourage more conservative, traditionalist, sectarian forms of religious community and practice.

I think that all seven of these hypotheses (and no doubt others) are true and operative in different contexts. Modernity generally increases pluralism, which typically causes a variety of diverse effects. Some of them reinforce each other. Some of them counteract each other. Some may "ricochet" off each other. Some of them may neutralize others, although those others may not neutralize them. And some of them may be "indifferent" to each other. The task of a critical realist sociology of religion is to conduct theory-informed research in order, first, to sort through which of these hypothesized causal influences is ever operative and, second, to better understand the more specific causal mechanisms that produce such operative effects of pluralism on religion, the specific kinds of social conditions that trigger different causal mechanisms, variance in the effects of different mechanisms on diverse populations and groups within the same contexts, and the configuration of different outcomes that may result from these causal dynamics. By contrast, when we stick to the positivist empiricism form of variables social science, these hypotheses get set up as if they were mutually exclusive competitors, and the research that sets out to test them ends up producing inconclusive conclusions and sometimes AMD: academic mutual destruction.

And what of the personalist part of critical realist personalism in this example? To begin, the very reason we are forced to a critical realist approach to variables social science is because human persons are what they are. Persons are not, contra Durkheim, "indeterminate material that the social factor molds and transforms."[36] Persons are naturally and powerfully capacitated agents of their own lives and of social engagement. As such, persons are endowed with immense faculties for symbolization, volition, creativity, understanding, interpretation, response, choice, anticipating the future, reflexivity, and more. This means that human social life never has entailed nor will entail the kind of law-determined relations of empirical observables operating in closed systems, which positivist empiricism assumed and hoped to master. Human social life always transpires in open systems of active, creative, responsive, relating persons existing within, perpetuating, and transforming a multileveled reality in patterned but often unpredictable ways. Persons comprise hosts of causal capacities to live in a world involving hosts of causal mechanisms that shape persons and the reality that persons inhabit. Reality, particularly human social reality, thus encompasses incredible amounts of complexity and dynamic interaction. In the midst of that kind of reality, what social science can do to enhance human understanding is not so much to discover correlated variables measured at the surface but instead to identify underlying causal

---

36. Durkheim, *The Rules of Sociological Method*, 106.

powers and mechanisms that recurrently exercise effective influences in shaping the experienced world. Variables social science can play a role in that pursuit. But the analysis of variables must take persons seriously, proceeding firmly with the commitment to the belief that persons and not variables are the causal agents of social life. Only such a view of persons can explain why the positivist empiricist version of variables analysis so often disappoints and why the critical realist alternative poses the most promising alternative.

Epistemological Humility

Critical realist personalism entails a fallibalist theory of human knowledge—meaning that our knowledge is always incomplete, endemically subject to error, and never certain. Critical realist personalism also takes seriously the fact that social scientists are persons and so are subject to all of the particularities, subjectivities, and limits of knowledge that personhood inevitably entails. Therefore, critical realist personalism commends epistemological humility in its scholarship. Some variables-oriented social scientists are well aware of the problems and their effects on our knowledge based on its findings. But many are not. Set in historical terms, as a research tradition, variables social science developed in the context of the larger positivist movement of the late nineteenth century.[37] This positivism launched the then-fledgling social sciences into academic research with an immense confidence in their ability to learn with certainty everything important there is to know about human social life.[38] Scientific knowledge about social life, it was believed, could be thorough and *positive* about itself (hence "positivism"). Unfortunately, a significant residual effect of that overly confident attitude remains in the variables paradigm today. Many variables analysts seem to believe confidently that they can get

37. Dorothy Ross, *The Origins of American Social Science* (Cambridge: Cambridge University Press, 1992); Christopher Bryant, *Positivism in Social Theory and Research* (New York: St. Martin's Press, 1985); Gillis Harp, *Positivist Republic: Auguste Comte and the Reconstruction of American Liberalism, 1865–1920* (University Park: Pennsylvania State University Press, 1995); Thomas Haskell, *The Emergence of Professional Social Science* (Baltimore: Johns Hopkins University Press, 2000).

38. See Christian Smith, *The Secular Revolution: Power, Interest, and Conflict in the Secularization of American Public Life* (Berkeley and Los Angeles: University of California Press, 2003), 54–56, 97–159.

social life figured out in detail through the application of sophisticated statistical methods. It is as if they were building a kind of social scientific Tower of Babel with the building blocks of variables paradigm findings. In response, the fallibalism of critical realist personalism calls our variables analyses to be more modest and realistic about what we can and will accomplish. We can learn several things about some features of human social life. But we will not learn most things or even all important dimensions of some things about social life. And we may find out that we are not entirely correct about what we think we have learned about human social life.

Here are some implications of this approach and examples of why it matters and what it might look like. The first implication of variables analysis operating in the mode of critical realist personalism embracing its fallible capacities for knowledge is that it needs to learn better to value sheer description. The first thing realism always wants to know is: what actually exists? The foremost task, therefore, is to describe what is. Quantitative social science is, as Stanley Lieberson reminds us, generally much better at telling us *what* exists and is happening in the social world than explaining *why* and *how* it exists and is happening.[39] As I have said above, social science generally wants to move beyond simple description to causal explanation. That is a legitimate aspiration. But it can only do us good to acknowledge that variables analysis is particularly limited in its ability to explain. What quantitative variables social science does best is to describe: to enumerate frequencies, chart distributions, measure observable changes, map relations, and estimate correlations between entities. Those are its real comparative advantages. And they mostly have to do with describing, not explaining. Explaining requires identifying causal mechanisms at work in social processes. And variables analysis is limited—not entirely debilitated, but definitely restricted—in its ability to do that. This admission does not need to be a huge disappointment, however. Providing accurate descriptions about the real social world—something that humans often work without—is one of the most valuable gifts that social science has to offer. It is a huge accomplishment that should not be undervalued, to know fairly accurately the extent of, distributions among, changes in, and correlations between things that matter to us. And this is true even

---

39. Lieberson, *Making It Count*, 219; David Zaret, "Statistical Techniques and Sociological Theory," *Sociological Theory* 5 (1987): 36–40. I agree with King, Keohane, and Verba: "Good description is better than bad explanation." King, Keohane, and Verba, *Designing Social Inquiry*, 45.

though we also always strive as best as we can to move beyond description toward causal explanation. In the end we need not always settle for description alone, but neither should we undervalue the importance of sheer description. Describing is central to our social science calling and we do well to accept that limited but important role in increasing knowledge and understanding.

Another aspect of epistemological humility is acknowledging that, even in much of our best variables analyses, we rarely do or perhaps can measure the most important things about our explanations, that is, the causal mechanisms at work in social processes. Most of what is of greatest importance about causal mechanisms is not represented by our variables themselves, but happens *between* the variables and so goes unmeasured. We may, for instance, find a statistical association—net of other relevant variables—between region and violent crimes, or between gender and frequency of prayer. But "region" does not cause violence and "gender" does not cause prayer. Some things about living in a particularly religious region or being a specific gender in a particular culture set into motion a variety of causal influences that result in greater acts of violence or prayer. Not only are such causal influences complicated, but also they usually are unmeasured. As for empirically demonstrating the real explanatory chains by which particular causes produce specific outcomes, most of our best variables analyses involve numerous missing links. In some cases, researchers do not know or think ahead of time to try to measure the key causal influences in their stories. In other cases, key causal influences are impossible to measure. So, the interpretive explanations of our statistical findings often require researchers filling in major explanatory gaps with inferred stories about causal relations and directions that are not actually demonstrated empirically by the data. Importantly, this often requires a heavy reliance by reviewers, editors, and readers on the *personal, subjective* plausibility of those stories to them in order for the causal explanation to make sense. Note that this is something variables analysts often disparage "qualitative" researchers for having to rely upon, but they themselves must rely upon the same personal, subjective sensibilities.

Usually the personal knowledge of reality that we participating knowers have about our social worlds suffices to sort through which interpretations are believable or not, to separate out better from worse explanations. But sometimes, in the absence of personal knowledge of or the presence of personal bias about a subject in question, reviewers, editors, and readers may reject an explanation that is correct—not because empirical evidence justifies the rejection but because personal subjectivity screens it out. For example, I have observed over the years that some personally irreligious journal reviewers can have a hard time believing that religious faith—which is alien to their personal experience—can actually motivate some people to engage in costly behaviors, and so they discount or reject a paper's causal interpretation that suggests that religious beliefs motivate costly action, insisting instead that some other factor must account for the findings. This is but one example—the general principle could just as easily apply to all sorts of other personal subjective dispositions, including personally highly religious reviewers being inclined to reject an (actually correct) interpretation of statistical findings suggesting that religious motives are neutralized or trumped by the interests of, say, race or social class or gender. The point here is not that the personal or subjective existence of scholars is a problem, any more than the time- and space-bound nature of the social world we study is a problem. Recall, as I argued above, that all human knowledge, including scientific knowledge, is inescapably *personal* knowledge, and necessarily and helpfully so. The point is more specifically that variables sociology rarely measures causal mechanisms at work directly, and so interpretations of findings usually require the filling in of explanatory narratives lacking immediate reference to empirical observations, the plausibility of which stories turn out to be heavily dependent upon the personal, subjective resonance they have with those evaluating them. This muddles the allegedly clear line between "hard," quantitative, variables analyses and "soft" qualitative research. We might respond by saying that survey researchers need to do a better job of measuring causal mechanisms more directly. Yes, we do. But critical realist personalism also tells us that what is real, including causally real, often does not exist "at the surface" of reality to be easily or directly observed. So we will regularly hit limits to our ability to measure causal mechanisms directly. And realizing this ought to engender humility about our analytical capacities.

The typical response by variables scholars to such causal problems is to turn to longitudinal studies, in which great faith is placed. If we can collect data over time, the argument goes, we will definitely be able to show causation at work. For many variables paradigm scholars, in my experience, longitudinal data is viewed as a kind of panacea, a supposed magic bullet solving our causation problems. Repeatedly I hear scholars looking to longitudinal analyses to overcome the limitations of causal explanations that we encounter when analyzing cross-sectional data. But longitudinal studies are no magic bullet. Longitudinal data are indeed a great improvement over cross-sectional data, improving our abilities to assess causal forces operating over time. Yet the fact remains that, even when we do have multiwave longitudinal data, we always still lack information about many significant facts and events occurring between waves that go unmeasured. We may, for example, know respondents' levels of alcohol consumption or sexual activities or church attendance at Time 1, Time 2, and Time 3. But, unless we specifically ask about it, we have no idea about those activities during the times *between* waves of data collection—and that is often no trivial matter. Furthermore, being able to show that differences in certain variables at Time 1 are associated with differences in other variables at Time 2 or Time 3—net of relevant control variables and perhaps lagged dependent variables—does little empirically to identify and verify causal mechanisms. Longitudinal data help to address the question of chronological causal order. And they can provide more complex descriptions of important observable changes over time. But they cannot make key causal mechanisms empirically accessible that were not directly measured—and many are not. Nor can they prove that an observed statistical correlation is the result of causal relations. Nor can they account for important processes, influences, and unobserved changes occurring between the points in time of data collection. The fundamental problems still remain. Again, it is not that longitudinal studies in the variables paradigm are not preferable to cross-sectional studies. They generally are. But we should not fool ourselves into overestimating their ability to provide the kind of definitive causal knowledge that many seem to believe they can. Even when using longitudinal data, humility and an understanding of their limits are needed.

Epistemological humility applied to variables analysis also suggests that sometimes, if not oftentimes, simpler statistical analyses of variables are more appropriate and helpful than highly complex ones. Simpler analyses often help to keep the data closer to the human actors they represent. Sometimes a handful of three-way elaboration cross-tabulations tells us everything we need to know. But for various reasons most variables analysts seem to want to increase complexity, as if more is always better. A simple example: it is well known that multivariate regression should really only control for variables that are associated with *both* the explanatory independent variables and the dependent variable. Yet the standard practice is to throw long lists of control variables into models without rationale. Such unnecessary and unjustified complexity creates the potential for statistical problems. But few journal article reviewers today will accept simple but solid models containing only handfuls of key variables. No, we have to feel that we have all of the ritualistic methodological bases covered, and then some. That is just the start of arguably unnecessary statistical complexity. Open up any issue of a top sociology journal, observe the hyperstatistical sophistication, and then ask yourself whether the findings and conclusions are any more accurate and believable than those simpler analyses based on more direct substantive observation and knowledge could have produced. Oftentimes not. Cranking up the complexity of the variables approach to manic levels may reinforce a general perception that our analyses are more "scientific" and, so, authoritative. It may also please the aesthetic sensibilities of scholars who love complex mathematics. But it does not necessarily tell us more truth about what is real and how that reality works. Sometimes it works against those goals. In response, critical realist personalism suggests this rule of thumb: we should as a default use the least complex analysis that is needed to answer our research questions well.[40]

Critical realist personalism recommends two additional maxims for the conduct of variables social science. The next is: Not every interesting and important question can be answered.[41] Many say that they know this. But I doubt most really believe it. Admitting such limits feels so, well, premodern, after all. Thus, many proceed in scholarship as if—aside from certain ethical challenges—every puzzle can be solved, every concept measured, every mystery explained, and every question answered. This is hubris, not in keeping with the real limits of human knowledge. The problem is not that we have not yet secured enough grant money, or that uncooperative respondents will not answer our long and intricate survey questionnaires, or that we have not yet fully developed our capacity to measure latent variables well. The problem—if indeed it even is a problem—is that human persons are creatures of immense personal depth and complexity, who are not fully transparent to themselves or others, and for whom certain concerns are not accessible and measurable. Add to that the "open systems" nature of human social life—compared to the "closed system" character

40. This advice—seemingly rarely given or heeded in the social sciences—was first offered to me by one of my excellent graduate school mentors, Steve Rytina—now of McGill University—who was and is, not incidentally, mathematically brilliant and personally capable of any amount of statistical complexity imaginable.

41. Lieberson refers to this as "The Doctrine of the Undoable" (*Making It Count*, 8–12).

of some natural science laboratories—and we quickly (ought to) realize the limits to our ability to understand and explain what we might want to know. Importantly, in other words, the problems involved are not all contingent upon situations but are often constitutive of the subject. Our very human personhood by natural character fixes limits on our capacity to know about ourselves, even given considerable resources and the best methods. Fully believing and embracing the fact that not every one of our interesting and important questions can be answered suggests to us quite a different self-image for the social sciences than the self-assured, true, and positive science of society that many of us have inherited from our professional forebears.

The other maxim that critical realist personalism recommends is this: Sometimes it is better simply to know nothing than to think we know something that may very well be flawed and erroneous. There are studies best not conducted, surveys best not fielded, papers best not published. If they cannot be done right, often it is best not to do them at all. This is because—being the kind of open, creative, self-reflexive, self-forming creatures that we human persons are—what we take to be true about social reality is not merely interesting, neutral information for our minds. Believed knowledge about reality can and does transform us, our inter-actions with social realty, and potentially, as a result, social reality itself. When the chemist makes a mistake in her laboratory, the chemistry she is studying does not change. But when the social scientist makes a mistake and publishes the mistaken findings, this holds the potential to change the reflexive human social world being studied. And if—because of, say, sample nonresponse biases, flawed survey questions, misspecified statistical models, or any number of other knowable flaws in our research—the findings of our studies are misleading or in error, then they can have pernicious practical consequences. In short, social science research, in a way that is not quite true of natural science research, holds the potential to alter what it studies. And social science research findings can be and sometimes are erroneous. So every publication of findings runs the risk of altering the social world on mistaken grounds and perhaps for the worse. Therefore, when we have reason to believe that the results of a research project or analysis may very well be flawed, epistemological humility suggests that we not conduct it or publish them. I have known surveys to be conducted with response rates so low and the probability of nonresponse biases so high that no claims about the sample's representation of the population it purports to represent are reasonably defensible—yet their investigators, upon questioning, have insisted, "Knowing something is better than know-ing nothing." Wrong. What critical realism asserts instead is that knowing something that is very likely to be true is better than knowing nothing (especially when we keep in mind that relative likelihood), but also that knowing nothing is also better than "knowing" something that could very well be incorrect—because a passive nothing will not mislead us as much as a positive error. This self-limitation raises the bar on what is required of published variables sociology to be valuable and responsible, especially insofar as variables sociology is particularly subject to statistical errors that are not checked by fieldwork in natural settings. Publish or perish be damned, in this case, because truth and reality are more important than curriculum vitae and careers.

Rules of Thumb

This chapter cannot advance an elaborate critical realist methodology for variables analysis. A great deal more thought and work needs to be done to sort through the relevant issues and possibilities. But it is worth noting certain rules of thumb that would likely be involved in an approach of critical realist personalism to variables sociology.[42] They include these:

- Focus on real causal mechanisms—remember that the goal is to understand how nonobservable social causal mechanisms produce types of outcomes and events, not merely to find significant correlations among variables.
- Assume that social reality is not uniform but complex, variegated, and open in nature and operation—no one principle, feature, or dynamic will explain it.
- Remember that what is general in sociological knowledge concerns analytically generalizable understandings of social mechanisms, not general "If X then (probably) Y" covering laws.

42. Existing works attempting to spell out some methodological implications of critical realism include Andrew Sayer, *Method in Social Science: A Realist Approach* (New York: Routledge, 1992); Pawson, *A Measure for Measures: A Manifesto for Empirical Sociology*; Bob Carter and Caroline New, eds., *Making Realism Work: Realist Social Theory and Empirical Research* (New York: Routledge, 2004); Porpora, "Do Realists Run Regressions?" in *After Postmodernism: An Introduction to Critical Realism*, ed. López, and Potter; Derek Layder, *Sociological Practice: Linking Theory and Social Research* (London: Sage, 1998).

- Remember that a statistically significant association between observed variables explains *nothing whatsoever*; it only presents a fact that needs explaining through a conceptual understanding of real causal mechanisms.
- Statistics cannot replace conceptualization—rigorously conceptualize and theorize about what exists and how it might work before ever touching a dataset.
- Engage literatures that address relevant causal mechanisms as they operate even in very different substantive fields—plural knowledge bases are assets.
- Do not use statistics to try to understand and explain social realities about which you do not already have extensive, personal, substantive knowledge—significant personal experience, fieldwork, and interviews should normally precede quantitative analysis.
- Pay close, critical attention to response rates and likely nonresponse biases in the data—do not ask a sample to validly represent a population when it cannot.
- Capitalize on description—statistics are best at describing reality, so describe and analyze thoroughly with simple statistics before jumping ahead to multivariate work.
- Consider all of the statistical methods options—do not automatically jump to multiple regression techniques to identify independent effects, as there may be better ways to get your questions answered (and methods to prod you to ask better questions).
- Employ multiple techniques to address the same explanatory concerns from different angles.
- Use variables to model causal mechanisms and processes as directly and explicitly as possible, not merely factors generally associated with mechanisms and processes.
- Use simpler methods available that solve your problem well, all else being equal—less is sometimes more.
- Direct independent effects alone are probably inadequate for explaining—investigate possible indirect effects, interaction effects, and conjunctural causes.
- Prefer culturally meaningful categorical variables over abstract continuous variables—create categorical dummy variables around person types based on culturally significant categories of respondents.
- Build models that include relevant measures of objective social structural dimensions as well as actors' subjective meaning-governed aspects of the realities in question, since both are aspects of the real.
- Believe that causation is real, even when nonobservable—do not be afraid to theorize causal dynamics and draw conclusions even when the data do not (because they cannot) "prove" cause and effect.

- Asterisks indicating "significantly more likely than" are not enough—always come clean on the substantive strength of any significant variable's associations and tell *how* much more likely than.
- Doubt and avoid the "findings" phrases "leads to" and "predicts"—either claim causal relations clearly or do not.
- No one analysis will be definitive—many cumulative studies will be needed not only to replicate and extend findings but also to examine different scope conditions and mechanism combinations in various settings; success in variables analysis involves a long-term, collective project.
- Not knowing is better than error—when we have good reason to doubt the validity or reliability of our data or findings, drop the project and settle for ignorance until more reliable data or findings can be obtained.
- Understanding and communicating the truth about reality is the ultimate goal, not accumulating publications—only publish that which genuinely helps to achieve the goal.

These are only a start. Critical realist and personalist sociologists have more work to do to rethink variables sociology. Critical realist personalism promises not to subvert variables sociology but to reframe it and improve its practice and contribution to knowledge. It should make a real difference. More important in this than changing specific techniques or running models in different ways, however, is first coming to the entire process with a different frame of mind about what social science and the social reality it studies are like, what social science ought to be seeking to accomplish, and what methods it has at its disposal to do that.

Conclusion

Critical realist personalism has something to say not only about theories and paradigms such as social constructionism and network structuralism. It also speaks to the more standard paradigm of variables analysis that has dominated most of the social sciences for decades. As it did with social constructionism and network structuralism, critical realist personalism finds both value and problems in the variables paradigm. Minimizing the problems and rightly capitalizing on that value requires that we reframe the variables approach within the terms of critical realist personalism. This demands that we first expunge the positivist assumptions and sensibilities that have long animated variables analysis. It means that we intentionally work to make not variables but persons the causal agents of the social world. It pushes us to develop specific person-centered methods of statistical analysis. It requires that we be clear in our own minds and scholarship about the nature and operation of causality. And it demands that we own up to and deal constructively with the inherent limits of our fallibalistic knowledge about social life as confronted in the variables approach. When variables social science is conducted in the wrong framework, making false assumptions, and with unrealistic aspirations, it is misguided and often misguiding. But when properly understood and used, variables analysis can serve as an important tool in our larger scholarly tool kit to help us better understand the truth about the reality of the social world of human persons.

PART III

Constructive Development

The Personal Sources of
Social Structures

"Social structure" is *the* central theoretical concept in sociology. It is also often an important idea implicitly and sometimes explicitly referred to in political science, economics, and history. And yet social structure is often only vaguely defined in these disciplines. The term *structure* is continually evoked in sociological analyses and debates. Often it seems to mean the opposite of *ideas* or *culture*. Yet not frequently do participants in sociological discussions seem to have a clear idea of what a social structure *is*. Recently, Pierre Bourdieu, Anthony Giddens, and William Sewell Jr. have taken steps toward clarifying the meaning of the idea. But I am not entirely persuaded that we have yet firmly grasped the nettle when it comes to understanding social structures. My aim in this chapter, therefore, is to contribute to theorizing social structures from the perspective of critical realist personalism, toward greater clarity and insight. In the following pages, I explore what social structures are ontologically, advance an account of their sources, and examine how they change. In keeping with the critical realist personalism elaborated in this book, I will, among other things, suggest that social structures are *real entities* of a particular sort and that possessing a thick notion of *persons* is essential for rightly understanding what social structures are and why and how they come to exist and change.

The Ontology of Social Structures

What *is* a social structure?[1] For many people, including some social scientists, it can be difficult to believe in the reality of social structures. That is

1. My discussion in what follows is significantly informed in various ways by Douglas Porpora, *The Concept of Social Structure* (New York: Greenwood Press, 1987); Porpora, "Four

because social structures are not tangible or directly observable. We can
see and inspect an architectural structure, such as a skyscraper. And we
can physically inspect communications infrastructures of, say, a corporate
computer network. But what about *social* structures? When we refer to
social class structures or the structure of a society's race relations or a
labor market structure, it is hard for some—given widespread empiricist
biases—to believe that such things exist, as buildings and computer systems exist. And yet without the reality of social structures, much of social
science loses its subject and raison d'être. One tradition in the social sciences, commonly called *materialist*, has addressed this uncertainty by emphasizing the tangible aspects of structures. Social structures are evident,
for example, in the material arrangements of managerial office and factory
floors, in the different amount of dollars in various workers' paychecks, in
flows of commodity imports and exports in a world system of trade, and
so on.[2] A different social science tradition, which we might call *cognitivist*,
has instead underscored deep mental categories that it says organize the

---

Concepts of Social Structure," *Journal for the Theory of Social Behavior* 19, no. 2 (1989):
195–211; Porpora, "Social Structure: The Future of a Concept," in *Structure, Culture, and History: Recent Issues in Social Theory*, ed. Sing Chew and J. David Knottnerus (Lanham, MD:
Rowman and Littlefield, 2002), 43–59; Porpora, "Cultural Rules and Material Relations," *So-
ciological Theory* 11, no. 2 (1993): 212–29; John Scott, "Where Is Social Structure?" in *After
Postmodernism: An Introduction to Critical Realism*, ed. José López, and Garry Potter (New
York: Continuum, 2001), 77–85; William Sewell Jr., "A Theory of Structure: Duality, Agency,
and Transformation," *American Journal of Sociology* 98, no. 1 (1992): 1–29; Neil Smelser,
"Social Structure," in *Handbook of Sociology* (Newbury Park, CA: Sage, 1988), 103–29; Sam
Porter, "Critical Realist Ethnography," in *Qualitative Research in Action*, ed. Tim May (Lon-
don: Sage, 2002); Peter Blau, ed., *Approaches to the Study of Social Structure* (New York: Free
Press, 1975); Steven Rytina, "Social Structure," in *Encyclopedia of Sociology*, ed. Edgar Bor-
gatta (New York: Macmillan Reference, 2000); José López and John Scott, *Social Structure*
(Philadelphia: Open University Press, 2000); Anthony Giddens, *The Constitution of Society*
(Berkeley and Los Angeles: University of California Press, 1984); Jeffrey Alexander, *Action
and Its Environments* (New York: Columbia University Press, 1988), 11–45; Charles Varela
and Rom Harré, "Conflicting Varieties of Realism: Causal Powers and the Problems of Social
Structure, *Journal for the Theory of Social Behaviour* 26, no. 3 (1996): 313–25; James House,
"Social Structure, Relationships, and the Individual," in *Sociological Perspectives on Social
Psychology*, ed. Karen Cook, Gary Fine, and James House (Boston: Allyn and Bacon, 1995),
387–95. I have also benefited from reading Jonathan Turner, *Human Institution: A Theory of
Social Evolution*, (Lanham, MD: Rowman and Littlefield, 2003).

    2. Already here, however, the inadequacies of such an approach begin to show themselves
for underappreciating the culturally and symbolically constituted nature of the meanings of
the material world—that is, of the centrality of institutional facts (see chapter 3) in composing social structures. There are, for instance, no nonculturally defined dollars actually "in" a
paycheck, just as managerial offices and factory floors mean nothing apart from the culturally

social world. The world of human relations, it believes, is fundamentally ordered by deep-seated, usually binary, cognitive classifications embedded in the brain or in some basic mental constitution.[3] Other social scientists, such as those we examined in chapter 4, conceive of social structure as the concrete networks of relationships that tie people together. Yet another conception of social structures is of stable multidimensional spaces of differentiated social statuses and positions in a society, defined, for example, by differences in sex, race, age, socioeconomic status, religion, education, and occupation.[4] These status differentiations, or "parameters"—whether they are categorical (e.g., religious positions) or ranked (e.g., income levels)—are said to structure social life, whether their occupants have direct relational ties or not.

Some accounts argue that social structures are governed by underlying principles existing in the "substratum" of society—whether they be the norms and values of society, as with Talcott Parsons's structural functionalism; or the means and relations of material production, as with Marxism; or some kind of deep mental structures, as with Claude Lévi-Strauss's anthropological structuralism. Other accounts view social structures as the empirical patterns of life that arise and accumulate as individual people interact—whether through rational exchanges, as, for example, with James Coleman's rational choice theory; or meaningful symbolic intercommunications, as with Herbert Blumer's symbolic interactionism. Yet other accounts identify social structures as the de facto orderings of social existence that materialize sui generis as societies evolve and differentiate into more complex systems of statuses, roles, positions, and rankings—as with, for instance, Peter Blau's theory of social parameters. Furthermore, some theories view structure as driven by rationally instrumental action and yet others by normative beliefs.[5] And certain theorists claim that social structures are real while others say that they are only "virtual."[6]

defined meaningful roles of manager and laborer, both of which are culturally defined by nonmaterial ideas and beliefs.

3. See, for instance, Marshall Sahlins, *Culture and Practical Reason* (Chicago: University of Chicago Press, 1978).

4. Peter Blau, *Inequality and Heterogeneity* (New York: Academic Press, 1977); Blau, "Parallels and Contrasts in Structural Inquiries," in *Approaches to the Study of Social Structure* (New York: Free Press, 1975), 1–20.

5. Alexander, *Action and Its Environments*, 18–30.

6. Compare the structurationist Giddens, *The Constitution of Society*, and the realist Margaret Archer, *Realist Social Theory* (Cambridge: Cambridge University Press, 1995).

What then are we to make of these different perspectives? Can we articulate a theory that ties together the best of the different approaches? I think it is possible to identify a core set of constituents involved in most interesting views of social structure with which to state a basic definition. We can then elaborate that definition by noting more complex features of social structures on which different theories shed light. With those in mind we can develop a more complicated and useful understanding of social structures.

Before moving into the abstractions of definitions, however, it may be useful to lay out some concrete examples from the social world that social scientists would typically refer to as social structures, to which we can refer in the discussion below. The following examples include structures operating at different levels of social reality,[7] as well as informal, formal, and legal types. Consider, then, the following conditions we might find in varying social situations:

- All of the agriculturally productive land in a region is owned by a few wealthy landowning families who employ some of the local landless peasants to labor in seasonal production for subsistence wages—this, as opposed to the widespread distribution of land ownership among yeoman family-farmers and homesteaders.
- Students in a school are divided into the different "crowds" of jocks, geeks, goths, burnouts, preps, band members, swimmers, and other groups and cliques—this, as opposed to relations in a school that consistently stresses standardization, solidarity, social participation in cross-cutting groups, and the wearing of uniforms.
- A society's religious institutions operate in a totally free-market system without any support from the state, creating competition among congregations as pure voluntary associations for individual adherents and support—this, as opposed to a monopoly enjoyed by one state-backed religion involving the suppression of other competing religious groups.
- A legislature is routinely inundated by lobbyists representing wealthy and powerful interest groups whose favors to lawmakers powerfully shape legislation and regulations to their own narrow benefit—this, as opposed to a decentralized participatory democracy that highly regulates and inhibits the influence of powerful special interests.

7. Which many of previous decades would have labeled micro, meso, and macro, but which are labels that a critical realist ontology questions as the best conceptual distinctions.

- Marriage partners are arranged in a mate-selection system by family elders based primarily on economic and status benefits to the elders' clans and with minimal concern for the desires of the marrying partners—this, as opposed to a romance-based system of mate selection in which family elders exert little control over the choices of individuals who are dating and courting.
- Childhood playmates in a neighborhood are divided into the working class, Catholic, Italian gang of kids versus the white collar, Anglo, Protestant children, each of which warily avoids the other—this, as opposed to a neighborhood where the children are highly stratified by age but integrated across all other social dimensions.
- Entrance requirements for elite universities are governed solely by principles of standardized merit and achievement—this, as opposed to admissions based on social class background, "old boy networks," and WASP status.
- A metropolitan area's residential and transportation pattern is, as a result of long-term development policies, sprawled out diffusely from the city center and connected only by networks of highways—this, as opposed to a planned high-density residential ecology replete with sidewalks, bicycle paths, a public bus system, and an army of taxis.
- A military conscription system drafts only men of a certain age through lottery, exempting those enrolled in an institution of higher education—this, as opposed to either mandatory conscription for all men and women or a purely voluntary recruitment system.
- Members of a utopian commune teach equality and humility, make decisions by consensus, and systematically rotate leadership—this, as opposed to a commune led by one charismatic leader who dominates all relations and decisions.
- Different public schools within larger regions receive unequal financial support per pupil, since their funding is provided through taxes levied at the local level, and since socioeconomic resources and property values vary significantly across local areas paying taxes—this, as opposed either to a pure free-market, nongovernmental system of families purchasing education or to a public education system funding individual students equally through a national taxation system and school vouchers.
- Marital divorces are governed by a no-fault legal system that allows either spouse to end a marriage for any reasons at any time—this, as opposed to a fault-based divorce system requiring the divorcing spouse to demonstrate with evidence a violation of the marriage contract through infidelity, battering, desertion, or the like.
- Employment in certain occupations subtly but effectively excludes women and members of certain racial minorities through informal hiring practices that

screen them out—this, as opposed to completely gender-neutral and race-blind job market and hiring practices.

- A populace enjoys a rich variety of voluntary associations in civil society in which most members participate—this, as opposed to a society in which a totalitarian government has removed most groups and associations existing between the state and individuals.

- University faculty and graduate students of various departments have over the years come to occupy offices that are spread out all over campus—this, as opposed to all offices being spatially clustered by department in single floors of shared buildings.

What is it that makes these situations "social structural"? Common to all of these examples and those in most theoretical approaches to social structures are three basic features. They all involve (1) human social relationships, (2) patterned systems comprised of parts, and, (3) temporal durability. Thus, something is not a social structure if it does not involve human social relations, is not some kind of arrangement of ordered components, and does not entail significant stability or continuity over time.[8] We can therefore begin by defining social structures ontologically as simply, "Durable systems of patterned human social relations." That is a good start. But it is a pretty blunt conceptual instrument. So what other crucial defining aspects of social structures might we tease out from the best of what we know and think about structures? I suggest eight additional features.

First, social structures, as broadly understood in social science, are always *actively sustained* by human behaviors, practices, and interactions. Structures are dynamic, continually maintained entities, not fixed or inert objects. Social structures do not have self-generating existences apart from human activity. Real human people must persistently act in ways that sustain social structures or else they cease to exist. Thus, to reference an example above, school students have continually to act like jocks, associate with other jocks, and symbolically distinguish themselves from other nonjock types of crowds in order to sustain the structure of high school identities and the consequences it produces for school cultures and individual student experiences. Likewise, the structure of no-fault divorce cannot stand on its own apart from human activity—it requires lawmakers, marriage partners, marital counselors, attorneys, and family relatives

8. See Smelser, "Social Structure," in *Handbook of Sociology*, 103–29.

to understand reality in a particular framework and act in ongoing ways to keep the no-fault divorce structure in place and functioning.

Second, social structures are not merely durable, but have specific *dynamic historical existences* involving generation, development, and change. By virtue of being dynamically sustained by human activity, they do not reflect properties of permanence but entail particular histories of emergence, evolution, and transformation. Durability is a crucial feature of social structures, but the kind of durability that also allows for development and change. Thus, the social structure of neighborhood playmates noted above might have evolved over previous years as newly upwardly mobile Italian Catholic families moved out of a city neighborhood and into a suburb that was previously occupied only by Anglo Protestants. But it is also true that the structure of playmate relations would change if black or Hispanic families began in large numbers to move in. Likewise, a particular military conscription system may have deep historical roots and longevity, but eventually social changes may make it irrelevant or inappropriate for new circumstances that require adjustments or reforms. The real durability of a structure is set within a larger dynamic of development, however slowly it evolves.

Third, social structures always involve human *bodily practices* of various kinds to be sustained and expressed. Composing and animating structures are not only abstract items like values and ideas and relations, but also the physical, corporeal objects of human bodies in place and motion. Always implicated in social structures, then, are issues of related embodied locations in space and time, bodily expressions of communication and meaning, recurrent bodily routines and habits, and other postures, ornamentations, disciplines, and behaviors that govern and express meanings and embody regularity. Humans are not angels or ethereal spirits, but instead have flesh and blood bodies—and much that is important about social structures derives from this fact.[9] Thus, social structures

9. Again, though not always consistent with my account here, a variety of scholars in different disciplines have encouraged us to take more seriously the embodied fact of human existence, including Elizabeth Teater, *Embodied Geographies: Spaces, Bodies, and Rites of Passage* (New York: Routledge, 1999); George Lakoff and Mark Johnson, *Philosophy in the Flesh: The Embodied Mind and Its Challenge to Western Thought* (New York: Basic Books, 1999); Simon Williams and Gillian Bendelow, *The "Lived" Body: Sociological Themes, Embodied Issues* (New York: Routledge, 1998); Evan Thompson, *Mind in Life: Biology, Phenomenology, and the Sciences of Mind* (Cambridge, MA: Belknap Press of Harvard University Press, 2007); Francisco Varela, Evan Thompson, and Eleanor Rosch, *The Embodied*

offered as examples above are constituted in different ways by the location (or nonlocation) of various kinds of bodies in church buildings, legislative chambers, war zones, urban downtowns, marriage beds, professional office buildings, bowling leagues, and faculty lounges.

Fourth, social structures always implicate *inanimate material objects* in their existence. While structures are never merely material things, they always rely on and express themselves through materiality. Physical matter provides resources for structures to be sustained and object expressions as products and representations of structures. The durability of the structure of urban ecology noted above, for instance, depends heavily on the blacktop in highways, the wood in suburban fences, the concrete in downtown parking garages, and the steel and plastic in cars. Likewise, the egalitarian utopian community mentioned above materially inscribes its social structure into concentric circles (not rows) of chairs set up for meetings, the unpretentious clothes that members wear, and the open communal dining hall lacking a head table. Materiality is at the heart of social structures as well insofar as a great many of them are driven by the need to address problems created by human strivings for scarce material goods and experiences and statuses related to the ability to access material goods. Scarcity, desire, insecurity, and rational egoism all play crucial roles in the formation of social structures.

Fifth, social structures are always constituted in part by *mental categories* that are culturally significant. Structures are much more than ideas. But they are never merely pure relations (whatever that might mean) or material objects. Social structures also always involve ideational, cognitive classifications and mental objects that are culturally and potentially personally meaningful. The unequal distribution of land in the first example above centers on agricultural material production, but also necessitates the culturally significant cognitive categories of legal ownership, peasant status, hourly wages, and the like to be sustained. Similarly, the society with many voluntary associations depends on the meaningful mental categories of government, citizen, community, freedom, membership, and so on to define and maintain that kind of life in civil society. Such mental categories are partly constitutive of the social structure in these and all cases.

Mind: Cognitive Science and Human Experience (Cambridge, MA: MIT Press, 1992); Chris Frith, *Making Up the Mind: How the Brain Creates Our Mental World* (Hoboken, NJ: Wiley-Blackwell, 2007); Shaun Gallagher, *How the Body Shapes the Mind* (New York: Oxford University Press, 2006).

Sixth, the human activities that generate and sustain social structures may be instrumental but they also always have significant *normative and moral* dimensions.[10] They are fraught with beliefs, motives, and intentions that involve oughts, obligations, visions of the good, commitments to the right, orientations to truth, and other aspects of normative and moral order. The example of systematic employment discrimination offered above does not simply entail some people wanting more money or status for themselves but also notions of proper gender roles, group superiority, symbolic pollution, the ideal employee image, and the like. Likewise, the religious free market (as opposed to state religion monopoly) system mentioned above inevitably involves committed beliefs about the nature of true religious faith, the proper role of government, individual conscience, features of a just and free society, and so on, which are clearly normative and moral by nature.

Seventh, support for, cooperation with, and conformity to the implicit and explicit bodily and cognitive practices prescribed by social structures are governed and encouraged by *normalizing sanctions*. Many forms of nonintentional "friction" are often naturally built into any resistance to social structural flows of action and thought. In addition, many human actors are invested in maintaining the social structures they inhabit and sustain, and so discourage and oppose those who would challenge or weaken them. Resisting the directives or flows of structures therefore normally results in various kinds of costs or punishments, just as cooperating and conforming tends to bring benefits and rewards. Consider the department chair whose faculty is sprinkled in offices located all around campus and who wants instead to centralize them in one building in order to increase departmental social density and intellectual community. She would very likely meet strong resistance from the faculty in the desired target building who would be displaced by the move and by her own faculty who do not want to move their offices because perhaps they would then have to begin interacting with certain detested colleagues they have previously managed to avoid. One would not be surprised if the department chair simply ended up abandoning her plan and left things as they were. Similarly, once established, structures of purely meritocratic standards of admissions to elite universities would have the effect of punishing new admissions officers who, for instance, attempted categorically to exclude qualified Jews who

---

10. See Christian Smith, *Moral, Believing Animals: Human Personhood and Culture* (New York: Oxford University Press, 2003).

applied, even though years earlier that was the common practice. Such persons would be labeled bigots and sanctioned for their lack of professionalism.

Eighth, for these and other reasons, social structures usually *encourage passive acquiescence if not agreeable adherence.* By nature, in many mutually reinforcing ways operating at multiple levels, social structures undercut the motivation and capacity of people involved in them to oppose or withstand their causally directive powers. Social structures exert real, compelling causal influences on human persons and thus powerfully shape and govern their mental and behavioral lives. It doesn't matter that children in some schools get underfunded educations while others enjoy relative educational luxury in their schools. Most families remain in the same areas in which they live, most children go to the schools to which they are assigned, most school budgets remain stably unequal, and different schools continue to produce inequitable educational experiences. It is hard to fight city hall. Likewise, most marriageable youth in strong arranged-marriage systems end up marrying the partner their family elders have chosen for them, even if they do not want to marry them because they harbor feelings for another person. Bucking the system is usually simply too difficult.

Having brought these additional features to our basic definition, how then might we elaborate our model of social structures? I propose that we theorize a more detailed definition of social structures as follows. Social structures are:

> durable patterns of human social relations,
>   generated and reproduced through social interactions and
>   accumulated and transformed historically over time, that are
>   expressed through lived bodily practices, which are
>   defined by culturally meaningful cognitive categories,
>   motivated in part by normative and moral valuations and guides,
>   capacitated by and imprinted in material resources and artifacts,
>   controlled and reinforced by regulative sanctions, which therefore
>   promote cooperation and conformity and discourage resistance and
>   opposition.

This more elaborate definition is a mouthful. But it includes numerous real characteristics of social structures that are definitionally important and analytically illuminating. With it we have a theoretical account that

ventures greater specificity in its understanding of the nature and operation of human social structures. This definition encompasses and makes
explicit ideas that most social scientists have in mind when they refer to
social objects as structures. It should therefore include all of those social
entities in the real world that we want to identify as social structures. Actual social structures, existing as particular cases of the concept defined
here, may operate at the macro-, meso-, or microlevels. They may also
be informal, organizationally formal, and even legally instituted. And
different empirical instances of structures may more clearly and strongly
embody and reflect certain elements contained in the above definition,
although we should expect that all social structures will entail all elements
of this elaborated definition. By working with such a definition—more
elaborate than simply "durable systems of patterned human social relations" yet still compatible with most compelling social science views of
social structures—we are able to connect it more clearly to other, broader
theoretical accounts of human persons and social life.

One intention in this chapter is to show how the view of social structures
just articulated flows from and connects with critical realist personalism.
So I want to point out at this stage some of its intellectual ties to critical
realist personalism.[11] For starters, this definition places human *bodies* and
bodily practices at the center of our understanding of social structures.
Critical realist personalism—unlike many more rationalist Enlightenment theories of the person—underscores the importance of embodied
personal existence for human social life. The durable patterns of human
social relations are expressed primarily through lived bodily practices. It is
up and out from the human body primordially that human life, experience,
and social relations emerge and are lived out. Human bodies are what
from the start define human causal capacities and their limitations. Even
spiritual dimensions of human persons are always rooted and embodied
in human flesh. Critical realist personalism thus naturally finds corporeal
embodiment and practices to be a central feature of social structures.

Second, the view of social structure elaborated here presupposes, with
critical realism, that *reality is stratified*, multileveled. Social structures as
defined here simply could not exist in a "flat" reality lacking multiple,
simultaneously connected levels of real existence. By virtue of being

11. What follows does not claim to be the exclusive perspective of critical realist personalism. Many of the following points are shared with other theoretical perspectives. But these are
in fact central points in critical realist personalism's approach and are worth noting here.

actual entities irreducible to acting human persons, social structures exist at a level other than and above personal human lives. That is the level of the distinctly social, constituted by interactive relationships, usually existent temporally for historical periods that transcend individual human lifetimes, and situated so as to be able to shape human mental and behavioral life.

Third and closely connected to the previous point, this view of social structures presupposes the reality of *emergence*. Human persons interact as distinct entities existing at one level. From those interactions, patterns of social relations emerge at another level of reality that are durable, historically continuous, and capable of exerting influence on other entities, including those from which they emerged. Social structures therefore entail emergent properties that cannot be reduced to the specific units from which they emerged through interaction. In this sense, this approach to social structure is also *antireductionistic*.[12]

Fourth, the view of social structures presented here is *causally realist*. Structures possess real causal capacities and powers to operate through various social mechanisms and processes to make changes happen in the world. The notion of causation embodied in this view of structures is not merely empiricism's probabilistically modified regular conjunction of events, the observed association between two variables. Instead, causation is the result of activated capacities naturally inherent to the real entities of social structures. Some known entity (whether directly observable or not) exerts real causal force (usually not directly observable) on another entity or entities that affects actual changes in or on them. Absent those real causal forces or others that affect the same outcome, the changes would not have happened. That is the power of social structures.

Fifth, to understand social structures thus conceived will inevitably require a degree of *hermeneutical* analysis. This is because all social structures involve the culturally meaningful components of cognitive categories, normative and moral orientations, expressive bodily practices, material objects fabricated with meaningful intentions, and significant purposive sanctions. No robust structural analysis, therefore, can proceed without engaging in at least some of the kind of interpretive work that critical realist personalism expects as normal in social science.

12. Another explicitly antireductionistic approach to social structure taking a different approach than mine here is Kyriakos Kontopoulos, *The Logics of Social Structure* (Cambridge: Cambridge University Press, 1993).

Sixth, this entire approach to social structural analysis reflects a commitment to discovering knowledge that equips us to make *generalizing* claims. The very definition is cast at a level of abstraction to facilitate general application to a variety of empirical instances of social structures. It is also intended to illuminate analytical similarities and comparisons across very different types of specific empirical cases. It therefore helps us make theoretical generalizations in social science. It does so not in the sense of identifying universally observable correlations between variables. It rather provides a key theoretical tool that facilitates the identification of real, general, underlying and manifest entities, principles, properties, mechanisms, and processes that exist and operate across a range of historical and empirical types of facts, circumstances, and events.

Finally, this account of social structures takes seriously the reality and causal agency of *human persons*. For social structures to be and do what they are and how they operate presupposes the activity of personal human agents of exactly the sort I am theorizing in this book. Social interaction, sustained relationality, embodied practice, meaningful signification, normative and moral motivations, and purposive engagement with the material world are all central to this view of social structures, and together reflect a specifically personalist theory of human beings. Numerous other theoretical approaches—including those that are purely materialist, utilitarian, fundamentally language-centered, rationally instrumentalist, strongly constructionist, or socially holistic—will inevitably fall short in explaining the kind of actors that are necessary to give rise to the type of social structures theorized here. To end up with the kind of social structures defined in the previous paragraphs, we also need to have the kind of human persons defined in the chapters above. And critical realist personalism gives us that kind of person.

The Sources of Structures

It is one thing to understand what social structures are. It is another matter to account for their generative origins. What brings social structures into being and why? What causes social structures to exist? I press the question of sources because I am not satisfied with received attempts to answer it. Structural functionalism, for example, explains social structures as the result of the natural evolutionary differentiation that societies experience as they grow and eventually modernize, on the one hand, and as the institutional expressions of the underlying norms and values of a society, on the other hand. Various microtheories—such as exchange theory, rational choice theory, and most versions of symbolic interactionism—explain social structures as the social accretions resulting from individuals interacting either for utilitarian benefits or to sustain meaningful definitions of identities and situation. By certain accounts, structures are empirical relations of exchanges in equilibrium. For yet others, structures are mere appearances, epiphenomena of reality generated moment to moment by interactive meaning makers. Relationalists and network structuralists (of the sort examined in chapter 4), either offer no account of the origins of relational structures or, similarly to microtheorists, assume them to be nothing but the configuration of empirical network ties established by social actors developing stable relationships. Various versions of conflict theory have located the origins of social structures in the purposive and systemic self-protective motivations of relatively wealthy and powerful actors who establish and promote ideological and institutional structures as social control mechanisms to defend their wealth, power, and status privileges; social structures—usually operating with large doses of "false consciousness" among those they subordinate—essentially serve the interests of rich and powerful minorities by keeping the social world unequal and tilted in their favor. Materialists of a more evolutionary and technological bent tend to explain the roots of social structural formations in the technological capacities that govern the means and relations of material production as societies evolve—the raw imperative of material survival interacting with the technological means at the actors' disposal generates social structures that reflect or correspond to the underlying productive infrastructure.

I cannot do justice to these accounts with a close and careful appraisal of their various merits and flaws. I can only briefly note in passing certain well-known problems with these views, toward moving on to a somewhat different approach. Some received explanations of the origins of social structures, such as structural functionalism, fail to provide an adequate account of the causal agents at work in processes of social development and change. Social systems, as distinct from people, are posited as having functional needs and evolving responsive structures. But exactly how a "society" experiences and generates those as a causal actor and how individual people fit into that explanation remains unclear. Other accounts unacceptably compress the range of motivations believed to be the elementary sources of human action into simplistic, one-dimensional purposes—often some version of self-interested utility maximization—that poorly reflect the human reality and so fail to explain significant swaths of social experience not explicable by those motives. Meaning and symbol-oriented theories often add helpful complexity to the nature of human actions but sometimes fail to explain the motives driving those actions. Moreover, many microtheories, even when arguably successful at their own level, have difficulty bridging from their microtheoretical starting points across to the macrostructural formations they seek to explain.[13] Conflict and social-control accounts of social structural origins tend to unrealistically overestimate the control that self-protective elites possess to institute structures that serve their interests. They also are liable to underestimate the knowledge, creativity, and normative investments that non-elite actors possess that compel them (apart from false consciousness) to support and reproduce the social structures that govern their lives—even those that sustain inequality and disadvantage. Furthermore, the reduction of the complexities of causal forces and dynamics in human social life to single driving factors, such as technological development or economic means of production, is unacceptably crude. We simply cannot explain the immense array of social structures that humans generate with appeals to simple materialist axioms. Suffice it to say that additional exploration of the sources of social structures is warranted. My thesis is that the approach of critical realist personalism will offer explanatory payoff—increased epistemic gain—toward answering the question of social structural origins.

Critical realist personalism points us toward the natural capacities and limitations of human persons and the creative tensions that arise between them. Human social life, I suggest, is the magma that erupts and builds up, so to speak, at the fault lines where natural human *capacities* meet and grind against and over natural human *limitations*. Human persons are endowed with immense causal powers to make and remake themselves, their relationships, their cultures, and the material world. But all such human powers operate within the confines of natural limits on human bodies, consciousness, and action.[14] This meeting of powers and limitations produces a creative, dynamic tension and energy that generates and fuels the making of human social life and social structures. Human existence is a naturally

13. See Jeffrey Alexander et al., *The Micro-Macro Link* (Berkeley and Los Angeles: University of California Press, 1987).

14. See Alasdair MacIntyre, *Dependent, Rational Animals* (Chicago: Open Court, 1999).

unstable compound, an ever-reactive mix of elements, out of which social structures solidify. It is real human persons living through the tensions of natural existential contradictions who construct patterned social meanings, interactions, institutions, and structures. It is also real human persons living through these tensions and contradictions who transform, reform, and sometime revolt against these very same patterns of social life. Society and history are thus rooted in the natural character of the human, specifically in the capacities and incapacities of persons. To understand the social, therefore, we need to attend not only to human capacities but also to human finitude and the natural limitations of persons.

Personalism begins with the body, and so our account of human limits must begin there as well. The human body is finite, first of all, in its natural indivisibility. Our bodies cannot be divided in order to be in two places at one time or, as far as we know, two different temporal moments simultaneously. The human body exists as a material singularity in limited space and time. Whatever other mental, spiritual, or interpersonal capacities persons enjoy, they must always deal with the fixed finitude of corporeal indivisibility. A second human bodily limitation on its other powers is the body's natural biological dependence on external sustenance. Healthy human bodies need to breathe oxygen regularly (damage sets in after mere minutes of asphyxiation), drink water at least every few days (death occurs after ten to fourteen days of not drinking), and eat food every few days (bodily damage from malnutrition begins after seven days and death by starvation occurs after about one month). Human bodies, in short, cannot autonomously maintain themselves but need constant nourishment from their environments, on which they are radically dependent. This creates a host of personal and social challenges for humans insofar as we live in a world of various forms of material scarcity and competition for access to physical goods, which has huge implications for the life of social structures. The normal, healthy human body is also naturally finite in that it also needs many hours of sleep per day, periods of rest during active behavior, and shelter from adverse environmental conditions. The body is highly vulnerable to damage or death by exhaustion and exposure and so must live within the limitations set by those natural restrictions. Furthermore, even healthy human bodies confront natural limitations from their great vulnerability to harm from accident and attack. It takes only moderate force to injure the human body. Skin and muscle are easily lacerated and bones easily broken. Eyes, noses, ears, mouths, and teeth can be injured without difficulty or intention. Heads and brains can be damaged with moderate blows, and internal organs can be ruptured. Every human who wishes to survive and prosper must carefully observe the boundaries and rules of bodily care, protection, and security.

Furthermore, the human body takes an extremely long time to come to physical maturity, which involves other kinds of limitations. While some animals are physically able to survive on their own soon after they are born or hatched, human bodies require many years to mature in physical structure, motor skills, and mental abilities enough to enable them not to be highly dependent upon their elders for care. This relates directly to the long years also needed to socialize new members of human societies, which concerns not simply bodily development but also mental, emotional, and cultural learning. Socialization, however, does entail a significant component of learning how to comport the body, given its natural, organic capacities, functions, and limits. Human bodies also impose socially relevant restrictions when it comes to biological reproduction: the DNA from only two embodied persons can be combined to generate a new human, which is nurtured in the mother's womb for most of a year, during which time care must be taken to protect the unborn person. Furthermore, over our entire human lifetimes, embodied people require physical sustenance, nurture, touching, and belonging in spatially located communities in order to thrive. Human bodies are also always at risk of disease and illness caused by a host of germs, bacteria, viruses, and different kinds of abnormal mutations and malignancies. Nearer to the end of life, human bodies exhibit other limitations to their natural capacities. Physical strength fails, the sharpness of perceptions declines, agility and coordination slip, and memory deteriorates. And, finally, all human bodies meet their ultimate finitude in death, when bodily existence cannot be sustained and flesh, organs, and bones decompose. Thus, humans in their bodies encounter profound limitations and vulnerabilities. All of these have consequences for the making of social structures that give form to human social life.

The line between human bodily life and human mental life is not exactly clear, since the latter emerges out of the former. But, wherever that line is to be drawn, human mental life is bounded by definite natural limits and restrictions on capacities, which also have implications for social life. For example, the embodied person participates in and interacts with his or her environment by way of natural senses of perception: sight, touch, taste, sound, smell. Yet we know that people are perceptually and cognitively incapable of taking in and processing all of the data that is available in what is actual, that is, what actually happens. Indeed, people cannot even take in and process the data available through their own personal experience. Instead, humans must narrow down to, take in, and mentally process only a small range of perceptions that pass the grids of their cognitive categories, sensory focuses, and cultural significations. All persons are thus dramatically restricted to being consciously in touch with severely limited aspects of the worlds in which they live. Most of reality and actuality passes people by unheeded. This fact is closely related to the natural limitations on human attention. People cannot mentally attend to much at one time. Attention requires focus, which, by definition, means concentration on certain objects. Most everything else is left in unfocused space, beyond consideration, out of attentive awareness. So we can only attend to one or a few things at a time. The number and extent of objects, among all potential objects, on which people can set their attention is highly finite.[15] This too has implications for how we live our social lives.

Closely related for understanding our mental finitude is the matter of the inevitable human need to *interpret* reality in order to know it. Humans are inescapably hermeneutical animals, creatures who actively make meaningful sense of our world and lives.[16] Interpreting reality is central for everything we believe and think that we know. On the one hand, reality presents itself with an objectivity that is autonomous from our consciousness of it—as I argued in chapter 3, we do not create whole swaths of reality by our knowing and speaking of it. On the other hand, as personal animals, our knowledge is always personal knowledge—finite, particular, and possessed from a specific perspective. Any significant knowledge we have of reality is attained through activities of interpretation. We must make inferences about best explanations. In order to comprehend reality in ways appropriate for personal human existence, we must interpret its character, operations, and meaning. We do not have a "God's-eye view," and so there is no other human way of knowing. And interpretation is always an active, social process.

Usually there is more than one plausible interpretation of reality. When our active, creative, representational, linguistic, and other amazing human capacities (enumerated in chapter 1) confront that immense richness and complexity of reality, we often find ourselves able to understand the same

15. See Eviatar Zerubavel, *Social Mindscapes* (Cambridge, MA: Harvard University Press, 1997), 23–52.
16. Charles Taylor, *Philosophical Papers*, vol. 1, *Human Agency and Language* (Cambridge: Cambridge University Press, 1985). Also see David Myers, *Intuition: Its Powers and Perils* (New Haven, CT: Yale University Press, 2002).

reality in more than one way. Whether it is the motions of the planets and stars, or an odd feeling inside of us, or the Bible, we have to actively interpret the given evidence in order to determine what it means, what we have good reason to believe about it. In some cases, we can believe and live with different interpretations without trouble—I believe, for instance, based on the trustworthy testimony of scientists, that light has properties that are both particle-like and wave-like, even though I don't know how light can have both. Yet our natural human capacities and drives for cognitive coherence and knowledge of truth, along with practical functional needs to know what really *is* in many cases, compel us to decide on what we believe are the *best* interpretations and live with them. We make our inferences to the best explanations and work with them. General agnosticism can only go so far. The funny noise in my car engine is either something that will cause a breakdown on my next road trip that needs fixing right away or it is not. The Book of Mormon is either a true revelation from God through the Angel Moroni to Joseph Smith or it is not. The time your girlfriend or boyfriend is spending with someone else should be threatening to you or not. Oftentimes we never do know for certain, until the facts have changed, but we have to interpret and believe one way or another, nonetheless. And for all of the incredible depths and complexities of understanding that personal, hermeneutical, interpreted knowledge gives us, our lack of unmediated and absolute knowledge and the need to interpret reality still functions as a cognitive limitation, a fact of our mental finitude. What we believe and know can be true—as explained in my excursus—in the real sense of truth that is genuinely veritable for human persons. But in the end we are profoundly limited by the fallibility and uncertainties of our interpretations, in our need to settle on some particular interpretations that inevitably exclude others, and the necessity to live out our lives on the basis of such interpretively grounded knowledge. And this inescapably hermeneutical nature of our human believing and knowing has implications for the socially structured character of our lives.

Human mental life, even at its sharpest, also confronts finitude in its capacities for memory. Human brains are amazing in their ability to remember. But they are neither unlimited nor infallible. The normal brain can only store and retrieve a certain amount of information, beyond which it is helpless to remember more. So, much if not most that is experienced in life is lost to the goneness of the past. Furthermore, our brains often only remember selectively, inaccurately, and inventively. Human memories are mostly reliable but they are hardly inerrant. Even to exercise well the functional capacities for focused attention, meaningful perception, mental processing, and reliable recall requires having been socialized cognitively at the start of life for many years by more experienced elders of society. New human persons do not begin to exercise their natural causal capacities effortlessly. They must be directed, stimulated, corrected, trained, disciplined, and rewarded by communities of older persons whose job it is to induct them into the functional expression of their personhood. Those are the natural limits that the structures and functions of the human mind impose upon social life. The same pertains to linguistic competence.

Further cognitive features exert limitations on human mental life. For example, humans are well known by social psychology to be cognitively biased toward their own selves. This means that people often do not see, think, and judge impartially. Their perceptions, thoughts, interpretations, and evaluations are distorted by their personal positions and interests.[17] For instance, people tend to attribute to themselves more credit than is warranted for outcomes that are positive, and discount their influence on outcomes that are negative. People also routinely see, consider, and judge differently among others who are like them and others who are different, even when what they are beholding is objectively the same. For instance, for the same observed behaviors, people are more likely to attribute good and sympathetic motives to others who are demographically similar to them and tend to attribute inferior and suspicious motives to others who seem alien. People also tend to form favorable judgments about phenomena when they personally are in positive moods and more critical judgments about the same phenomena when they are in bad moods.[18] Hence people's purportedly objective judgments are influenced by their personal subjective affective states. Human persons live in their worlds always grappling with the finitude imposed by numerous perceptual and mental limitations that set restrictions on the extent and quality of the performance of their capacities.

Finitude, vulnerability, and limitations also express themselves in other ways at different levels of personal existence. As linguistically capable but therefore also linguistically dependent animals, for example, humans can only communicate with other persons who share their same language.

17. Martha Augoustinos and Iain Walker, *Social Cognition* (London: Sage, 1995), 185–261.

18. Herbert Bless, Laus Fiedler, and Fritz Strack, *Social Cognition* (New York: Psychology Press, 2004), 183–95; Ziva Kunda, *Social Cognition* (Cambridge, MA: MIT Press, 1999), 246–62.

Communication across languages is difficult. Human life in communication even within the same language is also fraught with immense opportunities for and instances of error, confusion, misunderstanding, and misinterpretation. Intersubjective understanding is possible and actual. But it is often beset by miscommunication, ambiguities, and mix-ups. Human persons are also highly vulnerable as emotional creatures. The immense human capacity for emotional feeling carries with it positive and negative potential. On the negative side, all normal humans are susceptible to a host of kinds of personal hurts, disappointments, phobias, sorrows, turmoil, dejection, anxieties, despair, panics, and anguish. Humans can also be subject to emotional dysregulation, wherein expressed emotional reactions are not modulated and so fall outside the bounds of what is culturally considered normal. Although many philosophies and life practices encourage people to master their emotions, most normal human persons remain at risk of numerous kinds of emotional disruptions, grief, obsessions, and devastations. Many such emotional troubles are by nature intense, gripping, and only marginally controllable. Most people desire to avoid such experiences, although sometimes they are inescapable.[19] Human persons are ever subject to the threat of emotional pain and distress. Given the affective constitution of human persons, emotional turmoil or devastation is always only one mistake, one accident, one broken relationship, one tragedy away. Aside from emotional damage, many people spend a good deal of their lives wrestling with the challenges of less traumatic emotions, such as frustration, longing, anger, and anxiety. Emotions can be powerful and preoccupying. This too has implications for how persons work out their personhood in ways that matter in social and cultural life.

Human persons are also finite when it comes to their normative, moral, and existential lives. All humans must assume or adopt some particular set of moral beliefs, normative viewpoints, value commitments, and personal preferences. People simply cannot believe, value, prefer, and practice all of the possibilities or none of them. We cannot dodge committing to some options. And we cannot hold all of the options open. Many of the alternatives are incompatible if not mutually exclusive. In addition, human cognitive and emotional abilities limit the beliefs and commitments that any individual can even manage. This inescapably forces persons to come

19. For some more serious cases see American Psychiatric Association Task Force, *Diagnostic and Statistical Manual of Mental Disorders*, 4th ed. (Washington, DC: American Psychiatric Association, 1994).

down somewhere, to identify with some finite, particular positions. And, despite the great human capacity for living with cognitive dissonance, this logically and practically excludes a host of other prospects. One cannot be a hedonist and an ascetic, an atheist and a person of faith, a liberal and a conservative, a humanitarian and a selfish cynic, an elitist and an egalitarian. People in the end—even the most cosmopolitan and open minded—must and in fact do end up in particular places on a host of moral and ideological issues, even if those places are complicated. And this helps to define their specific identities and life practices.

Finally, human persons are finite and vulnerable in their existential being related to meaning systems. Since fundamental life meanings are rarely fixed and indubitable, our "ontological security"—that is, our basic sense of mental stability and trust that the natural and social worlds, including self and identity, exhibit continuity and are what they appear to be—remains vulnerable to the threats of destabilization and disintegration.[20] Humans rely on predictable routines and shared cultural "stocks of knowledge" to help reduce and control the potential anxiety and anomie of a precarious ontological security.[21] When such controls break down, people face the prospect of their worlds "falling apart." What one has always taken for granted suddenly becomes doubtful. What has always seemed real and hard becomes uncertain and weak. The experience can be unnerving, even terrifying. Part of the inescapable problematic human finitude is the human inability to gain a "God's-eye view" in order to know the absolute, certain truth about ontological reality to resolve such matters once and for all. Human knowledge in its entirety is conceptually mediated, culturally cast, perspectival, and fallible. That does not mean humans cannot know a great deal that well represents what is true and real. But it does mean that no human knowledge is absolute or indubitable. So every person's ontological security is susceptible to undoing. And that sustains a particular precariousness in the human existential condition.[22] This too

20. Giddens, *The Constitution of Society*, 50, 375.

21. Wendy Wood, Jeffrey Quinn, and Deborah Kashy, "Habits in Everyday Life: Thought, Emotion, and Action," *Journal of Personality and Social Psychology* 83, no. 6 (2002): 1281–97; Judith Ouellette and Wendy Wood, "Habit and Intention in Everyday Life: The Multiple Processes by Which Past Behavior Predicts Future Behavior," *Psychological Bulletin* 124, no. 1 (1998): 54–74; Peter Berger and Thomas Luckmann, *The Social Construction of Reality* (New York: Anchor Books, 1967), especially 92–104.

22. Calvin Schrag, *Existence and Freedom: Toward an Ontology of Human Finitude* (Evanston, IL: Northwestern University Press, 1970).

has implications for human social and cultural life and the making of social structures.

Much of the account of the human person that I have developed in this book until now has focused on human capacities and powers. More generally, academia has in the last decades taken some turns emphasizing human self-construction, creativity, emancipation, reinvention, and transformation. Sometimes the human possibilities seem endless. Sometimes academics have gotten carried away. There is some grain of truth in recent academic discourse about unlimited self-creation. But all of that needs to be contextualized in the larger truth about natural human finitude, vulnerabilities, dependences, limitations, and incapacities. Humans do exercise amazing powers and capabilities, but always within strict limits of ability and under multiple, sustained risks to body and self that are ultimately rooted in natural reality. And all of that matters both to human experience and for the nature of human social and cultural structures and institutions within which that human experience is lived out. Thus, in seeking to understand human persons and social structures we must recognize and account for natural human finitude.

How do social structures emerge from the confrontation of human capacities and limitations? Essentially, human capacities propel persons into world-engaging activities of bodily action, subjective experience, moral evaluation, material fabrication, and social interaction. Engaged in these activities, people quickly hit their many natural limitations. In order to continue to live out life as the kind of creatures they are—that is, as *persons*—humans work to develop a variety of solutions, tools, practices, procedures, and systems that nurture and advance their natural capacities, given the facts of their natural limitations. Some of these are material, others are cognitive and affective, and yet others are relational. In all cases, a central accomplishment of personal existence on behalf of capacities over limitations is the overcoming of a variety of forms of loss, discontinuity, instability, unpredictability, and disruption. The latter—which are directly tied to human capacities and finitude—not only make life instrumentally inefficient and sometimes impossible but also obstruct personal existence, the achievement of robust personhood. Continuity of being, practices, and relationships across time and space is a fundamental precondition for personal life. This is true not only about human physical survival but also of and for personal identity, self-understanding, sense of purpose, understanding causality, responsibly exercising agency, enjoying significant social relationships, exercising moral character, and developing and sustaining meaningful life narratives. Continuity and durability of and in life is central to the achievement of that about us which is most human: our personhood.

Recall again that a person is a conscious, reflexive, embodied, self-transcending center of subjective experience, durable identity, moral commitment, and social communication who—as the efficient cause of his or her own responsible actions and interactions—exercises complex capacities for agency and intersubjectivity in order to sustain his or her own incommunicable self in loving relationships with other personal selves and with the nonpersonal world. I am suggesting, by virtue of simply being what we are—persons—and by naturally pursuing the development of our personhood, given our limits, we humans engage in activities that give rise to social structures. We naturally establish social relationships. We naturally develop, in the experience of those social relations, systems of difference that organize actors. And we achieve in that process patterns of continuity and durability that make personhood possible. Because of the kind of personal creatures we are, those durable systems of patterned human social relations are conveyed through bodily practices, defined by culturally meaningful mental categories, motivated by normative and moral visions, resourced and expressed in material objects, and influenced and fortified by regulative sanctions. And all of this has the causal effect of encouraging cooperation and compliance by the people who constitute them. It is thus *the natural drive toward a sustained and thriving personal life broadly*—more so than motivations for, say, material advantage, relational dominance, or ontological security more exclusively—when confronted with our natural limitations, *that generates social structures out of human existence.*

To help grasp the larger point, consider what human life would look like in the absence of social structures. In fact, it could not exist. But imagine what something approximating it might look like. Individuals would traverse their existence as isolated animals. Physical survival would be precarious at best. Sources of sustenance and protection would be irregular and unpredictable. Sickness and disease would run rampant. Absent family structures to care for them, newborns would survive only a few hours, or perhaps days, past birth. No language would exist with which to communicate. Limited mental categories would keep thought to the most primitive levels. Bodily sensations that we interpret as meaningful emotions would remain amorphous and enigmatic. Human relationships would be undefined, fleeting, uncertain. People could never know what to expect of others. Competition and conflict would probably dominate human interactions. Any larger meanings about life and the world would be unknowable. The ends beyond sheer bodily survival toward which to direct the human will would be indefinite. Existence would be a bundle of fears, insecurities, and sufferings borne in stunted solitude. In short, human life without social structures, if it can be imagined, would resemble the worst of Hobbes's state of nature—being nasty, brutish, and short in the extreme. The personhood of humans would in most cases simply be extinguished and, for the few who survived, badly retarded. But that situation violates personal existence to the core. And so humans, by simply acting out their natural personhood, actively counteract those tendencies by developing—in both intentional and nonintentional ways—concrete patterns of social relations that are meaningful, stable, and durable over time and space. The very nature of human personhood thus generates the social structures it (at least sometimes in some ways) benefits from and in turn is nurtured and sustained (at least sometimes and in some ways) by the same social structures.

But what more precisely does this process look like? How does personal existence give rise to social structures? Take a primordial example: families. Where do families, of whatever particular form, come from and why? Humans, being the personal creatures that they are naturally, exercise capacities for agency and intersubjectivity to sustain their incommunicable selves in loving relationships with other personal selves and the physical world. To do so, we humans operate out of our conscious, reflexive, embodied, and self-transcending centers of subjective experience. From there, as the efficient causes of our responsible actions and interactions, we develop and live within and out from durable identities, moral commitments, and social relationships. All that this entails, however, quickly runs up against the many facts of our natural finitude and limitations. We swiftly confront our inescapable indivisibility, profound dependence on physical sustenance, realities of biological reproduction, vulnerability to injury and disease, need for protracted socialization, limitations on perceptions and learning and memory, emotional vulnerabilities, reliance on language and interpretation, and need for cultural narratives, moralities, and worldviews. When all these and related factors converge, the human imperatives of biological reproduction combined with the realities of economic production, along with the human drive toward relational community and communion, produce a need for and interest in durable patterns of social relations that can organize and regulate physical sustenance, sexual associations, household production, social identities, emotional nurturance, the socialization of new members, emotional stability, and related tasks. Through historical human activity addressing these needs and interests, the kind of durable systems of social relations that we call "families" emerged.[23] These can take many forms, each of which organizes and regulates differently, and can and do change over time. But in one form or another, in every place where humans are found, family social structure comes into existence, embodying all of the ontological features of social structures noted above and exerting powerful emergent causal capacities that shape personal human life at lower levels. In similar ways and for similar reasons, all of the other social structures that comprise human social life—political, economic, military, religious, associational, residential, educational, recreational, and so on—emerge out of the confrontation of natural human capacities and natural human limitations.

Note that at the most fundamental level, it is the needs and interests of human persons in a world of endemic objective and subjective scarcity and relentless competition that generate social structures that organize and regulate life. Structures are not the products of, for example, the "requisites of the social system," as structural functionalism would have it.[24] Instead they derive through human activity from the real, concrete requirements and desires of human persons, given their natural capacities and limitations. It is human persons, and not social systems, who are the ultimate actors in this account. Structured social systems are only the emergent products of ongoing personal interaction. Once emergent, those irreducible social structures can and do function to exert their level-specific causal influences on the persons existing simultaneously at the lower, personal level. But structures are not self-generating as social systems.

23. We do not have specific historical data on the emergence of the first, primordial families in protohuman societies, but empirical historical origins are not the point here. What matters is the conceptual account of how the stability and durability of culturally meaningful, patterned social relationships addressing sex, sustenance, child rearing, physical protection, relational identity, property ownership and inheritance, and the like grew out of the needs and interests of, and solved fundamental problems challenging the living of, personal human existence, in light of the given nature, capacities, and limitations of personhood.

24. If the framework is shifted from functionalism to evolution, then structures might more legitimately be thought of as requisites of systems, but only, in the end, because humans are persons of the kind I have described in this book—even a plausible evolutionary account of structures as required by systems depends on a reality of personhood like something advanced here.

They always depend upon the real interactions of related persons who are the primal agents of social activity. Furthermore, the generation of social structures, as I have described it here, cannot be reduced simply to the manipulation of arrangements to serve the interests of wealthy and powerful groups who wish to dominate and exploit subordinate groups, as various materialist and conflict-oriented theories would have it. This happens all the time in social life. But that is not the most fundamental causal origin of social structures. Both the complex, higher-level, historically emergent being in stratified reality and the inherited causal "momentum" of social structures in forming the lives of all of those who at any given time occupy them means that their existence cannot be attributed to that kind of instrumental intentionality on the part of affluent and powerful actors that various social theories assert. Nobody has that much control in social life. Moreover, as human persons in the full-orbed sense I have described here, all human actors, including the most prosperous and powerful, have a larger number of natural interests and concerns to pursue than simply gaining and protecting wealth and power. Personal self-transcendence and moral commitments often contribute to that multiplicity of focus. Yes, material resources and capacities to make thing happen in the world do, when deployed rightly, serve the achievement of personhood. But there is more to essential human existence than wealth and power. To think otherwise is to operate with an emaciated model of the human person, one that will not do for explaining the richness and complexity of social life.

Moreover, the nature of human personhood naturally generates people's *resistance* to the constraints of social structures. Although social structures tend strongly to induce cooperation and conformity, there is another side of people's relations to structures in which they persistently seek to resist, evade, subvert, cheat, defy, and oppose the downwardly causal structural forces. People cut corners on their taxes, disobey their parents, drag their feet on the job, experiment with new ways of relating to others sexually, cut classes, make fun of authorities behind their backs, convert to minority religions, move across segregated neighborhood boundaries, mobilize protests to challenge injustice, and sometimes even assassinate leaders and blow up buildings to try to topple regimes. Humans need and benefit from social structures. But they also recurrently find themselves aggravated, restricted, oppressed, and dehumanized by structures in ways that provoke them to rebel. What is the ultimate source of this persistent tendency toward resistance to and subversion of structural forces? It is not the transformation of the global world system, new linguistically

constructed ways of looking at the world, increased flows of material resources, the alteration of network structures, or the increasing importance
of some significant demographic or social location variable. The ultimate
source of people's continual propensity to resist and subvert social structures is the natural character of their human personhood. Persons are embodied, so structural forces that impinge on the well-being of their bodies
matter to them. Persons are reflexive and so possess the capacity to stand
outside of simple conscious awareness in order to investigate the causal
dynamics of their world and how they affect outcomes that matter from
different perspectives. Persons are self-transcending—they can get outside of what is in their strict interests and of their particular concerns in
order to examine the workings of the social world as it affects other people
and groups they may care about. Persons are centers of subjective experience, so they process ideas, emotions, and desires in deep and complex
ways that can lead them to stand against structural forces. Persons have
and hold strong identities and moral commitments that social structures
can violate. Persons are capable of intersubjective understanding, enabling
them to see and feel how social structures negatively affect other persons
beyond themselves. Persons are the efficient causes of their responsible
actions—they are significantly free—so when their personal freedom is
felt to be violated by certain social forces, they can purposefully choose
to set themselves in opposition to the violations of freedom, even when
those forces normally induce conformity. Most importantly, persons by
nature are oriented toward sustaining their incommunicable selves and
relationships of self-giving care with other persons and with the nonpersonal world. That is the core of human personal existence. So when social
structures exert influences that infringe upon personal incommunicability, harm other significant persons, distort social relationships, or destroy
or pollute the nonpersonal world they inhabit—which social structures
so recurrently do—the very essence of the personhood of human selves
revolts. The social conditions that hinder or facilitate opposition vary,
and so people's and groups' capacities to successfully resist differ. But the
resistance itself is not finally caused by social conditions. Opposition to
structures is not an anomalous or alien occurrence generated by forces
external to personal being. The resistance is directly rooted in the nature
of personal existence. Forests and rivers do not protest their own destruction. Cats and dogs in the animal shelter do not organize demonstrations
for better conditions. It takes persons to actively and intelligently resist
social structures. Hence, human personhood explains not only the genera-

tion of social structures but also their defiance, subversion, and sometimes demolition. Persons remain at the heart of social structural matters from beginning to end.

I could with more space continue to show that the personalist account of social structures developed here contrasts in important ways with other important approaches in social theory, including, for instance, language-centered, strong social constructionist, and utilitarian exchange theories. But I will not belabor the analysis. The point is that critical realist personalism's explanation of the sources of social structures offers an account that rivals a variety of other alternatives—while incorporating certain of those alternatives' strengths—and that those differences entail important theoretical implications that often head us in divergent intellectual directions. They also, I suggest, entail important practical moral and political implications that social scientists should not ignore. Still, critical realist personalism's view of social structural origins is not wholly unique. If its account of social structures comports best with an existing theoretical school, it probably is with certain versions of symbolic interactionism and purposive action theory combined with network structuralism—insofar as these explain the origins of social structures as the accumulated consequences of concrete human activities and interactions. Yet, beyond that shared general view, my account insists on the genuine existence of a stratified reality involving multiple levels of the real operating causally through emergence and downward causation, which symbolic interactionism, action theories, and network structuralism tend not to emphasize. My account also brings in a sense of moral orientation, identity concerns, embodied action, and even spiritual experience, which some of those theories tend to discount or ignore in various ways. In short, critical realist personalism shares affinities with certain important existing theories, yet also articulates an approach that is both distinctive and important in its assumptions, structure, and implications.

How Social Structures Work

Having examined what social structures are ontologically and why and how they originate, this chapter turns next to consider how structures work. I begin with the relatively simple though abstract observation that social structures engage in dialectical interplays of social similarity and difference. The strongest accent here is on difference. Social structures work by building upon and reproducing distinctions and differences between people and social groups. Structures are never about undifferentiated unity, but about generating and maintaining social dissimilarities. Insofar as my idea of social structures focuses on human social relations as systems comprised of patterned parts, this fact of difference is conceptually inherent. There must be distinctions in categories and actors to have meaningful systems of relations among or between them. Almost invariably, such social differences also mean social inequalities—social distinctions are rarely mere descriptions of objects that are not entirely alike, but typically also associate with unequal distributions of material goods, prestige, influence, power, comfort, advantage, and so on. And yet, social differentiation at one level also presupposes identity or solidarity at another level. Without some underlying basis of commonality, it would be impossible to hold together the differences that make up the unequal structural systems. At the same time, identity, association, and community depend upon difference to function. Without difference, there would be nothing needing similarity, solidarity, connection, or shared distinctiveness to bring together. Difference and solidarity operate in dynamic systems of interdependency. Human social life is never about one or the other. This, it is worth noting, reflects a fundamental fact of human personhood existent at a lower level: each person is truly an incommunicable self, a genuinely distinct personal being; yet each is also embedded in, fully dependent upon, and in some sense living in solidarity in social relations with other, distinct, incommunicable selves. Personal human being is thus constituted in part by the dialectical interplay of difference and identity, singularity and solidarity, contrast and community. That is the human condition. And that condition manifests itself in the higher-level social structures, of which it is the source.

Building on my account of the origins of social structures above, I argue next that structures work to define, pattern, organize, regulate, motivate, express, and control human life as powerfully as they do because they ride directly upon the human capacities and limitations out of which they emerge. The key question to answer for understanding how social structures work is: What is it about social structures that fosters durability? The answer reveals numerous mechanisms—and as they integrate and overlap with one another, they create overdetermining forces of stability and resilience. Recall, as a point of reference here, that social structures are durable patterns of human social relations, generated and reproduced through social interactions and accumulated and transformed historically over time, that are expressed through lived bodily practices, which are defined by culturally meaningful cognitive categories, motivated in part by normative and moral valuations and guides, capacitated by and imprinted in material resources and artifacts, controlled and reinforced by regulative sanctions, which therefore promote cooperation and conformity and discourage resistance and opposition. By considering first a single social structure analytically—as opposed to the interlocking of social structures, which I discuss below—we can see many distinct dynamics promoting durability. Let us work backward through this definition point by point.

First, social structures possess causal powers to promote cooperation and conformity and oppose resistance and opposition among those people involved in them. This causal capacity propels people in similar directions, engaging in patterned behaviors that align in common motion. In whatever specific form it takes, this fact of compliance generates mental-behavioral momentum, flows of action, and configurations of activity that become difficult to resist. Picture, for example, a crowded ice rink during a public skate session, in which everyone is flowing around the rink in a counterclockwise direction; latecomers who step onto the ice—I know as a regular and observant ice skater—even those who have never seen or skated on an ice rink before, always automatically skate with the flow of the crowd; to skate against it would be to invite chaos, friction, and collisions in the flow of bodies. Most of the movement of social life works similarly. Not to cooperate with the causal influences of social structures is, to mix in additional metaphors, to swim against strong social currents. This generates a hot relational "friction" by abrasively rasping against the grain of the directional surface of social practices. Few people ever sustain that for long. The normal result is either eventual cooperation with or exit from the social structure. None of this has to be conscious or intentional. It is simply the result of bodies of people acting in concert in ways that influence one another for significant periods of time. The larger outcome of this process is a current of temporal human activity sustained in space that tends—along with the force of other influences described below—strongly to reproduce itself across time. We might call this contribution to social structural durability *collective activity currents*.

Second, normally, at least some if not most of the people implicated in a social structure are invested in it operating in certain ways as it does. So they regulate and reinforce it with positive and negative sanctions. Under normal circumstances, most behaviors that challenge or oppose the social structure are actively discouraged or punished by variously subtle and obvious means. Those who cooperate and conform are rewarded. Costs must be paid by those who act in ways that resist or weaken the social structure. Consider, from the examples listed at the start of this chapter, the fate of scrawny high school geeks who try to join the swimming team, or that of youth whose draft lottery numbers are called but who refuse to enroll in college and to be drafted into the military. This dynamic tends again to produce cooperation and conformity, not simply in order to flow with the social current but specifically to avoid sanctions intentionally meted out to noncooperators. The larger outcome is the tendency for the practices of the past to be continued as the practices of the future—in short, to strengthen durability. Let us call this contribution to structural durability *socially enforced conformity*.

Third, social structures, I have said, are also capacitated by and imprinted in material resources and artifacts. This presents another quite different cause of structural durability. The material world possesses a robust objectivity to human life. Unlike ideas and institutional facts, most of the material world enjoys existence apart from human consciousness and activity. True, all material objects are subject through the larger forces of entropy to processes of decay, decomposition, transformation, and disintegration. But many material objects—particularly the kind that humans draw on to help build social structures—possess a fixity and sturdiness that enables them to outlast specific human thoughts, desires, beliefs, feelings, memories, and even lifetimes. Many human deployments of material objects to help create social structural worlds involve major "sunk" costs that are difficult if not impossible to reverse or erase. For instance, once the concrete, steel, and blacktop of an interstate highway system are laid down, there it is objectively, a material reality in physical space that cannot reasonably be retracted or redesigned, what environmental historians call the "built environment"—its sheer physical existence thereafter has real consequences for subsequent human transportation activities. Or again, once the professional belongings of a department's faculty are spread out in offices located all over campus, it becomes a major resource cost and logistical challenge to try to centralize them all on one floor of one building on campus—this then has important effects on departmental faculty relationships. Yet again, once the Italian Catholic kids have built their tree fort in one neck of the woods and the Anglo Protestant kids have settled into playing in their parents' in-ground swimming pools and billiard rooms, the prospects for altering that segregated playmate system are greatly reduced—compared to if all children played on one open sports field and playground. Thus, because of the physical autonomy and durability of material objects, the inscribing of human social relations into objects of the material world exerts in turn the causal effect of tending to perpetuate the nature of the social relations that the material objects facilitate and express. Were people who are implicated in those social relations to come to want to change the patterned relationships, in many cases they would in the process have also to change the material objects that are also implicated in those relations. Sometimes that is not hard, sometimes it is simply not feasible, usually it is possible but quite difficult. We might call this contribution of material objects to social structural durability *objective material fixity*.

Fourth, social structures are motivated in part by normative and moral valuations and guides. As particular kinds of causes of action, moral and normative motives often involve more consistent kinds of strength than instrumental motivations do. The latter operate on means-ends criteria and are therefore situationally guided—if one course of action produces some end, then that is good; if a different means works better, then that is preferable. There is no reason to stay with any given course of action. By contrast, most moral and normative motives reference standards believed to be higher and less situational than instrumental motives.[25] By nature they are harder selectively to follow or deny. Goths simply *are not* friends with jocks, even if jocks can help with homework. Youngsters secretly in love simply *do not* defy their family elders, whose moral right and responsibility it is to choose marriage partners, even if the partners they choose are repellent and their mutual love is crushed. Thus, when people really believe in (or are at least surrounded by others who believe in) the normative and moral standards that guide their actions, those activities gain a force and gravity that are arguably stronger than those of instrumental motives. It is one thing to decide that there are better ways to accomplish certain goals. It is quite different to discard a commitment previously believed to be morally right or normatively correct. This difference is not absolute. But it can be significant in governing behavior. Let us call this contribution to social structural durability *moral belief validation*.

Fifth, social structures are always defined by culturally meaningful cognitive categories. It is impossible to have any patterned elements in relationship without difference of elements to be related. In human social life it is impossible to have difference that is not conceptually mediated.

25. Smith, *Moral, Believing Animals*.

People know their world through conceptual categories that organize and make sense of it. Such categories are the basic cognitive building blocks of cultural meaning and institutional systems. So, for example, to have family social structures, one must have culturally significant cognitive categories such as mother, father, child, kin, nonrelatives, and so on, to define distinctions that the structure relates in patterned ways. Likewise, to have latifundia structures of massive agricultural estates in Latin America, one has to possess the meaningful categories of private property, landowner, peasant, wage laborer, labor boss, and so on, to know what is what and who is whom within the structured system. For this reason, there more generally cannot be a social structure without the embedded cultural meanings that help constitute it. Their relationship is interpenetrating and mutually reinforcing—the meaningful cognitive categories partly create the structure, even as the interactive relational practices of the structure simultaneously validate the meanings and reality of the cultural categories with which it is built. Meaningful cognitive categories or schemas enhance the durability of social structures because such categories are rooted in primal mental organizations of human consciousness. Since cognitive schemas are necessary for life and the world to be even minimally accessible, interpretable, and engageable, and since fundamental understandings of reality are imprinted early in life and rarely change dramatically, most cognitive categories with which people operate are highly stable. When they are implicated in social structural practices, they become even more ingrained in the fabric of practice, perception, and thought. Social structures normally are therefore highly durable because the culturally meaningful cognitive categories that help constitute them are deeply rooted in human consciousness and powerfully validated by the practices of the structures. We might call the contribution of enduring cognitive categories to the durability of social structures *cognitive category stability*.

Sixth, social structures are expressed and reinforced through lived bodily practices. Structures, I have said, do not entail simply abstract relations or thought systems. They organize and regulate physical bodily locations, treatments, appearances, postures, behaviors, contacts, disciplines, and interactions. Most of what social structures do with and to bodies has to do with repetition. Consistency in reiterations of bodily behaviors is a crucial part of what social structures accomplish. Some bodies stay on one side of the tracks, other bodies live on the other side. Some bodies are made proud, tall, and domineering in posture, while others shrink in meekness and submissiveness. Some bodies in some settings are almost entirely covered with clothing, while others in other settings are almost fully bared. Some bodies may meet in intimate contact, others may simply never touch. Some bodies are nourished and protected with every resource a social group possesses, while others are systematically neglected, deprived, or even intentionally put into mortal danger. In these and many other ways, social structures are constructed not only through shared mental schemes and material artifacts, but also through repetitions of bodily treatments and behaviors and appearances across space and time. This in part provides the corporeal dimension of the "collective activity currents" described above. It is important for present purposes to note that most bodily practices that structures shape are not conscious and intentional. In the first stages of learning, many bodily practices usually do require self-conscious attention. But no person has the capacity of attention and cognition to focus on every bodily concern that life entails. So, most bodily practices become highly routinized, automatic, habitual.[26] Think of what it takes in this way to drive a car, type a manuscript, or play sports well—it is as if, once learned, bodily motions know what to do on their own, apart from intentional directions from conscious attention. Involved is something like "muscle learning." Viewed from another perspective, consider how hard it is and how long it can take to break a deeply ingrained habit of unreflective bodily behavior. This relates closely to the "passive" or "involuntary human" capacity for living in a state of "practical consciousness," noted in chapter 1. Normal people have the ability to "go on" in life, executing a host of functional behaviors without consciously thinking about why and how they are doing them or perhaps even being consciously aware that they are doing them. It is this kind of corporeal, "tacit knowledge," in which our bodies "know more than we can tell"[27] and execute more than we could possibly attend to with conscious intention, that enables us to perform most socially structured bodily practices on "automatic pilot."

In short, the majority of what humans do with their bodies every day, although important, is not directly intentional. Our bodies perform a host of practices while our conscious awareness focuses on other matters. Our

26. Steven Vaisey, "Socrates, Skinner, and Aristotle: Three Ways of Thinking about Culture in Action," *Sociological Forum* 23, no. 3 (2008): 603–13; Giddens, *The Constitution of Society*, xxiii.

27. Michael Polanyi, *The Tacit Dimension* (1966; Gloucester, MA: Peter Smith, 1983), quote from p. 4.

bodies function primarily on learned routine and habit, most of which performs in continuity with and guided by the social structural contexts in which they operate. In turn, our automatic bodily practices operating on tacit knowledge reproduce and confirm the social structures that organize and regulate them. This fact—that the motions of most embodied practices are performed without conscious awareness or intention—provides social structures yet another reinforcement of their continuity and durability. That is because the "auto-pilot" character of those bodily practices can perpetuate the complex motions of embodied life that help to constitute social structures with relatively little effort. By contrast, to undermine the durability of social structures through the performance of uncooperative or contrary bodily practices requires a good deal of focused attention and directive mental effort. So, to illustrate, some people wake up on Sunday mornings, spend the next two hours thinking only about one event that happened the previous week, and yet somehow find themselves at ten o'clock dressed up and sitting in a pew at church with Bibles in hand. Their bodies just know how to do that, even if their minds are paying no attention. For those same people with the same histories to by contrast end up at ten o'clock meditating quietly in the woods or on their knees and faces at a mosque would require a good deal of focused attention, intention, and self-direction. The natural default is for human bodies to repeat what they have already learned as tacit performance knowledge. And the larger tendency, therefore, is for most people to continue enacting the embodied behaviors that their social-structurally governed and disciplined bodies have come routinely to perform. And that gives those social structures additional stability. Let us call this contribution to social structural durability *reiterated body practices*.

Seventh, according to my definition above, social structures are also accumulated historically. Social structures are not reinvented for every new situation and generation. They usually do not disappear simply because their "founders" have lost interest or died. They accrue to new generations as populations age and reproduce. And in this, as the kind of dependent objective realities described in chapter 3, they entail a kind of momentum or directional inertia acquired over time. Structures may with time be transformed or wither away, but usually that happens through slow, halting processes. Meanwhile, social structures are, through continued interaction—unless they are in unusual circumstances dramatically changed—sustained and passed on from day to day, person to person, and generation to generation. A person's experience of participating in social structures is not like sitting down with a group of friends to invent a new organization from scratch, but more like being thrown into a swim meet that is already underway or being pushed onstage into a complexly choreographed opera that is halfway through its performance. The best anyone can do is jump into the flood of activity already underway and try to join in as best as one is able. And that is what nearly everyone does with social structures. From the phenomenological perspective of new members of society, therefore, inherited social structures are "the way things are," the taken-for-granted nature of reality to which one has to adjust.[28] There is, under normal circumstances, by natural default, given the human condition, more reason for new members being inducted into society to accept and perpetuate than to question and discontinue the social structures—often even if they are not the obvious beneficiaries of the differences and inequalities the structures entail. This historical accretion and momentum of social structures across generations and the "naturalness" of structures that it tends to convey provide added reinforcement to their durable character. We might call this contribution of historical accumulation to social structural durability *accumulating temporal solidification.*

Finally, social structures are generated and reproduced through social interactions. This has important consequences for their durability. No single individual can generate or maintain a social structure. That takes ongoing social relations among interacting people. This means that multiple actors are involved in the making and sustaining of all social structures. And that takes full control over structures out of the hands of any of the persons involved. Interactions are multiparty productions. Each participant contributes his or her part, but the whole is a collective accomplishment. And we know from more than a century of research on social interactions that individual participants' contributions to interactions are powerfully influenced by the contributions of others. While most interactions are at some level culturally scripted, specific interactions are also open enough that all participants are dependent upon careful interpretations of the cues of symbolic meaning given off by interaction partners, to which they respond with their own communications of meanings in turn. Contributions of single persons are thus governed not only by their desires and intentions but also by the larger interactive contexts in which they are participating and sustaining. Again, this puts the interactions as whole

28. Berger and Luckmann, *The Social Construction of Reality.*

productions beyond the control of any given participant. We know from personal experience that, because of situational and intercommunicative factors beyond our immediate command—that is, what others for their parts are bringing to the interactions—our own roles in social interactions can turn out quite differently than we intended and wanted. We can end up acquiescing to ideas that we do not believe, agreeing to commitments that we do not want, reacting to others in ways we did not anticipate, and otherwise failing to present ourselves or our interests as we originally intended or might have desired in retrospect.

This makes all but the most micro and local of social structures difficult to get control of by any participant involved. Because many are engaged in its production, normally no single participant is positioned to be able to transform or terminate a social structure at will. The nature and impact of social structures usually stand beyond the grasp of any of the persons who interactionally sustain them. So, even when some people implicated in a social structure would prefer a different system of relations that produces different outcomes, rarely can they exert the influence to change the structure. That is in part because the other contributing participants are also their own distinct persons who bring their own beliefs and interests to the collective interaction. This dynamic of putting structures outside of the ready control of their individual constituent participants endows them with an autonomy to operate and persist at a level above and beyond those who might seek to transform or end them. And that contributes to their continuity and durability over time. Let us call this causal reinforcement of social structural durability *intractable interaction processes*.

We see, then, that there is no one reason why social structures are so durable. There are many, distinct, and interpenetrating reasons. The ontological nature of social structures entail varieties of combinations of what I am calling collective activity currents, socially enforced conformity, objective material fixity, cognitive category stability, reiterated body practices, accumulating temporal solidification, and intractable interaction processes. For any given structure, each of these causal forces tends to validate and reinforce the others. And they operate in a multiplicity of ways at various levels of human life that prevent simple summaries and counteractions. The durability of most social structures is in most cases profoundly overdetermined. Having understood what social structures are and how they come to be, it is hard to imagine how they could be anything but highly stable, persistent, and durable across time.

To return to our larger question, social structures work by drawing new participants into involvement in reiterated social interactions, which are grounded in and reproduce stable patterns of social relationships between differentiated groups. Normally these interactive relationships have already been established and set into motion by the time new participants merge in, so they have historical momentum and the appearance to new participants of natural self-existence. In the process, new members are, in various ways, inducted into the meaningful cognitive categories that help to constitute the social relationships, and into the moral and normative horizons that help to motivate and make meaningful sense of activities perpetuating the structures.[29] People are also drawn into social structures because life in a world of material scarcity, competition, and power relations means that not participating in the social structures would mean foregoing goods they value—food, security, status, sex, belonging, and more. The social structures not only engage human activity but also consume material resources as the sustaining means of their continuation in physical space—which also means they help to distribute those resources evenly or unevenly among the people involved. They also inscribe their particular imprints of meaning and purpose upon material objects in order to refabricate the physical world so as to facilitate and express their structural existence. To maintain behavioral conformity, actors constituting social structures also purposefully sanction the compliance and deviance of one another through rewards and punishments. As a result of these multiple, complex, and mutually reinforcing dynamics, the persons whose lives are drawn up into such social structures are powerfully compelled to cooperate with and collaborate in their routines, imperatives, and practices. Consequently, the lives of those actors are provided an orderliness, stability, continuity, and predictability that are preconditions for not only human physical survival but also the development and flourishing of personhood, which is the central purpose of human life. At the same time, those structures generate certain characteristic outcomes for the lives of their constituents, which usually vary for different groups engaged in the social structural relationships. Since such outcomes tend to involve variations in humanly valued goods, most social structures not only involve differentiation in the abstract but also foster the organization and

---

29. Douglas Porpora reminds us that "structures also motivate," in Porpora, "Do Realists Run Regressions?" in *After Postmodernism: An Introduction To Critical Realism*, ed. José López, and Garry Potter (New York: Continuum, 2001), 265.

reproduction of social inequalities of various kinds, many of which, paradoxically, also undermine flourishing personhood.

Important to underscore about this entire process is something like what Anthony Giddens calls the "duality" of social structures.[30] That is, that structures are the producers of the relational interactions in which people engage, and simultaneously and in the same process are the products of those very interactions. As Pierre Bourdieu puts it, we are dealing with structured structures that function as structuring structures.[31] The ordered, durable patterns of social relationships of which structures consist organize the subjective experiences and objective practices that direct people's lives. But those patterned social relationships are the outcomes of the organized practices and experiences through which people's lives are directed. Social structures are thus concurrently the causes *and* outcomes of real, sustained, patterned social interactions of human actors.[32] This means that, contra theories of social holism, structures are not ontologically preexistent or autonomous entities possessing their own purposes or logics that, for their own reasons, "push around" human beings. Structures are always and everywhere entirely the dependent, emergent products of ongoing human activity. But this also means, contra reductionistically individualistic theories, that social structures exist emergently as real entities above and beyond the level of personal being and, as such, possess irreducible, downward causal capacities to organize and direct human consciousness and action from a level above. This apparent paradox is the result of the duality of structures, derived from their emergent existence as real entities in a stratified reality operating at one level above that of personal actors. So, social structures are not, from a critical realist perspective, mere linguistic metaphors for describing the orderliness of social life. They are real existents with ontological being and causal powers, irreducible to social life lived. At the same time, social structures cannot be isolated and observed apart from the concretely patterned interactions of social life lived. For it is lived social life that is simultaneously the cause of and the causal consequence of existent social structures.

30. Giddens, *The Constitution of Society*, 25–29.

31. Pierre Bourdieu, *Outline of a Theory of Practice* (Berkeley and Los Angeles: University of California Press, 1977), 72.

32. Margaret Archer's discussion of temporally structured morphogenesis is helpful here. Archer, *Realist Social Theory: A Morphogenetic Approach*.

Interlocking Social Structures

In the previous pages, I have focused on how and why individual social structures—if we can conceive of them as particular units of reality— operate and durably sustain themselves across time. But the question of structural durability and functional operation is not fully answered by attending to the features of individual structures. Before turning to the next question, therefore, I need to elaborate the concept of "interlocking" structures. What we call *societies* consist of massive conglomerations of distinct but tightly linked social structures in larger *structural environments*. And every person's life is engaged in multiple social structures of many different kinds—familial, political, economic, residential, racial, occupational, educational, gender, friendship, and so on. I have argued in the pages above that particular social structures, when viewed as single cases, entail numerous features that overdetermine their continuity and durability. Just as importantly, however, the interlocking of multiple social structures, both vertically and horizontally, creates conditions that generate an even greater durability of—and openness to change in—structures.[33] What does this mean and how does it work?

In human social life, no social structure stands on its own. Most of the elements of any given social structure possesses *hooks*, so to speak, that link them to the elements of other social structures, just as the miniature hooks on Velcro bond together the two strips of attached material. To use a different image, if we think of individual social structures as molecules, then each of them possesses various positive and negative charges that bond them to other molecules into larger compounds or lattice structures. Analogously, human societies are comprised of vast assemblages of connected and interpenetrating social structures operating in a larger structural environment, which are linked together at various points in different ways. What do those links and bonds look like? Take the case of the structure of inequitable school financing, offered as one example at the start of this chapter. We might conceive of that analytically as an isolated structure. But such a structure cannot and never does stand alone. Rather, it is connected on all sides to multiple other social structures. Schools and their funding structures are tied, for instance, to family, residential,

33. Michael Mann also highlights "multiple overlapping and intersecting sociospatial networks of power" in *The Sources of Social Power* (Cambridge: Cambridge University Press, 1986).

occupational, social class, governmental, regulatory, education supplies, sports, cafeteria work, building maintenance, and communications technology structures. And each of these structures is in turn tied to a variety of others. For example, the occupational structures within which school students' parents in particular districts deal with jobs and work are linked to other, larger economic, educational, professional, labor market, union, tax incentive, global trade, transportation, real estate, race relations, gender, and other associated structures.

For present purposes, the key idea in this is that no single structure is able under normal conditions to dramatically transform its practices by accident or at will, in part because its practices are interconnected with those of multiple other, durable structures. So just as the nature and operation of any given social structure are characteristically beyond the definitive control of any particular person who helps to constitute that structure, the nature and operation of any given social structure is usually also beyond the definitive control of those who might mobilize against it, even of those with formal authority over it. That is because the social structures that some may want to challenge and over which authorities are designated to have control are integrated into much larger conglomerations of other social structures—the demands, expectations, regulations, and practices of which are largely beyond the capacity of challengers and authorities to command or influence. So, for instance, although the principals and school board are authorized to govern the schools and school system, they are not authorized to manage the multiple related social structures to which their schools are linked. They cannot alter the economic structures that produce geographically based systems of socioeconomic differences in their area. They cannot command the governmental institutions of public revenues to increase taxes or change their system of distribution. They cannot terminate the flow into their districts of non-English-speaking immigrants in need of costlier bilingual education. And they cannot change the fact that cultural expectations and human capital standards mean they must fund costly football programs and computer labs for their students. The list could go on and on. But the point is that, in normal circumstances, few particular structures enjoy tremendous latitude in other- or self-direction and transformation. Every structure, by virtue of being linked to multiple other structures, is significantly constrained in the degrees of freedom with which it has to function, change, and be changed. Too much attempted transformation generates problems in the linkages with other social structures. Thus, an intended change in school composition evokes protest by parents who do not want their children bussed to other districts. A proposed revision of class sizes and teacher deployments meets resistance from the teachers' union. Planned deferred building maintenance encounters objections from state environmental regulators. Efforts to increase voluntary parental involvement in schools fail because the two-paycheck schedules and high divorce rates among students' parents make the effort toward greater participation difficult. In short, the leeway that any given social structure enjoys to change itself intentionally or by happenstance or be changed by challenging outsiders is constrained by the many similarly constrained structures with which it is linked. And so relatively little change happens, and when it does, it happens slowly and haltingly. Individual social structures are thus like vehicles caught in a social structural gridlock in which, despite the fact that all engines are running and everyone wants to move, no vehicle is able to move far because no other vehicle is able to move far. The interdependence of compacted vehicles whose movements cannot be orchestrated in unison makes the movement of any of them difficult. And so stability and durability of structures prevails. Every social reformer and political maverick knows this fact well.

It is possible in this to distinguish conceptually between social structures that are *vertically interlocked* and those that are *horizontally interlocked*.[34] The vertical dimension of the linkages of structures refers to ties that link structures above and below one another in scale, function, or authority. The metaphor of reference here is of vertically integrated business production. For example, in such a case a firm not only sells a brand of coffee beans at the local grocer but also owns and operates the coffee plantations, roasting facilities, packing and shipping operations, and distribution systems ("below" the grocery store sales), as well as a national network of café chains that also sell a variety of other food and drink products built around the brand name ("above" the grocery store sales). From the rows of coffee bean plants at the bottom up to the chic café in the upscale shopping mall at the top, the firm has vertically integrated its production and sales of coffee and related products. In roughly analogous fashion, social structures can be vertically tied to or nested within one another. The particular social structuring of elite university admissions and recruitment, to give one example, is normally vertically linked with other

34. For a related discussion of distinct levels of social life, see George Ritzer, "Levels of Social Analysis and an Integrated Sociological Paradigm," in *Metatheorizing in Sociology* (Lexington, MA: Lexington Books, 1991), 139–59.

social structures of differentiated secondary education systems and institutional structures of national standardized testing systems below, and with graduate and professional school admissions and jobs recruitment above. Likewise, the ethnic and religious segregation of childhood playmates in a neighborhood is tied to similar relational structures of association and segregation operating among the kids' parents above, which, in turn, is linked to broader structures of social, theological, and organizational divisions between Catholics and Protestants nationally and worldwide, as well as broader cultural differences between working-class and white-collar Americans. As a result, structures at any given level are usually not free to be readily changed or to be transformed at will in part because they are hooked into related structures above and below that operate beyond the control of actors at any one level. Stability at one structural level tends to enhance stability at other, interlocked structural levels. And, given the overdetermined durability of social structures at all levels, the vertical interlocking of structures up and down levels serves to further reinforce the stability and durability of all structures at all levels. If one piece of chain mail in a suit of armor, so to speak, is hard to break apart, all of the pieces of chain mail interlocked together are all that much more so. Once again, and now for even more reasons, the durability of structures are robust and overdetermined.

Social structures may also be *horizontally* interlocked. The horizontal dimension of the linking of structures refers to ties that connect structures operating on a similar plane of scale, function, or authority. The general metaphor of reference here again is horizontally integrated business firms. These either tie together control over multiple companies operating in the same general market or else involve one company marketing a similar product in different ways to sell it in diverse and segmented markets. The first strategy pursues monopoly control, the second expanded market share. The horizontal interlocking of social structures does not usually involve business firms, markets, and sales. The conceptual parallel is more general, concerning the interconnection of social structures that serve similar functions or that operate on similar levels of scale or authority. Take, for instance, the free-market religious economy mentioned as an example at the start of this chapter. That is one social structure, analytically speaking. But it is likely also horizontally interconnected to other roughly parallel structures operating at a comparable level. The various denominations and congregations operating in this unregulated religious economy not only compete with one another as faith communities but are also likely tied in various ways to other nonreligious structures. These may involve counseling centers, mortuary and funeral services, voluntary associations, community service programs, health and social service agencies, recreational facilities, tutoring programs, sports leagues, food pantries and homeless shelters, retreat centers, moral reform or social justice movement organizations, and so on. Only the most sectarian of religious groups will maintain few ties to other such social structures. The larger point is that we should expect such horizontal integration to strengthen the durability of the original religious structures in question. For one thing, horizontal ties tend to lead to the stability of organizational and cultural isomorphism. As particular social structures relate to parallel structures operating at similar levels of function and scope, they tend to monitor and reference one another's criteria of legitimacy and evolve to share one another's characteristic features.[35] Moreover, increased interlocking ties between structures at this level also tend to fortify the stability and durability of each of the involved structures because they are apt to institutionalize various forms of joint communication, accountability, standardization, and coordination. So, when one college operating on the quarter system joins a consortium of colleges most of which happen to operate on the semester system, a host of new structural pressures suddenly arise—such as the ease of cross-registration, students transferring without losing credits, and shared participation in joint international programs—for the newly joining college to replace its quarter system with the more standard semester system. In which case, the larger system produces a short-term and limited change, which has the longer-term, more powerful consequence of solidifying similarity, continuity, and durability.

What more exactly are the hooks or links that interconnect or glue different social structures into larger conglomerations of structure? They can be many and various and are usually multiple in any given case. But the list of forces and activities that interconnect social structures together certainly includes monetary flows and resource dependencies, cognitive categories and cultural schemas, legal and regulatory directives, established behavioral routines and practices, normative and moral commitments, political influences, network relationship ties, and the alignment of material or physical configurations that are transposable, prescriptive, bridging, or

35. Paul DiMaggio and Walter Powell, "The Iron Cage Revisited: Institutional Isomorphism and Collective Rationality in Organizational Fields," *American Sociological Review* 48 (1983): 147–60.

isomorphic from one domain or structure to another. For instance, to return to some of the examples of structures presented at the start of this
chapter, the social structure of high school "crowds" and identity cliques
internal to a given school's culture and relational structure does not float
freely on its own. It is interlocked with and reinforced through horizontal
ties to similar social structures at other high schools and with and through
vertical ties to images, models, vocabularies, and aesthetics drawn down
from social structural features of the music industry, clothing products,
cable television, sports entertainment, Hollywood, shopping malls, the
advertising industry, and more. Likewise, the military conscription system drafting young men by lottery but exempting those enrolled in higher
education is analytically isolatable in theory but concretely enmeshed in
reality in a host of other structural systems that help to define, legitimate,
and enforce it—such as state laws that prohibit the hiring of employees
who are not or have not been registered with the Selective Service and university programs that provide reprieve from military conscription to those
who can gain admission and pay tuition. Any social scientific analyses of
social structural features and dynamics in particular empirical cases, therefore, need to pay attention to the larger social structural environments
that provide the forms and processes of structural stability and durability
through complex, vertically and horizontally interlocking dependencies
and interdependencies of various kinds.

   In order to grasp these complex forces generating social structural durability, it helps to approach the matter from the point of view of a group
wishing to alter one intentionally. This is the position in which social and
political movements for change find themselves. Suppose that you and
your comrades are social justice activists—inspired, let us say, by liberation theology and the social doctrines of the Catholic Church.[36] You want
to transform the latifundia land tenure system of your native Central
American country. In that system, immense estates of the most productive agricultural land, also sometimes known as haciendas, are owned by
a small number of elite, oligarchic families. The owners employ poor,
landless wage laborers on a seasonal basis who work for subsistence pay.
Production is supervised by demanding overseers, the wage laborers are
routinely exposed to toxic pesticides, the system is backed by local army

36. See Phillip Berryman, *The Religious Roots of Rebellion* (Maryknoll, NY: Orbis Books,
1986); Christian Smith, *The Emergence of Liberation Theology* (Chicago: University of Chicago Press, 1991); Penny Lernoux, *Cry of the People* (New York: Penguin Books, 1982).

militias that are "in the pockets" of the landowners, and the crops produced are sold on the agro-export market for overseas consumption. You
believe this social structure is unjust and you are determined to change it.
What are you up against? Perhaps more than you can imagine.

Within that individual social structure, you first confront the need to
change collective activity currents and undo accumulated temporal solidification. Across the entire region, flows of social activity follow the same
patterns they have for decades. The spatial location of landowners and
peasants, the regular migration of workers, the patrols of militias, the
movement of shipping trucks, the daily rounds of labor overseers, social
visits by shady politicians, and all the rest move in the steady current that
the social structure reflects and impels. You then have to challenge the socially enforced conformity processes not only of the armed militia groups
but also of the laborers' fatalistic family members and friends who discourage them from "making waves." You also have to deal with the force
of objective material fixity, in the form of the technology of the farming
equipment designed for this kind of labor system, the road infrastructure
built to carry produce to the nearest port city instead of to local markets,
the fences and patrol shacks set up to guard the haciendas, and so on. Furthermore, you have to address cognitive category stability, the automatic
thought assumptions, mental classifications, and cultural meanings—including *patrón*, *peones*, ownership, daily wages, debt, submission to God's
will, and much more—that those involved in the system readily refer to in
defining reality. You also have to challenge the reiterated body practices
implicit in the system, the bodily differences between cowering back and
standing tall, between shuffling into the fields every morning and picketing
at the gate in protest, between retiring to the bottle and spending evenings
learning to read and write. Finally, you must get a handle on intractable
interaction processes. Some *peones* may initially believe and support your
social change message. But word of mouth and spreading chains of communication and interaction can generate hosts of conversations, fears,
reactions, and oppositional responses that are difficult to anticipate or
control. Altogether, these factors operating analytically within one social
structure present a formidable challenge to overcome.

But the point of this section is that social structural durability is not
only fostered by factors internal to individual structures, analytically conceived, but also by interlocking ties and interdependencies with other
social structures in a larger structural environment. In our case, for example, the local militias have strong (upwardly vertical) personnel ties to

the country's National Guard (which in turn has upward international ties to the U.S. Department of Defense); the large landowners have long-term (upwardly vertical) export contracts with global multinational agribusiness firms; the labor shift overseers know enough to exploit long-running (downwardly vertical) rivalries and disputes among area kinship networks of laborers; and the region's landowners together belong (horizontally) to a National Growers Association comprised of their peers, which wields power to ensure that the nation's Congress enacts laws sustaining the established production system. Furthermore, the distribution of the area's educational funds for schooling, controlled by the local mayor, ensure (downwardly vertical) that peasant children get poor educations that limit them to working on the haciendas when they grow up; the old style priest at the local (upwardly vertical) Catholic Church teaches a heavenly reward for those who suffer patiently and that God ordains people to their social stations; and a few humanitarian assistance and self-help organizations distribute enough food and clothing (horizontally) to the landless workers to sustain their impoverished existences at a manageable level of deprivation. In short, your activist efforts to challenge and transform this system will meet not only the forces of internal structural continuity but also external forces of durability caused by a host of interlocking ties to other social structures in the larger structural environment. You in your activism will be fortunate therefore to affect only modest changes, if, in fact, you do not lose your life.

I have here emphasized the durability of structures. But structural interlocking also helps to explain structural change. Two or more interlocked social structures create opportunities in which the cultural logics of each may question, criticize, or provide alternative models for thought and action for the others. Universities whose business schools work closely with for-profit corporations, for example, may end up being rationalized or restructured by lessons learned and models observed about efficiency, personnel policies, or outcome-driven teaching that flow back from the corporate world into university organizations. In these kinds of ways, the interlocking of social structures that typically tends to promote structural durability also itself opens up doors for outside forces of social critique and change to exert structure-transforming influences.[37]

The empirical realities of interlocking social structures are complex, and the theoretical idea of interlocking structures is highly abstract. So we

37. Thanks to Steve Vaisey for pointing out the idea about structural change noted here.

are forced to use a variety of analogies and metaphors—things like Velcro hooks, molecule lattices, integrated business firms, vehicle gridlock, and various forms of social adhesives—to try to wrap our minds around this matter. Every good analogy and metaphor involves illuminating similarities but also entails potentially misleading dissimilarities. I trust that the case made here is now clear enough, without having been muddled too badly by the metaphors. The point is that social structures are normally highly stable and durable not only because of their internal characteristics, which certainly promote continuity and persistence, but also because of the constraining and influencing powers of the interlocking ties that connect extensive and complex conglomerations of social structures in the real social world. Each particular structure is hooked to, embedded within, and interpenetrated by many other different structures that tend to create "interstructural drag" or "friction" against change for any and all of them. At the same time, the adjoining nature of social structures also creates occasions for critiques of structures and their potential transformation—insofar as the logics or cultures of some structures can impinge critically or disruptively on those of others with which they are interlocked.

How Does Social Structural Change Ever Happen?

This chapter's focus on social structures has so far drawn our analytical attention to the problem of social order. Addressed primarily here has been the Hobbesian question of how, given the diverse thoughts, desires, interests, and actions of myriad individual humans, any kind of stability and order in human social life is ever possible. Why is the social world not one of sheer chaos, volatility, confusion, and mayhem? My answer, and that of all structuralist theories, is that social structures provide an organization, regulation, and stability to social life that pose a bulwark against such turmoil and instability (even if in other ways they also help to generate these). Good, so far as it goes. But all theories of social order must also confront and answer the opposite inquiry, the question of social transformation. That is, given the overdetermining structural forces that impose order and continuity on social life, how is it that the social world ever changes? What explains social transformation, evolution, development, reform, adjustment, innovation, and revolution? Social scientists have offered numerous explanations of social change over the decades, some helpful, some problematic. It is not my purpose here to sort through and evaluate the many existing theories of social change. That would be an undertaking beyond my present capacity. My task is more modest. I wish to develop from the definition of social structures elaborated above a theoretically coherent account of how and why social change occurs. Any theory of order should be directly complemented by a corresponding and compatible theory of social change. My purpose, then, is to explore an understanding of change that references the above theory of social structure in order to develop further my overall theoretical account and show its consistency with my more general theory of critical realist personalism.

Immediately we confront the difficulty of specifying the right level or proximity of causal influence. Every causal force or influence is caused by other causal forces or influences, creating great and complicated chains and webs of causal effects. Specifying which causes at which times were most important or decisive in producing some social change can be tricky. For example, suppose a specific college in Iowa became secularized and so lost its historic religious character. Was that because its president in 1896 decided to break its denominational affiliation and signed a document declaring that break? Or was it because higher education in Germany, where the college's faculty and president earned their degrees, had already secularized in the eighteenth and nineteenth centuries? Or perhaps was it because the Protestant Reformation of the sixteenth century set in motion certain key secularizing cultural and institutional influences that spread throughout the Western world? Or maybe was it the result of the radical monotheism that arose in the Ancient Near East millennia ago, which culturally created a deep cognitive gulf between sacred transcendence and mundane immanence that was the precondition of the possibility of subsequent changes like the Protestant Reformation and a secularized Europe? Arguably the college in Iowa secularized because of all of these reasons and many others. But to answer any question about the causes of cases of social structural change, we have to specify a proper level or proximity of the reasons for the social change in question in a way that actually satisfies the persons who are inquiring. It will not do, for instance, to explain the causes of the First World War by saying that the muscles of someone's index finger pulled a gun trigger that killed an archduke (too proximate). Nor will it do to say that human evolution has caused people to be prone to conflict (too remote). Both may be true, but neither is very illuminating. We have, instead, to exercise the faculties and judgments of personal knowledge to determine what kind of causal explanation will answer well the questions we persons raise. In what follows, I will enumerate a variety of kinds of reasons behind the occurrence of social transformations that override the normally overdetermined durability of social structures. For each reason offered, questions can legitimately be raised about what kinds of forces in turn cause those influences. Still, the explanation in any given case of social change will have to draw boundaries around the scope of its analytical account beyond which no explanation will be offered, in order to avoid an infinite regress of questioning and so to keep the original question from being lost in the process of fuller explanation. For present purposes, I wish only to focus on the analytical dimensions of causes of social change that tell us theoretically how and why social structures are transformed.

To begin, we might remind ourselves that, from the outlook of critical realist personalism, human persons are the prime agents of social life—not things at a reductionist level below, like "selfish genes," or impersonally above, like the "functional requisites of the social order" or the "imperatives of the world system."[38] We should always return to the natural character of persons for clues about how social life works. Crucial among them will certainly be the capacities for creativity, moral judgment, symbolization, meaning creation, truth seeking, valuation, and anticipation of the future. Furthermore, recall that personhood is in an important sense realized, it is not a static fixity. Our human capacities come as rich potentials that we must develop through life into fullness or some approximation of it. And this itself adds a questlike character to every human life well lived,[39] which also creates a dimension of change and instability in human life that can, under the right conditions, lend itself to social structural change. At the same time, critical realist personalism insists that reality is stratified into different yet simultaneously connected levels of existence, each of which operates according to its own principles and exerts its own causal dynamics irreducible to but emergently dependent

38. The strategies and structures developed by humans need to ensure their reproduction in their natural environments, otherwise the humans would cease to exist; but there are many possible strategies for reproductive fitness, so we need specifically personal and social explanations to explain the variation and transformations of the conditions that we actually observe.

39. Alasdair MacIntyre, *After Virtue* (Notre Dame, IN: University of Notre Dame Press, 1984), 204–25; Erizim Kohák, "Selves, People, Persons: An Essay in American Personalism," in *Selves, People, and Persons: What Does It Mean to Be a Self?* ed. Leroy Rouner, Boston University Studies in Philosophy and Religion (Notre Dame, IN: University of Notre Dame Press, 1992), 17–35.

upon and sometimes shaped through downward causation by the others. One of the important levels existing above that of the human personal is the social structural, which possesses its own emergent features and causal powers. In principle, then, we should recognize that the causes that transform social structures might arise, first, from human actors at the level below, from which structures are emergent. Second, they might be exerted by other social structures operating at the same level or other interlocked structural levels. And, third, they might operate downwardly as causal forces from even higher levels of reality, such as processes of global warming and climate change or devastating hurricanes or other "acts of God." In most cases of social structural change, the relevant causal influences come as the intentional and unintentional effects of purposive human actions operating in the context and under the influence of combinations of stable and shifting social structural forces, which in turn may be shaped by the influence of real causal powers operating downwardly from higher levels of reality. The trick in any good sociological explanation of change is to interpret the available evidence in a way that accounts for all relevant levels of influence and illuminates and satisfies people's personal curiosity and knowledge about how causal forces work on the real world.[40] Usually this means accounting for human purpose and agency as well as important social structural and contextual influences. And that is a task that sociological theories have been working for decades to learn how to accomplish well.

We might also remind ourselves that the "duality of social structures" means that, although social structures are real entities with genuine, irreducible causal powers, they do not exist independently of the specific, patterned social interactions from which they, through emergence, arise into being. Structures not only structure social interactions but also simultaneously are continually constituted and structured *by* social interactions. For this reason, they do possess an ontological reality at a different level that is distinct from the concrete human activities that generate them, but they do not enjoy an autonomously self-generating source of being. Consequently, the stability and durability of social structures are paradoxically constituted out of the dynamic motion of activity from which they arise

---

40. In the end, there is no test of proof, validity, or significance that can establish a good explanation of social change; all such fixed methodological tests are provisional and subordinate, serving only the final real test of good explanation: personal human judgment and intellectual satisfaction.

emergently—similarly, perhaps, to the hardness of solid material at the physical object level arising emergently from the motion of protons and neutrons spinning unimaginably fast around nuclei at the atomic level. In this sense, social structures do not exist "out there" as self-existent objects autonomous to human thought and action. All social structures are intimately connected to the lively, buzzing, humming realm of constant human activity that at another lower level appears to be highly fluid and open. Stated differently, social structures involve human activity that is highly patterned, but being patterned does not mean being static, rigid, or inert. Structures are stability and durability in motion. And that motion contributes to the potential for social structural change.

Returning, then, to our question: given that the continuity and durability of human social structures are normally overdetermined by multiple and complex forces of stability, how is it—other than through purely exogenous shocks like massive natural disasters, plagues, and so on—that any social change happens? Considering the definition of social structures elaborated above and their features promoting durability, we should expect social structural change to occur given the following, usually interdependent and mutually influencing kinds of conditions.

First, social structures are often transformed when new relationships between different groups are initiated and when old relationships are severely weakened or terminated. Social structures are fundamentally about patterns of human social relations. So when fundamental group relationships change for reasons extrinsic to the structures, those structures also tend to change. This happens, on the one hand, when new social relations are established. For example, the social-structural worlds of the Celts, Angles, and Saxons were transformed by direct contact with Romans through the Roman conquest of Britain in and after AD 43; just as those of native Americans and Pacific Islanders (e.g., Aztecs, Incas, Hawaiians) were altered by the arrival of Western conquerors and explorers (and vice versa). Likewise, the structures of local communities are altered when they are newly incorporated into national economic markets through the opening up of new transportation and communication infrastructures, such as canal and railroad systems.[41] Similarly, the arrival of a new racial or ethnic group in an established neighborhood or town will often restructure

41. George Thomas, *Revivalism and Cultural Change: Christianity, Nation Building, and the Market in the Nineteenth-Century United States* (Chicago: University of Chicago Press, 1989).

the patterns of relations among the existing residents. This process of relational-change-inducing structural transformation also happens, on the other hand, when established relations are ended. The collapse and disappearance of a historically rival tribe or civilization, for example, may very well alter the internal political, economic, or military structures of the remaining tribe or civilization. The termination of a relation of colonial rule of one country by another, for another instance, changes many of the internal structures of the newly postcolonial nation. Simple alterations of group relations driven by factors outside of a social structure can change the internal order of a social structure.

Second, social structures are often transformed when the basic cognitive categories that help to constitute and justify them are altered. For example, political and economic structures are changed when people stop thinking in terms of lords, peasants, and knights and imagine life instead in terms of burghers, citizens, traders, and entrepreneurs.[42] The same is true when a premodern cosmological Great Chain of Being is replaced in the popular cognitive imagination by a modern view, such as a Newtonian mechanistic cognitive picture of reality.[43] Further, when one conceives of the world as ruled by one, transcendent, almighty God rather than populated by myriad animistic spirits or competing anthropomorphized gods, the kinship and political structures that articulated with the animistic and polytheistic worldview will be altered in favor of alternatives more consistent with monotheistic beliefs.[44] Structures of gender and race relations are likewise changed when relevant people come to believe the idea that all humans are equal persons instead of the idea that some can be property or are naturally inferior types.[45] Sometimes the important cognitive change altering social structures is simply a new realization that traditions of the past do not have to determine practices of the future, that the momentum of history need not be controlling of impending outcomes—that, in short, is a mental challenge through "cognitive liberation"[46] to the power of "ac-

42. See, for instance, William Sewell Jr., "Ideologies and Social Revolutions: Reflections on the French Case," *Journal of Modern History* 57, no. 1 (1985): 57–85.

43. See Karl Polanyi, *The Great Transformation* (Boston: Beacon Press, 2001).

44. Rodney Stark, *One True God: Historical Consequences of Monotheism* (Princeton, NJ: Princeton University Press, 2003).

45. See, for example, Micheline Ishay, *The History of Human Rights* (Berkeley and Los Angeles: University of California Press, 2004); and Kirsten Sellars, *The Rise and Rise of Human Rights* (Stroud, UK: Sutton, 2002).

46. Doug McAdam, *Political Process and the Development of Black Insurgency, 1930–1970* (Chicago: University of Chicago Press, 1999).

cumulating temporal solidification." Examples could be multiplied. But the basic idea is that, insofar as social structures are inherently dependent on cognitive categories that help to constitute them, structures alter when the constituting cognitive categories change. Cognitive categories can change when new ones are invented, when defunct ones are revived, when the meanings of established ones are transformed, and when the established meanings of existing ones are transposed from one domain of life to a new domain. In any case, it is mistaken to conceive of social structures as "hard" or "material" entities, because in fact they partly consist of the ideas and mental types with which people think, perceive, interpret, and reason. And that has consequences for social change.

Third, social structures are often transformed when sustaining material resources are significantly reduced (and sometimes when they are increased). The resource mobilization theory of social movements and ecological theories of organizations have highlighted this for decades. Just as human persons cannot be sustained without food and drink, social structures cannot carry on without certain levels of material resources that maintain them. Political structures become vulnerable to instability and sometimes revolution, for instance, when their revenues and treasuries become depleted through reduced taxes or excessive spending.[47] The overall structure of faculty appointments and status in graduate school programs is altered when disparities in financial resources between public and private universities grow. Family elders can no longer control the mate selection of children through arranged marriages when they lose control over economic production and the provision of household services.[48] In some cases, by comparison, social structures may operate well on modest levels of resource consumption and then undergo transformation when resources *increase* dramatically. Structures of sectarian religions, for instance, may soften and adjust as previously poor members of those faiths enjoy upward socioeconomic mobility, leading to increased integration into and decreased tension with mainstream society.[49] Structures of the

47. Theda Skocpol, *States and Social Revolutions: A Comparative Analysis of France, Russia, and China* (Cambridge: Cambridge University Press, 1979).

48. Robert Coppinger and Paul Rosenblatt, "Romantic Love and Subsistence Dependence of Spouses," *Southwestern Journal of Anthropology* 24, no. 3 (1968): 310–19; Paul Rosenblatt and Paul Cozby, "Courtship Patterns Associated with Freedom of Choice of Spouse," *Journal of Marriage and the Family* 34 (1972): 689–95; William Goode, *World Revolution and Family Patterns* (New York: Free Press, 1963).

49. See, for instance, Laura Vance, *Seventh-Day Adventism in Crisis: Gender and Sectarian Change in an Emerging Religion* (Champaign: University of Illinois Press, 1999).

division of labor in premodern societies tended to modify as the agricultural productivity of the surrounding countryside increased dramatically, providing surplus production that sustained new classes of occupations.[50] The causes of changes in available material resources can be many, including technological developments and diffusion, political decisions, natural disasters, and military defeats. But they all tend to have structure-unsettling effects.

Still on the topic of the material constituents of social structures, to take a slightly different tack, sometimes structural changes occur in part because material objects that instantiate and express social structures deteriorate or become irrelevant to their future continuation. For example, when through mass urbanization most of the population of England migrated to cities, the contribution of the "objective material fixity" of the many church buildings and chapels owned by the Church of England—most of which were located in depopulated rural parishes—to the durability of its structural status and authority in British society declined precipitously, as those rural houses of worship still required costly ongoing maintenance yet were relevant to much less of the population. So, changes around material entities can help to transform social structures not merely as a result of alterations of sustaining resource flows but also as the consequence of growing deteriorations of or disjunctures between the specific material objects that express and represent structures and the larger structures themselves.

Fourth, social structures can be transformed as a result of changes in the moral and normative beliefs of affected people and in the practices, procedures, rules, and laws those beliefs underwrite. Whether or not there are absolute moral truths in the universe—for instance, that it is always and everywhere morally wicked to gratuitously torture babies and children for pleasure—it certainly is true that people's moral beliefs vary across time and place and sometimes change in the course of lifetimes. Because social structures are constituted by moral and normative beliefs and commitments, when those constituting elements are modified, the structures they help to compose tend to change as well. This is partly because moral and normative beliefs help to inform people's structures of motivation and partly because they add justifying reasons for the shared cognitive categories and behavioral practices that also comprise structures. So,

50. Stephen Sanderson and Arthur Alderson, *World Societies: The Evolution of Human Social Life* (Boston: Pearson, 2005), 49–81.

when, over the course of a few decades the youth of a culture switch from believing that sex before marriage is immoral to believing that it is not immoral, that change contributes to transformations in social structures of dating, courtship, marriage, and cohabitation.[51] When leaders of business corporations stop believing that they have a moral obligation in an implicit social contract to care for the health and employment well-being of long-term employees who have been loyal and industrious, that in turn has causal consequences reshaping structures of labor markets, career preparation, family employment decisions, and health care delivery systems.[52] When the majority of a people stop believing that a religious Sabbath or day of rest is a collective good to institutionalize for all of society and so stop prohibiting through legal ordinances commercial transactions on Sundays, larger social structures of shopping, recreation, worship, and family routines are transformed in due course.[53] When enough of the right people (at the right time and in the right circumstances) came to believe that slavery is not an inevitable part of natural human society but a reprehensible evil, global structures of slavery systems were transformed.[54] Morality and normative sensibilities are clearly not all-determining. But neither are they the mere epiphenomena of cultural superstructures wafting off of allegedly more "hard" and determinative social infrastructures. Morality and normative sensibilities are partly constitutive of all social relations and practices. They have the power, therefore, as they evolve and collapse, to help transform even the oldest and seemingly most durable of social structures.

One more point on the subject of moral and normative influences on social structural transformation: in some cases, social structures are altered

51. Charles Turner, Rose D. Danella, and Susan Rogers, "Sexual Behavior in the United States, 1930–1990," *Sexually Transmitted Diseases* 22, no. 3 (1995): 173–90; Judith Treas, "How Cohorts, Education, and Ideology Shaped a New Sexual Revolution on American Attitudes toward Non-Marital Sex, 1972–1998," *Sociological Perspectives* 45, no. 3 (2002): 267–83. Also see Mark Regnerus, *Forbidden Fruit* (New York: Oxford University Press, 2007), 83–118.

52. Peter Cappelli, *The New Deal at Work: Managing the Market-Driven Workforce* (Cambridge, MA: Harvard Business School Press, 1999).

53. Alexis McCrossen, *Holy Day, Holiday: The American Sunday* (Ithaca, NY: Cornell University Press, 2000); Paul Laverdure, "Canada on Sunday: The Decline of the Sabbath, 1900–1950" (PhD diss., University of Toronto, 1990); Craig Harline, *Sunday: A History of the First Day from Babylonia to the Super Bowl* (New York: Doubleday, 2007).

54. See, for example, Christopher Brown, *Moral Capital: Foundations of British Abolitionism* (Chapel Hill: University of North Carolina Press, 2006).

when moral and normative standards do not change but actually remain intact, when certain structural outcomes violate public or elite sensibilities sustained by those standards in ways that generate strong emotional reactions.[55] This is particularly likely when emotional responses result not from endemic problems, to which people often adjust, but from suddenly imposed grievance.[56] Outrage over those kinds of traumas and injustices can motivate people to challenge practices and the social structures that generate them in ways that routine self-interests could never motivate. When a terrorist organization attacks and kills thousands of innocent civilians, people react and massive structures of transportation, military defense, and homeland security are reformed.[57] When a nuclear power plant suffers a life-endangering accident amid people who had been assured by authorities that the plant was safe, the resulting emotional reaction of betrayed shock over the felt moral violation of trust can transform an entire nation's structure of energy planning and production.[58] Such is the power of human emotions in response to the violation of shared moral standards to alter established social structures.

Fifth, and closely related to the previous point, social structures can be transformed when enough of their participants simply—for whatever reasons—stop sanctioning noncompliance, deviance, and rebellion. This can happen when actors genuinely change their moral and normative views. It can also occur when such underlying views do not actually change but other considerations shift balances of interests in ways that reduce people's investments in rewarding believers and cooperators and punishing dissenters and nonconformists. Either way, when the cost of social friction to dissenters for their noncooperation with structural imperatives and flows is lessened, participants whose beliefs and interests are not served by the standard outcomes of structural arrangements have more room to resist. In such cases, more participants may also reconsider what their true interests are and whether alternative structures might

55. James Jasper, *The Art of Moral Protest* (Chicago: University of Chicago Press, 1997); Christian Smith, *Resisting Reagan* (Chicago: University of Chicago Press, 1996).

56. Jeff Goodwin, James Jasper, and Francesca Polletta, eds., *Passionate Politics: Emotions and Social Movements* (Chicago: University of Chicago Press, 2001).

57. See, for example, David Lyon, *Surveillance after September 11* (Cambridge, MA: Polity, 2003); Bashara Doumani, *Academic Freedom after September 11* (Brooklyn, NY: Zone Books, 2006).

58. Edward Walsh, "Resource Mobilization and Citizen Protest in Communities around Three Mile Island," *Social Problems* 29 (1981): 1–21.

serve them better. In effect, socially enforced conformity is weakened. For instance, when gays and lesbians begin openly displaying their affections in public without being immediately disparaged and attacked, and when church pastors begin performing same-sex blessing rites and ceremonies without denominational punishment, these open the door for a possible larger transformation of heterosexually normative social structures. Likewise, when fundamentalist and evangelical faculty at secular universities "come out" about their strong faith, church attendance, and financial support for groups like Campus Crusade without being ostracized by their less religious colleagues, the conditions of possibly acceptable academic identities, epistemologies, and lifestyles shift in ways that may contribute to longer-term shifts in the structural relations of religion, science, and higher education. Or again, when a military that previously backed an unpopular political dictator stops repressing oppositional demonstrators who are protesting in the streets, the chances of a popular revolt and political restructuring dramatically increase. In these and other myriad ways, the reduction of formal and informal positive and negative sanctions that previously helped to maintain social structures contributes to their possible transformations.

Sixth, social structures can change when new or newly mobilized systems of communication decrease the intractability of coordinated interactions. Part of what normally makes social structures durable, I have suggested, is the difficulty for any given involved actor in communicating with and coordinating the expectations and actions of enough other actors. I called this factor intractable interaction processes. But sometimes it is possible to increase the tractability of innumerable social interactions despite the otherness of the actors and their spatial diffusion. This can happen when existing means of communication are applied to new structural challenges. For example, the communication channels that were long embedded in African American churches and historically black colleges were employed to help coordinate communications in the black civil rights movement of the 1950s and '60s.[59] It can also occur through the diffusion of new technologies of mass communication that function to coordinate exchanges and actions. For instance, new Internet, digital video, satellite broadcasting, and cell phone technologies have helped to mobilize and sustain various uprisings, protests, and insurgencies since the

59. Aldon Morris, *The Origins of the Civil Rights Movement* (New York: Free Press, 1986).

1990s.[60] But the problem of ungovernable interaction processes is not all related to social movements and protests. Simple truces and cease-fire agreements, when properly communicated and enforced, can alter social structures of conflict by solidifying mutual expectations about social interactions across many members of opposing groups.[61] And "consciousness raising" among particular groups can enhance perceptions of common predicaments, social identities, and collective interests that can enable them to better coordinate their expectations and interactions in ways that resist status quo conditions.[62] Whatever the specific means, it is not impossible for some actors to try at least partly to overcome ungovernable interaction processes and so to increase their control over the coordination of social interactions that intentionally or unintentionally give rise to and perpetuate social structures. When social structures change it is often in part because some actors have succeeded in that communication and coordination effort.

Finally, seventh, social structures can be transformed as a result of disruptions of normal reiterated body practices and collective activity currents. Social structures are fundamentally about the patterning and regulation of bodily practices and flows of embodied activities. Mere behavioral changes of this sort, literally the doing by some people of unexpected things with their bodies, can exert significant causal forces of social structural change. A relatively small number of civil rights activists, for example, instigated havoc in the established structure of Jim Crow race relations in the American South by sitting their bodies at off-limits lunch counters, occupying certain unacceptable seats on public busses, and spending time standing their bodies in certain forbidden transportation terminals.[63] The normal locations and flows of bodies was upset, sending shock waves of attention and reconsideration into other dimen-

60. Michael Chase and James Mulvenon, *You've Got Dissent: Chinese Dissident Use of the Internet*, RAND digital download, 2002; Pippa Norris, *Digital Divide: Civic Engagement, Information Poverty, and the Internet Worldwide* (Cambridge: Cambridge University Press, 2001); Michael Dartnell, *Insurgency Online: Web Activism and Global Conflict* (Toronto: University of Toronto Press, 2006).

61. Virginia Fortna, *Peace Time: Cease-Fire Agreements and the Durability of Peace* (Princeton, NJ: Princeton University Press, 2004); Karen Umemoto, *The Truce: Lessons from an L.A. Gang War* (Ithaca, NY: Cornell University Press, 2006).

62. See, for instance, Anita Shreve, *Women Together, Women Alone: The Legacy of the Consciousness-Raising Movement* (New York: Ballantine Books, 1990).

63. Peter Levy, *The Civil Rights Movement* (Westport, CT: Greenwood Press, 1998).

sions of the racialized social structure—concerning established cognitive categories, moral and normative beliefs, socially enforced sanctions, and so on. Likewise, the taken-for-granted status of the deeply entrenched system of American public education is disturbed when a small minority of school-age children in home-schooling families place their bodies in their homes instead of public-school classrooms during the hours that are normally spent in school.[64] The systemic implications of such altered bodily routines are potentially immense for the legitimacy and practices of the larger educational system. Social structural changes may occur not only because of different placements of bodies in space but also because of altered practices of bodily discipline and inscription. The structure of Muslim orthodoxy, for example, is partly maintained by specific disciplines of the body—fasting, head coverings, prescribed bowing in prayer, and such—that, when dramatically changed, weakens the larger Islamic system of beliefs and practices.[65] Certain structures of established, Western bourgeois sensibility have been dramatically challenged by various generations of youth (hippies, punks, and the like) by the adoption of certain defiant bodily presentations and routines, such as unusual hairstyles and colorings, skin piercing and tattoos, wearing vibrant or black clothing, taking mind- and body-altering drugs, and so on.[66] The various doings of the body thus matter much for social structures, and changes in them can, under the right conditions, contribute to structural transformations.

To summarize, despite the various and complicated forces overdetermining social structural continuity and durability, structural change can and does happen. The factors that can cause social structural transformation are many—including purely exogenous shocks like natural disasters—but they certainly include (1) establishing new or terminating old relations between groups, (2) alterations in the basic cognitive categories that constitute structures, (3) changes in flows of material resources or bearings of relevant expressive material objects, (4) modifications of moral and normative orders implicated in structures and emotional reactions to

64. Bruce Cooper, "The Politics of Homeschooling," *Educational Policy* 21, no. 1 (2007): 110–31; Mitchell Stevens, *Kingdom of Children: Culture and Controversy in the Home School Movement* (Princeton, NJ: Princeton University Press, 2003); Paul Hill, "Home Schooling and the Future of Public Education," *Peabody Journal of Education* 75 (2000): 20–31.

65. See, for instance, Daniel Winchester, "Embodying the Faith: Religious Practice and the Making of a Muslim Moral Habitus," *Social Forces* 86, no. 4 (2008): 1753–80.

66. Daniel Wojcik, *Punk and Neo-Tribal Body Art* (Jackson: University Press of Mississippi, 1995); Barry Miles, *Hippie* (New York: Sterling Publishing, 2005).

the violation of established moral or normative beliefs, (5) the weakening of sanctions that police conformity to structural expectations and imperatives, (6) decreases in the intractability of dispersed interaction processes, and (7) disruptions of normal reiterated body practices and collective activity currents. Rarely do changes in only one of these factors transform social structures. In most cases, structures change because numerous of these forces work in concert to exert pressures for change. Rare, too, are cases where propitious sets of conditions that cause change are brought about primarily through intentional human actions. Even people acting collectively and in great numbers have limited control over the character of society and the course of history. Most often, the forces that transform structures are animated by other causal forces beyond anyone's purposive control or foresight. When the right causal "stars are aligned," so to speak, to change social structures, usually those favorable circumstances for change are the result of the unintended consequences of other groups of actors operating in many other social structures who are intending to achieve a variety of entirely unrelated goals. Nevertheless, no social structure is transformed without some purposive human action intending change. Even if it involves only a small group of well-placed actors, human purpose and agency is never absent from structural change. Many forces beyond their control may have created propitious conditions for the success of their purposive actions, but some intentional activities of some people are nevertheless necessary for the achievement of the structural change. Thus, human agency is implicated not only in the human activity that goes into generating the unintended structural forces that set contexts facilitating social change, when that happens, but also in the necessary purposive action that is required to achieve any intended social structural transformation.

I reiterate: no interesting social laws concerning social structures or structural change exist of an "if X then Y" kind—whether of a deterministic or probabilistic form. The expectations of positivist empiricism on this point have failed us, and we should stop trying to formulate such deductive-nomothetic statements for empirical testing. All events happen in the social world because of the operation and influence of real causal powers and mechanisms. But those powers and mechanisms do not operate as linear constants or even probabilistic predictives. They are only causal tendencies, dispositions to produce certain outcomes. Causal powers and mechanisms may often be real and present in different social situations yet remain untriggered because of particular configurations of conditions. And those configurations can be extremely complicated, operating according to complex sets of interactive, suppressing, and conjunctural causes. Furthermore, quite different combinations of causal tendencies and mechanisms can operate with and against each other to produce the very same or quite different outcomes. And all of this takes place for human social life in what are always open systems of real causal dynamics, not the closed systems of highly controlled experimental conditions. The real and important challenge of social structural analysis is not formulating and testing simple "if → then" social laws that attempt to sort out independent effects of variables—an exercise in futility—but of descriptively establishing the various constituent elements operative in any specific case of a structured event or outcome in question, identifying the underlying causal mechanisms that sustain the structure, analyzing how the elements and mechanisms work together to produce the relevant events and outcomes, and, if appropriate, identifying forces of agency and structure that operate to generate social structural change. This is essentially what the best of sociology already does. Better that we all be more reflective and intentional about it, by understanding the determinative underlying philosophical issues, embracing the intellectual framework that justifies and directs our work at its best, and carrying out the research program it commends more purposively and systematically.[67]

67. Before concluding, I wish to make a few comments comparing the approach developed in this chapter to those of four theorists whose work most closely bears on the questions addressed here, to situate my account of social structures in relation to other relevant accounts in the established literature, in order to enhance clarity about the position of my approach for those readers familiar with these theories. Pierre Bourdieu's theory of social structures (*Outline of a Theory of Practice*) as consisting of rules and resources in field-bounded practices was an important and helpful contribution to our thinking in the 1980s and '90s—particularly in his bringing in the rule-based, mental-structural character of social structural workings; decompressing the variety of semiautonomous fields of social life operating according to similar logics (which theoretical Marxism tended to compact); and showing, through concepts such as "habitus" and "doxa," how social reproduction occurs often without the conscious intention of the actors involved (for a critical realist interpretation of habitus, see Raymond Lau, "Habitus and the Practical Logic of Practice," *Sociology* 38, no. 2 [2004]: 369–87). William Sewell is arguably correct, however, in observing that Bourdieu's (especially early) theorized world is overly objectified, totalized, and so theoretically tends toward immunity to social change (Sewell, "A Theory of Structure: Duality, Agency, and Transformation," 13–15; although theoretical developments around duality of structure, mismatch between habitus and field, inherently turbulent fields, and social crises create more possibilities for social change). Furthermore, Bourdieu seems to presuppose a narrow motivational structure believed to impel human action—essentially an instrumentally driven, status and power-maximizing, egoist

psychology (Smith, *Moral, Believing Animals*, 128–33; but see George Steinmetz, "Bourdieu's Disavowal of Lacan: Psychoanalytic Theory and the Concepts of Habitus and Symbolic Capital," *Constellations* 13, no. 4 [2006]: 445–64). By contrast, I have in this chapter attempted to develop a more expansive, complicated, multidimensional theory of the ontology and operation of human persons and social structures. By starting with a richer personalist model of human beings, I have been able to elaborate a theory of structure that I think is more adequate to actual social life and capable of explaining historical social structural change. The kind of empirical social scientific analyses to which the theory developed in this chapter ought to give rise may be more messy than those animated by Bourdieu are likely to be. But the cost of that messiness should be more than offset by the value of being truer to what is real in the actual social life we live.

Anthony Giddens's work has also, in my view, been helpful for understanding the nature and functioning of social life (*The Constitution of Society*; GIDDENS, *Central Problems in Social Theory* [Berkeley and Los Angeles: University of California Press, 1979]. Also see John Parker, *Structuration* [Philadelphia: Open University Press, 2000]; Ian Craib, *Anthony Giddens* [London: Routledge, 1992]). His notion of the duality of structures is important, when properly understood. His insight into the "knowledgeability" of actors is crucial. His emphasis on the process character of "structuration," as opposed to structures being viewed as static entities, is essential, when rightly appropriated. And his emphasis on the importance of rules engaging resources is also an important contribution. Yet Giddens's theory is beset with some serious problems. Some of Giddens's key terms remain problematically underspecified; confusions arise about when something counts as a *rule* versus a *resource*, and Giddens sometimes confuses mental structures with lived procedures (Sewell, "A Theory of Structure: Duality, Agency, and Transformation," 1–29; also see Sewell, "Historical Events as Transformations of Structures: Inventing Revolution at the Bastille," *Theory and Society* 25 [1996]: 841–81). Giddens's understanding of basic human motivations—which focuses primarily on the drive for "ontological security"—is also too simplistic. Personalism can help us improve on that point. In addition, the key conceptual distinction Giddens introduces between "social structures" and "social systems" is unnecessary, confusing, and reflective of a serious theoretical flaw. Namely, Giddens is simply wrong in asserting that social structures are merely "virtual" instead of real. Here I agree with the realists Margaret Archer and Douglas Porpora that Giddens has been led astray on this point by the exaggerated emphasis on language in post-Wittgensteinian hermeneutical philosophies of science, found, for instance, in the thinking of philosophers like Peter Winch in the 1950s and '60s (Archer, *Realist Social Theory*; Porpora, "Four Concepts of Social Structure," 195–211; Porpora, "Cultural Rules and Material Relations," 212–29; also see Roy Bhaskar, *The Possibility of Naturalism* [New York: Routledge, 1998], 25–44; William Outhwaite, *New Philosophies of Social Science: Realism, Hermeneutics, and Critical Theory* [New York: St. Martin's Press, 1987]). This emphasis leads Giddens to explicitly deny the reality and autonomous causal power of social structures, distinct from their real-time "instantiation" by actors who sustain them through social interactions. The intellectual hinge swinging Giddens in the wrong direction is his open rejection of emergence as a real process generating multiple, stratified levels of reality with entities possessing irreducible characteristics and powers. Lacking an account of natural reality creation and differentiation through emergence, Giddens is forced back to a "flat" view of reality that entirely conflates human interactions and structural dynamics in one middle level of being. As a consequence, the usefulness of many of the conceptually valuable terms he introduces in his theory is lost through the compression effected in this error of "central conflation" (Archer, *Realist Social Theory*). In fact, we will never understand social structures if we cannot recognize them as possessing a reality and causal powers of their own. While there is a certain "virtual" quality to some aspects of social structures, they are not in the end and as a whole reducible to only virtual existence. Critical realism can rescue us from that fatal intellectual misstep. And when it does, we no longer need to create the distinction Giddens introduces between social structures and social systems. Finally, while Giddens generally is intellectually fascinating, in the end he leaves the reader with little idea of how his abstract system would be applied in actual empirical analysis and scholarship. By contrast, I have tried in this chapter to suggest how my theoretical approach can and should inform actual, empirical sociological investigations.

William Sewell Jr. has offered an extremely helpful reading of both Bourdieu and Giddens and has advanced a correction of certain weak points in their theories (Sewell, "A Theory of Structure: Duality, Agency, and Transformation," 1–29). Many sociologists have benefited from his helpfully clarifying and constructive work. Sewell's critiques of Bourdieu and Giddens are spot on. His reconceptualization of rules as "schemas" is sensible. His concern to theorize the bases of social structural change is important, and the four ideas he advances to do so—the multiplicity of structures, the transposability of schemas, the unpredictability of resource accumulation, and the polysemy of resources—are theoretically helpful and analytically useful. And his general insistence on the culturally constituted nature of all social structures is excellent. Nevertheless, I do not believe Sewell has taken us all the way to where we need to go to adequately understand social structures. His thinking too is not without problems. To begin, Sewell develops a theory of human agency—centered on the capacity to exert control over social relations—that is good as far as it goes. But it does not go far enough. His intention was to theorize structures, not develop a philosophical anthropology, so we might grant some leniency on this point. Still, to better work out the basis and implications of Sewell's theory of structures will require a much better developed model of human persons as agents, one that will entail the kind of complexities of capacity and finitude described in this book. More seriously, Sewell rightly criticizes Giddens for a lack of distinction and clarity of the key terms *rules* and *resources*. But, perhaps because he continues to follow Giddens closely in his constructive work, he also ends up in places confusing the two. In explaining the unpredictability of resource accumulation, for instance, he offers a joke told, a financial investment made, a marriage proposed, a cavalry attack, and crops planted as examples of the "enactment of a schema" (Sewell, "A Theory of Structure: Duality, Agency, and Transformation," 18). Yet schemas, he insists, are virtual, while the investments, cavalry attacks, and agricultural seeds referenced here are not. At best, Sewell has inadvertently introduced a third key analytical concept—"enactments" or schemas being "put into action"—that he leaves undertheorized and so which remains confusing in his argument. Perhaps worse, Sewell may simply be reproducing some of the same conceptual confusions he criticized in Giddens. Furthermore, Sewell misspeaks in perhaps a telling way when he says that "schemas are the effects of resources, just as resources are the effects of schemas" (ibid., 13). The word *are* here, to be accurate, needs to be changed to "partly constituted and often significantly shaped by," otherwise we end up with an ontologically confused position that attempts to resolve the idealist-materialist dilemma by simply conflating each into the other—a very Giddens-like move. This suggests that Sewell, no more than Giddens, has not grasped the crucial idea of emergence as necessary to address the core intellectual issues that are raised in his article. Moreover, Sewell's theory of structure claims that social structures empower, constrain, and reproduce action, but it does little to explain with terms native to the theory how or why that operates. A more adequate theory of structure needs to spell out not only what structures do but also specifically how and why they do it. Finally, Sewell's attempt to differentiate kinds of structures by the two dimensions of "depth" and "power" provides a suggestive start on that important question, but his idea remains woefully undeveloped (ibid., 22). The key terms here go largely unexplained, so it is not clear how they might be used.

How does a theory of social structures grounded in critical realist personalism address these concerns and problems? First, it presupposes a model of human persons and agency that is far more elaborate and complex, which better underwrites the theory of social structures that follows from it. Second, by disaggregating more finely specified, multidimensional elements that are compacted into Sewell's two-category theory of "schemas" and "resources"—such as moral beliefs, cognitive categories, material resources, expressive objects, reiterated body practices, activity flows, and so on—the theory developed in this chapter provides more conceptual tools for sorting through the relationships between ideal and material factors in social life. In fact, I think they lead us to see that structures do not actually consist of combinations of schemas and resources, as separate entities per se, but rather conglomerations of constituent parts that are mostly—like human persons themselves—both material and immaterial in unified nature. Third, the theory advanced in this book places the notion of emergence at the theoretical center of the task of understanding persons and human social life. Lacking this key idea, Sewell, like others, stumbles in crucial ways in trying to explain how action relates to ideas and objects; how structures are both external to and constituted by human activity; and, more generally, how ontological realities both persist and transform over time. Fourth, the theory developed in this chapter goes much further than Sewell does or even might be able to do on his own terms in explaining exactly what it is about social structures that causes the people who generate and sustain them to be so powerfully influenced by them, in ways that lead to the prevailing dynamic of social reproduction. Finally, this chapter's theory of social structures provides a toolkit filled with more conceptual instruments than Sewell's to help begin sorting through and organizing the various kinds of features and dynamics characteristic of different types of social structures. Overall, then, I say that Sewell has offered a valuable contribution to our understanding of social structures, but one upon which further theory needs to and can develop and improve. Critical realist personalism I think offers the most promising means to that end.

Finally, to round out my brief comparison with other theorists, Douglas Porpora has written extensively and with much deftness on sociological theories of social structure (Porpora, *The Concept of Social Structure*; Porpora, "Four Concepts of Social Structure," 195–211; Porpora, "Cultural Rules and Material Relations," 212–29; Porpora, "Social Structure: The Future of a Concept," in *Structure, Culture, and History: Recent Issues in Social Theory*, ed. Chew and Knottnerus, 43–59). Porpora is a critical realist whose arguments I find compelling (I quibble with Porpora on only a few points. For instance, I do not think that a critical realist theory of structures needs to be as closely tied to Marxist theory as he apparently does. And, if I am reading him correctly, I believe Porpora confuses objects as being "material" or not with having ontological being and causal power (see Porpora, "Cultural Rules and Material Relations," 222). All material objects have ontological objectivity and can exert causal

Conclusion

Humans live out their lives enmeshed in complex webs of social structures that they as personal agents sustain and that simultaneously sustain their lives as personal agents. The specific qualities of those social structures are generated by fundamental facts of human personhood, particularly the creative tensions arising between our capacities and limitations as persons. Without being the particular kind of persons that we humans are, we would not have the specific kinds of social structures we have. In short, in order to make sense of the social structures that social science studies, we need to account for the personal being of the human animal from whose active lives the structures emerge. It is not that only human persons can or do generate social structures. Wolves, honeybees, apes, and other animals operate within their own kinds of social structures. But the qualities of their structures are radically different from those generated by human persons. Only personally grounded human social structures involve the exercises of creativity, moral judgments, language use, complex meanings, symbolization, self-reflexivity, narratives, technologies, deep intersubjective understanding, and major change over history that makes them so distinctive and powerful. In this sense, embodied, spiritual human persons exist in solidarity with the rest of the material and animal world yet also transcend it in limited but dramatic ways. If we want to understand human social life and all that is distinctive about it, therefore, we need a solid underlying account of human persons and all that is unique about us.

---

forces; however, those two criteria do not make something material, since many entities are ontologically objective and possess causal powers yet are not material. But these are minor and isolated points. His analyses of alternative theoretical approaches—those of Durkheim, Marx, Blau, Homans, Giddens, Collins, Winch, Berger, and many others—are smart and perceptive. His insights and judgments about which theories do and do not make sense and why are incisive and persuasive. I will not spell out details about the valuable points of his work. I simply commend Porpora's theoretical arguments as powerful, illuminating, and potentially discipline changing, and so deserving of increased attention and engagement in sociological scholarship.

CHAPTER SEVEN

The Good

Sociologists today ought to feel dissatisfied with the typical disconnection between the moral and political commitments to which many of us and our colleagues appear to be personally committed, on the one hand, and the nature of the scholarly theories and analytical approaches that many of us and the same colleagues are invested in employing in their professional work, on the other hand. That disconnection arises from the fact that the moral and political commitments that many sociologists embrace entail a particular account of the value and dignity of human persons, which their working scholarly theories and analytical approaches often seem to ignore if not outright deny or violate. This gives rise to a kind of personal/scholarly schizophrenia that is neither appealing nor necessary. This chapter brings my descriptive and critical account of the nature and sources of human personhood as the starting point for sociologically understanding human social life, and its relation to the social structures that are a key object of sociological inquiry, back around to this question of the moral and political implications of our scholarly theories and analyses. The same account that best informs our explanatory concepts, theories, and analyses in sociology—critical realist personalism—also entails ramifications for knowing what is morally good in, about, and for human persons and, by extension, human societies.[1] My purpose is to overcome personal/scholarly schizophrenia by offering a single, coherent theory that

---

1. For another critical realist account addressing the good, see Andrew Collier, *Being and Worth* (New York: Routledge, 1999). In certain ways what I am attempting in this chapter and the next is similar to Martha Nussbaum's project in her 2006 book *Frontiers of Justice: Disability, Nationality, Species Membership* (Cambridge, MA: Belknap Press of Harvard University Press).

informs and underwrites good sociological scholarship and the right moral and political commitments.

My argument begins by blunting the standard "is-ought problem" that so habitually and unjustifiably undercuts the kind of moral thinking in which we need to engage. I will in this chapter argue that we can discern a normative understanding concerning moral *oughts* with regard to human persons and human society from descriptive realities about the *is* of human personhood. The *is* and the *ought* need not be separated by an unbreachable wall of difference. We can begin to understand normatively what in reality is good and bad in human life and society through an understanding of what descriptively is when it comes to the same. Because that is not an intellectual move that can be taken for granted, I first defuse standard but erroneous objections to it. I then turn to develop my argument, which follows an essentially Aristotelian line of reasoning focused on the notion of the realization of natural ends and the late twentieth-century revival of virtue ethics.[2] I begin by prioritizing the good over the right. Right and rights flow from substantive knowledge of the good, of what is good, not the other way around. Within that framework, I argue that the good for human persons is to flourish as persons, to realize our own nature, to develop in fullness what we actually are. I have described above what I think we human persons are, what that means, what it entails. Our human good,

2. The expansive literature on the revitalization of virtue ethics includes Alasdair MacIntyre, *After Virtue* (Notre Dame, IN: University of Notre Dame Press, 1981); Rosalind Hursthouse, *On Virtue Ethics* (New York: Oxford University Press, 2002); Philippa Foot, *Natural Goodness* (New York: Oxford University Press, 2001); Richard Kraut, *What Is Good and Why: The Ethics of Well-Being* (Cambridge, MA: Harvard University Press, 2007); Stephen Gardiner, ed., *Virtue Ethics, Old and New* (Ithaca, NY: Cornell University Press, 2005); Roger Crisp and Michael Slote, eds., *Virtue Ethics* (New York: Oxford University Press, 1997); Roger Crisp, *How Should One Live? Essays on the Virtues* (New York: Oxford University Press, 1996); Christine Swanton, *Virtue Ethics: A Pluralistic View* (New York: Oxford University Press, 2003); Daniel Statman, ed., *Virtue Ethics: A Critical Reader* (Washington, DC: Georgetown University Press, 1997); Stan Van Hooft, *Understanding Virtue Ethics* (Montreal: McGill-Queens University Press, 2006); Richard Taylor and John Donnelley, *Virtue Ethics* (Amherst, NY: Prometheus Books, 2002); Raymond Devettere, *Introduction to Virtue Ethics: Insights of the Ancient Greeks* (Washington, DC: Georgetown University Press, 2002). The roots go back of course to Aristotle, *Ethics* (Baltimore: Penguin, 1953 [circa 350 BC]). Crucial to the recent revival of virtue ethics were G. E. M. Anscombe, "Modern Moral Philosophy," *Philosophy* 33, no. 124 (1958): 1–19; and Philippa Foot, *Virtues and Vices* (Berkeley and Los Angeles: University of California Press, 1978). Also see Francis Fukuyama, *Our Posthuman Future* (New York: Farrar, Straus and Giroux, 2002), 105–77.

then, is to realize our nature as persons, as the particular kind of persons I have described. It is to be as fully alive and flourishing as persons as we are able to be in the context of the real world that we inhabit and of our natural limitations, finitude, and failings. What is the social good? The good for society is to facilitate and foster through its institutions and structures the development and flourishing of human persons as they are by nature. Good societies foster personal thriving; bad societies do not. The more that human societies do that, the morally better they are. The less, the worse. Finally, one particular feature of personhood bears importantly on the personal and social good, is much debated in moral and political philosophy, and has massive implications for morality and ethics: human dignity. I devote the next chapter to explaining the personal sources of human dignity and its implications for human morality and social ethics.

Reconsidering the Is-Ought Problem

"Everybody knows" that you cannot derive an ought from an is. The idea is commonplace that the descriptive "is" and the normative "ought" belong to two separate orders that should be kept apart. To mingle them is, we think, for those who were taught the term, to commit the *naturalistic fallacy*—that is, to pretend that a normative assertion (what ought to be) is or derives from a part of nature (what is) even though it really does not belong to nature.[3] What is concerns descriptive statements, while what ought to be, prescriptive statements, which are, the thinking goes, logically unrelated. This difference is also closely connected to the fact-value distinction that everybody also knows must be maintained—facts are one thing and values are quite different, such that the facts of a case tell us nothing about what our values concerning it should be. One cannot observe a society that is characterized by high levels of inequality (fact), for example, and know whether that inequality is good or bad (value). The inequality simply is.

---

3. By now I am using multiple definitions involving versions of the words *nature* and *natural*. Nature and the naturalistic fallacy as used here are not to be confused with the anti-naturalist phenomenology I described in chapter 2, neither of which should be confused with Moore's ethical nonnaturalism described below. I am all for rooting the social in nature, yet resist the reductionistic tendencies in scientific naturalism as Taylor defines it; do not believe the naturalistic fallacy needs to paralyze our ethical reasoning; and am opposed to ethical nonnaturalism.

Whether we think it is good or bad has to come from some other source of knowledge or evaluation. Or so says the is-ought problem.

But there are problems with the is-ought problem. One is that it seems to violate its own instructions. Note that, in the second sentence in the previous paragraph, the descriptive observation is first made that is and ought belong to different orders, from which is then derived the normative injunction what we *should* keep them separate. But if we really cannot get an ought from an is, where did that injunction come from? Presumably we had to bring in an additional normative premise: that one *should* not confuse different kinds of statements. But where did that come from? Well, it seems ultimately to derive from the nature of language and logic, which observe that descriptive and normative statements are simply different sorts of things and that there is something illogical or wrong about switching back and forth between them. But getting from that "is" to the eventual "ought" seems somehow to compromise the injunction of the is-ought problem.

A second difficulty with the is-ought problem concerns the practical oddity of cordoning off normative and moral knowledge about what ought to be from descriptive knowledge about what is. It seems right and simple enough to say, for example, that the fact that a desk is heavy tells us nothing about whether heavy desks are good or bad. But to apply such logic to all of life so that our normative and moral beliefs cannot be seriously informed by the way reality is seems perverse. Why should what is good and right not be primarily informed by what really exists, its known characteristics, and natural functional operations?[4] To not somehow root the ought in the is seems foolish. What good is a moral system in telling us how we ought to live in the world that is disconnected from the world as it is?

A third snag with accepting the standard conclusion of the is-ought problem is that it is not the case that "everybody knows" that you cannot derive an ought from an is. A number of very smart philosophers whose job it is to think carefully about such things do not think the is-ought

4. Daniel Dennett, with whom I do not often agree on specifics or ever on general perspective, nevertheless makes a similar point: "Ethics must somehow be based on an appreciation of human nature—on a sense of what a human being is or might be, and on what a human being might want to have or want to be. If that is naturalism, then naturalism is no fallacy. No one could seriously deny that ethics is responsive to such facts about human nature." Dennett, *Darwin's Dangerous Idea* (New York: Simon and Schuster, 1995), 468. Also see Hans Jonas, *The Phenomenon of Life: Toward a Philosophical Biology* (Chicago: University of Chicago Press, 1966).

problem is a problem or that the fact-value distinction is inviolable. These include not only the likes of Plato and Aristotle but also recent philosophers and other thinkers as diverse as John Searle, Ayn Rand, Ruth Anna Putnam, Richard McKeon, Marvin Zimmerman, Hilary Putnam, Murray Rothbard, and Alasdair MacIntyre.[5] In fact, it turns out that even David Hume, the philosopher thought to have first raised the is-ought problem, did not believe that one cannot derive an ought from an is. This being the case, we have reason to question the "everybody knows" idea that a normative ought cannot be derived from a descriptive is. I will argue that what is tells us a great deal about what ought to be by disclosing what is naturally good in, for, and by what is.

Let us return to the apparent source of the is-ought problem for a second look. The ostensible source, as I said, is the eighteenth-century Scottish philosopher, David Hume. He is commonly credited with establishing the teaching that one should never derive an ought from an is. The necessity of the complete severing of the is from the ought in this way has been dubbed "Hume's Guillotine."[6] But rereading Hume's argument is instructive. Here is the crucial passage:

> In every system of morality, which I have hitherto met with, I have always remark'd, that the author proceeds for some time in the ordinary way of reasoning, and establishes the being of a God, or makes observations concerning human affairs; when of a sudden I am surpriz'd to find, that instead of the usual copulation of propositions, *is*, and *is not*, I meet with no proposition that is not connected with an *ought*, or an *ought not*. This change is imperceptible; but is, however, of the last consequence. For as this *ought*, or *ought not*, expresses

5. John Searle, "How to Derive 'Ought' from 'Is,'" *Philosophical Review* 73 (1964): 43–58; Ayn Rand, *The Virtue of Selfishness* (New York: New American Library, 1964); Ruth Anna Putnam, "Creating Facts and Values," *Philosophy* 60 (1985): 187–204; Ruth Anna Putnam, "Perceiving Facts and Values," *Philosophy* 73 (1998): 5–19; Richard McKeon, *Selected Writings of Richard McKeon*, vol. 1, *Philosophy, Science, and Culture*, ed. Zahava McKeon and William Swenson (Chicago: University of Chicago Press, 1998), 429–46; Marvin Zimmerman, "The 'Is-Ought': An Unnecessary Dualism," *Mind* 71, no. 281 (1962): 53–61; Hilary Putnam, *The Collapse of the Fact/Value Dichotomy* (Cambridge, MA: Harvard University Press, 2004); MacIntyre, *After Virtue*. Also see Foot, *Virtues and Vices*, 99–105; A. Kenneth Hesselberg, "Hume, Natural Law, and Justice," *Duquesne Review* (Spring 1961): 46–47; Murray Rothbard, *Individualism and the Philosophy of the Social Sciences* (San Francisco: Cato Institute, 1979), 5.

6. Max Black, "The Gap between 'Is' and 'Should,'" *Philosophical Review* 73, no. 2 (1964): 165–81.

some new relation or affirmation, 'tis necessary that it shou'd be observ'd and explain'd; and at the same time that a reason shoul'd be given, for what seems altogether inconceivable, how this new relation can be a deduction from others, which are entirely different from it.[7]

What is Hume saying here? That descriptive and normative propositions are completely different kinds of statements. That he notices that moral writers regularly make a subtle shift from descriptive statements to normative statements, seemingly without noticing or explaining that move. That when writers do make such a move, they should be obliged to observe that they are doing so and explain to their readers their reasons justifying it. And that when such a move is not made properly, the relation of the ought flowing from the is seems inconceivable. This "observation" Hume offers as a "precaution" against conceiving and accepting what he calls "the vulgar systems of morality." But note what Hume is not saying. He is not saying that moral thinkers are always wrong to derive moral propositions from descriptive observations. He is not saying that it is impossible to move from the is to the ought. What he is saying is that moral arguments based on descriptive facts are too often done thoughtlessly and without explicit justification. The lesson to be learned from the is-ought problem according to Hume, therefore, is not that one can never derive an ought from an is. It is rather that when one does derive an ought from an is, one needs to be aware that one is doing so and explain one's good reasons—if one has them—for why one's argument works. An ought actually *might* be derived from an is, then, but that needs to be done with self-awareness and care.[8]

Does Hume really believe this? Well, yes. In fact, he derives an ought from an is in this very passage. Look at what he says again. First, a descriptive fact, what is: moral writers frequently move without adequate awareness or justification from descriptive claims to moral claims. Second, a normative claim: moral writers should not shift from is to ought

7. David Hume, *A Treatise of Human Nature* (1740; Oxford: Oxford University Press, 2006), Book 3, Part 1, Section 1, p. 302. Quotes in the rest of this paragraph are taken from the same page. It should be noted that Hume's central point here concerns not the is-ought problem but rather a larger argument against the idea that morality can be derived from reason, as Hume believes that morality concerns the passions or sentiments.

8. Alasdair MacIntyre, "Hume on 'Is' and 'Ought,'" *Philosophical Review* 68 (1959): 451–68; Black, "The Gap between 'Is' and 'Should,'" 165–81.

without observing that they are doing so and providing good explanations and reasons for it. The second he derives from the first without offering any intervening normative propositions, such as, "all intellectual moves in ethical writing should be clearly justified." So, in expressing his precaution about the is-ought problem Hume reveals by example that he thinks moving from is to ought is justified in at least some cases. Not only that, but Hume's entire moral philosophy—not only descriptive but also normative[9]—derives what he believes should be from what he believes actually is. This is not the place to unpack the logic of Hume's moral theory.[10] Suffice it for present purposes to quote here a few summary passages indicating that Hume believed—precisely because he was an empiricist arguing against rationalist and divine revelation viewpoints—that morality *must* be rooted in the nature of reality, especially human nature and particularly in natural human sentiments. Thus, his *Treatise of Human Nature*[11] declares:

> An action, or sentiment, or character is virtuous or vicious; why? Because its view causes a pleasure or uneasiness of a particular kind. In giving a reason, therefore, for the pleasure or uneasiness, we sufficiently explain the vice or virtue.

9. Although much of Hume's focus is on descriptively analyzing how and why humans have a moral sense, he also evidently believes himself normatively that certain things are actually morally right (and wrong), including justice, honesty, honoring property rights, keeping promises, and allegiance to government.

10. The major points of which are as follows: Reason alone cannot motivate the will but is rather the "slave of the passions." Morality is not derived from reason but rather from moral sentiments, that is, feelings of approval and disapproval felt by observers who contemplate a character trait or action. While some virtues and vices are natural, others, including justice, are artificial. Critiques of Hume's idea that practical reason begins with ends that are not rationally motivated—critiques that comport with the moral approach developed below—include Joseph Boyle, "Reasons for Actions," *American Journal of Jurisprudence* 46 (2001): 177–97; R. Jay Wallace, "How to Argue about Practical Reason," *Mind* 99 (1990): 355–87; John Finnis, *Fundamentals of Ethics* (Washington, DC: Georgetown University Press, 1983), 26–79.

11. Hume, *A Treatise of Human Nature*, 303, 367, 369. Francis Fukuyama rightly writes: "Like virtually every serious philosopher in the Western tradition since Plato and Aristotle, Human believed that the 'ought' and the 'is' were bridged by concepts like wanting, needing, desiring, pleasure, happiness, and health—by the goals and ends that humans set for themselves." Fukuyama, *Our Posthuman Future*, 115, referencing Robert McShea, "Human Nature Theory and Political Philosophy," *American Journal of Political Science* 22 (1978): 656–79—not that I find Fukuyama's book adequate as a whole.

[Some] virtues and vices . . . are entirely natural, and have no dependence on the artifice and contrivance of men. . . . Moral distinctions depend entirely on certain peculiar sentiments of pain and pleasure, and . . . whatever mental quality in ourselves or others give us a satisfaction . . . is of course virtuous; as every thing of this nature, that gives us uneasiness, is vicious.

Sympathy is a very powerful principle in human nature. . . . [I]t produces our sentiments of morals in all of the artificial virtues. From thence we may presume, that it also give rise to may of the other virtues.

[We] may pronounce any quality of mind virtuous, which causes love or pride; and any one vicious, which causes hatred or humility. . . . This reflection is self-evident.

Elsewhere, Hume wrote even more clearly, "I found that the moral philosophy transmitted to us by Antiquity, laboured under the same inconvenience that has been found in their natural philosophy, of being entirely hypothetical, and depending upon more invention than experience. Every one consulted his fancy in erecting schemes of virtue and of happiness, without *regarding human nature, upon which every moral conclusion must depend*."[12] We see, then, that morality for Hume is rooted in and derives from nothing other than the nature of things as they are. Human nature, Hume observes, has a particular character, and that is what enables us to understand why certain dispositions and acts are not only believed to be but also are moral and immoral. In short, far from prohibiting the deriving of ought from is, Hume relies squarely upon just that to develop his moral philosophy. Hume does not require us to use a guillotine to sever the normative head from the descriptive body. All Hume asked of moral theorists was to derive ought from is consciously and with explicit and justified good reasons.

So, if not from Hume, where did we get our widely accepted ideas about the is-ought problem? The answer is from certain early twentieth-century analytic moral philosophers who transmitted Hume's writings selectively through the lens of their own, different intellectual commitments and interests. A crucial figure in this history was the highly influential

12. From the letters of David Hume, as quoted by John B. Stewart in his work *The Moral and Political Philosophy of David Hume* (New York: Columbia University Press, 1963) at 343n16, italics added for emphasis.

Cambridge University philosopher G. E. Moore, mostly through his text, *Principia Ethica*.[13] Moore was an ethical nonnaturalist, meaning he believed that moral goodness cannot be defined by or reduced to natural properties, such as needs, wants, pleasures, evolutionary advancement, or the like. The predicate "good" cannot, Moore believed, be defined using natural terms (or divine or supernatural references, such as God's will). "Goodness," Moore claimed, was a simple, indefinable, nonnatural property. How, according to Moore, can we know moral truth if it is alien to the natural? Through the faculty of what he called "moral intuition," which, he claimed, instinctively tells us when something we observe is good or bad. In Moore's view, moral goodness consisted especially in "personal affections and aesthetic enjoyments." Therefore, to try to define moral good by relying on a definition of "good" that depends upon any natural property is to commit what Moore called the "naturalistic fallacy." That fallacy is to identify goodness with reference to any natural property, that is, erroneously to "naturalize" the good.[14] This entire set of presuppositions and arguments thus led Moore to deny the possibility of drawing any ethical conclusions from any natural facts. Nothing about the natural, descriptive "is" could say anything about the normative goodness involved in "ought" statements. So, we see, it is Moore, not Hume, who is responsible—along with the help of those who for various reasons subsequently restated his views[15]—for lodging into popular consciousness that an is can never give rise to an ought.

Fortunately, we have good reasons to ignore Moore's views, which carry little weight in mainstream moral philosophy today.[16] Moore's ethical nonnaturalism and intuitionism entail little to commend and much to

13. G. E. Moore, *Principia Ethica* (Cambridge: Cambridge University Press, 1903). Important too in Moore's program, but not worth detailing here, was his "Open Question Argument," which contributed to the case against natural bases of morality.

14. William Frankena, "The Naturalistic Fallacy," *Mind* 48 (1939): 464–77; Stuart Hampshire, "Fallacies in Moral Philosophy," *Mind* 58 (1949): 466–82; Casmir Lewy, "G. E. Moore on the Naturalistic Fallacy," *Proceedings of the British Academy* 50 (1964): 251–62.

15. Karl Popper, for instance, wrote: "Perhaps the simplest and most important point about ethics is purely logical. I mean the impossibility to derive [*sic*] nontautological ethical rules ... from statements of facts. Only if this fundamental logical position is realized can we begin to formulate the real problems." Popper, *Aristotelian Society Proceedings* 21 (1948): 154. For a more recent statement related to morality and genetics, see Paul Ehrlich, *Human Natures: Genes, Cultures, and the Human Prospect* (Washington, DC: Island Press, 2000), 309.

16. Even if they have profoundly influenced popular culture, assumptions, and thinking.

cast doubt on them. MacIntyre rightly judges Moore's ethical thought in retrospect as consisting of a combination of ideas that are "plainly false," "at least highly contentious," and "obviously defective," together leading to "great silliness" and opening the door to philosophical moral "catastrophe."[17] So, unless we approach the entire question of morality with ethical nonnaturalistic presuppositions and are prepared to believe in the existence of "moral intuitions" as the sole and sufficient guide to our ethical conduct—in which case there it little reason to continue engaging this chapter—we need not accept Moore's argument about radically separating is from ought, fact from value. If we are prepared to consider the possibility of ethical naturalism—as we ought to be—then we are justified in proceeding to explore how certain descriptive accounts of the real might help to provide normative accounts of the good and the moral.

Before proceeding, however, a few more observations about the fact-values distinction may be helpful, especially for social science readers. Can social science *really* legitimately employ such normatively loaded terms as the *moral good, flourishing,* and *dignity*? For present purposes, yes, it can. There are numerous tasks in social science for which issues of morality and dignity are not directly relevant. But the task at hand is to understand the real nature of human personhood for purposes of critical and constructive social theory. Doing so requires us to account for key aspects of the person as they relate to social life. The moral good and (as we will see in the next chapter) human dignity are, by my lights, two of them. To be clear, in what follows I am not making my own moral judgments, much less floating personal opinions. I am developing the internal reasoning of the

17. MacIntyre, *After Virtue*, 1–5, 16. The next move after Moore, crucial in the liquidation of substantive ethics, was when ethicists, also influenced by logical positivism—which taught that there are no means of knowing other than through empirical and logical procedures and no facts other than natural facts—took Moore's nonnaturalism another step and rejected his moral realism in favor of a "noncognitivist" theory of morality, claiming that moral statements are not matters that are true or false but rather merely emotivist expressions of personal attitude or prescriptive expressions of desired imperatives. "Twentieth-century British ethical theory is unintelligible without reference to *Principia Ethica*," writes Thomas Baldwin, "its history until 1960 or so being, in brief, that although Moore was taken to have refuted 'ethical naturalism,' Moore's own brand of 'ethical non-naturalism' was thought to make unacceptable metaphysical and epistemological demands; so the only recourse was to abandon belief in an objective moral reality and accept an emotivist, prescriptivist or otherwise anti-realist, account of ethical values." Baldwin, *G. E. Moore* (New York: Routledge, 1990).

personalist theoretical tradition out of which I am working.[18] I hope in the end to show how matters like the good and personal dignity are relevant to understanding human social life and structures.

For those who may continue to stumble over any normative language in social science theory—my deconstruction of the philosophical history behind the false is-ought divide notwithstanding—I point out first that the previous chapters have already employed numerous terms laden with normative associations to theorize personal existence: creativity, responsibility, agency, morality, reflexivity, and so on. Which of us does not regard "the empowered agent of responsible, creative actions engaging in reflexive self-understanding and communicative interactions toward intersubjective understanding" as a normatively *good* thing? If we are willing to accept those normative terms, why should we not be willing to consider others, like *goodness* and *dignity*? No social science theory, no matter how hard it tries to be objective and neutral, can ultimately avoid using concepts and vocabularies that are normatively colored or loaded. Humans, even scientists in their science, cannot escape being human. Humans, as persons, cannot escape, even temporarily, into a world of scientific value neutrality. It would be better to own up to our moral and value commitments, as they connect to our personal being and scientific work, and deal with them aboveboard, to achieve more coherent, integrated, and intellectually responsible theory and scholarship.

I also point the doubtful reader back to the antinaturalistic phenomenological approach presented in chapter 2. We have no good reason to eliminate from our theoretical explanations terms without which we cannot finally do in the living of our own, real lives. The observation, experience, and judgment that human persons encounter moral goodness and badness is something I, and I trust most readers, cannot live our ordinary lives without. Social science does not always have to acknowledge this explicitly to do its work. But there is no good a priori reason why in principle it may not bring in the reality of morality, if an account that takes it seriously helps better to explain theoretically the real nature of persons and human social life. The compulsion to expunge any such normatively tinged language from social science discourse is driven specifically by the dictates

18. Also see Thomas Williams, *Who Is My Neighbor: Personalism and the Foundation of Human Rights* (Washington, DC: Catholic University of America Press, 2005); Thomas Rourke and Rosita Chazarreta Rourke, *A Theory of Personalism* (Lanham, MD: Lexington, 2005).

of the often-presupposed philosophical paradigm of naturalistic positivist empiricism. I, for one, simply reject that paradigm as offering a starting point inferior to the alternative theoretical approach introduced in chapter 2. I reject it in part because the models of the human the paradigm typically produces are alien to our lived experiences and difficult if not impossible to connect to our real moral and political commitments—and that tells us a great deal of intellectual and practical importance.

Furthermore, the arguments following will be more palatable when we realize that (even positivist) science necessarily depends upon normative values. The injunction, for instance, to separate fact and value is, again, not a self-evident, fixed law of nature but a normative belief. It tells us not only that fact and value are different, but also that it is *good* for us to separate facts and values, that we *ought rightly* to separate the two. To proceed with "value-free" science under the banner of "the separation of fact and value" is, ironically, to admit that the whole approach of good science is governed by a normative commitment. This affirms a belief that a higher-level normative fact exists that properly should regulate the operation of science. In which case, facts have not escaped the connection to or control of values. Facts and values remain joined, because good science can only proceed on the basis of a commitment to at least one normative fact. The question becomes the more relevant one of which facts and which values most matter.

From a critical realist point of view, the aspiration to separate fact and value is not completely wrongheaded. It does contain one valuable insight, but one that was formulated badly and so needs to be restated in different terms. The right goal is not to separate fact and value, which is ultimately impossible anyway. The right goal is to know as well as possible what is true about reality. Truth is the value. And if and when our personal desires and biases prevent us from knowing as perspicuously as possible what is true about the real, they must give way to the higher imperative of the latter. But this is not so because fact and value are of a completely different order. Quite the opposite, it is because we are humanly committed to the normative value of knowing, as well as we are able, the truth about the real. So it is not the setting aside of value that enables us to isolate the facts. Rather, it is commitment to a higher value (knowing truth about reality) that drives us to subordinate lesser values (confirming our personal desires and biases). We do this in order to understand transitively as clearly and fully as we are able what is intransitively real. And there is nothing at all in this picture that dictates that the real cannot or does not comprise both normative and nonnormative dimensions in a single whole. What is and what is good need not automatically be divorced. Critical realist personalism claims that they normally should not be.

Finally, in the last century we came to see that belief in the radical separation of fact from value recurrently helped to serve as an ideological rationalization for an "autonomous" science conducting research that was in its effect at times destructive of human personhood, yet which washed its hands of moral responsibility even as it directly served obviously normatively driven political ends. Consider, for instance, the "Eugenics Science" movement, Nazi scientific experiments on living human "specimens," and the development of the atomic bomb. The separation of fact from value has not always served humanity well. We would do well to be open to alternative, realistic approaches that reconnect them.

Interpenetrating Descriptive and Normative Realities

It is one thing to be open in principle, based on the above considerations, to deriving an ought from an is, to reconnecting facts and values. It is quite another to see how that might be done. One key to reconciling is and ought as well as fact and value after their needless divorces is to modify the common assumption that is and ought (and fact and value) are totally different and unrelated sorts of things. This is a necessary, though flawed, premise of their separation that we too easily admit into our reasoning. Why should we? Many philosophers today have come to think, to the contrary, that normative ideas are often entailed in descriptive statements, and that descriptive ideas are often involved in normative statements. The two are often mutually implicated. Likewise, value statements presuppose whole sets of factual entities taken to be important, and factual propositions similarly presuppose concepts, categories, and focuses that can be laden with interests and values.

Consider the descriptive, factual statement, "The world is a difficult place within which to grow up to be a kind and generous person." This sentence is stated in the indicative, not the imperative, mode. It is a statement of (purported) fact. Nothing about it tells anyone what he or she ought to do or be. And yet in order to make this purely descriptive observation of fact it is necessary to employ multiple concepts and ideas with major normative import. Without the existence of a web of meaningful notions about the moral status of the world as a context, difficult tasks, growing up

well, kindness, and generosity, this indicative sentence is entirely meaningless. Furthermore, without a larger normative understanding about
what a good life should look like, the rhetorical purpose of the statement
as a whole is unknown. Is it the complaint of a concerned parent? The
celebration of a fiend? The argument of a recruiter for an ascetic commune in the desert? Or what? Embedded in a simple statement of fact,
thus, are assumptions, ideas, concerns, and interests that are profoundly
normative and moral. The two turn out not to be so absolutely different
after all. But what about a simpler descriptive statement, one that does not
introduce value-loaded terms like *kind* and *generous*. Consider the plain
observation, "This desk is very heavy." Again, there is nothing prescriptive on the face of this sentence. Yet, embedded in it too are normative
elements required to help it to make sense. "Very heavy," for instance, is
a relative idea. Heavy compared to what? That can only be answered in
the context of some prior expectations. What were we anticipating? That
depends upon the reason the factual observation is made in the first place.
It could be that two murderers are about to drop the desk from the roof
onto a victim and are confirming the probability of death upon impact.
Or it could be that someone has agreed to help move a friend from their
third floor apartment and is now regretting it. In either case, the larger
meaning of the indicative statement depends upon specific practices that
make it meaningful. And both the practices and meanings are infused with
normative and moral significance—whether it be cold-blooded murder or
reluctantly aiding a friend. What this shows is not that there is no difference between descriptive and normative statements as forms of discourse.
Of course there is. What it shows is that the composition, meaning, and
relevance of at least some descriptive statements of fact are dependent
upon that which is normative, moral, and value laden.

The relationship, being mutual, also works the other way. Consider,
for instance, the moral statement, "Young people should work hard to
grow up, despite the pressures of this world, to become kind and generous
people." Here we have a normative statement that intends to prescribe
what is good and right. But does it belong to a realm of speech that is alien
to that concerning descriptive facts? I think not. For it assumes and depends on descriptive facts to have any meaning or relevance. Most simply,
the moral statement presupposes the factual existence of things such as
young people, hard work, growing up, pressures, kindness, and such. For
its imperative meaning it also presumes descriptive facts about a world out
there and about normal life course development that function in such and

such ways, in order for the moral idea of the need to "work hard" against "pressures" to have any import. Furthermore, by simply adding the four words "It is true that" to the beginning of this moral statement, we turn this prescriptive statement of normative instruction back into a descriptive statement of fact that happens to be about normative ideas about morality, without changing the moral significance of the sentence. The new descriptive statement may be factually correct or incorrect, but it would still be a descriptive utterance about fact. We see again, then, that the normative and the descriptive are not so easily hermetically sealed off from each other. Finally, considering the normative statement, "It is good for friends to help other friends to load their heavy furniture when they are moving," we observe again—along the lines of thought developed here—that this moral declaration of what is good and therefore what ought to happen in such circumstances presupposes and employs numerous beliefs about purely descriptive, factual matters in order to be composed, expressed, relevant, and interpretable by and for anyone.

Consider further the following. The practice of medicine is premised on a close connection between is and ought observations and statements. We know in purely natural terms that some bodies are sick and diseased in certain ways but also that such bodies naturally work hard to restore their health. Were fact and value divorced, that is all we might know. Next subject. But because fact and value are normally closely connected and mutually implicated, we not only know that some bodies are sick and diseased and that they work to heal themselves, we also know that they *ought* to be healed, that we *should* assist bodies in their healing processes, that beyond doing no harm we have a moral *obligation* to practice medicine to promote recovery, healing, and bodily well-being as we are able. We know that life and health not only *are*, but also are *good*, and therefore that the practice of medicine is a worthy and noble devotion. We know that not because a unique revelation from heaven has told us so or because we have had some ethereal ethical insight that has no relation to the natural world. We know that and act upon it routinely because the nature of the "is-ness" of reality makes it plain. Of course, to state it in formal syllogistic terms we need to state explicitly a premise, "Life and health are good and should be promoted." But my point is that this premise has its origins in nature, that the "ought" it entails is derived from nowhere else but the "is" of human bodies and human life.[19]

19. Thanks to Bill Hurlbut for suggesting this example.

So, again, we see that it is not the case that is and ought statements are identical. They *are* different kinds of speech acts. But their mere difference does not mean they are or have to be disassociated—any more than, say, men and women must be disassociated because they are different. In fact, for each to be what it is normally requires a lot of truck and barter between the two. Descriptive and the normative statements are highly implicated in, dependent upon, and supportive of each other for accomplishing the various kinds of discursive work they achieve. When we say things like "is versus ought" and "separation of fact and value," we cannot mean the severance of the two as entirely dissimilar entities to be kept apart in disconnected realms of existence and use. We cannot mean that because each is implicated in the other. What we mean instead, I think, is something like, "For present purposes I want to focus exclusively on the descriptive dimensions of the matter under consideration," or "Here is something real that I believe makes moral demands of us." Those more humble and legitimate meanings are about emphasis and the speech use, not about distinguishing mutually alien sorts of verbal utterances.

Discerning the Good

How might we reasonably move from a descriptive and analytical understanding of the way reality is to a prescriptive, moral understanding of how persons ought morally to live in it? First, we need to describe reality as truthfully as possible. I have tried to do this in the previous chapters. After that we need to see whether that reality entails facts that give rise to an understanding of what is good. If it does so, then that understanding provides a basic normative orientation with which we can develop a more substantive moral vision for human life. All of this, I believe, can be done, and I attempt in the pages that follow to show what it looks like. The basic shape of this account of the good and the moral for human persons and societies tracks upon three central descriptive statements about reality. First, humans exist as a specific kind of creature, as persons possessing particular, natural characteristics, capacities, interests, purposes, and limitations.[20] Second, the good for humans consists of persons realizing or

20. Fukuyama rightly writes: "It is . . . impossible to talk about rights—and therefore justice, politics, and morality more generally—without having some concept of what human beings actually are like as a species." Fukuyama, *Our Posthuman Future*, 128.

achieving the essential nature of their true human personhood as fully as possible. Third, morality—both personal and social—concerns the dispositions, relationships, attitudes, desires, practices, and institutional structures that do and do not help persons to achieve the good. If those three statements are granted as accurate descriptions of the real, as I think they should, then we can proceed better to specify the morally good and right.[21] The following discussion further develops this case, building on five key themes: ends, challenges, quests, virtues, and community.

First, my account says that humans have a real end or purpose—a telos[22]—that derives from the nature of their personal being. What is *the good* for humans is to pursue that natural purpose toward flourishing[23] as the very kind of life form that human persons are.[24] This telos provides a broad but definite vision of what an excellent version of one's life looks like, a general model for persons of what kind of existence to aim for, what

21. This account is fundamentally a virtues or *aretaic* ethic (from the Greek *arete*, meaning goodness, excellence, or virtue in the attainment of a purpose), focused on the moral character of the acting person and the learning of virtues necessary to achieve one's telos. It incorporates reworked elements of consequentialist ethics (normally considered opposed to virtue ethics) that, as it deliberates about virtues and character formation partly in light of the kind of long-term ends or purposes, they are likely to produce. And this itself incorporates the virtue of prudence. It remains distinct from most forms of consequentialist ethics, however, insofar as the focus of outcomes is not on events or conditions but rather on the flourishing character of the personhood of personal actors—that is, on *eudaimonic* consequences (see footnote 23).

22. From the Greek word *telos*, meaning end, purpose, or goal.

23. The Greek word for flourishing is *eudaimonia*, which refers to a life objectively well lived, rather than to the subjective emotional state of the person experiencing it at any given time. Sometimes *eudaimonia* is also translated as "happiness," although this intends to indicate a long-term knowledge that one has lived a good and proper life of virtue leading toward one's telos, not a more transitory feeling of pleasure, cheerfulness, or contentment, which even immorality and perversity can sometimes produce for a time.

24. "Within the teleological scheme there is a fundamental contrast between man-as-he-happens-to-be and man-as-he-could-be-if-he-realized-his-essential-nature. Ethics is the science which is to enable men to understand how they make the transition from the former state to the latter. Ethics therefore in this view presupposes some account of potential and act, some account of the essence of man . . . and above all some account of the human *telos*. The precepts which enjoin the various virtues and prohibit the vices which are their counterparts instruct us how to move from potentiality to act, how to realize our true nature and to reach our true end. To defy them will be to be frustrated and incomplete, to fail to achieve that good of rational happiness which it is particularly ours as a species to pursue. The desires and emotions which we possess are to be put in order and educated by the use of such precepts and by the cultivation of those habits of action which the study of ethics prescribes; reason instructs us both as to what our true end is and how to reach it." MacIntyre, *After Virtue*, 52–53.

complete and thriving versions of the self they should become appear to be—in MacIntyre's words, an idea of the-person-as-she-could-be-if-she-realized-her-essential-nature.[25]

Second, the challenge. The reality of the world and of persons means that the pursuit of the personal telos is far from an effortless, straightforward task. Humans, I have already said, are limited and finite, the real social structural world is obdurate, and in some very basic way the world as we encounter it is something like broken. Things—people, groups, organizations, systems—are simply not what they are supposed to be, they do not work or act as we want and know they ought to. So, the purposeful pursuit of the real human telos, far from being easy, demands a lifelong struggle, serious learning, and continual effort to work against countervailing forces that prevent persons from moving closer to their telos. Something in the nature of things presents continual challenges and obstacles to the realizing of our personal nature. Achieving the true ends of personhood inevitably involves striving against external and internal forces of resistance, opposition, danger, setback, distractions, difficulty, and destruction. Furthermore, pursuing the end of personhood is challenging because the goods of personhood are multiple, complex, and often involve difficult judgments and trade-offs. Thriving personhood is not achieved by following simple formulas or regulations, but instead requires wisdom, discernment, prudence, and choices that in specific situations can be quite challenging to make and exercise.

The third key theme in my account of morality is human life as a quest. Despite the various forces of challenge, resistance, and difficulty just described, people can and often do move closer to the full realization of their purpose, of their inherent personal nature at its best. It is possible to advance significantly toward realizing the human purpose. By the same token it is also unfortunately possible to lose ground, to regress, to stall, badly to miss the mark, even to self-destruct. Nothing is determined. Nobody is promised a successful ending, a proper arrival. As they live their lives people can move either closer toward or further away from their telos.

---

25. I have intentionally mixed the singular and plural of *vision* and *versions*, since my account opens up multiple possible versions of the larger personal *telos* while maintaining that all of those possible versions are bounded by the broad outlines of the trajectory or vision of the natural purpose or end of personhood. The good life of a distinct person could thus take many different forms, though each form to be good would have to respect the parameters of the same *telos* of personal being. Ibid., 52–54.

In many cases, unless a person is actively pursuing his or her proper end, the natural default is to slip, however imperceptibly, away from it, toward a diminishment of personhood. A static position in this matter is difficult to maintain. Entropy and challenges take their toll. This movement toward or away from the telos thus gives every human life the character of a quest, of living out a story that is going somewhere significant, of enacting a real narrative the ending of which is not known or completed.[26] No person is therefore merely walking a treadmill or repeating endless cycles. Everyone is inescapably on an important and more or less successful or failing journey to the proper end of realizing their personhood.

Here again, the morally good and bad come into play with, fourth, the centrality of virtues. Succeeding in the quest of realizing one's natural purpose, as we are in this particular world, requires that we learn certain dispositions and practices that promote its realization. No humans can journey well and thrive as persons without having progressively formed sets of tendencies, qualities, habits, orientations, disciplines, and characteristics over the course of their lives that tend to promote flourishing personhood. We should think of these as virtues. Moral virtues are those dispositions and practices that foster the achievement of the telos of persons. Moral vices and evils—either exercised by persons themselves or by others around them—are those that deflect or frustrate persons from realizing their purpose, which compromise, damage, negate, endanger, deny, or tear down the true nature of people's personhood.

Finally, fifth, the human quest to realize one's own nature in flourishing human personhood is never pursued individually but always within larger social experiences in communities of persons. But communities are never mere necessary situations or environments for the pursuit of a personal telos, although they are that too. The very living as persons in social relationships, institutions, and structures is also constitutive of the telic quest for flourishing personhood. Communities of persons are the

---

26. This idea I draw from MacIntyre, who writes, "The unity of a human life is the unity of a narrative quest. Quests sometimes fail, are frustrated, abandoned, or dissipated into distractions; and human lives may in all these ways also fail. But the only criteria for success or failure in a human life as a whole are the criteria of success or failure in a narrated or to-be-narrated question. A quest for what? . . . [It] is not at all something already adequately characterized. . . . It is on the course of the quest and only through encountering and coping with the various particular harms, dangers, temptations, and distractions which provide any quest with its episodes and incidents that the goal of the quest is finally to be understood. A quest is always an education both as to the character of that which is sought and in self-knowledge." Ibid., 219.

necessary means to and partial ends of the natural purposes of persons. In moral terms, good societies facilitate well the pursuit of the natural personal ends of all of its members. Bad societies damage the personhood of humans, obstruct people's pursuit of personhood's natural ends, or systematically exclude some of its members (or persons in other societies whose lives they influence) from participating in the quest toward the personal telos. Those are the objective moral standards by which social relationships, groups, communities, institutions, systems, societies, and structures should be judged as good or bad.

That is the sum of the matter. The remaining tasks are first to further unpack this approach and its implications. Then, if it is embraced, we need to work out—as part of the very quest for personhood—in conversation with other persons, past, present, and future, how more specifically it works and what it looks like. Many millennia of historical experience of human life on earth provide treasures of resources on which to draw—but also rubbish to be discarded. We have much to learn from the past, both appreciatively and critically. At the same time, even the valuable riches of tradition need to be worked out in ever-new contexts of developing history. Further, critical realism suggests that we can improve and hopefully have improved the truthfulness of our transitive knowledge about intransitive reality. We therefore must be prepared to acknowledge that some of what we believed in the past to be true, good, and right must subsequently be amended or reformed in light of what we take to be more truthful accounts of reality. We have mostly learned this lesson already about slavery and patriarchy. No doubt there will be other similar lessons to be learned.

Before moving on to further develop some of the substantive moral implications of this approach, I think it worth noting even at this stage some of its comparative advantages. First, this personalist teleological account sits squarely on the ground of moral realism, affirming that moral facts are real and rooted in the nature of reality. With that we steer clear of moral skepticism, antirealism, and relativism, which do not lead to where most of us want to go in terms of the kind of world we believe in and want to live in. Second, this account understands morality as working for the real good and happiness of people, not finally as a coercive force depriving, controlling, or alienating people from their true interests. The more people learn and practice moral virtues, the closer they move toward the realization and flourishing of their essential natures and therefore toward their true long-term happiness. This helps to solve a serious motivational problem that besets so many other theories of morality, since, by this account, one's true, informed self-interest rightly compels one to learn to live morally.[27] Third, the present account accommodates an appropriate amount of historical and cultural difference without losing its basic parameters as rooted in the nature of reality. Moral virtues are not always expressed the same way everywhere and at all times; but neither is "the sky the limit" when it comes to morality.[28] In some times and places, the pursuit of personhood will entail certain particular kinds of life, in other times and places, others. But in all human places and times the moral good is always bounded and significantly defined by the real, objective nature of human personhood. This approach thus affords cultural flexibility and accommodation without the serious troubles inherent in cultural relativism and the related meltdown of moral judgment making across differences.

Fourth, the present account balances well the diversity of human gifts, interests, and personalities in given communities with the corresponding fact of the unity of people's common personal humanity. It neither demands a strong conformity that crushes personal distinctiveness and the richness of diversity nor sanctions attempts at a moral "anything goes." This general approach observes somewhat broad boundaries rooted in the nature of personhood that establish a distinct trajectory toward its fulfillment, within which distinctiveness and diversity are not only tolerated but also, for the sake of personal flourishing, nurtured and celebrated. Fifth, this personalist teleological account is not fundamentally rules-based, which I take to be an advantage. Morality here is not essentially about specifying and obeying rules and regulations, whether divine or human— except insofar as the latter operate as subordinate parts of the learned dispositions and practices that serve as means toward achieving the end of flourishing personhood.[29] We thus avoid sticky problems explaining where

27. In philosophical terms, my account provides for "motivational internalism," since the right moral beliefs are intrinsically motivating of right moral behavior.

28. Fukuyama agrees: "Human nature does not dictate a single, precise list of rights; it is both complex and flexible as it interacts with various natural and technological environments. But it is not infinitely malleable." Fukuyama, *Our Posthuman Future*, 128.

29. The teleological personalist account that I am developing here is not incompatible with a divine command theory of morality, which appears to be the vague background view of many if not the majority of Americans. But compatibility would require a version of that theory in which God commands out of a prior knowledge of and loving commitment to what is good for human persons, given the nature of the (presumably divinely created) reality in which persons live, and because it is God's loving will that human persons flourish. By contrast, the present account would not be compatible with a version of divine command theory charac-

freestanding moral rules come from, who or what rightly declares and authorizes rules, and how they should be applied in complicated situations that mix shades of moral grays. Sixth, this approach provides a greater depth and richness of personal participation and meaning than that of, say, utilitarianism's thin calculations of mere pleasures and pains. The achievement of our true personal nature turns out to be a challenging, complicated matter, the pursuit of which cannot be reduced to computations of empirical utilities and pain. Sometimes the path toward our telos can involve disciplines, hardships, even at times sufferings—though not for their own sakes but rather for the realization of our larger personal good and that of others—and that fact can be understood and accommodated within the present account.

Seventh, this personalist teleological account advances an ethic that is about more than devotedly executing one's rationally understood duty. Morality is about much more than mere responsibility and obligation performed as rational beings to enact imperatives that in theory all rational people should know to perform. We thus gain a richness and earthiness to morality that the Kantian tradition typically lacks. Eighth, the present case avoids a thin, proceduralistic approach to rights and ethics by offering a substantive vision of the human good, natural ends, and necessary virtues. The good is not finally a matter of methods, procedures, and due processes—although it certainly involves those when and as they are appropriate—but of realizing the nature of what we as living beings are. Ninth, this approach embodies something like the existence of a natural law—in that reality is objectively structured in a certain way such that various moral dispositions and actions have their normal, characteristic consequences—without having to posit (or deny) the metaphysical existence of a natural law, traditionally understood. Morality is rooted in and

---

terizing God's commandments as arbitrary expressions of divine will, capricious or random legislative decrees seeking to test human obedience per se and apart from outcomes of human flourishing, the mandates of which could just as well have commanded some quite different moral imperative had God so willed. Apart from the compatibility issue mentioned here, the latter view also runs into other significant problems, including the "Euthyphro dilemma" posed by Plato—namely, having to choose between the belief that an action is morally good because God commanded it (which raises the problem of whether God could have commanded something entirely different and, if so, whether divine morality is entirely arbitrary) or the belief that God commands certain actions because they are morally good (which raises the problem of God being subordinate to a higher and independent [nondivinely established] law of morality and so being not ultimately God)—which the former version of divine command theory avoids, in my view.

governed by the nature of reality—particularly of the human person as existent in this world—and cannot be constructed differently at will or wished away. A larger fabric of reality provides a given structure, order, predictability, and consistency within which human quests are either well or badly pursued. I take this to be a strength of this theory. Tenth, my account of morality includes, integrates, and necessitates personal morality and social ethics within one coherent system of thought and explanation. Unlike some moral systems, which either emphasize individual morality but fall silent on issues of social ethics, or which speak to ethical concerns at the collective level but hold few moral expectations of specific people, this account offers a unified moral vision for each and every living person as well as every social relationship, group, community, and institution in society. Eleventh and finally, this teleological personalist approach to goodness and morality involves not only the assertion of moral rights that others must respect but also the undertaking of moral responsibilities that each person must fulfill.[30] We are thus informed about who may reactively do what to whom, and also proactively about who is responsible to live in such and such ways in order to live a good life.

The Good of Others as One's Personal Good

In the following section I draw out a range of what seem to me to be some of the moral implications of the personalist teleological approach I am developing here. Before doing so, however, it is essential to establish a crucial moral truth on which personalism insists: the promotion of the realization of the personhood of other persons is always included in the natural telos of every person pursuing the realization of his or her personhood. In other words, an innate part of any person's quest to achieve the flourishing of his or her personal being is—given the relational nature of personhood—to likewise advance the flourishing of the personal being of other persons. The achievement of the natural human end of flourishing personhood is not like an individual sport in which distinct contenders compete in zero-sum games of elimination. It is like a team sport in which the victory of each player is dependent upon the success of the other players, such that being a member of an excellent athletic squad requires not only excelling as an individual athlete but also doing all one can to foster

30. See Williams, *Who Is My Neighbor?*

the athletic accomplishments of one's teammates. So it is impossible to
work to develop one's personal self without also working to help other
persons develop their personhood. Performing the latter is *intrinsically a
part* of achieving the former. For this reason, striving toward the natural
human telos involves a profound mutuality and synergy in which interacting persons-moving-toward-their-true-ends necessarily encourage and
advance the progress of *each other* toward their telos.[31]

The underlying model of the good of personhood is therefore one of
gift giving and exchange[32]—that, as opposed to zero-sum competition, conflict, or domination. Persons moving-toward-the-natural-human-telos, as
an intrinsic part of that movement, give to other persons the gifts involved
in caring about and promoting their distinct personhood. And those other
persons do the same in return and to others for the same reasons. Those
gifts are not and need not be given out of pure altruism, because the giving of such gifts enhances the personhood of both the receiver and the
giver. One may give in part in order to become the person in fullness that
is one's true best end. Self-fullness is thus achieved in part by selflessness.
By giving to others in this way, one also receives what is most important:
progress toward achieving one's telos. That is simply the fact of the good
concerning human personhood. It is also a fact that mounds of empirical
social scientific evidence have been corroborating in recent years.[33]

Having said that, a crucial clarification is in order. We must not mis-
understand the right motivational and dispositional character needed in
living to enhance the good of others as an intrinsic part of our personal

31. For related though distinct approaches, see Emmanuel Levinas, *Totality and Infinity:
An Essay on Exteriority* (Pittsburgh: Duquesne University Press, 1969); and Paul Ricoeur,
Oneself as Another (Chicago: University of Chicago Press, 1992).

32. Marcel Mauss, *The Gift* (London: Routledge, 1990); Allen Markman, "The Importance of Gifts in Marriage," *Economic Inequality* 42 (2004): 483–95; Pierre Bourdieu, *The
Logic of Practice* (Cambridge: Polity, 1990). Much theorizing about gift giving—including
that by Mauss and Bourdieu—leans, however, toward a more obligated, pressured view of
exchange than the view I develop here, which more emphasizes caring reciprocity.

33. The relevant literatures here are various and massive. For a small sample, see Stephen
Post and Jill Neimark, *Why Good Things Happen to Good People* (New York: Broadway,
2007); Michael Argyle, *The Psychology of Happiness* (New York: Routledge, 2001); Jonathan
Haidt, *The Happiness Hypothesis* (New York: Basic Books, 2005); B. D. Robbins, "What Is
the Good Life? Positive Psychology and the Renaissance of Humanistic Psychology," *Hu-
manistic Psychologist* 36, no. 2 (2008): 96–112; C. R. Snyder and Shane J. Lopez, *Handbook of
Positive Psychology* (New York: Oxford University Press, 2001); Daniel Gilbert, *Stumbling on
Happiness* (New York: Random House, 2006).

development. Seeking to develop the personhood of others cannot be instrumentalized into a means/end calculus driven by the purpose of enhancing our personal good. That kind of self-serving calculating turns the other from a person into a means that is useful for our own benefit. That itself is a moral violation of their personhood, to which personalism objects. It automatically spoils the entire life-building process of loving gift giving toward mutual personal flourishing. Virtue ethics, we must remember, are concerned centrally not with rules and duty, but with the kind of persons we are and are becoming, with the formation and living out of good, moral personal character. Counterfeit virtues, instrumentalized morality, and manipulative care for the good of others are inherently self-defeating. One finds real love in a relationship when one truly *loves* the other for his or her own sake and for the sake of the good of love, not when one only acts *as if* one loves the other merely because doing so would be good for oneself. Likewise, one reaps psychological and physical benefits of religious faith[34] only when one actually *believes* in the faith, not when one pretends one believes in order to enjoy its psychological benefits.[35] Similarly, the kind of seeking of the good of the personhood of others that actually does enhance our own personhood is in the end that which we do and would do *whether or not* it does or will enhance our personhood—primarily, that is, for the good of the other and the goodness of the act of caring for their well-being, period. There is no substitute for the genuine article—in the long run only learned and enacted concern for the genuine welfare of others will enhance our personhood. Stated differently, the development of our personhood is typically an indirect and unintended consequence of helping to develop the personhood of others—not direct and intended. Stated differently yet again, a morality set within an ontology of realism requires that concern for the personhood of others be genuinely *real*, an authentic fact of *reality*, not merely an "as if" imitation or appearance of concern for others. And for that to be the case, it cannot be primarily

34. The literature on such benefits are voluminous; see, for a few examples, Robert Hummer et al., "Religious Involvement and U.S. Adult Mortality," *Demography* 36 (1999): 273–85; Howard Koenig and David Larson, "Use of Hospital Services, Religious Attendance, and Religious Affiliation," *Southern Medical Journal* 91 (1998): 925–32; Kenneth Pargament, *The Psychology of Religion and Coping: Theory, Research, Practice* (New York: Guilford, 1997); James Wells, "Religion and Mental Health," *British Journal of Health Psychology* 8 (2003): 359–76.

35. In sociological jargon, we can be tripped up here by adding too many layers of self-reflexivity, which introduces the problem of the double hermeneutic.

motivated by concern for the good of one's own personhood. Honoring the personhood of others only in order to enhance our own personhood is like working extremely hard to fall asleep—it doesn't work. Such things are not achieved instrumentally and directly. Just as we have to stop trying to fall asleep in order to fall asleep, we also have to take our eyes off ourselves and learn sincerely to care for the genuine well-being of others if our attention to others is to actually do us good. As Aristotle noted, a great many virtues are first learned by behaviorally imitating role models of moral maturity and excellence. And people normally begin practices of care for others with their own well-being in mind. But in the end, a virtue is a real virtue only if, when, and because it has become part of the moral character of the person who embodies and lives it.

Who then are the others whose personal development a person ought to labor to promote? Is it possible to specify at the outset exactly which other people belong to the set of persons whose personhood any given person should seek to advance? The teleological, virtues-based, personalist approach to morality I am developing does not readily lend itself to such rules and instructions. The point is not to fulfill a specific obligation. The point is to cultivate and realize one's essential nature as fully as possible through a kind of art of living. The general orientation of this view on this point would therefore be to say something like the following. Prudent and just persons will in general accept and work with their personal finitude and limitations—mental, emotional, bodily, financial, and so on—as they go about seeking the good of others, and so not try to be or do more than reality allows, which is not good for anyone. In this, most persons have particular, prior moral commitments and promises to especially protect and serve the personal well-being of specific others—spouses, children, parents, friends, neighbors, students, and other sorts of intimates and collaborators—to whom good persons will devote their first and best resources. Nevertheless, achieving the flourishing of human personhood happens to require extending oneself to others beyond one's natural in-groups, reaching out to strangers, the needy, even sometimes offenders and enemies. The movement toward personal development and enrichment entails a concurrent movement outward in wider and wider concentric circles of relation and association. As the core or heart grows stronger in personhood, it naturally reaches beyond what is close in order to engage and enhance what is further beyond. In this, in principle, there is no fixed boundary or limit beyond which the person-on-the-way-to-their-telos ought not or cannot reach, as long as they are fulfilling their already established promises and commitments and not neglecting or abusing their personhood. Absolute strangers, people on the other side of the world, the completely alien—these, too, are persons whose natural personal ends every person can come to the aid of, simultaneously for their own good and that of the other. The simple answer to the question is: most definitely certain other persons but potentially any number or type of other persons. The specifics appropriate for any given case—which will also change over time and across circumstances—must be judged through discernment, relying on prudence, wisdom, justice, and courage.

Of course, lamentably, with people and the world the way they are, life does not always or even often work out so well. There are powerful forces at work to distract, derail, and destruct people's realization of their true personhood. People are limited and finite. In our perceptual and cognitive fallibility we often do not know and understand what is really true about reality. Furthermore, the relations and structures of the social world often do not function for the human good but operate for lower, lesser, and more limited purposes that often prove to be stunting and dehumanizing of persons in various ways. For these and other reasons, I have described persons and the world as reflecting a kind of brokenness—a lack of integration, functionality, or devotion to the good that is present in people and in social systems. This brokenness does not seem to be a matter of lack of information or of frustrating bad luck. Sometimes the diminishment of people's personhood happens through unexpected misfortunes, tragedies, and devastations. But there are also elements of brokenness that involve capacities of human volition and cognitive intention. The brokenness of persons and the world sometimes appear to involve willful turnings against the good, deliberate injury to self and others, determined refusals to speak and accept what is true, and purposeful structurings of social systems that exclude and exploit. People's integrity is met with deceit, caring hits walls of indifference, self-giving love coexists in a world of hate and murder—and not always among the desperate, unaware, and misled, but often among the secure, the equipped, the cunning. As a consequence, although gift giving is essential to realize the true human good, it occurs far less often than the right pursuit of personhood commends that it should. All too often it is replaced with clutching, snatching, and breaking.

Nevertheless, gift giving between persons happens. This is not only because human life would be functionally impossible without it. It is also in part because persons only in the rarest cases can completely forsake their natural telic end of personhood to embrace the fullness of potential inhumanity. Most people will at least seek to get by with minimal gift giving. Numerous causes work to encourage gift exchange, especially among people of equal status. In such cases, for instance, unbalanced dependence and potential threats to esteem are avoided, so ongoing, mutually beneficial, reciprocal exchanges are sustained. At the same time, persons often impart gifts in relationships of unequal status. Parents give to children. Teachers give to students. Mentors give to those they mentor. Adult children give to failing parents. Volunteers give to the needy. Donors give to recipients. And here I venture a hypothesis: it could very well be that the personhood of gift givers is especially enhanced by their giving gifts to those who are least able to reciprocate. Many personalists suggest—and much accumulated wisdom of the best of our broad human experience confirms the notion—that the giving by the able of gifts that strengthen the personhood of others who are especially weak, poor, and vulnerable does more to propel and enrich the personhood of the giver toward its true end than their giving of gifts to those who need them less.[36] It very well may do more for the personhood of someone to give generously of themselves to help provide for the health and well-being of marginal and excluded persons who cannot repay them in kind, than for the same someone to give the same things to comfortable and secure others who will reciprocate to maintain equity and equilibrium. There is nothing wrong with the latter. But there may, personalism suggests, be something better about the former. Of course, the risk of the moral hazards of paternalism, smugness, condescension, guilt relief, and the desire to control others may be increased in such cases. But the potential for the greater learning of virtues and exceptional progress toward one's telic good through genuine selflessness would seem to be amplified as well.

The matter of moral goodness is fraught with profound *social* import. Morality is not primarily a matter of distinct individuals doing the right thing on their own. Its central concern is not for individual agents to, for instance, follow the rules or observe the right procedures or simply not step on the toes of other people. The pursuit of human goodness does not elevate or isolate people above or away from other people. The good of personhood is pursued and realized primarily in and through social relationships—through reciprocal and selfless exchanges of good gifts of myriad kinds; through shared efforts to advance the strengthening of the common good of all; and through communion and love among friends

36. See, for example, Jean Vanier, *Becoming Human* (Toronto: Anansi, 1998).

and intimates—all of which are crucial for achieving the true, good end of flourishing personhood. Necessarily, it is impossible to split personal morality from social ethics. The good of distinct persons is inextricably bound up in the existence and functioning of good, right, and just social relations, institutions, and structures—just as the latter, since structures are indeed emergent from persons, are significantly dependent[37] for existence and function upon the personal moral qualities of the persons from whom they emerge.

Moral Deliberation

The present argument hinges on the idea of the human good being the realization of the essential nature of human personhood. But what is that? Here we need again to refer to the model of the person developed in the first chapter. A person, according to that account, is a conscious, reflexive, embodied, self-transcending center of subjective experience, durable identity, moral commitment, and social communication who— as the efficient cause of his or her own responsible actions and interactions—exercises complex capacities for agency and intersubjectivity in order to develop and sustain his or her own incommunicable self in loving relationships with other personal selves and with the nonpersonal world. To realize the essential nature of human personhood, therefore, involves nurturing, protecting, and sustaining healthy human bodies out of which personhood is emergent. It also entails developing the many human capacities from which the personhood of persons emerges. Realizing our essential nature means exercising personal agency in responsible actions and social interactions. It means learning intersubjective understanding as well as developing and maintaining our unique, incommunicable personal selves among other selves. It involves living well as physical animals among other animals and inanimate objects in a complex, interdependent material world. And it means building and nurturing loving relationships with other persons in a variety of kinds of associations and communities toward the building up of the common good of the flourishing personhood

37. Although not directly and entirely so, insofar as social structures, as I say in the previous chapter, possess emergent properties and capacities that are irreducible to their constituent parts, such that the effects of social structures cannot be fully explained with reference to the nature of their components. Nevertheless, the constituent parts do shape the quality of the emergent entities from which they arise and so cannot be dismissed as irrelevant.

of all, up to the limits of actual possibilities. It is the good of we human beings as persons to achieve these ends and realize our own nature. Ways of thinking, feeling, acting, and structuring social life that encourage, support, and promote progress toward those achievements are morally good. Ways that deny, frustrate, obstruct, or ruin those achievements are morally wrong and sometimes evil.

So, I have said that the good for humans is to develop our personhood as much as we are able and that morality concerns the personal and social attitudes, desires, dispositions, habits, and practices that foster the achievement of that good. But what does this look like more specifically? Again, the answer does not immediately involve a set of rules and procedures that must be followed and obeyed—although rules and procedures eventually do become important in morality.[38] The first task is to engage in sustained reflection and deliberation about requirements and means for achieving the good, on the one hand, and dispositions, desires, behaviors, and practices that frustrate or spoil the achievement of the good, on the other. I cannot spell out the details of such a reflection, nor is that my purpose. My intent is to sketch a vision for how such a teleological personalist moral inquiry might proceed and how it provides a coherent account of the sources of moral and political values and commitments I believe we should want to affirm and defend. Most of the virtues involved will engage both personal and social aspects, so it is difficult to consider personal versus social ethics in this approach. Moral reflection will often weave in and out of both.

The crucial starting point for human moral life is for persons to grasp the truth about what they are and in what their true good consists. It is possible to misconstrue what a human or a person is and so to head in wrong directions. If we, for instance, understand ourselves to be animals up to little more than pursuing bodily and psychological pleasures and avoiding all forms of pain then our moral quest has gotten off on an entirely wrong foot. We have also headed in the wrong direction from the start if we understand ourselves to be autonomous individuals seeking our self-defined happiness and bound only by the imperative to not obstruct the happiness-seeking of other individuals; as materialistic consumers of experiences and products trying in essence to satiate our preferences and desires; as mere duty-bound centers of rationality diligently carrying out

38. See, for instance, Stephen Gardiner, "Seneca's Virtuous Moral Rules," in Gardiner, ed., *Virtue Ethics, Old and New*, 30–59.

self-evident or pregiven imperatives and obligations; or as social animals ultimately conforming to the constructed cultural norms, beliefs, and dictates of society. No, we must start from the right place to get headed in the correct direction.[39] Persons—as I have suggested in this book—are emergently complex and powerful agents of a particular kind engaged in self-development and the formation of relationships and structures according to means and toward ends that are embedded in the nature of personhood. Always entailed in that are dimensions of personal identity, self-transcendence, moral vision, responsibility taking, intersubjective understanding, incommunicable self-existence, and fellowship, love, and communion among persons. This picture of persons and moral life is more complex and open-ended than many alternatives. It requires persons to act as responsible participants, not merely obedient followers, rational calculators, or compliant conformists in moral living. It also means that the intentional pursuit of the moral good and rejection of the moral bad by persons becomes a key part of the kind of personal life-on-a-meaningful-quest that in turn intrinsically helps to constitute the moral good that is the human personal telos. The deliberate pursuit of the good is part of the good being pursued. Moral life that is tuned to reality thus begins with a correct understanding—whether intuitive or reflexive—of the real human condition, actual human potentialities, and the right telos of personhood.

The next step in reflection and deliberation about the good and morality for any person is working to imagine in specifics what a good end looks like. We ask the question: If you and I singly and we together succeeded in reaching our personal telic ends, what would that look like? What would robustly developed, healthy, flourishing versions of persons—ourselves included—look like if that were achieved? And what would a social order look like that would foster that end? Insofar as this moral approach is teleological, it gains essential leverage of thought, vision, and motivation by

---

39. "The good is not exhausted by the experiential—the key tenet of hedonism. Real understanding of the ways things are, for example, is pleasurable because it is fulfilling or perfective of us, not vice versa. . . . Our desires are not purely arbitrary: we are capable of desiring certain things while other things leave us unmoved, uninterested. So, prior to being desired, the object desired must have something about it that makes it *fitting*, or *suitable*, to be desired. What makes it fitting to us is that it would *fulfill* or *perfect* us in some way or other. Thus, what makes a thing good cannot consist of its being enjoyed, or in its satisfying desires or preferences. Rather, desires and preferences are rational only if they are in line with what is genuinely good, that is, genuinely fulfilling." Patrick Lee and Robert P. George, "The Nature and Basis of Human Dignity," in *Human Dignity and Bioethics* (Washington, DC: President's Council on Bioethics, 2008), 419, italics in original.

drawing a contrast between what currently is and what eventually could and should be—between the status quo and the quest fulfilled. We are thus drawn to determine what we need to do now by a telic vision of where we are trying to go, of an imaginable destination, of a purpose or end or goal of personhood that is good, worthy, admirable, compelling. Only by knowing what we ought to be and the qualitative and quantitative distance standing between that potential good *ought* and the actual less-than-fully-good *is* can we ever learn about the virtues and moral dispositions and practices we need to learn in order to get to our destination. Growing in virtue means learning to distinguish between our current empirical desires, thoughts, feelings, habits, and reactions and the kind of desires, thoughts, feelings, habits, and reactions that would help us more fully realize our essential nature as persons or that would be reflected in fully realized personhood. Having distinguished that difference, when and where it exists, learning moral virtues involves disciplining desires, transforming thought patterns, adjusting feelings, reforming habits and reactions, and so on in ways that enhance rather than diminish our personhood and that of others. In these kinds of ways, growing in moral virtue is similar to improving one's performance as an athlete, artist, or musician. In all cases, objective standards of excellence exist toward which the learner aspires; an understanding of and submission to those standards is a precondition for improving one's growth and performance; training by teachers and role models is crucial for making progress; and a commitment to engaging the hard work of practice, practice, and more practice is required to unlearn tendencies and habits that impede and learn the new skills and habits that advance performance toward the goal of excellence.

I must step aside here in this and the next paragraph in order to head off two possible misconceptions about my notion of a telos by better specifying my meaning. The first misconception is that a telos is conceptually too individual and restrictive, charging that there is no one, single telos that works for all people. The second misconception is that this idea is too expansive and empty of instructive content—that the substance of my definition of personhood is so general it cannot tell anyone, beyond offering vague platitudes, how to live. I think we can avoid these misconceptions by distinguishing between the shared human telos, a personal telos, and a life plan. The shared human telos is the more general end toward which all humans ought to move, given the nature of what they as persons are, and that helps to define the right boundaries within which all humans should move forward toward any end. I use the word *the* here because there is only one shared human telos in virtue of there being one shared human personhood. A personal telos, by comparison, concerns the more specific ends that are good and appropriate for a particular person, given their unique biographies, talents, interests, and social situations. I use the word *a* here instead of *the* because each person has their own personal telos, which means that there are a multiplicity of personal teloi across many people. Finally, a life plan—as I mean it here—consists of a set of specific intentions and commitments about relationships, activities, education, vocations, locations, and other existential and practical matters that together comprise much of the long-term content of any given person's life as they do and expect to live it. My life plan, for instance, involves being married, having children, having earned a PhD, being an academic, researching, publishing, being on the faculty at Notre Dame, and so on. Most elements of people's life plans are not morally good or bad in and of themselves, but they can become morally significant in terms of promoting people's personal flourishing as life plans begin to work together either to promote or deflect movement toward personal teloi. These three distinct concepts range in character from great-though-not-absolute generality (the shared human telos) to biographically specific ranges of possible life ends (a personal telos) on down to highly particular intentions and choices by which specific lives are lived (life plans). These three are also linked in specific ways. For example, a person's life plans must be appropriately nested within their personal telos, which in turn must be nested within the shared human telos. Many different life plans may fit one person's personal telos. For example, the same person with the same proper personal telos could appropriately choose to become a writer or a filmmaker, to marry or not marry, to live in Tuscaloosa or Los Angeles, and to take up knitting or judo for a hobby. Furthermore, many quite different personal teloi can fit well within the more expansive, single, shared human telos. But every person's life plan must fit within the boundaries of their personal telos, just as every distinct personal telos must fit within the trajectories and ends of the shared human telos. No life plan, in other words, can be good if it does not work toward achieving a personal telos, just as no telos can be personally good and proper if it is humanly bad or improper. Thus, one ought not to include in one's life plan going to medical school, for instance, if one's proper personal telos entails the calling to devote oneself to becoming a world-class athlete. Furthermore, one ought not to decide that one's proper personal telos is to engage in the modern slave trade or to become a drug addict—even if for some particular reason one feels compelled because of one's biography or interests to engage in human trafficking or be addicted to drugs—because slavery and drug addiction fall outside of the proper shared human telos. People can and do participate in slavery and drug addiction, but they are teleologically wrong in so doing by virtue of those violating the larger shared human telos.

By making these distinctions among the shared human telos, a personal telos, and life projects, we are able to make sense of the problem of specificity and generality in proper ends. All persons ought to be living so as to pursue the human telos in one way or another, for that helps provide the moral vision that ought to be guiding every human person. Every person ought also to be living so as to pursue their own personal telos, for that defines the right direction and end of their lives as distinct persons. Finally, every person ought to carry out life plans that suit their own highly particular interests, gifts, needs, opportunities, and constraints. Note the inverse relationship in all of this between scope of generality and range of options. The human telos entails the greatest scope of generality and yet the smallest range of proper options, namely, one. At the other end, life plans concern the most specific scope of identity and behavior possibilities and yet the largest range of potential choices that might count as good and proper for any given person's life. Here is what this comes down to. The ends in terms of which we think about the good for persons can be specified at three different levels. All persons seek the good most broadly by pursuing the single human telos, which has moral implications—but that human end is broad in scope and therefore properly encompasses a broad range of possible personal teloi and life plans. All persons also ought to seek the good more specifically by pursuing their personal telos, based on their particular histories, abilities, interests, callings, and so on—which is necessarily constrained by the parameters of the human telos and dramatically narrows down the range of possible life plans that might be considered. Finally, all persons seek the good by making and deploying life plans that carry out the pursuit of their personal telos. Different life plans may achieve one personal telos, just as many personal teloi can properly achieve the one human telos. Again, there are few precise rules or obligations, the fulfilling of which specify what the living of a good life looks like for any given person. The approach instead is that of grasping what the good is; imagining what a specific life in pursuit of the good could, would, and should look like; learning virtues that promote and instantiate that good in actual life; and putting all of that together in a coherent life story and project in ways that pursue the personal flourishing of oneself and those whose lives one touches. Prudence, self-understanding, insight, discernment, and readiness to continually learn are all essential here. In sum, when we see that the vision of the good advanced as a teleological approach to morality in this chapter is grasped as involving the three nested levels just described, we can address the challenge of providing an account of the telos that is both general and specific enough to include all people appropriately. There actually is one telos that fits all persons, but it allows for a variety of paths and expressions in pursuing it, while at the same time—because of the given nature of human personhood—providing real content that can guide the choices and disciplines every person makes in moving toward or away from the shared human telos and their own personal telos.

Back to the larger argument now. Having realized something of the truth about what we are, in what our actual good consists, and developed a vision of the difference between where we now stand and what we ought to achieve, we stand prepared to begin to specify some substantive moral arguments. Morality and the virtues, thus conceived, function as a kind of plan of action, as a smart trip itinerary and reliable travel guidebook, as ways to get where we believe we need and ought to go in order to become our real and best selves. But morality and the virtue are not merely a means. Living morally and virtuously is also a part of the good end they seek to achieve. For, to be a flourishing person is constituted in part by living a moral and virtuous life. Thus the distinction between means and ends begins to break down.

My purpose is not to elaborate a new moral system. The last thing the world needs is a new moral system. My purpose is to explain why there are intellectually coherent reasons—which also comport with insightful social scientific theory and inquiry—to be committed to the old moral system that many of us admire, to which we find ourselves recurrently drawn back, whether through hard knocks or intuitive understanding, which is presupposed in the kind of scholarship and activism in which so many social scientists engage. So why is murder morally wrong? Because it is the destruction of the personhood of the murdered and the desecration of that of the murderer. Why is stealing morally wrong? Because stealing violates the personhood of the victim as well as that of the thief. Why is lying normally morally wrong?[40] Because it denies what is reality,

40. The present account recognizes exceptional circumstances in which it may be morally necessary to lie to people who are intent on damaging or destroying the personhood of others

destroys the trust needed for relations in which persons flourish, and so diminishes the personhood of the lied to and the liar. The same operation can be performed on the many moral goods and bads to which we subscribe. Why are love, justice, kindness, peacefulness, understanding, patience, forgiveness, generosity, equity, faithfulness, and the like moral goods? Because they nurture and protect human personhood. Why are selfishness, injustice, meanness, exploitation, revenge, oppression, hate, exclusion, indifference, and such ills moral bads? Because they frustrate and damage human personhood. Why is it morally wrong to break promises, deprive people of their rights, cheat in committed relationships, perpetuate poverty, vandalize property, commit pedophilia, demean people's identities, engage in terrorism, or commit a host of other harms, injustices, and crimes? Because they tear down rather than build up the personhood of the people involved. Why is it morally right to care for the sick, to pay just wages, to honor people's privacy, to observe due processes in judicial proceedings, to share with the needy, to respect people who are different, and a multitude of other forms of integrity, benevolences, and justice? Because they build up the personhood of all of the people involved. Why ought we to admire and seek to learn courage, wisdom, prudence, temperance, honesty, charity, mercy, dignity, loyalty, humility, perseverance, self-control, and the like? Because they are virtues that, when judiciously exercised, are important for the development and flourishing of human personhood. Why ought we to disdain and reject selfishness, vanity, envy, greed, hatred, laziness, foolishness, despair, callousness, bigotry, and the like? Because they are vices that tend to retard and damage the development of human personhood. Why do relationships of love matter? Because love nourishes personhood. Why is social injustice reprehensible? Because injustice poisons social relations and corrodes the personhood of the dominant and the oppressed.

We can be even more specific. Why does a good society ensure and protect the basic safety and lawfulness of the social order? Because those are preconditions for the prosperity of human personhood—in their absence, personhood is stunted and sometimes ruined. Why is a good society one that provides for the nutritional and health-care needs of all of its members? Because a healthy body is normally a foundational building

---

in order to protect those others. Lying to the Nazi SS about the presence of Jews hidden in one's house would be an example of such unusual circumstances. The exceptions, however, are entirely consistent with the larger approach developed here.

block of flourishing personhood, and all members of society in the pursuit of their flourishing personhood should be rightly interested in the bodily well-being of others. Why is a good society one that provides universal educational opportunities for its members? Because the development of personal capacities requires an education not only in "practical," technical matters but also broadly in the arts and sciences that expand the horizons and enrich the personhood of those educated—it is this, and not some calculated economic rationale, that rightly justifies our investments into liberal arts education from elementary school through college. Why is a good society one that maximizes participation by all of its members in employment, associational life, and politics? Because social participation is an essential means to and constitutive element of thriving personhood. Why is a good political system one that entails significant freedom for, involvement by, input from, and accountability to its citizens? Because those systems respect the personhood of its citizens in matters of the common good and public justice and tend to foster social conditions allowing for the greater development of personhood. Why is a good society one that does not destroy the natural environment on which its life depends but cares as a responsible steward for the healthy ecology of the living and material world it occupies? Because persons are material, embodied beings whose good it is to exist in flourishing relationship not only with other persons but also with the material world they inhabit. By contrast, why are totalitarian states, racial segregation, complete social chaos, radical individualism, collectivist economies, slavery, repressive military regimes, grinding poverty, concentration camps, categorically exclusionary institutions, environmental degradation and destruction, oppressive patriarchies, exclusive state religions, infringements of freedom of speech, tolerance of domestic violence, judicial and political corruption, fascism, full-time child labor, mass executions, and such systems and practices objectionable if not immoral and repulsive? Because they oppose, undermine, diminish, and sometimes destroy the personhood of persons.

In sum, what is personally moral and interpersonally excellent is driven by the interests of flourishing personhood. What is socially, politically, culturally, and institutionally good, fair, just, and worthy are also driven by the interests of flourishing personhood. All human persons are, or at least should be, on a telic quest—whether largely successfully or not—to enhance their personhood. What is good and moral and virtuous is succeeding in that quest. What is good is flourishing personhood. What is moral fosters flourishing personhood. What are virtues are those dispositions and practices that tend to promote flourishing personhood. What by contrast is for humans wrong, bad, immoral, offensive, and evil are those things that oppose, thwart, diminish, retard, and destroy thriving personhood. That, in any case, is the account offered by critical realist personalism.

None of this, however, is to suggest that moral decision making is always clear and easy. Sometimes it is not. That is because the paths to the realization of our essential nature as persons can be multiple, involve uncertainties, and entail trade-offs and the prudent balancing of apparently competing goods and alternative bads. No one faces a single, unambiguous, predetermined pathway to personal flourishing. A teleological personalist approach to morality does not specify in advance a fixed lists of rules or procedures or imperatives that need to be followed to do the right and achieve the good. The good is a quest to pursue. And the very purposeful pursuit of the good itself becomes part of the realization of the good. Working toward the good requires learning from those who know better, wisdom from experience, prudence in making judgments, and courage to choose the right ends and means. The good can also be learned by observing the bad in history. Again, learning virtues is part of the achievement. In addition, there is regrettably something wrong with life and the world that I have described as brokenness, which generates confusion, obstructions, tragedies, and the active will to resist what is good and right. The larger context of the quest for the good is not an open, easy, facilitating environment in which everyone coasts downhill on smooth tracks toward its realization. Achieving the good is an uphill struggle against multiple and confusing obstacles and forces within and without that would prevent its realization. Successful quests require overcoming, learning from failure, correction, and courage and perseverance in the face of opposition and despair. Finally, in this broken world we recurrently find ourselves in difficult situations at the margins—at the start and end of life, in the tragic damaging and radical deformation of life—where the prospects for personhood seem dim to nonexistent. What then? Again, answers are often not clear and easy. I take up such matters in greater length in the discussion of dignity in the following chapter.

At the same time, this recognition of the obscurities and difficulties involved in our quests for the good of personhood does not entitle us to collapse into moral subjectivism, antinomianism, or relativism. The quest for the good, for moral living, and for the learning of virtues is structured and driven by the objective nature of the human condition, by the given character of personhood. And we cannot simply reconstruct those at will or wish them away. Merely because movement toward the realization of our good has the character of a quest does not mean that a good life is only finally about the journey. To believe otherwise is to have lost sight of our personal human nature and our shared good. No, there is a given, proper, substantive end that gives the journey its entire point. Without a destination, journeys collapse into aimless wandering, into pseudo-quests. The process of pursuit of the good does indeed get caught up in the telos. But it is not only about process. The telos also provides an objective end, crucial moral bearings by which to pursue it, and definite virtues to be learned and practiced that are necessary to ever hope to achieve it. As persons we do enjoy a bounded freedom within which to exercise prudent judgments in the pursuit along possible multiple pathways of our good. But we are never free to construct from scratch as we wish the good itself, our human nature that established it, or the means by which it is characteristically realized. Those are given by the objective nature of reality.

To summarize, if we wish to know what is morally good and right, we need a proper telos toward which to be moving, and we need to deliberate wisely about what attitudes, behaviors, dispositions, desires, practices, relationships, and social structures will help us get there. Given the nature of personhood, the range of possibilities concerning the latter is not rigid and preset. But neither is it wide open. Millennia of human experience give us many reliable clues, though no exact blueprint we can thoughtlessly follow. And what will motivate us to pursue the difficult quest toward our proper telos? Our informed interest in realizing our highest good of robust and flourishing personhood within thriving communities of other flourishing persons.

Objections and Replies

My account thus far raises numerous possible objections that I need now to engage. The first is that I have in this discussion done little more than to draw out moral conclusions that were implicit in my definition of personhood. The objection is that I planted a set of moral commitments into my descriptive account of personhood at the start of this book, which I am now "discovering" there. Is my account a sleight-of-the-hand magic trick pulling a normative rabbit out of a descriptive hat? Have I unfairly defined a descriptive reality in terms that inevitably lead to the normative, moral conclusions I want to deduce? The problem with this objection is that it presupposes the rigid is-ought distinction and fact-value separation that my account has already rejected and that no reader needs to accept. *Of course* I am drawing out moral conclusions from the descriptive account of persons that I have advanced. That is precisely my intent and procedure. And nothing about that is misleading or circular or erroneous—assuming that my account of personhood is on the mark. The question is not whether one can draw prescriptive conclusions from descriptive facts. We cannot ultimately avoid that. The question is whether our understanding of the descriptive facts is correct or not, and whether or not the conclusions rightly follow from them. In this case, the key issue is whether my description of persons in chapter 1 and throughout this book is essentially true or not. If it is not, then my case folds. If it is, then the moral conclusions I have drawn are essentially valid and reliable. So if one objects to my account of the good, morality, and virtues in this chapter, one needs to go back to the account of personhood from which they derive and show where that account got it wrong. Otherwise, merely to notice the fact that my moral conclusions derive from my definition of personhood is to offer no real objection. It is to understand what I am intentionally doing in developing my argument, and confirms the cogency of the connection between the descriptive and prescriptive.

Another possible objection to my account is to suggest that I have imported without explanation or justification the stipulation above, namely that one cannot pursue one's good without that also involving the pursuit of the good of others. That stipulation is the belief on which the features of social responsibility, concern, benevolence, and charity entailed in my account depend. Lacking it, the pursuit of individual personal goods degenerates into a zero-sum competition of each self-seeking individual against the others. On what grounds, then, ought we to believe that achieving the good of other persons is an intrinsic element of achieving our own good? The answer is that it simply is so by virtue of the nature of reality. *If* my descriptive account of personhood in this book is essentially correct, then it is the case that no person can pursue their good without also and as part of that seeking the good of other persons. Persons by nature are—as I have described them—interdependent, inescapably tied up in webs of social relations, dependent for their personal good on the common good, and oriented in their proper ends toward meaningful, loving, and just relationships and social structures.[41] The Hobbesian world in its "state of

41. See Amitai Etzioni, *The Common Good* (Malden, MA: Polity, 2004).

nature"—a nasty, brutish, and short existence in a war of all against all—accurately depicts certain aspects of our broken human existence; but in the end it misrepresents the true nature, potential, and end of our personhood. Likewise, the autonomous individualism assumed by liberal political theory—that of human atoms emancipated from every encumbrance except the mutual agreement not to encumber other emancipated human atoms—attempts imperfectly to describe what is true about human freedom, responsibility, and incommunicability; but in the end it too misrepresents the profoundly relational and social character of personhood. I could go on, but enough said. Every person ought for his or her own sake to be invested in the good of other persons, not by virtue of some externally coercive duty or constraint but because—by the nature of reality and their own existent being—enhancing the good of others is naturally a constitutive feature of enhancing the good of each person. This is not because I say so. It is because of reality. I am only saying so because (I believe) this is reality. Those who cannot see or believe that simply do not, by my account at least, understand or accept reality as it is. When we do understand and accept reality, we know that the personal good and the common good, our own well-being and that of other persons are inextricably tied up together in ways that provide us with substantive moral direction.

Nevertheless, the objection may persist: in the real world as we encounter it, what is good for one person is often bad for another. One person or group's flourishing often comes at the expense of another person or group's flourishing. Zero-sum situations are often not so easily avoided. Is not my portrayal of mutual benevolence mere utopianism? My reply is that as a description of life as it happens, this is accurate. People and groups often do seek what they believe to be their good at the expense of others. But we need to bring some nuance to this observation, which the difference between the transitive and the intransitive in critical realism provides. First of all, what people believe to be their good is not necessarily their true good. For example, it is not, according to a teleological personalist account, the true good of people to benefit through the exploitation, oppression, slavery, and exclusion of other persons. That may appear to be their good, as visions of the good can be distorted by insecurity and fear. It may yield short-term forms of pleasure and happiness. It may produce what other circumstances might have borne out to be true goods. But under these conditions, the violation of the good of others inevitably violates the true good of the "beneficiaries" and engenders longer term ills and evils that entrap everyone—resentment, mistrust, enmity, violence, estrangement, vengeance, murder, and war. In a teleological personalist perspective, happiness and fulfillment are hard-won, long-term, shared achievements, not easy and immediate pleasures to be enjoyed at the expense of others. So, yes, people do take advantage of other people all the time. But this does not show my account to be wrong. It shows those people to be wrong in their implicit account of the reality of their personhood and its proper ends. This is part of the brokenness that such people need to face and overcome. Second, this "realistic" objection about incompatible goods dramatically underestimates the extent of investment by persons in the good of others that needs to and does happen in our world, as broken as it is. Love happens. If many parents were not investing selflessly in the good of their children, for instance, we would soon face a war of all against all. But they do, so we normally do not. Good teachers teach well because they genuinely care about and invest in the good of their students. The same is true about good friends, neighbors, spouses, coaches, employers, mentors, colleagues, and a host of other important social relationships. Even in many interactions among strangers, people often—not always, but still often—express various forms of kindness, equity, empathy, respect, and consideration that are not warranted by the logic of short-term, rational egoism. We must keep in perspective a balanced view of the actual, extensive seeking by persons of the good of other persons that counters, although does not erase, the similarly extensive pursuit of people's (false) good at the expense of others. Too jaded or cynical a view distorts rather than makes clear our understanding of the fullness of reality.

I would also counter the critical suggestion that the good of others is not entailed within every person's own good by placing the burden back on the objector to explain what is good and right and virtuous if they are correct and how that could be so. The responsibility and motivation to seek the good of others and not only oneself seems to be an ineradicable part of any morality worth the name. We cannot live without that. Suppose that it is not the case that the realization of every person's good involves their investing in the good of others. Where does that leave us? We might try utilitarianism. But utilitarianism, based entirely as it is on calculations of aggregate pleasures and pain, possesses no account of the natural rights of any given person—if the greatest good for the greatest number requires the sacrifice of some, then so be it, as a moral principle. Moreover, utilitarianism is no more successful at overcoming the is-ought and fact-value divides than any other approach, and less able than the present account to explain how and why we ought to get from the descriptive facts (of pleasure and pain) to normative prescriptions (that maximizing pleasure is good and minimizing pain is bad). Utilitarianism is another version of deriving an ought from an is. In the end it will not help us here. Well, then, we might try some kind of socially constructed social contract ethic. Let us suppose, for instance, that we agree to allow each other to live as each wishes, with the only constraints being that, first, living as one wishes does not obstruct others living as they wish and, second, that certain common investments in security and order (national defense, police, roadways, etc.) are required and so justify a minimal common government to provide them. First, we should notice that this is not a moral system but an exchange contract. It may *allow* for the living of moral systems within it, but it does not tell anyone what is actually good or right to do. As an exchange contract, as Durkheim pointed out long ago, it could never have been generated in the first place and could not be sustained over time without the preexistence of a deeper moral order providing for the kinds of agreement, trust, and mutuality required for any exchange contract to function.[42] Successful exchange contracts are always and only built within contexts of shared moral commitments. Furthermore, it remains unclear how a socially constructed social contract ethic could produce a genuine concern for the good of other persons—especially those outside one's most intimate relatives—that was not easily reducible to calculated self-interest. Under some conditions, when it would serve our interests, we might want to invest in the good of others. But under other conditions we might not. And we would be perfectly entitled not to seek the good of others if we so wished. Their own good would be their own concern. Finally, because such a social contract ethic would not be rooted in nature, in the given facts of reality, but would be the cultural product of a social construction, there would be no intrinsic reason why any social contract could not be reconstructed by enough bargaining partners to exclude, exploit, oppress, or even eliminate the weak, the unproductive, the ugly, the inconvenient, the rival. There is no reason why the logic of benefiting at others' expense could and should not overwhelm the logic of responsible benevolence, inviolable rights, or benefiting together in a common good. In order to secure the latter, if we wish to do so, morality needs to be grounded not in variable social constructions but in the objective nature of

---

42. Émile Durkheim, *The Division of Labor in Society* (1893; New York: Free Press, 1997)—against Herbert Spencer's individualistic theory.

reality. A coherent account of how and why the latter is the case is exactly
what teleological critical realist personalism attempts to provide. Without
belaboring the point, if morality does entail a genuine and active caring for
the well-being of other people, the burden falls on those who object to the
present account's explanation of how and why that is so to demonstrate
through an alternative account how and why that could be.

Modernity and Morality

Before concluding it seems worth addressing a set of questions raised by
this chapter's argument. Does the human race ever make moral progress?
Or does every generation have to strike out on the quest for personhood
from the same starting line? More specifically, has modernity brought
with it significant moral improvement? Or is modernity morally neutral?
Or has modernity in some sense brought about significant moral decline?
Some scholars with a bent toward virtues and communitarian ethics with
perhaps some tendencies toward personalism—here I think of Alasdair
MacIntyre, Stanley Hauerwas, and Robert Bellah[43]—tend to interpret
modernity, and the liberal capitalism it often involves, in quite a negative
light. Others with similar intellectual leanings—such as Charles Taylor
and Amitai Etzioni[44]—are more positive about the prospects of a coherent
morality within modernity. What might my account suggest?

At the purely intellectual level of moral philosophy, I tend to agree
with MacIntyre that modernity has entailed a kind of catastrophe destroying coherent moral thought and practices.[45] This catastrophe—which we
have a difficult time seeing, precisely because we are in it and of it—was

43. See, for example, MacIntyre, *After Virtue*; Aladsair MacIntyre, *Three Rival Versions
of Moral Enquiry: Encyclopaedia, Genealogy, and Tradition* (Notre Dame, IN: University
of Notre Dame Press, 1990); Stanley Hauerwas, *A Community of Character* (Notre Dame,
IN: University of Notre Dame Press, 1981); Stanley Hauerwas and William Willimon, *Resident Aliens* (Nashville, TN: Abingdon Press, 1989); Robert Bellah et al., *Habits of the Heart:
Individualism and Commitment in American Life* (Berkeley and Los Angeles: University of
California Press, 1985).

44. Charles Taylor, *Sources of the Self* (Cambridge, MA: Harvard University Press, 1989);
Taylor, *Modern Social Imaginaries* (Durham, NC: Duke University Press, 2004); Charles
Taylor and James Heft, eds., *A Catholic Modernity* (New York: Oxford University Press,
1999); Amitai Etzioni, *The Spirit of Community: The Reinvention of American Society* (New
York: Touchstone, 1994); Etzioni, *The Common Good*.

45. MacIntyre, *After Virtue*, 1–22.

the direct result of the abandonment, for understandable but unfortunate reasons, of the notion of teleological purposes in human life. The reasonable analytical rejection of telic purposes in nature that the scientific revolution instigated was extended—needlessly and misguidedly—to the realm of human life. When, as a result, moral reasoning was stripped of any legitimate notion of an objective moral end or purpose or standard, it was simply a matter of time and repeated failed efforts of nonteleological philosophical alternatives to drive us into moral subjectivism, emotivism, and relativism. The end of that road has been a dead end. I am persuaded that the reclaiming and refurbishing of a teleological morality in the Aristotelian tradition offers the most promising way forward and away from that intellectual debacle.

At the same time, intellectual moral philosophy is not the entire game. In some sense, the experience of moral life on the ground is just as important as the coherence of the justifying theories operating in the intellectual background. And the potential for the realization of the flourishing personhood of persons is not a sociohistorical constant. Different social orders more or less facilitate movement toward the personal telos. How has modernity fared on that account? The record is mixed. Modernity, it turns out, has multiple faces.[46] On the positive side, the material prosperity of modernity has brought unprecedented capacities for expanding human health, longevity, education, vocational specialization, travel, scientific understanding, and artistic expression—all of which create huge opportunities to enhance human personhood. I think there is no question that the potential for us humans to realize our essential personhood is significantly greater in most modern societies than in hunter-gatherer, horticultural, and in at least some ways most agricultural societies. Infant mortality drops spectacularly with modernity, as do death rates for mothers in childbirth.

46. S. N. Eisenstadt, "Multiple Modernities," *Daedalus* 129, no. 1 (2000): 1–29; S. N. Eisenstadt, *Comparative Civilizations and Multiple Modernities*, 2 vols. (Leiden: Brill Academic, 2003); Peter Wagner, "Modernity—One or Many?" in *The Blackwell Companion to Sociology*, ed. Judith Blau (Oxford: Blackwell, 2000); Luis Roniger and Carlos Waisman, eds., *Globality and Multiple Modernities: Comparative North American and Latin American Perspectives* (Brighton, UK: Sussex Academic Press, 2002); Peter Berger and Samuel Huntington, eds., *Many Globalizations: Cultural Diversity in the Contemporary World* (New York: Oxford University Press, 2003). Also see Gerard Delanty, *Social Theory in a Changing World: Conceptions of Modernity* (Malden, MA: Polity Press, 1999); Peter Taylor, *Modernities: A Geohistorical Interpretation* (Minneapolis: University of Minnesota Press, 1999); Bernard Yack, *The Fetishism of Modernities: Epochal Self-Consciousness in Contemporary Social and Political Thought* (Notre Dame, IN: University of Notre Dame Press, 1997).

Many diseases have been cured and others can more readily be prevented. Nutritional knowledge and availability of healthy foods has increased dramatically. Modern medicine, surgery, and pharmacology work miracles of bodily and mental health and well-being. Antibiotics and anesthetics have reduced widespread suffering and death. Parents who live longer can build loving relationships with grandchildren. The spread of universal education and global travel has radically expanded the horizons and prospects of the minds and spirits of billions of people. The modern division of labor enables people to pursue meaningful careers that use and sharpen their particular personal gifts, skills, and interests. Modern technology greatly reduces multiple forms of drudgery and danger previously required simply to survive. In these and myriad other ways, the potential for enhancing the personhood of billions of persons has increased dramatically. New forms of social and geographic mobility have opened up prospects for personal development of which humanity could not before have dreamed.

Not only has the potential for good increased, but major advances in substantive moral understanding and practices have also come with modernity. It took the arrival of modernity for human slavery to be seen by the majority of people as the evil that it is and for major social movements to emerge to try to eradicate it. Modernity birthed the reality of inalienable and legally protected civil and human rights. The writing and adoption of the UN Universal Declaration of Human Rights is undeniably a gigantic landmark in human moral understanding and commitment.[47] Religious freedoms and the rights to life, property, assembly, expression, organized labor, and equality before the law have been major modern achievements. Modernity has also produced a variety of agreements and conventions constraining some of the worst practices of warfare.[48] In modernity many have come to embrace gender equality and do away with some of the worst practices of patriarchy. Modernity has also resurrected the ancient idea and practice of democracy and the personal goods of participation, responsibility, and accountability it entails. For these and other reasons we cannot judge modernity to be an unambiguous source of

47. Also see the Convention on the Prevention and Punishment of the Crime of Genocide (1948); the International Covenant on Civil and Political Rights (1966); the International Covenant on Economic, Social, and Cultural Rights (1966); the United Nations Convention against Torture (1984); among many other international agreements and conventions.

48. Such as The Hague Conventions (1899, 1907), the Geneva Conventions (1864–1949), the U.N. Convention on Certain Conventional Weapons (1980), and the Chemical Weapons Convention (1993), among others.

moral decline and corruption. Modernity has produced numerous moral achievements of tremendous significance that only ingrates could ignore or discount.

Yet the story is more complicated than that, for modernity also bears its own barbarisms and horrors.[49] Colonialism, the Atlantic and Indian Ocean slave trades, the Reign of Terror, the genocidal conquest of native America, maiming factory machines, eugenics science, Jim Crow, chemical weapons, biological warfare, dehumanizing mass-production labor, blitzkriegs, U-boats, carpet bombing, Auschwitz, Hiroshima, the Iron Curtain, apartheid, the Gulag, the Great Leap Forward, McCarthyism, the Tuskegee Syphilis Study, napalm, Pol Pot, the killing fields, toxic environmental pollution, 9/11, and the threat of global thermonuclear warfare are also the distinctive progeny of modernity. What we have learned from these moral extremes is that the astounding increases in human control over the natural world afforded by modern, advanced technologies and organizational systems have amplified not only the potential for moral good but also for shocking evil. To repeat, power in the hands of humans is largely neutral.[50] Power can be put to good, neutral, or dreadful moral ends, depending on the purposes of the humans exercising it and the constraints of the social structures through which the power is deployed. All human capacities potentially cut in two directions. Every human faculty for constructive good implies a converse ability for destruction and evil. Every explicitly declared "Yes!" necessarily predicates a potential "No!" Every fact of love inherently opens up a possible not-love. Thus the more persons have power to do, the more their doings may exercise power for either good or bad. As such, modernity is not necessarily a force for either moral good or ill. Modernity drastically enhances our human powers to do both good and evil. We therefore witness modernity producing impressive moral achievements and horrific moral atrocities.

49. S. N. Eistenstadt, "Barbarism and Modernity," *Society* 33, no. 4 (1996): 31–39; Leszek Kolakowski, *Modernity on Endless Trial* (Chicago: University of Chicago Press, 1990).

50. This is strictly speaking and meant to apply to human capacities and powers generally, not necessarily to technologies specifically. Concerning the latter, specific technologies can only accomplish certain activities, were designed with certain purposes in mind, and lend themselves to accomplishing some tasks better than others—hammers can be used for many purposes but the functional possibilities for intercontinental ballistic missiles is more limited. Nevertheless, whether, when, why, and how any given technology is (developed and) employed remains finally within the power of (powerful) human actors to direct. In any case, my larger point here is simply that even good powers can be put to wrong uses.

More subtly, modernity has eroded some of the social conditions that facilitate the pursuit of a coherent moral life of virtue, teleologically conceived. Virtue ethics going back to the Greeks emphasizes the importance of participation in the civil life in communities—the Greek polis or city-state—for learning and practicing the virtues that develop moral character. But the social and cultural life of modernity seems to make that experience more difficult. Modernity absorbs local sociopolitical communities and regional ecologies into national and global megainstitutions and markets. Modernity's division of labor and various forms of subcultural and spatial segregation often fosters participation in "lifestyle enclaves" more than the fully orbed life of communities. The social and geographical mobility of modern life and structural weakening of families makes sustaining long friendships, family, and other relationships that serve as the crucibles in which virtues are learned more challenging. Furthermore, modern liberal individualism erodes the ideas of an objective proper end of human life, the common good, and the moral interdependence of persons. Modernity's emancipatory impulses reject notions of external authorities, objective standards of excellence, learning from role models, the self-disciplining of thoughts, and desires and emotions, the pedagogical value of historical experience, and the rationality of submission of oneself to the disciplines of a historical tradition.[51] And modernity's surveillance and social controlling impulses tend to rely more on technology, formal process, bureaucratic procedures, and legal regulations than on trust in the virtuous character of the people involved in situations in question. Moreover, the mass consumer capitalism on which modernity's prosperity is built and the media and advertising industries that sell its goods tend to displace traditional concerns with the good, the right, and the true with more functional interests in consumer-defined tastes and preferences, the satiation of felt desires, and the continual accumulation of material products. Modern pluralism and liberalism also cultivate public institutional cultures that downplay moral particularities that function as authorities by which to judge our progress toward our telos in favor of least-common-denominator inclusiveness and the simple avoidance of judgment making and conflict. Altogether, these do not present social conditions conducive

51. James Hunter provides an incisive analysis of the impossibility of character education in communities lacking shared, particular moral visions. Hunter, *The Death of Character: Moral Education in an Age without Good or Evil* (New York: Basic Books, 2000). Also see Alan Wolfe, *Moral Freedom: The Search for Virtue in a World of Choice* (New York: Norton, 2001); MacIntyre, *Three Rival Versions of Moral Enquiry.*

to people pursuing difficult, life-long quests toward realizing their essential and proper ends as persons in communities of character by the learning and exercise of moral virtues taught by traditions and role models that specify or exemplify objective standards of excellence. What modernity most effectively promotes is individual autonomy, institutional immensity, and material abundance—or, in the words of Peter Wagner, freedom and control, autonomy and mastery.[52]

More generally we can observe that humans can make and have made significant moral progress over the course of historical experience, if by that we mean the cultural recognition and social and political institutionalization of real moral truths about or to which previous generations were uncertain or oblivious. It is simply not true that humanity is stuck in a moral trap or is treading through inexorable cycles of moral repetition. The moral awareness and practices of humankind are at least in some ways getting better—if nothing else than in shared reaction to moral horror. That is largely due to the fact that social institutions can organize ideas and purposes that outlive individual lives.[53] At the same time, the moral condition of *specific human persons* does not seem to be noticeably evolving toward perfection. Most of the same challenges, temptations, and vices appear to afflict and beset people today that have for all of human history. Single lives provide only so much time to learn and the socialization of following generations is, given the nature of persons, only somewhat effective. And, again, something like a brokenness of persons and the world plagues human efforts at moral understanding, character, and life. In this sense, it would seem to be naive in the extreme to expect specific humans, given their evident condition, to progressively evolve into natural models of moral goodness and integrity anytime soon. And before and until such a day comes, the best we can do with the moral challenges we confront will be to engage in the discernment and struggle around our real ends, challenges, quests, virtues, and communities.

52. Peter Wagner, *A Sociology of Modernity: Liberty and Discipline* (New York: Routledge, 1994); Peter Wagner, *Theorizing Modernity* (London: Sage, 2001). Also see Stephen Toulmin, *Cosmopolis: The Hidden Agenda of Modernity* (Chicago: University of Chicago Press, 1990).

53. Social solidarity is only ever possible in the presence of moral communities; see Steve Vaisey, "Structure, Culture, and Community: The Search for Belonging in 50 Urban Communes," *American Sociological Review* 72, no. 6 (2007): 851–73.

Conclusion

While some of the moral account of this chapter sounds progressive and humanistic and therefore compatible with some of contemporary academic culture, a great deal of my case will also grate abrasively against many modern and postmodern sensibilities and attitudes. The teleological discourse, for example, seems absolutely premodern. Wasn't Aristotle sidelined from scholarly inquiry after the scientific revolution? What is he doing back at the table? And who could seriously entertain the idea of a natural human purpose or end—or even a "human nature?" Furthermore, this talk about quests and virtues and goodness will likely strike many contemporary academics as having snuck out of some medieval ballad or Sunday school classroom. Does not the contrast between what people currently are and what their end says they ought to be imply a negative judgment on people as they are? Who are we to judge? And whatever happened to de-centering the subject, the objectivity of science, the rejection of Eurocentrism, empirical data collection, cultural relativism, disbelief in master narratives, materialism, historicism, pragmatism, statistical significance tests, Nietzsche, Dawkins, Rorty, and the rest? Can an academic scholar really take teleological personalist morality seriously? Well, I hope so. I do not see a better alternative. It is, I think, our best account. I for one am prepared—especially in light of the breakdown of foundationalist epistemologies and the recent resurgence of Aristotelian virtue ethics—to bring an open mind to the possibility that a careful retrieval and reworking of ancient notions such as a human telos, brokenness, quest, virtues, and the like may help us to understand ourselves, our experiences, our social condition, and our moral good better than nonnaturalistic ethics, empiricism, positivism, strong constructionism, anthropological relativism, pragmatism, and other current options in the intellectual and theoretical smorgasbord fare typically offered up in contemporary academia.

CHAPTER EIGHT

Human Dignity

The dignity of all human persons has been a hallmark of the theory and movement of personalism, a commitment on which it has always insisted. As a feature of personhood human dignity also bears on the personal and social good, is much debated in moral and political philosophy, has major implications for morality and ethics, and is arguably related to the work of social science. In a book about personalism—even one primarily engaging sociological theory such as this—I must do more than obliquely refer to human dignity, as I have in previous chapters. This chapter discusses the reality of dignity in human personal life, explores some problems concerning the sources or groundings of dignity, and offers some arguments that I hope will help to resolve some of those problems.

The Reality of Dignity

Personalist theory insists that human persons possess an inherent dignity by virtue of the properties of their existent personal being. Simply by being the kinds of creatures they are ontologically, persons are characterized by real dignity. Dignity is not an extra benefit conferred upon persons by social contract or positive law. Dignity is not the culturally relative invention of some people who socially construct it in their minds and discourse. Dignity is a real, objective feature of human personhood. The question is not whether dignity exists, any more than whether the Grand Canyon exists. The question is whether human minds understand, acknowledge, and respond to the fact that human persons possess dignity. Human dignity therefore is not to be regarded as simply an ethical or theological or philosophical opinion or assertion that is superimposed post hoc upon hard scientific knowledge about humans—as if a humanistic do-gooder has spray-painted a glossy, flesh-colored coating onto the surface of an otherwise unpleasant looking metal statue of a human body. Dignity inheres in the emergent constitution of human personhood, including in the personhood of people who are ignorant of or deny its reality. It is inalienable. It cannot be thought or wished away. It cannot be sold or negated by legal judgment. Dignity exists as a real and ineliminable dimension of human persons, just as liquidity does of water and growth and reproduction do of living organisms. This is not to say that nonhuman animals or perhaps other objects do not possess a kind of dignity—but, if so, from a personalist perspective, that would be a different kind of dignity from the dignity that inheres in human persons.

By "dignity" in this context I mean an inherent worth of immeasurable value that is deserving of certain morally appropriate responses. Dignity makes persons innately precious and inviolable.[1] Because of this dignity, human persons are naturally worthy of certain kinds of moral treatment by themselves and in their mutual relations—in particular, of respect, justice, and love.[2] The ontology of personhood makes it morally true that persons are creatures worthy of being treated with respect, justice, and love. In the nature of things, persons should give other persons the recognition and honor of respect. Persons ought to provide other persons what

1. Leszek Kolakowski writes, "It is difficult to define what human dignity is. It is not an organ to be discovered in our body, it is not an empirical notion, but without it we would be unable to answer the simple question: what is wrong with slavery?" Kolakowski, "What Is Left of Socialism," *First Things* 126 (2002): 42–46.

2. To be clear, by *dignity* I do not mean the other, common meaning of the word, denoting seemliness in decorum, self-esteem, or acting in a noble or dignified manner. It is true that some people are concerned with such matters, precisely because dignity, in the way I mean it here, is real in human persons and gives rise for some to such concerns. But the real existence of dignity as I mean it is not dependent upon people acting dignified, reflecting self-esteem, behaving properly, or projecting nobility. Even the poorest (or richest!), dirtiest, least attractive, most foul, and repulsive human person possesses a dignity of the kind I mean here, according to personalism. This distinction Aurel Kolnai, for example, confuses, it seems to me, by writing that dignity "can actually be impaired and destroyed, temporarily or irreversibly, like any real 'quality,'" that human dignity is simply "a kind of half-way house between a set of prescriptive claims and the basic quality of being-a-person: a semi-fictitious, semi-real status 'ascribed' to the person as such." Kolnai, "Dignity," *Philosophy* 51 (1976): 258, 259. For a revealing history of the matter, see Carlos Ruiz Miguel, "Human Dignity: History of an Idea," unpublished paper, University of Santiago de Compostela (Spain), n.d.; also see Adam Schulman, "Bioethics and the Question of Human Dignity," in *Human Dignity and Bioethics* (Washington, DC: President's Council on Bioethics, 2008), 3–18.

they rightly deserve in justice. And persons should care for the genuine well-being of other persons in love. All of this pertains by virtue of the nature of human personhood, not because the state or "society" says so. If these do say so,[3] it is because they rightly recognize what is objectively true in reality, not because governments or societies have the power by declaration to make it true or untrue.

A number of important moral facts, which can be stated for present purposes as reliable prescriptions, proceed from this reality.[4] One, echoing Kant, is that persons ought not to treat other persons as things. Persons and things belong to two different ontological orders of reality, with their own distinct, naturally proper characteristics and moral statuses. To treat a person as a thing is to violate that order of reality, to try to turn a "you" into an "it." It is a denial of personhood. This is why, among other reasons, slavery, for instance, is a categorical evil—because it treats persons as property rather than as real persons with dignity. A related reliable prescription, echoing Kant again, resulting from the moral imperatives of respect, justice, and love, is that persons should not be treated purely as means but rather as ends. This is why the pure instrumental manipulation of other people for one's own purposes is morally wrong; it treats persons as functional objects, not valuable ends. That violates the personhood of both the actor and the mistreated other. Good, virtuous people do not do that. A third reliable prescription flowing from personalist theory is that persons have natural, inalienable rights that other persons must honor to properly pursue the flourishing of their own personhood. Persons are endowed with identifiable rights: the right to life, security, liberty, just process, conscience, association, participation, and so on. These are facts of moral entitlement and responsibility generated by the ontology of personhood, which all persons are right to honor and entitled to receive. A fourth reliable prescription is that persons are responsible to develop and

3. As does the German constitution, for instance, which states in the first paragraph of Article 1 that, "Human dignity is inviolable. To respect and to protect it is the duty of all state authority." Examples of other states that explicitly refer to the inviolability of human dignity in their constitutions include Spain, France, Finland, Greece, Portugal, and Sweden.

4. It might appear that I am shifting from the teleological ethics of the previous chapter to a deontological ethics here, though that is not so, since, as we will see, I intend to contextualize the rule statements about dignity's implications here within a larger moral approach centered on the human *telos*, the good, virtues, and character. See Stephen Gardiner, "Seneca's Virtuous Moral Rules," in *Virtue Ethics, Old and New* (Ithaca, NY: Cornell University Press, 2005), 30–59.

exercise their personal capacities to enhance their own well-being and that of other persons. Freedom in personalism does not mean the license to do whatever one wants, but rather the ability to flourish as the person one is and should become and to help other persons to flourish in who they are and ought to become—and this lays moral responsibilities in addition to rights and freedoms on persons. A fifth reliable prescription is that all social institutions and practices should exist and function to serve the development of the people whose lives they touch. The center and purpose of every society is not the power of the state, the growth of the economy, or any other nonpersonal end, but the well-being and development of the personhood of all of its members and hopefully those beyond. All other purposes are subsidiary and instrumental to this person-serving purpose.

Recognizing the dignity of human persons and the reliable moral prescriptions that follow from it is hardly an original achievement of personalism. In this, personalism follows a long lineage in philosophy, ethics, and theology, whatever else we make of any of their other specific positions. The ancient Hebrew creation story, for instance, states that God declared, " 'Let us make humans in our image, in our likeness, and let them rule over the fish of the sea and the birds of the air, over the livestock, over all the earth, and over all the creatures that move along the ground.' So God created humanity in his own image, in the image of God he created humans; male and female he created them."[5] The Greek and Roman Stoic philosophers believed in dignity as a genuine possibility of all human beings, regardless of their empirical life situations, by virtue of their reflective reason.[6] The Roman statesman and philosopher Cicero (106–43 BC) wrote, "It is vitally necessary for us to remember always how vastly superior is man's nature to that of cattle and other animals: their only thought is for bodily satisfaction. . . . Man's mind on the contrary is developed by study and reflection. . . . From this we may learn that sensual pleasure is wholly unworthy of the dignity of the human race."[7] Saint Leo the Great, Pope from 440 to 461, insisted on the dignity of all human persons, Christian or not, by virtue of being made in God's image and of the incarnation of

5. Genesis 1:26–27.

6. Martha Nussbaum, "Kant and Stoic Cosmopolitanism," *Journal of Political Philosophy* 5 (1997): 1–25; Nussbaum, "The Worth of Human Dignity: Two Tensions in Stoic Cosmopolitanism," in *Philosophy and Power in the Graeco-Roman World*, ed. Gillian Clark and Tessa Rajak (Oxford: Clarendon Press, 2002), 31–49; Nussbaum, *The Therapy of Desire: Theory and Practice in Hellenistic Ethics* (Princeton, NJ: Princeton University Press, 1994).

7. Cicero, *De Officiis*, I (circa 44 BC; New York: Oxford University Press, 1994), 30.

God in Christ, teaching, "Everyone, not only the baptized, has a dignity."[8] In the twelfth century, the Italian jurist Burgundio of Pisa asked of "man" in his treatise *De Natura Hominis*, "How can we exaggerate the dignity of his place in the creation?"[9] The humanist scholar of the early Italian Renaissance, Giannozzo Manetti (1396–1459), wrote eloquently of human dignity in his *On the Dignity and Excellence of Man*, as did the humanist Pico della Mirandola (1463–1494) in his *Oration on the Dignity of Man*. Pierre Boaistuau wrote similarly in France in the sixteenth century in his *Brief Discourse on the Excellence and Dignity of Man*.[10] Furthermore, Immanuel Kant taught famously that human beings have "an intrinsic worth, that is, dignity" that is "beyond all price," such that all persons should "act in such a way that you treat humanity, whether in your own person or in the person of any other, always at the same time as an end and never simply as a means."[11] Similar examples could be multiplied. The preamble to the *Charter of the United Nations* (1945), for instance, declares its determination "to reaffirm faith in fundamental human rights [and] in the dignity and worth of the human person." Likewise, the Universal Declaration of Human Rights (1948) states that the recognition of "the inherent dignity and of the equal and inalienable rights of all members of the human family" are "the foundation of freedom, justice, and peace in the world." According to the Buddhist Dalai Lama, "We are all basically the same humans beings. We have common human needs and concerns. . . . Human beings . . . have the right to pursue happiness and live in peace and freedom."[12] None of this means that all people or cultures have perceived, acknowledged, and given voice to the reality of human dignity. Nor does it mean that many who recognized and affirmed human dignity have been

8. Sancti Leonis Magni Romani Pontificis, *Tractatus Septem et Nonaginta, Sermo XXI, Sermo XXVII, Sermo XXVIII* (Turnhout, Belgium: Brepols, 1973).

9. Johannes Burgundio of Pisa, *De Natura Hominis* (1194; Leiden: Brill, 1975), 21.

10. Giannozzo Manetti, "On the Dignity of Man," in *Two Views of Man*, ed. Bernard Murchland (1452; New York: Frederick Ungar Publishing, 1966); Giovanni Pico della Mirandola, *Oration on the Dignity of Man*, trans. A. Robert Caponigri (Chicago: Regnery Publishing, 1956); Pierre Boaistuaua, *Bref discours de l'excellence et dignité de l'homme*, ed. Michel Simonin (Geneva: Droz, 1982).

11. Immanuel Kant, *Grounding for the Metaphysics of Morals*, trans. *James W. Ellington* (1785; Indianapolis: Hackett, 1993), 36.

12. Dalai Lama, "Human Rights and Universal Responsibility," talk given at the "United Nations World Conference on Human Rights," Vienna, Austria, June 15, 1993. Any number of quotes by Martin Luther King Jr. affirming dignity could also be produced here.

consistent in working out and acting on its implications. The point is that many different observers from various backgrounds have noted the native dignity of human persons that personalism also seeks to highlight and preserve.[13]

The reason why such a wide range of thinkers from such varied social contexts and operating out of such different traditions would converge on a similar view of human dignity, personalism suggests, is because they have articulated an objectively real, though intangible, feature of persons that rational, reflexive minds can recognize. And the reason why other thinkers in other traditions—including Nietzsche, Skinner, Foucault, and Singer—have been able to conclude, in disagreement, against the dignity of persons is, ironically, because they as persons possessed the properties of personhood that, personalism theorizes, entails dignity—including reflexivity, rationality, self-causality, creativity, and freedom—and have misguidedly used those capacities to think themselves into corners that involve the denial of an aspect of reality that is integral to a larger mode of personal being on which they were fully dependent to come to their argued denials of the same.[14] Had their conclusions been right, they probably could not have come to them in the first place, nor would they have been internally consistent in seeking to advance them as important truths that other people should embrace. If Skinner were correct about the illusions of freedom and dignity in behavioristic human life,[15] for instance, he had no good reason to conduct the kind of research and publish the kind of scholarship he did, which presupposed the dignity and freedom of its audience in deploying reasoned arguments with evidence to persuade it. Stated differently, reasoned cases against human dignity are arguably self-undermining insofar as, if they are valid, nobody is obliged to pay their

13. See Robert Kraynak, "Human Dignity and the Mystery of the Human Soul," in *Human Dignity and Bioethics* (Washington, DC: President's Council on Bioethics, 2008), 61–82.

14. Recent ethicists who seriously question the reality of human dignity include Ruth Macklin, "Dignity Is a Useless Concept," *British Medical Journal* 327 (2003): 1419–20; Dieter Birnbacher, "Human Cloning and Human Dignity," *Reproductive BioMedicine Online* 10, Suppl. 1 (March 2005): 50–55; and Peter Singer, *Rethinking Life and Death: The Collapse of Our Traditional Ethics* (New York: St. Martin's Griffin, 1996).

15. "The hypothesis that man is not free is essential to the application of the scientific method to the study of human behavior. The free inner man who is held responsible for the behavior of the external biological organism is only a pre-scientific substitute for the kind of causes which are discovered in the course of a scientific analysis." B. F. Skinner, *Science and Human Behavior* (New York: Macmillan, 1953), 447.

proponents the respect of listening to and answering them—if we humans truly lack an innate dignity as persons, we are free to disregard any others at will with whom we do not wish to engage, without having to offer, even in principle, any account justifying our indifferent and dismissive treatment of them. Without dignity, common truth and accountability get lost to the overriding concerns of individual desire and preference. There are reasons why chimpanzees do not try to convince each other that their members of their species do not possess personal dignity. One is because they do not possess it, at least as humans do. They are not persons and so by nature are not concerned with such matters.[16] What is more mysterious is why certain persons are devoted to persuading other people that human persons lack dignity and freedom.

Because human dignity is objectively real, it does not require that people recognize it in order to exist. Someone's denial of personal dignity does not alter its reality. A government's violation of human dignity does not mean that no dignity existed to be violated. The dignity of persons is reality. Even so, although cognitive belief in dignity is not dignity's ground of existence, in the phenomenological experience of most normal human people, dignity is nevertheless validated.[17] I, for instance, experience myself—even in my most self-disesteeming moments—as embodying a dignity I cannot deny or renounce. Indeed, it is only against that personal dignity that disesteem can gain any meaningful traction in the first place. I wager that the phenomenological experience of most readers is similar. Human dignity exists objectively and cannot be reduced to something else with a property or quality that does not have to do with dignity.

Because human dignity is part of the fabric of reality, it does not require embracing one particular philosophy or ideology or theology to under-

16. This does not mean that chimpanzees are not valuable, important, and deserving of kind treatment; they simply are not persons. Although I do not have the space or mandate to develop it here, I believe that, in the long run, personalism will lead to much more caring treatment of animals than alternative worldviews generated by naturalism, positivism, or utilitarianism.

17. It is legitimate and important to distinguish the normal from the not normal in such analyses. Cases of severe abuse and neglect have left some humans in such a state of negative self-regard that they may not be able properly to discern their own inherent dignity. But those are anomalous cases that should not be allowed to determine for most of us what we know phenomenologically about human dignity. What those cases do tell us is that the brokenness of human personhood is capable of pathological destruction of the normal. In any case, the distinguishing between normal and abnormal mental states is itself a human universal—see Donald Brown, *Human Universals* (New York: McGraw-Hill, 1991), 135.

stand. Dignity inheres in the nature of things and can be phenomeno-logically evident to beings possessing dignity. For this reason, there are atheistic, pantheistic, and theistic accounts as well as Muslim, Jewish, Con-fucian, Buddhist, Hindu, and Christian accounts of human dignity.[18] What is real gets recognized and expressed in different ways through a variety of traditions. Different particular theorists, personalist or otherwise, also emphasize different aspects of personhood as the basis for human dignity. Some emphasize the human capacity for reason.[19] Others point to the hu-man ability to act as the cause of their own actions.[20] Others emphasize the capacity to act morally.[21] Yet others stress the incommunicability of each person, to choose our ends, or to think systematically.[22] Still others

18. Paul Weithman, "Two Arguments from Human Dignity," in *Human Dignity and Bio-ethics* (Washington, DC: President's Council on Bioethics, 2008), 435–67; Mohammad Hashim Kamali, *The Dignity of Man: An Islamic Perspective* (Cambridge: Islamic Texts Society, 2002); Göran Collste, "Islam on the Sanctity of Human Life," in *Is Human Life Special?* (New York: Peter Lang, 2002), chap. 7; Doron Shultziner, "A Jewish Conception of Human Dignity," *Jour-nal of Religious Ethics* 34, no. 4 (2007): 663–83; Qianfan Zhang, "The Idea of Dignity in Clas-sical Chinese Philosophy: A Reconstruction of Confucianism," *Journal of Chinese Philosophy* 27, no. 3 (2000): 299–330; Perry Schmidt-Leukel, "Buddhism and the Idea of Human Rights," *Buddhist-Christian Studies* 26 (2006): 33–49; Arvind Sharma, *Hinduism and Human Rights* (Oxford: Oxford University Press, 2004); R. Kendall Soulen and Linda Woodhead, *God and Human Dignity* (Grand Rapids, MI: Eerdmans, 2006); James Dalton, "Human Dignity, Hu-man Rights, and Ecology: Christian, Buddhist, and Native American Perspectives," in *Made in God's Image: The Catholic Vision of Human Dignity*, ed. Regis Duffy and Angelus Gamba-tese (New York: Paulist Press, 1999); Carlyle Marney, *The Recovery of the Person* (Nashville: Abingdon, 1979); John Carman, "The Dignity and Indignity of Service: The Role of the Self in Hindu Bhakti," in *Selves, People, and Persons: What Does It Mean to Be a Self?* ed. Leroy Rouner, Boston University Studies in Philosophy and Religion (Notre Dame, IN: University of Notre Dame Press, 1992), 107–22; Henri de Lubac, *Catholicism: Christ and the Common Dignity of Man* (San Francisco: Ignatius Press, 1988).

19. For instance, Borden Parker Bowne, *Principles of Ethics* (New York: Harper and Brothers, 1892); Bowne, *Personalism* (Boston: Houghton Mifflin, 1908). Also see Henry Veatch, *Rational Man* (Indianapolis: Imagi, 1962); Patrick Lee and Robert P. George, "The Nature and Basis of Human Dignity," in *Human Dignity and Bioethics* (Washington, DC: President's Council on Bioethics, 2008), 409–33.

20. For example, Karol Wojtyla, *Person and Community* (New York: Peter Lang, 1993).

21. Susan Shell, "Kant's Concept of Human Dignity as a Resource for Bioethics," in *Human Dignity and Bioethics* (Washington, DC: President's Council on Bioethics, 2008), 333–49.

22. John Crosby, "A Neglected Source of the Dignity of Persons," in *Personalist Papers* (Washington, DC: Catholic University of America Press, 2003), 3–32; Christine Korsgaard, *Creating the Kingdom of Ends* (Cambridge: Cambridge University Press, 1996); Allen Wood, *Kant's Ethical Thought* (Cambridge: Cambridge University Press, 1999).

of a more theological bent stress dignity conferred on humanity by God in creating people in his own divine image and, for some, because of the incarnation of Christ.[23] It is not necessary for present purposes to choose among these accounts. The crucial point for the moment is that dignity is an objectively real characteristic of human personhood that people can recognize and theorize from a variety of perspectives.

Again, proponents of a positivist, empiricist science of the human fail to see this, because their unnecessarily parochial presuppositions blind them to some of the fullness of reality operative in human life. Here again, it is helpful to return to Charles Taylor's larger argument about granting explanatory legitimacy to the terms that we must employ within our overall best account in order to live our lives. When it comes to dignity, Taylor observes:

> Proponents of reductive theory may congratulate themselves on explanations which do without these or those terms current in ordinary life, e.g., "freedom" and "dignity." . . . But even if their third-person explanations were more plausible than they are, what would be the significance of this if the terms prove ineradicable in first-person, non-explanatory uses? Suppose I can convince myself that I can explain people's behaviors as an observer without using a term like "dignity." What does this prove if I can't do without it as a term in my deliberations about what to do, how to behave, how to treat people, my questions about whom I admire, with whom I feel affinity, and the like?[24]

The burden is on personalists attempting to engage social science to cash out how dignity matters for understanding and explaining human social existence in social science terms and how that matters for human life. I believe that can be done, for moral as well as theoretical reasons. What is it that most powerfully justifies moral commitments to things such as human rights, freedom of speech, the abolition of slavery, religious liberty, universal education, due process, racial nondiscrimination, the prohibition of torture and genocide, outrage against rape, the freedom of conscience, protections against starvation, and care for refugees? Not a utilitarian cal-

23. For example, Deotis Roberts, *A Philosophical Introduction to Theology* (Philadelphia: Trinity Press International, 1991), 162–64; Roberts, "Black Consciousness in Theological Perspective," in *Quest for a Black Theology*, ed. James Gardiner and J. Deotis Roberts Sr. (Philadelphia: Pilgrim Press, 1971); Regis Duffy and Angelus Gambatese, eds., *Made in God's Image: The Catholic Vision of Human Dignity* (New York: Paulist Press, 1999).

24. Charles Taylor, *Sources of the Self* (Cambridge, MA: Harvard University Press, 1989), 57.

culation. Not a social contract. Not the interests of the wealthy and power-ful. Not the findings of naturalistic, positivistic, empiricist social science. What justifies these moral commitments is the recognition of the natural dignity of persons, which is ontologically real, analytically irreducible, and phenomenologically apparent. In naming the real about humans in this way we continue to pull back together fact and value, the *is* and the *ought*. What flows from our sociological analysis stands a chance of making sense of many of our political commitments, and vice versa. And yet, because in all of this we are most highly committed to the truth about reality, what-ever that turns out to be, regardless of its consequences for our current desires and leanings, this need not degenerate into propaganda and ideo-logical manipulation operating under the cloak of science and academia. Critical realism's emphasis on truth seeking provides a firewall against the intellectual flames and meltdowns of individualistic subjectivism, relativism, and the politicization of scholarship.

In all of this, we must acknowledge that not all people or cultures or philosophies have recognized or understood the fact of human dignity or often treated ordinary people with dignity. Quite the contrary. History is replete with failures to understand, affirm, and respect human dignity. Treating humans as possessing the dignity that is rightfully theirs by virtue of the ontology of personhood may be the exception, not the rule in hu-man history. Does this disprove the personalist belief in human dignity? How can we affirm real, objective, universal human dignity in the face of such massive misrecognition and violation of it? Does this not suggest that the idea of human dignity is actually a recent cultural invention of dubious ontology and relative value? No, I think not. Nothing whatsoever in a realist theory requires that people recognize and understand some-thing in order for it truly to exist. Bacteria and germs existed and wreaked havoc on human bodies for most of history without anyone realizing they were real—it was not until the nineteenth century that the germ theory of disease became widely known and accepted. The objectively real moral fact that slavery is a categorical evil was likewise not widely appreciated throughout most of human history, yet in the United States people's com-mon erroneous moral understanding of slavery until the nineteenth cen-tury did not mean that slavery was not evil. It *was* evil—whether or not anyone realized it. Human dignity does not become real "for us" simply because we start believing in it, any more than our heliocentric solar sys-tem became real when people started believing in it. It always was true. What needed to happen was simply for people to conform their hitherto mistaken minds to what was already true about the real. This was the case with Copernican astronomy. This is the case with human dignity. As noted in chapter 3, there are certain "institutional facts" that are real social things and made so precisely by people believing in them, through "social construction"—things like money, representative government, and sports.[25] But human dignity is not an institutional fact. Dignity is, in Searle's terms, a "brute fact" of ontological reality that is a characteristic and ineliminable property of emergent human personhood.[26] Dignity is rooted in the nature of things personal, not in ideas or discourse. So the fact that not all people or cultures or philosophies have recognized or understood or respected human dignity does not touch the question of its existence.

This nevertheless compels us to recognize the historically conditioned nature of humanity's awareness of its own dignity. The recognition of human dignity has not been a historical constant. Various people, cultures, and philosophies have at different times throughout history explicitly articulated the reality of personal dignity.[27] But the clear understanding of the inalienable, universal nature of human personal dignity that emerged in the twentieth century—especially in the wake of Nazi Germany and World War II—and that is now expressed in many national constitutions, the Charter of the United Nations, and the Universal Declaration of Human Rights, was the outcome of long historical developments shaped by a variety of different religious, ethical, philosophical, and cultural traditions unfolding over time. Like most of human knowledge about people and the world, knowledge of human dignity has also been historically dynamic and progressive. People today can say more about dignity that really is true than they used to be able to say—just like we can say more now about physics, medicine, ocean life, the brain, the moral status of child labor, and the origins of the cosmos than we could centuries ago. Personalist theory is entirely comfortable with this notion.[28] The twentieth century saw a rejection of widespread nineteenth-century ideas about evolutionary progress and the superiority of colonizer nations. This rejection might

25. John Searle, *The Construction of Social Reality* (New York: Free Press, 1997), 27–29.

26. Some philosophers may be more comfortable saying that dignity "supervenes" on human persons, that the relation of dignity to the features of personhood by virtue of which the dignity exists is one of "supervenience." Here, however, I intend to advance the stronger though perhaps more controversial claim, that dignity is a real emergent property of personhood.

27. See Peter Berger, "On the Obsolescence of the Concept of Honor," in *Revisions: Changing Perspective in Moral Philosophy*, ed. Stanley Hauerwas and Alasdair MacIntyre (Notre Dame, IN: University of Notre Dame Press, 1983), 172–81.

28. See, for example, Wojtyla, *Person and Community*, 209–17.

make us wary of the idea that we humans have learned more about our natural dignity and its moral and political implications as the centuries have unfolded. But nothing in the personalist understanding of our historically increasing self-understanding needs to involve any of the self-congratulatory, naively optimistic faith in progress or colonial superiority that was so characteristic of much of the West before World War I. On the one hand, personalism's recognition of the brokenness of persons and the world helps to avert this. On the other hand, to deny the idea of real human dignity on the grounds that people have not always explicitly recognized or affirmed dignity would be silly. For one thing, that would by implication deny the fact of the long-term history of the growth of scientific knowledge. It would also have the effect of endangering our current moral and political commitments to universal human dignity, opening up the door to a future in which dignity was no more important or protected institutionally than it was centuries and millennia ago.

We should not overstate the degree to which real, existent human dignity was ignored in times past and still is in the present. If personalism is correct, normal individual persons, whenever and wherever they lived, would have sensed phenomenologically, in certain primal ways at least, their own personal dignity. They might not have had a language with which to identify and express it. They might not have been embedded in social structures and cultural practices that honored and underscored dignity. But, even so, the Babylonian warrior, the Greek wife, the Mayan farmer, the medieval Chinese peasant, the precolonial African Serengeti child should have sensed internally that they were not mere things, but persons with an innate value and worth qualitatively distinct from inanimate objects and other animals. Anthropological accounts provide clues to the universality of human dignity. For example, studies of human universals—an idea that for what turn out to be flimsy intellectual reasons is now out of fashion in much of academia—show that humans at all times and everywhere, as far as we know, are concerned with modesty, feel shame, attend to etiquette, are able to feel pride in self, have shared standards of courtesy, feel responsible for their actions, understand that people have private inner lives, symbolically mourn their dead, use the same facial expressions to convey disgust and contempt, and engage in rituals of respect for one another.[29] These are marks of personal beings in

29. The best work on this issue is Brown, *Human Universals*, especially pages 134–35, 139 on these particular points. Also see, for instance, Clyde Kluckhohn, "Common Humanity and Diverse Cultures," in *The Human Meaning of the Social Sciences*, ed. Daniel Lerner (New

possession of their own dignity. Nonpersonal animals that do not share in human dignity do not feel compelled to cover their genitals and to copulate in private, for instance, or to honor their dead through ceremonial funeral rites of respect and mourning. But humans universally do. The dignity of persons gives these practices weight and meaning. Unique human emotions, too, clue us into the universality of dignity—the most obvious is indignation. Nonpersonal animals can get frightened, upset, angry, and headstrong. But only humans get genuinely indignant. Indignation is not frustration or rage. Indignation is a particular kind of feeling of anger, one that results from the perception of having one's dignity violated by injustice, disrespect, or meanness. The quality of indignant anger indicates the presence of a real personal dignity that has been violated. And it is not only modern, Western people who feel indignation. The experience of indignation is universal because human dignity is universal. Different cultures surely conceptualize and express human dignity and personhood somewhat differently,[30] but this does nothing to undermine the ontological facts of dignity and personhood.

In sum, human persons posses dignity—a quality of worth deserving respect that is ineliminable and irreducible, and that has consequences for the scientific understanding and the moral and political ordering of human personal and social life. This we need to take into account as we seek to understand the nature of human personhood.

The Problem of Dignity's Grounds

Where does dignity come from? Most philosophical discussions of dignity, as varied as they are, tend to take one of three general positions. The first is that human persons possess dignity by virtue of certain specifiable dignity-conferring capacities that they have, such as a rational nature or purpo-

York: Meridian, 1959), 245–84; Irwin Altman, "Privacy Regulation: Culturally Universal or Culturally Specific?" *Journal for Social Issues* 33, no. 3 (1977): 66–84; Robert Redfield, "Social Science among the Humanities," *Measure* 1 (1950): 60–74.

30. Richard Shweder and Joan Miller, "The Social Construction of the Person: How Is It Possible?" in *The Social Construction of the Person*, ed. Kenneth J. Gergen and Keith E. Davis (New York: Springer, 1985), 41–69; Michael Carrithers, *Why Humans Have Cultures: Explaining Anthropology and Social Diversity* (New York: Oxford University Press, 1992), 3–5; Eliot Deutsch, "The Comparative Study of the Self," in *Selves, People, and Persons*, ed. Rouner, 95–105.

sive agency. These we might call capacities-based accounts. The second approach focuses on the divine conferral of dignity on humans, arguing that dignity has its source in a human relationship with God or some human feature bestowed on humans by God, such as being created in God's image. We can call these theistic accounts.[31] The third position finds the first and second accounts unpersuasive and so abandons the notion of human dignity altogether. Let's be honest, this view says, we have no good reason for believing that humans possess the particular kind of dignity that previous theorists have imagined, so we should stop claiming such an unrealistic, self-important status for ourselves. For some, such a belief in dignity is merely an unwarranted assertion of "speciesism."[32] We should recognize that humans are animals among other animals and that what really matters is not some fictitious dignity but rather the physical well-being, pleasure, reduction of suffering of all sentient creatures. Having abandoned the search for the grounds of dignity, this approach changes the question to something else, such as the putatively unprejudiced making of utilitarian calculations of pleasure and pain across all sentient living creatures. This we might call the skeptical account.

This triad of positions in the debate has led to a stalemate, as far as I can see, since each account has its characteristic problems that prevent it from being able to overcome the challenges of the others. For example, the capacities-based position has difficulty explaining how any human should be thought of as possessing dignity, who permanently and perhaps even temporarily lacks the capacities, such as rationality or agency, believed to confer dignity. Certain humans in whom some theorists want to recognize dignity do not possess the specific capacities said to produce dignity. Consider, for instance, unborn and newborn babies, the seriously mentally deranged and disabled, advanced Alzheimer's disease patients, those in comas from which they have little chance of recovering, perhaps even sleeping people—by the logic of capacities-based accounts, these arguably lack dignity because they do not or cannot exercise the capacity or capacities said to confer dignity. The capacities thought to ground dignity are not coextensive with all members of the human race, at least at any given time. The difficulty becomes determining exactly to which humans

---

31. These first two positions need not be mutually exclusive. Both might be right and mutually affirming. But most accounts defending dignity do tend to gravitate to one or the other of these approaches.

32. Peter Singer, *Animal Liberation* (New York: Avon, 1990).

dignity can be ascribed and which not, or of which it must be recognized and which not.[33] Most theistic accounts want to recognize dignity in every human regardless of his or her ability to exercise capacities of rationality and free will—thus, even the Down syndrome preterm newborn and the senile nursing home patient possess dignity by virtue of, according to one version, God's love for them.[34] But human capacities-based accounts do not appeal to such a transcendent, inclusive justification of dignity, only to specific human capacities. The problem is how to recognize the dignity of specific humans who do not possess or cannot exercise those capacities. If dignity derives, say, from our human rationality or free will, are we prepared to conclude that humans incapable of exercising rationality and free will in various ways possess no dignity? It is difficult, given standard capacities-based accounts, to see how to avoid that conclusion. We may be morally obliged to respect and defend the dignity of rational people with

33. Leon Kass also writes about a different kind of threat to human dignity arising not from the limits of medicine but from the successes of biotechnology. This threat does not concern the "marginal" or "life and death" issues raising questions about what Kass calls "the basic dignity of human being." It rather involves challenges arising from the growing bio-technological potential to "improve," "enhance," and even "evolve beyond" ordinary *Homo sapiens* life through reproductive feature-selection, cloning, man-machine and man-animal hybrids, the manufacture or trafficking in human body parts, person-transforming chemical and pharmacological interventions, agency-ignoring behavior modification, performance-enhancing and performance-transforming drugs, and so on—which Kass says raises the distinct issue of "the full dignity of being human." Kass, "Defending Human Dignity," in *Human Dignity and Bioethics* (Washington, DC: President's Council on Bioethics, 2008), 297–331.

34. See, for instance, Nicholas Wolterstorff, *Justice: Rights and Wrongs* (Princeton, NJ: Princeton University Press, 2008); Michael Perry, *Toward a Theory of Human Rights* (Cambridge: Cambridge University Press, 2007); Perry, *The Idea of Human Rights* (New York: Oxford University Press, 1998), 11–41; Perry, "Morality and Normativity," unpublished paper; Emory University, n.d.; Christopher Eberle, "Basic Human Worth: Religious and Secular Perspectives," in *New Waves in the Philosophy of Religion*, ed. Eric Weilenberg and Yujin Nagasawa (New York: Palgrave, 2009); David Gelernter, "The Irreducibly Religious Character of Human Dignity," in *Human Dignity and Bioethics* (Washington, DC: President's Council on Bioethics, 2008), 387–405; Glenn Tinder, *The Political Meaning of Christianity* (Baton Rouge: Louisiana State University Press, 1989), esp. 19–52; Christian Smith, "Can Naturalism Sustain Universal Benevolence and Human Rights?" in *The Believing Primate: Scientific, Philosophical and Theological Perspectives on the Evolution of Religion*, ed. Jeffrey Schloss and Michael Murray (New York: Oxford University Press, 2008); and chapters by Robert Kraynak, David Walsh, and Kenneth Grasso in *In Defense of Human Dignity*, ed. Robert Kraynak and Glen Tinder (Notre Dame, IN: University of Notre Dame Press). Also see Marc Guerra, "The Affirmation of Genuine Human Dignity," *Journal of Markets and Morality* 4, no. 2 (2001): 295–301.

free will. But, it seems to many critics, there is no intellectually coherent reason, based on a capacities account, why we should treat the severely mentally impaired young adult, for instance, or the motorcycle accident patient "living" on artificial life support in a permanent vegetative state as having dignity, since they do not seem to possess and exercise that which confers dignity.[35] We might also be forced to think of other people who exist between the extreme states of fully operational capacities and radically impaired capacities as enjoying, in the words of ethicist James Walters, only "proximate personhood"—that is, accepting the idea that humans are only persons to the extent that their lived experience approaches the life of a normal, fully functioning adult in society.[36]

Furthermore, some critics observe, other kinds of people do not behave empirically in ways that suggest the presence of any real dignity in their

35. Patrick Lee and Robert George attempt—not entirely successfully, I think, because they do not incorporate the crucial idea of proactive emergence from capacities to personhood—to make the move from capacities to dignity even for the radically incapacitated of "marginal cases" through the idea of a human "substantial nature" that "entails the capacity" for rationality and so involves the "being of a certain kind of thing": "From the time [humans] come to be, they are developing themselves toward the mature stage at which they will . . . perform such acts [of conceptual thought]. Moreover, they are structured . . . in such a way that they are oriented toward maturing to this stage. So, every human being, including human infants and unborn human beings, has this basic natural capacity for conceptual thought. . . . The criterion for full moral worth is having a nature that entails the capacity (whether existing in root form or developed to the point at which it is immediately exercisable) for conceptual thought and free choice—not *the development* of that natural basic capacity to some degree or other. . . . The criterion for full moral worth and possession of basic rights is not *having* a capacity for conscious thought and choice, but *being* a certain kind of thing, that is, having a specific type of substantial nature." Lee and George, "The Nature and Basis of Human Dignity," 423–24, 429, italics in original.

36. "A developing individual's right to life increases as he or she approaches the threshold of indisputably personal life, the life of the normal adult in any society. . . . Likewise, the further beyond the threshold of incontestably personal life an adult individual is (such as a patient with advanced Alzheimer's disease), the less clear is that individual's moral status and claim to morally valuable and legally protectable life. . . . The proximate personhood approach offers three pivotal criteria for making decisions: (1) the *potential for* gaining or regaining personal being, (2) the *development toward* becoming a personal being or development beyond such being, and (3) the *bonding of* an individual and significant others or society at large. These criteria are, respectively, intellectual, physical, and social." James Walters, *What Is a Person? An Ethical Exploration* (Urbana: University of Illinois Press, 1997), 63, italics in original. Walters suggests, however, that once an individual human rises above the "threshold of personhood," they become as much a person with moral rights "as the president of the United States" (63).

lives. Examples of the latter include humans we think of as totally morally degenerate, who seem consistently to employ their reason and free will to achieve ends that are debased, destructive, despicable, and abhorrent. Can we ascribe and protect dignity for the Idi Amins and Jeffrey Dahmers of the world? Further, can we honor dignity in some ordinary people who lead thoughtless, conformist, apathetic existences, buying what they are told by others to buy, stuffing themselves on what they are told to eat, passively watching the insipid television shows playing in their faces? Are these really creatures who because of certain capacities possess immeasurable value and inviolable worth that other people and societies are morally and unconditionally obliged to protect and defend? The purpose and value of a theory of universal human dignity is to protect dignity not especially among those in whom it seems obvious but those in whom it is most vulnerable and expendable. Can an account based on mere empirical human capacities, of which there is immense variability and sometimes complete lack and breakdown, really sustain a strong commitment to universal human dignity? Many critics doubt it. I doubt it.

Yet many thinkers concerned with dignity do not believe in a dignity-conferring God and find the theistic account no more compelling than one that would appeal to unicorns or leprechauns. This is part of the reason why some capacities-based theorists seek to locate the source of dignity in some feature of humanity, because they do not believe in God or because they do but nevertheless want an account that is not dependent on belief in God in order that it might be universally compelling to all humans, including nontheists.[37] If dignity depends upon God, the concern runs, and if many people were to come not to believe in God, then dignity would be jeopardized.[38] The theistic case, they say, even if perhaps intellectually in-

37. See, for example, Alan Dershowitz, *Rights from Wrongs: A Secular Theory of the Origins of Rights* (New York: Basic Books, 2005); Ronald Dworkin, "Life Is Sacred: That's the Easy Part," *New York Times Magazine,* May 16, 1993, 36; Alan Gewirth, *Human Rights: Essays on Justification and Applications* (Chicago: University of Chicago Press, 1982); Immanuel Kant, *Groundwork for the Metaphysics of Morals* (Cambridge: Cambridge University Press, 1998). Also see Collste, *Is Human Life Special?*

38. For example, Martha Nussbaum writes: "I think we ought to seek political principles that have a moral content but that avoid contentious metaphysical notions (for example, the notion of the soul) that make them incompatible with some of the many reasonable comprehensive doctrines that some citizens hold. To make a dignity-based approach appropriate to the basis for political principles in a pluralistic democratic society . . . we must first work to develop it in a non-metaphysical way, articulating the relevant idea of dignity in a way that shows the ethical core of that idea but that does not insist on linking it to involved metaphysical or

ternally coherent, given its premises, is practically risky. All it would take is enough nontheists around and the recognized basis of dignity goes down the drain. Furthermore, some nontheists view the theistic account of dignity as not intellectually defensible, as having no epistemic merit. Theism, for such, is incredible and cannot serve as the basis for human dignity.

As to skepticism about dignity, both capacities-based and theistic accounts reject it. If dignity exists, as both views believe, the simple fact that attempts to explain it run into difficulties does nothing to make dignity not exist. Difficulties in *explaining* real facts do not turn those facts into illusions. They mean we need to continue to work harder to better explain the facts. The skeptical account is a resort to a kind of intellectual "nuclear option" to which many—myself included—do not wish to give quarter. That is not because we do not like it as a view. It is because, as a misdescription of reality, it is wrong. What is needed in response is continued work to provide a better transitive theoretical account of the intransitive reality of human dignity.

As it stands, however, none of the three accounts seems able in the end to emerge from this debate with a case compelling enough to win over adherents of the other accounts. So the dignity discussion remains stuck and the intellectual condition of its defense unstable. That does little to lend the weight of reason to the practical defense of human dignity in real cultural, social, and political life. What, then, can and ought we to make of these disagreements and difficulties? For starters, critical realist personalism clearly rejects the skeptical viewpoint, as I have indicated. Human dignity is real and consequential. If this is "speciesism," then so be it. I plead guilty, along with other personalists and defenders of human dignity, without apology. But that position does not resolve the apparent difficulties with the capacities-based and theistic accounts of dignity. What of them?

I do not propose to resolve the matter in this chapter by developing a fully worked out theory of dignity. I am not capable of doing so here. But I do hope to contribute a set of what I hope are insights that might help to move the discussion forward toward a more satisfactory resolution. My position is that capacities-based accounts are vulnerable to the kind of critiques noted above and so need to be modified to protect the dignity of

psychological doctrines concerning which the major religions and secular conceptions differ." Nussbaum, "Human Dignity and Political Entitlements," in *Human Dignity and Bioethics* (Washington, DC: President's Council on Bioethics, 2008), 361.

humans who lack the capacities believed to confer dignity. I think critical
realist personalism helps us there. As to theistic accounts, I find some of
them persuasive. But I also hope for a coherent account of dignity that
does not depend exclusively on theistic beliefs. My own reasons for believing in dignity are at rock bottom theistic. But the defense of human dignity
today and in the future will require more than only believers in God to
support the cause. I am interested in a defensible account of dignity that
bridges across as many people of good will as possible, one that includes
as many discussion partners as it is able who believe in and want to protect
human dignity.[39] I think that if a good theistic account of human dignity
is valid, we should expect the truth it explains on the human side of the
divine-human relationship to show up and be discernible in lived human
life. Human dignity, even *if* its ultimate source is in God, should disclose
itself in various this-worldly experiences, signs, and evidences that even
people who cannot believe in God may observe and about which they
might rationally theorize.[40] My intention is to offer a few hopefully useful
ideas and arguments to contribute to these larger, shared, bridge-building
observations, discernments, and reflections toward the articulation of a
more adequate account of the grounds of human dignity than we have today. Coming to a more adequate account of dignity will require a process
of ongoing deliberation over time, involving thinkers who do not now entirely agree. We may not achieve a better account today or tomorrow, but
hopefully we will in due time. Intellectual breakthroughs like that typically happen not when people hammer away harder at the same questions
within the same terms of the debate, but instead when they ask different
and more helpful questions, reframe the terms of the debate, and shift presuppositions and perspectives to see the problems in somewhat different
lights. I believe doing that will be necessary to advance our thinking about
human dignity. My purpose in what follows is to contribute to revising the
questions, reframing the terms, and altering the perspectives regarding
dignity by suggesting what I hope will be helpful ideas and perspectives on

39. This readiness to affirm the reality of dignity and rights, even while lacking consensus
about their bases, was the strategic agreement behind the success of the 1948 Universal Declaration of Human Rights. It may be intellectually unsatisfying to live with the incoherence,
but it is preferable to putting the affirmation of dignity and rights on hold until theoretical
consensus about their justification is reached.

40. One possible account from a religious perspective of how this might work is John
Macquarrie, "Rethinking Natural Law," in *Three Issues in Ethics* (New York: Harper and
Row, 1970), 82–110.

the matter. Again, this chapter will not settle the debate about dignity and tie up all of the intellectual loose ends. It does not even offer a fully packaged proposal that addresses all of the intellectual challenges involved. What follows simply asks to be put on the table as considerations worth contemplating in our efforts to better understand and explain the reality of human dignity and toward the end of better honoring it in practice.

The Dignity of Emergent Personhood

Dignity, I suggest, is an emergent property of human personhood, not a quality of one or more of the specific capacities out of which personhood emerges. Capacities-based accounts locate dignity's ground in specific human characteristics, such as rationality or purposive agency, and in this I think are looking in the right general direction. But, from the perspective of critical realist personalism, capacities-based accounts do not take adequately seriously the stratified nature of reality and the fact of emergence. The wetness of water is an irreducible, emergent property of an emergently entity (H_2O) existing at one level as a result of the interactions of other entities (H and O) existing at a lower level. Wetness is not a property of H or O but of H_2O. Analogously, dignity is not a property of any one specific human capacity operating at a lower level of human being (rationality, choice, agency, etc.) but is an emergent property of the proactively[41] emergent reality of personhood that has being at a higher level than the lower level capacities from which it emerged. Humans have dignity as a natural, brute fact because they are persons, not simply because they are rational or act according to purposes. Furthermore and importantly, for reasons and by ways I attempt to explain below, the reality of proactively emergent personhood can survive the nascence, dormancy, or impairment of various specific capacities from which it ordinarily emerges (in a way that water, in this simple analogy, can*not* "survive" the absence of H and O). In pondering the grounds for the recognition and defense of the dignity of human beings, then, the correct question is not whether we can empirically observe people exercising reasoned decisions, agency toward a goal, self-awareness, or some other specific capacity. The question is whether the human lives under consideration are persons. If they are persons, they possess dignity—because dignity is an emergent and

---

41. For the distinction between proactive and responsive emergence, see pp. 86–88.

ineliminable property of personhood—regardless of their exercise or not of certain empirically observable capacities at any given point in time.

Earlier in this book, I developed a three-level system of human being.[42] At the "bottom" level are human bodies—organic, material entities of a particular configuration and being. Human bodies then give rise through specific relations and interactions of their parts through emergence to a "middle" level of specific human causal capacities. I elaborated a list of numerous specific capacities, including the capacities for mental representation, language use, abstract reasoning, creativity, reflexivity, being the efficient cause of one's own action, and so forth. But my account of personhood did not stop at this "middle" level. Instead, human personhood, I observed, exists in reality at a next higher level up. Personhood is the emergent fact at the "top" level of human being, proactively emerging out of the complex interaction of the causal capacities operative at the level below it. Through the interaction of capacities, the new, ontologically distinct, higher order, emergent reality of the human person exists. Being "centers of" is a crucial element of personhood. Persons therefore are not the sum total collection of human capacities but distinct and higher ontological realities proactively emergent from capacities irreducible to them. Through the generativity of emergence, new properties, capacities, and qualities come to exist that are characteristic of the higher emergent entity but not of the lower level components out of which it emerges. Dignity, I am claiming here, is one of them. We need not make any claims about dignity residing in or deriving directly from middle level human capacities—such as rational agency or free will—in order to ground the reality of human dignity. That is because dignity is an attribute of personhood, and personhood exists as a different reality at a different level from the specific capacities out of which it emerges.

Exactly how and why this might be so—that is, how the new fact of personal dignity comes into being emergently out of lower-level entities not possessing dignity—is a mystery, admittedly. But it is no more mysterious than the wetness of water emerging from interacting hydrogen and oxygen atoms that possess no wetness; or amazing, living human bodies emerge out of the interactive combination of twenty-seven different chemical elements such as carbon, nitrogen, and sulfur. These things occur in various

---

42. As a clarifying reminder, these levels are neither spatially nor temporally separated, but are rather ontologically distinct stratifications of reality existing coherently and concurrently in identical space-time locations.

ways by virtue of the way our reality so happens to work. We sometimes understand the mechanisms giving rise to certain emergent qualia, but often we do not. In any case, to attempt to deny or refute emergence and its consequences is simply to beat our heads against the wall of reality. Relocating dignity in the higher-level, more comprehensive fact of personal being rather than particular, lower-level human capacities will, I believe, produce a phenomenologically more plausible account of dignity than a capacities-based view—insofar as it does not have to explain exactly what it is about the specific ability to reason or make free choices or act with agency that itself bestows agency on people. Dignity is a natural, irreducible, brute-fact property of personhood, not the result of the exercising of some capacity or other.[43]

Understood in this light, the misstep made by capacities-based accounts of dignity is in trying to locate the basis for dignity at the "middle" level of human being, the level of distinct capacities. This or that specific capacity, they suggest, legitimates or confers dignity on people. But the full weight of dignity cannot be hung on the single pegs of capacities for rationality or free will. And the level of individual capacities is the wrong stratum of reality at which to explain dignity. No one or even handful of capacities gives humans the possession of dignity. It is at the proactively emergent reality of personhood existent at a higher level of human being where the dignity that characterizes human life is to be found. Dignity is an ontologically real, emergent attribute of human persons, not a feature of one or more of the lower-level capacities out of which personhood emerges. For this reason, when critics question the intellectual soundness of trying to derive dignity from specific empirical human capacities, they are not mistaken. Capacities accounts have hitched their dignity wagons to the wrong and insufficient level of reality. The correct level of reality we need to apprehend is not the middle level of capacities but the higher level of personhood.

---

43. Unpersuaded readers with an inclination toward a capacities-based account may claim that I have not explained why and how personhood entails the property of dignity, but only offered assertions and metaphors. I reply that neither have capacities-based theorists explained why and how rational agency or free will explains dignity. My personalist account here has not stopped at a more superficial level of explanation than Kant or anyone else. We all at such a point simply hit the bedrock of our premises and logic of explanation at which place, as Wittgenstein said, our "spade is turned" (Ludwig Wittgenstein, *Philosophical Investigations*, Sec. 217 [1953; Upper Saddle River, NJ: Prentice Hall, 1958], 85).

What has this proposed theoretical move, shifting the basis of dignity from capacities to personhood, accomplished? First, it has eliminated the need to identify which specific human capacity or capacities endow people with dignity. We need not decide whether it is agency, free will, rationality, self-reflexivity, or something else that bestows dignity. Focusing on those items pitches our gaze at the wrong level. We need to look instead at personhood at a higher level to understand the real grounds of our human dignity. Second, this approach also eliminates the need to have to explain what it is about rationality or agency or some other capacity that bestows dignity on those who exercise it. I, for one, confess that it is not rationally or phenomenologically clear to me how or why it is that exercising reason, for instance, makes me or anyone else a creature endowed with immeasurable dignity. Where in or what about rationality does dignity reside or derive from? I can believe that certain nonhuman animals possess primitive capacities to reason, yet I am not persuaded that they possess dignity. Then again, I have spent significant time with preemie and infant humans in hospital neonatal and pediatric intensive care units (NICU and PICU) who, because of their developmental state and paralyzing and sedating medications, exercised no powers of consciousness, much less reason—and, if they did not develop into health, never would exercise powers of reason—yet who, it was clear to me, possessed a dignity and value of immeasurable worth. What is more understandable to me and, I suspect, most people reflecting in depth on their own phenomenological experience, is the idea that persons, by virtue of their having *centers* in personhood—and not specific capacities giving rise to personhood—possess an irreducible dignity that they and other persons must respect. Third, as hinted at by my anecdote about hospital NICU and PICU infants, this account of dignity creates the possibility of successfully addressing the challenge of including in the community of those possessing dignity those humans who do not have or exercise certain capacities believed by capacities-based accounts to grant someone dignity.

One may not understand how dignity could characterize the emergent reality of personhood. But then again we do not understand how wetness characterizes the emergent reality of water. And we have no good reason to hold double standards of acceptance because we are more obviously familiar with certain kinds of emergent ontologies (the wetness of water) than others (the dignity of persons), about which we might be tempted to be more skeptical. Life, including science as one dimension of life, has its mysteries. In this case, however, the readiness to live with a partial mystery involved in emergence may open up the door to a much greater explanation and understanding of what have heretofore been perplexing. It will also not do to insist that somebody show us dignity emerging from the capacities that give rise to personhood before we are willing to believe it. Again, such an insistence betrays a naive faith in positivist empiricism. That faith will make it difficult for anyone to understand more generally what is most real and important about human persons. It will make it impossible to understand anything about human dignity that has any connection to our scientific understanding of reality. Again, we need to discard positivist empiricism (as well as postmodern constructivism) and embrace instead, as a general framework of knowledge, the critical realism, personalism, and phenomenological epistemology I presented in chapter 2 and the understanding that flows from them.

Ontological Dignity versus Variable Realization

What I have not yet explained, however, is how the dignity of personhood exists in emergent being through the interaction of lower-level capacities that, in situations of less than fully normal humans, are undeveloped, damaged, or deteriorating. The wetness of water relies on the existence and interaction of hydrogen and oxygen to produce water characterized by wetness. Remove either the hydrogen or oxygen, and water and its wetness are gone. Does the removal or impairment of any of the human capacities noted in chapter 1 mean that personhood is undercut or non-emergent, bringing us back around to the problem of capacities-based accounts of dignity? I think the answer is no, for several reasons. First, the fact that personhood is *proactively* emergent, not responsively emergent, means that personhood adheres in each human from the start with everything needed to develop and unfold itself—in nourishing environments, of course—through natural processes of becoming. Persons do not emerge out of capacities and bodies at some chronologically delayed time, only after some crucial development has taken place. Persons exist at the start of life and are their *own* agents of development and emergent being across their entire life course. Various forms of underdevelopment, injuries, and degeneration may and sometimes do impede a mature expression of the development of normal personhood—but those do not eradicate or compromise the being of personhood. Second, my account never specified an exact model stipulating the precise number of capacities that must interact in specific combinations and ways to give rise to personhood. As I have repeated, the general model developed in the first chapter described very robust personhood possessing a well-rounded array of capacities. But not every human person emerges into being with every capacity functioning at full capacity, every capacity "piston" firing in a complete system. Different persons—even normal persons—are often stronger and weaker in certain of the functioning capacities out of which their personhood emerges. Some persons significantly lack the functioning of some capacities. But they are still persons. From a personalist perspective, especially given the proactive nature of personal emergence, although Helen Keller, for example, lacked certain basic perceptual and communicative capacities, she still was a person—her personhood existed emergently from the capacities she did possess. As she was able to learn alternative means of language use, she was able to more fully develop the telos or expression of her personhood. But she did not become "more" of a person.

Personhood as a particular form of existent being is not a variable commodity—like the number of cereal boxes in the pantry—of which one can have more or less. Personhood is a matter of ontological being that either exists or does not exist. However, once personhood *does* exist, the extent to which its fullness is realized *is* a variable fact of development, health, maturity, enhancement, and progress. The teleological morality of the previous chapter is entirely dependent on this fact. The potential states of the existence of personhood, in other words, are either 0 or 1—either personhood has being in any instance or it does not exist. There are no varying degrees or partial states of the being of personhood. However, once personhood *is*, once it exists, its development or realizations may, and always does, reflect varying states of difference. Persons—who if they exist at all, do so at 100 percent of their being—may in their variable development or realization of potential ends be nascent, infantile, immature, promising, budding, growing, progressing, advancing, maturing, improving, burgeoning, thriving, or flourishing. In their development as persons they may also be undeveloped, impaired, retarded, wounded, stunted, distracted, damaged, declining, or deteriorating. But no matter what the developmental state the realization or fulfillment of one's personhood and its proper ends may be, the personhood itself as a matter of being is fully existent until and at which time it is ended.[44] And insofar as dignity is a property of person-

44. Other scholars who insist on this distinction between what I am calling *being* and *actualization* include Holmes Rolston III, "Human Uniqueness and Human Dignity: Persons in Nature and the Nature of Persons," in *Human Dignity and Bioethics* (Washington, DC:

hood generally, and not of certain capacities specifically, humans possess dignity for at least as long as they are persons—regardless of the variable state of their realization of the ends of or the exercise of the expressions of their personhood. This is the reason why persons who are very deeply asleep, thoroughly drunk, or under the full sedation of anesthesia still possess the same fullness of dignity as those who are fully awake, functioning, subjectively aware, and socially engaged. They are still fully persons. The functioning of most of their expressive capacities of personhood is temporarily suspended or dramatically impaired. Yet the ontological being of their proactively emergent personhood remains fully real, existent, and actual. And so we rightly protect the dignity of persons who are asleep, stone drunk, or anesthetized, even though in such conditions they hardly look or act empirically like functioning persons.

Two analogies may help to illustrate the larger point. The first is drawn directly from the critical realist theory of causal powers. Empiricism, which critical realism opposes, can only recognize causality when it is manifest in the empirical making of events that happen in the world. Causation is thus equated with its operation to produce observable outcomes. For the empiricist, the idea of a cause that makes nothing happen is ludicrous. For a critical realist, however, causes are not fundamentally about making events happen but most essentially about the natural powers or capacities that various entities possess. Recall that critical realism distinguishes among the real, the actual, and the empirical. Causes are the function of natural powers of elements in the real sometimes performing through various mechanisms what they by nature are able, sometimes producing outcomes and sometimes not. Observable events are not produced until the causal powers of entities are initiated, engaged, or triggered—even though the same causal powers always exist as an innate aspect of the entity. Causal being is distinguished in this way from causal realization. So, for example, human eggs and sperm have the joint causal powers to create zygotes, embryos, fetuses, babies, and so on when they are joined together to form a new entity, but their existent causal powers often go unrealized because they are not joined together.[45] The causal power exists in being,

---

President's Council on Bioethics, 2008), 147; Kass, "Defending Human Dignity," 326; Lee and George, "The Nature and Basis of Human Dignity," 409–33.

45. The activated egg has a certain limited momentum of development, due to its huge supply of preset biochemical stores, but without the penetrating sperm the egg will die around the blastocyst stage at the fourth or fifth day—the egg thus has a certain potential, but it is a passive, verses an active, potential. A human zygote is not merely an activated egg, but a

whether it is ever acted upon, initiated, or manifest in observable reality. Similarly, normal five-year-old girls have the natural, indwelling power to bear children even though that real power has not yet been activated through the hormonal triggers of puberty and realized through intercourse and conception—we do not call normal five-year-old girls "infertile," because it is not true that they do not have powers of fertility; rather, they have such powers even though they are for a time unrealized. Likewise, to shift subjects, superior military units normally possess the causal powers to destroy enemies. Whether or not that existent causal ability is ever realized by triggering conditions so that the destructive causal power is empirically manifest is a different question. A superior military unit can sit undeployed for its entire existence, its causal force unrealized. Yet that does not mean a causal reality does not exist. It does, but in an unrealized state of being. Thus, causality is real by virtue of existent being, is sometimes actual by virtue of being realized, and when actual is sometimes empirical by virtue of being observed. By analogy, by differentiating the being from the realization of the personhood of persons—and locating human dignity in existent personhood instead of in exercised capacities—we can establish the grounds of dignity as existing in all persons as beings, regardless of how fully or not that personhood is developed and realized, much less empirically observed.

A second analogy, to shift back to fertility images, concerns a pregnant woman and the developmental state of her unborn child. Whether or not a woman is pregnant is famously not a matter of degrees. She either is or she is not. It is a 0/1 reality when it comes to the living progeny within her uterus. However, if and when a woman is pregnant, the development and realization of the offspring within her is not a 0/1 fact but one of varying degrees—of developmental variation in age, complexity, size, weight, organic functioning, and physiological normalcy. If the natural end of the unborn in its condition is to grow and be born, any given case of the offspring in a pregnancy stands in some varying position between its starting point and its proper end. Moreover, while most pregnancies involve developmentally normal offspring physiologically, in some cases the brokenness of the world is manifest in abnormal and malformed offspring. Things go wrong. The fetus does not develop as it should. The unborn offspring in one way or another does not realize its natural, proper end. Analogously,

new substance established by the joining of distinct and essential components. Thanks to Bill Hurlbut for his expertise on this example.

human persons as a matter of their being (like being pregnant) either are persons or are not; personal existence is not a matter of degrees but of belonging to the real or not real in any given case. However, the actual and empirical *realization* or *development* of the personhood of persons in relation to their proper end is a matter of variation, of different amounts. No matter how far along in gestation a pregnant woman is and how normally or not her offspring within her is developing, as long as she is pregnant that woman is as pregnant as any other pregnant woman. She is entirely pregnant in reality and so has to deal with the implications of what that means in her life. Likewise, no matter how undeveloped or malformed people may be in the development or realization of their personhood, if they are persons they exist every bit as much as persons as any other person. They all possess personhood and are caught up in the implications of that, including the possession of natural dignity.

In short, human persons possess dignity by virtue of their given personhood, even when their ability or status in realizing the proper end of flourishing personhood is variably undeveloped, impaired, suspended, or deteriorating. Dignity is to personhood, regardless of its variable state of actualization, as pregnancy is to being pregnant, regardless of its variable state of development, even as real causal powers are to the entities that possess them, regardless of their triggering and actualization in observable events. The real is not the actual, and neither, in turn, is the empirical. Real personhood entails real dignity in fact and apart from whatever specific state of actualization that personhood may stand in, in relation to the fullness of its realizaton, whether in actuality or as empirically observed.

The Supply Side of Dignity

One unfortunate consequence of the dominance, by liberal individualism, of the history of the theorizing of human dignity in the West is its almost complete focus on the right of persons possessing dignity to make moral demands on other individuals, who are obliged to honor their dignity by respecting their associated rights. This "demand side" focus of thought attends almost exclusively to the question of which individuals rightly possess dignity and what that entitles them to demand of other individuals whose status is uncertain with regard to their respecting the dignity of others. Those others who are morally obliged to supply the responses appropriate to dignity are viewed as secondary, duty-bound parties whose role it is to fulfill for others the requirements of dignity once the latter has been established in those dignity bearers. The part of these "respondents" in the process is taken as unproblematic while the basic issues around the claimants of dignity are being sorted out. In short, most of our debates focus primarily on the bearers of dignity and little on the moral fulfillers of the obligations dignity demands of others. The practical work of the latter only really begins, it seems, once the key theoretical questions about dignity's bearers have been settled. The presupposition here also appears to be that by default individuals have no natural reason to honor the rights of other individuals and therefore often will not do so unless externally compelled. Dignity becomes a moral possession; its rightful holders can demand respect from individuals who would not otherwise be forthcoming with respect. The philosophical anthropology operating in the background here is rational egoism of a sort informed by Thomas Hobbes and Adam Smith.

There is some truth in liberal individualism on this matter, at least as seen by critical realist personalism, otherwise it could not have sustained the compelling adherence among so many that it has. It is true that something about humans involves or reflects a natural quality—dignity—that deserves to be respected by others. It is also true that the honoring of others' rights cannot be entirely left up to the voluntary goodwill of people, but needs stronger moral, cultural, and legal guarantees. It is likewise true that specific people, not simply abstract ideas about people or whole collectivities of people, are the bearers of dignity. But what is lopsided in this liberal individualistic account of human dignity is its nearly exclusive focus on the demand side of dignity. Missing is a vigorous account of the real, moral self-concerns of the personhood of the respondent and the associated motivations that persons may or do have proactively to treat other persons with dignity—and not only when they are obliged to do so by the compulsion of the demand-side claims for the respect of others on the basis of their asserted dignity. If we are to move the discussion about the grounds of dignity beyond its current seeming impasse, I think we will need to develop such a supply-side account. I believe that critical realist personalism offers such an approach.

In the prior chapter, I argued that the promotion of the realization of the personhood of other persons is always included in the natural telos of every person pursuing his or her personhood. An innate part of our quest to achieve the flourishing of our personal being—given the relational nature of personhood—is to advance the flourishing of the personal being of other persons. This observation, if true, has major consequences for how we think about human dignity: it provides a "supply-side" rationale for desiring to treat other persons as creatures in possession of dignity. The Hobbesian rational egoism underwriting liberal individualism's account of dignity and rights is misguided on the question of people's true natural interests. The reality about real humans is not that each is oriented solely toward their own pleasures, happiness, security, and well-being; that individuals engage other people primarily to obtain those goods for themselves; and that dignity is needed as a means to protect the rights of each individual against their likely violations and encroachments by other individuals. People may believe that, particularly if they have been trained by liberal individualism to do so, but in believing it they are wrong. Rather, first—following the account of the prior chapter—it is in the true interest of persons to work toward the realization of their proper telos as persons; and, second, a necessary part of working toward the flourishing of one's personhood is to work toward that of others. The genuine good and well-being of others becomes a part of one's own good and flourishing. Persons thrive by successfully seeking to develop themselves as persons and moving toward the realization of their proper telos—and an innately necessary aspect of doing that is helping others also successfully to develop themselves as persons and realize their own telos. The good of others is thereby inescapably implicated in the real good of each. In short, dignity is not simply about the rights some humans possess and enact, but also the human good and the virtuous means by which the good is achieved.

For the present discussion of dignity this means: It is in the true interest of every person to seek out, to recognize, and to honor the dignity of other persons to the extent that they are able. Dignity is not merely a claim that some use to make demands for rights against reluctant others. Dignity is a property of personhood that calls for self-realization through the recognition and honoring of the dignity of other persons. One cannot fulfill one's own dignity while simultaneously violating or even ignoring the dignity of others. It is by appreciating, honoring, and working to enhance the dignity of others that every person moves closer to the realization of their own dignity and personhood. The relation between persons when it comes to dignity—at least those who understand and act upon the truth of their personhood—is therefore one of an ongoing, internally motivated supply of the honoring of the dignity of others extended out from each person. Sometimes those relations involve strong reciprocity and mutuality, in which the supply is continually offered in both or all directions. At other times, given the asymmetrical relationships often involved in human social life, the persons whose personhood has developed relatively more fully toward the natural telos of flourishing recognize, honor, and privilege the dignity of others whose personhood is less developed or more impaired in ways that mean they cannot and will not reciprocate. The parent devotes her full self to the care of her ill newborn. The teacher expends himself to develop the believed-in potential of a student who is as yet entirely unappreciative and unmotivated. A mental health system, at great cost, cares for, protects, and invests in the well-being of a severely disabled population. Communities of people distribute their resources to meet the essential needs of hapless disaster victims on the other side of the world. In such cases of asymmetrical social relations, the more robustly developed persons involved enjoy a greater opportunity to recognize and honor the dignity of the weaker, more helpless, less capable, undeveloped, damaged, and declining persons in the relationship. And, if I am correct, they also reap a greater personal reward of growing even further into the flourishing of their personhood. Any person engaged in the pursuit of his or her good will not seek to minimize their labors to honor the dignity of other persons, will not shirk opportunities to respect the personhood of others, and will not seek to find cases of undeveloped, damaged, or declining actualizations of personhood and dignity in order to exclude them from the community of persons deserving to be treated as bearers of dignity. The person engaged in the pursuit of his or her own good will go out of his or her way to assure the dignity of the most nascent, marginal, vulnerable, damaged, and excluded persons.

Consequently the "difficult cases" that appear to lack the basis for the claim to dignity are not left vulnerable to being denied dignity and rights, because, when properly understood, the good of the personhood of the persons who are related to these difficult cases means that they naturally have the interest of honoring the life and dignity of the vulnerable ones. The zero-sum game of one person's "cashing in" on their dignity resulting in a corresponding cost to others obliged to honor their dignity is potentially replaced by a positive-sum game of proactive gift giving in respect, justice, and love, in which the honoring of the dignity of even the most impaired and vulnerable of human persons works to increase the actualization of the personhood of those who do the honoring. Dignity becomes not merely a duty to fulfill but more importantly an essential path toward the realization of our own good in human personhood. Such actions, again, do not create the existence of the dignity of anyone involved. But they do recognize and enhance the development toward the realization of the dignity of every person involved, those who honor and protect the dignity of others and those whose dignity is honored and protected. All of this turns the tables on the typical question. The issue is no longer only the basis upon which certain people can or cannot make dignity-based claims of others. The issue also becomes the honoring of human dignity by others that is entailed in their simply pursuing their own good in personhood.

This case flows naturally from the virtues-based, teleological theory of the good developed in the prior chapter. Many accounts of dignity, in particular those developed in a Kantian mode, take a "deontological" approach—from the Greek word *deontic*, meaning "necessary," "binding," or "duty"—stating that respecting the dignity of others is morally right and obligated by duty, regardless of the consequences or character of the one doing the respecting. What follows from that view is the elaboration of various rules that must be followed as they apply in specific situations. Such a view is not completely without merit, especially when contextualized in a teleological, virtues-based account.[46] The virtues-based approach advanced here, however, emphasizes the moral character of the actors over the intrinsic rightness of rule-specified actions. What matters is that actors of a particular kind (persons) are pursuing their natural good ends (flourishing personhood) and are learning in well-ordered communities to practice the kinds of virtues that characteristically help to achieve those good ends. Each person is on a quest to realize his or her true nature in flourishing personhood and—in doing so, by my account—is naturally and internally drawn to help other persons also realize their true nature in flourishing personhood. In such a system, individuals are neither inevitably pitted against each other, with a semblance of peace kept through the assertion of the rights inherent in dignity; nor are they left to be motivated by the belief that the honoring of the dignity of others is the inviolable duty of all rational agents. Persons naturally and proactively seek to perceive, respect, and enhance the developed expression of the dignity of other persons because, properly understood, that is what it means to be a person, what is involved in learning to become more fully and authentically

46. Francis Fukuyama notes rightly that deontological ethics "cannot escape making certain judgments about what is naturally best for human beings. . . . In default of a substantive theory of human nature or any other means of grounding human ends, deontological theories wind up elevating individual moral autonomy to the highest human good." Fukuyama, *Our Posthuman Future* (New York: Farrar, Straus and Giroux, 2002), 122, 123.

the kind of "thou" for others that one really is, and what is the path toward and the partial ends of flourishing personhood for oneself—and, by
implication, for others.

In sum, what one ought to want, what one finally must want, is the
good. Wanting, pursuing, and achieving the good is good for the persons
seeking it. Seeking the good for oneself means also seeking the good of
other persons. Seeking the good of others means recognizing and respecting their real personal dignity—whether the relationship is symmetrical
or asymmetrical, whether others can reciprocate or not. Recognizing, respecting, and promoting the actualization of the dignity of others enhances
one's own dignity and personhood. The honoring of dignity thus forms the
moral character of persons seeking to realize their essential nature and
also helps constitute the good life appropriate to their essential nature.

The Temporal Continuity of Personhood

Much of the difficulty in recognizing real dignity in some humans is caused
by the dubious tendency of viewing human lives in distinct temporal slices
that supposedly are ontologically unrelated. The typical way this happens
is by identifying "difficult situations" in the case-study approach to moral
decision-making. For instance, it is claimed that human dignity has something to do with some feature of human life, such as rational agency or
free will. Cases are then found where that feature is limited or absent
(prematurely delivered babies, Alzheimer's patients, victims of severe
fetal alcohol syndrome, and such) yet for which we would still want to
claim dignity. The argument becomes stuck. Participants think they have
to admit either that humans in such cases do not possess dignity, or that
dignity must be regrounded in theism, or perhaps that they have to abandon the idea of dignity altogether because of the lack of consistency of
applicability of a capacities-based theory across a full range of cases. But
the line of reasoning leading to these problems seems to presuppose that
human lives consist of distinct segments that can be viewed and evaluated
as isolated snapshots detached from one another in existence, identity,
and meaning. How we might think about the status of one person's dignity,
therefore, might be radically different at different times and in different
associated conditions, depending on whether we consider their life when
they are a toddler, a mature adult, or a failing nursing home resident. The
very same person may be viewed as having dignity at one time but not

another, depending on the condition of their health and bodily and mental capacities.

Yet it is not clear that this view of a human life is helpful or warranted. In fact, viewing single human lives as isolated snapshot fragments requires the imposition of a static and disjointed perspective on personhood that treats people's lives in time as moving in discontinuous lumps. If we insist on considering human lives in this way we will have difficulty explaining dignity in many difficult cases. But that suggests that we should perhaps view human lives in alternative terms. Specifically, I suggest we consider understanding human lives as continuous and evolving wholes that cohere at the "centers of" the particular personhood of those lives dynamically lived in time. The logic of proactive emergent realities—as opposed to responsive ones—leads us to believe that personhood adheres in human life from beginning to end. Such a perspective grasps the major experiential and capacity differences between persons as babies, children, youth, adults, and elders. Yet it connects these differences in start-to-finish flows of full, coherent lives. The kind of person one is in a coma is and should not be disconnected from the person one was before the coma and the kind of person one might be if one were to awake from the coma.[47] If it were otherwise, then there would be no reason for family members to come and visit and care for their son or sister or aunt in the coma, since that would be "another (non?)person." Each distinct phase of every life—whatever the quality reflected or capacities exercised at any given segment—is linked to the integrated whole of life that is centered in the dynamic reality of the person. Empirically, the stages of a life can look very different. But ontologically the personal life exists as a sufficiently coherent unity in which each stage—but especially the stages of greatest personal realization and fulfillment—is related to and so helps to define the others.

Such a holistic view of human lives is hardly odd. In fact, it is the natural, default viewpoint adopted by most people as they consider their lives. I, for instance, can remember and picture myself at very different points in my life—as a child, teenager, young adult, in middle age—and, while

47. During the writing of this chapter, the Reuter's News Service reported that a sixty-five-year-old Polish man awoke from a coma of nineteen years that was caused by an accident in 1988 after which doctors gave him only two to three years to live; cared for daily by his wife, he awoke in 2007 surprised to find that communist rationing of food had been replaced by capitalist cell phones and other consumer products. Reuters, "Democracy Stuns Polish Coma Man," *Reuters News*, June 2, 2007.

I know I looked and was capacitated quite differently than I look and am now, I nevertheless know myself to be the same person I was at those other ages. Much has changed. But through all of the changes the sufficient continuity of my life as a distinct person has sustained itself. I am certain that most readers experience their lives similarly. Indeed, it is precisely when people's lives suffer dramatic ruptures in the continuity of their singular personhood that we know something has gone deeply wrong. Schizophrenia, multiple personality disorder, traumatic and psychogenic amnesia, advanced Huntington's disease, and the like we take not as normal differences of experience but as injurious, pathological breakdowns of normal existence.

Furthermore, in various obvious ways we normally view human lives as continuous, integrated wholes in possession of dignity, even when the exercise of capacities and functions thought responsible for dignity are inoperative at particular times. Consider, for starters, people who are asleep. They are not conscious or actively exercising their powers of rationality or free will or purposive agency. They often are, as we say, "dead to the world." Yet despite those facts, most of us do not say that while they are asleep people's dignity recedes, retires, or disappears. We do not think we are entitled to dispose of sleeping people simply because during those times of their lives they cannot exercise the capacities or exhibit the traits we believe otherwise ground their dignity. No, we view their lives as larger, continuous wholes flowing through time, and consider the one-third of their lives spent sleeping as connected to and defined by the two-thirds spent awake. The same can be said of people who have been knocked unconscious or anesthetized. If we believe a person should not be, for example, involuntarily sexually fondled because of the dignity they possess, we do not conclude that he may be involuntarily sexually fondled if he is found knocked unconscious by the side of the road from having fallen off of his bicycle or she is found fully sedated in a private hospital room recovering from surgery on the leg. During those temporal slices of their lives, such unconscious and anesthetized persons exercise few capacities connected to that which many associate with human dignity. Yet we nevertheless understand their temporarily insensible selves as ontologically connected to their normally conscious and active selves by virtue of the unifying personhood that constitutes their selfhood and identity through time. The continuity of the whole person overrides the dramatic differences in the person's experience and functioning across time.

Our normal acceptance of this holistic, start-to-finish perspective on the integrity of people's lives is also evident at the temporal extremes of human existence. Thus, at the starting line, the best of our understandings do not assign dignity to human persons in degrees according to their exercise of the capacities and properties thought by many to ground dignity. Whenever we believe that personhood begins—whether at conception, during some trimester of pregnancy, or at birth—most of us believe that the new human person possesses dignity that morally deserves to be fully if not especially protected and nurtured. This, importantly, is *despite* the fact that at that stage of life and for a long time to come the new person is incapable of exercising or expressing the fullness of their potential capacities of personhood. At that temporal stage, the expression or actualization of the personhood that grounds the dignity of newborn babies exists as terrifically valuable bundles of potentialities yet to be much realized. But we do not, if we have any good moral bearings, discount the new human person's dignity or consider it more eligible for violation than that of an adult existing in the greater fullness of the realization of personhood. To the contrary, the morally sound person cherishes and protects the dignity of the undeveloped and helpless new human person, understanding that its life also belongs to a much larger single life that, barring tragedy, it does and will possess and unfold as a coherent whole from the center of its personhood. In this way, again, it is clear that we do not typically view the dignity of people's lives by considering them as isolated snapshot segments that shift from one disconnected, sequenced stage to another. Rather, we rightly think of people's lives over time as integrated and connected wholes that differ in experience and capacities temporally, but that exist as integrated unities more profoundly across those temporal changes in and through the continuity of personhood.

We can make a similar observation at the opposite end of human life. Ethicists may argue about the dignity of physically and mentally degenerate seniors.[48] But it is worth observing that even after people die we ordinarily treat their dead bodies with dignity. Even in death, there seems to remain some significant *vestige* of personal dignity in the mere corpse of the person that once was. That is, I suggest, because of the real continuity of personhood existent from start to finish across single lives, trailing off to

---

48. For a brief overview of this history of the bioethics debate about dignity, see F. Daniel Davis, "Human Dignity and Respect for Persons: A Historical Perspective on Public Bioethics," in *Human Dignity and Bioethics* (Washington, DC: President's Council on Bioethics, 2008), 19–36. John Evans provides a more in-depth look at bioethics in his 2002 book, *Playing God? Human Genetic Engineering and the Rationalization of the Public Bioethical Debate* (Chicago: University of Chicago Press).

completion even in the dead bodies of the deceased. It is not the case that the dead body, considered at the time after death, exhibits the features of developed personhood from which dignity derives. What we see is a deceased corpse of flesh in early stages of decomposition. And yet we know or believe that the corpse even in death retains some last links to the single personal life it once emergently gave rise to by virtue of the capacities and personhood it bore. We normally treat the bodies of the dead with sacred reverence.[49] The precise way to explain this might be to say that human dignity is an independent objective reality that gives rise to and is overlaid by a dependent objective reality of our understanding about dignity that sees traces of the former true dignity even in dead bodies. But my point here is simpler: most people in existential reality understand that the dignity of a person cannot be sliced into phase-by-phase temporal segments but holds together in whole lives and—insofar as the dependent objective reality operates—even as we honor corpses with care and respect. This is not simply the view and practice of "civilized" moderns. All known human cultures in history and across space engage in funeral rituals to honor and mourn their dead and deal respectfully with their bodies.[50] If it made sense to conceive of human lives as disconnected phases occupying distinct steps in time that lack the ontological continuity of personhood, there would be little reason to so consistently recognize the fading dignity of the dead by honoring them in the treatment of their corpses through funeral rituals. We might instead mentally and emotionally appreciate the lives they lived and unceremoniously dispose of their essentially useless dead bodies, which we would have every reason to believe had little to do with (especially the possible dignity of) their previous lives. But we do not normally do that.[51] This is because we understand the personhood of human lives

49. Sentimentalized versions of funeral rituals can also be operative, in which mourners focus, for example, entirely on the "memory" of the deceased; these often have more to do with the affective dispositions of the living and their emotional needs than with their honoring the personhood of the dead—my argument here, to be clear, does not refer to such sentimentalized versions of funeral rites but to more robust reverencing of the persons and bodies of the deceased.

50. Brown, *Human Universals*. The specific treatment that is considered respectful differs across cultures, but the underlying intent to be respectful is universal.

51. Thus, news reports of a cremation business that was actually stacking corpses in storages sheds, scattering them in nearby woods, and burying them in unmarked shallow graves on its property, rather than properly cremating them, evoked howls of outrage not only from family members of the uncremated deceased but also from the general public. Dirk Johnson and Vern Smith, "Unearthing a Grim Tale: The Woods of North Georgia Hid a Terrible

as continuous-though-changing and integrated-though-developing wholes
that do not suddenly dissolve, even when life has left dead bodies. To be
sure, dead bodies do not represent lingering personhood, since with death
persons are fully deceased. That is part of the grief and sometimes horror
of death—the full termination of personhood. Yet even corpses, which
were the preconditions of the emergence of the personhood of persons,
are still there, and so seem to retain some kind of final vestiges or traces of
the dignity of personhood that once was and so deserve a final treatment
of dignity.

What might we conclude about the reality of the continuity of personhood across temporal changes for thinking about human dignity? I have
suggested that human dignity is an irreducible attribute of persons, proactively emergent as an ontologically real property at the level of personhood, not the lower level of individual capacities. Even so, at different
times of their lives, human persons are, by nature of their constitution as
embodied creatures that exist in time, more or less capable of actualizing
and expressing the fullness of their personhood. Sometimes the breadth
and depth of the personhood of a human life enjoys full realization and
thrives. At other times, the personhood of a life is merely potential, nascent, undeveloped, slumbering, damaged, trampled, corroded, faint, or
deteriorating. Some of this is part of the natural life course of embodied, historically situated, temporally finite human personhood. Some of it
has more tragically to do with the brokenness and injustices of the world.
In our efforts to understand the dignity of persons, we do not serve our
purposes well by dissecting single human lives into disconnected segments, some of which appear to warrant dignity and some of which do
not. We should view human lives in the way we normally experience our
own fundamental personal selves and how we treat the lives and bodies of
people who are asleep, unconscious, sedated, and newly born: as single,
integrated, continuous personal wholes existing in significant continuity
as personal centers across the changes of time. By taking this approach,
even in considering the "marginal" or "difficult cases" of fetuses, helpless
infants, coma patients, the Alzheimer's diseased, and the like, we need not
assess the dignity of such humans strictly in terms of their selves in those

---

Secret: A Family Business Devoted to Cremating the Dead Was Not Doing Its Job. A Haunted
Community Wonders Why," *Newsweek*, March 4, 2002; also see, for instance, Shaila Dewan,
"Disasters and Their Dead," *New York Times*, October 16, 2005; Dave Scheiber, "The Wrong
They Could Not Bury," *St. Petersburg Times*, February 25, 2001.

segmented points of time viewed in isolation. Rather, we can recognize the dignity of their personhood as it is connected to all of the other temporal points of their lives, past and future. And this helps us to avoid erroneous conclusions about the lack of dignity in such difficult cases. We are, I hope, one step closer to a personalist theory of human dignity that is inclusive of all of humanity and not merely those humans who most clearly express the powers of personal life or who happen at the time of observation to occupy proximity to the prime of their lives.

A Social Ontology of Species Solidarity

We often have difficulty thinking clearly about human dignity, particularly in "difficult cases," because of the atomistic individualism that has come to permeate modern, Western culture and that often frames our thinking about dignity. Atomistic individualism is not our natural—that is, given inherently by nature—human social ontology. It is a particular cultural worldview that has developed in specific places under unique historical circumstances and in the context of the formation of particular social institutions, such as market capitalism and liberal democracy. It is perfectly legitimate to ponder questions of dignity within the ideological framework of atomistic individualism in order to see what results that may provide. But there is no reason why we need automatically to do so or to limit ourselves to thinking in its terms. Yet most philosophical and legal works that address the question of dignity do appear to bring atomistic individualism to the discussion as the governing background assumption about personal and social ontology. However, thinking about human dignity primarily through the lens of atomistic individualism can create unnecessary problems and generate misleading conclusions. We set ourselves up for trouble when we take for granted the dominant modern, Western cultural definition of social ontology in trying to make sense of the dignity of human persons.[52] We will therefore do well, I think, to surface atomistic individualist assumptions, consider their problematic tendencies, and supplement or replace them with a perspective that takes seriously our real, ontological social solidarity as a species. I am aware that many megainstitutions that dominate our lives—mass-consumer capitalism, liberal democracy, free

---

52. Recall that personalist theory makes an important conceptual distinction between the "individual" as atomistic, which it resists, and the "person" as relational, which it promotes.

labor markets, and national and global communications and transportation systems among them—powerfully reinforce and reproduce the "reality" of atomistic individualism as institutional facts. But that does not mean we have to understand the real nature of human personhood, social ontology, and personal dignity within its framework.

It can be difficult for modern Westerners to conceive of a nonatomistic ontology of persons and society. Many of us far too easily assume something like the social ontology asserted by the former British prime minister, Margaret Thatcher, when she declared, "There is no such thing as society. There are individual men and women and there are families." Such a viewpoint leaves individual persons in solitary isolation when it comes to the question of possibly possessing dignity. The ideas of people belonging to an organic human family, participating in the ontology of human social being, and existing in solidarity with the human species simply disappear from sight.[53] We are stripped of possible resources for thinking more

53. Theistic theorists of human dignity who are Christians, at least, have every reason to take an ontology of human social solidarity seriously. Much of American Christianity—especially Protestantism, and particularly evangelicalism—has admittedly evolved into a highly individualistic version of faith focused on the forgiveness of individuals' sinful behaviors through penal satisfaction theories of atonement toward personal admission to heaven. But a review of Christian scripture and historical theology with the individualistic lens removed reveals powerful affirmations of collective responsibility and solidarity from beginning to end of the Christian story. Adam as primordial human was representative of the entire human race, choosing the spiritual and moral fate of all descendants thereafter (Romans 5:12–14; 1 Corinthians 15:22). Jesus is said to have existed in the loins of Abraham through some mystery of bodily solidarity thousands of years before his birth (Hebrews 7). The people of Israel are recurrently praised and condemned not for their individual righteousness and sins but for those of the nation (e.g., Judges 2:20; Isaiah 1:4; Amos 6:1), such that arguably innocent children and adults were punished through the Babylonian captivity for the failures of previous generations (e.g., Ezra 9:7; Daniel 1:1–3; also see Deuteronomy 28:41; 2 Chronicles 29:9). God similarly judges the wickedness not only of individuals but also of other nations, such as the Assyrians, and Babylonians (Jeremiah 48:46; Ezekiel 39:25). Through his incarnation and death, Jesus Christ united himself with the entire human race (Romans 6:5; 2 Corinthians 5:14) and, just as the "First Adam" plunged the cosmos into and under the power of sin and death, so Christ as the "Second Adam" through obedience to God and solidarity with humanity freed the cosmos from sin's power (Romans 5; 1 Corinthians 15:22, 45; 2 Corinthians 5:21; see Romans 8:3–4). Christ's redemptive sacrifice provides for the forgiveness of not only individual sins but also for the sins of the whole world (2 Corinthians 5:19; 1 John 2:2). Christian believers are members of Christ's body and comprise subsidiary parts of the church as a body (Romans 12:5; Ephesians 5:30; 1 Corinthians 12; Colossians 2:16–19). Christians are rarely referred to in scripture as saved souls but rather as members of a particular nation, a people, a priesthood (1 Peter 2:9). That few American Christians seem to emphasize these collectivist biblical

fruitfully and in ways less culturally bound about the nature and extent of human dignity. Attempting to do so in what follows may feel unnatural or forced in certain ways. But that may be, not because human solidarity is an ontological fiction, but because we have so deeply absorbed our culture's individualistic social ontology despite its being inadequate to reality. Taking social solidarity seriously can help us account for a more inclusive view of human dignity in personalist terms.

In this book I have emphasized the personhood of the distinct person. But the distinct person is not the highest level of reality in the realm of the human. Emergent from—and acting back down upon—the interaction of persons is the real realm or level of the social, which includes emergent social structures. Personhood is not simply constituted by the upwardly moving human physiological facts and causal capacities that exist at lower levels. It is also developed through downward causation by the real level of the humanly social that exists at a higher level of stratified reality than do persons. A full understanding of personhood, therefore, requires viewing it as existing between and shaped by levels of reality both below and above. For present purposes, what matters is attention to the level above, to the reality of human sociality, community, communion, and solidarity. How might attention to human species and social solidarity help us to better answer our knotty questions about the basis and extent of human dignity?

The definition of persons that I have elaborated in this book is socially and relationally oriented. Humans literally cannot develop as persons without other persons with whom they share and sustain their personhood. To be a person is not to be an incommunicable self, distinct from other selves.[54] It is also to be related to, communicating among, and in communion with other personal selves. Inherent to a personalist understanding of the human being is a strong dimension of relational connection and solidarity.[55] Only by living in communities of other personal selves can anyone become a distinct personal self. Thatcher was dead wrong; it is not

themes only highlights the power of (Western, individualistic) culture to shape the reading and interpretation of sacred texts.

54. See chapter 1, note 59.

55. John Macmurray, *The Self as Agent* (1957; Amherst, NY: Humanity Books, 1991); Harold Oliver, "The Relational Self," in *Selves, People, and Persons*, ed. Rouner, 37–51. Personhood thus has nothing to do with "autonomous viability" or viable autonomy, which none possess; all are dependent and interdependent on others from start to finish in different and important ways.

existent individuals who aggregate into (allegedly fictional) communities but communities that emerge as real institutional facts from individual interactions. It is also as much existing emergent communities of persons that make possible the developed reality of distinct people, as it is people who interactively form emergent communities.[56] This is an important point to grasp, as it has significant theoretical and moral consequences. For example, from a personalist perspective, people enjoy certain rights in society—but not because they, per liberal political theory, are ontologically separate individuals with negative freedoms ("freedoms from") that other individuals have no business infringing. People enjoy rights because they are real persons naturally and always in relationships of solidarity with other persons and communities, all of the members of which in the seeking of their own telic ends must honor the dignity and rights of others in order to be good persons and, through the exercise of virtues toward their proper purposes, to sustain their mutual personhood. In short, any personalist theory instinctively precludes atomistic individualism and instead recognizes the natural centrality of human social solidarity for personhood.

Beginning with a proper social ontology of species solidarity and interdependence, one that maps perfectly onto personalism, enables us to see that all humans are bound together in membership in a common species that shares among all of its members the central feature of personhood. Specific members of the species can, as I have said, be found anywhere on the spectrum of the *actualization* of personal powers in experience, between the extremes of the most nascent or damaged expressions of personhood to the most developed and robust realizations of personhood. But, wherever they fall on that continuum, each belongs with all of the others within the largest social community of shared humanity. And so each possess an organic tie to the emergent personal dignity proper to the personhood of humanity, whether or not their particular empirical state of the actualization of human life at a given time represents the fullest, most developed expression of personhood. Consequently, even physically and mentally undeveloped, impaired, or declining members of humanity share

---

56. As always from a critical realist perspective, as discussed in the previous chapter, human collectivities are actually composed of the "parts" of distinct persons, but also cannot in their emergent properties as collectivities simply be reduced to the sum of their parts. Social entities such as structures, communities, and institutions possess ontologically real, emergent properties with powers of downward causation.

a stake in and hold a claim on the dignity that is proper to shared personhood and to the moral responses for which that dignity calls.

Two analogies may help to convey this idea. First, all U.S. citizens enjoy
certain civil rights by virtue of their common membership in the class of
people known as American citizens. There are certain features of identity
and practice that normally represent the most developed, robust expressions of national citizenship. These include residing in the United States,
faithfully voting in political elections, flying the flag appropriately, paying taxes in full, honoring national holidays, obeying laws, a willingness
to fight to defend the Constitution, singing the national anthem before
sports events, and so on. In this sense there are "ideal type" U.S. citizens
who we might consider the most entitled to the enjoyment of their civil
rights. Some real Americans instantiate that ideal type in their lives. But
many U.S. citizens do not express or reflect those features of identity and
practice that define good citizenship. Many cut corners on their taxes, do
not vote, do not sing the national anthem, and so on. Some even live overseas as expatriates, sometimes even alienated from their own culture and
society. And yet, the civil rights of these not-ideal citizens are not abridged
by their undeveloped or even undetectable expressions of good citizenship. However well they do or do not empirically embody the model of the
good citizen, they normally still retain the same civil rights as every other
citizen. If no U.S. citizen at all instantiated the "ideal type" citizen, then
the entire national project would collapse and with it the basis of the civil
rights enjoyed by all. But so far, enough have done and currently do so to
prevent that from happening. In effect, some citizens empirically "do the
work" to create and maintain the reality of "citizenship," which is then
enjoyed by the broader population of all U.S. citizens. Note too that the
civil rights of citizenships are not apportioned out according to the degree
to which one has instantiated the role of good citizen ("You've flown the
flag regularly, so you get an extra portion, let's say 8 percent more, of civil
rights"). Citizenship, and the rights pertaining thereto, is not a matter of
varying degrees but of categorical status. It is membership in the class
of people to whom a certain status pertains—and not the empirical instantiation of the fullest development of expression of the role attached
to that class membership—that is the basis of the claim to the rights attached to that membership. Similarly, now back to the question of dignity,
mere membership in the human species may confer upon every one of its
members the status of dignity that is grounded in the personal being that is
the hallmark feature of the species—regardless of how well actualized or

damaged the empirical expression of that personal existence is. Might others who actualize more fully developed and robust expressions of personal being be doing the "heavy lifting" of human personhood that sustains the collective reality of humanity-with-dignity for all? Perhaps that is part and parcel of the larger reality of solidarity and interdependence that is the real social ontology of human existence.

Critical readers may object that the analogy just given suggests inappropriate parallels, insofar as U.S. citizenship is a legal status created through social construction as an institutional fact, whereas the dignity of human personhood I am claiming to be a natural and inherent human status created through natural processes of emergence as a brute fact. Those dissimilarities are real, though every analogy involves insightful similarities and unsuitable differences. In response, I offer a second analogy that, like my claims about dignity, involves inherent status, natural process, and brute fact. That is the analogy of family belonging and its genetic reproductive implications. There are some very large extended families, containing numerous generations with many offspring. As a natural fact, the genetic composition of each family member is determined by his or her relation to other family members. And those genetic ties influence the physical features and personality traits of the various people in question. The genetic inheritance of each person is—short of an advanced technological genetic intervention—fixed and inalienable. Now, it sometimes happens that some full biological members of the family turn out not to look or behave much like most of the other family members. They do not have the blond hair that everyone else has, they are covered with freckles when nobody else is, they are uniquely serene and peaceable among characteristically wild and tempestuous kin, and so on. It also sometimes happens that certain family members can behave in ways that create distance and even alienation between themselves and the rest of their families. They can move far away, try hard not to think and act like their parents, change their family name, and undergo plastic surgery. However, for better or worse, no amount of visual or behavioral dissimilarity or distancing or alienation can alter the fact that every one of those people are blood relatives of the rest of their family, embody the genetic makeup of their two parents, and possess an objective biological relational status—such as daughter, nephew, and grandson—to their kin. Simply by virtue of their natural biological membership in their families, resulting from the brute fact of their genetically reproduced inheritance, whether they like it or not, these people possess natural, objectively given, and inalienable blood

ties, attributes, and statuses in relation to their families. I do not wish to
stretch and apply every point of the analogy to the issue of human dignity.
My point is that—in virtue of the nature of the reality we humans inhabit
and help to compose—certain characteristics of particular entities may
pertain to all members of the class of those entities regardless of how
well or clearly specific members of the class express, instantiate, reflect, or
embody the typical features of that class.

That is the general principle. Its specific application to human dignity
may be this: given the realities of human personal being as described in
this book, dignity is a status and attribute naturally and inalienably possessed by every member of the human species regardless of the degree to
which they have, can, or do actualize, express, and instantiate the features
of personhood empirically. Humanity exists most fundamentally not in
atomistic solitude but in species solidarity, the doctrines of liberal individualism notwithstanding. Personhood is the hallmark feature of human being, and dignity is an ineliminable feature of personhood. Therefore, every
member of the human species, regardless of the extent of the actualization
of its personhood, may be thought to claim a share in the dignity that is
the natural birthright of personhood, by virtue in part of his or her natural
solidarity with the other members of its kind. Thus, just as the one family
member who does not share any of the typical empirical traits or behaviors of the rest of the family nevertheless possesses objective relations and
fixed genetic materials of the family, so the fetus, newborn infant, seriously disabled teenager, coma patient, and senile widow who actualize
very little if any of the fullness of developed personhood nevertheless may
possess the same dignity as those of their shared species who do. In order
to see this possibility, we need to disabuse ourselves of the social ontology
of atomistic separation that is mistakenly promoted by the doctrines of
liberal individualism that dominates modern Western culture. Doing so
may help us to recognize and defend the real dignity of persons comprising the "difficult cases" with which philosophy and ethics struggle.

Taking Stock

To where have we come in our exploration of human dignity in this chapter? My purpose has been to help provide an account of dignity that primarily references the nature of human persons. Yet I have sought to avoid
risking the exclusions from the community of humans who are ascribed

dignity those who appear to lack the specific functioning capacities on which capacities-based accounts ground dignity. My goal has further been to develop an approach that is compatible with but not dependent upon a theistic account of dignity, in order to create inclusive grounds for discussion and possible agreement between theists and nontheists who are committed to the reasoned defense of human dignity, insofar as that is possible. I have pursued this purpose by advancing the following arguments.

First, I have relied upon critical realism's concepts of stratified reality and emergence to shift the source of dignity from specific capacities operating at the middle level to emergent personhood existing at the highest level of personal being. Dignity is a proactive emergent property of personhood as a whole, not a result of the possession or exercise of some specific given human capacities. I have indicated that the exact factors and processes by which multiple human capacities interact to give rise through emergence to personhood cannot be spelled out in a precise recipe or formula. Nevertheless, it appears that real personhood can exist in the absence of the functioning of all of the capacities that I have in this book enumerated—meaning that we can and do have emergent persons even in the absence of certain capacities important in the existence of a very robust realization of personhood. I have argued from the proactive nature of the emergence of the person that personhood adheres in human life from start to finish. Furthermore, I have distinguished between the natural being of personhood, which is a categorical given in and for all persons, and the development of the potential and expression of aspects of personhood, including dignity, that are matters of variable, empirical differences of amount and degree. Persons are ontologically fully persons, not more or less so, although the extent to which the potentialities of their personhood can be actualized, developed, and realized varies according to numerous factors. I have suggested that this viewpoint helps to avoid the problem of not being able to recognize dignity in humans who do not possess the functional capacities said by capacities-based approaches to be the sources of dignity, without having either to deny the empirical differences in manifestations of capacities across real humans or to jettison the belief in the dignity of all or any human beings. As long as people are persons—and all living humans are inclusively persons by my account—they possess the dignity of personhood in its fullness, as described in the first section of this chapter. Different persons will stand in varying positions and statuses with regard to the development and limitations of their capacities to actualize or realize the experiential fullness of dignity. Some persons fulfill the potential of their dignity in extensive, vigorous, and highly elaborated ways. Others—through unfortunate chances, bad choices, exploitive and excluding social structures, and the failing health of old age—are stuck with stunted or damaged or declining expressions or realizations of their personal dignity. But in all cases, the same ontological dignity of person-hood exists and warrants for each the kind of moral responses of respect, justice, and love from self and others that such dignity deserves.

Furthermore, critical realist personalism and the larger teleological moral system it animates draws equal if not greater attention to the rec-ognition that dignity is a feature of the persons who proactively engage the lives of others in ways that could potentially help or harm them. The dignity of the active personal subject as well as the demanding personal object concerning the respect of rights—when combined with the teleo-logical, virtue-based morality advanced in this book—provides all people with a rational motivation for seeking not only their own narrow good but also the good of others. The seeking of their true good necessarily entails seeking the good of others, meaning specifically that the honoring and cultivation of one's personal dignity voluntarily compels one also to honor, promote, and defend the dignity of other persons. In part by giving to oth-ers their rightful due, persons come to be their rightful selves. Moreover, not all such proactive payings of respect to the dignity of others involves relationships of equality and reciprocity. Some crucial relationships in hu-man life are highly asymmetrical. In those cases, the more robustly devel-oped persons involved enjoy a greater personal opportunity and calling to recognize and honor the dignity of the weaker, more helpless, less capable, undeveloped, damaged, and declining persons in the relationship—and, I think, reap a greater personal reward of growing even further into the flourishing of their personhood by doing so. The introduction of this cru-cial supply-side dimension of the honoring of dignity shifts the grounds on which the entire discussion is carried on, by explaining why ultimately every person must recognize and respect the dignity of others. This is es-sential to recognizing and respecting the true nature of their own being and self. And pursuing and realizing one's true nature and telos is the only good that is good for human persons. Any person engaged in the pursuit of his or her good will go out of his or her way to assure the dignity of the most marginal, the most vulnerable, the most damaged, the most excluded.

I continued my development of personalist perspectives on human dignity by arguing that we would be mistaken to view human lives as fragmented snapshots of discrete, temporal segments that possess no ontological continuity across time. Human lives and the personhood they express are single, continuous, and organic wholes. The various phases of those wholes are bound together significantly, though not perfectly or seamlessly, at the "centers with purpose" of which personhood consists at the core. When we therefore behold the prematurely delivered preemie weighing 1,000 grams, the twenty-year-old hospitalized with traumatic brain injury, the chemical factory worker whose health has been destroyed by toxic compounds, the war veteran whose body is irreparably burned and maimed, the senile parent who can no longer remember the face of his or her daughter, we must consider their dignity in that moment in light of the real personhood of the larger personal life they have lived from the start and will continue to live until death.

Finally, I suggested that a properly realistic social ontology of social solidarity—rather than the individualistic atomism reflected in the erroneous doctrines of liberal individualism—could helpfully inform our understanding of the dignity of all humans. Regardless of how much dignity any one human case appears empirically to possess, we are not wrong to understand every case as organically connected to the entire human family from which its body, life, being, and personhood has arisen. The biological and social ties between all people are strong, indispensable, and morally meaningful. We have every reason to doubt the social ontology of atomistic individualism and to think instead in terms of social solidarity as the context and basis for real human personhood and its associated dignity—including perhaps that of the members of the human family whose personhood and dignity seem most undeveloped, impaired, and deteriorated. Such an approach will not establish the dignity of every living human being. But as part of a broader personalist understanding it should contribute a significant intellectual part to that end.

Reprise: What Has Dignity to Do with Sociology?

This and the previous chapter seem to have wandered far from the central concerns of sociology. Why are we discussing the human good and dignity in a book about sociological theory? The answer is that the two are never as distinct as most sociologists believe. Every sociological thought and activity is framed and guided by some philosophy of social science or other, whether the sociologist realizes or understands that or not. All important sociological work is also ultimately motivated and informed not by the arbitrary choice or directionless attractions of the sociologist but by larger personal and social interests rooted in normative visions of the good life and the good society. Most often in American sociology that normative vision is concerned with social equality, inclusion, and justice—moral and philosophical issues driven by mainstream political liberalism. The empiricist bent of most of American sociology may obscure the moral and philosophical sources of its work, but that does not make them irrelevant—it only means that many sociologists work unaware of, or at least reticent about acknowledging, the larger moral and philosophical ideas and commitments that drive and shape their efforts. Furthermore, as I suggested in the introduction, every sociologist is also more fundamentally a person and so ought to be concerned with the nature and purpose of his or her self and—I believe—the possible relationships between personal knowledge and academic understanding. If reality and persons are as I have described them here, then intellectual coherence and integration are good, and fragmentation and contradiction are bad. We should wish what we believe to be true about ourselves as persons to have coherent connections to what we do and how we think as sociologists.

Beyond these larger framing, governing, and integration issues—that is, the role of philosophy of social science metatheory, moral and philosophical backgrounds to sociological scholarship and teaching, and the coherence of our personal and scholarly lives—how else might attention to the human good and dignity inform good sociological work? This question is not often asked. So we may not feel equipped to offer well-developed answers. But I will venture one here. To start, it is helpful to recognize the extent to which human social life is driven by concerns with dignity and the good. I have already elaborated in a previous book the centrality and ubiquity of visions of the moral good in constituting and shaping human interests, identities, relationships, cultures, and social institutions—so I will not restate that here.[57] What then of dignity? If human dignity were not real, then human social life would look dramatically different than it does. Significant dimensions of every social relation and institution and certain social institutions in their entirety are centrally about recognizing and respecting human dignity. I am not speaking only about things such as formal hospital ethics review boards. Consider, for instance, microsocial

57. Christian Smith, *Moral, Believing Animals: Human Personhood and Culture* (New York: Oxford University Press, 2003).

interactions. In them—as Erving Goffman, among others, has so cleverly shown—actors are acutely attentive not only to opportunities to win material advantage or gain new instrumental knowledge. They are also keenly attuned to subtle yet pervasive interactive dynamics concerning the moral credibility of interactive performances and self-presentations around respect, poise, esteem, reputation, honor, and the avoidance of embarrassment and discrediting. "Any projected definition of the situation . . . has a distinctive moral character," Goffman observes.

> Society is organized on the principle that any individual who possesses certain social characteristics has a moral right to expect that others will value and treat him in an appropriate way. Connected with this principle is a second, namely that an individual who implicitly or explicitly signifies that he has certain social characteristics ought in fact to be what he claims he is. In consequence, when an individual projects a definition of the situation and thereby makes an implicit or explicit claim to be a person of a particular kind, he automatically exerts a moral demand upon others, obliging them to value and treat him in the manner that persons of his kind have a right to expect.[58]

Dignity is a necessary part of this picture, as is a background commitment to reality and truth. If human persons were not creatures for whom dignity is central and essential, then a great deal of what Goffman has revealed about interactions everywhere would be pointless and enigmatic. Were we somehow able to remove the reality of dignity from human being and consciousness—which we cannot—we would observe people interacting very differently from what we in fact do. Human interactions might resemble those of apes or chimps, which involve relations of helping, dominance, and submission and reflect traces of awareness of other minds, but fundamentally lack a concern with ongoing reciprocal self-definitions, the credibility of moral identities, or the mutual recognition of personal worth, propriety, and integrity.[59] "Man," Mark Twain observed, "is the only animal

58. Erving Goffman, *The Presentation of Self in Everyday Life* (New York: Doubleday, 1959), 13.

59. Richard Wrangham et al., eds., *Chimpanzee Cultures* (Cambridge, MA: Harvard University Press, 1994); Richard Byrne, *The Thinking Ape: Evolutionary Origins of Intelligence* (New York: Oxford University Press, 1995); Peter Richardson and Robert Boyd, *Not by Genes Alone: How Culture Transforms Human Evolution* (Chicago: University of Chicago Press, 2005); Terrence Deacon, *The Symbolic Species: The Co-Evolution of Language and the Brain*

that blushes. Or needs to."[60] In all of this, sociological analyses may take dignity for granted, as a background fact presupposed by the interpretations of our observations. But we in sociology have no good grounds on which to deny it. And our explicit inclusion of it in our thinking may enhance our sociological insight and deepen the richness of our scholarly, theoretical accounts of social life.

At an institutional level, the reality of human dignity explains a great deal about commitments to certain activities, allocations of resources, forms of institutional legitimacy, and the establishment of routines and practices. Human persons are not simply concerned about physical survival, material comfort, political security, social psychological contentment, and tangible relational benefits. Human social life is about much more than those concerns. Notions of dignity and the good are ubiquitous and important in human social life.[61] Again, if dignity were somehow expunged from human life and consciousness, our political, economic, civic, and cultural practices and institutions would function very differently than they do. Very many of our laws would be pointless, never legislated in the first place. Many social movements never would have materialized. Social service and health and social security entitlement programs would work quite differently, if they existed at all. Judicial systems in their entirety—the fundamental raison d'être of which being the virtue of justice as respecting the fact of human dignity—would also work radically unlike they attempt to do now in most cases. In economic production, human resource departments, management practices, employment regulations, compensation systems, property transactions, and much more would operate quite differently in the absence of the reality of human dignity. Experiences within and the behaviors of militaries would be different if the human dignity of soldiers and enemies were not real. Hospitals, orphanages, nursing homes, foster care systems, funeral homes, and even cemeteries might not exist in the absence of human dignity and, if they did, certainly would operate in other ways than they do; likewise with pris-

---

(New York: Norton, 1997); Ian Tattersall, *Becoming Human: Evolution and Human Uniqueness* (New York: Harcourt Brace, 1998).

60. Mark Twain, *Following the Equator and Anti-Imperialist Essays* (1897; New York: Oxford University Press, 1996), 256, quoted in Rolston III, "Human Uniqueness and Human Dignity: Persons in Nature and the Nature of Persons," 129–53.

61. See, for example, Michel Lamont, *The Dignity of Working Men: Moralities and Boundaries of Race, Class, and Immigration* (Cambridge, MA: Harvard University Press, 2000).

ons and other penal, detention, and reform systems. If dignity in human life were not real, family relations, parenting practices, rules of sexual behavior, and our most fundamental conceptions of family existence and obligations would also function in ways different than they do in human life. Of course, exactly how dignity is worked out in different cultures and societies varies significantly. Human dignity can be and is recognized and honored in many ways—depending upon the particularities of history, culture, and circumstance. In some cultures, what constitutes respect for dignity would violate it in others. But that does not negate the fact that in all cases dignity exists and normally is in some ways or other recurrently recognized and responded to.

The skeptic may point out at this juncture that few if any societies do a very good job of respecting the alleged dignity of persons, and that the institutions of some or many societies routinely violate the supposed dignity of persons. If dignity were such a definite fact about human persons, then how or why could this be so? Does not the fact that dignity appears to be flagrantly violated with impunity in some societies and institutions prove that dignity is a social construction believed in by some people in particular times and places and not a natural fact of human personhood?

A few points are needed to reply to this objection. First, critical realism does not claim that all humans always fully understand the truth about reality. Human knowledge is incomplete and fallible. But not rightly grasping the truth about reality does nothing to make it untrue. What is real, outside of institutional facts, is not dependent upon our consciousness of it to be real. For this reason a major task of all sentient animals, particularly humans, is to learn from reality how to conform our minds to understand as well as we are able what is true about reality. But we never do that perfectly. My point is not that all people everywhere fully grasp the reality of human dignity and its implications. If that were true, I would not need to write this chapter. My point is that the reality of dignity is sufficiently inextinguishable from human life and phenomenologically apparent to actual people such that it plays a significant and pervasive role in the character and functioning of many social institutions in human societies—though in some more than in others and certainly differently across all of them.

Second, I have described in this book the reality of existence and the world as it actually is as something like broken. That means, among other things, that people can and do recurrently pursue that which is not the good and, even when they do, social systems often do not function in ways that produce the intended outcomes of the persons operating them. The failure of social structures (as institutional facts) to adequately recognize and honor the dignity of human persons (as a natural brute fact) should not be taken to mean that dignity is not a natural fact. It means that social structures are broken, that they function in ways inadequate to the real world in which they operate. If airplanes are inventions honoring the physical laws of gravity and force in the interest of rapid human travel through space, the empirical fact that some planes fail and crash does not mean that the laws of gravity and force are mere variable social constructions that might be believed in some places but not others. It means that some things about some airplanes or their pilots are dysfunctional and therefore are not successfully responding to the laws of gravity and force. Human dignity is not a socially constructed institutional fact. Dignity is a natural brute fact of emergent human personhood. So if some cultures and societies do not adequately understand and honor that institutionally, it is they, and not dignity, who have the problem with reality.

Third, the teleological approach to the good, virtues, and morality discussed in the previous chapter entails a clear understanding of a gap between what is and what ought to be. As a normative system, this teleological approach is naturalistic in the sense that it expects to understand the *ought* as arising from the *is*; but it is not naturalistic in the sense of morally authorizing as ought that which is.[62] The idea of a telic human purpose presupposes a difference between where we are and where we ought to be, what we need to become. The good life involves a process of learning virtues that enable us to move toward what we ought to become and the actual living of it as we move closer. So, because human histories, cultures, and circumstances are diverse and because human persons are the creative agents and the efficient causes of their own actions, it is not surprising that some societies have constructed social institutions that do not respect human dignity as well as those of other societies; or that some institutions in any society do not do so as well as other institutions in the same society. Different social structures help to realize our telic ends more or less well. Judgments about such differences are exactly what provide the basis of any social ethics. The recognition that human social institutions across time and space vary in their success in honoring human dignity—indeed, that some are quite broken in their respecting of dignity—should not cause us to deny the reality of dignity. It should cause

62. Philosophers call this the "appeal to nature" problem or the fallacy of relevance.

us as persons to name the broken institutions as "broken" and work as the creative and efficient causes of our actions to socially reconstruct them to better honor the reality of human dignity.

This brings us back to another crucial connection between dignity and sociology. A central purpose of sociology as a discipline should be to help achieve the human good by providing reliable knowledge and understanding about what kinds of social institutions and structures tend to lead toward the thriving of human personhood, on the one hand, and that tend to obstruct or diminish it, on the other. The proper, ultimate purpose of human life—its telos—is the thriving of personhood for all persons. Flourishing personhood, given its profoundly social nature and formation, can and does thrive more or less well under different social conditions—it is fostered by certain social practices, institutions, and structures and hampered and damaged by others. Constructive social ethics is about discerning which practices and institutions promote flourishing personhood. Virtue ethics' teleological approach says that those that do should be judged morally good, those that do not morally neutral or bad. But the question of which social conditions, practices, and institutions promote which kinds of outcomes is not primarily a moral or philosophical issue. It is largely an *empirical* question, one concerned with learning chiefly through observation—as well as rational conceptualization, retroduction, and theorizing—about what social reality is and how it works. In order to complete the larger ethical task of knowing what makes for a good society, toward carrying out informed social reforms and structural changes that are effective in advancing the flourishing of all human persons, it is essential that everyone involved knows what kinds of social arrangements promote that goal and which do not. Sociology is the discipline best equipped to produce exactly that kind of empirically based knowledge. The idea is not to turn sociology into a political advocacy movement or the intellectual handmaiden of policy studies and social work. The idea is that sociology—when well-conducted on its own terms as a distinctive discipline employing the best methods available—can provide the kind of knowledge, understanding, and insight needed to complete the larger, informed, moral and political process of discerning which social arrangements are good and bad or better and worse toward implementing social changes that move everyone more closely to the good society that best promotes flourishing personhood. This is a major dimension of the "critical" in *critical* realist social science. There is nothing necessarily utopian about this, at least from a critical realist perspective, which recognizes that knowledge is fallible and the world is broken. Furthermore, this disciplinary "calling" to serve the good of personhood by informing social ethics need not displace the more fundamental disciplinary task of producing basic, empirically informed, generalizable theoretical knowledge and understanding about the nature and functioning of human social life. The two purposes are distinct yet can be mutually enriching. In short, sociology stands well positioned to be, not an "objective science of society" or to act as merely one among many disciplines competing for inter- and intra-university status and resources, but to serve as an essential contributor to the larger, shared moral and political project of pursuing the telic social good of institutionally and structurally promoting human dignity.[63] In short, this *service on behalf of human dignity is part of the discipline's teleological end*, defining for it what is the true good of sociology.

Further exploring the ways that a more explicit acknowledgment of the dignity of human persons might enhance our sociological understanding takes us into largely uncharted territory. My purpose here is not fully to explicate a "sociology of dignity" or to conduct a thorough archaeology of the dignity hidden in, behind, and beneath existing social life and sociological scholarship about it. My more limited purpose is to defend the reality of dignity as part of a theory of the human person that has theoretical and analytical relevance in sociology. I am confident that the scholarly fruits of better accounting for human dignity in sociological scholarship will prove significant and rewarding. Accounting for dignity would force us to reconsider some academic theoretical perspectives that have difficulty accommodating dignity. It would help us to overcome the odd split frequently evident between our professional scholarship and our personal moral and political commitments. It would position us to move toward a single, more coherent and integrated account of the reality in which we live. And it would help to define a clearer moral calling for sociology as a discipline. All of those possibilities belong to the good and so should be ends toward which sociologists work.

63. For related though not identical (particularly not consistently teleological, virtues-ethics based) arguments, see Bent Flyvbjerg, *Making Social Science Matter: Why Social Inquiry Fails and How It Can Succeed Again* (Cambridge: Cambridge University Press, 2001); Alan Wolfe, *Whose Keeper: Social Science and Moral Obligation* (Berkeley and Los Angeles: University of California Press, 1989); Robert Lynd, *Knowledge for What? The Place of Social Science in American Culture* (1939; Middletown, CT: Wesleyan University Press, 1967).

Conclusion

What academic scholars do in their professional lives is not finally disconnected—and therefore should not in practice be disconnected—from
who they are and what they do in their personal, moral, and political lives.
If we believe in the dignity of human persons, in our own dignity as people,
there is no reason why that belief in dignity should not have bearing on
what we believe social scientifically about what society is and how and why
it exists and operates as it does. If so, a crucial question is: What metatheoretical framework best enables us to bring the two together? Positivist
empiricism cannot. Aside from misconstruing the nature of causality,
among other key ideas, it is inherently unable to recognize or account
for anything like real dignity, values, morality, or the good. Postmodernism also cannot. Postmodernism in the end is the abandonment of social
science, actually, in favor of antirealist storytelling and identity postur-
ing. That is a dead end. Hermeneutical interpretivism can go a long way
toward bridging the personal, the professional, and the political. But that
approach also significantly distances itself from the social scientific challenge of providing causal understandings, preferring instead to take on
the more underachieving task of interpreting the meanings of actions and
texts for actors. And so with it our moral and political commitments are
never finally linked with robust social scientific scholarship.

So far as I can see, the one and only viable metatheoretical framework
that underwrites and links good social science and robustly humanistic
morality and politics is critical realism. "Critical realism alone," writes
Douglas Porpora, compared to positivism, postmodernism, and traditional sociological humanism, "recovers both scientific causality and—not
just agency—but morally responsible, ontological agents."[64] This is where
contemporary social science needs to go. The alternatives have all been
tried—some for far longer than they have deserved—and been found
wanting. Critical realism provides the best account of what reality and human knowledge are like and what we as scholars need to be doing. When
fused with philosophical personalism—producing critical realist personalism—we discover a more comprehensive framework of understanding
that explains our human selves to ourselves in a phenomenologically most

64. Douglas Porpora, "Do Realists Run Regressions?" in *After Postmodernism: An
Introduction to Critical Realism*, ed. José López, and Garry Potter (New York: Continuum,
2001), 264.

sensible and morally most bracing way.[65] In critical realist personalism we thus find a promising basis upon which to construct a coherent understanding of personal being, interpersonal relationships, social structures, the moral good, and human dignity. Fulfilling that promise would be a major achievement for the good.

65. This book has only begun to explore the relevant issues and has left numerous unanswered questions and intellectual loose ends to be addressed in continued work. In my mind, these include exploring the relationship between critical realist personalism and the American pragmatism that has influenced some in American sociology recently, particularly the work of Hans Joas; further developing critical realist personalism's understanding of power and inequality; better engaging the literature in social psychology, which often directly engages questions of the nature and function of human personhood; and further exploring questions about the origins and social and institutional perpetuation of the brokenness of reality, including the sources of recurrent tendencies to deny and violate human dignity. Obviously, too, more work needs to be done to press out the practical methodological and analytical implications of critical realist personalism for empirical research.

Postscript

What is the practical payoff? That is what most American sociologists want to know straight away about any new theory or method. And rightly so, for if a new idea does not promise to change our thinking and practices in ways that increase our epistemic gain, then it is not clear why the idea deserves serious consideration. In the case of the critical realist personalism that I have begun to describe in this book, I think the positive practical payoffs for American sociology in fact are big—though they will come with some costs. Some readers may be cautious of the approach advanced in the preceding chapters or the broader philosophical frameworks underwriting it. But little promise of it making a practical difference ought not to be among the reasons why. If anything, an understandable reason might be because this book's approach—when its implications are unpacked—entails the disruption or adjustment of a host of well-established assumptions, tendencies, beliefs, habits, boundaries, practices, methods, standards, and systems upon which a great deal of mainstream American sociology is built—on which many have built their careers. On the one hand, a good part of the best scholarship that American sociology produces is, whether its authors know it or not, tacitly and de facto critical realist in approach. Reality simply pushes in that direction. Good scholarship can be made even better by being more self-reflexive and corrective about its philosophical moorings in order to be to be more consistent with the directives and fuller implications of critical realism. On the other hand, a great deal of scholarship produced in American sociology is inadequate if not flawed in various ways. That is because it is driven by often-unrecognized philosophical assumptions and commitments that are deeply problematic. By correcting much of our sociological meta-theory, we can realize valuable payoffs in our more specific sociological research, writing, and teaching.

That is not to say, however, that one can jump straight from reading some orienting books about critical realism or personalism to a long list of specific, "practical" instructions, techniques, and methods that will immediately change how we do business. All forms of social business-as-usual—including sociology's business-as-usual—are governed by the kind of social structures described in chapter 6, which lend them resilience and stability over time and space. That is what helps make them "as usual." Change is not easy. Realizing the practical payoffs that critical realism, personalism, and antinaturalistic phenomenological epistemology have to offer will require scholars to invest in new learning, thinking, and imagining; to develop new practices of research; and to reform structures and routines to better match the kind of scholarship for which critical realist personalism calls. Those are some of the costs I mentioned above. It is not that everything will change. Much that we do now will remain in place. But how we think about what we are doing, how we go about doing it, what counts as a valuable contribution, and the tools we use to accomplish it all will be revised—for the better, I believe. Figuring that out will have to be a collaborative process engaged by many interested sociologists. It will require patience and determination, not simply demands to tell immediately what the practical payoff is. In the end, it will involve change in some of the status hierarchies within sociology, the structure of graduate student training, the constitution of research programs, the format of typical journals and articles, and more.

The preceding chapters have discussed the beginnings of a variety of ways that critical realist personalism could and should make a difference in the doing of sociology. The discerning reader will have seen many of the implications already. Obviously, key matters at issue include our dealings with causation, explanation, mechanisms, unobservables, generalization, agency, temporality, hermeneutics, narrative, retroduction, personal knowledge, truth-seeking, antireductionism, the importance of conceptualization, the role of description, accounting for emergence, methodological pluralism, achieving cumulative knowledge, and the relation between academic scholarship and visions of the good in human personal and social life. While these have been running themes in this book, I have not systematically identified and elaborated these practical implications. I am afraid that to draw out those lessons more thoroughly will require another book, which I hope will be forthcoming in due time. In the meantime, interested scholars can work with what has been started here, and with the many other publications referenced in the notes, toward further developing and modeling the practical significance and implications for doing sociology in the mode of critical realist personalism.

In addition, a variety of relevant topics either hardly or not at all touched upon in this book require further consideration in any development of critical realist personalism. This book, for instance, barely mentioned the human unconscious, although that is an issue of importance in the matters at hand. It also did not engage models of the human person implicit or explicit in various approaches in social psychology, a field that would seem to provide a wealth of insights and grist for the theoretical mill. Conversations with those who work in the more pragmatist theoretical tradition would also likely be fruitful, as well as scholars in Weberian sociology and feminist theory. More work needs to be done in a critical realist mode to consider how ethnographers can better observe causal mechanisms in process, how surveys and statistics can better isolate and test directly unobservable causal mechanisms at work, and the relevance and limitations of natural and artificial laboratory experiments for understanding causation in social life. The substantive matters of power and inequality are also clearly central to the approach of this book, although I did not develop them as much as they need to be. The nature and role of culture and morality also could use better connection and development. The same is true about scholarship in normative legal and political theory, cultural studies, moral philosophy, medical ethics, and bioethics. The issue of the nature of the human person is also central to visions concerning the purpose and structure of higher education, which I fear are becoming increasingly more blurred and distracted, in part as a result of problematic understandings of personhood. In short, much more intellectual work needs doing to advance the lines of thought introduced in this book both for sociology and beyond it. But it is not enough simply to have some intellectually stimulating ideas and debates. In the end what finally matters for sociology will be the development of better criteria for knowing what good sociology looks like; illuminating practices of sociological research that are more adequate to the actual humanly social subject of study; and the publication and teaching of better sociological descriptions, analyses, and explanations of structured social life.

It is all too easy for American sociology to fall victim to a particular social causal mechanism that it observes in other groups and organizations, namely, goal displacement. We in this collective sociological enterprise too easily forget about the true, long-term, substantively worthy goals of our discipline. We easily end up instead spending most or all of our time, attention, and energy focused on mere means. The means thus displace the goals. What were once means become the new goals. We become consumed with writing papers, publishing articles, landing jobs, building curricula vitae, securing positive teaching evaluations, earning tenure, increasing the number of undergraduate majors, producing graduate students, reviewing papers and books, attending conferences, protecting budgets, maintaining our courses in curricula, applying for grants, upgrading computer equipment, interviewing and recruiting faculty, countering external offers to colleagues, building and maintaining departmental rankings, and on and on. To what end? Often, because we get lost in means, we need to refocus our vision on the most important end goals. This book is, among other things, an attempt to encourage that refocusing. To get sociology right, we need to start with a most helpful general approach and correct metatheory about social science that rightly tells us what good sociology is and how the results of sociological scholarship relate to the larger project of pursuing the good in personal and social life. What are the available alternatives? Positivist empiricism does not get us there. Hermeneutical interpretivism gets us part of the way, but not nearly far enough. Postmodern deconstruction takes us somewhere, but no place we should want to go. How to proceed? The way forward for sociology is critical realist personalism.

Index

Lightning Source UK Ltd.
Milton Keynes UK
UKOW04f2153180315

248096UK00002B/18/P